D0456350

CHRISTOLOGY IN CULTURAL PERSPECTIVE

WITHDRAWN

To Haren:

Wishing you every blessing
in your journey of faith

Colin.

DATE DUE

Christology in Cultural Perspective

MARKING OUT THE HORIZONS

Colin J. D. Greene

William B. Eerdmans Publishing Company

Grand Rapids, Michigan / Cambridge, U.K.

First published 2003 in the U.K. by
Paternoster Press, an imprint of Authentic Media
P.O. Box 300, Carlisle, Cumbria CA3 0QS U.K.

This edition published 2004 in the United States of America by
Wm. B. Eerdmans Publishing Co.
255 Jefferson Ave. S.E., Grand Rapids, Michigan 49503 /
P.O. Box 163, Cambridge CB3 9PU U.K.
www.eerdmans.com

Printed in the United States of America

08 07 06 05 04   7 6 5 4 3 2 1

Library of Congress Cataloging-in-Publication Data

ISBN 0-8028-2792-6

'Dr Greene draws on a wide variety of theological, historical, and conceptual resources to explore a constructive approach to Christology and successive cultures. He rightly avoids exclusive alternatives between cosmological, anthropological, and political trajectories, and underlines their complementary character as indicating continuities with biblical and historical formulations relevant to our own day. This book repays careful study.'

Canon Anthony C. Thiselton, Emeritus Professor of Christian Theology in Residence, University of Nottingham.

'Colin Greene's magisterial work is far more than a conventional survey of what theologians have done with Christology, though it takes that in on the way. It is a challenge to several of the major assumptions that underlie the work not only of theologians but also of cultural critics, politicians, and opinion-formers in today's world. It is, in other words, doing for today something of what the gospel writers did for their day: telling the story of Jesus in such a way as to blow open existing worldviews and propose fresh, startling perspectives in their place.'

Canon Tom Wright, Westminster Abbey, London.

To Valerie, Peter, Kathryn and Naomi
(we have one life but we carry each other)

In memory of Henry Greene
1923–1998

and

Richard W.A. McKinney
1938–1996

(the road has risen to greet them)

Contents

Foreword

The figure of Jesus is a fascinating theological and cultural study, as he moves through every one of the past twenty centuries and is now present in every part of the world. I remember when giving a seminar on Jesus in the University of Beijing how very difficult it was to be sure that the main categories and concepts I was using really linked up with the students and staff present. There was a sense of the need for long, patient conversation about a wide range of matters, not all of them directly related to theology. In this book, Colin Greene has wisely not tried to cover all cultures. His main focus, the ways Jesus figured in the early centuries of Christianity and later in Western civilisation, is quite vast enough. He patiently enters into one period and theology after another, and sets up a wide-ranging conversation that centres on Jesus as the Christ of God.

The subject matter of the book is multifarious and many of the thinkers discussed are complex, but again and again Colin Greene manages to draw out the key issues and lays them out in a form that acts both as an educational introduction and a theological discussion. There are a number of basic cultural paradigms, whose differences set the scene for a confrontation between the diverse ways in which Jesus Christ has been understood. There is also the historical approach, examining how Jesus has featured in premodern, modern and postmodern theologies and cultures. Colin Greene describes the book as a journey, and it is one that faces the big problems, crossing the rough country and making the necessary detours.

One of the strengths of the book is that, for all its large scale, it continually engages in critical dialogue with specific thinkers. Colin Greene has read widely, and offers not just analyses and descriptions but also assessments of one theologian after another. As someone who tries to do Christology, I found myself repeatedly stimulated to think in new ways, either with or against particular thinkers. One of my own preoccupations is with the way the Bible is interpreted in Christology and, even though this is not a leading theme for Colin Greene, he continually provokes further thought about it.

The culmination of the book comes when a series of recapitulations of the previous chapters leads into suggestions for the reconstruction of Christology in the aftermath of postmodern deconstruction. This is one of the great challenges to contemporary theology, and Colin Greene has taken it up with energy, learning and insight.

David F. Ford
Regius Professor of Divinity
University of Cambridge

Preface

The most profound, disturbing, prophetic and enduringly significant theological exploration is usually born out of a confrontation with specific cultural and historical contexts. From the apostle Paul to Tertullian, Ambrose and Augustine struggling with the idolatrous pretensions of the Holy Roman Empire, to the Reformers resistance to the heteronomy of the Roman Catholic Church, to Karl Barth and the Barmen declaration and the martyrdom of Dietrich Bonhoeffer, theology and successive theologians made a stand against cultural hegemony in the name of the crucified and risen Christ. Nothing pushes Christology back into the centre of theological concerns more than the threat of cultural domination and nothing removes Christology to the margins more than the scourge of cultural accommodation. Such insights have penetrated the theological convictions that lay behind both the conceiving and the writing of this particular book.

What began as an attempt to critically investigate and reconstruct the genesis and development of Christology from the biblical sources to the modern era, quickly moved on to an exploration of the specific cultural contexts that have dominated these concerns. It was then a short but nevertheless disconcerting step to discover the ideological subtext that undergirds such cultural referents and which often masquerades in the guise of human emancipation and progress. While thorough immersion in the biblical and Christological tradition may alert one to this unpalatable reality it does not protect one's own deliberations from similar dangerous liaisons. It is only when one has come to the conclusion that what largely distinguishes modernity and postmodernity from previous historical and cultural contexts is that they are almost entirely cultural and ideological constructs that one feels an invigorating liberty to propose new Christological and theological alternatives.

Inevitably in a project of this nature and duration some of the thinking has been aired in other contexts. Chapter five, 'Christology and History', first appeared as 'In the Arms of the Angels: Biblical Interpretation, Christology and the Philosophy of History', in C.G. Bartholomew, C. Greene and K. Möller (eds.), *Renewing Biblical Interpretation* (SAHS Vol. 1; Paternoster/Zondervan, 2000), 198–239. Similarly, an earlier and shortened version of the concluding chapter appeared as 'Starting a Rockslide: Deconstructing History and Language via Christological Detonators', in C. G. Bartholomew, C. Greene and K. Möller (eds.), *After Pentecost: Language & Biblical Interpretation* (SAHS Vol. 2; Paternoster/Zondervan, 2001), 195–223. My only major regret is that another planned chapter on Christology and the religions had to be omitted due to the projected length of this study.

In undertaking a journey of this nature one is constantly indebted to a range of conversations and insights gained from colleagues and associates. I am grateful to Rev Dr Martin Robinson, Neil Crosbie and Linsi Simmons, and other colleagues (past and present) at the British and Foreign Bible Society, for the encouragement and intellectual stimulation they provided throughout this project. Similarly, I wish to thank Canon Tom Wright, Professor David Ford, Professor Colin Gunton and my close friend Canon Tom Smail who have all helpfully challenged some of my basic assumptions and critically probed some of my conclusions. I am also grateful to Tony Graham, my editor, who has doggedly stuck with me throughout all the twists and turns of the journey. Most of all, I am profoundly grateful to my wife and three children and indeed my wider family who have supported and encouraged me unstintingly throughout this particular venture.

1.

Christology – The Nature of the Task

At the centre of Christianity stands not a timeless truth, nor a principle, not even a cause, but an event and a person – Jesus of Nazareth experienced and confessed as the Christ. Through the diverse genres, titles, confessions of the New Testament there is the constancy of a confession, constituted by the community's present experience of its Crucified and Risen Lord to this person Jesus of Nazareth.[1]

Introduction

Alex Wright asks, what for many of us today, both inside and outside the academy, is an obvious question, why bother with theology?[2] Another question, which has direct bearing on the subject matter of this book, could be added, why bother with Christology, which is, after all, merely a subset of the theological task? Why bother indeed when increasingly the marginalisation of the Christian church, and theological and christological exploration from the wider realities of culture, society and the rampant consumerism of modern life in general is all but complete?

It could be argued that this statement applies only to the fate of the Christian church in Western Europe and some parts of North America, where, according to a recent statement, Christianity has 'almost been vanquished' as a force for spiritual, moral and cultural renewal in the public life of society.[3] Elsewhere, in the Two-Thirds World, the church continues to grow and expand at an astonishing rate. Furthermore it may be that this fact is an expression of the internal dynamic of the Christian faith itself. A faith that is in essence a diaspora

---

[1] D. Tracy, *The Analogical Imagination: Christian Theology and the Culture of Pluralism*, 317.

[2] A. Wright, *Why Bother with Theology?*

[3] Remarks made by Cormac Murphy O'Connor, Roman Catholic Archbishop of Westminster, at a National Conference of Priests in Leeds, UK, Sept 2001 that were picked up by the BBC and gained national media coverage. The Archbishop subsequently pointed out that this was not so much an admission of defeat as a clarion call to action and thoughtful missional engagement.

movement, a centrifugal force that always moves away from its heartland and flourishes again on the margins.

In response to this observation two comments should be made. First, the rapid numerical growth of the Christian church, for instance the spread of Pentecostalism in Latin America, is not necessarily synonymous with the emergence of a Christian vision of human flourishing which leads to a renewal of public life and social imagination. Secondly, although we might welcome the growth of Christianity elsewhere in the world this still leaves us with a lacuna in terms of how we understand the decline of the public significance of Christianity in its historic heartlands of Europe and North America. In recent years, attempts have been made to explain this startling decline in terms of a collective case of religious amnesia[4] or a preference for a vicarious form of religious practice[5] or the loss of the discursive power of the Christian story.[6]

Wright adds to this the fact that theology in the West at least, is too far removed from the real world of human relationships, popular culture and the public life of society to be able to offer a counter cultural vision of human life and destiny. This state of affairs, however, was not always the case. Arguably, for at least seventeen hundred years of its existence, Christianity offered to society in general a broader practice of religion that was based largely on a christological vision of reality that assured the Christian faith a central role in the cultural heritage of its native Europe and beyond.

In this book we seek to trace the development of this christological vision, and define and examine its constituent elements. We do so because Christology adumbrates a conviction that there was and is more significance to the man Jesus of Nazareth than just a first-century Palestinian itinerant rabbi, peasant or religious leader who met an untimely death at the hands of the Roman authorities. On the contrary, both the NT and the later creeds of the church claim that Jesus stands in a unique relationship to the God whose coming kingdom he proclaimed, the history of Israel and, indeed, the whole history of humanity, the very existence and destiny of which he is believed to have rescued and redeemed:

> The assertion 'Jesus is the Christ' is the basic statement of Christian belief, and Christology is no more than the conscientious elucidation of that proposition. When we say that Jesus is the Christ, we maintain that this unique, irreplaceable Jesus of Nazareth is at one and the same time the Christ sent by God: that is, the Messiah anointed of the Spirit, the salvation of the world, and the eschatological fulfilment of history.[7]

---

[4] G. Davie, *Religion in Modern Europe: A Memory Mutates.*
[5] G. Davie, *Europe: The Exceptional Case: Parameters of Faith in the Modern World*, 19–20.
[6] C. Brown, *The Death of Christian Britain: Understanding Secularisation 1800–2000.*
[7] W. Kasper, *Jesus the Christ*, 15–16.

It is such theological claims and convictions that Christology sets out to explain and to test, because such momentous statements amount to a particular truth claim that warrants universal significance and relevance.

In the light of this analysis we then offer our own interpretation of why that vision ceased to grasp the public imagination and attention of European and North American society in general. Moving beyond mere diagnosis we offer particular suggestions of how to re-ignite that vision in the context of postmodern deconstructionalism which, like all cultural episodes in human history, is both a threat and an opportunity to the continued credibility of Christian faith and belief to society in general. In our account we combine theological, philosophical, historical, sociological and cultural analysis in recognition of the fact that the Christian faith always receives its distinctive ecclesial existence downstream from broader cultural and historical affiliations and concerns. To begin with, however, we must briefly examine the story (or stories) that underpinned that christological account of how things are in the created order.

The Gospel Story – A Pre-critical Look at the Evidence

Before the advent of historical critical scholarship in the eighteenth century, which largely borrowed its methodology from the natural sciences, scholars, preachers, evangelists and ordinary believers alike viewed the Gospels as history like narratives.[8] A pre-critical reading of the NT attended to the plain literary sense of the Gospels and epistles, and concluded that here was a real story, involving real historical occurrences based on a number of accounts of the life of a real historical person. For Martin Luther and John Calvin, the biblical world and the world of their own experience were one and the same reality.[9] There was little concern about an apparent critical distance or dislocation between the world of the NT and that of seventeenth-century Europe. Indeed, the latter was judged and appraised in the light of the former, because it was the biblical world that attested to the coming of the Saviour into our midst. Consequently, it would have been of no surprise to the reformers that the question of the true significance or identity of Jesus is raised in the Gospel records themselves and not just by the christological controversies that beset the early church in the fourth and fifth centuries.

---

[8] H. Frei, *The Eclipse of Biblical Narrative: A Study in Eighteenth and Nineteenth Century Hermeneutics.*

[9] Cf. Neil B. MacDonald, 'Illocutionary Stance in Hans Frei's The Eclipse of the Biblical Narrative: An Exercise in Conceptual Redescription and Normative Analysis', in C. Bartholomew, C. Greene & K. Möller (eds), *After Pentecost: Language & Biblical Interpretation*, 312–27.

The uncertainty and curiosity over Jesus' identity originates in the encounter between Jesus and those to whom he speaks and ministers. For instance, John the Baptist's question, 'Are you he who is to come, or shall we look for another?' (Mt. 11:3), expresses the conundrum that Jesus' person and ministry posed to his contemporaries. Was this the promised Messiah or was Jesus merely another itinerant cynic, charismatic rabbi or prophet, or, indeed, as some postulated, was he the agent of Beelzebub, the prince of the devils? The same enigmatic quality occurs during Jesus' triumphal entry into Jerusalem: 'the whole city was stirred and asked, "Who is this?" ' (Mt. 21:10). Even Satan seemed unsure of Jesus' identity, hence the repeated interrogation 'if you are the Son of God' before the equally determined attempt to test out Jesus' credentials (Mt. 4:1–11; Lk. 4:1–13).

If the Gospels are not simply the carefully edited credo of the early church, but contain some genuine evidence of the enigma Jesus presented to his contemporaries then part of the difficulty was no doubt due to the fact that he did not seem to fit with previous patterns and expectations of what constituted a messenger of God, a prophet, or teacher of religion. He was not a priest; unlike his cousin John the Baptist, he did not come from a priestly family. Neither was he a bona fide prophet in the OT sense of the word, because his preaching was not couched in the idiom of a reiteration of the word of God. Nor was he simply an apocalyptic seer or visionary whose main concern was to interpret the signs of the times and proclaim God's judgement upon society in general. He was most definitely not a teacher of the law in the Pharisaical sense of the word; indeed, he was opposed to the casuistry that typified their profession.[10] Nor was he merely a teacher of wisdom, although he did speak in parables, aphorisms and proverbs. He was not a politically motivated Zealot,[11] nor was he simply another itinerant magician, wonder worker or charismatic

---

[10] One of the factors that distinguishes what is referred to as the third quest for the historical Jesus is a dispute over just how radical and noticeable was Jesus' conflict or controversy with the Pharisees. For instance, M. Borg in *Conflict, Holiness and Politics in the Teachings of Jesus* views Jesus as advocating a new holiness agenda based on a politics of mercy over and against the traditional purity code preferred by the Pharisees. E.P. Sanders, on the other hand, minimises the significance of the supposed conflict between Jesus and the Pharisees because he wants to stress the continuity between Jesus and his contemporary Jewish *Sitz im Leben*. See *Jesus and Judaism* and *The Historical Figure of Jesus*.

[11] The third quest has sought to re-open what were previously regarded as almost standard theories of NT exegesis. J.D. Crossan denies that there was a Zealot movement before or during Jesus' ministry; see *The Historical Jesus: The Life of a Mediterranean Jewish Peasant* and *Jesus: A Revolutionary Biography*. M. Hengel and J.K Riches argue vehemently to the contrary. See *Judaism and Hellenism: Studies in their Encounter in Palestine During the Early Hellenistic Period* and *The World of Jesus: First Century Judaism in Crisis*, respectively.

miracle worker. In all respects, Jesus broke apart previous categories and expectations. As Eduard Schweizer commented, Jesus was 'the man who fits no one formula'.[12]

To a certain extent this was also the case in terms of his intimate address of God as *Abba*, his message that the future rule of God had already broken through in his own person and ministry, his predictions concerning his own suffering and fate, and his table fellowship with women, the poor and those who were considered to be the social outcasts of contemporary society. There can be no doubt therefore that, 'the question of Jesus' identity, role, or relationship to the divine forced itself on those who came in contact with him – either he was a blasphemer, a fool, or one who spoke with divine authority', indeed,[13] all three possibilities are entertained in the Gospels (Mk. 1:22, 27; 2:7; 3:21).

Such uncertainty and speculation concerning the true identity and status of Jesus reflects 'the encounter quality of the first christological reflections'[14] (i.e. the issue of Jesus' identity did not arise first and foremost as a theoretical problem). It was not the problem of how this person can be said to both express and unite the essence of humanity and divinity in a way that is unique or unparalleled in the history of religion. In fact, this is an issue with which the Gospels are not concerned. Rather, it was in the actual, concrete, everyday interaction of Jesus with individuals and the multitudes – his compassion for the poor, the sick and the marginalised members of society; his proclamation of the coming kingdom of God and his demonstration of the saving and healing reality of that kingdom in individual lives – which produced the first examples of christological reflection and confession.

The Gospels affirm both the mysterious and enigmatic quality of Jesus' life and ministry, as well as an apparent witness to his unique status as the promised Messiah. Peter's famous confession at Caesarea Philippi is understandably a turning point in the Gospels. Here Jesus raises the question of his own identity in the face of public speculation and uncertainty. The answer he received constitutes 'the first example of a dogma understood as a public confession':[15] 'You are the Christ, the Son of the living God' (Mt. 16:16). However, this form of confession was not confined to those of the house of Israel or to those who knew Jesus intimately. The centurion who witnessed the terrible and

---

[12] E. Schweizer, *Jesus Christ: The Man from Nazareth and the Exalted Lord*, 86.

[13] R.H. Fuller & P. Perkins, *Who Is This Christ?*, 24. Kasper makes the same point: 'Who was Jesus of Nazareth? On the one hand he is regarded as the messianic bringer of salvation, on the other as a blasphemer and false prophet or as a rebel. Herod derides him as a fool (Lk. 23:6–12) and his closest relatives regard him as mad (Mk. 3:21).' Kasper, *Jesus*, 68.

[14] D.J. Hall, *Professing The Faith*, 373.

[15] B. Lohse, *A Short History of Christian Doctrine*, 9.

tumultuous events of the crucifixion exclaimed, 'Surely he was the [or a] Son of God!' (Mt. 27:54).

As we have intimated previously, however, the Gospels also tell us that Jesus came under suspicion as either a messianic impostor, a political revolutionary, or a blasphemer because he appeared to put himself above the authority of the Mosaic Law; or indeed a combination of all three because his own subversive re-telling and re-enactment of the central narrative of his native Judaism afforded to him a crucial role as the personal representative of YHWH, i.e. the Messiah.[16] Consequently, it was also the case that, 'he came to that which was his own, but his own did not receive him' (Jn. 1:11). The issue of who Jesus was and is still stands at the heart of Jewish-Christian relationships. Much of the anti-Semitism that has bedevilled the history of Christianity stems from the unequivocal testimony of the Gospels that Jesus was rejected by his own people and suffered an ignominious fate. The explanation and interpretation of Jesus' suffering and death later promulgated by the nascent Christian Church reflects those Jewish origins, namely that this was an atonement for the sins of the people.[17] Although nowhere does the NT provide a complete theological explanation of what that atonement actually involves or means.

How much such affirmations reflect the faith of the early Church and how much they can be attributed to the immediate response of Jesus' contemporaries is a central and pressing issue. The one incontrovertible fact that modern scholarship has forced us to accept is that the Gospels do not present us with the biographical account of the life of Jesus. Rather, they introduce us, to a certain extent, to the variegated strands of the credo of the early Church and it is to this issue that we must now turn.

The Critics' Story – Searching for the Historical Jesus

It would not be a gross generalisation to claim that since the eighteenth century the Jesus story has tended to be supplanted and indeed, at times all but obliterated, by the critics' story, particularly as that concern has manifested itself in the seemingly endless search for the so-called 'historical Jesus'. So called because it is this elusive figure, it is contented, that lies behind the different and diverse christological titles we find scattered around the NT. Rarely, therefore, does any scholar nowadays commence christological investigation with a simple lexicographical method that seeks to delineate the implicit meaning of the

[16] This indeed is the central emphasis of N.T. Wright's fine study, *Jesus And The Victory of God*.
[17] See for instance M. Casey, *From Jewish Prophet to Gentile God: The Origins and Development of New Testament Christology*.

various christological titles. Rather, it is assumed that the christological titles (such as *Logos*, Wisdom, Messiah, Son of God, Son of Man and the new Adam) actually amount to post-resurrection, public professions of faith that tell us as much about the social, cultural and religious context of the early Christian communities as they do about the person of Jesus. The more favoured route, particularly by many now involved in the latest episode of Jesus research, is to draw a firm line between the historical and the theological, and contend that what the NT scholar can legitimately concern him or herself with is the former and not the latter.

N.T. Wright argues for a fourfold classification of the main stages of this movement. The first quest, he asserts, began with Reimarus and ended with Albert Schweitzer; the new quest began with Ernst Käsemann and ended with Eduard Schillebeeckx; the third quest was dominated by E.P. Sanders and Geza Vermes; and the 'renewed new quest', as Wright labels it, is probably best represented by J. Dominic Crossan and the Jesus Seminar.[18] Ben Witherington, on the other hand, opts for a simpler schema, which he refers to as the first, second, and third quests, incorporating Sanders and Vermes into the latter movement.[19] It is Witherington's classification we will adopt as we briefly survey some of the major findings of the third quest for the historical Jesus.

Jesus the cynic

One of the more fashionable trends proffered by representatives of this burgeoning industry of Jesus research is the attempt to equate the original Jesus with other discernible contemporary religious figures or types. Thus we have the notion of Jesus the cynic, a thesis intriguingly ventured by Crossan, Burton Mach and Gerald Downing.[20] Bold and at times overtly historicist and unsubstantiated claims are made that Jesus was one of a variety of the popular philosophers who roamed the Greco-Roman world, offering their own brand of cynical withdrawal from a corrupt and decadent society. The difficulty here is that Jesus' worldview and preaching appear to be permeated with an essentially Jewish eschatological expectation concerning the impending judgement brought about by the proximity of the kingdom of God, a theme which is almost wholly absent from the message of the cynics.

---

[18] Wright, *Victory*, 13–121; cf. also M. Goodacre, 'The Quest to Digest Jesus: Recent Books on the Historical Jesus', *RRT* 7.2 (April 2000), 156–61.

[19] B. Witherington, *The Jesus Quest: The Third Search for the Jew of Nazareth*.

[20] Cf. Crossan, *Historical Jesus*; also B. Mack, *A Myth of Innocence: Mark and Christian Origins*, Cf. also M. Borg, 'A Temperate Case for a Non-eschatological Jesus', in *Foundations and Facts Forum* 2(3): 81–102; *Jesus: A New Vision*; also *An Orthodoxy Reconsidered: The 'End-of-the-World' Jesus*, 207–17; also F.G. Downing, *Cynics and Christian Origins*.

Jesus the Spirit-filled mystic or Spirit-possessed healer

Outside the rarefied atmosphere of the Jesus Seminar, Marcus Borg, Vermes and Graham Stanton offer a more restrained thesis that in Jesus we find a charismatic prophet with unusual healing gifts.

Borg claims that the Spirit-filled person is a well-known religious type with two distinguishing characteristics. First, frequent and vivid experiences of God of a mystical or visionary nature that correspond to Jesus' acknowledgement of God in intimate terms as *Abba*. Secondly, such a person easily becomes a conduit, or a living embodiment of the Spirit's power, manifested in healings, miracles and exorcisms.[21]

Stephen Davies, although constructed from very different historical premises, offers a similar argument.[22] Building on the earlier work of James Dunn and Geoffrey Lampe,[23] Davies concludes that Jesus was a spirit-possessed charismatic healer and that this is the link between the Jesus of the Gospels and the Christ of the NT communities, i.e. 'Christology grew out of Pneumatology'.[24]

---

[21] M Borg, *Conflict, Holiness and Politics in the Teachings of Jesus*.

[22] S. Davies, *Jesus the Healer: Possession, Trance and the Origins of Christianity*.

[23] J.D.G. Dunn, *Jesus and the Spirit*; cf. also G.W.H. Lampe, *God as Spirit*.

[24] Davies, *Jesus the Healer*, 187. To a certain extent, all attempts to identify the historical Jesus with other recognisable religious itinerants of the time suffer from similar flaws and weaknesses. At worst they demonstrate a tendency to manipulate, or at best show an unwarranted preference for, certain dubious historical sources. For instance, in the case of Crossan and those involved in the Jesus Seminar, the denigration of Marcan priority in favour of an exaggerated over-reliance on extra-canonical sources such as the Gospels of Peter and James despite the latter's obvious Gnostic influences; and an equally imaginative reconstruction of Q. Cf. Witherington's comments on methodology in *Jesus Quest*, 79, 208. Also problematic is the dissolution of the old eschatological consensus dominant in NT studies since Schweitzer, and the consequent virtual abandonment of any apocalyptic or eschatological context to Jesus' life and ministry, or the translation of eschatology into ethics. Finally, the inability to take seriously or examine rigorously the passion and resurrection traditions. As Witherington comments, 'We do not believe that the Gospel writers were badly mistaken when they concentrated half or more of their Gospels on the last week of Jesus' life; most if not all that Jesus said or did prior to Passover would have been long forgotten had it not been for the events of that week. In Acts, the early Christian preachers focus on the death and resurrection of Jesus and, like Paul, rarely quoted Jesus' parables or aphorisms.' Cf. Witherington, ibid., 92; NT scholarship may well change in this regard as R.E. Brown's *The Death of the Messiah: From Gethsemane to the Grave: A Commentary on the Passion Narratives in the Four Gospels* is fully absorbed and sifted.

Jesus the Hasid

Vermes seeks to reconfigure Jesus as essentially a charismatic Galilean holy man in the tradition of the *hasids*, despite the fact that the Gospels contain little evidence of Jesus as a prayer warrior and an abstemious observer of the law.[25] Vermes has modified his former notions only in so far as Jesus is now seen as a prophet-like holy man and charismatic leader cum exorcist, whose character and charm exceeds by far the normal credentials of the *hasidim*. However, he still holds to the old development thesis that, largely because of the influence of Paul and John, Jesus the holy man was gradually elevated to the status of incarnate Lord.[26]

Jesus the Jew: prophet or reformer

Not surprisingly, there has been a counter trend in the third quest to firmly situate the historical Jesus within a first-century Jewish context. Sanders, whose work has been highly influential in this regard, sought to underscore the link between the historical Jesus and the early Christian communities by portraying Jesus as essentially an eschatological prophet who preached and expected the imminent arrival of the kingdom of God. In Sanders' case, a restoration eschatology, rather than any particular social or political reform, takes centre stage. He argues that Jesus, like the Qumran community, waited for the judgement of God upon a corrupt temple and the restoration of Israel as the covenant people of God which were also discernible concerns of the early church:

> Jesus looked for the imminent direct intervention of God in history, the elimination of evil and evildoers, the building of the new and glorious temple, and the reassembly of Israel with himself and his disciples as leading figures in it.[27]

In a rather different vein, Gerd Theissen, Richard A. Horsley and R. David Kaylor[28] have sought to depict Jesus as a radical social prophet initiating a renewal and reform movement within contemporary Galilean Judaism. Concentrating their corporate efforts on exploring and detailing the religious,

---

[25] G. Vermes, *Jesus the Jew: A Historian's Reading of the Gospels*.

[26] G. Vermes, *The Changing Faces of Jesus*.

[27] Sanders, *Jesus and Judaism*, 153.

[28] G. Theissen, *Sociology of Early Palestinian Christianity* and *The Shadow of the Galilean: The Quest of the Historical Jesus in Narrative Form*; R.A. Horsley, *Sociology and the Jesus Movement*; R.A. Horsley and J.S. Hanson, *Bandits, Prophets and Messiahs: Popular Movements at -the Time of Jesus*; R.A. Horsley, *Jesus and the Spiral of Violence: Popular Jewish Resistance in Roman Palestine*; R.D. Kaylor, *Jesus the Prophet: His Vision of the Kingdom on Earth*.

economic and socio-political setting of first-century Galilee and Judea, they draw comparisons between Jesus and his disciples and the Jewish reform movements of the time. Theissen maintains the Schweitzerian consensus that Jesus expected the imminent arrival of the kingdom, whereas Horsley prefers a Jesus with a radical social agenda who sought to challenge the power structures of his native land, particularly patriarchy, and reorder Galilean society along essentially egalitarian lines. Maintaining the egalitarian theme, Kaylor discovers a Jesus who sought to return to pre-monarchical covenant theology based on peace and justice for all.

A purely reformist Jesus and, indeed, even a Jesus with an acute eschatological expectation, does not necessarily maintain a strong connection between Jesus of Nazareth and the later full-blooded christological affirmations of the NT. Indeed, many biblical scholars are still inherently suspicious of any such connections, so it is refreshing to find those who acknowledge the crucially important nature of this question, because to leave it as a mere historical lacuna is to effectively barter away some of the essential capital of early Christianity.

Jesus the sage

In line with these comments it is perhaps more profitable to look at the efforts of those scholars who are unafraid to investigate the 'Christology of Jesus'.[29] Here again we can refer to two recent works, both of which have different emphasis but put Jesus firmly within the hinterland of first-century Jewish expectation.

Ben Witherington and Elisabeth Schüssler Fiorenza view Jesus as essentially a prophetic Jewish sage, 'standing at the confluence of prophetic, apocalyptic and wisdom traditions',[30] and so offering a counter wisdom to the Judaism of his day.[31] Fiorenza prefers a Jesus who is a radical prophetic figure standing in the line of the more egalitarian tradition of Judaism, and so opposed to both the hierarchical and patriarchal structures of contemporary Judaism. In the name of the *Sophia* God, Jesus created a 'discipleship of equals', an essentially reformist movement within Judaism that connected with the equally anti-patriarchal Christian movement of the early church, situated as it was within Greco-Roman structures of domination.[32] In this way Fiorenza endeavours to overturn what she and other feminists concur is a baleful history of 'androcentric' bias in biblical scholarship and so valorise a Jesus who is a

---

[29] B. Witherington, *The Christology of Jesus*.

[30] B. Witherington, *Jesus Quest*, 163.

[31] B. Witherington, *Jesus the Sage: The Pilgrimage of Wisdom*.

[32] E.S. Fiorenza, *In Memory of Her: A Feminist Theological Reconstruction of Christian Origins*, 99–159.

liberator of women and other marginalised and oppressed groups within his native Judaism.[33]

Jesus: Personified Wisdom

Witherington goes further than Fiorenza and unearths a very important strand for modern Christology. His investigation of the wisdom tradition found in the Old Testament and other apocryphal sources concludes that wisdom was already personified in this tradition as an attribute of divine agency distinct from God. Relying heavily on the material referred to as Q, Witherington suggests that Jesus understood himself not simply as a prophetic sage, but as the personification of God's wisdom on earth. This helps to explain 'some of the key elements in Jesus' teaching: his emphasis on the kingdom, Son of Man, God as Father, creation theology, the lack of *halakic* material, the absence of any "thus says the Lord" formulas and the stress on justice and the reversal of fortunes'.[34] Similarly, such convictions are taken up in the christological hymns of the epistles (Phil. 2:6–11; Col. 1:15–20; 1 Tim. 3:16; Heb. 1:2b–4), brokering a transition from the sapiential messianology of the teachings of Jesus to the high Christology of the later Christian church.[35]

Jesus the Messiah

In terms of those who want to develop, what Wright refers to as a pincer movement in NT studies, both moving forward from an analysis of early Judaism and backwards from the Gospels and the witness of the early church, a number of scholars have somewhat surprisingly happened on a Jesus who is only understandable as in some sense a Messianic figure.[36] Here special mention should be made of the meticulous and painstaking scholarship of John P. Meier.[37] He

---

[33] See chaper 8 for a full discussion of these and similar issues.

[34] Witherington, *Jesus Quest*, 244.

[35] Ibid., 270.

[36] See for instance, P. Stuhlmacher, *Jesus of Nazareth — Christ of Faith*; J.D.G. Dunn, *Christology in the Making: A New Testament Inquiry into the Origins of the Doctrine of the Incarnation*, and 'Messianic Ideas and Their Influence on the Jesus of History', in J.H. Charlesworth (ed.), *The Messiah: Developments in Earliest Judaism and Christianity*, 365–81; M. Bockmuehl, *This Jesus: Martyr, Lord, Messiah*; I.H. Marshall, *The Origins of New Testament Christology*; P. Pokorny, *The Genesis of Christology: Foundations for a Theology of the New Testament*; M. de Jonge, *Jesus, the Servant-Messiah*; Witherington, *Christology*; Wright, *Victory*, and *Who Was Jesus?*. This surprising consensus moves us beyond the impasse that dominated the older quests for the historical Jesus.

[37] J.P. Meier, *A Marginal Jew: Rethinking the Historical Jesus*. Vol. 1, *The Roots of the Problem and the Person*. Vol. 2, *Mentor, Message and Miracles*.

demonstrates that even in the postmodern world of hermeneutical pluralism, a scholarly application of the historical critical method to the canonical material can reap surprising dividends.[38] Meier cautiously but deliberately constructs a basic life of Jesus that offers few surprises but establishes Jesus as both a marginal Jew and so a mere blip on the radar screen of the larger Greco-Roman world, yet, nevertheless, a Messianic figure in the line of Moses, Elijah and Elisha:

> Whatever his precise relationship to the Elijah of old, Jesus the eschatological prophet was acting out the role of the eschatological Elijah as he both proclaimed the imminent coming of God's rule and made the rule a reality even now by his miracles. It was this convergence and configuration of different traits in the one man Jesus ... that gave Jesus his distinctiveness or "uniqueness" within the Palestinian Judaism in the early first century AD.[39]

Meier creatively explores the similarities and the differences between the respective persons and ministries of John the Baptist and Jesus concluding that Jesus was initially a disciple of John. Consequently, it would be highly unlikely if Jesus abandoned or radically altered the eschatological tone of John's message.

One of the most helpful aspects of Meier's work is his rigorous and detailed examination of Jesus teaching concerning the kingdom of God. It is helpful and judicious because it demonstrates just what historical critical scholarship can and cannot establish. He concludes that kingdom of God, an expression that was sparsely used in early Jewish literature, formed the centre of Jesus' teaching and was not a metaphor for socio-political reform. Instead, it refers to the coming of God in person to reverse the tide of injustice, suffering and poverty in favour of God's just and inclusive reign and rule. Less helpful is Meier's tendency to return to the old Jesus of history/Christ of faith distinction that once again drives a wedge between history and theology, and creates a bifurcation that, as we shall see, leaves Christology outflanked as far as its biblical basis is concerned.

Even though Meier and other scholars quite rightly want to take seriously the fact that Jesus was crucified under the epithet 'King of the Jews', it is as well to keep in mind James H. Charlesworth's comment that we should distinguish Christology (the affirmation that Jesus was the Christ, the anointed viceroy of God) from messianology (the disparate notions concerning various messianic figures we find in post-exilic Jewish literature).[40] We will leave a

---

[38] The same could be said of N.T. Wright as he seeks to deploy his particular brand of critical realism in regard to historical scholarship.

[39] Meier, *Marginal Jew*, 1045; quoted in Witherington, *Jesus Quest*, 205.

[40] J.H. Charlesworth, 'From Messianology to Christology: Problems and Prospects', in J.H. Charlesworth (ed.), *The Messiah: Developments in Earliest Judaism and*

fuller discussion of these and other related issues to our penultimate chapter, however, it is sufficient to say at this stage that the consensus of scholarship appears to be that there was no single coherent or normative Messiah figure that most Jews were expecting at the time of Jesus.[41] Similarly, the phrase 'the Messiah' rarely occurs in the Old Testament and only very rarely in early Jewish literature generally, so not surprisingly the origins of messianology are extremely fluid, going back to the Son of Man figure we find in Daniel 7:13–14 and 1 Enoch, as well as the expectations of another king in the Davidic lineage.

Jesus the eschatological prophet

In a rather different but equally important vein, Wright claims that both the symbolic import and practical impact of Jesus' ministry was directed at changing Israel's whole worldview. Narratival worldviews — represented by Jesus, the Qumran community, the Pharisees, the Zealots and the Sadducees — revolved around certain central questions and typical responses, although they all differed in how to effect the necessary change. Wright outlines the range of questions concerned:

1. *Who are we?* — the normal and almost universal answer was, 'We are Israel, the chosen people of the Creator God.'
2. *Where are we?* — 'We are in the Holy Land focused on the Temple, but, paradoxically, we are in a sense in exile.'
3. *What is wrong?* — 'We have the wrong rulers; pagans on the one hand, compromised Jews on the other, or halfway between Herod and his family. We are all involved in a less-than-ideal situation.'
4. *What is the solution?* — 'Our God must act again to give us the true sort of rule, that is, his own kingship exercised through properly appointed officials (a true priesthood; possibly a king) and in the meantime Israel must be faithful to his covenant charter.'[42]

Consequently, it was not for nothing that Jesus was likened to Elijah, John the Baptist and Jeremiah, because the Gospels provide a profile of Jesus as essentially a prophet whose message and praxis intertwined in 'a new way the prophetic styles of oracular prophets on the one hand and leaders of renewal movements

---

[40] *(continued) Christianity*, 3–35. Although it is interesting that N.T. Wright takes issue with Charlesworth on this point, cf. *Victory*, 486.

[41] See for instance, J. Neusner, W.S. Green and E. Frerichs (eds), *Judaisms and their Messiahs at the Turn of the Christian Era.*

[42] Wright, *The New Testament and the People of God*, 243; cf. also Witherington, *Jesus Quest*, 221.

on the other'.[43] Wright discerns four interrelated themes in Jesus' message and revolutionary praxis:

1. His invitation to Israel to embrace eschatological repentance and faith at the expense of Zealot revolutionary zeal and insurrection.
2. The unconditional message of forgiveness expressed in the welcome of sinners to table fellowship that symbolically expressed the return from exile predicted by the prophets.
3. The challenge to live as the new covenant people of God with a particular lifestyle epitomised in the Jubilee principle.
4. His redefinition of Messiahship according to his kingdom praxis.

> Jesus' journey to Jerusalem, climaxing in his actions in the Temple and the upper room, and undertaken in full recognition of the likely consequences, was intended to function like Ezekiel lying on his side or Jeremiah smashing his pot. The prophet's action *embodied* the reality. Jesus went to Jerusalem in order to embody the third and last element of the coming of the kingdom. He was not content to *announce* that YHWH was returning to Zion. He intended to enact, symbolise and personify that climatic event.[44]

In a manner reminiscent of Schweitzer, Wright claims Jesus went to Jerusalem intending to force the issue. He sought to take upon himself the testing that preceded the coming of the kingdom of God, defeat the Satan by letting it rent its fury on him, and allow YHWH to act redemptively through him. Not everyone would agree with Wright's interpretation of the eschatological dimensions of Jesus' message and ministry. Similarly, there is a hint that Wright prefers the Lucan Jesus. Some would also quarrel with his basic thesis that Jesus personified and symbolised in his teaching and actions the long-awaited return of YHWH to Zion. However, enough has been said to indicate that located here could be fruitful foundations for a full-blown Christology.

What this brief review of some of the main strands of recent Jesus research demonstrates is that however the move is made from the historical to the theological, they cannot and should not be separated in the name of so-called objective historical research.[45] The NT eschews any such distinction between the historical and the theological because both are inextricably intertwined and form what we might refer to as the basic ecology of salvation.[46] Jesus only becomes accessible to us not when we try and detach him from the witness

---

[43] Wright, *Victory*, 169.

[44] Ibid., 615.

[45] Such apparent objectivity is now seriously questioned. Cf. I. Provan, *Ideologies, Literary and Critical: Reflections on Recent Writings on the History of Israel*, 585–606.

[46] In this regard see Wright, *Victory*, 8–9.

of the early church – which, as we shall see, is what much modern critical scholarship from Reimarus to Adolf von Harnack and Johannis Weiss; and now of course, the Jesus Seminar, has endeavoured to do – but when we apprehend him through this particular context. The light that shines forth from Jesus, as it is refracted through this particular lens, offers a more multi-dimensional image than the often rather bland stereotypes that emerge from historical-critical reconstruction of the original Jesus.[47]

In conclusion, everything that has been said so far alerts us to a basic affirmation that the Jesus of the Gospels can only be understood in terms of his own religious, historical and cultural context, and that of the early Church. Jesus was a Jew and those who first sought to understand and interpret his significance did so within the context of Jewish spirituality, imbued as it was with apocalyptic and eschatological expectations. It seems clear, for instance, that the infancy narratives reflect something of the '*anawin* piety' – the piety of the poor – which the Judaism of that time espoused and which expressed a belief that God would intervene for the sake of the poor and oppressed. In a similar vein, the story of the disciples meeting the risen Jesus on the Emmaus road and the confession of Peter at Caesarea Philippi appear to reflect the yearnings for political liberation and justice that typified the Zealot cause. As we shall see, despite the disputes and refutations of NT scholars, the enduring significance of Jesus is that both these traditions can be nurtured and transformed into contemporary christological hopes and expectations.

The early church was soon propelled beyond these particular cultural boundaries into a confrontation with the Greek and Roman worlds. In many ways one of the earliest christological slogans, *Jesu Christos Kyrios* (Jesus Christ is Lord; 1 Cor. 12:3; 8:6) reflects the dual allegiance to Jewish and Greek thought which was to prove so decisive to the missionary success of the first Christians.

The Biblical Story – Discerning the Logic of the Christological Narrative

It is entirely appropriate for New Testament scholars, such as James Dunn and Frank Matera,[48] for instance, to distance themselves from a purely historical analysis of the Gospel traditions, preferring instead a more canonical approach that underscores the pluralism of christologies present in the New Testament (e.g. the Son of God christologies of Matthew, Luke, Acts and the Pauline corpus; the Son of Man and last Adam christologies of Mark and Paul; and the

---

[47] So for instance G. Bornkamm, *Jesus of Nazareth*.
[48] Dunn, *Christology*, and F.J. Matera, *New Testament Christology*. See also R.W. Wall and E.E. Lemcio, *The New Testament as Canon: A Reader in Canonical Criticism*.

Wisdom/*Logos* christologies of Hebrews, John and Revelation). The central issue all such christologies raise is Jesus' relationship to the God whose kingdom he proclaimed. Underlying the pluralism of the New Testament witness to Jesus is the unitary conviction that Jesus stands in a unique relationship to the future God of the kingdom:

> To be sure, the several writings of the New Testament do not present Jesus' relationship to God in the same way, even though most of them identify him as the Son of God. For example, if we only possessed the Synoptic Gospels, it would be difficult to argue that Jesus is the preexistent Son of God. But if we only possessed the Fourth Gospel, we might seriously question Jesus' humanity. Or, if we only possessed the Pauline writings, we would hardly appreciate the earthly life and ministry of Jesus. The genius of the New Testament canon is its ability to hold the diversity and unity of the New Testament in a creative tension that requires each generation to correct and deepen its understanding of Christ.[49]

Is it possible to discern the logic of the christological narrative as it develops in the NT witness to Jesus as the eschatological prophet to Jesus the incarnate Son of God? This was the substance of the thesis advanced some years ago by John Knox.[50]

Knox focused on the question of how the early Church sought to affirm both the humanity and the divinity of Christ as complementary aspects of Jesus' destiny and calling. In so doing, he isolated three distinct yet interrelated patterns of christological reflection that are an essential part of the NT witness to Jesus as the Christ of God.

The first pattern he regarded as the most primitive; it is best described as an adoptionist Christology that takes as its primary reference point the incontrovertible reality of the resurrection. In Acts 2:6, for instance, we read, 'God has made this Jesus, whom you crucified, both Lord and Messiah'. Here the inference seems clear: God exalted the Jesus who was crucified – God's holy servant, an extraordinary human being but nothing more – to a new position of power and messianic status. Such a basically adoptionist form of the Christ story was soon recognised as inadequate. While it may have concurred with the actual experience of Jesus' disciples, who knew and remembered him in the flesh, it did not accord with the recognition, contained already in this passage from Acts, that what happened to Jesus was part of God's divine foreknowledge and plan, and not some unfortunate mistake. This raised the question of Jesus' pre-existence:

> It would have followed ineluctably upon the primitive Church's acknowledgement of Jesus as the Christ that God should have known him as such before the

---

[49] Matera, *Christology*, 255.
[50] J. Knox, *The Humanity and Divinity of Christ*.

foundation of the world. But there is obviously only a short step from the idea of this kind of pre-existence in the mind of God to the conception of a pre-existing hypostasis, a pre-existent being more personal and objective.[51]

Here Knox raises a point that Wolfhart Pannenberg has also emphasised: reflection on the resurrection and post-resurrection status of Christ led almost imperceptibly to an affirmation of the pre-existence of Jesus as the one ordained before the foundation of the world to fulfil the saving purposes of God.

Such retrospective considerations produced the second stage of christological reflection, which is found particularly in the Pauline corpus. Knox referred to this as a *kenosis* (self-emptying) Christology, citing Philippians 2 as his example. The human Jesus is understood to be the result of the self-emptying of a previously divine figure. Knox discerned both of these stages in some of the earliest NT traditions concerning the status of the man Jesus. They were subsequently incorporated into a larger perspective, which Knox labelled incarnationalism.

Kenosis Christology raised a problem that soon began to dominate the christological concerns of the early church. How could a previously divine figure actually become a real human person? One answer was docetism, which Knox believed was implicit in the high Christology of John's Gospel. Jesus' humanity was a disguise or a mere appearance of the real thing; he was a divine person masquerading in human form. Docetism was deemed inadequate by the early church because, to use the formula first adopted by Gregory of Nazianzus, 'that which he did not assume he did not redeem'. Our salvation is only secure if the humanity of Jesus was the same as our own in all respects, except that it was not polluted by sin and egotism.

Knox claimed that incarnationalism (found in various forms in John's Gospel, the Pauline corpus and Hebrews) was a more diverse and variegated form of the Christ story. He concluded, however, that asserting the notion of Christ's pre-existence put an intolerable strain upon the affirmation of the full humanity of Jesus. Consequently, Knox retreated into a functional Christology that simply concentrated on the activity of God in Christ and avoided the apparently intractable issues that he believed incarnationalism bequeathed to the later church. He was, however, able to point, albeit inadequately, to a genuine christological logic that forms an essential part of the NT witness that towards the end of the first century, the person Jesus of Nazareth was, in fact, identified with the pre-existent *Logos* of God.

Pannenberg's answer to the christological issue moves in a similar direction.[52] While he agrees that Christology must begin with the history of Jesus, he

---

[51] Ibid., 10.
[52] W. Pannenberg, *Systematic Theology*, Vol. 2, 282–8.

believes that its primary task, as Knox sought to demonstrate, is to discern the logic or narrative of christological development that is presents in the NT. Adopting a more naunced approach to Knox, Pannenberg explains that this can only be done on the supposition that there is a complementary relationship between the gospel *of* Jesus and the gospel *about* Jesus. In other words, as we shall see in due course, what the originators of the new or second quest for the historical Jesus set out to demonstrate – namely, that there is an inner consistency between the proclamation of Jesus and the primitive Christian confession that Jesus is the *Christos* and *Kyrios*, – is implicit in the NT itself:

> We can develop such a theory only if we assume that the christological confessional statements of primitive Christianity may be understood as an explication of the content and meaning implicit in the appearance and history of Jesus.[53]

Crucial to this correspondence between Jesus' message and the *kerygma* of the early church was the historical event of the resurrection, an event to which all the NT writings give prominence.[54]

> Only by his resurrection from the dead did the Crucified attain to the dignity of the *Kyrios* (Phil. 2:9–11). Only thus was he appointed the Son of God in power (Rom. 1:4). Only in the light of the resurrection is he the pre-existent Son. Only as the risen Lord is he always the living Lord of his community.[55]

It is the resurrection that establishes the reality of the divine action of God in the person of Jesus; it affirms the unity of the person of Jesus with the God whose kingdom he proclaimed and inaugurated; it identifies Jesus with God's eschatological saving will and purpose for the whole cosmos; it makes it possible for Christology to move from below to above and affirm that he who is now one with God was always so. For Pannenberg, the resurrection also makes it possible to demonstrate that both Christology from above and below tend to dissolve into one another because both imply the other.[56]

---

[53] Ibid, 283.

[54] Dunn, *Christology*, 254.

[55] Ibid.

[56] Christology from above begins with the pre-existent divine Son and his relationship to God; it ascertains the basis of the Son's relationship to creation and his incarnation in terms of this primary relationship. In the second century, *Logos* Christology emerged as a way of describing how God both created the world and redeemed it through the same agency. This inevitably entailed that the history of the man Jesus was understood in terms of the earthly realisation of the mission of the divine *Logos* or pre-existent Son. The main criticism of the 'from above' approach to Christology is that it assumes what Christology must substantiate, i.e. the divinity of Jesus. It also

The centrality of the resurrection to christological theory has often been overlooked in the past, but both Jürgen Moltmann and Pannenberg have put it firmly at the centre of their respective christologies. This is an interesting similarity given their divergent approaches to the christological question. It would seem that any Christology worthy of the name must look to the resurrection as the crucial event in Jesus' career because it facilitates the link between Jesus the prophet of the kingdom to Jesus the mediator of the kingdom and Lord of all.[57]

The Church's Story – The Continuity of the Incarnational Narrative

In a recent book that has been largely ignored by the world of biblical scholarship, C. Stephen Evans argues for the historical veracity and philosophical cogency of the church's story:

> [It] is an account of how the divine Word took on human flesh was born as a baby, lived a life characterized by miraculous healing and authoritative teaching, died a cruel and voluntary death for the sake of redeeming sinful humans, was raised by God to life, and now abides with God, awaiting the time of his glorious return and ultimate triumph. So much at least seems common ground among orthodox Christians, be they Catholic, Orthodox, or Protestant.[58]

In seeking to debunk the epistemological distinction between the Jesus of history and the Christ of faith, Evans directs our attention to a crucial issue: is our only access to Jesus via historical-critical research? History separates us from

---

[56] (*continued*) tends to overlook the historical particularity of the man Jesus, his relationship to the God whose kingdom he proclaimed and his setting within the Judaism of his time.

The phrase Christology 'from below to above' was first coined by Albrecht Ritschl in the nineteenth century. He developed this approach in opposition to the speculative Christology of G.W.F. Hegel and F.W.J. Schelling. Ritschl put the historical Jesus at the centre of christological concerns. The problem emerges, however, which aspect of Jesus' life and ministry do we take as the basis of such christological statements? Jesus' self-understanding in relation to the kingdom of God (Ritschl); the preached *kerygma* about Jesus (R. Bultmann, for whom interest in the historical Jesus was of no real theological value), Jesus' authority in relation to the past traditions of Israel (P. Althaus), or both Jesus' proclamation and his praxis of the coming kingdom of God (E. Schillebeeckx)?

[57] Dunn, *Christology*, 267.

[58] C.S. Evans, *The Historical Christ and the Jesus of Faith: The Incarnational Narrative as History*, 5.

those who knew him 'after the flesh', so how do we encounter Jesus today? What role should we allow to the church as both custodian and mediator to successive generations of the basic incarnational narrative concerning the coming of the Son of God in human flesh?

These issues lie at the heart of christological concerns and they help us to distinguish two quite distinctive approaches to Christology: one concentrates on the experience of the present and the other relies on the testimony of the past. One of the earliest christological confessions, 'Jesus Christ our Lord' articulates this distinction because it 'designates, not primarily an historical individual in the past, nor yet a character in a symbolic story, but a present reality actually experienced within the common life'.[59] Moltmann describes these two approaches to the issue as the difference between 'therapeutic Christology' and 'apologetic Christology'[60] (because of the pejorative connotations often associated with the word apologetic, we prefer the term theoretical Christology). Clearly, both approaches are not mutually exclusive, but they do reflect a difference in emphasis that is still crucial to how christological enquiry is conducted and approached.

Therapeutic Christology

By deciding to opt for a therapeutic or practical Christology, Moltmann stands in the tradition of those who claim that we come to acknowledge the divinity of Jesus through the reality of the salvation he alone can offer. Phillip Melanchthon astutely summarised this position when he claimed, 'We only know Christ through his benefits' (*Christum cognoscere, eius beneficia cognoscere*).[61] Moltmann puts it in his own inimical fashion: 'Therapeutic Christology is soteriological Christology. It confronts the misery of the present with the salvation Christ brings, presenting it as a salvation that heals.'[62] This statement is based on two fundamental presuppositions. First, the person and the work of Christ, or Christology and soteriology, cannot be separated either theoretically or practically. The question whether or not Christology must precede soteriology, which is the arrangement we will follow, is a real one. In other words, must we first establish a credible basis to acknowledge and assert the divinity of the Saviour, before the offer of salvation can become one that is universally applicable to the human condition? While this may be theoretically

---

[59] Knox, *Humanity and Divinity*, 3. To a certain extent, the NT expressions 'according to the flesh' (*kata sarxa*) and 'according to the Spirit' (*kata pneuma*) (cf. 1 Tim. 3:16; 1 Pet. 3:18) express the same distinction.

[60] J. Moltmann, *The Way of Jesus Christ: Christology in Messianic Dimensions*, 44.

[61] Melanchthon, *Loci Communes Theologici*, 7.

[62] Moltmann, *Way*, 44.

the case, the point that Moltmann makes is that the person of Christ and the salvation he proclaims is only meaningful if it addresses the concrete wretchedness and situatedness of people in today's world. This constitutes, as Dietrich Bonhoeffer recognised, the pro me or *pro nobis* (for us) structure of christological confession. It could well be the case that we only know Jesus as Lord and Saviour because the reality of his saving grace and love actually changes concrete situations in human life and community. 'A Christology which does not put at the beginning of the statement, 'God is only God *pro me*, Christ is only Christ *pro me*, condemns itself'.[63] Secondly, this does not mean we can restrict the salvation and liberation Christ offers to the religious sphere. We cannot claim that we only know Jesus as the Christ through the individual awareness of the forgiveness of sins, or through participation in the eucharistic life and witness of the church, where the real presence of Christ is still to be experienced.

While this is obviously true in terms of our Christian experience and heritage, we cannot restrict christological reflection to the domain of the individual Christian or the church. For Moltmann, this is to condone the corruption of religion that has taken place as a product of the Enlightenment:

> In a society which has declared 'religion' to be 'a private affair', the salvation Christ offers can be presented as the private salvation of the individual soul if, and only if, Christianity assents to this confining of the religious question to 'the human heart', emancipated from social ties. But then the economic, social and political sins of human beings which have led to this personal isolation and spiritual loneliness are left without liberating criticism and without the saving hope of the gospel.[64]

The kind of Christology that Moltmann seeks to espouse[65] has laudable antecedents in the Eastern and Western traditions of Christian thought and practice. It is to claim that we know Jesus primarily not through our own religious experience or through membership of the Church, important as both these may well be, but through a life which is conformed to his search for righteousness and infused with his love and compassion for his fellow human beings ('christopraxis'). We only really know the Messiah when we are committed to, and immersed in, his Messianic mission to the world. This entails that we recognise that Christology is eschatologically determined. The mission of the Messiah to reconcile, restore and redeem is still underway. There is an inevitable eschatological proviso to all our Christology. No christological confession can finally grasp the full significance of Jesus because

---

[63] D. Bonhoeffer, *Lectures on Christology*, 48.
[64] Moltmann, *Way*, 54.
[65] See chapter 11 for a fuller discussion of Moltmann's Christology.

his own history of engagement with the world is not yet finished. He is, as the title of Moltmann's book implies, still 'on the way' toward the full realisation of his reign in the affairs of the world. Not surprisingly, this also implies that every Christology is contextualised. We join him on the way in the context of one particular episode of history and we seek to interpret him to our contemporaries as the one who still heals our diseases and infirmities.

The question of how Jesus as Lord and Saviour relates to our human predicaments and dilemmas both personal and social has, as we shall see, been interpreted differently in the history of christological debate and also appears in different cultural guises. Nevertheless, theologians as diverse as Friedrich Schleiermacher, Rudolf Bultmann, Paul Tillich and Schillebeeckx all viewed the concrete experience of salvation – the saving grace which brings a new wholeness, meaning and integrity to human existence – as the way in which the unique status of Christ as both the divine Son and the new Adam could be affirmed and acknowledged.

Theoretical Christology

Theoretical Christology seeks to provide an adequate *apologia*, or intellectual foundation, to the belief in Jesus as the divine Son of God and Saviour of the world. Those who take this particular route would claim that we cannot do this task properly by appealing to, or basing our defence of Christology on, our present experience of salvation, however it is understood. While many who are committed to christopraxis might not want to go as far as Tillich and assert that 'Christology is a function of soteriology', therapeutic Christology, it is claimed, always runs the risk of degenerating into wish-fulfilment. Is there any guarantee that we have not projected onto the historical figure of Jesus human desires for liberation and meaning, which, as we have already acknowledged, inevitably take different cultural shape and form?

This is the substance of Pannenberg's critique of all forms of Christology that take as their starting point some aspect of the soteriological concern.[66] Pannenberg claims that to safeguard against such a possibility of projection, we must locate the saving significance of Jesus in the biblical and doctrinal record to him as the one who reconciles and redeems. While our sympathies will remain with Pannenberg in terms of the two divergent approaches to Christology, it is sufficient to note at this point that it is the continuity of the incarnational narrative that unites both approaches, because the church embodies this story and offers it to the world as the eternal word of life.

---

[66] W. Pannenberg, *Jesus–God and Man*, 39–49.

The Cultural Story – Discerning Another Important Lens of Interpretation

In a fascinating and illuminating study, Jaroslav Pelikan develops a number of distinctive and evocative images or cameos portraying Jesus' place in the history of human culture.[67] He discusses the correspondences and analogies that one finds between the figure of Jesus and the domain of high culture. We will draw upon his considerable insights in a number of ways. At this stage, however, it is important to note how Pelikan demonstrates that each age constructs an image of Jesus out of the cultural hopes, aspirations, biblical and doctrinal interfaces that both make Jesus accessible and simultaneously illustrate something of the genius of the particular age in question. This is because 'For each age, the life and teachings of Jesus represented an answer (or, more often, *the* answer) to the most fundamental questions of human existence and of human destiny'.[68] Tillich articulated a similar point when he contended that every age embodies in cultural and religious form the many ways in which human beings express 'a state of being grasped by an ultimate concern, a concern which qualifies all other concerns as preliminary, and which itself contains the answer to the problem of the meaning of life'.[69]

Common culture

The study and investigation of human culture is a relatively recent arrival on the intellectual scene. It emerged as a major feature of German Romanticism and came to be understood as: 'a shared spiritual force that is manifest in all the customs, beliefs and practices of a people. Culture, they held, shapes language, art, religion and history, and leaves its stamp on the smallest event.'[70]

Similar approaches and definitional stances can be seen in more recent studies concerning the relationship between religious faith and culture. So, for instance, Aidan Nichols comments:

> A culture is … a system of inherited conceptions (intellectual), a set of common standards of behaviour (morals), a pattern of meanings embodied in symbols (material), and a series of conventions governing human interaction (institutional), by which human beings communicate and perpetuate, but also modify and develop, their knowledge about attitudes to life.[71]

---

[67] J. Pelikan, *Jesus through the Centuries: His Place in the History of Culture*.

[68] Ibid, 2.

[69] P. Tillich, *Christianity and the Encounter of the World Religions*, 4.

[70] R. Scruton, *An Intelligent Person's Guide to Modern Culture*, 1.

[71] A. Nichols, *Christendom Awake*.

This notion of common culture was later taken over by anthropologists in the their investigation of different tribes and societies.[72]

High culture

The Romantics unearthed an alternative viewpoint. For many, culture referred to what we would term high culture, the primary forms of which are art, music and literature. On the other hand, Immanuel Kant's threefold distinction of transcendentals into truth, goodness and beauty corresponded epistemologically to science, ethics and art. Utilising this concept, Matthew Arnold defined culture as 'the pursuit of perfection', which required 'an inward condition of the mind and spirit'.[73] Even to this day, high culture is often understood as the domain of the elite, those who involve themselves in the pursuit of intellectual and aesthetic attainment. As we shall see, since the Enlightenment theology has often been confined to this rarefied domain.

Popular culture

In modern times, particularly with the advent of the human sciences, culture has come to refer mainly to that which we designate as popular culture. For the contemporary sociologist, or exponent of cultural studies, popular culture often provides a mass marketed strategic and fluid identity – a sense of belonging if you wish – for the great mass of ordinary people often in the face of oppression or social exclusion. In the mind of the exponent of popular culture any artefact, system of values, political ideology or media-induced reality are all the simulacra of particular cultural aspirations and beliefs which are there to be deconstructed and analysed at will.

It is Roger Scruton's fascinating contention that all three forms of culture find their unity and common basis in religion. This is similar in some ways to Tillich's understanding. Common culture, expressed and articulated in a common language, values and beliefs, adheres in common religion. The social, moral and political function of all religion is to offer and sustain an ethical view of human life and destiny:

> The ethical vision endows human matter with a personal form, and therefore lifts us above nature, to set us side by side with our judge. If we are judged then we must be free, and answerable for our actions. The free being is not just an organism: he has a life of his own, which is uniquely his and which he creates through his choices. Hence he stands above nature in the very activities which reveal him to be a part of it.

---

[72] Cf. K. Tanner, *Theories of Culture: A New Agenda For Theology*, 25–38.
[73] Cf. M.P. Gallagher, *Clashing Symbols: An Introduction to Faith & Culture*, 11.

He is not a creature of the moment, but on the contrary a creature extended through time and compromised forever by his actions. You are answerable now for the deeds of yesterday and accountable tomorrow for the deeds of today.[74]

Pelikan also acknowledges that Christology continually informs and sanctions such an ethical vision of human nature and destiny, even though that ethical vision will take different cultural forms. The difficulty with Scruton's conclusions is that they come perilously close to that reduction of religion to ethics and morality which has been characteristic of all those theologians who deduce their philosophical presuppositions from Kant. Scruton's eventual conclusion that the only way to rescue the ethical vision from extinction in a postmodern world is to live against the grain in Confucian like Stoicism and restraint would bear this out.

Christ and culture

Perhaps the classical study in the modern period of the relationship between Christianity and culture was Niebuhr's *Christ and Culture*. Niebuhr defined culture as the,

> 'artificial, secondary environment' which man superimposes on the natural. It comprises language, habits, ideas, beliefs, customs, social organisation, inherited artefacts, technical processes and values. This 'social heritage', this 'sui generis', which the New Testament writers frequently had in mind when they spoke of 'the world', which is represented in many forms but to which Christians like other men are inevitably subject, is what we mean when we speak of culture.[75]

Niebuhr's synopsis is but another attempt to define common culture. He understands the essential significance of culture as the attempt to develop, nurture and sustain human values.[76] Consequently, culture relates to 'the conservation of values', although Niebuhr did recognise that such values were relative to different cultural forms and hence were inevitably disparate, pluriform and at times mutually contradictory.[77] The difficulty here is that the reduction of the culture issue to the problem of competing values effectively surrenders a christological approach to culture to that of ethics.

Niebuhr is remembered more for the typology he articulates in terms of how the relationship between Christ and culture can be expressed – namely, Christ against culture, the Christ of culture, Christ above culture, Christ

---

[74] Scruton, *Guide*, 11.

[75] H.R. Niebuhr, *Christ and Culture*, 46.

[76] Ibid., 50.

[77] Ibid., 52.

and culture in paradox, and Christ the transformer of culture.[78] However, Niebuhr's typology has a tendency to pit Christ and culture over and against each other as 'two complex realities', whereas we wish to argue for the inevitable interaction and interdependence of both realities within a more comprehensive hermeneutical and intellectual framework.[79]

The emphases and importance we allow for successive cultural contexts aligns our analysis with George Lindbeck's cultural-linguistic model of doctrinal and religious formulation:

> A religion can be viewed as a kind of cultural and /or linguistic framework or medium that shapes the entirety of life and thought ... It is not primarily an array of beliefs about the true and the good (although it may involve these), or a symbolism expressive of basic attitudes, feelings or sentiments (though these will be generated). Rather, it is similar to an idiom that makes possible the description of realities, the formulation of beliefs, and the experiencing of inner attitudes, feelings and sentiments. Like a culture or language, it is a communal phenomenon that shapes the subjectivities of individuals rather than being primarily a manifestation of those subjectivities.[80]

While we would agree with Lindbeck's emphasis on the cultural embeddedness of doctrinal discourse and language, we would not agree that christological statements or beliefs are reducible to this context alone. There is always the question of how such christological language was acquired or

---

[78] Niebuhr's classification has rightly been applauded for its comprehensiveness and scope, nevertheless, it is our contention that the problem with this analysis, at least as far as Western culture is concerned, is that historically there have really only been three mainstream manifestations of the relationship between Christ and culture: (1) the apostolic model, which approximates to Niebuhr's Christ against culture; (2) the Christendom model, which obviously moves close to Niebuhr's second type, i.e. the identification of Christ and culture; (3) the pluralist model, which is unfortunately the capitulation of Christ to culture. Niebuhr is aware of this capitulation, but he handles it with notable equivocation when he assesses Ritschl; ibid., 100–22. We would also argue for a new model – the critical interaction of Christ and culture; this is similar to, but critical of, Niebuhr's Christ the transformer of culture type. This new model includes the postmodern experience of fragmentation and multiculturalism, which Niebuhr's study could not address. Cf. C.J.D. Greene, 'Consumerism and the Spirit of the Age', in C. Bartholomew & T. Moritz (eds), *Christ and Consumerism*, 13–33.

[79] Cf. C. Schwobel, 'Once Again, Christ and Culture: Remarks on the Christological Bases of a Theology of Culture', in C. Gunton (ed.), *Trinity, Time, And Church: A Response to the Theology of Robert W. Jenson*, 103–26.

[80] G.A. Lindbeck, *The Nature of Doctrine: Religion and Theology in a Post-Liberal Age*, 33. See also A.E. McGrath, *The Genesis of Doctrine: A Study in the Foundation of Doctrinal Criticism*.

learned. In that sense, the 'grammar of assent', to use Cardinal Newman's phrase, is a more polymorphous form of discourse than Lindbeck's analysis allows: 'Theology forever remains a fallible, unfinished, and constructive task and not simply the reassertion of a single cultural-linguistic system'.[81] In other words, there is always the reality of that conversation or mutual interaction of the Jesus story, the critics' story, the biblical story, the church's story and the cultural story that continually witnesses to the enduring power of this particular religious narrative. We might wish to assent to the epistemological priority of the biblical witness to the risen Jesus, but it is often the cultural story that is allowed to predominate, and this raises another concern.

The perennial problem: cultural accommodation or isolation?

A full-blown theology of culture is an exercise yet to be successfully explicated in Christian theology and we will not be attempting this enormous task here.[82] However, we will be addressing that crucial issue by observing and, at times, radically disagreeing with how successive theologian's tackle this question, especially if they do so from a normative christological perspective. At this juncture, however, we can say that Lindbeck's analysis alerts us to that pressing and at times vexing dilemma we will encounter constantly in our explorations: the attempt to tread a fine line between cultural accommodation and cultural insensitivity. There can never be any guarantee of success in this endeavour; it is always something of a delicate balancing act.[83] It may come as a surprise to those who invoke the standard interpretation of the theological orientation of Karl Barth, but he stood in the same tradition when he contended that the changing contours of our historical and cultural contexts demanded that theological reflection continually begin afresh.

It is our conviction that we are presently immersed in a vast cultural transition. This study represents an attempt to seek to learn from the successes and the failures of the past, so as to equip us for the inevitable pilgrimage of theological reconstruction that awaits us in the future. To commence such a

---

[81] W.S. Johnson, *The Mystery of God: Karl Barth and the Postmodern Foundations of Theology*, 35.

[82] For just a hint of what such endeavours might involve, see R.W. Jenson, *Essays in Theology and Culture*.

[83] The dilemma is not new. The Apostle Paul recognised both dangers in his letters to the Corinthian church where he described the uncompromising message of the crucified Christ as a stumbling block to the Jews and foolishness to Gentiles (1 Cor. 1:23). Nevertheless, he upheld the essential *Logos* or truth of the Christian faith to those who would forsake the dialogue with culture altogether. See C.J.D. Greene, 'Is the Message of the Cross Good News for the Twentieth Century?', in J. Goldingay (ed.), *Atonement Today*, 222–39.

journey is not only to rejoice in the community of the saints, it is to be continually amazed and grateful for the theological versatility and perspicacity of
one's former and contemporary companions along the way.

We contend that in the history of Christology there have been three main
christological trajectories that continually witness to the fertile debate between
the biblical horizons of faith and belief, the christological tradition and successive historical and cultural contexts. In what follows we will examine the
cosmological and political Christology of the patristic and Byzantine era,
which occupied the minds and souls of theologians from at least the second to
the twelfth centuries of Christian faith and devotion. Both are examples of
Christology from above and they not only changed the way theology was
understood and practised, but simultaneously transformed the cultural contexts
in which they were situated. We will then investigate an alternative approach,
one which has been called anthropological Christology,[84] a branch which grew
out of the same stem of orthodox Christology but which came to its full
flowering in the Medieval and Reformation periods. At the same time, we will
take particular note of the critical reduction of scale of this form of Christology
which not only guaranteed its survival into the modern era but also bore major
consequences for that continual dialogue between culture and theology to
which Hans Küng refers:

> Whoever (as often still happens) sees in the development of the modern conception
> of Christ since the Enlightenment mere apostasy not only undervalues the fertile
> impulses that emerged here, but also fails to appreciate the many flashbacks that are
> made to the representations of Christ from earlier ages.[85]

The flashbacks to which Küng refers alert us to the 'fertile impulses' of
christological reflection that preceded the Enlightenment and postmodernity.
They also underline the importance of the cultural perspectives we will explore
in this study, because they are fundamental and crucial stages of transition in the
history of christological deliberation.

We will endeavour to build our case accumulatively. In some chapters we
will encounter specific issues and concerns that will demand a fuller analysis
and exploration at a later stage in our journey. Similarly, we will arrive at our
conclusions and perspectives from detailed investigation of the christological
perspectives and reflections of particular theologians. The latter are not chosen
at random, but are viewed as important representatives of particular cultural
paradigms that have dominated christological reconstruction particularly in the
modern era. Consequently, such strategic thinkers take their place as worthy

---

[84] Cf. Moltmann, *Way*, and Kasper, *Jesus*.
[85] H. Küng, *The Incarnation of God*, 19.

representatives in the history of that engaging, enriching and potentially dangerous dialogue between Scripture, theological and christological interpretation, and culture; a dialogue that continually rescues the person of Christ from the emasculation and obstification of Christian propaganda and control. Perhaps then all that is required at this stage is to remind ourselves that it is the eschatological dimensions of the Christian faith that inject an inevitable provisionality into all of the historical and cultural perspectives that continually influence Christology, simply because we are rather forcibly reminded of the ontological priority of the future.[86] In that sense, as Moltmann contends, we join the risen Christ on the way to the full realisation of his kingdom and we wait to see what further wisdom each succeeding epoch brings to our endeavours.

---

[86] Pannenberg, *Jesus—God and Man*, 53–108.

2.

Three Christological Trajectories

By the fourth century it had become evident that of all the various "titles of majesty for Christ" adapted and adopted during the first generations after Jesus, none was to have more momentous consequences than the title *Logos*, consequences as momentous for the history of thought as were those of the title King for the history of politics.[1]

Introduction

In his search for a new christological paradigm that more readily befits the exigencies of the contemporary era, Jürgen Moltmann reviews the two models which he thinks have dominated the history of Christology – the cosmological and the anthropological. Earlier, Walter Kasper had identified the same basic schema with the addition of a third contender – Christology within the perspective of universal history.[2] Although Kasper was right to identify three dominant christological perspectives, he attached too much importance to the third. It is our contention that while successive theologians have often identified the fundamental legacy to the Christian faith of both cosmological and anthropological Christology, they have equally frequently undervalued the importance of the political Christology that surfaced early in the fourth and fifth centuries. In this chapter we will endeavour to explore the development and impact of the cosmological, political and anthropological christological trajectories, whilst recognising that they represent diverse yet complementary ways of explaining the central Christian belief that Jesus of Nazareth was 'Son of God, begotten before all ages, sent from heaven to become flesh in or as the son of Mary'.[3] In other words, they are all expressions of the basic continuity that underlies the incarnational narrative.

---

[1] Pelikan, *Centuries*, 58.

[2] The main advocates of this third position he claimed were G.W. Hegel and Pannenberg. See, Kasper, *Jesus*, 17–20.

[3] Dunn, *Christology*, 251.

Part 1

Cosmological Christology: Jesus the Eternal Logos

We begin with an examination of the reasons why the concept of the *Logos* began to dominate christological concerns from the time of the early apologists. Our primary concern is not to rehearse the christological debates that took place in the fourth and fifth centuries, engrossed as they were by the *Logos–sarx* (word–flesh) or *Logos–anthropos* (word–man) alternatives. Instead, we will examine the intellectual and philosophical antecedents that produced this form of Christology from above.

The Cosmological Worldview

From the second century onwards, the burgeoning Christian church was still a minority religion in the Roman Empire.[4] As it spread throughout the Gentile world, Christianity faced the new cultural and intellectual challenge of an alternative *weltanschauung* (worldview). The Jewish/Christian worldview, with its salvation–historical schema, emphasised the eschatological difference between the present age and the age to come. The Gentile worldview, on the other hand, was dominated by 'an instinct for cosmology' that made an ontological distinction between the immutable, eternal world of the divine and the changing, transient world of humanity.[5]

Philosophical enquiry and speculation were rife in the Greek academy. A more educated population was already forsaking the old pagan polytheistic religions in favour of a more credible and nuanced view of the world; one that leaned towards what we would refer to nowadays as a unified field theory of knowledge (the attempt to find an underlying unity and purpose to everything that exists). This cosmocentric world was the product of a number of philosophical and religious influences – Platonism, Stoicism, Neo-Platonism, Gnosticism and the Hellenistic Judaism of Philo of Alexandria. These tended

---

[4] Until the third century the most widespread religion was the cult of Mithras, a sun cult derived from the Indo-Iranian sphere, which was compatible with the emperor cult, but not Hellenism.

[5] Moltmann notes: 'Compared with the modern world, the world of antiquity may be described as cosmocentric. Human beings saw themselves and their civilisation as embedded in the orders of the cosmos which wrapped them round'; cf. *Way*, 46.

to coalesce into a vision of reality that viewed the cosmos in terms of a graded ontological scale of being:

> When he compares himself with the gods, the human being perceives the funda-mental ontological difference between divine and earthly being: the divine being is eternal, one, infinite, immutable, immortal, impassable, and exists of itself; whereas what is human, like all earthly being, is temporal, manifold, finite, changeable, capable of suffering, mortal, and exists not of itself but out of something different from itself.[6]

The fundamental difference between the transcendent world of the eternal and the finite world of humanity would easily have degenerated into an ontological chasm if it were not for some principle of unity that held both worlds together. This cosmological link was the *Logos* (Word), a term signifying that which gave shape, reason, structure and purpose to the universe.

As the church expanded, Christology began to make a distinctive contribu-tion to the Gentile *weltanschauung* it inherited. Not surprisingly, the move from a predominantly Jewish, historical and eschatological way of thinking to a Greek mindset – put simply, the replacement of one dualism by another – had major consequences for Christology. As David Bosch notes:

> The "low" Christology of early Jewish Christians, who had put a high premium on the historical Jesus, gave way to Hellenistic Christianity's preoccupation with the exalted Christ, who became identified with the timeless Logos, an approach which led to a radical spiritualization of the Christ event. The interest shifted from eschatology to protology, to Christ's eternal pre-existence, his relation to God the Father, and the nature of his incarnation. It became more important to know *whence* Christ came than *why*.[7]

It would be wrong, however, to suggest that the early Christian apologists, and the theologians who were to build on their creative endeavours, simply borrowed the concept of the *Logos* from the philosophers. The prologue to John's Gospel already referred to the creative, revelatory *Logos* who was there with God in the beginning; hence the notion of the *Logos* as the second God which began to appear in the writings of some of the apologists.[8] Similarly, the Pauline epistles spoke of the cosmic Christ and his mediatorial role in creation (e.g. 1 Cor. 8:6).

Nowhere are the cosmic dimensions of Christology stated more unequiv-ocally than in the christological hymn of Colossians 1:15–20. Here we find the

---

[6] Ibid, 46–7.
[7] D.J. Bosch, *Transforming Mission: Paradigm Shifts in Theology of Mission*, 197.
[8] For instance Justin Martyr and Origen.

Christ who is both *pantocrator*, the first born over all creation, the one through whom all things were made; and the one who is the first born from among the dead, the eschatological fulfilment of the created order. The beginning and the end, *alpha* and *omega*, are his domain because in him is found all the fullness of God (cf. Heb. 1:1–3). The cosmic Christ easily became identified with the personified Wisdom of the Old Testament who was also there with God before all things (Prov. 8). Thus, as Moltmann remarks and as the New Testament scholar Ben Witherington has sought to argue, 'Logos Christology is originally Wisdom Christology, and is as such cosmic Christology'.[9]

The relationship between the *regula fidei* (the rule of true faith) and the worldview of a particular culture is one that is complex and fraught with potential dangers. The theologians of the first five centuries show us that between the extremes of hostile repudiation and *laissez-faire* accommodation lies the route of continual dialogue and immense intellectual endeavour. Their corporate endeavours began to break apart some of the limitations of the philosophical system they inherited. As Jaroslav Pelikan notes:

> the identification of Jesus as Logos also made intellectual, philosophical and scientific history. For by applying this title to Jesus, the Christian philosophers of the fourth and fifth centuries who were trying to give account of who he was and what he had done were enabled to interpret him as the divine clue to the structure of reality (metaphysics) and, within metaphysics, to the riddle of being (ontology) — in a word, as the Cosmic Christ.[10]

The *Logos* as the Divine Word

The Word active in revelation

It is possible to trace the route whereby the concept of the *Logos* operated simultaneously as an apologetic, epistemological, philosophical and soteriological principle of unity between God and the world. To begin with, second-century Greek apologists such as Justin Martyr, Tatian and Aristides tended to present the Christian faith as the fulfilment of the search for truth upon which both Jew and pagan had embarked.[11]

Both Judaism and paganism valued tradition highly. As a consequence, any religion that purported to be new could not be true. For Justin, the solution to this dilemma was the identification of Christ with the *Logos*. The latter was not

---

[9] Moltmann, *Way*, 282; cf also Witherington, *Christology*.

[10] Pelikan, *Centuries*, 58.

[11] Cf. B. Studer, *Trinity and Incarnation: The Faith of the Early Church*, 45.

understood as solely the mediator of creation (cf. Athenagoras and Tatian), but as God's spoken word, a revelatory principle of education through whom God had spoken to both Jew and pagan (Moses and Socrates) before the coming of Christ into the world. The apologetic motive is clearly discernible:

> We are taught that Christ is the first-born of God, and we have shown above that He is the reason (Word) of whom the whole human race partake, and those who live according to reason are Christians, even though they are accounted atheists. Such were Socrates and Heraclitus among the Greeks, and those like them.[12]

This affirmed the accessibility of God's revelation to all people or their participation in the *Logos* before the coming of Christ. The divine *Logos* sows seeds throughout human history. Consequently, the seed-bearing logos (*Logos spermatikos*) is known, albeit only partially and inadequately, in pagan and Jewish religion. This, in turn, guarantees the universality of God's revelation in Christ, because we find the fulfilment of all God's dealings with humankind, both before and since, in the Word made flesh.[13]

The Word active in creation

The opening words of the prologue to John's Gospel (Jn. 1:1) are a conscious re-echoing of the first verses of Genesis. In the beginning God spoke and the world was brought into being (Jn. 1:3). This automatically links the Word, or *Logos*, ontologically with both the creator and the creation. The Platonists, middle-Platonists (such as Philo of Alexandria), and the early Christian apologists shared this much in common. However, the former adhered unswervingly to a doctrine of the inaccessibility and impassability of God.[14] The distinction between God and the world was preserved by the use of a hierarchical or graded scale of being. The eternal forms, of which the *Logos* is one, were derivatives of God, through which all that was came into being. This model firmly tied the ontological link between the *Logos* and the created world, and raised potentially disastrous consequences for the Christology of the early apologists.

Justin, Irenaeus and Origen
Justin consciously tried to tread a middle road between the monotheism of the Monarchians and the affirmation of the divinity of Christ. His solution was to

---

[12] Justin c.150:I.xlvi. 1–4.

[13] The idea that the *Logos* is the self-manifestation of God found in other religions and in the philosophical quest for truth has been prominent this century in the apologetic theology of Tillich.

[14] Cf. J. Pelikan, *The Christian Tradition: A History of the Development of Doctrine*, Vol. 1, 230–2.

view the *Logos* as something between the pure divinity of God and the non-divinity of the creation. Such a hierarchical ontology automatically ensured that the *Logos* was an intermediary between God and the world. Thus, the mediatorial *Logos*, who became incarnate, could not actually be conceived as God present in person (a view that took Justin perilously close to the Gnostics who would not countenance a God actively involved in the created order).

The natural heir of the teaching of Justin was Irenaeus, Bishop of Lyons and native of Smyrna. He was not at ease with the notion of the mediatorial *Logos*, because it appeared to cut God adrift from the world and introduced an intractable dualism into the being of God. Irenaeus replaced the notion of the go-between Son with the principle that it is the actual incarnation that creates the mediation between God and the creation. He contended, against Gnosticism, that God takes a real 'hand' in the affairs of the world, through his Son, because the divine Son takes on, or assumes, our humanity:

> It was necessary that "the mediator between God and human beings" [1 Tim. 2:5], through his sharing in the life of both, bring the two together in friendship and harmony and bring it about both that humanity is made over to God and that God is made over to human beings.[15]

For Irenaeus, Word and Spirit (the 'two hands of God') were always active in the history of salvation; and they find their culmination in the event of the Word becoming flesh.

Some relief for the inherent tensions in this schema arrived with the philosophical theology of Origen of Alexandria, the illustrious pupil of Clement of Rome. With Origen we move beyond apologetics to a full-blown systematic theology that attempted to build a metaphysics that could unite the middle-Platonism of his native city of learning with the Christ attested to by Scripture.[16]

In Origen's thought the *Logos* is, for the first time, clearly delineated as the Wisdom, or Word of God who is eternally begotten. There never was a time when the *Logos* did not exist. In this way, Origen connects with the theme of the pre-existence of Christ, which permeates John, the Pauline corpus and Hebrews. The Word or Wisdom is the complete expression of the unseen God. He is both 'of one being' (*homoousious*) with God and also a separate *hypostasis* ('a second God'). He is God in another form of being, the Son, who is united with the *arche*, the divine source of being, and yet because he is begotten, is subordinate to God the Father. The Holy Spirit proceeds from the

---

[15] Irenaeus, *Against Heresies*, Book III, quoted in R.A. Norris, *The Christological Controversy*, 54.

[16] Küng, *Great Christian Thinkers*, 48.

Son and so is a third *hypostasis*, again subordinate to the Son. So, at the same time as Tertullian, in the West, deployed the language of God existing in three persons (*personae*), Origen spoke of the one God who is nevertheless three *hypostases*.

But how does the incarnation actually occur? Through the agency of the *Logos* God brings into being an immaterial cosmos of rational spirits, the *logikoi*. Set on the loving contemplation of God through his Wisdom and yet in possession of freedom, finitude and changeability, these spirits fall away from God. In his providence, God creates for them an ordered world of materiality, not as Wilhelm Leibnitz later claimed, the best of all possible worlds, but a lower second-order world designed as the process of God's pedagogy with human beings whereby they can return to their divine origin.[17] The *Logos* accomplishes this return or redemption because there was one rational spirit who did not fall away from the freedom to love God in obedience and adoration, the soul of Jesus. The unfallen soul is united with the eternal image of God, the *Logos*. Both the disclosure of this pure rational spirit to the world of fallen humanity and the means of redemption of all the fallen spirits takes place when this *Logos*, already united with the soul of Jesus, becomes incarnate in a human body, a body which can itself be transfigured by the glory that resides in it:

> [The] soul ... a rational substance ... [was] receptive of God ... it had already entered into God in God's character as *Logos* and Wisdom and complete truth. Consequently, in view of the fact that it existed totally in God's Son, or else received God's Son wholly into itself, that very soul, together with the flesh which it had assumed, is correctly called Son of God and Power of God, Christ, and Wisdom of God.[18]

In the assent of the rational soul from bondage to freedom, Origen can envision a process of redemption that eventuates in the 'restoration of all things' (*apokatastasis ton panton*).[19]

The speculative nature of Origen's Christology is both impressive and deceptive. It is impressive because here both theology and mysticism are united through the twin notions of divine indwelling and the soul's ascent to God.[20] It is deceptive because Origen's Christology does not have a clear conception of

---

[17] Norris, *Controversy*, 14–17.

[18] Origen, *On First Principles*, Book II; quoted in Norris, *Controversy*, 76.

[19] This solution to theodicy, with its implicit universalism, probably prompted the disfavour of Demetrius, the bishop of Alexandria, and the later denunciation of Origen as a heretic.

[20] Cf. A. Grillmeir, *Christ in Christian Tradition*, Vol. 1, 141. It was this form of mystical theology that Origen bequeathed to his pupils, Gregory of Nyssa and Evagrius Ponticus, the latter particularly introducing such mysticism to Egyptian monasticism. Cf. Pelikan, *Christian Tradition*, Vol. 1, 344.

what constitutes either the unity of Christ's person or indeed his full humanity. Both these problems he bequeathed to later christological reformulation.[21]

Similarly, Origen, like many of the early apologists (eager as they were to emphasise the compatibility between the *Logos* of the philosophers and the logos of the New Testament), did not perceive clearly enough the dangers inherent in such a view until they surfaced with all their problematic consequences in the Arian controversy. The explicit subordinationism of Arianism not only threatened the unity of the Godhead but also turned the second person of the Trinity into a demiurge that was neither truly God nor human. The achievement of the Council of Nicea and of the doctrine of the Trinity was to tie the ontological link the other way round: the *Logos* was co-eternal, one in being, or as Origen suggested, *homoousios* (of one substance) with the Father. The divinity of the *Logos* was secure which meant that he could be both the creative and revelatory word of the creator. He could in some genuine manner make God accessible to us, reveal him to us, because he was one with the Father in essence. The eternal *Logos*, the second person of the Trinity, became the revelatory key to the Godhead and this established an apologia for the doctrine of the incarnation. What better way for God to become intelligible to us than through the *Logos* becoming *enhypostatos* in human form (the *Logos* as the personal centre of the man Jesus)? Before we explore this in greater depth, there was one other crucial factor that the Christology of the apologists had already made explicit.

The **Logos** *as the divine reason*

The *Logos* was also conceived as the divine mind or reason of the cosmos. As Pelikan notes, to be without *Logos* in classical Greek meant to be without reason.[22] Those who denied the eternity of the *Logos* were accused of teaching that God had once been insane! *Logos* as divine reason insured that there was an inherent rationality to the cosmos. There was a structure and order to things that could be studied and observed. But how could this be unless there was also within humanity a similar capacity for rationality and reason? If the greatness of humanity was the fact of our creation in the image of God, did this not point to an analogy between the divine reason that became incarnate in Jesus Christ and that capacity for rationality already inherent in human nature?

> The Greeks asked the question how the human word and human language are able to grasp reality. Their answer was that the *Logos*, the universal form and principle of

---

[21] CF. D. Farrow, *Ascension and Ecclesia: On the Significance of the Ascension for Ecclesiology and Christian Cosmology.*

[22] Pelikan, *Centuries*, 62–3.

everything created, is both in reality as a whole and in the human mind. The word is meaningful when men use it because it can grasp reality. The opposite is also true. Reality grasps the human mind, so that men can speak to and about reality.[23]

Again, important christological principles came to the fore.

First, if Christ was the incarnate *Logos*, understood as the reason of God, this became a useful foil to those who wished to regard the Christian faith as irrational, absurd or even some inferior form of knowledge. While there would always be something mysterious to the ways and wonders of God, this did not entail that there was an inevitable anti-intellectualism about the Christian faith. Here is the basis to the Catholic vision of the Christian faith clearly articulated in the respective theologies of Clement of Alexandria, Origen and Tertullian.[24] Because the universe already possessed an essential rationality through the mediation of the *Logos*, and if that same *Logos* became incarnate in Christ, then in principle there was no conflict between faith and reason or, indeed, science and theology. Both would have to learn to tread warily between the acknowledgement of mystery and the affirmation of true wisdom.

Secondly, if the *Logos* was the reason of God, it was possible to view the *Logos* as the ontological ground and structure of the universe. This entailed two further consequences:

1. It was the *Logos* who brought order and harmony to the cosmos, the one through whom God ordered chaos into a rational system.
2. The *Logos* could consequently be described as the ontological cement of the cosmos. So to slip away from the *Logos* was to slip back into non-being. This was precisely how sin was understood in the Eastern church. It was a turning away from God and therefore a relinquishing of one's hold on reality. It was a slipping into the abyss of non-being, becoming subject again to impermanence, transience and decay. This was how, since Origen, the fate of a fallen creation was understood, it was always in danger of falling back into the chaos and anarchy from which it was first formed.

The **Logos** *incarnate, Saviour and Lord*

Why did the *Logos* become incarnate? In terms of Origen's metaphysics, we could say precisely to avert the danger to which we have just referred – the cosmological principle that viewed the *Logos* as the ground of being tied together the purpose of creation and redemption. If the *Logos* as the Father's co-partner, created out of nothing a cosmos of order, design and beauty, then it

---

[23] P. Tillich, *Perspectives on 19ᵗʰ and 20ᵗʰ Century Protestant Theology*, 30.
[24] Cf. Pelikan, *Christian Tradition* Vol. 1, 48–50.

was the *Logos* incarnate, still the Father's co-partner, who could save and redeem and so prevent a return to disorder, disintegration and chaos caused by human sin and evil:

> Not only, therefore did "all things hold together" in Christ the *Logos* as the structure of the cosmos but it would also be in the *Logos* as Saviour that the universe itself is to be freed from the shackles of mortality and enter upon the liberty and splendour of the children of God.[25]

In the theology of the Eastern Church, death was not regarded as primarily the result of sin and guilt, as it was in the West, but as a manifestation of the transience of all things. We could say then that the *Logos* incarnate came to repair the ontological fabric of the universe and so allow humanity 'to become partakers in the divine nature' (2 Pet. 1:4).

Logos–sarx *Christology*

It is from within the metaphysical framework of this way of conceiving of the drama of salvation that Athanasius, the anti-Arian bishop of Alexandria, asks the same question, 'Why did the *Logos* become incarnate?' His *Orations Against the Arians*, written during the period of his third exile, answered the question by clearly distinguishing between the *Logos* in himself and the *Logos* enfleshed, or in human form. The suffering and the humiliation of Christ belong to the *Logos* only by virtue of his incarnate state. They are the real experiences of the flesh that the *Logos* assumes. At the incarnation the *Logos* became the experiencing subject or personal centre of the human Jesus. Athanasius argues that it is wrong to conceive of the *Logos* indwelling a whole human being understood as an independent human subject or self.

Immediately the Achilles' heal of this Christology becomes apparent. Based on these premises it is extremely difficult to attribute full humanity to the person of Jesus, something that became abundantly clear in Athanasius' strained attempt to account for the apparent human ignorance of Jesus in the light of the *Logos*' perceived omniscience.

Apollinarius of Laodicea, a close friend of Athanasius, drew the logical conclusion. In the spirit of both Origen and Athanasius, Apollinarius views the incarnation as the enfleshing of a rational spirit, i.e. the *Logos*. There could not be an independent experiencing subject or human soul as far as Jesus was concerned. There is only 'one composite nature' in which the *Logos* becomes the single life principle of the human Jesus. Both *Logos* and *sarx* indwell each other, the human characteristics of Jesus belong to the *Logos* and the divine

---

[25] Ibid, 67.

characteristics of the *Logos* are conferred upon Jesus. There is a proper sharing
of properties (*communicatio idiomatum*). So, in effect, the incarnation produces a
hybrid figure constituted by the amalgamation of divinity and humanity in
bodily form. The inadequacies of Apollinarianism were only overcome
when in dispute with the Antiochene tradition of Christology (particularly
the christological dualism of Nestorius) Cyril of Alexandria conceded that the
hypostatic union entailed that the *Logos* was in possession of two natures that
could not intermingle.

  Within the framework of *Logos–sarx* Christology the basic soteriological
motif remains the same. The *Logos* assumes human nature so that we might be
restored to our original state of union with the divine nature. Salvation was
understood as deification, the way our perishable, mortal humanity could
partake of the imperishable, immortal divine nature:

> Human beings ... find themselves in God. Their true selfhood lies in their
> assimilation to God and their sharing in his way of being. For Athanasius, therefore,
> redemption can occur only through God's active presence with people. The incar-
> nation is and must be the incarnation of one who is fully and truly God. Inevitably
> ... Athanasius repudiated the teaching of Arius on christological, and not merely
> theological, grounds. His understanding of redemption made no sense if the *Logos*
> was a being "between" the divine and the human. It made sense only if the
> *Logos* was God's way of being personally present and active in the world.[26]

All this could be so only if the ontological re-grounding of the cosmos took
place through the incarnation, death and resurrection of the Christ, the divine
Logos. The great achievement of cosmic Christology was to link creation
with incarnation, incarnation with resurrection and resurrection with the
consummation of the whole created order. The divine *Logos* was the alpha and
the omega, the origin and the goal of the cosmos. The incarnate *Logos* had
entered the sin and sickness of a fallen creation to redeem and to restore it. The
resurrected *Logos* had become the first fruits of the new creation and finally,
when he had subjugated everything to his just and gentle rule, including death
itself, God would be all in all.

Logos–anthropos *Christology*

In terms of both Christology and soteriology, the Antiochene tradition (represented at its best by Theodore of Mopsuestia) moved in another direction. The
Antiochenes could not accept the Apollinarian thesis of the *Logos* resident in

---

[26] Norris, *Controversy*, 19.

'one composite nature'. This, they claimed, was to corrupt the divine nature making the *Logos* the subject of human passions and limitations. In other words, Apollinarianism dangerously infringed upon the Neoplatonic belief in the impassability of the divine nature. The Antiochenes postulated that the *Logos* was in possession of two separate natures.

This *Logos–anthropos* Christology, allowed for the full humanity of Jesus but once again only at a price, i.e. how to conceive adequately of the union of the two natures in the person of Jesus. For Theodore of Mopsuestia this was achieved through the notion of *prosopic*, rather than *hypostatic*, union. He conceived of a union of will rather than a genuine ontological or substantial union. The *Logos* accordingly unites himself to Jesus at the moment of his conception. As Jesus matures and takes on his unique vocation as the Messiah, that union achieves fuller expression, until, at the resurrection, the *Logos* and the human Jesus show that they have always been, to all intents and purposes, one functional unity.

The *Logos'* gracious identification with the human Jesus takes place through the adherence of the *Logos* in two natures, which seemed to suggest two personal centres or two subjects occupying the same human form. It was only a short step from here to the heresy probably wrongly attributed to Nestorius, that Jesus was two personalities or two sons.

It is important to recognise that the Antiochene insistence on the full humanity of Jesus produced a different soteriological emphasis. Attention was given to Jesus' struggle with the principalities and powers, and his resultant victory over the devil. Here was a Saviour who won for us a new humanity, whose goodness and moral energy could also become our possession.[27] This attention to the full humanity of Jesus was to reappear latter in the history of Christology accompanied by a rigorous christopraxis the centre of which was the believer's vocation to emulate the Son of Man in similar victory over the ruler of this present world.

Chalcedon

The apparent intractable division between the two traditions of Christology and the resultant hostility between the sees of Constantinople and Alexandria led to a protracted and bitter political and theological struggle. This was only resolved when, after the inconclusive results of the Council of Ephesus (AD 431), and at the behest of the emperor Marcian, the Council of Chalcedon (AD 451) brought together bishops from the East and representatives from the bishop of Rome. Together they sought to embrace the essential

---

[27] Cf. Theodore of Mopsuestia, *On the Incarnation* Book VII; quoted in Norris, *Controversy*, 118.

insights of both traditions, producing the definition of Chalcedon, which remains the acid test of christological orthodoxy to this day:

> Following, therefore, the holy fathers, we confess one and the same Son, who is our Lord Jesus Christ, and we all agree in teaching that this very same Son is complete in his deity and complete – the very same – in his humanity, truly God and truly a human being, this very same one being composed of a rational soul and a body, coessential with the Father as to his deity and coessential with us – the very same one – as to his humanity, being like us in ever respect apart from sin. As to his deity, he was born from the Father before the ages, but as to his humanity, the very same one was born in the last days from the Virgin Mary, the Mother of God, for our sake and the sake of our salvation: one and the same Christ, Son, Lord, Only Begotten, acknowledged to be unconfusedly, unalterably, undividedly, inseperably in two natures, since the difference of the natures is not destroyed because of the union, but on the contrary, the character of each nature is preserved and comes together in one person and one hypostasis, not divided or torn into two persons but one and the same Son and only-begotten God, *Logos*, Lord Jesus Christ – just as in earlier times the prophets and also the Lord Jesus Christ taught us about him, and the symbol of our Fathers transmitted to us.[28]

We would agree with George Hunsinger that Chalcedon offers a minimalist hermeneutical reconstruction of the essential mystery of the incarnation.[29] Nevertheless, the strains and stresses of trying to accommodate the essential considerations and distinct emphases of two virtually incompatible christological traditions are apparent in the highly technical Chalcedonian definition and, some would add, a christological formulae that is insufficiently grounded in Scripture.[30]

Chalcedon and beyond

Chalcedon may have represented the triumph of good sense over ecclesiological strife and division, but it tended to obscure rather than illuminate the enduring appeal of *Logos* Christology. Cosmological Christology may pay scant attention to Jesus the Jew and his antecedents in apocalyptic Judaism, but it is born out of a marriage of metaphysics and mysticism that, together with the political settlement we will shortly investigate, was to ensure its survival for at least another thousand years.

Chalcedonian orthodoxy, however, proved difficult to sustain. Indeed, throughout the sixth and seventh centuries further refinements were added.

---

[28] The Chalcedonian Definition; cf. Norris, *Controversy*, 159.
[29] G. Hunsinger, *Disruptive Grace: Studies in the History of Karl Barth*, 132–3.
[30] For a useful discussion and analysis of these issues see Piet Schoonenberg, *The Christ*, 50–105.

Three distinct christological positions emerged, all with competing doctrinal emphases, ecclesiological bias and political representation. They were (a) the Nestorians, who understood the incarnation in terms of a duality of *hypostases* in one person simply because hypostases designated both the individuality and the distinct properties of both the divine and human natures; (b) the monophysites, who upheld the notion that Christ was one hypostasis in one incarnate nature; and (c) the orthodox Chalcedonians.

In all of this we can see the inherent tensions of Chalcedonian orthodoxy being exposed and exploited particularly the difficulties caused by the assertion of a duality of natures which always appeared to threaten the unity of the person of Christ. Not surprisingly, the Chalcedonians began to seek other terminology that could overcome this obstacle, hence the emergence of the monergism (one action) and monotheletism (one will) tendencies, both of which were condemned as heretical at the third council of Constantinople in AD 681 and the Lateran synod in Rome in AD 649. Instead, the duality of natures was reaffirmed with the consequent notion of each nature in possession of a separate will and centre of action.[31] As Pelikan admits, the search for christological and soteriological consistency led to a level of theological abstraction that was far removed from the suffering servant of God described in the Gospels. Indeed, 'practically the whole of Byzantine religion could have been built without the historical Christ of the Gospels'.[32]

Part 2

Political Christology

If political theology cannot perform its task by striking out on its own into Jesuology, it must learn how to perform it christologically, making its way along that stream which flows from the apostles proclamation of Christ as 'Lord' to the later, ontologically developed definitions of the ecumenical creeds. But in order to perform its own special task, it cannot simply draw from that stream at its most convenient points of access, the Chalcedonian doctrine of the Two Natures, for example. It has to show how the Christological tradition belongs to the proclamation of the Kingdom of God.[33]

---

[31] Ibid., 61–75.

[32] G.P. Fedotov, *The Russian Religious Mind*; quoted in Pelikan, *Christian Tradition*, 75.

[33] O. O'Donovan, *The Desire of the Nations: Rediscovering the Roots of Political Theology*, 123.

Introduction

As we have already noted, the relationship between the Christian faith and the diverse cultures to which it continually has to adjust is a complex one. Should uncompromising allegiance to Christ also be accompanied by an equally uncompromising vigilance in regard to any politicising of the Christian faith? Such vigilance appears to lie behind Jesus' refusal to identify his own mission with the imperial expectations of the Jewish messiah. The Christian faith, however, is inherently political because absolute allegiance to Christ automatically relativises the authority and jurisdiction of all other earthly principalities and powers. Colin Gunton makes this point:

> There is a political Christ: not only the one depicted in the Gospels as coming to grief in the political-religious cauldron of first-century Judea, but also the one crucified by "the rulers of this age" (1 Cor. 2:8), however those ambiguous entities be conceived.[35]

The changing political and social fortunes of the early church show us that christological considerations cannot remain immune from such developments. It is to such a political Christology that we now turn. The roots of this development are to be found in the preference for a particular christological affirmation that is part of the New Testament witness to Jesus as the Christ.[35]

Jesus Lord of Lords and King of Kings

Is there an underlying unity to the diverse christological confessions we find in the New Testament? As long ago as 1990, James Dunn attempted to demonstrate that there is a common core to the early Christian *kerygma* about Jesus of which there are three components.

1. Most important for our purposes, the proclamation of the present Lordship of Christ by virtue of his resurrection and exaltation.
2. The call for a response of faith and commitment to Jesus as the risen Lord.
3. The promise of a continuing relationship between the one who believes and the exalted Christ, i.e. the experience of salvation.[36]

---

[34] C.E. Gunton, *Yesterday and Today: A Study of Continuities in Christology*, 199.

[35] For a fuller discussion of the issues that concern us see C.J.D. Greene, 'Revisiting Christendom: A Crisis of Legitimization', and the response by Oliver O'Donovan in C. Bartholomew et al. (eds.), *A Royal Priesthood: The Use of the Bible Ethically and Politically. A Dialogue with Oliver O'Donovan*, 314–43.

[36] J.D.G. Dunn, *Unity and Diversity in the New Testament: An Inquiry into the Character of Earliest Christianity*, 30.

Jesus is Lord is the principle confession of faith in the Pauline corpus. It occurs some 230 times in Paul's epistles alone.[37] The expression also appears many times in Luke-Acts; for instance it is the basic content of the gospel Peter preached to his contemporaries in his Pentecost sermon (Acts 2:36). While it is true that in the Gospels, where it occurs infrequently, the title may signify nothing more that an honorific address, the post-resurrection use of the confession denotes a person who both possesses divinely given authority and shares God's divinity itself (e.g. Phil. 2:11). Jesus acknowledges that his authority is a delegated one given to him by the Father: 'all authority in heaven and earth has been given to me' (Mt. 28:18; Jn. 17:1–5). That authority invested in him by virtue of his resurrection and exaltation.

There are of course different ways in which such a delegated authority can be understood. John Macquarrie, for instance, acknowledging his debt to Graham Stanton, asserts that because the title *kyrios* is one denoting rank or worth, it expresses Jesus' authority over the individual or the Church, and consequently is best understood as an existential Christology.[38] Such a conclusion is only possible if we forget that associated with the idea of authority is the notion of kingship or reign, well expressed in Revelation 11:15: 'the kingdom of the world has become the kingdom of our Lord and of his Christ, and he shall reign for ever and ever'. It is for this reason that Jesus can be hailed as 'Lord of lords and King of kings' (Rev. 17:14), which 'must be the primary eschatological assertion about the authorities, political and demonic, which govern the world: they have been made subject to God's sovereignty in the exaltation of Christ'.[39]

This conviction informed the millenarian hopes of the early Church. In 1 and 2 Thessalonians, for instance, the dignity and authority of Jesus the *kyrios*, was that of the returning eschatological Judge, which is a conscious re-echoing of the Son of Man figure we find in Psalm 110:1 and Daniel 7:13.[40] N.T. Wright convincingly argues that the Pauline confession of Jesus as *kyrios* is the essential core of the gospel of salvation, which was deliberately framed in Romans (with similar emphases in Philippians and Thessalonians) in such a way as to counteract the essentially idolatrous politico-religions aspirations of imperial Rome.[41] One makes such audacious claims from within the white heat of eschatological expectation and the imminent threat of martyrdom.

---

[37] Ibid, 50.

[38] J. Macquarrie, *Jesus Christ in Modern Thought*, 45–6; cf. also G.N.S. Stanton, *Incarnational Christology in the New Testament*, 155.

[39] O'Donovan, *Desire*, 146.

[40] Cf. Marshall, *Origins*, 102–4.

[41] N.T. Wright, 'Paul and Caesar: A New Reading of Romans', in C.G. Bartholomew et al (eds), *A Royal Priesthood: The Use of the Bible Politically and Ethically. A Dialogue with Oliver O'Donovan*, 173–93.

Indeed, such millenarian hopes – that Jesus the heavenly king would soon establish his kingdom here on earth – carried on well into the second century, and it was such expectations that could not fail to be interpreted by the representatives of Caesar as a political threat.

The Early Church

In Roman society the religious cult of either a local deity or later of the emperor himself was a guarantor of political and social stability; only to be interfered with on pain of death. In the second century, Christians were accused of being atheists because they had forsaken belief in the traditional pagan gods. Justin acknowledged the charge: 'Thus, we are even called atheists. We do confess ourselves atheists before those whom you regard as gods, but not with respect to the Most True God.'[42] However, Christian allegiance to Jesus as the *kyrios* inevitably relativised the absolute authority of the Roman emperor and resulted in a recurring cycle of indiscriminate persecution and social ostracism.

The account of the Martyrdom of Polycarp of Smyrna stands as irrefutable evidence of such persecution. When faced with the demands of the Proconsul, 'Swear by the genius of Caesar [i.e. acknowledge Caesar as lord and king], and I will release you: curse the Christ.' He replied, 'For eighty-six years I have been the servant of Jesus Christ and he never did me any injury. How then can I blaspheme my King who has saved me?'[43]

Moreover, recent research has conceded that the imperial cult functioned as a kind of dominant ideological metanarrative drawing all other religions and cultures under its sway and rewarding its devotees with Roman citizenship. Christians who refused to adjust their belief system accordingly risked economic and political isolation and alienation.[44]

Clearly, the early Christians were not political revolutionaries engaged in a plot to overthrow the empire from below and they protested their innocence on numerous occasions.[45] Similarly, the antimillenarians spiritualised the kingdom claiming it was a kingdom not of this world and pointed to their custom of demonstrating loyalty to the empire through prayers for the safety of the empire and protection of the imperial house. But even they could pledge only loyalty and obedience, not worship, for that would be to accept the emperor as divine. Indeed, *kyrios* was a title reserved for king Jesus alone.

---

[42] Justin Martyr, *First Apology*, 6 (see M.J. Buckley, *At the Origens of Modern Atheism*, 4).
[43] H. Bettenson, *Documents of the Christian Church*, 10.
[44] See W. Howard-Brook and A. Gwyther, *Unveiling Empire: Reading Revelation Then and Now*.
[45] H. Bettenson, *Christian Loyalty to the Emperor*, 7.

Inevitably, therefore, the central Christian confession of Jesus as *kyrios* came into conflict with the imperial claims of Caesar for absolute sovereignty and rule. Christians could sanguinely acknowledge, if not fully participate in, the socio-economic benefits of the empire, but they could not bow the knee in political and religious homage to the emperor. The sovereignty of Rome had to give way to the absolute sovereignty of Jesus as Lord of lords and King of kings.

Accordingly, the faith of first- and second-century Christians could not remain a private, individualised, personal religion. Rather, it was a public acknowledgement that the rule of Christ encompassed every domain of life. Christians could not afford to the emperors the absolute loyalty and allegiance they demanded in return for political stability and protection because all such powers and rules were subordinate and subservient to Jesus' reign. This explains why some of the most morally and politically astute of the emperors (e.g. Marcus Aurelius and Diocletian) persecuted Christians with a ferocity not previously experienced.

Christ and Christendom

In the annuls of church history and Christian doctrine, nothing has provoked a more ambiguous reaction than the emperor Constantine's endorsement of the Christian faith with the Milan Protocol of AD 313. Whether or not Constantine really accepted the Christian faith in a personal sense it is clear that:

> From Constantine's perspective the state needed a religion which was strictly monarchical in its view of God and the world, and which was represented and continued on earth in the political monarchy of the absolutist emperor.[46]

Christianity clearly fitted the bill in this regard and the later imperial Christology of Eusebius effectively absolutised the emperor's position. Eusebius perceived the emperor as a copy or image of the divine *Logos* who rules in the heavenly spheres. As the *Logos* rules in subordination to the Father's kingdom, so the emperor rules and prepares his subjects for the rule of the Saviour. As the *Logos* fights against principalities and powers in the heavenly realm so the emperor defeats the rulers of this present age in the power of the symbol of the conquering Saviour.

> The one who is God's 'priorly-existing and unique Word ... older than all time and every age ... holds a supreme dominion over the whole cosmos ... from whom and

---

[46] N. Brox, *A History of the Early Church*, 48.

by whom our emperor, beloved of God, bearing a kind of image of the supreme rule as it were in imitation of the greater directs the course of all things upon earth.[47]

The whole universe was in effect *logikos*, sustained by the Word and his image on earth, the emperor. It is clear how Jesus' claim to divine authority in Matthew 28:18 is here being understood. God the Father, King of the universe, has conferred authority on Jesus the representative of his kingship on earth, that authority has now been transferred to Jesus' vice-regent the emperor. This was the system of deferred or dual authority that evolved over three centuries in Byzantine Christendom at least from the time of Constantine to Justinian the Great and well expressed in the Byzantine ceremony of coronation.[48] Here the intermingling of a religious and political settlement amounted to a re-authorisation of secular government that could hardly concur with that limitation of secular political power the resurrection and exaltation of Jesus demanded.

If Christ the King had elected to exercise his sovereignty over the world through the emperor to whom he had appeared in visions and given victory in battle, then it was incumbent upon the emperor to call the first ecumenical council at Nicea for the purpose of restoring concord to both the church and empire alike. According to Eusebius, the inclusion of the formula that Christ was of one being or substance with the Father was the result of a direct intervention by the emperor (which explains why a second-rate, semi-Arian theologian like Eusebius would have accepted the *homoousios* clause in the first place). Constantine then wrote to all the churches in the provinces explaining that 'whatever is determined in the holy assemblies of the bishops is to be regarded as indicative of the divine will'.[49] He then issued an edict against heretics forbidding them to gather and confiscating all their church buildings.

Not surprisingly, such a political use of Christology led to the emergence of imperial Christology. A transference took place where titles originally given to the emperor where attributed to Christ, who became *Christus Imperator*, ruler or Lord of the world. Correspondingly, the emperor was given titles that originally had a christological meaning, such as servant of God, shepherd, and peace-maker. The title Lord of Glory, which originally held an apocalyptic meaning was also politicised. With the continuation of the Holy Roman Empire, Christ was viewed as the *Rex Gloriae*, the triumphant Lord who continues to subdue the kingdoms of this world by the power of the emperor.

Quite apart from the issues of political expediency, it is clear, as is so often the case in christologies from above, that the *Christus Imperator* is one who has

---

[47] Eusebius, *In Praise of Constantine*; quoted in L.G. Patterson, *God and History in Early Christian Thought: A Study of Themes from Justin Martyr to Gregory the Great*, 78.

[48] Pelikan, *Centuries*, 54.

[49] Eusebius, *Life of Constantine*, 3.20, 64–5.

been surrounded by an ever increasing weight of divinity, almost to the total exclusion of the real humanity of Christ. If more attention had been paid to the latter, then it would have been clear that the cross of Christ is the symbol of one who forsook political aggrandisement, and refused to extend the Father's kingdom through the use of battalions and armies. Similarly, the *Rex Gloriae* is the one who, it was claimed, would, 'rule the nations with a rod of iron' (Rev. 2:27; 12:5; 19:15). However, little or no account was taken of the original reference to Jeremiah (1:10; 23:29) where it is clearly the Word of God that will rule in this manner. Nor was any real allowance made for the fact that the one who is worthy to occupy the throne of heaven is also the Lamb who was slain before the foundation of the world. These and other considerations show us that:

> The imperial Christ was a product of dogmatic divinity abstracted from the gospel accounts of the human Jesus. When the divinity was separated from the humanity it became possible to adapt the doctrine of the divinity of Christ to the political needs of the day.[50]

Such a separation of Christ's divinity and humanity is precisely what was forbidden by Chalcedon: 'We confess ... one and the same Christ, Son, Lord, Only Begotten, to be acknowledged of two natures, without confusion, without change, without division, without separation ...' It is doubtful, however, as both Moltmann and Gunton claim, that the imperial Christ was simply modelled on secular and worldly notions of political power.[51] Eusebius viewed Constantine as the royal man. As Oliver O'Donovan contends, the Emperor chosen by God to establish a viable political alternative to warring national factions, which was in turn the product of polytheism. The victory of Christ over the principalities and powers in the heavens was expressed on earth by a corresponding political settlement. The more insidious error in Eusebius' political Christology was the conflation of the imperial office with the notion of divine rule, with the consequent loss of the eschatological tension between this present age and the consummation of the divine rule that is yet to come.[52] In that sense, Moltmann is correct to contend that in such a situation salvation was internalised as the business of establishing the *imperium sacrum* was left to the emperors and the political processes over which they held sway.

---

[50] Gunton, *Yesterday*, 198.
[51] Gunton, *Yesterday*, 195; Moltmann, *Way*, 54.
[52] Cf. O'Donovan, *Desire*, 197–8.

Christ and the Church

It is, however, possible to draw the lines of connection between the eternal Kingship of Christ and the temporal kingship of earthly rulers in several different ways. In the East the chain of command was understood to run from the Father to the Son or *Logos* and hence to the emperor who is the Son's vice-regent on earth. This is one possible way of interpreting Jesus' words in the great commission: 'All authority in heaven and earth has been given to me' (Mt. 28:18). The model adopted by Constantine and Eusebius, however, was not the only alternative.

It was possible to interpret Jesus' words in the great commission in a rather different sense and this was the way things were understood in the Christian West. Christ's authority was given first of all to the apostles, an authority to make disciples and therefore ensure the spread and survival of the Christian Church. Peter had been given the authority to bind and loose sins, which included, so the theory went, the authority to bind and loose political power. In this model the line is drawn from God to Christ to Peter, the first pope, and from Peter to his successors and then to emperors and kings.[53]

The origins of this viewpoint can be seen in Ambrose of Milan's uncompromising attitude to successive Roman emperors. A classic example was his attitude to Theodosius the Great, who was hailed as the champion of Nicene orthodoxy at the Council of Constantinople in AD 381. Ambrose refused communion to Theodosius until he repented over his use of excessive force in the retaliatory measures taken in the case of a riot against the imperial garrison at Thessalonica. Ambrose clearly regarded the emperor, hailed as the saviour of the Catholic faith, as simply another lay Christian who must submit to Episcopal discipline like everyone else.

> The emperor, refused the privilege of interfering in the church's affairs, was himself by no means immune from interference. In a case of faith, Ambrose reminded Valentinian, he was subject to the bishop's jurisdiction. The church expected the emperor to act like a Christian, and when he failed to do so it claimed the right to censure him. On several occasions Ambrose withdrew communion from emperors, sometimes for moral, sometimes for doctrinal causes.[54]

It is easy to see how such an attitude led to another expression of Christendom, where the imperial Christ sanctioned a particular doctrine of the Church, once again modelled on the lines of imperial Rome. In the later Byzantine and medieval period Christ was the King of kings, the church was a monarchy, the

---

[53] Cf. Pelikan, *Centuries*, 53–6.
[54] O'Donovan, *Desire*, 200.

pope was a monarch and it was by his authority that earthly monarchs exercised their own divinely derived authority and right to rule.[55]

Since the disillusion of Christendom that took place as a direct consequence of the religious wars of the sixteenth and seventeenth centuries, it is clear that neither of these two models are now open to us. The question remains: How are we to work out the parameters of a political Christology in the context of a radically secularised culture, where the separation of church and state is regarded as both expedient and essential to the proper exercise of political power? We will return to this question at a later stage, but we can be certain of one thing: the political theology of Eusebius, the so-called emissary of Byzantianism, where monotheism and monarchy were conflated in the interests of absolutism and where the emperor functioned without impunity as Christ's vice-regent on earth, is precisely the kind of imperialist ideology modern political Christology seeks to overthrow.

Part 3

Anthropological Christology – Jesus Lover Of My Soul

Anthropological Christology is simply Jesuology and nothing else. Jesuology is not the opposite of Christology. The term is used for the modern Christology, which is also called 'Christology from below'. The centre of this Christology is the human being Jesus of Nazareth, not the exalted or pre-existent Christ. That is why we talk about Jesuology.[56]

Introduction

Moltmann's assessment of anthropological Christology is that it is simply a particular form of Jesuology. By this he means the post-Enlightenment concentration of Christology on the historical Jesus.[57] However, the antecedents to Christology from below actually go back long before the Enlightenment to Byzantine theology and the emergence of what became known as Christ mysticism in the sixth century. Here we find a theology of negation or an

---

[55] Pelikan, *Centuries*, 55. O'Donovan charts the course that led from Ambrose's insistence on two authorities to Augustine's notion of two societies and to the later medieval insistence on two rules. Cf. *Desire*, 196–206.

[56] Moltmann, *Way*, 55.

[57] Ibid.

apophatic theology that in the East formed part of the dogmatic and philo-sophical tradition of the church. The full flowering of Christ mysticism, however, took place in the West between the eleventh and fourteenth centuries, partly as a consequence of the demise of scholasticism and partly as an offshoot of medieval monasticism.

This type of Christology from below flourishes on the immensely fertile ground of religious experience and, although divided by the historical schism of the Reformation, takes a distinctly Catholic and Protestant form. In this section we will examine the rise of what became known as Christ-mysticism and its corresponding development into christopraxis, which takes as its starting point the real humanity of Jesus as the example of divine–human union. Like all forms of Christology, however, anthropological Christology has its roots in a particular biblical tradition that concentrates on the represen-tative status of the risen Christ.

Jesus the Representative of the New Humanity

The New Testament proclaims Jesus as the unique Saviour of humanity because he is the representative of a new relationship between God and our-selves: 'In his person, Jesus has become the fulfilment of the human destiny to community with God'.[58] Jesus is affirmed as the representative prototype or perfect example of that new humanity destined to live in fellowship with God and one another. Pannenberg delineates three areas where this is so:

1. Jesus' dedication and commitment to his vocation or office to bring people into the kingdom of God represents personal existence lived in faithful obedience, trust and openness to God (Mt. 6:25–34).
2. In his submission to his fate and acknowledgement of the vicarious nature of his death (Mt. 16:21), Jesus is the paradigm of a life of self-con-scious subordination to the will of the Father (in Rom. 5:19; Phil. 2:8; and Heb. 5:8 this is described as an obedience demonstrated through suffering).
3. In his resurrection from the dead Jesus is the eschatological fulfilment of human destiny to live in nearness to God and in conformity to his will and purpose.[59]

---

[58] Pannenberg, *Jesus–God and Man*, 195.
[59] Ibid, 19.

Christ the new Adam

The representative nature of Christ as the one whose personal destiny established a new relationship between God and humanity is perhaps best expressed in the Adam typology we find in 1 Corinthians 15:45f. and Romans 5:12f. In both contexts Jesus is the new Adam, the prototype (*prōtos*) of a new, reconciled humanity. In contrast to the first Adam who brought death and disobedience, Jesus is the heavenly man, the life-giving Spirit who brings grace, righteousness and life everlasting. In Romans, Jesus' pre-Easter path of suffering and obedience is linked with his resurrection as evidence of his sonship. Again, these texts affirm three ways in which Jesus is the representative of a new humanity:

1. The old humanity (the first Adam) was a life of disobedience dominated by sin and death. The new humanity (the second Adam) is a life marked by obedience that overcomes our mortality and morbid fear of death.
2. The Adam typology links the new humanity with the old, thereby showing that God's creative purposes for humankind, which were marred by sin and death, have been brought to completion in Jesus. His personal existence was not fractured by sin and his resurrection demonstrates his victory over death.
3. The fact that we will all bear 'the image of the man of heaven' establishes a social dimension to this new humanity. These considerations are taken further with the affirmation that through the Spirit we can have a share in the divine sonship and can be transformed into his likeness (Rom. 8:12–17; 2 Cor. 3:17–18).

In his more recent work, Pannenberg notes the important link in the New Testament between the second Adam theology of Paul and John's doctrine of Jesus as the incarnate *Logos*. Both traditions establish the necessary link between anthropology and Christology and both do so by affirming the unity of creation as salvation history directed by God towards its eschatological fulfilment in Jesus Christ.[60] These connections and associations were explored most fruitfully through the recapitulation theology of Irenaeus.

Irenaeus and Athanasius

Irenaeus affirmed that humanity was created through the *Logos* in the image of the Creator. However, this was not, as the Genesis story recounts, a perfect humanity. Rather, it was humanity with that propensity or potential. Irenaeus

---

[60] Pannenberg, *Systematic Theology*, Vol. 2, 297–315.

developed a distinction between the divine image and the divine likeness (cf. Gen. 1:26) The history of humanity was destined to mature from one made in the image of God to one that could bear the divine likeness. Because of the Fall, however, this only became possible with the coming of the divine *Logos* in the form of a real human being. Consequently, the incarnation becomes the great act of recapitulation in the history of salvation, where what was begun with the *Logos* as the second person of the Trinity is brought to completion by the *Logos* incarnate.[61]

Religious Experience

The link between the Adam typology and the Christian's participation in the Spirit of sonship is one, which, as we have noted already, becomes explicit in Romans 8. We bear the image of the heavenly man when we receive the Spirit of freedom and life and so become part of that new creation which Jesus' death and resurrection inaugurated. This immediately directs us to the soteriological dimension of Christology and its basis in religious experience.

Whenever Christology wishes to retain an epistemological privilege for religious experience, we need to be sure that we know what we mean by the notoriously generalised term 'experience'. In common parlance, the term refers to that accumulated body of knowledge and information that is part of our life history. Its theological usage is more nuanced, and is often understood as a sense or feeling of the 'numinous', or the subjective encounter with the divine, which may be accompanied by other heightened emotional states such as joy, peace, or an eruption of meaning and personal worth.

Sometimes the claim is made that such religious experience forms a common core present in all religions. This assertion has been substantially criticised by George Lindbeck.[62] The problem with this view of religious experience is that it is incorrigibly vague and hopelessly uncontextualised. If, ultimately, religious experience means nothing more than the unmediated presence of the divine, how is it classified, corroborated or indeed even properly described? And in what way does such experience bear the marks of the distinctive historical and cultural contexts through which it is mediated?

In Christology, however, we are referring to experience that has the person of Christ as its essential content or core element. We are not referring to undifferentiated religious states or feelings, but the way in which the

---

[61] Ibid. 298–9. Athanasius followed Irenaeus' lead and linked the Adam typology with *Logos* Christology. See, Athanasius, *The Incarnation of the Word of God: Being the Treatise of St. Athanasius, De Incarnatione Verbi Dei*, 41.

[62] Lindbeck, *Nature of Doctrine*.

believer actually encounters, is united with, or related to, the person of Christ, however that can be concretely described.

Moltmann's claim that anthropological Christology represents the reduction of Christology to Jesuology carries with it the implication that the post-Enlightenment obsession with the historical Jesus is another example of that generalised pious devotion to the person of Jesus, which has appeared at regular intervals in the history of the church and has very little to do with the doctrinal considerations of orthodox Christology. Such a claim can, however, be seriously challenged, particularly when we look at the origins of this approach in the mystical theology of the East.

Christ mysticism

'In Christianity, Christ-mysticism is what emerged when the figure of Jesus of Nazareth became the object of mystical experience, mystical thought, and mystical language'[63] Paul Tillich asked whether 'mysticism can be baptised by Christianity'. His answer to his own rhetorical question was 'yes', provided a distinction was maintained between the abstract mysticism of Hinduism and the concrete mysticism of the Christian faith. The latter is Christ-mysticism, which, when removed from Christianity, allows it to degenerate into the kind of intellectualism or moralism found in the theologies of Albrecht Ritschl and Immanuel Kant, respectively.

According to Tillich, the Christian tradition would have become a sterile intellectual wasteland without its enrichment by Christ-mysticism. For Tillich, and indeed Karl Rahner, mysticism is not the opposite of rationalism. Quite the contrary, a proper rational grasp of the divine presence within us develops out of mysticism. Put simply, we learn to speak correctly about God when first we have learned to be silent in the face of the mystery of God.

While there is a mystical tradition within Judaism (e.g. the visions of Isaiah, Ezekiel and Daniel) the origins of Christ-mysticism are most closely associated with what Gregory Dix referred to as 'the de-Judaisation of Christianity'.[64] In other words, its full-flowering took place in the Greek soil of Neoplatonism. Here, in the writings of Plotinus and Proclus, we find a particular way of relating to the divine reality understood in terms of a threefold assent. The way of knowing ceases to be a purely rational or cognitive process and becomes instead spiritual union between the believer and Christ. The three steps are purification (*katharsis*), illumination (*ellampsis*) and union (*henosis*), all of which are refinements of the basic Neoplatonic notion of participation in the divine forms or heavenly archetypes. Pelikan notes that there were three fundamental

---

[63] Pelikan, *Centuries*, 123.
[64] Ibid, 123.

influences that contributed to the development of this form of Christology,[65] although there are clear echoes of this type of approach to Christology in the thought of Origen.

Pseudo-Dionysius

The first was the enormous influence in the sixth century of the writings of *Pseudo-Dionysius*. In the medieval church he was believed to be Dionysius the Areopagite mentioned in Acts 17:34. It was not until the nineteenth century that the author was identified as an unknown late fifth-century inhabitant of Syria. In this corpus of writings we find the attempt to bring together Neoplatonic speculation and Christianity in one great synthesis. In his treatises *The Heavenly Hierarchy* and *The Mystical Theology*, Dionysius describes the soul's assent to the Trinity achieved by means of the apophatic procedures of purification, illumination and, finally, union with the divine or deification.[66]

The status of Christ in this mystical schema is difficult to determine. Jesus often appears as a mere exemplar or cipher of the universal presence of the *Logos*. Virtually no connection is made with the earthly vocation of Jesus of Nazareth. Indeed, although Dionysius could speak of Christ's mediatory role in creation and in the consummation of all the hierarchies, the apophatic impulse of such mysticism tended to relegate all discriminatory doctrinal language to that of mere appearance as opposed to a higher reality where God was essentially Oneness.[67] Utterly remote and ultimately monistic Oneness was preserved at the cost of rendering both the Trinity and the incarnation mere conventions of theological language.[68]

Maximus Confessor further developed this subtle synthesis between Neoplatonic and biblical elements in the seventh century. Maximus began his work in Constantinople but spent most of his life in exile in the East. He is regarded by modern historians as 'the most universal spirit of the seventh century and perhaps the last independent thinker among the theologians of the Byzantine church'.[69]

---

[65] Ibid., 122–32.

[66] Pelikan, *Christian Tradition*, Vol. 1, 344.

[67] H.R. Mackintosh is less generous in his assessment of the situation: 'Here can be traced the malign influence of the pseudo-Dionysius, that unknown Christian theosophist of (probably) the sixth century, whose Neoplatonic and more than half-docetic conceptions did so much to colour mediaeval religious thought, and to infect it with a mysticism which had nothing Christian about it save the name.' See, *The Person of Christ*, 226.

[68] Ibid., 345–8. In regard to the implications for religious language from such a apophatic mysticism see D.R. Stiver, *The Philosophy of Religious Language: Sign, Symbol & Story*.

[69] H.G. Beck; quoted by Pelikan in *Christian Tradition*, Vol. 2, 8.

Maximus shared with his illustrious predecessor the belief that everything in creation participates in the *Logos* and that deification was the goal of the Christian life. He also embraced the link between the Adam typology and the mediation of the *Logos*. The first Adam united in himself the destiny of the human race as that established in creation by the *Logos*. The beginning implies the end; the human being is a microcosm of the universe. But where Adam transgressed casting the whole creation into the power of sin and evil, the second Adam prevailed reuniting the creation with its eschatological destiny.

The Neoplatonic elements of this view of the nature of salvation are easy to discern. It was assumed that humanity was originally created for a mode of existence that was non-material and consisted of sharing in the divine. The Fall was not just a fall from a life infused with the divine grace. It was also a fall into another mode of existence, where humanity became trapped in materiality, dominated by its passions and carnal appetites. The reason the divine *Logos* became incarnate was to set humanity free from this slavery to human passion and to restore us to the condition for which we were originally created. Deification was the gift of God's grace at work in us whereby we share once again in the divine nature.

The Song of Songs

In medieval monasticism another biblical tradition emerged as a potent contributor to mystical theology, i.e. the allegorical interpretation of the Song of Songs. Originally intended as a poem celebrating the reality of human love, in Christian antiquity this poem was interpreted as an allegory of Christ's union with the believer, and in the medieval cloister it was the book most read and commented upon. The greatest commentary is that of Bernard of Clairvaux. He, more than any other theologian of the period, cultivated a particular form of adoration and worship based on a renewed interest in the humanity of Jesus:

> No writer of this time approaches Bernard of Clairvaux in the intensity with which he realised the manhood of Jesus. Besides the mysterious and half-unknown Christ of the sacrament, he grasps and clings to the Man whose mind and deeds and passion are the medium of Divine life to the world.[70]

As Pelikan acknowledges, Bernard's allegorisation of the Song of Songs portrays the human Jesus as 'the Bridegroom of the Soul'.[71]

Before such a relationship of mutual love and adoration can be achieved the Christian needs to follow the three stages of mystical assent. First of all, the soul needs to be purged of all carnal desire and preoccupation with self. It was for

---

[70] Mackintosh, *Person of Christ*, 227.
[71] Pelikan, *Centuries*, 126.

this reason that the *Logos* became incarnate, so that he could purify our flesh from its bondage to carnality.[72] The next stage, expressed most succinctly in the writings of Julian of Norwich, is to allow the soul's natural darkness to be illuminated by the light of Christ. The human soul is caught fast bound in the night of sin and selfish desire. So only the revelation of the suffering Christ can bring the illumination that overcomes the natural blindness of the soul. Finally, only after the assent of the soul through these preliminary stages will come that state of *unio mystica*, mystical union between the believer and Christ, that state of blessed joy and communion, where, in the language of John, we learn how to abide in Christ and he in us (Jn. 15:4). The lives of the saints in the medieval period were often depicted in terms of this ecstasy of divine love and union that could at times be described in frankly sexual imagery.

Hesychasm

The link between Christ-mysticism and the revival of monasticism has already been alluded to and this directs us to the third facet of this form of devotion, the monastic tradition of Hesychast spirituality, which came to the fore in the East between the eleventh and the fourteenth centuries.

It had long been recognised in the East that practice was the basis of theory. Right doctrine, orthodoxy or right glory can only be attained through right practice and that means primarily the discipline of Christian devotion. It was Symeon, surnamed 'The New Theologian', who developed an interpretation of Christian doctrine as that which was based on the contemplative tradition of prayer and silence. This tradition found its most fertile soil in the monasteries because there the monks had both the time and the practical framework of living to give attention to the evangelical imperatives of the faith.[73]

The contemplative tradition was nourished through regular participation in sacramental worship. Symeon reminded his fellow Christians that it was essential not only to possess a dogmatic knowledge of Christ, to believe in him, but to have a personal knowledge of Christ. Using the terminology of Chalcedonian Christology, Symeon asserted that, just as Christ enjoyed a personal union with the Father through a shared divinity, so it was possible for us to enjoy a personal union with the risen Lord as we were assimilated into his body the Church. This identification with Christ became a summons to a life of holiness and love. The two marks of authentic Christianity were orthodox belief and a life of humility and obedience in conformity with the will of God.

Symeon also stood in the tradition of Pseudo-Dionysian and Maximus Confessor, acknowledging that God was utterly incomprehensible. True theology is apophatic theology, a theology of negation. Genuine knowledge

---

[72] Bernard of Clairvaux, *Sermons on the Song of Solomon*.
[73] Pelikan, *Christian Tradition*, Vol. 2, 255.

of God is not found in the scholastic organisation of concepts and theorems but in the contemplative practice of prayer and silence that takes us beyond words into the realm of the ineffable, i.e. mystical union with Christ, who is the revelation of the divine nature.[74]

Christopraxis

Closely related to the mystical theology of both the East and the West, nurtured as it was by the tradition of asceticism and contemplation developed in the monasteries, was a particular form of christopraxis, a 'school of service of the Lord', which kept the fire of Christian faith burning in the midst of Europe's Dark Ages. It took shape as a communal life of order and discipline modelled on the human life of Jesus.

The intense interest in the humanity of Jesus, encouraged by theologians such as Bernard of Clairvaux and his arch-opponent Peter Abelard, was a feature of the monastic tradition. Jesus was worshiped and venerated because he was understood to be the perfect example of a human life lived in conformity to the will of God. His humanity became the icon of the divine love always seeking those who will respond to the example of the suffering servant of God.[75]

The monks portrayed an exemplary lifestyle: 'He who says he believes in Christ ought to walk as Christ walked, poor and humble and always preaching the truth.'[76] In the monasteries, ordinary men and women embraced a life of poverty, humility and chastity as they sought to live in conformity to Jesus' life and teachings.[77] This union with Christ was manifested in a number of distinctively practical ways.

First, it was evident through a radical renunciation of worldly wealth and the embrace of poverty as a positive good. Following the Son of Man who had nowhere to lay his head involved a willingness to accept voluntary poverty, which, for Francis, was the Queen of the virtues because it was the way of identification with Christ and the Virgin Mary.

---

[74] Cf. Ibid, 259.
[75] Cf. Bernard of Clairvaux, *Letters*, 190.9.25; quoted in McGinn, Meyendorff and Leclercq (eds), *Christian Spirituality Origins of the 12th Century*, 258.
[76] Quoted in Bosch, *Transforming Mission*, 232.
[77] St Francis of Assisi probably embodied this tradition more profoundly than anyone else. His devotion to Christ 'took the form of a deliberate conformity to the details of his life in all things'. Pelikan, *Centuries* 135. In many ways the same could be said about St Benedict who had such a profound influence on the more orthodox monasticism of the West. There is the same moral seriousness, the same emphasis upon personal discipline, the same concern that a life of work and worship should mean that in all things God may be glorified.

Secondly, David Bosch refers to the 'patience, tenacity and perseverance' of the monks as the Saracens, Huns, Lombards, Tartars, Saxons and Danes attacked the peasants and destroyed the monasteries.[78] The extraordinary resilience of monasticism was in part due to a practical acceptance that to follow Christ was to share in the sufferings of the one who was crucified for the sins of the world. All through his life St Francis identified himself with the suffering Christ and it was while he spent forty days on retreat in the mountains near Florence that he experienced his famous vision of the crucified Christ and received in his body the actual stigmata (wounds) of Christ.

In these and other ways, monasticism exhibits a Christology from below that can be summarised in the words of Thomas à Kempis: 'for whoever will understand the words of Christ plainly and in their full savor must study to conform all his life to His life'.[79] Monasticism was a pilgrimage of radical identification with the humanity of the historical Jesus in such a way that the life of the believer became another embodiment of the suffering servant of God. This intense engagement with the vicarious humanity of Christ is well summarised by Frederick W. Dillistone:

> It may be dangerous to characterise any era as a whole but those who lived in the Middle Ages seem to have been peculiarly aware of the transience of things temporal and of the suffering which belongs to the ordinary human lot. The exceptional individuals therefore were those who mastered the conditions of earthly existence by showing contempt for the worse that these conditions might impose upon them. And no way of achieving this end was surer than to be identified with Christ in his self-humbling, his obedience, his passion, and his death.[80]

Assessment

Cosmological and political christologies

In parts 1 and 2 we examined two closely related forms of 'Christology from above'. It is often not recognised that the political or imperial Christology of Byzantium develops almost imperceptibly from the cosmological Christology of the patristic era. Both conflate the biblical Christ with the divine *Logos* understood as a mediating principle between God and the world. In cosmological Christology, the *Logos* is the ontological bridge between the eternal, transcendent, immutable, immortal and ultimately inaccessible world of divine reality and the finite, changing, corruptible and all too accessible world

---

[78] Bosch, *Transforming Mission*, 232.
[79] Thomas à Kempis, *The Imitation of Christ*, 56.
[80] F.W. Dillistone, *The Christian Understanding of Atonement*, 328.

of material reality. In political Christology, the *Logos* is the mediating power of divine government, stability and authority who rules in both the heavenly and earthly spheres.

The soteriological concern of cosmological Christology is not just the salvation of the individual; it is also concerned about the restoration of the whole created cosmos. The *anakephalaiosis* or recapitulation of the universe has not yet taken place but is an eagerly expected eschatological hope. The soteriological concern of political Christology is the restoration of the social and political order to the image of its heavenly prototype. Both forms of Christology express the Eastern Orthodox approach to mission, which takes the possibility of the conversion of the empire seriously.[81]

The deduction that there is no neutral political sphere does not, however, permit a notion of mission understood simply as the territorial expansion of the empire nor acquiescence to the 'peril of negative collusion', the failure to prophetically challenge the rulers of this present age in the name and authority of the ruling Christ.[82] The theological and, consequently, political failure of both forms of Christology, is that they concentrate on the divine exalted Christ to the virtual exclusion of the historical Jesus. Their epistemological focus is the incarnation, why the divine *Logos* became incarnate, rather than the actual historical vocation of the man Jesus, or indeed, the unity of his person and destiny revealed in the cross and resurrection.

The Christendom ideal has been the subject of much modern disputation and denunciation. Before we judge the endeavours of these representatives of Christendom too harshly, we should keep in mind the wise words of Lesslie Newbigin:

> Much has been written about the harm done to the cause of the gospel when Constantine accepted baptism, and it is not difficult to expatiate on this theme. But could any other choice have been made? When the ancient classical world … ran out of spiritual fuel and turned to the church as the one society that could hold a disintegrating world together, should the church have refused the appeal and washed its hands of responsibility for the political order? It is easy to see with hindsight how quickly the church fell into the temptation of worldly power. It is easy to point … to the glaring contradiction between the Jesus of the Gospels and his followers occupying the seats of power and wealth. And yet we have to ask, would God's purpose … have been better served if the church had refused all political responsibility?[83]

Some of this criticism is clearly justified because the church was not immune from the temptation to succumb to the acquisition of worldly power and

---

[81] Cf. A. Schmemann, *The Missionary Imperative in the Orthodox Church*, 256–7.

[82] Cf. O'Donovan, *Desire*, 212–3.

[83] L. Newbigin, *Foolishness to the Greeks: The Gospel and Western Culture*, 100f.

wealth. There is, however, a very modern tendency to read this important
era of Christian mission and expansion through the eyes of liberal democracy
or indeed, through a decidedly Nietzscherian assessment that Christendom
represented nothing more than the naked will to power and domination.

Such would appear to be the case with Stanley Hauerwas who conflates the
Christendom idea with Constantinianism, which he regards quite starkly as
the mistaken attempt to forward the influence and extent of the kingdom by
the use of worldly power and violence.[84] In contrast to Hauerwas, however, O'Donovan believes that this view is both historically inaccurate
and theologically naïve. O'Donovan is surely correct when he asserts that
Christians reasonably fresh from the vocation of martyrdom were not
prepared to return to the catacombs and indulge in a false quietism, rather,
they actively sought to realise in astute political form the 'triumph of Christ
among the nations'. The rule of Christ while clearly an eschatological reality is
based, nevertheless, on the actuality of the resurrection:

> It was the missionary imperative that compelled the Church to take the conversion
> of the Roman Empire seriously and to seize the opportunities it offered. These were
> not merely opportunities for 'power'. They were opportunities for preaching
> the Gospel, baptising believers, curbing the violence and cruelty of the empire and,
> perhaps most important of all, forgiving their former persecutors.[85]

Alan Kreider and Ramsay MacMillan have entered this debate on the side of
Hauerwas. Kreider claims that O' Donovan's view of Christendom over-
looks two vital failings. First, there was a general accommodation of Christian
teaching by the preachers and catechists of the post-Constantine era to the
more favourable political circumstances that existed.[86] Secondly, it was largely
'inducement and compulsion' that implemented the Christendom ideal. The
persecuted Christian church became the persecutor of other sects and pagans;
consequently, dissent and heretical convictions were no longer tolerated.[87]
Hauerwas' critique is therefore more ideological or ecclesiological. He believes
the church failed to become in its own community life a radically subversive
political reality and so accommodated itself to the advantageous political
climate of the empire. Kreider sees the same thing happening but interprets it as
a failure of nerve and vision in terms of the practicalities of Christian mission

---

[84] S. Hauerwas, *After Christendom: How the Church is to Behave if Freedom, Justice, and a Christian Nation are Bad Ideas*.
[85] O'Donovan, *Desire*, 212.
[86] Cf. A. Kreider, 'Changing Patterns of Conversion in the West', in *The Origin of Christendom in the West*, 3–46.
[87] Ibid., 3–46; see also MacMullen, 'Christianity Shaped Through its Mission', 97–117.

and initiation. O'Donovan accepts that abuses and irregularities existed but applauds the attempt to fashion a genuine vision of theocracy, 'the homage of the Kings to the Lord of the martyrs'.[88]

However, the Christendom ideal was not simply based on political expediency, or its later degeneration into ecclesiastical rule rather it was the persuasive combination of popular mysticism (how can human beings participate and share in the divine), and metaphysics (how can we properly delineate the relationship between the human and the divine) and a pragmatic political settlement (how can we model proper social, moral and political relationships of divine governance), which was to secure the enduring worth and success of cosmological, and its corollary, political Christology for over a thousand years. In other words, a common culture was established and the Christendom era held sway in the popular mind and imagination at least until the final parting of the ways between the East and the West in the fifteenth century. So from its biblical origins in the notion of Christ's pre-existence to the full-blown metaphysics of Eusebius' imperial Christology, the fecundity of the concept of the *Logos*, linked as it was with the honorific title of the *kyrios*, was to prove nearly invincible in establishing both the viability and the versatility of a christological vision of the world. This achievement has never since been repeated and it is both tendentious and demonstrably superficial to denigrate this period as the era when Christianity traded the lordship of Christ for that of the empire.

Antropological Christology

The slide toward exemplarism
As we have noted, Dillistone offers a useful historical and cultural analysis of why medieval Christology moved in this direction. Another fundamental reason, however, was the disillusion of that subtle synthesis between metaphysics and mysticism present in the Neoplatonic notion of ontological participation in the divine. The gradual loosing of this connection was a distinctive feature of medieval Scholasticism. In the considerable theological achievement of Thomas Aquinas, for instance, a clear break with the epistemology of Neoplatonism can be discerned. In place of the notion of mystical participation and the resultant direct illumination of the human mind from the transcendent Ideas, Aquinas sanctioned the value of direct sensory experience and the ability of the intellect to investigate the empirical reality of the world. Most certainly this was to lead to the apprehension of God via the philosophical investigation of the natural world's relationship to the creator, but nevertheless he did grant a relative independence to the empirical world as the domain where both human freedom and natural reason could find legitimate expression.

---

[88] O'Donovan, *Desire*, 193.

For Aquinas, like Aristotle, we apprehend universals via their concrete manifestation in the world. For Plato and Augustine, the reverse was the case. We know particulars because the mind is illuminated directly through knowledge of the heavenly archetypes. Aquinas sought to resolve the scholastic dispute between realism and nominalism by affirming that the eternal ideas possessed three kinds of existence: (a) as exemplars in the mind of God independent of things; (b) as intelligible forms in things; (c) as concepts in the human mind arrived at by abstracting from things. What is obvious is the epistemological move towards the ability of the human mind to interpret direct sensory experience.[89]

This process was to be taken further by both Duns Scotus and William of Occam. The latter was an early manifestation of that peculiarly British orientation towards empiricism that was to find its fulfilment in David Hume and John Locke. Ockham simply denied the reality of universals outside of their apprehension by the human mind and their description by human language. The concepts of the mind possessed no necessary metaphysical foundation beyond concrete particulars. God requires no pre-existing ideas in order to create a world of his own choosing. Since all human knowledge is consequently based on sensory intuition of concrete particulars, knowledge of God and his purposes for creation must be based on revelation:

> Thus with the fourteenth century, the long-assumed metaphysical unity of concept and being began to break down. The assumption that the human mind knows things by intellectually grasping their inherent forms – whether through interior illumination by transcendent Ideas, as in Plato and Augustine, or through the active intellect's abstraction of immanent universals from sense-perceived particulars, as in Aristotle and Aquinas, was now challenged ... With the displacement of abstract speculation by empirical evidence as the basis of knowledge, the earlier metaphysical systems seemed increasingly implausible.[90]

This whole process was aided and abetted by the tendency of theologians like Augustine and Aquinas to stay very firmly within the formal boundaries of

---

[89] R. Tarnas, *The Passion of the Western Mind*, 179–90. See also Fergus Kerr, 'Thomas Aquinas', in *The Medieval Theologians: An Introduction to the Theology of the Medieval Period*, 201–22.

[90] Tarnas, *Passion of the Western Mind*, 207–8 A very similar point is made by Roger Lundin, 'Interpreting Orhans: Hermeneutics in the Cartesian Tradition', in R. Lundin, C. Walhout & A.C. Thiselton (eds), *The Promise of Hermeneutics*: 'By demystifying the world, nominalism opened the way for the modern scientific study of nature and human experience. In rejecting formal and final causes, it left only material and efficient causality as plausible modes of explaining movement and development', 8.

orthodox christological doctrine and so, paradoxically, increase the distance between theological reason and practical faith. For instance, Aquinas raises the interesting question whether or not it was only the *Logos* who could become incarnate? Clearly, he can speculate in such fashion because divinity, which is obviously already complete in itself, must remain uncontaminated from too close proximity with humanity. Consequently, not only is the theology of the incarnation abstracted from the actual historical career of the man Jesus of Nazareth, but christological considerations degenerate into mere formal philosophical logic concerning how to conceive adequately of the union between the finite and the infinite.

It is clear what effect such intellectual developments had on medieval Christology. It was to undermine the Neoplatonic metaphysical basis to *Logos* Christology and to allow both Christ-mysticism and its corollary, Christo-praxis, to float free from their moorings in the christological tradition. As Pelikan notes, for instance, medieval mysticism easily blurred the distinction between Creator and creature embracing in the process a form of pantheism which lost touch with the necessary New Testament eschatological tension between the already and the not yet.[91] The inherent danger with Christopraxis was that it inevitably produced an exemplarist form of anthropological Christology that took as its starting point some aspect of the life, ministry and death of Jesus. From Bernard of Clairvaux onwards the summons to be 'conformed to the image of the Son' (Rom. 8:29) or the traditional theme of the *imitatio Christi* was regarded as the main goal and purpose of both christological considerations and the whole *ordo salutis* (order of salvation).

The twelfth-century theologian Peter Abelard is often regarded as one of the chief exponents of just such an exemplarist Christology, an outlook for which he received substantial criticism from Bernard of Clairvaux. But not all of this criticism is entirely fair and there are aspects of Abelard's Christology that appear to move beyond mere exemplarism. For Abelard there is no inner or outer necessity to which God must conform; rather, Jesus came to reveal to us the extent of God's love and reconcile us to him through his death:

> There is only one possible motivation that Abelard can find for the Son of God to redeem us through the particular means of 'such numerous fastings, insults, scourgings and spittings, and finally that most bitter and disgraceful death', that motive is the sheer love of God.[92]

As Paul Fiddes points out, in moving from the example of love that Christ shows us to the notion that through this example he also repairs our

---

[91] Pelikan, *Centuries*, 131.
[92] P.S. Fiddes, *Past Event and Present Salvation: The Christian Idea of Atonement*, 143.

nature, Abelard is seeking to move beyond the limitations of an exemplarist approach.[93]

The problem remains, however, that Abelard never really explained how this could happen in a sufficiently objective sense. Consequently, it seems that Jesus' example is merely a kind of subjective influence upon us as we seek to emulate his life of faithful obedience and love for God and his fellow humanity. This intense concentration or devotion to the image of the suffering Christ and the attendant piety of quietism and mortification of the flesh also had an adverse effect on the viability of the christological vision of reality for the ordinary populace, based as it was on the Lordship of Christ over every domain of life. Drawing on the fascinating study of the late medieval period by Delumeau, Zygmunt Bauman notes:

> The monks, preachers and other 'artists of religious life' set standards of piety which collided not just with popular sinful inclinations, but with the maintenance of life as such, and thereby placed the prospects of 'eternal life' out of reach of all but a few saints; the care for salvation rapidly became a luxury for the chosen few, able and willing to opt out of normal life, and practice otherworldly asceticism, and by the same token ceased to be a viable proposition for ordinary people who wished or were obliged to carry on their business of life as usual.[94]

This observation probably applied less to the Celtic form of monastic life the theology and praxis of which were more in touch with the ordinary rhythms of life. However, after the Synod of Whitby (663–4) it was the Latin monastic tradition of asceticism which dominated in Britain at least.

The critical reduction of scale
With the gradual erosion of the metaphysical basis to Christology and the severing of the intimate connection between metaphysics and mysticism, Christology was inevitably dominated by soteriological concerns. This was another distinctive feature of that critical reduction of scale in Christology that accompanied the disillusion of medieval scholasticism. From Anselm, Bernard of Clairvaux and Abelard, right through to Luther, Melanchthon and Calvin, the work of Christ in securing our salvation dominated christological reflection. With the unquestioning acceptance of the two natures Christology of Chalcedon, the doctrine of the atonement took central stage. In that sense, Schleiermacher was correct when he noted that the Reformers simply left the old formulas of christological dogma intact, without any attempt at critical reconstruction.[95]

---

[93] Ibid., 141–5.
[94] Z. Bauman, *Postmodernity And Its Discontents*, 173.
[95] See for instance Articles 1 and 3 of the Augsburg Confession (1530).

Ironically, the prominence of atonement theories in this period was also linked to the fact that successive theologians extracted the narrative of the Jesus tradition from its rootage in the story of the election of Israel. This not only led to an insipid anti-Semitism which sullied the witness of the church but rendered an account of the gospel as right belief or correct doctrine rather than the practice of the Lordship of Christ.[96] To a certain extent, this tendency had always been a distinctive feature of the Western tradition in Christology. Anselm was the natural heir of Tertullian and Cyprian.[97]

It was Tertullian and Cyprian who first moved away from what Gustaf Aulen called the classic doctrine of the atonement, with its central notion of Christ triumphing over the forces of sin and evil, to a view of atonement which essentially viewed the death of Christ as a work of supererogation, a sacrifice which earns an excess of merit paid to God to compensate for human sin and evil.[98]

Accordingly, Anselm's fundamentally anthropological question, 'Why did God become man', received different answers from the eleventh century onwards. For Anselm writing within the cultural framework of medieval feudalism, the answer was that Christ became incarnate, and suffered cruelly on our behalf to satisfy the demands of God's violated honour and justice. For Bernard and Abelard, influenced more by monastic life and tradition, the vicarious humanity and death of Christ expressed in exemplary form the condescending love of God for the whole creation. With the advent of the Reformation, these issues were reconceived within another cultural context. One dominated now by the problem of human sin and guilt. Luther's anguished question 'where could a gracious saviour be found', reverberated throughout the theological agenda of the Reformation and insured that the essential *pro nobis* character of christological reflection remained intact.

The Reformers
Luther found his gracious saviour in that 'happy exchange' whereby Christ's alien righteousness was imputed to the justified sinner. The way to true knowledge of Christ was through personal appropriation of the salvation he had won

---

[96] Cf. Hauerwas, *After Christendom*, 169.

[97] 'Here, as in almost all departments of activity in the Latin Church, it was of the highest moment that Tertullian, the jurist, and Cyprian, the ecclesiastical ruler, were the first Latin theologians. Disinclined for philosophical and strictly religious speculation, and dominated by a prosaic but powerful moralism, the Latins were possessed from the first of an impulse to carry religion into the legal sphere.' A. Von Harnack, *History of Dogma*, Vol. 3, 310.

[98] G. Aulen, *Christus Victor: An Historical Study of the Three Main Types of the Idea of the Atonement*, 86–9.

for us, and this was nowhere more succinctly expressed than in Melanchthon's reformulation of the christological issue:

> The knowledge of Christ is to know his benefits, taste his salvation, and experience his grace; it is not as the academic people say, to reflect on his natures and the modes of his incarnation. If you do not know the practical purpose for which he took flesh and went to the cross what is the good of knowing his story?[99]

In the christological considerations of John Calvin, the central theme is the use of the term mediator. It is only through Christ's mediator role that true knowledge of him, i.e. saving knowledge is to be found. We require such a mediator not just because of our sin but also due to our creaturely finitude. Christ as mediator is the double mirror, in his divinity representing God to us and in his humanity representing us to God.[100]

Calvin developed a more systematic approach to the saving work of Christ in terms of the threefold biblical office of prophet, priest and king. In his prophetic office, Christ is anointed by the Spirit to be the herald and witness to the coming kingdom of God. That which he proclaims, however, he also inaugurates in his own person, thus fulfilling his kingly vocation. Finally in his priestly function Jesus both appeases the wrath of God toward human sin and expiates our sins through the obedient substitution of himself in our stead.

Calvin's doctrine of penal substitution has justly received much criticism, but to his credit, and unlike Anselm, he recognised that the saving efficacy of Jesus the mediator encompassed the whole of his life and not just the events surrounding his death and resurrection. The concept of the mediatorial offices of Christ as the way the reconciliation of the world to God was achieved was superior to the medieval notion of expiatory satisfaction because it clearly delineated the role of the Father in sending the Son. Similarly, the work of reconciliation is not limited to the event of the cross but also encompasses the whole course of Jesus' life and indeed the apostolic proclamation of Jesus as the exalted Lord (2 Cor. 5:11–21). We cannot, however, attribute a direct consciousness of the threefold mediatory office to the historical Jesus of Nazareth. Rather, this is a typological rendition of the significance of Jesus, as he is understood to fulfil the kingly, priestly and prophetic roles of the old covenant in his own mission and passion.[101]

However, the question remains: How are we to understand the union between Christ and the believer? For Martin Luther, this was conceived in essentially dialectical terms in his famous designation of the Christian as

---

[99] P. Melanchthon, Preface to the *Loci Communes Theologici*.
[100] Cf. Pelikan, *Centuries*, 158–9.
[101] Cf. Pannenberg, *Systematic Theology*, Vol. 2, 446–9.

simultaneously a saint and a sinner. With Calvin, a more considered doctrine of the inner illumination of the Spirit actually constituted a return to classical mysticism:

> To "know" Christ, however, does not mean speculative knowledge, but enjoying "the sacred and mystical union" between us and him; but the only way of knowing this is when he diffuses his life into us by the secret efficacy of the Spirit.[102]

Once again this raised the issue of the epistemological validity of religious experience. With Calvin, however, as was true for Melanchthon and the later Reformers, this was mysticism reconceived in terms of the distinctively Reformation emphasis upon the *ordo salutis.* Mystical union with Christ proceeds through the totality of the Spirit's work in us, namely, illumination, regeneration, justification, election, sanctification and finally eschatological transformation. Knowledge of Christ can only be based on the way he has chosen to make himself known to us and that knowledge comes, not through a process of mystical assent, but through a personal experience of the grace of the living Christ. At its best, reformed theology has always contended that the objective and subjective dimensions of this relationship must receive equal weight.[103]

P.T. Forsyth

It is such convictions that have remained at the centre of all forms of Protestantism. Later Puritanism, Pietism and Evangelicalism regarded the fundamental experience of repentance and conversion as the only way a person could attain to real knowledge of Christ. The legitimacy or otherwise of this approach to Christology is expressed cogently by Peter Taylor Forsyth:

> But am I really forbidden to make any use of my personal experience of Christ for the purposes even of scientific theology? Should it make no difference to the evidence for Christ's resurrection that I have had personal dealings with the risen Christ as my Saviour, nearer and dearer than my own flesh and blood? Is his personal gift of forgiveness to me, in the central experience of my life, of no value in settling the objective value of his cross and person?[104]

Forsyth's justification of personal faith was threefold:

---

[102] J. Calvin, *Commentary on John 14:17*; quoted in E.A. Dowey, *The Knowledge of God in Calvin's Theology*, 199.

[103] C.E. Braaten, *Justification, the Article by which the Church Stands or Falls*, 83.

[104] P.T. Forsyth, *The Person and Place of Jesus Christ*, 196.

1. There is the incontestable reality of moral transformation; the Christian is a changed person and that is only brought about by the regenerative power of the risen Christ.
2. The transformative power of the witness of Christ in the Church and beyond, which has so visible influenced human history and the whole process of civilisation.
3. The basic conformity of the church's gospel about Christ and the gospel that Jesus preached. Jesus was in his own person and proclamation the route of access to the Father. That was also the experience of the early church and it remains the experience of countless generations of Christians after them.

Forsyth was in many ways a theologian ahead of his time. In this third point, for instance, he anticipates some aspects of the new quest for the historical Jesus that has dominated twentieth-century New Testament scholarship.

Forsyth delineates clearly three arguments that point to the epistemological priority of personal knowledge of Christ as Saviour before we can acknowledge him as the universal Lord. In that sense Tillich's infamous statement that 'Christology is a function of soteriology' might appear to have some substance to it, although, as we have noted already, this view is not without its opponents. As we have noted, Pannenberg has remained an unswerving critic of all attempts to build Christology from soteriological concerns. He recognises that it is our inherent interest in Jesus as Saviour that so often provides the driving force for our personal engagement with the Jesus of the Gospels. However, without an adequate answer to the question, 'Is Jesus God', Jesus the Saviour could remain just one of any number of saviour figures which have appeared in the history of religion imparting their own particular brand of wisdom, illumination, freedom from guilt and sin, or in more modern vein, personal satisfaction and fulfilment. The real Achilles' heel of anthropological Christology, both in its medieval and Reformation manifestations, is the inherent tendency towards individualism. Jesus the Saviour becomes essentially, Jesus the lover of the individual soul. In all such forms of piety, the move from the erotic to the egocentric is never far away.

The next major surge in christological reconstruction was to take place with the advent of the Enlightenment. As we shall discover, however, this critical reduction in scale with its inevitable tendency towards exemplarism and individualism was to reappear in what can only be viewed as the christological reductionism of the major exponents of this new enlightenment. In that sense, they were the natural successors of their Reformation forebears:

> The reformers had very thorough answers to the question "why did Jesus die?"; they did not have nearly such good answers to the question "why did Jesus live?"

Their successors to this day have not often done any better. But the question will not go away. If the only available answer is "to give some shrewd moral teaching, to live an exemplary life, and to prepare for sacrificial death", we may be forgiven for thinking it a little lame. It also seems ... quite untrue to Jesus' own understanding of his vocation and work.[105]

To conclude, and in anticipation of the issues that will concern us in our next chapter, the skilful application of Occam's razor that effectively severed the connection between mysticism and metaphysics inevitably created an anthropological Christology based solely on the mystical union of Christ with the believer. This, in turn, thrust soteriological issues to the forefront of theological reflection and produced an exemplarist, humanist form of christological praxis and discipleship. The christologically constructed political settlement of Christendom remained intact, but not for much longer. As we shall see, the bitter and apparently intractable religious wars that followed in the wake of the Reformation effectively demolished the last major bulwark upon which both the credibility and the validity of Chalcedonian Christology was based. Mysticism on its own and its imaginative manifestation in either medieval christopraxis or Reformation evangelical conviction could not sustain the christological vision of reality that Christendom had maintained. The purveyors of the new Enlightenment were to construct their own secular humanist alternative to the vision that undergirded Christendom. In the process they would contend that both metaphysics and mysticism belonged to the old cultural regime and should be repudiated. At the same time they would endeavour to provide a new epistemological foundation for ethics, politics and religion that required only the most minimalist of christological convictions and beliefs. A new rationalism took hold of the popular imagination and, not surprisingly, a new Jesus appeared on the scene.

---

[105] Wright, *Victory*, 14.

THE ENGAGEMENT WITH MODERNITY

THE SEARCH FOR CULTURAL PARADIGMS

3.

Christology and the Enlightenment

The Enlightenment began with the rise of modern science, culminated in the French Revolution and then dwindled in wave after wave of yearning, hope and doubt. It was characterised by a scepticism towards authority, a respect for reason, and an advocacy of individual freedom rather than divine command as the basis of moral and political order.[1]

Introduction

The turn inwards to the human subject as the sole arbiter of our experience of the external world and ourselves – this so-called process of human emancipation or liberation – began with the Enlightenment, and its intellectual, socio-political and cultural consequences continue to reverberate throughout the exigencies of the modern world. According to some sociologists and cultural commentators, this process is still moving inexorably onwards, carrying everything before it, engulfing more ancient agrarian societies and making our world a deeply disturbing and equivocal place. It is nothing short of a vast, monolithic, intellectual, cultural and social reconstruction of the nature of the world and our place in it as credible participants in the drama of creation. As Moltmann explains, 'the phenomenon of the modern world is in fact unique and unparalleled in human history'.[2]

The Enlightenment marked a final break with the medieval worldview. The move away from a theocentric world to one centred on human concerns and achievements had already begun with the new humanism of the Renaissance and the rediscovery of religious freedom awakened by the Reformation. With the Enlightenment, however, human beings replaced God as the makers of their own destiny, the masters of their own fate. Not surprisingly, all the external authorities – be they the church, the Bible or the dogmas of revealed religion – were replaced by the final arbiter of truth, omnicompetent human reason:

---

[1] R. Scruton, *Guide*, 21.
[2] Moltmann, *Way*, 56.

Man begins with himself in his search for understanding. The Bible is treated primarily as a human product; the world is explored by human investigation, and only what can be established rationally and scientifically is to be believed; religion itself must be validated by reference to human experience, human values and human reason. Here lies the key to the outlook of the Age of Reason.[3]

Similarly, the more restrained and pessimistic view of human nature as incontrovertibly corrupted by sin and evil was replaced by a more optimistic and elevated view: 'The Christian sense of Original Sin, the Fall, and collective human guilt … receded in favour of an optimistic affirmation of human self-development and eventual triumph of rationality and science over human ignorance, suffering, and social evils.'[4]

This new emphasis on intellectual advancement and moral achievement inevitably changed the direction of modern Christology. Jesus ceased to be regarded as the *Logos* incarnate, or the Divine Son of the Father and became instead the great example of moral excellence, or the simple teacher of common sense religion. Exemplarism and humanism once again took centre stage.

The Causes of the Enlightenment

Whenever a new epoch in human culture and self-understanding emerges, the reasons for such a development are often complex and difficult to discern. In the case of the Enlightenment, socio-political, historical, theological and philosophical factors all contributed to the dissolution of Christendom and the emergence of the modern project of 'scientific and technological civilisation'.[5] Science replaced religion as the final arbiter of truth and the natural sciences were accepted as the most effective way to understand the world and manipulate it for our own purposes.

---

[3] A.C. Heron, *A Century of Protestant Theology*, 11. Similarly, Martin Heidegger commented: 'Christianity is bereft of its power it had during the Middle Ages *to shape history*. Its historical existence no longer lies in what it is able to fashion for itself, but in the fact that since the beginning of and throughout the modern age it has continued to be that *against which* the new freedom – whether expressly or not – must be distinguished.' *Nietzsche*, quoted in B. Ingraffia, *Postmodern Theory and Biblical Theology: Vanquishing God's Shadow*.

[4] S. Tarnas, *Passion of the Western Mind*, 290. See also R.A. Harrisville and W. Sundberg, *The Bible in Modern Culture: Theology and Historical-Critical Method from Spinoza to Käsemann*, 29–30.

[5] Moltmann, *Way*, 56.

The rise of the natural sciences

It is now widely recognised that the originator of modern science was Francis Bacon, and not Isaac Newton. It was Bacon who advised his contemporaries to eschew speculation and collect facts.[6] He rejected the imposition of external authority as a basis of knowledge and replaced it with the right to free enquiry and investigation, and provided succeeding generations with a method of experiment and inductive reasoning that appeared to offer an infallible means of distinguishing between truth and error.

Bacon's confident empiricism implied a direct criticism and rejection of the way knowledge was thought to be obtained. He saw no need of a world that was founded on Aristotelian final causes, or Platonic hidden essences. Such deductive reasoning, based on preconceived philosophical premises, obscured rather than illuminated the essential nature of the real world. Only science, which was upheld as a new utilitarian, developmental and material counterpart to God's plan of redemption for humanity and was therefore in it's own way a religious quest, could unlock nature's secrets.

Bacon's enthusiasm for applied science as a source of true knowledge seemed to be vindicated by the discoveries of Newton, especially the law of gravity, which had a profound effect on Newton's generation. The scientific ideals of careful investigation, experiment and mathematical calculation were greatly enhanced. More importantly, the discovery of gravity changed peoples' view of the world. Nature ceased to be regarded as a mysterious hotchpotch of influences and semi-occult forces, supernaturally held in check by divine providence. In their place emerged the notion of indubitable scientific laws of nature. Nature was disclosed as a precise system of intelligible laws and energies accessible to human reason, and obviously constructed by a God who was rather like an omnipotent technologist.

Deism

Deism was the religion of the Enlightenment. God was upheld as the 'First Cause' and 'Supreme Architect' of the universe, who constructed a universe analogous to a vast machine that, because of the internal laws of causation, was self-sustaining:

> The new image of the Creator was ... that of a divine architect, a master mathematician and clock maker, while the universe was viewed as a uniformly regulated and fundamentally impersonal phenomenon. Man's role in that universe could best be judged on the evidence that, by virtue of his own intelligence, he had penetrated

---

[6] A.C. MacIntyre notes that the notion of fact in the English language is a folk concept with an aristocratic ancestry! See, *After Virtue: A Study in Moral Theory*, 76.

the universe's essential order and could now use that knowledge for his own benefit and empowerment.[7]

Deism could not find a place for the biblical account of revelation, inter-spersed as it was with the problem of miracles. The mechanical orderliness of the universe, sustained by the laws of nature, appeared to be put at risk by the notion of miracle as supernatural incursions into the realm of nature.[8] So, for instance, as there were no contemporary analogies to an event like the resurrection, it followed that the accounts of such events were based on unre-liable human testimony. The French rationalist Denis Diderot expressed this contemporary incredulity toward the miraculous when he declared that if the entire population of Paris were to claim that a man had just risen from the dead, he would not believe a word of it.[9] Deism did not lead to the promised renewal of the Christian faith; it did, however, pave the way for the eventual denial of Christianity by the philosophy of modern atheism.

Natural religion
If Christianity could not be sustained by recourse to the miraculous or the authority of the Bible (given that the new sciences were already begin-ning to conflict with the Genesis account of creation), what could it be founded on? The Deists proclaimed a natural religion that had no need of the miraculous or the supernatural. Instead, religion was regarded as an inte-gral element of human nature that possessed a largely moral and rational character. Publications such as John Locke's, *The Reasonableness of Christianity*, John Toland's *Christianity not Mysterious*, Anthony Collins' *The Grounds and Reasons of the Christian Religion*, and Matthew Tindal's *Christianity as Old as Creation* or *The Gospel, A Republication of the Religion of Nature* all espoused the same belief in a Jesus who was the exemplary manifestation of common sense religion.

Jean-Jacques Rousseau perhaps best expressed the main tenets of this natural religion in *The Social Contract*. They were:

---

[7] Tarnas, *Passion of the Western Mind*, 271. The French astronomer Laplace best expressed this essentially pragmatic view of science and cosmology. When asked by Napoleon what place God had in his theory of the cosmos, his reply was 'Sire, I have no need of that hypothesis'.

[8] David Hume was widely believed to have demonstrated the impossibility of miracles: 'No testimony is sufficient to establish a miracle unless the testimony be of such a kind that its falsehood would be more miraculous than the fact which it endeavours to establish.' See, D. Hume, *Essay on Miracles*.

[9] Quoted in A.E. McGrath, *The Making of Modern German Christology: From the Enlightenment to Pannenberg*, 24.

1. Belief in an omnipotent, benevolent and intelligent deity.
2. The immortality of the soul.
3. The necessity to embrace the common good, to punish the wicked and to preserve the sanctity of the social contract.[10]

The irony of such a natural religion was that it tried desperately to manufacture a compromise between faith and reason so that at least some of the ethical teaching of the Judeo-Christian faith could be rescued from oblivion. The inexorable forward march of science was later to make such a compromise seem more untenable. 'Knowledge is power' was Bacon's great slogan (Nietzsche later espoused it in a somewhat revised form). Science became the handmaiden of technology, i.e. the way in which human beings could manipulate the natural environment for their own ends. The 'superman' capable of self-mastery, who would ultimately go beyond the values of a defunct Christianity, had arrived on the historical stage.[11]

Socio-political evaluation

The sociological achievement of the Enlightenment was the emergence of the new middle classes.[12] The Enlightenment commenced that great trek from the countryside to the cities (still a determining feature of modern life) and eventuated in the replacement of a largely agrarian, subsistence economy with that of an urbanised, industrial, free-enterprise society. Andrew Walker describes this period of enormous social change, which began with the Reformation, as the inevitable process that led to the 'transformation of feudalism to capitalism, communitarianism to individualism, traditionalism to rationalism, and of oral culture to literary culture'.[13] The beneficiaries of the Enlightenment, the new intelligentsia, were the educated middle-classes: bankers,

---

[10] Kant's reduction of religion to practical morality, which similarly required a benevolent deity, the after life and the moral autonomy of the individual, was an expression of the same moralising tendency that exemplified Deism.

[11] 'Science, particularly the physical sciences ... acquired unrivalled intellectual prestige in the modern academic world, and in society as a whole. It is widely believed to be the most reliable method open to us of finding out how things are in every sphere of reality. What is not scientific, at least in method, is thought to be unreliable, or to have abandoned the encounter with reality ... Thus both philosophy and religion, which once had the prestige today enjoyed by science, have been discredited as sources of information about reality.' Nicholl, *Guide to Modern Theology*, Vol. 1, 18.

[12] Paul Tillich refers to this as the bourgeois character of the enlightened individual. He notes, in passing, that the French word *bourgeois* is derived from the German *burger*, which means 'he who lives inside the walls of the town'. See, Tillich, *Perspectives*, 45.

[13] A. Walker, *Telling the Story: Gospel, Mission and Culture*, 40.

businessmen and merchants. They no longer accepted the old divinely instigated order of things. They wanted to know in order to control, and they needed to calculate in order to progress. It was out of this new matrix of commercialism, based in part upon the Protestant work ethic, the efficacy of science and the value of exchange, that capitalism was born. Productivist societies organised in and around the industry and technology of mass production emerged in the place of former 'symbolic societies', which were based on guilds, patrons, festivities and religious rituals.[14] Not surprisingly, all of this was to eventuate in one of the first celebrated works of economic theory, Adam Smith's *The Wealth of Nations*.

Such achievements were based on a new political vision. The old sacred order of things ordained by the gods gave way to Jean-Jacque Rousseau and John Locke's carefully crafted myth of the social contract. Inherited tradition was deemed too restrictive for the new emancipatory politics. Whether it was the revolutionary idealism of Voltaire and Denis Diderot, the Romantic liberalism of Rousseau, or the inevitable conservative reaction to the excesses of the French Revolution epitomised by Edmund Burke, none were to dissent from the fundamental tenet of the new modern world that inherited status and privilege must ultimately give way to common consent and contractual politics.

Both the newly emancipated peasants of the French Revolution, or Rousseau's inherently problematic notion of the noble savage, were in their own way another manifestation of Thomas Hobbes' insistence that at the heart of the civil society stood the self-interested, autonomous individual.[15] Whatever the nature of the contract, it was a manifestation of self-interest and self-preservation, i.e. the alienated human will. The new contractual politics based on the myth of the enlightened self-interest of the autonomous individual led to the rise of the nation state. The right to life, liberty and the pursuit of happiness, which became the manifesto of the new emerging liberal democracies proved unsustainable unless it was bolstered by the sovereignty of the nation state. However, the question can legitimately be asked:

> 'Who is under obligation to honour the claim?' In the Middle Ages the answer was found within the network of reciprocal rights and duties. The man farming the land had a duty to provide troops to fight his lord's battle and a corresponding right to his lord's protection. Duties and rights were reciprocal. One could not exist without the other, and all were finite. But the quest for happiness is infinite. Who, then, has the infinite duty to honour the infinite claim of every person to the pursuit of happiness? The answer of the eighteenth century, and of those who have followed,

---

[14] J. Baudrillard, *The Mirror of Production*.

[15] Cf. J. Sachs, *The Politics of Hope*, 58–60; cf also A. Giddens, *Modernity and Self-Identity: Self and Society in the Late Modern Age*, 210–14.

is familiar: it is the nation state. The nation state replaces the holy church and the holy empire as the centrepiece in the post-Enlightenment ordering of society. Upon it devolves the duty of providing the means for life, liberty, and the pursuit of happiness. And since the pursuit of happiness is endless, the demands upon the state are without limit. If, for modern Western people, nature has taken the place of God as the ultimate reality with which we have to deal, the nation-state has taken the place of God as the source to which we look for happiness, health, and welfare.[16]

It is at this juncture that the political economy of modernity founders. Society is not the same as the nation state, and the former never was and never could be founded on a spurious notion of social contract. Instead, the myth of the social contract helped to construct the ideology of the nation state.[17]

Historical evaluations

The historical roots of the Enlightenment go back to the Peace of West-phalia (1648), which brought an uneasy truce to the long and bitter religious wars of that era. In effect, this also hastened the end of Christendom. No longer did the one, holy catholic and apostolic church guarantee the political stability of Europe. Instead, each state now became responsible for its own confessional stance.

Pluralism in religious belief produced an important intellectual develop-ment. Was the fact that Europe could tear itself apart in the name of religion an indication that the Christian faith was not based on divinely inspired dogmas and doctrines after all, but was a human construct, which obscured rather than illuminated the essential truths of human nature?

> The Enlightenment systematically exalted the natural reason against the positive doctrines of the warring confessions, and regarded Christianity as a way of life, an ethic, rather than a system of revealed truths.[18]

A new intellectual impulse was released that sought to reformulate the basic concepts of politics, morality, economics, philosophy, science and religion upon that which was understood to be common to human nature, thereby guaranteeing a more humane society. In the place of a divinely inspired, revealed and providentially sustained universal common religion, which had been the basis of political, social and cultural hegemony, there emerged a new-found faith in a naturalistic, secular, but nevertheless, equally common and universal human nature.

---

[16] Newbigin, *Foolishness*, 27.

[17] J. Thornhill, *Modernity; Christianity's Estranged Child Reconsidered*, 3–56.

[18] A. Nicholl, *The Pelican Guide to Modern Theology*, Vol. 1, 36.

The chief proponents of the Enlightenment always measured the particular in terms of the universal. As Jürgen Habermas has indicated, there was good reason for doing so because only in this way could they refashion society according to humanisitic ideals and aspirations.[19]

Philosophical evaluation: religion within the bounds of reason

The Enlightenment produced a new investigation into the limits, boundaries and foundations of human knowledge. Human reason, untrammelled by received tradition, was given the right of free enquiry and investigation.[20] How do we know and what can we know with any degree of certainty about God, the world and ourselves? Three personalities dominate the intellectual horizons of this debate and they all, in their own way, narrow down the limits of religious faith and belief to that which is accessible to reason alone.

Descartes
René Descartes lived at a time when the findings of the new science, which meant mainly the discoveries of Copernicus and Galileo, were beginning to unsettle people. People had always thought, according to received wisdom endorsed by the church, that the earth was at the centre of the universe. The discovery that the sun, and not the earth, is at the centre of a much bigger planetary system gave rise to a certain epistemological flux; uncertainty and a new scepticism began to emerge, as exhibited by the French essayist Michel Montaigne. Things are not what they seem: the earth is rotating yet the ground beneath our feet seems stationary. People no longer felt secure or at home in the world, old verities were being challenged and undermined.

Descartes set about the task of finding certain knowledge.[21] He resolved to doubt everything until he found a bedrock of knowledge altogether resistant to the corrosive effects of uncertainty. Descartes claimed to have discovered this Archimedean point in the famous *cogito ergo sum* ('I think, therefore I am'). Even when he was uncertain about the very fact that he doubted, he was aware of himself as a thinking being. But suppose he was being deceived? Suppose there were a malevolent genius controlling the universe? At this point Descartes brought in the idea of God to overcome this theoretical possibility. If

---

[19] J. Habermas, *Modernity Versus Postmodernity*, 9.

[20] This is epitomised by Alexander Pope: 'Know then thy-self, presume not God to scan. The proper study of mankind is Man.' Cf. *Essay On Man*.

[21] Descartes is usually attributed with the dubious honour of being the first philosopher to introduce the principle of methodological doubt into the quest for certainty. In fact, this approach to the search for truth had already been espoused and encouraged by the medieval theologian Peter Abelard.

there is a God and if this God is good and true then we have no need to fear such metaphysical deception. The route to knowledge of God is no longer via the existence of the external world, as was the case with the medieval proofs for God's existence, but via our own inner subjectivity. The existence of God is a presupposition of our own self-awareness, i.e. when the thinking subject examines the certainty of their own existence. We only arrive at a sustainable belief in God when we reflect on our own self-consciousness.

Descartes was, in fact, replacing the medieval cosmological proofs for God's existence with an anthropological alternative based on the reality of the thinking subject. In the process, he was inevitably privileging the epistemological scope of the individual subject and creating the basis for the fateful subject–object dichotomy that dominated the history of philosophy that ensued from his labours.

At the same time, Descartes was trying to establish a rational basis for the objective existence of the external world. He uncovered a dualism, an epistemological disjunction between *res cogitans* (thinking substance, subjective self-awareness, soul or mind) and *res extensa* (extended substance, the material cosmos, and objective reality). Only in the human persona do the two realities come together as mind and body, and both find their common source in the presupposition of a benevolent deity. Utilising the principle of methodological doubt, the human reason establishes first the certainty of its own existence, then God's existence, out of logical necessity, and finally the God-given certainty of the objective world, and its inherent rational order susceptible to scientific observation and investigation.

> In Descartes' vision, science, progress, reason, epistemological certainty and human identity were all inextricably connected with each other and with the conception of an objective, mechanistic universe; and upon this synthesis was founded the paradigmatic character of the modern mind.[22]

In the end, Descartes initiated a Copernican revolution in epistemology that was soon to be completed by Kant. However, the route from one to the other went via the enigmatic figure of David Hume.

Hume

In his *Essays Concerning Human Understanding*, Hume effectively debunked the so-called argument from causation and the argument from design; two of the most persuasive of the cosmological arguments in favour of divine initiative in the world. This amounted to a demolition job on both the proofs for God's existence and the medieval synthesis of faith and reason. As an empiricist,

---

[22] Tarnas, *Passion of the Western Mind*, 280.

Hume claimed that all our knowledge is derived from our experience of the world. When it comes to causation, for instance, Hume argued that there is no necessary connection between cause A and effect B. In our observation of such events all that we perceive is the regular occurrence of B due to the instrumentality of A. When it is claimed, as was the case in the argument from causality, that there cannot be an infinite regress of causes and, consequently, we arrive at God the uncaused Causer, what we are doing, in fact, is wrenching the law of cause and effect out of its natural habitat in the real world and providing it with a quite unnecessary and erroneous metaphysical basis.[23]

The same was true, claimed Hume, for the argument from design. This argument rests on the claim that the universe displays the hand of its architect in much the same way as a human artefact is recognisable as the work of a human designer. But our awareness of design in real experience is based on encountering repeated instances of the same artefact. Suppose we discovered something of which there was no other example? How could we be sure that is was an artefact or someone had designed it? The universe is just such a one-off; we are not in a position to experience other worlds or world designers. How then can we assume that the universe is the product of divine design and intention?[24]

Once again, traditional religious certainties, this time the so-called foundation to natural knowledge of God, had been subject to the scrutiny of critical reason and was found wanting. Not surprisingly, traditional orthodox Christology, which spoke of a human person bearing both a divine and human nature, began to look like another illegitimate violation of the limits of human reason. Instead, the rationalism of the Enlightenment developed a preference for a Jesus who was basically a moral educator.

Kant

Immanuel Kant went further than either Descartes or Hume in mapping out the boundaries of human knowledge. Kant's celebrated book, *Religion within the Limits of Reason Alone*, declared his express intention of criticising the religion of reason, and not Christianity, in order to make way for genuine faith. He outlined the groundwork for this endeavour in his major philosophical works.[25]

Kantian epistemology put the human subject firmly at the centre of the cognitive process. He built on the empiricism of Locke and Hume, making a distinction between *noumena* (things in themselves, which we cannot know) and *phenomena* (things as they appear to us), which form the basis to all human knowledge. Kant, however, went beyond his august predecessors in claiming that knowledge is not just random experience of the world around us. The

---

[23] See D. Hume, *A Treatise on Human Nature*, 247–9.
[24] See D. Hume, *Dialogues*, Part XII.
[25] See, I. Kant, *The Critique of Pure Reason* and *The Critique of Practical Reason*, 74–82.

knowing subject is at the centre of the process. Our experience and under-standing are shaped by our minds or, more precisely, the a priori categories or concepts that are part of the mental furniture of our minds which enable us to make sense of the manifold of experience. Take, for instance, the concepts of space, time and causation. These are essential prerequisites for our under-standing of the world. This does not mean that there are such entities existing objectively in the world beyond our experience. We do not know time and space in themselves. Rather, it is through these concepts or categories of understanding that we bring order and coherence to the world of phenomena.

On the basis of this epistemology, knowledge of God could only be guaran-teed if either God himself was part of our experience of the world or an a priori category necessary for our ordering and shaping of the world. As neither of these were the case, was atheism inevitable? Not at all! Although God is not a necessary condition for the exercise of pure reason, the situation changes when it comes to practical reason. Practical reason has to do with the business of moral choices and actions. The core of morality is the categorical imperative, the unconditional demand upon us to do what is right for its own sake. This, however, must be founded on three other conditions:

1. The moral autonomy and responsibility of the individual person.
2. The acceptance of immortality as the basis for both reward and punishment.
3. The existence of God as the supreme Good, the ultimate guarantor of the moral order of the universe.

While the existence of God cannot be proved by the exercise of critical reason, it is a necessary presupposition to the exercise of practical reason. In effect, religion functions as the interior presupposition of moral action and religious doctrines can therefore be understood as 'value judgements', which are not grounded in any-thing over and above our moral experience. In a manner similar to Descartes, God is brought into the system via the back door, as the ultimate justification for moral action. Remove the categorical imperative and God is not required either. In the *Critique of Judgement*, Kant sought to find a mediating position between the other two critiques and was forced to recognise that the reality of God must be presupposed if morality is to possess a consistent rationale.

> In order to set ourselves a final purpose in conformity with the moral law, we must assume a moral cause of the world (an author of the world); and to the extent that setting ourselves a final purpose is necessary, to that extent (i.e. to the same degree and on the same ground) it is also necessary that we assume [that there is] a moral cause of the world, that is, that there is a God.[26]

---

[26] I. Kant, *Critique of Judgement*, 340.

Theological evaluations

Explanations concerning the theological causes of the Enlightenment are many and varied. Karl Löwith, a German historian and theologian, suggested that the Enlightenment was the product of a fundamental change in the way people experienced history. Instead of history being understood as a teleological process controlled by God's providential action, it became the arena of arbitrary human self-realisation.[27] Hans Blumenberg, on the other hand, regarded the Enlightenment as a necessary process of spiritual emancipation. It was an inevitable act of human self-assertion against the repressive and authoritarian theological absolutism of Christian theism. Karl Barth took an opposite view and described the origins of modernity, especially the eighteenth-century view of human nature, as but the expression of human self-assertion and hubris in the face of the Christian God, i.e. nothing more than a peculiarly modern manifestation of the sin of Adam. G.W.F. Hegel, the father of German idealism, viewed the Enlightenment as the worldly or secular realisation of the idea of Christian freedom rediscovered at the Reformation and expressed in different forms by both Enlightenment rationality and Romanticism.[28]

Dietrich Bonhoeffer provided much later another more positive assessment. He claimed that secularisation was the emergence of 'man come of age'. It was the inevitable abandonment of an outmoded metaphysic, the *deus ex machina* (the God outside the machine), and emancipation from the tutelage of the God of the gaps.[29] We should also take note of Immanuel Kant's candid assessment of the situation: 'The Enlightenment is the emergence of man from immaturity that he is himself responsible for. Immaturity is the incapacity to use one's own intelligence without the guidance of another person.'[30]

In their different ways, both Bonhoeffer and Kant were referring to the disestablishment of the Christian faith by secular, political and religious alternatives to the vision that upheld Christendom. In old Christendom both philosophy and theology were deployed to prove the existence of God, and the authority of the church sanctioned all attempts to suggest otherwise. The world became a different place when theology and authority were discredited. Gone was the old metaphysic that viewed the universe as the inevitable product of divine omnipotence and benevolence. Reformation Protestantism replaced the authority of the church with the authority of the Bible, but both were to prove susceptible to the corrosive acids of modernity. Consequently, a new

---

[27] Lesslie Newbigin noted the importance of this recent development in *The Gospel in a Pluralist Society*, 68–9.

[28] Cf. W. Pannenberg, *Christianity in a Secularized World*, 6–7.

[29] D. Bonhoeffer, *Letters and Papers from Prison*, 129.

[30] I. Kant, *Was ist Aufklarung: Aufsätze z. Geschichte u. Philosophie.*

situation emerged where the church ceased to be the bond that held society together; it became instead a voluntary organisation for those sections of society that still took an interest in religion.

Romanticism

Not surprisingly, Enlightenment rationalism spawned its counter-ego. Romanticism can be described as a diverse philosophical and cultural movement that endeavoured to unite what Enlightenment rationalism had rent asunder. Humanity and nature, subject and object, teleology and history, divinity and culture were all to be reunited in one great cosmic synthesis. The religion of reason and the religion of the Spirit, however, shared some common presuppositions:

- Both were deeply humanist in their high regard for humanity's cognitive and aesthetic capacities.
- Both prescribed our relationship to nature as the fundamental domain of human creativity and advancement.
- Both probed deeply into the nature and structure of human subjectivity and consciousness.
- Both looked to a renewal of classical culture as a source of contemporary values and aspirations.
- Both exhibited the spirit of Prometheus in their rebellion against imposed authority and their valorisation of individual freedom.

There were, however, fundamental differences that are worth noting.[31] First, Enlightenment scientific rationalism locked onto nature as an object to be investigated, subjugated and ultimately made to conform both to the pattern of the human mind and the force of the human will. Romanticism sought to rescue nature from such manipulative manhandling listening to and evoking its own inner depths of aesthetic vitality and subliminal spirituality. Secondly, where Enlightenment scientific explanation and epistemology focused on the cognitive, the empirical and quantitative behavioural studies, the Romantics – as evidenced by Rousseau's *Confessions*, a self-conscious re-echoing of Augustine – turned towards imaginative self-awareness and the intuitive depths of feeling and emotion. Thirdly, the Enlightenment penchant for the universal, the grand overarching ideologies and unitive scientific theories,

---

[31] Whereas the Enlightenment temperament's high valuation of man rested on his unequalled rational intellect and its power to comprehend and exploit the laws of nature, the Romantics valued man rather for his imaginative and spiritual aspirations, his emotional depths, his artistic creativity and powers of individual self-expression and self-creation. Tarnas, *Passion of the Western Mind,* 367.

a new, but no less intimidating jealous monotheism, was opposed by the radical perspectivism of the Romantics. Divergent explanations located in the multiplicity of particulars were accepted as legitimate apperceptions of a magnificently pluriform and inherently complex world. Fourthly, the positivistic naturalism of the Enlightenment that sought to pluck objective truths and facts from the dumb matter of nature and history was countered by the profoundly disturbing awareness of each interpreter's horizon of meaning and experience. This was lucidly expressed by Nietzsche: knowledge was candidly accepted as value laden, or exposed as nothing more than the naked will to power and ideological domination. Accordingly, humankind replaced the gods as the source of all innovative, recuperative possibilities and imaginative fiction. Fifthly, the Enlightenment's inherent scepticism toward tradition and all similar advocates of past superstition was replaced by the Romantics' appreciation of tradition as a repository of collective wisdom, the social memory of the world soul with its own inner evolutionary entelechy. Finally, where Enlightenment rationalism replaced religion with science as the final arbiter of truth and source of all genuine public knowledge, the Romantics diverted religion into art and aesthetics. High culture now opened a new route to transcendence. Art, literature and music became the inevitable nostalgia for God, the heroic possibility of re-entering the Garden of Eden, but this time accepting that there might just be no possibility of divine superintendence.

> Thus while Romanticism in this most general sense continued to inspire the West's 'inner' culture – its art and literature, its religious and metaphysical vision, its moral ideals – science dictated the 'outer' cosmology: the character of nature, man's place in the universe, and the limits of his real knowledge. Because science ruled the objective world, the Romantic perception was by necessity limited to the subjective. The Romantic reflections on life, their music and poetry and religious yearnings, richly absorbing and culturally sophisticated as these might be, in the end had to be consigned to only a part of the modern universe.[32]

The philosophical roots of Romanticism go back to the great disciple of Kant, J.G. Fichte. Fichte endeavoured to overcome the Kantian dualism between the thing in itself (*noumena*) and the thing as it appears to us (*phenomena*) through the idea of an all-encompassing self-positing Subject or Absolute Ego. Thus we have productive, cosmic, divine Subjectivity realised in the world of nature. Nature is no longer the realm of brute facts or mechanical self-regulating laws, but the self-realisation of the divine in another form, where beauty and harmony can be discerned and enjoyed for its own sake.

---

[32] Ibid., 375–6.

This principle of the relation between the finite and the infinite is the first principle of Romanticism on which everything else is dependent. Without it, Romanticism and a theologian like Schleiermacher become completely unintelligible.[33]

Such ideas were taken further by Friedrich Schelling. In his *System of Transcendental Idealism*, Schelling put forward the idea that nature is the unconscious product of subjectivity. As such it possesses a drive to realise itself in subjective form, i.e. the historical and moral life of humanity. It was these philosophical ideas that inspired the poetic vision of nature as slumbering spirit advocated by the Schlegel brothers (Wilhelm and Friedrich) accompanied by Novalis (von Hardenberg). Thus the most basic idea of Romanticism, which is present in thinkers as diverse as Goethe, Schelling and Hegel, is the idea of humanity as the microcosm of the universe. The human being is not merely part of the universe; rather, the creative self-positing cosmic Spirit, externally realised in nature, comes to conscious self-expression in ourselves.

Hegel

For Hegel the evolution of the cosmos is the product of a dialectical process of opposition and synthesis. Each stage in the process brings forth its antithesis that is then resolved through the synthesis, or overcoming of such inbuilt contradictions. Dialectic was the driving force of nature and history. Each cultural and historical epoch posited its own contradiction. However, in the resolving of that dichotomy truth moves on encompassing a larger whole. While Kant argued that the human mind was unable to penetrate beyond the world of phenomena to things as they are in themselves without becoming hopelessly trapped in irresolvable antinomies and contradictions, Hegel viewed this process as indicative of a higher reality. The human mind was analogous to the divine Mind or Spirit (*Geist*) and so in principle was capable of transcending such apparent contradictions. This could only be so if the a priori categories of the human mind were not fixed, timeless entities, but part of a historically conditioned process leading eventually to consciousness possessing an absolute knowledge of itself. The evolutionary process of the Absolute's self-realisation would supersede each generation's critical philosophical self-awareness. The genus of Hegel's whole system rests on three inherently problematic metaphysical principles that, by and large, were rejected by the subsequent history of philosophy, but paradoxically continually infiltrated the world of theology.

Like Fichte, the first is the notion of the Absolute that first posits itself in the immediacy of its own self-consciousness. The second is the supposition that that condition is then negated as the Absolute moves out into its other, which

---

[33] Tillich, *Perspectives*, 78.

is the finite world of time and space. In that sense, the Absolute is both *in itself* and *for itself* in and through the Other. The third is the negating of the negation whereby the Absolute recovers its own inner essence. The notion of the self-abnegation of the Subject both Absolute and finite in the other; the self-estrangement or self-alienation of this irreducible plenitude until it recovers its own fullness of being in an even greater potency of self-consciousness, was to exercise a particular and, some would add utterly detrimental, influence upon theology and Christology which entailed that Hegel was never expunged from the theological agenda of modernity.[34]

How then is this harmony of finite beings with the world of nature achieved? We can only know and understand nature when we commune with it through our more intuitive or aesthetic senses of feeling, imagination and self-awareness, not when we seek to dissect or dominate it through critical reason. The most original and influential purveyor of German Romanticism in England was Samuel Coleridge. His *Aids to Reflection* and the posthumously published *Confessions of an Inquiring Spirit* gave philosophical and theological expression to ideas first present in his poetry. The more pantheistic form of Romanticism can be discerned in the poetry of William Wordsworth. The Romantics eschewed the domination of reason and embraced the dynamic of imagination and intuition. Harmony with nature, the divine and ourselves was achieved through intuitive reason (Coleridge), the aesthetics of art, music and poetry (the Schlegels) or the religion of *das Gefühl*, inadequately translated in English as feeling or emotion (Novalis and Schleiermacher).

Assessment

The intellectual, socio-political and cultural consequences of the Enlightenment still reverberate throughout the exigencies of the modern world. 'The Enlightenment, we discover, is part of us. It belongs to the archaeology, rather than the pre-history, of modern consciousness';[35] and we the enlightened beneficiaries of this great cultural and social revolution still live in abject fear of it. More than anything else, it is this immense intellectual and cultural ferment that has produced the 'crisis of modern Christology'. The reasons for this are not hard to discern.

---

[34] So, for instance, Hegel's famous announcement of the death of God was by no means a precursor to the nihilism of Nietzsche, rather it referred to the death of Christ the second person of the trinity. However, here the theological is understood philosophically as the self-abnegation of the transcendent God into the immanence of history and human community.

[35] Scruton, *Guide*, 26.

The Christology of the Patristic, Byzantine, and medieval period found a home within a perception of the universe that was theocentric, replete with an inbuilt teleology that revealed its divine origins. A universe that was continuously contingent upon God and directly governed by him through the agency of his omniscience and omnipotence. By contrast, the Newtonian cosmology reduced God to a distant cognitive possibility, or heavenly potentate, rather than a dynamically active force and reality. God was more the metaphysical ground of the universe's existence, the original architect or first Cause, rather than one who was directly and redemptively involved in the world, or, indeed, historically revealed in the freedom and contingency of the created order. The universe consequently became an altogether more impersonal place – vast, sinister and silent, governed by mechanically ordered, self-regulating universal laws. The gods gave way to a scientific version of fate and inscrutable destiny, and were only assigned a place on the margins of human existence. This inevitably contributed to the increasing secularisation of the modern world and the growing sense of existential dislocation and alienation.

The intellectual maelstrom of the Enlightenment greatly enhanced the cause of human advancement and achievement. New sciences brought with them new knowledge, which in turn further released the creative energy of the human spirit to investigate, explore and eventually, it was hoped, conquer the natural environment. The inherited religious view of the human drama as but a temporary sojourn in a fallen world to prepare us for our eternal destiny receded from view in favour of a secularised notion of human progress and individual self-determination. In a world where science and technology were increasingly pushing back the boundaries there no longer appeared to be the same need for a saviour:

> From the emergence of physics and calculus at the turn of the eighteenth century to steady advances thereafter in botany, zoology, chemistry and geology, the natural sciences had, by 1830, reached a level of prestige in Western culture that it has yet to relinquish.[36]

The epistemological success of science, the sheer explanatory power of the new disciplines fuelled by the same intoxicating brew of inductive reasoning and empirical investigation, effectively dethroned theology as the queen of the sciences. Empirical observation, mathematical calculation and verifiable hypotheses replaced biblical revelation and theological explanation as the means to true knowledge of the world and ourselves. Within such a scientific and secular mindset it became possible to doubt the theological and religious veracity of the Judeo-Christian worldview and eventually reject it altogether.

---

[36] Harrisville and Sundberg, *Bible in Modern Culture*, 89.

Rationalists and materialists such as Hume, Diderot and Baron d'Holbach poured scorn on the foundational elements of Christian belief and doctrine.[37]

From within the parameters of a naturalistic explanation of the world, miracles, exorcisms, a virgin birth, a divine human saviour, a resurrection from the dead and ascension into heaven, together with the assurance of eschatological return, all began to look like superstitious mythology or legendary accretions to a religion now systematically beating a hasty retreat from the mainstream of human culture and intellectual endeavour. Few people actually rejected religion because of the advances in science; it was simply that science gradually constructed a new *plausibility theory* as far as the known world was concerned.[38] This hastened the process, so determinative of the modern world, referred to as the privatisation, marginalisation or compartmentalisation of religious faith and belief:

> Faith and reason were now definitively severed. Conceptions involving a transcendent reality were increasingly regarded as beyond the competence of human knowledge; as useful palliatives for man's emotional nature; as aesthetically satisfying imaginative creations; as potentially valuable heuristic assumptions; as necessary bulwarks for morality or social cohesion; as political-economic propaganda; as psychologically motivated projections; as life-impoverishing illusions; as superstitious, irrelevant or meaningless.[39]

Rationalism enthroned reason as the measure of all things and empiricism opened up a route from a traditional religious worldview to one of secular humanism or scientific materialism.

Essential to both a biblical and classical Greek outlook was the concept of divine order, one that was not self-regulating but informed and directed by the divine will. Whatever order was now perceived to reside in the natural world was either the innate regularities or inbuilt structures of its essential elements – or, if one preferred Kant's account, the order imposed on the phenomenal world by the a priori categories of the human mind. Both perceptions virtually eliminated the concept of purpose from the natural order and replaced it with power, control and domination.

The new role occupied by the human subject as master of his or her own fate and primary agent in the investigation and control of the objective world, was accompanied by a corresponding inflation of the cognitive and rational

---

[37] For a helpful and informative survey of the inevitable trend towards atheism which dominated the latter stages of the Enlightenment see J.M. Byrne, *Glory, Jest and Riddle: Religious Thought in the Enlightenment*, 124–49.

[38] P.L. Berger, *The Heretical Imperative: Contemporary Possibilities of Religious Affirmation*, 136–48.

[39] Tarnas, *Passion of the Western Mind*, 268.

elements of human nature. Although briefly challenged by Romanticism in the hope of rehabilitating the aesthetic, relational, ethical and emotional components of the human psyche, scientific materialism was to prove more hard-nosed and ultimately more durable.[40]

The final deathnell to the uneasy alliance between the natural religion of the Enlightenment and the new scientific outlook was ushered in by the arrival of the Darwinian theory of evolution in the nineteenth century. While Darwinanism greatly enhanced the apparently ubiquitous nature of scientific explanation, it introduced another altogether more difficult paradigm into the scheme of things. The Cartesian-Newtonian universe still retained a place for God as the divine originator of the whole created process. Those of a more religious nature could see in the self-regulatory order and harmony of the universe, a further manifestation of the divine nature. The theory of evolution, which was constructed upon the twin notions of random selection and the survival of the fittest, appeared to be a downright rebuttal of the biblical account of creation.

> The human mind was not a divine endowment but a biological tool. The structure and movement of nature was the result not of God's benevolent design and purpose, but of an amoral, random, and brutal struggle for survival in which success went not to the virtuous but to the fit. Nature itself, not God or a transcendent Intellect, was now the origin of nature's permutations. Natural selection and chance, not Aristotle's teleological forms or the Bible's purposeful Creation, governed the processes of life.[41]

If the underlying structure of the natural world appeared to be a form of egocentric determinism, what place was there for the altruistic, self-sacrificing and voluntaristic virtues inherent in the biblical story?

Finally, with the apparently inalienable right to individual self-determination now ensconced in the intellectual, cultural and political fabric of the new world order, the Christian doctrine of redemption was replaced with the secular notion of progress. Humanity's chief end was no longer 'to glorify God and enjoy him for ever'. Rather, it was to be emancipated from such imperialistic religious restraints. In place of a covenantal framework, which was essentially communitarian, orientated towards justice, love and reconciliation, we find the modern dependency upon utilitarian and expressive individualism.[42]

Clearly, what is at issue here is not the debate about the genesis and development of modernity, however that is conceived. We have already conceded that

---

[40] Cf. Scruton, *Guide*, 44–50.

[41] Tarnas, *Passion of the Western Mind*, 289.

[42] R.N. Bellah, *Habits of the Heart: Individualism and Commitment in American Life*, 142–63.

modernity probably originated in the sixteenth century with the rediscovery of religious freedom and the rejection of the ubiquitous power and authority of the Roman Catholic Church, ushered in as it was by the Reformation as well as the valorisation of humanistic scepticism which typified Renaissance figures such as Erasmus and Montaigne. The seventeenth-century scientific revolutions of Galileo, Bacon, Descartes, Leibniz and Newton greatly enhanced the dynamic of this vast cultural transformation. This, in turn, eventuated in the republican political theories and revolutions of the eighteenth century that swept aside traditional political allegiances in Europe and America. Finally, the industrial revolutions and social Darwinanism of the nineteenth century ensured that in the early twentieth century the social, political and intellectual capital of modernity was everywhere in evidence throughout Europe and America and their respective colonies in the Two-Thirds World.

Such a vast process of cultural change and transformation was only made possible because of the positive self-image modern Western culture had often bequeathed to itself. An image that, noticeably 'places the highest premium on individual human life and freedom, and believes that such freedom and rationality will lead to social progress through virtuous, self-controlled work, creating a better material, political and intellectual life for all'.[43] Consequently, the Enlightenment did not just set new challenges for Christology and theological reconstruction; it literally rewrote the textbook as far as our self-understanding in relation to the world was concerned. As such, it created a number of fundamental new paradigms against which all subsequent theological endeavours would have to contend.[44]

---

[43] L. Cahoone, *From Modernism to Postmodernism: An Anthology*, 12.

[44] Thomas Kuhn's theory of paradigm shifts in the natural sciences has been taken over into theology by Hans Küng and David Tracy, in relation to the major epochs of theological development, cf. H. Küng and D. Tracy (eds), *Paradigm Change in Theology: A Symposium for the Future*; also H. Küng, *Christianity: The Religious Situation of Our Time*; and by David Bosch in relation to the history and theology of mission, cf. Bosch, *Transforming Mission*. Kuhn sought to show how one scientific paradigm, or model of interpretation, could be completely supplanted by, or sublimated in, another. He defined 'paradigm' as 'an entire constellation of beliefs, values, techniques, and so on shared by the members of a given community', cf. T.S. Kuhn, *The Structure of Scientific Revolution*, 175. The use of the term paradigm or model of interpretation moves away from a purely history of ideas approach to the development of knowledge re-establishing the link between scientific advances and their socio-historical contexts. In this regard other sociologists such as S.E. Toulmin, *Human Understanding, The Collective Use and Evolution of Concepts*, and Berger, *Heretical Imperative* have been quick to see what theologians tended to ignore. In that sense, the idea of a constant search for new paradigms refers to the continual dialogue and interchange that takes place between Christology and the changing historical and cultural contexts it seeks to address.

The first and arguably most tendentious of the new paradigms was the general uncertainty and equivocation that now surrounded the role and status of religion in the modern world. We noted how significant Enlightenment thinkers replaced the notion of a universal common religion with that of a universal common humanity. Subsequent theologians, such as Schleiermacher, Tillich, Rahner and Pannenberg, would respond to this paradigm shift by arguing that religion itself was an essential and irreducible part of our common humanity, from the basis of which could be constructed a plausible and culturally sensitive Christology. While such essentially apologetic approaches might appear laudable and commendable, they do tend to miss the more central issue that is bound up with the public or socio-political significance of Christology in the context of a modern, pluralist and secular culture. On the whole, Western theology has been either mute or ineffective in responding to this challenge.

Secondly, religion manifests itself in historical and cultural form. The Enlightenment invented another theory of history, replacing the conviction that the purpose and *telos* of history was maintained by the providential activity of God, with the notion that history was effectively the story of human progress and self-realisation.

> Instead of an unchanging, static, eternal world order with a hierarchical ordering (*ordo* as understood by Plato, Augustine and Thomas) instead of a Reformation two-realms doctrine of the kingdom of God and the kingdom of the world, there is now a new unitary view of world and history in the sense of a lasting progress: this is the second leading value of modernity.[45]

This new paradigm, or myth,[46] referred to as the secularisation of history, has tended to dominate christological issues throughout the modern period. Only in the light of more recent arguments in literary and political theory has some of this obsession with history appeared passé and unconvincing.

Thirdly, we have noted how the onslaught of Darwinianism effectively destroyed the uneasy truce between the Christian faith and the natural religion of the Enlightenment. Darwin's theory of evolution as a scientific explanation of the origin of the species was preceded by the all-encompassing myth of evolution, a new metaphysic spawned by Idealism that can ultimately be traced to Fichte and Hegel and has often appeared to offer new possibilities for christological reconstruction. It is this paradigm that has probably been most ardently addressed by Roman Catholic theology of the post-Thomistic variety.

---

[45] Küng, *Christianity: Religious Situation*, 680.
[46] By myth I mean a socially constructed interpretative model that may or may not lose its interpretative power and status.

Fourthly, at the heart of the new story or metanarrative constructed by the proponents of the Enlightenment was the self-postulating, self-determining, morally autonomous individual. In that sense, the personal identity of the modern person has been reduced to 'the reflexive project of the self'.[47] Such an abject reduction and erroneous notion of human personhood could only be founded on another pernicious myth that claimed the Enlightenment opened up a new and glorious route to human emancipation:[48]

> emancipation came to mean the self-determination of men and women generally in the face of an authority which demanded blind obedience and a rule which was illegitimate: freedom from natural compulsion, from social compulsion and the compulsion of those who have not yet achieved their own identity.[49]

Science, technology and economics – the harbingers of the new age – were inevitably the means through which such freedom could be gained. Liberation christologies take issue with how such freedom should be defined, but their genre is a reflexive reaction founded on a new social myth.

Finally, the pathos, irony, and at times, despair, of postmodernity is that the socio-political myths and paradigm shifts of modernity are no longer generally believed. Christologies constructed on these foundations consequently appear increasingly culturally disingenuous and herein lies the present crisis of modern Christology. So, it is to this fascinating story that we now must turn.

---

[47] A. Giddens, *Modernity*, 5.

[48] This point is barely recognised in the otherwise informative and thorough analysis of these issues in A.C. Thiselton, *Interpreting God and the Postmodern Self: On Meaning, Manipulation and Promise.*

[49] Küng, *Christianity: Religious Situation*, 686.

4.

Christology and Religious Experience

PARADIGM ONE:
WHAT PLACE FOR RELIGION IN THE MODERN WORLD?

[The Enlightenment] dispensed with Christology because first it had virtually dispensed with faith in Christ as Saviour. Jesus is indeed the Teacher of a perfect morality and the pattern of character for all time; but there is nothing supernatural about Him. To call Him in any metaphysical sense God's Son is irrational, for His personality was the product of natural gifts directed by an energetic will.[1]

By reducing mystery to reason and by flattening transcendence into common sense, the rationalism of the Enlightenment had dethroned superstition only to enthrone banality.[2]

Introduction

One of the fundamental judgements of modernity upon its own religious history was that the 'sacred canopy' of the Christian faith was largely redundant. The transition from Christendom to the modern world of the Enlightenment either consigned religion to the intellectual dustbin or reduced it to morality, apart from a brief period of Romantic fervour when religion was redirected into aesthetics. The familiar dictum, 'he who marries himself to the spirit of the age will soon find himself a widower', was most certainly the case for those who espoused the religion of the Enlightenment. Deism and the natural religion of reason represented the accommodation of the Christian faith to the intellectual and cultural trends that convulsed Europe between 1670 and 1790. The limitations of the universal religion of reason were evident in the unequivocal and at times absurd reductionist tendencies of Enlightenment Christology. Christianity stands or falls by the adequacy or otherwise of its Christology; during this

---

[1] Mackintosh, *Person*, 249.
[2] Pelikan, *Centuries*, 194.

era Christology degenerated into a Jesuology that was exemplarist, rationalistic, anti-supernatural and thoroughly moralistic.

Two theologians who understood implicitly the nature and magnitude of the crisis that engulfed the role of religion in the modern world were Friedrich Schleiermacher, hailed as the father of modern theology, and Paul Tillich, his natural successor. The central driving apologetic of both theologians was their passionate desire to rehabilitate an intellectually defensible and ethically inspirational view of religion within the cultural aspirations of their contemporaries. This laudable concern necessitated a search for appropriate philosophical categories through which the conversation with culture could be conducted. As a result, a new christological paradigm came to dominate the modern period.

Part 1

Friedrich Schleiermacher

The Search for a Paradigm

The stature and importance of Schleiermacher was due to his unique ability 'to reweave religion, threatened with oblivion, into the incomparably rich fabric of the burgeoning intellectual life of modern times'.[3] Schleiermacher was a disciple of the religion of reason. He had a profound respect for the new scientific worldview, which would not allow him to return to the old supernaturalism of Protestant orthodoxy. Like Kant, Schleiermacher accepted the limits of critical reason, which meant religion could not venture into metaphysical speculation; unlike his predecessor, Schleiermacher refused to reduce religion to morality – God could not be pushed to the background as the divine guarantor of moral duty and obligation. Rather, God must occupy the foreground of our innermost being and religious sensibilities.

Schleiermacher also had a profound sense that the Christian faith was founded on the sheer givenness of the grace of God, mediated through the redemption Christ offers to the believer and made concrete in the community of the church. He appropriated this from his Moravian Pietist background, with its emphasis upon the grace and love of Christ personally experienced through justification and the sanctifying work of the Holy Spirit, as well as a rediscovery of the church as the evangelical community of faith.[4] But

---

[3] P. Otto, 'Preface' to F. Schleiermacher, *On Religion: Speeches to its Cultural Despisers*, vii.

[4] See B.A. Gerrish, *A Prince of the Church: Schleiermacher and the Beginnings of Modern Theology*, 21–39. This was also Barth and Brunner's assessment of the situation.

Schleiermacher left behind Pietism's literalist interpretation of Scripture, preferring instead the historical and critical exegesis of the biblical texts, thereby becoming the founder of the modern discipline of hermeneutics.

Scleiermacher took from the Romantics their distrust of cold, detached, analytical reason, their love of art and culture, their conviction that reality is a living, dynamic, organic whole, and the belief that the essence of religion was to be found in the affective and intuitive dimensions of human existence. However, he rejected the idealism of Fichte, Schelling and Hegel, and dispensed with the idea that everything is the product of the self-positing divine Subject. In that sense one could say that the discernment of Schleiermacher was that he refused to be seduced by the pretensions of transcendental idealism; on the other hand, this inevitably made his whole theological programme vulnerable to the criticism that it was an indefensible reduction of theology to anthropology. In Schleiermacher's defence, while it is true that he believed our knowledge of God must be grounded in human experience, the charge that he was guilty of a subjective reduction of theology to experience failed to take adequate account of the Platonic structure of his later work. The philosophical realism of Plato enabled Schleiermacher to think of God not just as the necessary divine presupposition to our awareness of absolute dependence, but as disclosed and present in that experience. To accept that there is a fundamental religious intuition that constitutes our essential humanity is also to realise that we are in relationship with the God who so formed us.

What About Religion?

Schleiermacher rigorously addressed the fundamental question of the nature and function of religion in the context of the modern world:

> Generally speaking there was no one on the church theological scene who in these stormy times between revolution and restoration, Enlightenment and Romanticism, could ask the question 'What about religion?' as urgently, credibly and effectively in public as [Schleiermacher] could.[5]

What is the status of religion if it no longer functions as the unifying bond of society or the arbiter of truth in the field of human knowledge? What public role could religion sustain in a post-Christendom society? Is religion simply a private belief system for those who find it impossible to cope with the rigours of the modern world without recourse to some notion of divine benevolence? Or is religion an indispensable component of human nature itself?

---

[5] Küng, *Great Christian Thinkers*, 165. Note also Karl Barth's recognition of Schleiermacher's importance in this regard, in *Protestant Thought: From Rousseau to Ritschl*, 306.

Schleiermacher recognised that the situation he faced in the modern world was similar to that which confronted the early Christian apologists. There was a need for a new *apologia* which could demonstrate that religion is *sui generis* – it belongs to it's own sphere and cannot be reduced to something else, be it morality (Kant), or truths about ourselves and the world (Deism), or supernaturally guaranteed dogmas and propositions (Protestant Orthodoxy). Few theologians in the modern era have recognised so acutely that the first and most crucial paradigm of modernity was the relativisation or privatisation of religion from exercising any public role or significance in the modern secular state. To accept such a domestication of the socio-political role of religion is to connive in a political conspiracy that now threatens the very existence of liberal democracy, particularly in the West.

The Essence of Religion

Schleiermacher first began to address the issue of the nature and function of religion in the context of the modern world in *On Religion; Speeches to its Cultured Despisers*, originally published in 1799. His audience were contemporary intellectuals imbued with the modern spirit of critical rationalism or metaphysical disdain, who had supposedly given up on religion. Schleiermacher, on the other hand, sought a more enduring rapprochement between religion and the exigencies of modern culture. He endeavoured to demonstrate that embracing the modern world did not necessarily entail an anti-religious agnosticism or secularism; neither did an appreciation of religion immediately construct an intellectual trajectory back into the pre-modern period. Religion could not be identifiable solely with metaphysics or morality; neither was it reducible to the aesthetic gaze, nor could it be encapsulated in dogma, doctrine or theological theorems. 'To seek and to find this infinite and eternal in all that lives and moves, in all growth and change, in all action and passion, and to have and to know life itself only in immediate feeling – that is [the essence of] religion.'[6]

Schleiermacher derived his conceptuality from Hegel and Fichte.[7] The subjective dimension of religion is, consequently, 'a sense and taste for the infinite'.[8] It is clear that Schleiermacher was, in his own way, trying to overcome Kant's bifurcated vision of reality, split between pure and practical reason. As the Romantics had complained, Kant had banished humanity from the ancient vision of the unity of all things. Schleiermacher accorded to religion the

---

[6] F. Schleiermacher, *On Religion: Speeches to its Cultural Despisers*, 79.

[7] Küng, *Christianity: Religious Situation*, 698.

[8] Schleiermacher, *On Religion*, 82.

function of reuniting the cognitive and volitional dimensions of human existence and so mediating to us a fundamental sense of personal identity.

So one could say that religion is both morphological and ontological prior
to knowing and doing. The affective dimension of life lies at the root of all
human existence. It is there in the infant, before the child becomes a knowing
or willing subject. Our intellectual and volitional capacities can operate
independently of each other, but underlying and accompanying both is
'the innermost sanctuary of life',[9] where we receive ourselves as gift. The ontological foundation of this primary intuition is that sense that our whole
existence is related to and dependent upon the infinite ground of all that exists:

> The infinite in the finite or God as the eternal absolute being that conditions all
> things – this, we can say, is the modern understanding of God and not (as
> Schleiermacher adds in the second edition at the end of the excurses on the idea
> of God) 'the usual conception of God as one single being outside of the world and
> behind the world'.[10]

Religion, Metaphysics and Reality

While Schleiermacher was understandably concerned to emphasise the independence of religion from metaphysics and morality, in the *Speeches* at least, he
struggled to maintain any complementary relationship between them. To find
the Absolute in the immediate self-consciousness of our inner subjectivity
moved perilously close to severing any connection between religion and the
praxis of ethical and humanitarian concern. In response to this (in the

---

[9] Ibid, 41.

[10] Küng, *Great Christian Thinkers*, 167. Macquarrie, in his analysis of Schleiermacher's
thought, prefers the definition of religion as 'a sense and taste for the infinite', to that of
'the feeling of absolute dependence', which Schleiermacher later advocated in *The
Christian Faith*. Cf. Macquarrie, *Modern Thought*, 197. To a certain extent, this more
adequately communicates the bipolar nature of Schleiermacher's '*das Gefühl*'. It is not
to be reduced to mere emotion, subjective feeling or stirrings of the heart towards
the divine. Rather, it refers to the co-givenness of the infinite in the reflective self-
consciousness it calls forth. There is within humanity an awareness, or a subjective
disposition, that feels itself in relation with the transcendent ground of being.
Schleiermacher later described this feeling or subjective awareness more concretely as
the feeling of absolute dependence, which he claims is the same as being in relation
with God. He regarded this situation as universal to human nature and therefore
it obviates the need for the traditional proofs for God's existence. In reality,
Schleiermacher replaced the old cosmological and teleological proofs for God's
existence with an anthropological proof based on the conviction, which located in the
inner-subjectivity of the human personality is an innate sense of God–dependency.

Speeches and most certainly in his later book *Monologues*) Schleiermacher, like Kierkegaard (although for different reasons), showed that he was fundamentally opposed to the state church, which he viewed as a corruption of the inherent freedom of the religious disposition and its expression in the genuine charity of the Christian community.

In terms of the development of his thought, a further counter to this criticism was Schleiermacher's preference for the definition of religion as the feeling of absolute dependence. While Hegel's acerbic remark that this renders a dog the most perfect manifestation of religion clearly misses the mark, Schleiermacher was concerned to demonstrate that such dependency is in fact the very essence of religious freedom and manifests itself in the works of faith and love, which characterise the Christian church.

How then is Schleiermacher's theology of religion to be classified? Was it a genuine Christian theology of religion or did it constitute the reduction of theology to speculative philosophy? The answer to this question depends on how one views the relationship between theological and philosophical enquiry. If all philosophy is to be denounced as an illegitimate infringement upon the incomparable majesty and sovereignty of God's revelation (Barth), then Schleiermacher's considerations at this juncture appear to be just another form of natural theology. If, on the other hand, philosophical investigation is to be embraced as a necessary companion in the theological attempt to delineate the necessary ontological and epistemological conditions that might render such a revelation of God possible, then this is what became known in later Roman Catholic theology as fundamental theology (Küng and Rahner).

Religion and the Religions

However we describe this attempt to define the essence of religion, it is clear that a more precise delineation of the relationship between the infinite and the finite was needed. Here the influence of Hegel upon Schleiermacher is clearly discernible. A bad infinity, according to Hegel, was where the finite and the infinite are juxtaposed in a metaphysical dualism that does not allow one to come to expression in the other. Accordingly, Schleiermacher referred to the 'positive' element in all religions as the manifestation of the infinite in the various myriad forms of the actual concrete religions. He discerned two fundamental criteria whereby the other religions could be classified in relation to Christianity. The first was how closely a particular religion could actually be described as monotheistic. The decisive test here was the ability of a particular religious system to distinguish between the feeling of absolute dependence upon God and the feeling of relative dependence and freedom in relation to the world of finite realities. The second was how closely the said religion could approximate to the teleological ideal. In other words, how well could a particular religion instil within its exponents a sense of participating in the wider spiritual goal and purpose of history?[11]

So, Schleiermacher opened up the possibility of the study of the religions in and for their own sake. Despite their inevitable corruption, distortion and misrepresentation in the institutions and belief systems that define them, the positive element in all religions is this coming to expression, with the Christian religion being its fullest form, of the infinite in the finite. Consequently, it should not be a surprise to us that:

> If there is still so much talk of 'experience' in religious studies and theology this is essentially because of Schleiermacher, and if religion is no longer understood merely in private terms but as the affair of the 'community', this again is largely due to him. If Christianity can be understood as the best and supreme individualisation of religion and so can be included in a comparison of religions, this too finds its legitimisation, at least in principle, in Schleiermacher.[12]

Schleiermacher was, in principle, working out a theology of other religions, one that accepted that religion could not be reduced to the natural religion of the Deists. The particular historical religions could not be deduced out of some vague notion of a common essence. In both respects he anticipated much of the debate that was to ensue a century later when the religious question was subsumed within the attempt to construct a plausible theology of the religions.

The Phenomenology of Religion

John Macquarrie highlights what he regards as a serious problem in Schleiermacher's philosophy of religion. He believes the definition of religion as the feeling of absolute dependence is too passive and therefore incapable of being universalised in today's world.[13] There are many nowadays who do not feel such a sense of absolute dependence at the heart of their being. Rather, they feel abandoned amidst the unfeeling immensity of an empty universe. This profound sense of cosmic alienation was well expressed by Pascal when he exclaimed: 'I am terrified by the eternal silence of these infinite spaces.' There are others who think we have the ability to be masters of our own destiny and therefore dependent on no one other than our own capacity for creative and technological advancement. This kind of criticism only hits the mark if we

---

[11] Schleiermacher, *Christian Faith*, §7, §8, §9, §11.
[12] Küng, *Christianity: Religious Situation*, 703.
[13] Macquarrie, *Modern Thought*, 202–3.

accept with Brunner and the early Barth that Schleiermacher's attempt to define the essence of religion clearly represents the subjectivisation of theology or its reduction to anthropology. As Küng indicates, starting with the human subject does not necessarily imply the anthropologising of theology if this is not where one ends up.[14] Schleiermacher had no intention of making the human subject the measure of all things and indulging in that 'infantile omnipotence' which typified some forms of idealism.

In defence of Schleiermacher, there is more to say at this juncture than Küng allows. For instance, Schleiermacher does not view religious intuition as that sense of the numinous or the encounter with the *mysterium tremendens et fascinans*, which is how Rudolf Otto later defined the nature of religious experience.[15] Rather, the feeling of absolute dependence is something that is part of our normal experience of the world. It is a reflective self-consciousness, determined and influenced by our essential relatedness to the wider world of persons, nature, culture and society. In the second of the *Speeches*, Schleiermacher went to considerable lengths to define carefully the nature of this interrelatedness. In every perception of an object or a person external to ourselves there is a fleeting moment of encounter where we are one with that object in our self-consciousness. That is the nature of religious experience, the feeling of being united with the whole of finite reality which is simultaneously a freeing of ourselves from the limitations of our own self-awareness and also a sense of being dependent upon the total realm of the finite that ultimately adheres in the infinite. So it is the real world of history, community, society, family and culture which is the medium through which the infinite is mediated to us, and it is here where Schleiermacher takes leave of Hegelian metaphysics.

The relationship between the infinite and the finite is not one of metaphysical negation. The infinite does not need to negate the conditions of its own self-consciousness in order to posit itself in the other. Rather, it is our participation in a wider community of reality mediated through human language and culture which allows us to perceive a relationship between the finite and the infinite that is not dependent upon the power of reason to intuit abstract metaphysical principles. It is this kind of analysis (i.e. the enquiry into the fundamental structures of reality as they are mediated to us via our own self-consciousness) that permitted Scleiermacher to anticipate, in some measure, the philosophy of phenomenology pioneered by M. Scheler, E. Husserl and M. Heidegger.

Macquarrie's criticism does raise a crucial issue for Schleiermacher, although not the one he intended. If the sense of God-dependency cannot be

---

[14] Küng, *Christianity: Religious Situation*, 704.

[15] R. Otto, *The Idea of the Holy: An Inquiry into the Non-Rational Factor in the Idea of the Divine and its Relation to the Rational*.

regarded as an unequivocal part of our basic humanity, then the universal significance of Jesus will also be called into question. This is because Schleiermacher's Christology appears to present a Jesus who is distinguished from the rest of humanity simply by the unremitting potency of his own God-consciousness

Schleiermacher's Christocentrism

Given that Schleiermacher went to considerable lengths to define the universal substance of religion, how does he define the distinctiveness of Christianity? One of the most important theses of *The Christian Faith* states his view unequivocally:

> Christianity is a monotheistic faith, belonging to the teleological type of religion, and is essentially distinguished from other faiths by the fact that in it everything is related to the redemption accomplished by Jesus of Nazareth.[16]

From this terse description certain general factors about Christianity can be deduced.

First and foremost, Christianity is a religion of redemption, which entails liberation from evil by some other agent than the one who is redeemed. Similarly, because Christianity is a teleological religion, the purpose of such redemption must be moral rather than aesthetic and this inner experience of salvation must entail, 'the passage from God-forgetfulness to God-consciousness, so that the latter awareness predominates in all the states and activities of life'.[17]

The agent of redemption is the person of Jesus. This essentially positive assessment of the distinctiveness of the Christian faith must be contrasted with Schleiermacher's misunderstanding of Judaism, which was to have a baleful effect upon his Christology. In his view, Christianity, as the universal religion of redemption, superseded Judaism the particular religion of retribution.[18] Schleiermacher ignored the Old Testament witness to the election of Israel and the continuing history of God with his people. He could not locate the origins of Christology within Judaism and Jesus the Jew was all but forgotten. Instead, Schleiermacher developed an essentially idealised picture of the founder of Christianity that was largely based on John's Gospel.

---

[16] Schleiermacher, *Christian Faith*, 52.
[17] K.W. Clements, *Friedrich Schleiermacher: Pioneer of Modern Theology*, 40.
[18] F. Schleiermacher, *On Religion*, 239.

If everything in Christian doctrine and discipleship is to be focused intensely around the redemptive relationship with Jesus, then here is a radically Christocentric vision of the Christian faith.[19]

> A particular element had been made the hub of all thinking and activity, and a quite new understanding of the corpus of doctrine results. The various doctrines – creation, redemption, sanctification, church and so forth – are no longer self-contained items touching each other at their edges. Each of them, now, has to be seen as in some way a reflection upon the new consciousness given by Jesus to the believer within the believing community.[20]

No doubt due to the collapse of traditional metaphysics that talked of a natural knowledge of God, Schleiermacher knew of only one criterion of justification as far as the Christian faith was concerned, i.e. the person of Jesus and the redemption he makes possible. Jesus defines God and humanity for us and it is this all-embracing Christocentricity that allows Schleiermacher to dispense with the normal criteria of justification upon which the distinctive, unique and normative nature of Christianity was traditionally founded (i.e. the inspiration of Scripture, the proof of miracles, the historicity of the resurrection, the reality of the Incarnation and the promise of the eschaton). In truth, Schleiermacher payed scant attention to any of these and so left some aspects of his Christology dangerously unsubstantiated.

The Historical Jesus

Given the orientation of Schleiermacher's vision to the present experience of redemption, it is surprising that he refused to lose touch with the historical Jesus:

> The pure historicity of the person of the Redeemer, however, involves also this fact, that he could develop only in a certain similarity with his surroundings, that is, in general after the manner of his people. For since mind and understanding drew their nourishment solely from this surrounding world, and his free self-activity too had in this world its determined place, even his God – consciousness however original its higher powers, could only express or communicate itself in ideas he had appropriated from this sphere and in actions which as to their possibility were predetermined in it.[21]

---

[19] J. McIntyre and I.T. Ramsey preferred to use the term 'Christo-Morphic Theology', see R. Niebuhr (ed.), *Schleiermacher on Christ and Religion*, 210–14.

[20] Clements, *Schleiermacher*, 41.

[21] Schleiermacher, *Faith*, 382.

The redeemer for Schleiermacher was not Kant's moral hero or ideal. The redeemer's ideality was expressed through his real historical existence. He must be understood within his own cultural situation and not just by his superlative God-consciousness.

Schleiermacher also attempted to sketch out in his Berlin lectures the narrative form of *The Life of Jesus*, which was the first of this genre of nineteenth-century 'lives' emanating from the stable of liberal Protestantism. Schleiermacher believed that it was possible through historical-critical research to discern Jesus' own sense of self-identity, and that this was not fundamentally at odds with the New Testament writers' witness that Jesus was uniquely the Son of God. Not only did Schleiermacher endeavour to set the real Jesus within his own historical context, he also anticipated a particular christological issue that was to dominate the theological agenda of his contemporaries:

> If we are not permitted to tear any man loose from the general condition of his individual existence, therefore not from his rootage in the life of his people and not from his age, then this appears again to put an end to that application which we postulate is to be made of the knowledge of Christ, for we are in another age and belong to another culture. If therefore we cannot extract Christ from his historical setting in order to think of him within that of our people and our age, it follows again that the knowledge of him has no practical value, for he ceases to have exemplary character. But we can raise the question from another angle. If we are to think of him under the conditions of a definite age and a definite setting in the life of his people, does this not imply a greater diminution of the specific dignity of Christ?[22]

The issue of the relationship between the historical Jesus and the Christ of faith was to exercise a pertinent fascination for those scholars and historians who shared many of Schleiermacher's liberal presuppositions.

While Schleiermacher was clearly aware of the importance of the historical Jesus for Christian doctrine and the life of faith, his systematic explication of both these factors does not begin with Jesus, but with a rigorous investigation of the nature of piety. Piety is distinguished from both knowing and doing because its essence is feeling and more particularly the feeling of absolute dependence. Clearly, all that will ensue will be closely related to the nature of that specific religious self-consciousness.

---

[22] F. Schleiermacher, *The Life of Jesus*, 11.

Schleiermacher's Christology

Schleiermacher's Christology was momentous because he unashamedly espoused a Christology from below. There is a direct line of descent from Schleiermacher to all that is typical of modern Christology, simply because he attributed fundamental importance to the preservation of Jesus' humanity in the face of any docetic tendency to render him less than a complete human being with his own particular historical vocation and destiny.

> Schleiermacher's critique of orthodoxy laid the foundation for future christological reformulations throughout the nineteenth century. His was a half-turn to the new direction of attempting to construct Christology from below, an assumption that all doctrines of Christ must begin with his humanly historical existence. [23]

Why did Schleiermacher decide to follow this particular route? First, he could not have done otherwise, given the presuppositions of his general anthropology of religion. Given that, for Schleiermacher, the essence of religion was the universal sense of God-dependency, then every human person has the potential for union with God. Consequently, the incarnation does not have to be viewed as the supernatural entry into the human sphere of the divine *Logos*:

> It must be asserted that even the most rigorous view of the difference between Christ and all other men does not hinder us from saying that his appearing, even regarded as the incarnation of the Son of God, is a natural fact ... As certainly as Christ was a man, there must reside in human nature the possibility of taking up the divine into itself, just as did happen in Christ. So that the idea that the divine revelation in Christ must be something in this respect absolutely supernatural will simply not stand the test.[24]

For Schleiermacher there is within all of us a potential for uninhibited God-consciousness (*Gottesbewusstsein*), which Jesus actually brings to expression. This guarantees his identity as the second Adam, the one who represents the ideal of humanity in perfect communion with God. It is this natural rather than supernatural view of the incarnation that led Schleiermacher to reject the doctrine of the virgin birth.

The second major consideration was the way Schleiermacher sought to reinterpret the language of Chalcedonian Christology. He endeavoured to remain true to the basic insights of Chalcedon: Jesus is both *God* with us, thus he deserves our, 'unconditional adoration'; and he is also God *with us* and

---

[23] M.S.G. Nestlehutt, *Chalcedonian Christology: Modern Criticism and Contemporary Ecumenism*, 182.

[24] Schleiermacher, *Faith*, 64.

thus we enjoy his 'brotherly companionship'.[25] Nevertheless, Schleiermacher showed himself to be a child of the Enlightenment in his rejection of the two-nature language. In a post-Kantian world the term 'nature' can only be understood as a summary of the characteristics that make up a finite reality and cannot without impunity be applied to God. Similarly, we cannot talk of the same person sharing or uniting two natures because this simply no longer makes epistemological sense. We must therefore look for other non-metaphysical categories that are capable of affirming Jesus' unique status as the Redeemer.[26]

Thirdly, the theological problem with the language of Chalcedon is that it is non-experiential. We cannot experience the divinity of Christ directly. Consequently, the way is blocked which moves from above to below. The only access we have to Jesus is our experience of the salvation he alone can grant as the Redeemer. There is at the centre of Schleiermacher's Christology a real human and historical Jesus, one who is no mere example of moral perfection, nor a divine *Logos* concealed in human flesh. He is the manifestation of a human being filled with a superlative God-consciousness. In all of these respects Schleiermacher affirms the full humanity of Jesus and constructs a Christology from below.

The Divinity of Jesus

The accusation is often made that Schleiermacher advocated an exemplarist degree Christology. He presents a Jesus who is the prototype or perfect exemplar of God-consciousness. Such a misunderstanding can easily arise due to his use of the German word *urbildlichkeit*, which roughly translated means 'the ideal'. Jesus is the ideal of human God-consciousness, the one perfect example of a human being completely infused with awareness of our absolute dependence upon God. However, when Schleiermacher spoke of the ideality of Jesus he did not mean just a model of perfection, but something more akin to the Platonic 'form', i.e. the universal that actually imparts reality to that which participates in it.

Similarly, Schleiermacher was clear that this ideality cannot be surpassed because such a view 'clearly marks the end of the Christian faith, which on

---

[25] Ebionite christologies stumble at the first hurdle and docetic christologies at the second. Cf. ibid, 397–8.

[26] Wolfhart Pannenberg has accepted Schleiermacher's criticism of the two-nature language. Cf. Pannenberg, *Jesus–God and Man*, 343; Gunton unearths a implicit dualism in Schleiermacher's understanding of the term nature. However, he is unable to contest the main point that Chalcedon struggled to maintain a clear notion of the unity of the person of Christ; see *Yesterday*, 88–92.

the contrary knows no other way to a pure conception of the ideal than an ever-deepening understanding of Christ'.[27] Jesus' perfect God-consciousness constitutes his sinlessness and, given that sin is endemic to the human race, this constitutes a difference in kind from the rest of humanity and not simply a difference of degree: 'Christ was distinguished from all other men by his essential sinlessness and His absolute perfection.'[28] At the same time, Schleiermacher did not reduce Jesus to the one archetype, or one human instance, of the union of humanity with God. He saw Jesus – the ideal of human God-consciousness – as uniquely capable of increasing the God-consciousness of others.

This type of Christology holds together the person and the work of Christ: 'The peculiar activity and the exclusive dignity of the Redeemer imply each other, and are inseparably one in the self-consciousness of believers.'[29] However, soteriological concerns inevitably come to the fore, because Jesus is also the *Vorbildlichkeit*, the one who is capable of transmitting his God-consciousness to others: 'The Redeemer assumes believers into the power of his God-consciousness, and this is his redeeming activity.'[30] As we have noted already, we have no awareness of Jesus' divinity apart from the knowledge of having been saved and redeemed by him; consequently, 'these two aspects of Jesus, which Schleiermacher calls his *Urbildlichkeit* and his *Vorbildlichkeit*, cannot be seperated. By virtue of the former, he is the redeemer; by virtue of the latter, he communicates redemption.'[31]

Schleiermacher did not view this influence in a purely individual sense. The impact of Jesus is found in the collective remembrance and experience of him in the Christian community. The way Schleiermacher viewed this creative influence could be understood in terms of a vigorous doctrine of the Holy Spirit, although that is not how he describes it. Rather, he seemed to view this union in essentially mystical terms:

> [T]he share of the Redeemer in the common life, viewed as continuing, we are fully justified in calling soul-bestowal (*Beseelung*), primarily with reference to the corporate life – as indeed the church is called his body. In just the same way, Christ is to be the soul also in the individual fellowship, and each individual the organism through which the soul works.[32]

---

27 Schleiermacher, *Faith*, 378.
28 Ibid, 413.
29 Ibid, 374.
30 Ibid, 425.
31 Niebuhr (ed.), *Schleiermacher*, 226.
32 Ibid, 428. Barth recognised that if Schleiermacher had developed a theology of the Holy Spirit at this juncture, his whole theological system could have moved in another direction more conducive to Barth's own theological position. Cf. K. Barth, *Church Dogmatics*, 3/3, 330.

Finally, it is clear that Schleiermacher believed that the category of God-consciousness is capable of translating into modern parlance what Chalcedon affirmed, i.e. that there should be no separation or division in Christ's person of divinity and humanity. For Schleiermacher, God-consciousness defines the essence of both natures. The essence of humanity is to participate in the perfect God-consciousness that Jesus exemplifies; the essence of divinity is the same thing, i.e. 'the constant potency of his God-consciousness, which was a veritable existence of God in him'.[33]

Schleiermacher was trying to conceive of Jesus unity with the Father in relational terms without recourse to the traditional ontological categories of nature and substance. He conceived of Jesus' divinity in terms of his perfect fellowship with the Father. He believed that 'to ascribe to Christ an absolutely powerful God-consciousness, and to attribute to Him an existence of God in him, are exactly the same things'.[34] As Jacqueline Marina notes, this is how Schleiermacher ensured that there is no dualism of a merely human ordinary nature juxtaposed against a divine supernature in his Christology; and this allowed him to dispense with the troublesome doctrine of the *commuicatio idiomatum*.[35]

Part 2

Paul Tillich

> Like … Friedrich Schleiermacher, Tillich sought to address both church and culture, though he was perhaps less interested than was Schleiermacher in defending religion against its 'cultured despisers'.[36]

Paul Tillich lived, preached, lectured and wrote as a Christian theologian more than one hundred years after Schleiermacher. In that time, European civilisation and culture had changed dramatically. Schleiermacher represented the full flowering of what Barth referred to, in entirely derogatory fashion, as *Kulturprotestantismus* (cultural Protestantism). The theological attempt to reunite religion, culture and ethics in one impressive synthesis in such a way that the foundations of European culture, self-understanding and self-belief stood once again on the cornerstone of the Christian faith.

---

[33] Schleiermacher, *Faith*, 385.

[34] Ibid, 386–7.

[35] J. Marina, 'Schleiermacher's Christology Revisited: A Reply to his Critics', *SJT* 49.2 (1996), 194.

[36] M.K. Taylor, *Paul Tillich: Theologian of the Boundaries*, 17.

Tillich – like Barth, Bonhoeffer, Bultmann and Niebuhr – recognised that this culturally conditioned liberal ideal perished irretrievably in the trenches of the First World War. All of these theologians reacted to that crisis in different ways engaging in alternative forms of theological reconstruction. Tillich's initial flirtation with the neo-orthodoxy of Barth and Bultmann was short lived and he, more than any other of his contemporaries, took up the mantle of Schleiermacher and endeavoured to 'interpret the evolution of the world – against its will – in a religious sense, to give it its whole shape through religion'.[37]

Towards the end of his life, Tillich provided his own explanation of what he had sought to achieve:

> My whole theological work has been directed to the interpretation of religious symbols in such a way that the secular man – and we are all secular – can understand and be moved by them.[38]

So, despite the radical change in their respective intellectual and cultural situations, Tillich shares with Schleiermacher a deep apologetic concern to re-interpret the basic axioms and symbols of the Christian faith in such a way that it could once again address the deepest existential concerns and anxieties of his contemporaries. His first lecture in Berlin was entitled *On the idea of a Theology of Culture*. Again, like Schleiermacher, this was to remain a central concern to all Tillich's theological endeavours because he recognised, as did his august predecessor, that the theologian must operate 'on the boundaries' between church and culture if religion was once again to be rehabilitated within the modern worldview. In terms of the earliest and most seminal influences upon the development of Tillich's thought, we can also discern surprising similarities between both theologians: with Tillich, we find another theologian in search of a new paradigm to help him address the most pressing theological issue of his and our day, i.e. is religion a redundant, or a socially repressed, or a potentially life-transforming category in the context of the modern world?

In Search of a New Paradigm

The similarities between Tillich and Schleiermacher extend to the philo-sophical roots from which both theologians drew most nourishment. Tillich stood firmly within the tradition of classical German idealism; although, unlike Schleiermacher, he had the benefit of reviewing and appropriating

---

[37] Bonhoeffer, *Letters*, 108.
[38] P. Tillich, *Ultimate Concern: Tillich in Dialogue*, 88–9.

the later developments of that tradition in the phenomenology of Edmund Husserl, the existentialism of Søren Kierkegaard and Martin Heidegger, and the political philosophy of Karl Marx.

Tillich has often been criticised for the seemingly eclectic nature of his philosophical reflections. However, early on in his career he recognised that to be a theologian on the boundary there could be no mutual juxtaposition of philosophy and theology. Rather, both would need to be conjoined in a process of cross-fertilisation, which later informed both his theological method and the structure of his systematic theology.

A fractured idealism

Tillich defines philosophy as 'that cognitive approach to reality in which reality is the object'[39] and ontology as the 'analysis of those structures of being which we encounter in every meeting with reality'.[40] We should note two things from this assessment. First, in terms of his philosophical ontology, Tillich is positioned in a philosophical trajectory that originates with Plato and Parmenides, and runs through Augustine, the medieval mystics to Kant, Fichte and Hegel. The central metaphysical concern of this tradition was always how to understand the nature of being and, as such, it was dominated by what Jacques Derrida termed, 'a metaphysics of presence'. That tradition suffered a critical fracture, or rupture,[41] in the criticism of Hegel which originated with Schelling, developed through Kierkegaard and Marx, and culminated in the radical perspectivism of Nietzsche and Heidegger and their combined attempt to expunge once and for all the remaining vestiges of the 'metaphysics of presence' from the philosophical agenda.[42] Tillich undertook his early doctoral research on Schelling and his understanding of the ontology of existence remained deeply influenced by this fractured idealism, which eventually dissipated altogether in the existential nihilism of Sartre and Camus.[43]

Secondly, on his own admission, the centre of Tillich's philosophical concern was the subject–object dichotomy first explored by Descartes and Kant, which formed the historical foundation of the idealist tradition. Once it is acknowledged that the human subject is an interpretative factor in the act of cognition then the phenomenology of the human subject becomes a

---

[39] P. Tillich, *Systematic Theology*, Vol. 1, 18.

[40] Ibid., 20.

[41] Nicholl, uses the suggestive phrase 'a ruptured idealism' to describe the philosophical tradition that most influenced Tillich; see *Modern Theology*, Vol. 1, 243.

[42] 'But there are no facts (*Tatsachen*) only interpretations and no world (*an sich*) apart from an interpretation: As though a world would be left over apart from interpretations', F. Schelling, *Nachlass* 705, 769.

[43] See J.P. Clayton, *The Problem of God in Modern Thought*, 467–71.

legitimate area of exploration and not, as the empiricists maintained, just the world of finite objects. In exploring the relationship between subject and object, Tillich was deeply indebted to the dialectical idealism of Hegel and Schelling. The dialectical structure of Tillich's own theological system continually bore witness to their abiding influence.

Hegel resolved the bifurcation of subject and object present in Kantian idealism through the notion of the dialectical self-realisation of Absolute Spirit in the self-consciousness of humanity. This effectively achieved a reconciliation of the subject–object relationship in his philosophical system. His critics simply denied that such a resolution of the subject–object dichotomy was possible, at least not through the iron grip of historical necessity.

Kierkegaard opposed the hubris of a system that claimed to have solved both the problems of history and knowledge through the rationalism of conceptual analysis, particularly one that postulated a historical determinism that obliterated the genuine freedom of the individual. Marx replaced Hegel's transcendental idealism with his own dialectical materialism, claiming that Hegel missed the true cause of human alienation and estrangement, which is the misuse of private property brought about by the class struggle. Schelling denied that the meaning of history could be reduced to a rationalist dialectic. Rather, what was required was a genuine existentialist dialectic that fathomed the depth of our existential and historical estrangement from our unity with the divine and yet recognised that the overcoming of this alienation can only take place through the embrace of divine love and human freedom.

Tillich appropriates Schelling's notion of the existential estrangement between essence and existence, but views dialectic as the intellectual sojourn that will not allow this dichotomy to persist but, instead, penetrates to the genuine *ousia* or essence of reality, which, ultimately subsists in the inexhaustible ground of being itself. It is at this juncture that Tillich truly revealed his idealist credentials: 'I am an idealist ... if idealism means the assertion of the identity of thinking and being as the principle of truth.'[44]

The Kähler connection

In his autobiographical work, *On the Boundary*, Tillich expressed his debt to Martin Kähler:

> Kähler was a man whose intellectual ability and moral and religious power were overwhelming. As a teacher and writer he was difficult to understand. In many respects, he was the most profound and most modern representative of the nineteenth-century theology of mediation. He was an opponent of Albrecht

---

[44] P. Tillich, *The Interpretation of History*, 60.

Ritschl, a proponent of the theological doctrine of justification, and a critic of the idealism and humanism from which he was himself intellectually descended. I am indebted to him primarily for the insight he gave me into the all-embracing character of the Pauline-Lutheran idea of justification.[45]

If Schleiermacher required the influence of his Moravian pietist background combined with the philosophical realism of Plato to move away from the pretensions of Romantic idealism, then Kähler served the same function with regard to Tillich's relationship to the idealist tradition.

Tillich took from Kähler a basic conviction that theology should continue to mediate between religion and culture, church and philosophy, but it should do so under the sovereignty of the great Protestant principle of justification by grace through faith. The application of this principle beyond the domain of Christology and soteriology to an understanding of religion and culture, allowed Tillich to avoid what he regarded as the two extremes facing any theology of mediation. The first he discerned in the great liberal tradition of eighteenth- and nineteenth-century theology. While acknowledging his own debt to this tradition, particularly with regard to its analysis of the nature of religion, he saw at the heart of liberalism the critical accommodation of the Christian faith to the vast cultural currents which threatened to sweep aside the institutional churches and their influence upon society. The opposite danger he discerned in the emergence of the new *kerygmatic* or dialectical theology associated with Barth and F. Gogarten. Here the dialogue with culture and the wider phenomena of religion was simply repudiated altogether as an idolatrous exercise which continually polluted the revelation of God in the Word made flesh.

While Tillich conceded that Barth and his colleagues were able to recover the *kerygmatic* function of contemporary theology, he maintained that they did so at the expense of a new *supranaturalism*; this entailed that 'the message must be thrown at those in the situation – thrown like a stone'.[46] The Protestant principle was justifiably opposed to any idolatrous identification of God and the world which allows the self-seeking hubris of human nature to construct its own religion, however that may be conceived, summed up, as some have concluded, in the indiscretionary folly of the idealist tradition:

Idealism supposes it possible to pass in a unbroken line from spirituality of the self, the intelligibility of the world, the meaningfulness of culture, the general development of religion, to the ultimate reality who is God Himself; but this philosophy of

[45] Tillich, *On the Boundary: An Autobiographical Sketch*, 47.
[46] Tillich, *Systematic Theology*, Vol. 1, 7. Similarly, Bonhoeffer accused Barth of a positivism of revelation.

religion makes God relative to self and world, religion relative to culture, and revelation relative to general history of religion.[47]

Granted this salutary reminder, the Protestant principle speaks of justification through the grace of Christ and, therefore, for the sake of the incarnation will not allow a total severing of the relationship between God and the mediating realities of culture, church and religion. It was such convictions that entailed that Tillich would not leave the boundaries, nor give up the cause of a mediating theology.

War experiences

'Hell rages around us. It's unimaginable.' So wrote Tillich to his father from the battlefields and grim sodden trenches of the First World War. Like many of his contemporaries, Tillich entered the Kaiser's war a nationalistic Prussian. He served as an army chaplain amid 'the sound of exploding shells, of weeping at open graves, of the sighs of the sick, of the moaning of the dying'.[48] The experience changed him irrevocably:

> At the beginning of the war Tillich was a shy, grown boy, truly a 'dreaming inno-
> cent'. He was a German patriot, a brave Prussian, as eager to fight for his country as
> anyone else, but politically naïve. When he returned to Berlin four years later he was
> utterly transformed. The traditional monarchist had become a religious socialist,
> the Christian believer a cultural pessimist, and the repressed puritanical boy a 'wild
> man'. These years represent the turning point in Paul Tillich's life – the first, last
> and only one.[49]

The First World War represented the collapse of European bourgeoisie civilisation and with it, the traditions of idealist philosophy and liberal theology that had sought to undergird this great flowering of cultural and intellectual optimism. 'The experience of those four years of war revealed to me and to my entire generation an abyss in human existence that could not be ignored.' Tillich sensed the 'end of the old and the beginning of the new'[50] – as did his contemporaries Barth, Brunner and Karl Jaspers. From then on Tillich would be forced to think differently about God and the apparent 'abyss of meaning-lessness'[51] which he diagnosed as the human condition. At the end of the War,

---

[47] W.M. Horton, 'Tillich's Role in Contemporary Theology', in C.W. Kegley and R.W. Bretall (eds), *The Theology of Paul Tillich*, 28–9.
[48] W. & M. Pauck, *Paul Tillich – His Life and Thought*, 49–50.
[49] Ibid., 41.
[50] Taylor, *Tillich*, 54.
[51] H. Zahrnt, *The Question of God: Protestant Theology in the Twentieth Century*, 296–7.

Tillich endeavoured to contribute to the reconstruction of Germany through participation in the religious socialist movement. He and his colleagues sensed a new *kairos*, a right time, to develop a new theonomous form of cultural engagement. Later, Tillich would concede that there was more than 'a slight tinge of romanticism' in the establishment of the new 'Kairos Circle'. Nevertheless, it is in the midst of his theological and political reflections at this time that we can discern a more critically nuanced view of the relationship between religion and culture.

Religion and Culture

Tillich claimed that religion always exercises a dual role in relation to culture: 'It contains within itself a "No", a *reservatum religiosum*, and a "Yes", an *obligatum religosum*'.[52] The 'no' occurs when the prophetic element in religion discerns 'the demonically distorted and conditioned forms of an epoch'.[53] Here there is an inevitable withdrawal as religion falls back upon its own sacred communities and prophetic figures, examples being the attitude of early Christianity to its pagan environment, the mysticism of the late medieval period and Reformation Lutheranism. However, because religion expresses its relationship to the 'Unconditioned' in cultural forms any complete withdrawal contributes to the demonisation of culture and society. The opposite extreme, the naïve identification of culture and religion results in exactly the same consequences. Here, Tillich both distanced himself from his liberal forbearers, and issued a warning to his contemporaries:

> [C]ulture is right in renouncing culture-Protestantism, and religion is right in rejecting the identification of religion and socialism. The only proper attitude toward culture and also toward socialism is that characterised by the double demand of *reservatum* and *obligatium religionsum*.[54]

Tillich later claimed that he endeavoured to exhibit the same dialectical relationship towards the influence of Marx on religious socialism. There was a 'yes' to Marx's realistic and humanitarian analysis of the abuses of capitalism but a firm 'no' to the propaganda and calculating materialism of Marx's rejection of religion.[55]

---

[52] P. Tillich, 'Basic Principles of Religious Socialism', in Taylor (ed.), *Tillich*, 59.
[53] Ibid., 59.
[54] Ibid., 60.
[55] P. Tillich, 'Autobiographical Reflections', in Kegley and Bretall (eds), *Paul Tillich*, 13.

Towards a theology of culture

If one accepts the traditional division of labour between philosophy and theology, then it has been the task of the former to address the exigencies of culture in an appropriate language and conceptuality that endeavours to focus that particular culture's sense of self-identity. Theology, on the other hand, reiterates and interprets the language, symbols and narratives that maintain the integrity and self-identity of the Christian church. However, a theologian on the boundary does not accept such a division of labour and consequently tries to correlate the questions, anxieties and self-awareness of a particular culture with the answers and symbols of divine revelation he finds in the Christian tradition. He or she must do so without compromising the integrity of the original Christian message, while at the same time concretely addressing in a relevant, vital and engaging fashion the genuine concerns of modern secular people. Tillich's famous method of correlation, which he later deployed throughout his theology, began to emerge in his attempt to sketch out a theology of culture.

> We have to remember that in Tillich's theology the question does not determine the answer any more than the answer determines the question, but the two are correlated, so that the question determines the form and not the substance of the answer. Perhaps the substance of the answer can affect the form of the question.[56]

This apparent equivocation concerning the relationship of existential questions to the answers obtained from revelation later threatened the integrity of Tillich's whole system.

Alisdair Heron quite rightly detects here the influence of Schelling and Hegel on Tillich. Like his predecessors, Tillich explored the realms of art, literature, sociology and psychology and discerned signs of that *estrangement* which he diagnosed as a fractured relation to Being-itself. So, like Schleiermacher, Tillich replaced a traditional natural theology independent of revelation with a phenomenological analysis of the relationship of religion to culture. Similarly, for a 'supranatural theology' of the kind he believed was present in Barth; he offered instead a theological answering of these questions and issues, which did not simply come 'vertically from above', but met and connected with the questions arising from the human side.[57]

Tillich's theology of culture followed a broadly Hegelian pattern. His cartography of cultural evolution bore witness to three crucial stages of cultural form: 'autonomy', 'heteronomy' and 'theonomy'.[58] In the early and high

---

[56] Nicholl, *Modern Theology*, Vol. 1, 264.

[57] Heron, *Protestant Theology*, 139.

[58] Cf. P. Tillich, *The Protestant Era*, xvi–xvii.

Middle Ages, Tillich discerned a theonomous form of culture, a culture where the ultimate meaning of life became transparent in the various finite structures of thought and action. On the other hand, Tillich defined the later Middle Ages as heteronomous, because of the attempt by ecclesiastical institutionalised power to curb and dominate genuine human autonomy and self-expression. The Renaissance witnessed to the triumph of the human spirit over such ecclesiastical heteronomy, permitting a new flowering of human creativity and responsible self-reliance.

This newfound autonomy soon gave way to another form of heteronomy with the emergence of Enlightenment scientific rationalism, which obscured our relationship to the ultimate ground of reality, in favour of a manipulative technological mastery of nature and a competitive individualism. The domination of 'technical' reason in turn gave way to that of 'planning reason'. Exploitative bourgeois capitalism created its counter ego, totalitarian oppression, the tyranny of the absolutist state. Western culture has accordingly encountered three 'faces' of the Leviathan. The ecclesiastical face of the late Middle Ages, the technological face of the age of the machine and the political face of totalitarian ideology, Fascist, Nazi and Communist. If such an analysis is accurate, what is the cultural situation of the modern person?

> The man of today … is aware of the confusion of his inner life, the cleavage of his behaviour, the demonic forces in his psychic and social existence. And he senses that not only his being but also his knowing is thrown into confusion, that he lacks ultimate truth, and that he faces, especially in the social life of our day, a conscious, almost demonic distortion of truth. In this situation in which most of the traditional values and forms of life are disintegrating, he often is driven to the abyss of complete meaninglessness, which is full of both horror and fascination.[59]

If it is true, as indeed Tillich concluded, that the immediate post-war years constituted a new spiritual wasteland, European civilisation caught in the throws of a vast cultural disintegration, then the positive side of such an apparent abyss is the possibility of a 'sacred void'. It might transpire that out of the depths of our existential despair, irrationality and meaninglessness, we cry out for manna from heaven and that a new theonomous culture could in fact emerge. Theonomy is the answer to the question implied in autonomy, not the subjugation of the human spirit under some rule of terror, be that ecclesiastical or political, but the acknowledgement that at the heart of our quest for existential meaning and significance is a proclivity for religion. There is need of a new self-transcending realism that will relocate nature and history in the context of what is the true character of our 'ultimate concern'.

---

[59] Ibid., 202.

The essence of religion

It is extremely difficult to avoid the conclusion that Tillich's conception of religion is but a twentieth-century equivalent to Schleiermacher's. In place of idealist's concepts borrowed from Fichte and Hegel, we have existential equivalents borrowed from Schelling, Kierkegaard and Heidegger, and, noticeably, there is the same evolution of thought that moves from the more objective grounding of religion in a concept of the infinite to the subjective dimension of religion located in the self-awareness of the human person.

In his early lecture *On the Idea of a Theology of Culture*, Tillich defined religion as 'experience or directedness toward the Unconditional':

> Religion is the experience of the unconditioned, and this means the experience of absolute reality founded on the experience of absolute nothingness. One experiences the nothingness of entities, the nothingness of values, the nothingness of the personal life. Wherever this experience has brought one to the nothingness of an absolute radical 'No', there it is transformed into an experience, no less absolute, of reality, into a radical 'Yes'.[60]

So, like Schleiermacher, Tillich viewed our experience of the Ultimate as that which is mediated through our experience of finite reality. However, this time it is not a sense of the groundedness of the totality of finite things in the infinite, which mediates this relation to the divine, but an experience of the fracturedness, the nothingness, the essential estrangement of finite reality from its eternal source.

The difference came from Tillich's conception of the relationship between essence and existence that he ultimately derived from Schelling. The human situation, according to Tillich, is one characterised by the estrangement of existence from essence. In true Platonic fashion, Tillich viewed the essence of being as an ontological reality, but not actual existence, rather it is the 'potential, unactualised perfection of things'.[61] When that essence is actualised, it becomes existence, but because existence is both finite and fallen, it is imperfect and therefore estranged from its perfect essence. Existence is disrupted and distorted due to this fracture from true essence. Tillich regarded the symbol of the *Fall* as an existential, rather than a genuinely historical expression, of the transition from essence to existence:

---

[60] P. Tillich, 'On The Idea of a Theology of Culture'; in Taylor (ed.), *Tillich*, 40. See the note providing a more accurate translation by Victor Nuovo, 40–1.

[61] S. Grenz and R.E. Olson, *20ᵗʰ Century Theology: God & the World in a Transitional Age*, 122.

Thus *estrangement* is the result of the transition of man from essence to existence, separated from the "ground of being" (God) and therefore from the origin and goal of his life. He is also separated from himself and from others, which leads to a rift through all being. Tillich proposes that this is what the Bible calls *sin* – not merely a subjective attitude and personal guilt, but always a tragic destiny and misfortune, shared by our actions, so that it is always a guilt for which we are personally responsible. Therefore, to live under the circumstances of existence means to live in sin.[62]

The Phenomenology of Religion

If finite, sinful existence is characterised by a radical sense of *estrangement* from our true essence then not surprisingly its psychological manifestation is an equally radical sense of fear and anxiety. Tillich's analysis at this juncture owes much to Kierkegaard and Heidegger. Finitude is characterised by anxiety about non-being of which there are three forms.[63]

First, non-being threatens the very ontological foundation of our existence and manifests itself in absolute terms as fear of *death* and in relative terms as fear of *destiny*. Secondly, non-being threatens our moral integrity and identity and is expressed in absolute terms as fear of eternal *damnation* and in relative terms as fear of *guilt*. Thirdly, non-being threatens the intellectual dimensions of our existence and manifests itself in absolute terms as fear of *meaninglessness* and in relative terms as fear of *emptiness*. To experience the vulnerability of our existence as that which is caught on the cusp between being and non-being is to intuitively know that 'religion is more than a system of special symbols, rites and emotions, directed toward a highest being; religion is ultimate concern; it is the state of being grasped by something unconditional, holy, absolute'.[64]

God is the focus of our ultimate concern and religion is the state of being ultimately concerned. Because every finite reality is threatened or conditioned by its negation to non-being it cannot be the focus of our ultimate concern. So ecstatic self-transcending reason arrives at the notion of God as the '*Unconditioned*' infinite ground or depth of everything that exists. This is not another Being among other beings. Rather, this is '*Being-itself*'. To avoid anthropomorphic projection we can only speak symbolically of God not as Person nor as the Supernatural but as the ultimately mysterious, infinite ground of the personal and the natural. In other words, as the transcendent in the immanent, the spiritual power and reality that mends the fracture between being and non-being and who is manifested supremely in the appearance of the '*New Being*'.

---

[62] Zahrnt, *Question*, 313.
[63] P. Tillich, *The Courage to Be*, 37ff., 135ff.
[64] P. Tillich, 'Religion and Secular Culture' in Taylor (ed.), *Tillich*, 123.

In true idealist fashion, Tillich viewed the dichotomy between object and subject as that which finds its ultimate resolution in the 'Unconditioned' and this process of reconciliation which overcomes our estrangement and alienation from being and essence remains the ultimate concern of the religions. The problem with the latter, as Thomas Luckmann indicated, is that 'matters that come to be of "ultimate" significance for the members of later generations are likely to be congruent only to a limited extent with matters that were of "ultimate" significance to earlier generations'.[65]

Christology Reconsidered

This is the picture of the New Being in Jesus as the Christ. It is not the picture of a divine-human automaton without serious temptation, real struggle or tragic involvement in the ambiguities of life. Instead of that, it is the picture of a personal life which is subjected to all the consequences of existential estrangement but wherein estrangement is conquered in himself and a permanent unity is kept with God. Into this unity he accepts the negativities of existence without removing them. This is the New Being as it appears in the biblical picture of Jesus as the Christ.[66]

Most of the main features of Tillich's Christology are contained in this statement. First, at the root of all christologies is a real historical event. The incarnation, however we understand it, occurred and forms the real, factual basis both to the man Jesus and how his significance was grasped and interpreted through the witness of Scripture.

The accusation is often levelled at Tillich that he takes no interest whatsoever in the real historical person Jesus of Nazareth and, like Bultmann, there is a near total divorce in his theology between existential faith and the historical Jesus:

Tillich's 'theology' is actually a philosophy of existence which attaches itself to the existence of Jesus of Nazareth in the most tenuous of manners, and which is not significantly disadvantaged if the specific historical individual Jesus of Nazareth did not exist.[67]

In fact, Tillich specifically denied that such could be the case in Christology. In terms of his concept of the New Being, Tillich had good reasons for doing so:

---

[65] T. Luckmann, *The Invisible Religion*, 82.
[66] Tillich, *Systematic Theology*, Vol. 2, 154–5.
[67] McGrath, *Modern German Christology*, 176.

[T]he mistake of supposing that the picture of the New Being in Jesus the Christ is the creation of existential thought or experience. If this were the case, it would be as distorted, tragic and sinful as existence itself, and would not be able to overcome existence. *The religious picture of the New Being in Jesus is a result of a new being: it represents the victory over existence which has taken place, and thus created the picture.*[68]

In true Kähler fashion, however, Tillich contended that it is 'the biblical historical Christ' which is the real object of christological enquiry. Behind the real person of Jesus stands a history of revelation, namely Jewish apocalyptic and prophetic expectations of the messiah. It is this expectation that forms the interpretative context to Jesus' life history and the only Jesus we therefore have access to is the biblical picture of this man who was understood to be the Christ:

> Christianity is what it is through the affirmation that Jesus of Nazareth, who has been called 'the Christ', is actually the Christ, namely, he who brings the new state of things, the New Being ... Christianity was born, not with the birth of the man who is called 'Jesus', but in the moment in which one of his followers was driven to say to him, 'Thou art the Christ'. And Christianity will live as long as there are people to repeat this assertion. For the event on which Christianity is based has two sides: the fact which is called 'Jesus of Nazareth' and the reception of this fact by those who received him as the Christ.[69]

Tillich contended that it is not possible by means of historical critical method to get behind the biblical portrait of Jesus as the Christ and reconstruct the so-called historical Jesus. All that historical research can attest is the powerful influence of Jesus upon his contemporaries and therefore the inherent probability of his existence.

The powerful reality of Jesus caused the image or the expressionistic portrait of him we have in the New Testament, but that in itself is not salvific. As was the case for Schleiermacher, so also for Tillich, the only access we have to the real Jesus is through coming to real existential faith in Jesus as the Christ. This is achieved, 'partly as a member of the church which is the actual continuation of the history of revelation, and partly as an individual who is grasped by the revealing event and becomes "contemporaneous" with it'.[70] This truth does not nullify the value of critical investigation of the scriptures.

---

[68] P. Tillich, 'A Reinterpretation of the Doctrine of the Incarnation', *Church Quarterly Review* 147/294 (1949), quoted in A.T. Mollegen, 'Christology and Biblical Criticism in Tillich', in Kegley and Bretall (eds), *Paul Tillich*, 232.

[69] Tillich, *Systematic Theology*, Vol. 2, 97.

[70] P. Tillich, 'The Bible and Systematic Theology', note 12; quoted in Mollegen, 'Christology', 236.

On the contrary, such investigation reveals how the biblical writers used and transformed the religious and cultural categories and symbols of their day and so aids the whole interpretative process whereby Jesus continues to be received as the Christ.

The new being

1 Corinthians 15 speaks of Jesus as 'the man from heaven'; this is a symbolic rendition of the meaning of the incarnation. In ontological terms, it is to be understood as the coming of the divine *Logos* in human form and substance. For Tillich, it was the manifestation of the New Being, the coming into the realm of estranged and alienated existence of essential *Godmanhood*:

> The life of Jesus at every point contradicts the life of existential estrangement and bears witness to and confirms him as the New Being. In the life of Jesus there are no traces of unbelief or self-evaluation. In the temptations he rejects unlimited desire for food, knowledge and power. When one speaks of Jesus' sinlessness and goodness these are but ways of describing the New Being as it overcomes the estrangement of existence.[71]

Jesus accordingly exhibits the New Being in two ways:

1. Through the continual maintenance of his unity with God, which is the identity of his essential manhood and *Godmanhood*.
2. Through his power to negate himself without loosing himself in his self-surrender to the will and purpose of God.

The two central representative symbols of the New Being are the Cross and resurrection of Christ. The cross is the most radical symbol of the depth of human estrangement and alienation from essential Godmanhood. There is enmity at the core of this relationship and only a victory over estranged existence and restitution of our essential community with God permits the genuine breaking in of the power of the New Being. The cross exposes the full extent of that sin and tragedy that characterises estranged existence, however, through his willing self-surrender Jesus sublimates finite estrangement within the divine love and through his resurrection negates the separation of existence and essence. If there is one crucial area concerning their respective theologies where Tillich and Schleiermacher diverge, it is located in the centrality Tillich gives to the cross and resurrection as the basis for his soteriologically orientated Christology.

---

[71] J.P. Newport, *Paul Tillich*, 119.

Tillich reinterpreted the traditional symbols of atonement and salvation according to his underlying ontology of existence. We are saved from the negativity of estranged and alienated existence, finite being which is always perishing. Jesus atones because he participates in existential estrangement and all its destructive consequences and he saves because the resurrection permits essentialisation. This rather cumbersome term means:

> [T]hat the new being which has been actualised in time and space adds something to essential being, uniting it with the positive which is created within existence, thus producing the ultimately new, the "New Being" not fragmentarily as in temporal life, but wholly as a contribution to the kingdom of God in its fulfilment.[72]

As others have noted, here we have the interrelationship of a number of key theological and philosophical concepts that reveals the extent to which Tillich's ontology dominates his Christology and, like Schleiermacher, threaten to translate the biblical terminology into an alien conceptuality.[73] The eschatological tension between the first fruits of the new creation and that which is still to be realised is not easily translated into the notion of essentialisation.

How did Tillich understand the traditional creedal christological formulations? Within the three volumes of Tillich's *Systematic Theology* we can discern an evolution of thought which was never satisfactorily resolved:

In Volume I, Tillich strongly defended the *Logos* Christology first clearly worked out by Justin Martyr and the attendant necessity to retain a clear doctrine of the incarnation.[74] His own method of correlation clearly required a *Logos* Christology that can be understood as the correspondent to the logos that is immanent in creation and human nature.

In Volume II, Tillich was critical of the traditional understanding of the doctrine of the incarnation. The incarnation cannot be understood in a mythological manner as the transmutation, or metamorphosis, of a previously divine figure into a human being, which is in fact common in polytheism. On the contrary, we must accept the transformational Christology that states that the *Logos became* flesh, although Tillich was clearly uneasy with how such a notion of *becoming* is to be protected from degenerating into superstition. If on the other hand, the quest for the New Being appears universally in all religions, then the universality of the Christian answer to this quest can only be maintained through the doctrine of the Incarnation.[75] Tillich viewed the

---

[72] Tillich, *Systematic Theology*, Vol. 3, 427.

[73] Cf. A. Thatcher, *The Ontology of Paul Tillich*, 146.

[74] Tillich regards the apologetic theology of Justin Martyr as an ancestor to his own method of correlation.

[75] Tillich, *Systematic Theology*, Vol. 2, 86–7.

cosmic Christology of the Pauline corpus and the Johanine *Logos* Christology as capable of being understood in this fashion. In Volume II, Tillich also claimed that to be true to the synoptic picture of the Christ and to maintain the dynamic of development that is present in this picture, we must seek to rehabilitate the older adoptionist Christology as a counter balance to the domination of *Logos* Christology.[76]

In Volume III, Tillich's clear preference for a Spirit Christology emerged. He believed that Spirit Christology breaks the static ontology of the two-nature doctrine and allows the divinity of Christ to be understood in terms of Spirit possession. Tillich's concern to develop a Spirit Christology was no doubt influenced by his growing interest in the dialogue between Christianity and the other religions. However, it leaves some fundamental questions in regard to his own Christology completely unanswered.

Assessment

It is clear that both Schleiermacher and Tillich were, in some manner, christocentric theologians. Christology played a central, interpretative and integrating role in their respective theological systems. Similarly, both decided to take the soteriological route to christological reformulation. The significant and crucial Jesus is not the Jesus of history but the Jesus who mediates to us the experience of God-dependency or that of the New Being. The former is the genuine historical basis of the latter, but it is our contemporary encounters with Jesus, however that is mediated, which validates his historical reality as that is mediated to us through the biblical witness to Jesus as the Christ of God. The cultural situation of both theologians is inevitably reflected in their respective reinterpretations of the nature of religion and indeed the cultural assumptions they bring to their respective endeavours. That laudable concern necessitates a search for appropriate philosophical categories through which the conversation with culture can be conducted. Whether it was Schleiermacher's phenomenology of God-consciousness or Tillich's ontology of essence and existence, already, a prior decision had been taken concerning the fundamental nature of religion, which tends to create a new Procrustean Bed for their respective christologies. Similarly, the fact that both theologians cannot in the end do justice to the inherent demands of traditional Christology should caution us in regard to both the desirability and the effectiveness of this approach to christological reconstruction.

---

[76] Ibid., 149.

Schleiermacher

Schleiermacher's concept of religion reflected an inevitable nineteenth-century bourgeois optimism in human progress. Did he, however, correctly address the paradigmatic question that the spirit of modernity raises concerning the role and status of religion in the modern world? Was his phenomenological analysis of the nature of religious feeling able to slow the slide into practical atheism and widespread unbelief that has typified European culture since the Enlightenment? In one sense, the judgement of history will be that he obviously failed to convince the cultured despisers of religion to think again about the religious question. However, in his defence, Schleiermacher, by placing the Christian faith within the wider ambit of what has become known as the 'dialogue with the other religions', did anticipate the crucial issue of religious pluralism and he did so without embracing an evolutionary view of religious development.

Schleiermacher, however, succumbed to the spirit of the age in two crucial respects. First, he exhibited that universalising tendency which greatly inhibited post-Enlightenment thinkers from taking the historical, cultural and ideological nature of human knowledge sufficiently seriously. It is clear that despite his disclaimer that we must start with the particular cultural and historical embeddedness of each religious system, the feeling of absolute dependence does function as a universal maxim against which all religions will be judged. Secondly, this fervent Prussian nationalist, both welcomed the nation-state as a divinely given ordinance, and bolstered this particular ideology through an acceptance of the Lutheran doctrine of the 'two kingdoms'. It is precisely this stark separation of church and state that accepts the modern strategy of privatising religious faith and so denudes all faiths of their real socio-political significance. In both respects, Schleiermacher reinforced the modern elevation of the state with its corresponding dependence upon capitalist expansionism that continued to inoculate its subjects against the claims of religion.

Is it also the case that because of his general philosophy of religion explicated in terms of God-consciousness or God-dependency, a prior decision has already been taken in regard to the content of this Christology that, despite Schleiermacher's intention to pay sufficient heed to the christological trajectory of the New Testamant, leaves too little room for a proper investigation of the biblical traditions concerning the significance of Jesus? This is certainly the case in terms of his inability to find clues to Jesus' self-identity within the eschatologically orientated hinterland of first-century Judaism. It is this concern, which, despite his appreciation of Schleiermacher's achievement, formed the heart of Barth's continual unease with Schleiermacher's basic theological presuppositions. Barth found in Schleiermacher's morphology of religious consciousness concepts and principles drawn from philosophy, psychology and anthropology which appeared to him, at least, to threaten the primacy of God's revelation in Christ because the Word of God can no longer impinge upon us as the Wholly Other.[77]

Does the Christology of a superlative God-consciousness present an idealised picture of the historical Jesus, which pays insufficient attention to his identification with the alienated and marginalised members of society, or his confrontation with the religious establishment? Even more to the point, is there any room within this schema for the experience of godforsakenness and abandonment, which appeared to interrupt Jesus' sense of God-dependency as he underwent the personal dereliction of the cross? This remained at the heart of David F. Strauss's criticism of Schleiermacher:

> Strauss notes Schleiermacher's refusal to assign to Jesus any inner turmoil prior to or during his crucifixion. And in fact, in the Jesus of Scheiermacher the conflicts of sensible human consciousness are so transcended by the unity of being with becoming that all conflict and struggle is relegated to the periphery.[78]

While Schleiermacher certainly picked up Calvin's threefold description of the work of Christ in terms of his prophetic, priestly and kingly functions, he is unable to accord to the cross and resurrection the central role they have within the New Testament in determining Jesus' identity as the divine emissary of God. Consequently,

> in contrast to the synoptic evangelists, he sees death and resurrection as a seamless transition of an ideal figure of cheerfulness and pure love from the physical to the spiritual present, which makes possible direct access to him for all those who live after him.[79]

Schleiermacher's inability to develop an adequate *theologia crucis* (theology of the cross) is clearly seen in his doctrine of the atonement. Jesus' atoning work is simply to actualize or exemplify the new prototype of the fully God-conscious human being. It is in this area of his theology where the charge of exemplarism does hit the mark. It is also here that Schleiermacher's

[77] K. Barth, *The Theology of Schleiermacher: Lectures at Göttingen, Winter Semester of 1923/24*, 205 (note 1 in Marina's article). Barth's criticism is similar to that of George Lindbeck who notes that what he refers to as the 'experential-expressive' form of religious thought inevitably privileges the philosophical, psychological and social sciences as mediatory discourses that help the church in its apologetic task. Cf. Lindbeck, *Nature of Doctrine*.
[78] Harrisville and Sundberg, *Bible in Modern Culture*, 86.
[79] Küng, *Great Christian Thinkers*, 181–2.

Christology marks another crucial transition – the virtual abandonment of the traditional sacrificial –substitutionary schema of atonement by nineteenth-century Protestant theology in favour of a Jesus who becomes the great moral example of the self-sacrificing love of God.

Finally, did Schleiermacher simply abandon ontological concerns in favour of a psychological interpretation of Jesus' unity with God, utilising the category God-consciousness?

> [Schleiermacher] started, not from Jesus' divine being, but from the special power of his divine consciousness; for him this was the real Being of God in Jesus. The attempt has always aroused the suspicion of ambiguity. For the starting point in human subjectivity only makes it possible to state the Chalcedonian dogma unambiguously in a new way if it is interpreted, not merely from categories of consciousness, but with categories of being as well.[80]

At the very least, he has failed to develop a satisfactory ontology of person-hood. This means that his own use of the terminology of God-consciousness cannot serve the purpose of offering an adequate christological alternative to that of the two-nature language. To put the issue even more pointedly: 'Schleiermacher's substitution of power, or God-consciousness, for two natures doctrine lacks the metaphysical clarity that he so desires in substituting an experiential for an ontic understanding of the divine presence in Christ'.[81]

Tillich

As early as 1952, J.H. Randall Jr suggested that post-war 'cultural conditions' determined Tillich's 'ontological anxiety of finitude' which pervades the first two volumes of the *Systematics*.[82] 'To Tillich finitude is a prison, existence a predicament, man an alienated unit, and all forms of being empty unless trans-parent to their essence.'[83] Tillich's description of the nature of existence as that which is fractured by a radical sense of estrangement and alienation could be seen as simply a return to the biblical realism of his Lutheran and Augustin-ian heritage; however, his preference for a philosophical rendition of this situation in terms of an ontology of essence and existence creates insuperable problems for his Christology.

---

[80] W. Kasper, *Theology and the Church*, 101.
[81] Nestlehutt, *Chalcedonian Christology*, 183.
[82] J.H. Randall Jr., 'The Ontology of Paul Tillich' in Kegley and Bretall (eds), *Paul Tillich*, 193.
[83] R. Page, 'The Consistent Christology of Paul Tillich', *SJT* 36 (1983), 207.

N. Ferre argues that Tillich's ontology distorts his Christology because it is controlled by the relation of essence to existence.[84] For instance, Tillich will not countenance a reduction of Christology to Jesuology because he claims that the existential Jesus sacrifices himself in favour of the essential biblical Christ. If this is the case then Jesus does not enter into the conditions of estranged existence at all. Rather, as Ferre points out, Jesus' essential manhood negates, or obliterates, his existence.[85]

Tillich utilised a dialectic which asserted that the essential Jesus as the Christ can only become manifest when the existent Jesus is negated, yet elsewhere he insisted that the New Being is manifest precisely as essential *Godmanhood* within the conditions of estranged existence in such a way that the alienation between essence and existence is overcome.[86] Clearly both these eventualities cannot be true. If we translate the first dialectic into the two-nature language, we would have to say that Jesus' humanity is negated in order that his divinity may be revealed. Or if we use the language of personal identity, then one person, the historical Jesus, is nullified in order that the real person, presumably the *Logos*, can emerge. The difficulty, as Adrian Thatcher indicates, is that Tillich's ontology continually oscillates between a two-term largely Platonic-Aristotelian dichotomy, where essence which is mere potentiality is realised in the actuality of existence, and a three-term Hegelian/Schelling dialectic where the antimony between essence and existence is resolved in the reality of the New Being.[87] On both counts idealist–existential–philosophical categories create as many logical difficulties as did the traditional Chalcedonian terminology.

Tillich's equivocation over the relationship between the *Logos* Christology of the first and second volumes of his *Systematics* and the Spirit Christology of the third volume also destabilised the apparent christocentrism of his theology. The pneumatology of the third volume emphasised the universality of the Spiritual Presence that, Tillich claimed, is present in all religions. However, if that also entails an adoptionist Christology where Jesus is the prototypical Spirit-filled individual, then the inevitable consequences can be drawn. There could be other Spirit-filled individuals who function as Saviour figures for the exponents of that particular religious system. The inherent relativism of this position can only undermine the 'high' *Logos* Christology that maintains both the uniqueness and the universality of the Christ event.

---

[84] N. Ferre, 'Three Critical Issues in Tillich's Philosophical Theology'; quoted in Thatcher, *Ontology*, 149.
[85] Ibid., 150.
[86] Tillich, *Systematic Theology*, Vol. 2, 108ff.
[87] Thatcher, *Ontology*, 155–7.

Tillich defended himself against the charge of relativism by claiming that the criteria by which every religion should be judged, including Christianity, is the appearance of Jesus as the Christ,[88] but it is at this point where another problem in Tillich's theology is clearly registered. Who exactly is the Jesus who is the Christ? Tillich was not in favour of the radical demythologising of the New Testament undertaken by Bultmann in order to restate biblical faith in essentially Heideggerian existential terms. However, his own preference for an existentialist interpretation of Jesus as the bearer of the New Being radically dehistorises the biblical narrative. As a number of critics have noted, there is a lack of specificity at the core of Tillich's Christology, which effectively and decisively bypasses the sense of narrative and story that is at the heart of the biblical portrayal of Jesus' life and destiny.[89]

This impression is further corroborated by the way in which Tillich collapses many of the essential events in Jesus' life history into a system of symbols that prefigure the central symbols of the cross and resurrection. In fact, the distinct impression is given that what is ultimately important about Jesus is that he symbolizes, expresses and manifests the new being: 'It is not the actualisation of the "New Being" in Jesus that matters, but its manifestation in us. And this does seem to be the main drive of Tillich's thought on the matter.'[90]

In a similar fashion, John Clayton objects that Tillich's argument makes the historical facticity of Jesus largely irrelevant to theological claims about his significance.[91] If this is the case, then the following is also true:

> To say that the experience of the reality of the New Being guarantees the factual element of the biblical picture of Jesus as the Christ, is tantamount to making the truth of a religious experience the norm, or criterion, for establishing the truth of a historical fact.[92]

Similar queries and criticisms surround Tillich's infamous method of correlation. As he explains the theological basis to his method of correlation, it all seems clear enough:

> It is the task of apologetic theology to prove that the Christian claim *also* has validity from the point of view of those *outside* the theological circle. Apologetic theology

---

[88] Tillich, 'Dialogues, East and West: Conversations between Paul Tillich and Dr. Hisamatsu Shin'ichi. Part 1; quoted in Taylor (ed.) *Paul Tillich*, 33.

[89] A.J. McKelway, *The Systematic Theology of Paul Tillich: A Review and Analysis*, 177.

[90] Heron, *Protestant Theology*, 141.

[91] See J.P. Clayton, *The Concept of Correlation*. Also D. Kelsey, *The Fabric of Paul Tillich's Thought*, 89–101.

[92] G. Richards, *Towards a Theology of Religions*, 65.

must show that trends which are immanent in *all* religions and cultures move toward the Christian answer.[93]

Consequently, the most important task of apologetic theology is to argue for the universality of the Christian message for people of other faiths and cultures, or to put the matter in familiar christological terms, the universal logos that indwells all people and cultures comes to fullest expression in the *Logos* 'who became flesh'. The problem, however, is the lack of interdependence between the form of the question and the content of the answer. Clayton discerns a total lack of reciprocity in this relationship that effectively nullifies the validity of the method:

> Despite Tillich's persistent talk about the 'mutual dependence' of questioning and answering in the method of correlation, reciprocity is finally illusory. There is no mutual interaction on the same 'level' or in the same 'dimension': form does not mutually effect form; content does not mutually effect content.[94]

Others have argued for a much looser and dialectical arrangement. For instance, David Tracy asserts that the method of correlation can be reformulated to allow for a loose configuration of questions and answers endemic to culture aligned with questions and answers resident in the tradition.[95] Such a more dialogical approach would be more conducive to Tracy's own preferences and certainly surfaces in Tillich's attempt to sketch out a theology of the religions.

Toward the end of his life, Tillich began to take a deep interest in the history of religions. His last public lecture delivered at Chicago in 1965 was entitled *The Significance of the History of Religions for the Systematic Theologian*. Mircea Eliade the renowned historian of religions with whom Tillich shared a seminar on the subject remarked, 'Paul Tillich did not die at the end of his career ... he died at the beginning of another renewal of his thought'.[96]

In his study of the religions, Tillich developed what he referred to as a dynamic-typological approach to religious experience; an approach that was much influenced by Otto's, *The Idea of the Holy*. He discerned three interconnected elements found to some degree in all religions, which together constituted what he called the Religion of the Concrete Spirit.[97] These

---

[93] Tillich, *Systematic Theology*, Vol. 1, 15.

[94] Clayton, *Concept of Correlation*, 226.

[95] D. Tracy, 'Tillich and Contemporary Theology', in J.L. Adams, W. Pauck & R.L. Shinn (eds), *The Thought of Paul Tillich*, 260–277.

[96] M. Eliade, 'Paul Tillich and the History of Religions', in J.C. Brauer (ed.), *The Future of Religions*, 35–6.

[97] Pan-Chiu-Lai draws out the similarities between Tillich's proposals regarding the religion of the Concrete Spirit and the more recent world theology of Cantwell Smith. Both develop a theology of the history of the religions which presupposes

foundational aspects of religion he called the sacramental, the mystical and the prophetic all of which form the parameters of our encounter with the Holy. The dynamic interaction of these three types of religious experience clearly represented the ideal form of religion for Tillich and here again he connected with Schleiermacher.

> [Tillich's] position ... is not far removed form that of Schleiermacher, for whom the essence of religion, the primordial form, pre-exists historical manifestation as an a priori condition, and is comprehended in and through the language and traditions of particular, historical religions.[98]

In many ways Tillich was an early pioneer in the field of inter-religious dialogue and his book, *Christianity and the Encounter of the World Religions*, both reflected his personal engagement with the Buddhist and Shinto traditions he experienced in Japan, and demonstrated his affinity for the inclusivist position which aligned him with modern Roman Catholic thinking in the field of religious studies.

Tillich reflected the mood which was soon to engulf the whole field of religious studies, which was to transfer the religious question out of its setting in the evolution of modernity, to the dialogue with the other great religious traditions or world faiths, which had hitherto been relatively unexplored by mainstream Christian thinkers. While this is a necessary and laudable concern it left unanswered one of the most fundamental questions of the modern era: how was it possible in the space of only two hundred years for a civilisation founded and nurtured on the Judeo-Christian faith to abandon its heritage in favour of a relatively new and untenuated religious judgement, i.e. that of modern atheism? Does interfaith dialogue shed any light on this perplexing phenomenon or does it merely evade the issue? We learn from both Schleiermacher and Tillich that when Christology becomes subservient to a phenomenology of religion, then something of the uniqueness and distinctiveness of the Christian faith is surrendered in favour of other cultural, philosophical and religious concerns. The question of the role, significance and function of religion in the modern world is, however, a question to which we will have to return at a later stage in our investigation.

---

[97] (*continued*) some unitive element which permits the possibility of inter-religious dialogue; see *Towards a Trinitarian Theology of Religions: A Study of Paul Tillich's Thought*. Also see W.C. Smith, *Towards a World Theology: Faith and the Comparative History of Religion*.

[98] Richards, *Theology of Religions*, 67.

5.

Christology and History

PARADIGM TWO: THE MYTH OF PROGRESS

From the seventeenth century onwards, the comprehensive paradigm 'History' was developed in Europe, as a way of interpreting human beings and nature, God and the world. In this paradigm time ceased to be conceived of in terms of the cycle of the recurring seasons; it was now thought of as the line of human goals and purposes.[1]

Anyone who would think or write about Christology today must face the considerable disarray that has arisen over the historical question. What do we know with reasonable certainty about the historical figure Jesus of Nazareth? And how much do we need to know in order to evaluate the claims that have been made for him?[2]

Introduction

We have already noted that one of the distinguishing characteristics of the Enlightenment was the way people understood and experienced history. Moltmann draws attention to the notable changes in the conception of history. For instance, both the ancient and oriental worldviews were dominated by a cyclical view of history analogous to the cycles of the seasons in nature. This largely pessimistic view of history regarded the rise and fall of civilisations and nations as a cycle of growth and decline from which nothing new was to be expected or gained. During the Patristic period – particularly due to the influence of Tertullian, Eusebius, Athanasius and Augustine – this notion of history was replaced by the Judeo-Christian conception of history as basically a linear straight line, running from creation to the eschaton with the Christ event understood as the crucial mid-point of salvation history.[3] This more optimistic

---

[1] Moltmann, *Way*, 227.
[2] Macquarrie, *Modern Thought*, 348.
[3] Pelikan, *Centuries*, 21–34.

idea of history incorporated the notion of divine superintendence, (the doctrine of providence), as well as the eschatological fulfilment of the historical process in the future kingdom of God. The Enlightenment school of history preserved the Christian schema of linear succession but removed the theological infrastructure. In other words, God as the controlling agent in history was replaced with the notion of human progress.[4] In the eighteenth century, the historicist school of thought, which developed out of Romanticism and the influence of Hegel's philosophical rewriting of the history of civilisation, began to take root, particularly in Germany. Historicism abandoned the idea of history as a progressive development with a beginning and an end. Instead, history was understood as the story of the growth of distinctive societies and cultures. The historian's task was to understand and enter into cultures different from their own through the technique of empathy.[5]

Not surprisingly, the issue of the historicity of past events and their accessibility to us today – particularly the foundational events surrounding the person, ministry, mission, and the cross and resurrection of Jesus – have dominated the christological horizon. The metaphysical background to Christology – the question of Jesus' divinity and his relation to the God he represents – have taken second place to the concern to retrieve the historical Jesus as the primary focus of Christology.[6]

In this chapter we will investigate how the modern consciousness of history in the post-Enlightenment era, has dominated Christology. We will consider the diverse and troublesome issues surrounding the hermeneutical recovery of the person of Jesus in the context of contemporary culture, examining how significant theologians answered the vexing question, what is the relationship between the Jesus of history and the Christ of faith?[7]

---

[4] This is admirably expressed in the words of one of the chief representatives of this Deist notion of history, A.N. de Condorcet; 'emancipated from his shackles, released from the empire of fate and from the enemies of progress, advancing with a firm and sure step along the path of truth, virtue and happiness'. See, *Sketch for a Historical Picture of the Progress of the Human Mind*, 201.

[5] The main exponents of this view of history were Von Herder and Leopold Von Ranke. See D.W. Bebbington, *Patterns in History: A Christian Perspective on Historical Thought*.

[6] There are obviously exceptions to this general trend, for instance Barth, Tillich and, to a certain extent, Rahner. The difference between all of these, and Pannenberg and Moltmann is that the latter only arrive at metaphysical concerns when they have endeavoured to settle the historical and hermeneutical issues that necessarily pertain in any modern discussion of Christology.

[7] See also C.J.D. Greene, ' "In the Arms of Angels": Biblical Interpretation, Christology and the Philosophy of History', in C.. Bartholomew et al. (eds.), *Renewing Biblical Interpretation*, 198–239.

The Secularisation of History

There were theological, political and cultural antecedents to the Enlightenment concept of history, which centred on the interpretation and understanding of the Bible, and contributed greatly to the genesis of modernity. The story began with the emergence of a new historical critical approach to the Bible that sat very uneasily alongside the older doctrine of the perspicuity of Scripture.

The beginnings of an inchoate understanding of the nature of history can be found in the Reformers' radical engagement with Scripture and the advancement of the doctrine of *sola Scriptura*. Luther's distinction between law and gospel gave precedence to a thoroughgoing Christocentric interpretation of Scripture. The law referred to the moral ordering of society ordained by a righteous God to stem the flow of human sin and wrongdoing. The gospel was the divine antidote to sin and lawlessness, that 'happy exchange' whereby our sin and trespass was expunged by the cross of Christ. The primacy of the gospel of grace allowed Luther to dispense with the medieval system of allegorical exegesis and attend instead to the literal sense and historical context of the text. Luther thus refused to allow the liberating voice of Scripture to be silenced or circumscribed by the magisterium of the Roman Catholic Church.[8]

Spinoza

The secularization of history received renewed impetus from the political processes of emancipation, which were set in motion by the deleterious effects of the Wars of Religion. Here, one figure dominates, Baruch Spinoza. As a native Jew of Holland and a victim of anti-Semitism, Spinoza had just reason for wanting to curb the excesses of religious enthusiasm which had convulsed Europe and traumatised so many of her citizens. In his *Theological-Political Treatise* we discover the beginnings of a defence of liberal democracy, which develops via a thoroughly modern and ultimately rationalist hermeneutic of suspicion concerning the Bible. There were four basic ingredients to his new method of exegesis:

1. The various books of the Bible, like all other books, must be 'explained in relation to the mundane causes, historical conditions, and cultural presuppositions of the times in which they were written'.[9] Here Spinoza anticipates one of the revered tenets of modern historical biblical criticism

---

[8] This emerging sense of the historicity of the text was silenced by later Protestant orthodoxy, which, unfortunately, retreated into a scholastic view of Scripture as a repository of doctrine and proof texts, replacing the infallibility of the Pope with that of the Bible.

[9] Harrisville and Sundberg, *Bible in Modern Culture*, 44.

that permits the opening up a gap between the horizon of the contemporary interpreter and the original historical context of the biblical writings.
Furthermore, he interprets the past anachronistically as a reality fundamentally different from a contemporary viewpoint. Thus, the biblical perspective of attributing everything to the activity of God does not cohere with a
modern understanding of reality as controlled by the dictates of reason.

2. Divine agency is replaced by human advocacy. This is a secular rather than
a literal understanding of the biblical texts. Thus, the Bible is unshackled
from the fetters of ecclesiastical control and treated like any other document
of literary merit. The Bible may be inspirational and divine in origin, but it is
subject to the same canons of rationality as any other form of literature.

3. The truth of Scripture is that which is accessible to reason and is manifest in its
correspondence to what is regarded as normal moral sensibilities. The Bible
teaches true virtue and wisdom, but it is virtue accessible to the rational
mind and its corollary the natural moral conscience.

4. The proper interpretation of Scripture is the domain of the intellectual
elite. The masses swayed by religious fervour and prejudice must be held in
check by the scientific and historical study of the Bible undertaken by the
intelligentsia.

Taking all four principles together it is clear why Strauss upheld Spinoza, rather
than Reimarus, as the father of modern historical biblical criticism:

> The motivation for historical criticism of the Bible is clear. It is a primary means to
> free society from the destructive force of religious passion. That is to say, the purpose
> of this new exegesis is not proclamatory or dogmatic, but political. The content of
> the Bible is investigated with an eye firmly fixed on its social effect. By undercutting
> religious passion, Spinoza encourages doubt. From doubt, Spinoza believes there
> will spring the social good of tolerance.[10]

Deism

Similar cultural and political factors came to the fore with the development
of English Deism and its preference for a natural religion wholly accessible to
and explicable in terms of reason. This is best illustrated in John Tolland's
Christianity not Mysterious, although, to a certain extent, the scene had already
been set by John Locke's *The Reasonableness of Christianity*.

Tolland deploys Lockean epistemological principles to draw a decisive
parallel between the progressive knowledge of finite realities and the concepts
and doctrines of the gospel, understood in a largely ethical and moralistic sense.
Both are open to rational investigation because reason is the only basis for

---

[10] Ibid., 45.

certitude and truth. In a manner that is entirely reminiscent of Locke's clear and distinct ideas derived from sense experience, divine revelation is reduced to a means of imparting information that complies with our moral sensibilities.[11] Accordingly, Deist exegesis operates with the same fundamental hermeneutical principle as that of Spinoza, i.e. that the normal rules of interpretation apply to the Bible, as they do for any other secular literature. Once this is recognised, the apostolic message is reducible to 'Piety towards God and the Peace of Mankind',[12] both of which can become the basis for a new political settlement.

This is exegesis in the humanist and Puritan tradition whereby the gospel is purloined as that which entirely complies with the canons of scientific rationality. In order to achieve this Tolland makes a distinction between the pure unsullied ethics of the gospel and the degenerative superstition, legalism and clericalism of the post-Apostolic period. Thus history emerges in the distinction between the gospel of moral rectitude and the doctrinal mystification of later Christianity. Almost unwittingly, Tolland anticipates Adolf von Harnack's equally positivistic conclusion that Christology represents the Hellinisation of the original gospel of Jesus. At the same time, Tolland exhibits a fundamental feature of liberal Protestant exegesis: 'Roman Catholic Christianity was a false development of primitive Christian faith that distorted the clarity of the gospel.'[13]

The Dogma of Human Progress

The Enlightenment's deep and abiding fascination with the myth of progress and self-advancement was another crucial factor in the development of an essentially secular philosophy of history. Significant advances in science, technology, medicine and public health helped to fuel the belief in the notion of human progress. Ably incorporated into the philosophical empiricism of Hume[14] and the political theory of Adam Smith,[15] history began gradually to be understood as the inevitably forward march of human achievement and civilisation. In England the doctrine of progress later became associated with what Herbert Butterfield called the 'Whig interpretation of history', the tendency to interpret the past in terms of the progressive ideas of the present.[16]

---

[11] In this regard see H.G. Reventlow, *The Authority of the Bible and the Rise of the Modern World*, 294–308.

[12] Ibid., 299.

[13] Harrisville and Sundberg, *Bible in the Modern Culture*, 52.

[14] D. Hume, *An Enquiry Concerning Human Understanding*.

[15] A. Smith, *Inquiry into the Nature and Causes of the Wealth of the Nations*.

[16] Butterfield, *Christianity and History*.

The same ideas were vigorously pursued on the continent by such thinkers as the Marquis de Concorcet,[17] Henri de Saint-Simon[18] and Auguste Comte.[19]

Comte's views easily coalesced with the social Darwinism of the nineteenth century, which directly developed out of the theory of evolution. The moral and social advancement of humanity were viewed as analogous to the progress of evolutionary development taking place at the biological and natural level. The evolutionary paradigm continued to gain ascendancy in the natural sciences and cosmology. However, the idea of the upward progress of humanity continued to be associated with the new science of historical research and investigation. Not surprisingly, modern, critical, historical biblical scholarship could not remain immune from such developments in the wider field of historiography.[20]

The development of the progress paradigm contributed to the success of the human project of a 'scientific and technological society', because it enabled human beings to detach themselves from the world of nature and view themselves as masters of their own destiny and fate. Similarly, it produced the modern science of history with its reliance upon historical-critical skills of investigation and interpretation. Our consciousness of time as a dynamic historical process was broken up into the sequence of past, present and future. Our awareness of temporal distance from past events, traditions and cultures became one of the significant new features of our worldview.[21]

In both respects, the Enlightenment forced upon every succeeding generation the liberal ideal of reverence before history. During the eighteenth and nineteenth century this was optimistically conceived in terms of the forward march of civilisation and progress. However, two world wars and the human

---

[17] Condorcet, *Sketch*.

[18] H. de Saint Simon, *On the Reorganisation of European Society*.

[19] A. Comte, *The Positive Philosophy*. Comte was the founder of the philosophy of postivism, which spawned the development in analytic philosophy known as 'logical positivism'. He combined an epistemological positivism with an evolutionary view of social dynamics. Thus we have the *theological age* when early civilisations attributed all natural causation to the direct intervention of God. Then comes the *metaphysical age* with a corresponding search for natural causes. Humankind then reached the *scientific age* when all knowledge was based on observation, deduction and the discovery of scientific laws.

[20] Cf. E.W. Nicholson, *Interpreting the Old Testament: A Century of the Oriel Professorship*, 16.

[21] Raimundo Panikkar views the Christian preoccupation with history with notable equivocation, precisely because it easily became aligned with the secular notion of linear progress and so contributed to the rise of Western imperialism with the consequent destruction of other indigenous cultures. Cf. *The Trinity and the Religious Experience of Man: Icon-Person-Mystery*.

slaughter of numerous other conflicts have tarnished this ideal in the twentieth century, some would claim, beyond repair. The relationship between the Christian faith and the new paradigm of history has shown the same ability to swing from naïve fraternity to open warfare, to the present situation of an uneasy truce.

Not surprisingly, it was the rationalist, progressive and anti-supernatural view of history (a product of Enlightenment Deism) that first struck a discordant note in the relationship between the Christian faith and history. Historical-critical investigation of the Bible and the Christian tradition began to redefine the fundamental nature of the christological question, and it seemed that any liaison between the modern paradigm of history, heremeneutics and Christology was doomed to failure.

The Quest for the Historical Jesus

Lessing and the ugly broad ditch

> If no historical truth can be demonstrated, then nothing can be demonstrated by means of historical truths. That is: accidental truths of history can never become the proof of necessary truths of reason ... That, then is the ugly broad ditch which I cannot get across, however often and however earnestly I tried to make the leap.[22]

Religious faith, according to the canons of critical reason must rest upon so-called necessary truths that are true for all time and cannot, therefore, depend upon the contingencies and vagaries of historical probability. G.E. Lessing's well-known dictum,

> [brings] us to the place where the nature and value of historical inquiry is judged in terms of its relation to the interpreter's present horizons. Lessing urges the limitations of historical inquiry not because history cannot speak to these horizons, but because it cannot provide the kind of truth that rationally compels assent.[23]

Understandably, the weakness of history as a means of acquiring knowledge, when compared with the natural sciences, seemed only too evident for many in the seventeenth and eighteenth centuries. History could only deal with contingencies and probabilities. How reliable is the evidence of the miracle of the resurrection, upon which much of the Christian faith is founded,

---

[22] G.E. Lessing, *Lessing's Theological Writings: Selections in Translation; With an Introductory Essay by Henry Chadwick*, 53–5.

[23] A.C. Thiselton, *The Two Horizons: New Testament Hermeneutics and Philosophical Description*, 65.

given that the Gospel accounts appear to flatly contradict each other?[24] What actually took place? More to the point, how does the historian accurately gain access to the past? How do they interpret events and what role does their judgement play in making sense of past events? The historian does not simply record brute facts; they interact with the evidence, some of which may already have been subject to interpretation and disputation:

> The historian's craft is ... as much an art as a science. [They are] seldom dealing with material that can furnish [them] with a clear Yes or No to [their] questions. It is always a matter of probability, and in the assessment of this kind of probability personal factors, such as intuition, or having the feel of the period enter in. Given the same evidence and the same method, one [historian] will be better than another at reconstructing the past.[25]

Even knowledge of the recent past is the subject of much contentious argument, because we are dealing with human agents whose motives and reasons for taking a particular course of action are often far from clear. How do we gain access to what people thought about themselves and their world? More particularly, how are we to assess the claim that one particular individual is the unique revelation of the eternal God?

Reimarus

These and many other issues surfaced between 1774 and 1778 when, under a pseudonym, Lessing published the famous *Wolfenbüttel Fragments*, which were originally written by Reimarus, erstwhile Professor of Oriental languages at Hamburg. Two of the seven fragments of Reimarus' *Apology* were more controversial than the rest – 'On the Resurrection Narratives' (1777) and 'On the Intentions of Jesus and His Disciples' (1778).

Reimarus' thought continually ebbed and flowed between a public acceptance of the tenets of Protestant orthodoxy and a private imbibing of the new rationalist religion of Deism. Consequently, he was the first exponent of the Enlightenment to postulate a radical dichotomy between the Jesus of history and the Christ of faith. Wielding the reductionist canons of critical reason, Reimarus dispensed with both miracles as legendary additions to the biblical text and any notion of historical revelation as being incompatible with the necessary and universal character of truth. More importantly, he argued that Jesus was an apocalyptic visionary teacher who mistakenly believed himself to be the promised messiah who would free the Jews from foreign occupation.

---

[24] David Hume contended that any evidence that relied on eyewitness accounts was inevitably flawed. Hume, *Essay on Miracles*.

[25] Nicholl, *Guide to Modern Theology*, Vol. 1, 56.

Jesus never intended to invent a new religion. Indeed, Jesus' message was pure Jewish eschatological and political expectation: the earthly realisation of the kingdom of God that would involve the defeat of Israel's Roman oppressors, was imminent. Reimarus claimed that the disciples invented the story of the resurrection to conceal the real truth and concocted the theory of the atonement as a way of giving saving significance to Jesus' death:

> The real Jesus of history has thus been concealed by the apostolic church, which has substituted a fictitious Christ of faith, the redeemer of humanity from sin, in the place of a thoroughly human figure, whose failure to live up to his followers' expectations led to their preferring a glorious invention to a failed reality.[26]

Reimarus' radical scepticism gained few admirers at the time. However, his trenchant rationalist criticism of the Gospel tradition unearthed all the main dilemmas of modern biblical criticism.[27] He was the first biblical critic to take serious note of the eschatological context of Jesus' message, even if he wrongly interpreted this solely in terms of the Davidic political expectation of the messiah. Reimarus thus raised the central issue of Jesus' relationship to his native Judaism and the even more thorny issue of Jesus' relationship to the early Christian communities. His distinction between the self-understanding of Jesus and that of the early church was based on the conviction that the delay of the *Parousia* caused a real problem for the apostles and the early church, which necessitated a radical reappraisal of the Jesus tradition. In all respects Reimarus initiated the first serious attempt to erect a bridge across Lessing's ditch.

The bridge under construction

It is clear that the early practitioners of historical criticism overvalued the epistemological scope of the new science. The aim was to get at the facts, uncover what really happened, and separate fact from fiction. As Van Harvey points out, underlying this endeavour was 'an almost Promethean will to truth'.[28] Almost all of the early contributors to the new science –Wellhaussen, de Wette and Wrede included – unwittingly fell victim to a form of historical positivism.[29]

---

[26] McGrath, *Modern German Christology*, 35.
[27] See Harrisville and Sundberg, *Bible in Modern Culture*, 62–3.
[28] V.A. Harvey, *The Historian and the Believer: The Morality of Historical Knowledge and Christian Belief*, 4.
[29] Cf. J. Rogerson, *Old Testament Criticism in the Nineteenth Century: England and Germany*, also W. Brueggemann, *Theology of the Old Testament: Testimony, Dispute, Advocacy*, 1–61 and Wright, *Victory*, 1–25. Regarding de Wette, W.A. Howard notes: 'In christological matters, de Wette remained fully committed to the underlying

This new endeavour was greeted with hostility by many, particularly in England, because Spinoza's and Lessing's supposition that the Bible could be investigated like any other collection of ancient literature appeared to conflict with the belief in its supernatural inspiration. For others, the issues were couched in a way that typified the ethos of the Enlightenment, namely, freedom of enquiry versus dogma and critical investigation against superstition and obscurantism.[30]

In this respect, the battle lines between the church's public profession of Jesus as the Christ and the scholars' increasing private uncertainty and scepticism were already being drawn up. For the latter, the tools of the trade were the so-called lower and higher criticism, the application of which began to yield surprising results. In Old Testament studies Wellhausen's thesis gained ascendancy. Moses was not the author of the Pentateuch as had been previously believed. Rather, historical critical analysis reveals the development of Israelite religion from its early primitive form, through ethical monotheism to 'degenerate legalism'. In New Testament studies, Wrede's radical re-presentation of Reimarus' scepticism rapidly became the new orthodoxy.[31] The Gospels were not straightforward eyewitness accounts; neither were they conceivable as biographical accounts of Jesus' life. Rather, we actually know very little about Jesus, except what the early church allows us to glimpse between the layers of fiction and fabrication. So began the refinement and development of historical-critical techniques which dissected and scrutinised the biblical documents in an attempt to lay bare the historical sources, origins, literary forms and early redactions that gave rise to the early church's confession of Jesus as the Christ.

The nineteenth-century quest for the historical Jesus (initiated by Schleiermacher and undertaken by various representatives of German Protestantism) was a consequence of this progressive and positivistic view of history. In the process, the prevailing philosophy or philosophies of history underwent some notable changes. The Deist rationalist preference for natural religion rapidly gave way to the Kantian moralist equivalent, which was often combined with the Hegelian idealist alternative; ironically, the new science of biblical criticism could not escape the philosophical undercurrents that continually pulled it in different directions.

---

[29] *(continued)* Kantianism of Fries' categories, which forbade rapproachment between *Wissen, Ahnung* and *Glaube*. Yet de Wette's ambiguous phraseology attests to the difficulty he had as a biblical critic wrestling with the Christ-history problem. For this reason, the category of "mystery" became almost a necessary refuge.' See, *Religion and the Rise of Historicism: W.M.L. de Wette, Jacob Burckhardt, And the Theological Origins of Nineteenth Century Historical Consciousness*, 88. See also H.G. Reventlow & W. Farmer (ed), *Biblical Studies and the Shifting of Paradigms, 1850–1914*.

[30] Nicholl, *Modern Theology*, 51–61.

[31] W. Wrede, *The Messianic Secret*.

Strauss

This was apparent in the controversy that surrounded the publication of David F. Strauss' *Life of Jesus* in 1834.[32] Strauss subjected the New Testament to the rigours of historical-critical analysis in an attempt to separate fact from fiction, and reality from legend and myth. His basic conclusion was the writers of the New Testament shared a non-scientific, mythical worldview that was typical of more primitive cultures. In such societies, events and circumstances were attributed to the agency of supernatural beings. Strauss interpreted myth (*mythos*) in a Hegelian sense as a primitive stage in the self-realisation of Spirit (*Geist*) in the course of history. He detected the evidence of myth in most of the traditions surrounding the birth, life, ministry and death of Jesus, and argued that the supernatural expectations surrounding the Old Testament belief in the messiah were simply transposed on to the historical Jesus by the New Testament writers. While some of these interpretations may have a basis in the actual history of Jesus, that is in itself of no theological import. At the end of his book, Strauss resorted to a Hegelian interpretation of Jesus as the realisation of the Absolute in the realm of history. His work, however, stimulated others to continue the quest for the original Jesus, much of which was influenced by studies in the synoptic problem. The Hegelian influence in biblical studies continued unabated and formed the philosophical background to the brilliant scholarship of Ferdinand C. Baur.

Baur

It appears, at times, as if Baur was largely unaware of how much he systematically imbibed the high-octane vapours of the Hegelian religion of the Absolute, and, correspondingly, the notion of the self-realisation of the Universal Spirit in the historical process. So, for instance, while he was critical of the negative strain of historical criticism present in Strauss' work, Baur nevertheless exhibited the same rationalist tendency to exclude miracle, eschatology, and dogma from the proper scientific study of the biblical texts. For instance, in true positivist fashion Baur denied that the resurrection could ever be the object of empirical investigation, a strategy repeated again and again by his successors. Similarly, Baur broke with the Reformation understanding that it was the doctrine of justification that formed the heart of Pauline theology. Consonant with his insistence on finding objective grounds for faith, rather than subjective dispositions, Baur located the centre of Paul's thought in the overpowering reality of the cross of Christ:

---

[32] According to Albert Schweitzer, 'Scarcely ever has a book let loose such a storm of controversy; and scarcely ever has a controversy been so barren of immediate result. The fertilising rain brought up a crop of toadstools.' Cf. *The Quest for the Historical Jesus: A Critical Study of its Progress from Reimarus to Wrede*, 96.

> A death which ran so directly counter to all the facts and presuppositions of the Jewish national consciousness ... must have a scope far transcending the particularism of Judaism. There can be no doubt that this was the thought in which the apostle first discerned the truth of Christianity.[33]

Although Baur attributed a genuine messianic consciousness to the historical Jesus – expressed particularly through Jesus' interiorisation of the Mosaic law – he, like Wrede, tended to interpret the genesis of Christianity in terms of the disputes and controversies that beset the early Christian church. In that sense, it was Baur, rather than Strauss, who bequeathed the greatest debt to subsequent New Testament scholarship. He became convinced that early Christianity was racked by a bitter controversy between Jewish particularism and Gentile universalism, which was epitomised by the dispute between Peter and Paul. Finally, Baur argued that there is a fierce antipathy to Judaism in the Johannine corpus, which the Fourth Gospel resolves by designating Jesus as the enfleshed *Logos*. Consequently, Baur came to the conclusion that the idealised picture of Jesus as the incarnate *Logos* should be rejected in favour of a Jesus made accessible by historical analysis. However, Baur's Hegelian idealist presuppositions would, however, never have allowed him, unlike Wilhelm Bousset, to draw the inevitable empiricist conclusions from this analysis, i.e. that on the basis of such research all that remained was to construct a 'life-like portrait which, with a few bold strokes, should bring out clearly the originality, the force, the personality of Jesus'.[34]

Rather, those who were motivated and inspired by idealist presuppositions, possessed an altogether more ambitious exegetical intent:

> One finds among idealists an inclination to interpret the identity of Jesus Christ by locating his significance, not in the transcendence of human consciousness, but in the notion that an individual known as Jesus Christ somehow became an indispensable, exemplary expression of all human consciousness, one who embodied the experience of human nature and instigated a cultural process to inspire and improve humanity – beginning with the European peoples.[35]

There were two major presuppositions that controlled the corporate endeavours of those who tried valiantly to traverse Lessing's ditch. Both were exemplified in the theology of the two main representatives of liberal Protestantism, Albrecht Ritschl and Adolf von Harnack

---

[33] F. Baur, *Die Tübinger Schule*, AW, 5:28f., 33, 35, 36; quoted in Harrisville and Sundberg, *The Bible in Modern Culture*, 117.

[34] Quoted by Harvey, *Historian*, 11.

[35] Howard, *Historicism*, 92.

Ritschl

The first presupposition was that endorsed by Ritschl, a close friend and former pupil of Baur. Like Schleiermacher, Ritschl espoused a soteriological approach to Christology, but he replaced Schleiermacher's reliance upon the religion of feeling with a more ethical approach.[36] It was at this point that Ritschl most fiercely disagreed with Baur. Access to Christ is not to be found in mystical union, but through the concrete and largely ethical experience of redemption and reconciliation mediated to us through the Christian community of faith founded by the historical Jesus. It was, therefore, essential to establish the Gospel tradition concerning Jesus as trustworthy. This could be achieved, and here is the nub of the issue, through historical investigation that uncovered the religious convictions of Jesus (i.e. the ethical ideal of the kingdom of God and the universal fraternity of humanity). Ritschl interpreted these in a distinctly Kantian sense,[37] which ensured at the same time the domestication of the Christian faith to his bourgeois cultural landscape.

Von Harnack

The second presupposition was found in the influential work of von Harnack on the history of Christian dogma. He concluded that the early church's christological dogmas represent the Hellenisation of the original gospel message concerning the person of Jesus: 'Jesus does not belong to the gospel as one of its elements, but was the personal realisation and power of the gospel, and we still perceive him as such.'[38] What von Harnack actually perceived, however, was 'a de-Judaized Jesus with a social programme'.[39] Not surprisingly, the person of the historical Jesus becomes accessible to us when he is divested of the metaphysical accretions imposed on him by the dogmaticians of the early church. Only then is it possible to discover a Jesus who is the personal realisation of the fatherly love of God towards humanity.[40]

In all of this we find the virtual domestication of the Christian faith, the elimination of all that is odd, controversial, angular and inimical to a progressive idea of religion and culture, which is exactly the nature of the dispute that was to break out subsequently between von Harnack and Barth.[41] Similarly, we find

---

[36] As Robert Jenson notes: 'liberal theologians derived their analysis of human existence and the location therein of religion from Immanuel Kant: religion was understood as the interior presupposition of moral action and religious doctrines as "value judgements".' See 'Karl Barth', in D. Ford (ed.), *The Modern Theologians* Vol. 1, 30.

[37] Cf. Niebuhr, *Christ and Culture*, 107–8.

[38] A von Harnack, *What is Christianity?*, 145.

[39] Wright, *Victory*, 58.

[40] Cf. G.S. Jones, *Critical Theology*, 15.

[41] Ibid. 11–37 for an informative, interesting and relevant review of this dispute.

the nineteenth-century obsession with the teachings of Jesus in order to characterise him as a teacher of religion of a decidedly post-Kantian ethical variety.

The bridge collapses

This whole edifice of historical-critical investigation, based as it was on these
positivist premises, was to collapse under the combined assault of three
notable theologians of this era. For two of them, the assault was embodied in
the publication of a particular book.

Kähler

The first attack was the publication in 1896 of Martin Kähler's seminal study,
The So-called Historical Jesus and the Historic, Biblical Christ. He demonstrated that
the historical sources did not yield the kind of information about Jesus that both
Ritschl and his predecessors had assumed:

> The Jesus of the 'Life of Jesus' is merely a modern variety of the products of human
> creative art, no better than the infamous dogmatic Christ of Byzantine Christology;
> they are both equally far removed from the true Christ. Historicism is at this point
> just as arbitrary, just as humanly haughty, just as pert, and as 'faithlessly gnostic' as the
> dogmatism which in its own day was also modern.[42]

Kähler asserted that the Gospels pay scant attention to the life of Jesus or his
own inner religious life. Rather, the real Christ is the preached Christ. The
Gospels were written from faith to faith; they are kerygmatic documents that
contain the faith convictions of their writers. The attempt to circumvent the
Christ of faith in some misguided search for the historical Jesus was doomed
to failure, because the real intent of the gospel writers was to witness to the
crucified and risen Lord.

Schweitzer

The second point of attack was the publication in 1906 of Albert Schweitzer's
study of the 'life of Jesus movement', *The Quest for the Historical Jesus*. He
accepted that the nineteenth-century quest for the historical Jesus had 'loosed
the bands by which he had been riveted for centuries to the stony rocks of
ecclesiastical doctrine, and rejoiced to see life and movement coming into the
figure once more'.[43] Schweitzer, however, also exposed the inadequacies and
inner tensions of the attempt to isolate the historical Jesus from the interpretative context of the early church. In words later immortalised by the Roman

---

[42] M. Kähler, *The So-called Historical Jesus and the Historic, Biblical Christ*, 43.
[43] Schweitzer, *Quest*, 397.

Catholic modernist George Tyrrell, those who had undertaken the quest for the historical Jesus had merely caught a glimpse of their own reflection at the bottom of the hermeneutical well.

Building on the work of Johannis Weiss, Schweitzer also recovered the essential eschatological context of Jesus' teaching and self-understanding. This similarly served to discredit the idealised Jesus of liberal Protestantism, portraying Jesus instead as essentially a disillusioned apocalyptic, a strange enigmatic and wholly otherworldly figure who threw himself upon the wheel of history in a vain attempt to force God's hand. However, the wheel eventually turned and crushed Jesus, leaving him the victim of an ambiguous religious fate.[44]

The combined assault of Kähler's and Schweitzer's work effectively demolished the bridge Protestantism had endeavoured to construct across Lessing's ditch. It became clear that consecutive theologians had been labouring under a mistaken ideal of historical objectivity failing to take into account the presuppositions or dogmas that historians bring to their studies. As Gadamer notes, the Enlightenment continually exhibited 'a prejudice against prejudice'.[45] Not surprisingly, as the writers of a recent symposium demonstrate, the authority and validity of the Enlightenment legacy of historical critical exegesis of Scripture is still an issue that divides the contemporary church:

> Biblical critics frequently claim that their use of the historical-critical method is free of confessional assumptions and theological motivations, that their approach enjoys the status of objective historical science. Upon close scrutiny, however, it is possible to show that historical critics approach the texts with their own set of prior commitments, sometimes hiddenly linked to ideologies alien or hostile to the faith of the Christian church.[46]

Troeltsch

The third attack on the progressive positivists' beleaguered positions came from Ernst Troeltsch. His contribution to the debate has proved the most difficult to refute. H.G. Drescher, for instance, notes that Troeltsch recognises 'like no other theologian of his time, the upsetting and urgent features of

---

[44] Schweitzer's suspicion that the historical Jesus may be irretrievable, and that those who attempt this particular task inevitably end up with a Jesus of their own making, has remained a central concern of modern Christology. William Hamilton, for instance, concludes that the modern search for a political Jesus is just as elusive. It always remains a pointless and fruitless exercise because there 'is no Jesus as he really was. What we find, wherever we look, is always fiction, and usually ideology.' See, W. Hamilton, *A Quest for the Post-Historical Jesus*, 72.

[45] H.-G. Gadamer, *Truth and Method*, 241–5.

[46] C.E. Braaten and R.W. Jenson, *Reclaiming the Bible for the Church*, xi.

the relation between faith and history'.[47] As a representative of the history of religions school, which embraced the historicist view of history, Troeltsch sought to demonstrate how all religious ideas must be understood within their original historical *Sitz im Leben*. To achieve this, the historian must use the three principles of historical enquiry:

1. *Criticism* – all judgements about the past cannot be claimed as either true or false but are mere probabilities always liable to revision and refutation.
2. *Analogy* – we are able to make such probable judgements only if we presuppose that our own experience of events is not radically dissimilar to the experience of people in the past.[48]
3. *Correlation* – all historical events are interdependent and inter-related, so every event must be understood in terms of its historical antecedents and consequences.

Troeltsch believed that these principles were incompatible with Christian faith because they necessarily excluded from the field of historical enquiry any event, such as the resurrection, that could only be understood as a unique act of God.[49]

> Rather than trying to locate some ahistorical 'essence of Christianity', one must look to the whole continuum of Christian history in order to comprehend Christian identity. In this way, Troeltsch's historicism removed all bastions for protecting religious dogma, subjecting every aspect of religion to the cold light of critical historical scrutiny.[50]

Troeltsch embraced a form of historical relativism that tended to view Christianity as the point of convergence of all other religions. Whether Christianity could be viewed as absolute or not required a criterion of judgement that was not yet available to the historian.[51] Interestingly, Troeltsch's historicism could not satisfy his own religious yearnings and aspirations. In the end he invoked his own brand of transcendental metaphysics to account for the enduring

---

[47] Quoted in S. Coakley, *Christ Without Absolutes: Study of the Christology of Ernst Troeltsch*, 191.
[48] The principle of analogy was for Troetsch the direct opposite of Spinoza'a principle of anachronism. Spinoza, in fact, postulated a radical dichotomy rather than a similarity between the experience of ancient peoples and that of his contemporaries.
[49] E. Troeltsch, 'Historical and Dogmatic Method in Theology' ('Uber historische und dogmatische Methode in der Theologie'), in R. Morgan and M. Pye (eds), *Religion and History. Ernst Troeltsch: Writings on Theology and Religion*, 11–32.
[50] Johnson, *Mystery*, 16.
[51] E. Troeltsch, *The Absoluteness of Christianity and the History of Religions*.

and, therefore, 'unconditioned', aspects of religious faith: 'Our engagedness [*Zugewandtheit*] with the majesty of God has nothing to do with history. God is immediately present, and in the movements of our feelings rests a permanent self-relation to him.'[52]

Progressive liberalism

Progressive liberalism had its heyday between the end of the Napoleonic Wars and the outbreak of the First World War. The development of European culture and economic expansionism, coupled with the intellectual freedom of enquiry epitomised by the German university system, permitted the three ideals of Enlightenment scholarship to appear almost unassailable. The triumph of reason, the realisation of political autonomy and the obvious sense of progressive intellectual and economic development saturated the mores of liberal bourgeois society. It was this cultural and intellectual climate that allowed critical-historical scholarship to flourish. However, cracks were already appearing in the edifice:

> During the nineteenth century, the apologetic effort of liberal theology had been directed toward the identification of Jesus with modern culture as the prototype of universal religious experience. As God entered the heart of Jesus, so he enters our hearts, directing us to the just life. The kingdom of God was understood to be the key biblical symbol for this experience. In the latter decades of the century, historical scholarship began to cut the nerve of this apologetic by locating Jesus firmly in the context of apocalyptic expectation.[53]

One of the dilemma's of historical scholarship isolated by Reimarus (i.e. the relationship of the historical Jesus to Second Temple Judaism) was beginning to be conceived in a decidedly Schweitzerian fashion. The second fundamental issue for Christology, the relationship of the historical Jesus to the Christ of faith of the early Christian community, was to prove an even more elusive issue, one upon which there is still no scholarly consensus.

With the outbreak of the First World War, the progressive development of European civilisation gave way to hell on earth. The resilient doctrine of progress was temporarily buried in the trenches and human slaughter of a war fought with new technologically advanced weapons. The sad irony of a war conducted between the irresolvable tensions of old strategies and new weapons was not lost on journalists, political commentators and historians. The young theologians who lived through the carnage and ensuing heartache were to subsequently turn their own considerable intellectual armoury against the

---

[52] Troeltsch, 'Glaubenslehre'; quoted in Johnson, *Mystery*, 17.
[53] Harrisville and Sundberg, *Bible in Modern Culture*, 204–5.

bridge liberal historical scholarship had valiantly endeavoured to construct across Lessing's ditch. In fact, many of them were to abandon it altogether.

The bridge abandoned

The legacy of Troeltsch was never expunged from the theological agenda, even in the midst of the extreme theological reaction to liberal Protestantism, the consequence of which was the new theology of crisis spearheaded by Karl Barth.

> A half-century ago Barth and Bultmann hailed the collapse of the quest of the historical Jesus. The one positive gain of the quest, in their view, had been to demonstrate its own sterility for the life of faith.[54]

Dialectical theology, as it became known, returned to the radical existential-ism of Søren Kierkegaard. It was inherently sceptical of any attempt to ground the divinity of Christ upon historical investigation of his life and ministry. Kierkegaard, in a manner reminiscent of Lessing, asked: 'How can something of a historical nature be decisive for an eternal happiness?'[55] His own solution to the problem of Lessing's historical ditch was to attempt to cross it by means of an existential leap of faith. However, Barth and his colleagues (Friedrich Gogarten and Rudolf Bultmann) railed against the three ideals of liberalism – history, ethics and religion – in the name of God the wholly transcendent Other, who is separated from us by an 'infinite qualitative distinction' which no historical bridge can traverse.

> If I have any system, it is restricted to bearing in mind, as much as possible, what Kierkegaard called the 'infinite qualitative distinction' between time and eternity, in its negative and positive aspects. 'God is in heaven, and you are on earth'. For me, the relation of this God and this person, the relation of this person and this God is, in a nutshell, the theme of the Bible and the totality of philosophy.[56]

Barth

Karl Barth is attributed with the honour of recovering normative biblical exegesis in the face of the positivist and reductionist tendencies of liberal historical scholarship. He subjected the rationalist canons of modernity to his own fearsome epistemological critique that involved the reestablishment of the autonomy of theology as essentially a discipline that operates within its own fiduciary framework, i.e. 'faith seeking understanding':

---

[54] Meyer, *The Aims of Jesus*, 107.
[55] S. Kierkegaard, *Concluding Unscientific Postscript to Philosophical Fragments*.
[56] K. Barth, *The Epistle to the Romans*, Introduction.

Since Barth exposed objective scholarship as theory-laden, it does not follow that his theological premise would be granted any privilege. It does, however, make inescapable the recognition that there is no innocent or neutral scholarship, but that all theological and interpretative scholarship is in one way or another fiduciary. Barth's sustained polemic against religion is that all such practice of meaning that eventuated in liberalism must be critiqued, not because it is neutral, but because it flies in the face of the subject it purports to study – namely, the work and presence of the Holy God who cannot be grasped in such conventional and autonomous categories.[57]

Barth later went on to construct the christological metaphysics of the *Church Dogmatics*, which involved a return to the *Logos* Christology of Athanasius and the Alexandrian tradition. However, both the architectonic structure and scope of the *Dogmatics* continued to demonstrate the fecundity and versatility of his newly liberated biblical theology.

Bultmann

Rudolf Bultmann, with the help of Kähler and Heidegger, continued to maintain a radical scepticism towards history as a reliable foundation for personal faith in Christ, preferring instead a Christology based on the existential encounter between the believer and Christ in the preached *kerygma*:

> the salvation-occurrence is nowhere present except in the proclaiming, accosting, demanding, and promising word of preaching. A merely 'reminiscent' historical account referring to what happened in the past cannot make the salvation-occurrence visible. It means that the salvation-occurrence continues to take place in the proclamation of the word.[58]

A radical scepticism toward the search for the historical Jesus can stem from theological motives. In Bultmann's case, it was an application of the Reformation doctrine of justification by grace through faith without recourse to reason, historical science or dogma. Similarly, his own commitment to form critical analysis was based on the conviction that there was no material continuity between the synoptic tradition and the *kerygma* of the early Christian communities. Rather, the only connection was the mere historicity of the Christ event about which, Bultmann claimed, we can know virtually nothing. His own answer to what we might possibly ascertain from the biblical material about the historical Jesus left no doubt that this was not a figure on which to stake one's life!

> With a bit of caution we can say the following ... Characteristic of him are exorcisms, the breech of the Sabbath commandment, the abandonment of ritual purifi-

---

[57] Brueggemann, *Old Testament Theology*, 18.

[58] R.K. Bultmann, *Theology of the New Testament*, 302.

cation, polemic against Jewish legalism, fellowship with outcasts such as publicans and harlots, sympathy for women and children: it can also be seen that Jesus was not an ascetic like John the Baptist ... but gladly ate and drank a glass of wine. Perhaps we may add that he called disciples and assembled about himself a small company of followers ... We can only say of his preaching that he doubtless appeared in the consciousness of being commissioned by God to preach the eschatological message of the breaking-in of the kingdom of God ... We may thus ascribe to him a prophetic consciousness ... The greatest embarrassment to the attempt to reconstruct a portrait of Jesus is the fact that we cannot know how Jesus understood his ... death ... What is certain is merely that he was crucified by the Romans, and thus suffered the death of a political criminal ... It took place because his activity was misconstrued as political activity. In that case it could have been – historically speaking – a meaningless fate. We cannot tell whether or how Jesus found meaning in it. We may not veil from ourselves the possibility that he suffered a collapse.[59]

What then of the early Christian *kerygma* with its obvious high christological affirmations? Here we encounter the Bultmannian category of myth, i.e. statements that objectivise the divine reality and activity and therefore already witness to a process of Hellenisation. All such statements must be demythologised and translated into Heideggerian existentialist categories in order that the saving significance of the *kerygma* may be heard and understood in the context of the modern world.[60] Here we encounter, yet again, what inevitably takes place when Christology is reduced to soteriology or philosophical existentialism, i.e. that critical reduction of scale whereby the only significant Jesus is the Jesus *pro nobis*, the one who meets me in my existential need and despair. Once this route is taken, history, indeed any wider appreciation of the significance of society, culture and nature, is dissolved into anthropology.

Bultmann's critics could discern the Achilles heel of his system. If the living Word who meets us in the preached *kerygma* is loosed entirely from the Word made flesh, have we not undercut the doctrine of the incarnation at source and left ourselves with a mere historical lacuna, a Christ idea about a suffering and justifying saviour who could just as easily have been the invention of the apostle Paul?[61]

Bultmann's disciples were deeply vexed by the dilemma. Ernst Käsemann, Gunther Bornkamm and Ernst Fuchs all differed in their respective approaches to the problem. However, they all agreed that if faith in the preached Christ were allowed to float free from any anchorage in the synoptic tradition then

---

[59] R.K. Bultmann, 'The Primitive Christian Kerygma and the Historical Jesus', in C.E. Braaten & R.A. Harrisville (eds), *The Historical Jesus and the Kerygmatic Christ*, 22–4.

[60] Cf. R. Schnackenburg, 'Christology and Myth', in H.W. Bartsch (ed.), *Kerygma and Myth: A Theological Debate*, 336–55.

[61] This formed the basis of Joachim Jeremias' objections to the Bultmannian position. See, *The Problem of the Historical Jesus*.

Christology must pay the ultimate price. Might it be the case that, in some sense yet not clearly determined, the story and history of Jesus is subsumed within the *kerygma* of the early church and, therefore, a new quest for the historical Jesus should and could begin?

A myth returns

What then of the ubiquitous dogma of progress that had been conspicuous by its absence during the bloody inferno of two world wars? With the newfound optimism and prosperity of the post-war period, the myth of progress found its way back into the mental furniture of ordinary people, historians and dare we assume, biblical scholars.[62] It emerged from the turpitude and dying embers of nineteenth-century bourgeois European civilisation, manifesting two distinct ideological forms, Marxism and capitalism. Both fixed their gaze on the future through the lens of historical determinism and both sought to revisit history through the mechanisms of their own prejudices and presuppositions. Incorporated into their respective systems was the same well-worn secular notion of the inevitability of human progress, although this time given a decidedly economic twist.[63] It is significant that in this cultural context a new quest for the historical Jesus should once again take root.

The bridge revisited

Käsemann

It was Ernst Käsemann who inaugurated the new quest with a lecture specifically on this issue delivered in October 1953. The old quest for the historical Jesus had been based on the presupposition of a radical discontinuity between the Christ of faith and the historical Jesus. That discontinuity Käsemann accepted as real, but not absolute. Rather, he suggested that the kernel of the *kerygma* about Jesus was already there in embryonic form in the ministry of Jesus himself.[64]

Käsemann's approach reflects what Wright has discerned as the preference amongst New Testament scholars since Schweitzer for the silhouette and icon rather than the concrete historical reality of the man Jesus.[65] We peer through a glass darkly, this time the New Testament *kerygma*, for any reflection or image of the enigmatic rabbi from Nazareth, hoping that by some stoke of luck we might happen upon that hidden continuity between the earthly Jesus and the exalted Lord.

---

[62] Cf. Bebbington, *Patterns in History*, 89.
[63] See Newbigin, *Foolishness*, 106.
[64] Quoted in Pannenberg, *Jesus–God and Man*, 56.
[65] Wright, *Victory*, 1–27.

Käsemann found that link in the interconnecting substratum of primitive apocalyptic. Apocalyptic, however it is understood, links Jesus' message about the present and coming kingdom of God and the early church's proclamation concerning a risen and exalted Saviour. Contra Bultmann, Käsemann insisted that the Pauline doctrine of justification was informed by this eschatological tension between the already and the not yet, and therefore could not be reduced to a mere existentialist anthropology. With the delay of the *parousia*, however, it was inevitable that the legitimisation of the leadership of the early Christian communities would become a real issue. In that sense apocalyptic was displaced, largely neutralised and eventually removed from the later development of the Christian faith into what Käsemann, like Baur, designated as 'early catholicism'.

Käsemann's antipathy toward this development stemmed as much from his conviction that the apolitical, bourgeois, twentieth-century equivalent, was his own Wurttemberg Church tradition! Käsemann located the necessary corrective to such parochialism in the Pauline proclamation of the cross of Christ. Here we discover Christian existence lived in obedience to the continuity between the mission of Jesus to seek and save the lost, and the Pauline conviction that through the cross God was reconciling the whole cosmos to himself. The cross and resurrection of Christ therefore become the non-negotiable *sine qua non* of the Christian faith:

> What for me may under no circumstance go overboard is this one single thing: The message of the justification of the godless ... Our God is not chiefly concerned with strengthening, bettering or preserving of the pious and the victory of religiosity in the world, but with freeing people and the earth from the demonic power of godlessness.[66]

In his dispute with Bultmann, Käsemann had virtually single-handedly set the agenda for the important and considerable theological endeavours that were to ensue from his labours. Apocalyptic now became the way to advance a full-blown theology of history, which endeavoured, in a radically inclusive manner, to lay the ghost of Lessing to rest, the contours of which were sketched out by Wolfhart Pannenberg.[67] Similarly, an equally inclusive theology of the cross advanced the cause of a new political theology whereby the righteousness of God is revealed in the justification of the godless and the godforsaken, an agenda which eventuated in a book which took the theological world by storm, Jürgen Moltmann's, *The Crucified God*.

---

[66] Käsemann, *Widerstand im Zeichen des Nazareners*, 29–30; quoted in Harrisville and Sundberg, *Bible in Modern Culture*, 249.

[67] W. Pannenberg, 'Redemptive Event and History', in *BQIT* 1 (1959), 15–80.

The bridge reinstated

Pannenberg

> History is the most comprehensive horizon of Christian theology. All theological questions and answers have meaning only within the framework of the history which God has with humanity, and through humanity with the whole creation, directed towards a future which is hidden to the world but which has already been revealed in Jesus Christ.[68]

This concise statement outlined the parameters of Pannenberg's theology of history, and signalled his return to the Idealist tradition, which viewed history as essentially the self-manifestation of the Absolute. Pannenberg has consistently advocated the need to forge a new theology of history and thus anticipates a lot of the present discussion about the need to develop a new theological biblical hermeneutic.[69] It is instructive to outline the main components in this agenda because at this stage in the story we find a theologian who embraces a particular philosophy of history, where christological issues are no longer merely tangential to the plot, but are utterly crucial and central to how we understand both the nature of history and religion. Here another important chapter in the narrative begins.

History is the arena of God's self-revelation and interaction with the world. God is revealed indirectly through the reflex of his action in the public field of human history. There can be no separation between salvation history and ordinary history. History is a seamless robe that defies such arbitrary distinctions. It is an interrelated nexus of events that only receives its unity, and therefore its ultimate meaning and significance, from the perspective of its end.

This notion of universal history was akin to that developed by Hegel and later espoused by Wilhelm Dilthey.[70] Pannenberg differs from Hegel, however, in his affirmation of the eschatological dimensions of the biblical view of history, and in his refusal to subordinate the biblical material to a speculative philosophy of history. In this respect, Pannenberg builds on the work of biblical scholars such as Gerhard von Rad, Käsemann, and his former colleagues Rolf Rendtorff and Ulrich Wilckens, in seeking to demonstrate the importance of the apocalyptic and eschatological framework of meaning for a new theology of history.

---

[68] Ibid., 15.

[69] Cf. F. Watson, *Text and Truth: Biblical Interpretation in Theological Perspective*, and K. Vanhoozer, *Is There a Meaning in the Text?: The Bible, the Reader, and the Morality of Literary Knowledge*.

[70] See W. Pannenberg, 'Hermeneutic and Universal History', in *BQIT* 1 (1959), 96–136.

Revelation is no longer understood in terms of a supernatural disclosure or of a peculiarly religious experience and religious subjectivity, but in terms of the comprehensive whole of reality, which, however, is not simply given, but is a temporal process of a history that is not yet completed, but open to a future, which is anticipated in the teaching and personal history of Jesus.[71]

Consequently, history is eschatologically determined which corresponds to the biblical perspective that creation is a historical process moving towards its consummation in the coming kingdom of God. As history is also the story of God's self-revelation (indeed, his trinitarian self-realisation) it follows that his complete self-unveiling will only take place at the end of history as well.[72] The end of history and, therefore, the definitive self-revelation of God, have occurred proleptically in Christ's resurrection from the dead. This is so because this event can only be properly understood within the context of apocalyptic Judaism, as a foreshadowing of the general resurrection from the dead that was expected at the end of history.

The statement 'existence anticipates essence' summarises this ontology of history. Everything exists in anticipation of its fullness of being and meaning, which is, as yet, hidden in the undisclosed future of God:

> Since the emergence of historical consciousness, the unity of all reality is conceivable only as a history. The unity of truth is still possible only as a historical process, and can be known only from the end of the process ... The unity of truth is possible only if it includes the contingency of events and the openness of the future.[73]

The exegetical and dogmatic bases to this theology of history were laid out in a book that provoked a storm of controversy and criticism, *Revelation as History*, published in 1961. The book represented the interdisciplinary work of a group of scholars who became known as 'the Pannenberg circle'. Their corporate endeavours were designed both to construct a more comprehensive category of revelation from the basis of biblical apocalyptic, and to find an alternative to what they regarded as the limitations of the Word of God theologies of both Barth and Bultmann. In doing so, they fully embraced a particular philosophy of history that had deep affinities with the Hegelian Idealist tradition.

---

[71] Pannenberg, *Revelation as History*, Preface to the American Edition ix.

[72] While the trinitarian schema of Pannenberg's theology of history was anticipated to a certain extent in *Revelation as History* it was only fully worked out in the first volume of the *Systematics* where he constructed his own highly original trinitarian doctrine of God.

[73] W. Pannenberg, *What is Truth?*, in *BQIT*, 2, 27.

Christological Considerations

The christological implications of this theology of history were fully developed by Pannenberg in his *Grundzuge der Christologie* (*Jesus–God and Man*) and later in the second volume of the *Systematics* (1994).

First, the christological affirmation of Jesus' unity with God must be firmly anchored in Jesus' proclamation of the coming kingdom of God and the resurrection. The historicity of both must be cogently demonstrated and maintained. This constitutes Pannenberg's endorsement of the new quest for the historical Jesus, namely, that the message *of* Jesus and the message *about* Jesus are linked by the eschatological horizon of the coming kingdom of God.

Secondly, Jesus' proclamation of the nearness of the kingdom of God implied a claim to unique authority, in that Jesus in his own person was the mediator of the future rule of God. That claim to authority was ambiguous and brought Jesus into conflict with the religious establishment which led to his execution.

Thirdly, Jesus' message looked to a future confirmation that the early church discerned in the resurrection. As noted already, the resurrection is an apocalyptic concept that refers to the general resurrection from the dead awaiting the end of history. To claim that this has proleptically taken place in the destiny of one man is to make two further christological affirmations:

1. The resurrection was a divine confirmation or validation of Jesus as the personal realisation of the saving rule of God.
2. The resurrection consequently becomes the basis for affirming Jesus' personal unity with God.

Fourthly, the resurrection is a real event in history. Consequently, its historicity must be maintained against all attempts to dissolve it into the religious subjectivity of those who supposedly witnessed the event. This point has been well expressed by Dale Allison: 'Belief in the resurrection of Jesus is not likely to be explained away by the sociological fact that faith can, despite everything, declare the fulfilment of its hopes. The mystery of the resurrection is not dissolved so easily.'[74] Consequently, Pannenberg stands by the validity of the resurrection appearances and the tradition of the empty tomb, both of which, he claims, are open to historical investigation.

This immediately brings Pannenberg into conflict with Troelsch's three canons of historical research. Pannenberg's basic point is that these three criteria represent an unwarranted anthropological constriction or secularisation of

---

[74] D. Allison, *The End of the Age has Come: An Early Interpretation of the Passion and Resurrection of Jesus*, 168.

the field of historical enquiry. Take, for instance, the principle of analogy or the belief in the homogeneity of all events. This is only so from the standpoint of the human observer whose perspective is always a limited one. Why, if the possibility of a unique event is not ruled out in the natural sciences, should it be disqualified from the probabilities of history? Pannenberg asserts that coming to the biblical texts with the prior presupposition that the dead do not rise is an approach to history that is controlled by a predetermined worldview. Why not let the evidence, based on a worldview that is always open to the contingencies and novelties of history, speak for itself?

> As long as historiography does not begin dogmatically with a narrow concept of reality according to which 'dead men do not rise', it is not clear why historiography should not in principle be able to speak of Jesus' resurrection as the explanation that is best established of such events as the disciples' experiences of the appearances and the discovery of the empty tomb.[75]

Fifthly, on the basis that the resurrection was actually the breaking in of the future kingdom of God, then this event has unique ontological significance:

1. It links Jesus ontologically to the future of God's rule and, therefore, with the deity of God.
2. It shows that the resurrection also has retroactive ontological power, taking up Jesus' pre-Easter life and ministry as that which was also linked with the being of God. From the perspective of the resurrection, then, we can move backwards to the incarnation and view this as a valid summary statement concerning Jesus' pre-existent unity with God.

Sixthly, the way to approach the contentious issue of Jesus' unity with God, i.e. his divinity, is not through his relationship to the pre-existent *Logos*, but indirectly through Jesus' relationship to the Father. Jesus is one with the Father whose kingdom he proclaimed because he differentiates himself from him. This self-differentiation forms the basis of their unity. Jesus perceives his vocation as a giving of himself away to the mission of the Father. As he differentiates himself from the Father, so Jesus makes room within his own life and ministry for the will and rule of the Father, mediated to him through the Spirit. This constitutes his divinity.

Pannenberg asserts that this is the only way to avoid the logical difficulties of Chalcedonian Christology. The central problem that faced both Alexandrian and Antiochene Christology was how to conceive of the unity of the *Logos* and the man Jesus through the incarnation. This led to all the difficulties of

---

[75] Pannenberg, *Jesus—God and Man*, 109.

whether the *Logos* was the personalizing element in the incarnation, or whether the *Logos* united with the already existing man Jesus of Nazareth. Reformation Christology sought to circumvent the two-nature impasse through the concept of the *communicatio idiomatum* (each nature communicates its attributes to the other), and later eighteenth- and nineteenth-century Christology explored the possibilities implicit in the notion of kenosis. Pannenberg's answer is to say that Jesus' unity with the *Logos* can only be approached indirectly through Jesus' primary relationship to the Father.

Finally, Jesus' claim to equality with God was interpreted as blasphemous and led to his crucifixion. The separation from the Father experienced on the cross was the ultimate expression of Jesus' self-differentiation from the Father in his act of total obedience and self-surrender: 'This obedience led him into the situation of extreme separation from God and his immortality, into the dereliction of the cross. The remoteness from God on the cross was the climax of his self-distinction from the Father.'[76]

In light of the resurrection, Jesus is confirmed in his mission and vocation as the unique Son of God. His awareness of his own finitude and, therefore, the need to differentiate himself from the Father is seen as the paradigm of the relationship of the finite to the infinite. By any standards, the theological integration of Pannenberg's christological considerations is impressive. He demonstrates how historical-critical interrogation and interpretation, systematic theological analysis and philosophical perspicuity can rescue the Christian religion from its reduction to morality, as was the case with Kant, or a speculative philosophy of history, as pertained with Hegel. However, in the process Pannenberg constructs a theology of history that remains deeply indebted to both a critical realist and idealist perspective. For Pannenberg, history remains the most reliable foundation to the dialogue that must continually pertain between the Christian faith and the exigencies of contemporary culture. It is at this point where his whole theological edifice appears most vulnerable to those of a postmodern disposition.[77]

Assessment

Few modern theologians have had the temerity to object to the dominance of the modern paradigm of history in every area of theological concern. Pannenberg consistently advocated that there is no other form of human

---

[76] Pannenberg, *Systematic Theology*, Vol. 2, 375.

[77] F. LeRon Shults seeks to deflect this criticism of Pannenberg by reinterpreting his theology as a precursor to postfoundationalism. See *The Postfoundationalist Task of Theology: Wolfhart Pannenberg and the New Theological Rationality.*

knowledge, other than that which is embedded within the traditions and events which history seeks both to preserve and interpret.[78] He also refused to be unnerved by the so-called distinction between Christology from below and above, opting for one in favour of the other. Rather, he endeavoured to show how both imply the other and how it is possible to build a Christology that takes this relationship seriously.[79] We can criticise Pannenberg's impressive endeavours, for instance did he correctly understand the nature of apocalyptic?[80] But this immediately brings us to the nub of the issue: given the fact that there is no objective, value neutral or non-ideological history, has anyone yet correctly understood the precise nature of apocalyptic expectation or is this inevitably a historical construct?

To a large extent philosophy, as the traditional partner in dialogue with theology, has given way to history, and particularly hermeneutics, as the new focus of attention. It is only now at this late stage in the evolution of the modern 'scientific and technological project' that dissenting voices are being heard which seek to subvert the continued ascendancy of the paradigm of history. They come from the advocates of postmodernity who are suspicious of the claim that history can, or ever did, represent, or interrogate reality.

---

[78] Edward Schlillebeeckx and Hans Küng are examples of two theologians who agree with the fundamental premise that our access to the real Jesus is via the route of critical historical investigation, but because of the secular and postivistic historical stance they adopt are forced to make other moves to guarantee the divinity of the saviour. Cf. H. Küng, *On Being a Christian*, and E. Schillebeeckx, *Jesus: An Experiment in Christology*.

[79] It is certainly the case that Pannenberg appeared to be advocating a Christology from below in the first edition of *Grundzüge der Christologie*. However, in the postscript to the fifth German edition he sought to not only acknowledge this deficiency but also began to raise doubts concerning the validity and logic of the distinction as an elucidation of the christological issues: 'It seems to me that the limitations of the present book lie in other places. These are connected with the limitation within which the history of tradition approach "from below" is carried through here by treating the reality of God as a *presupposition* of Christology. This point has not really become thematic in the discussion so far. There is, to be sure, a section about the doctrine of the Trinity in my book. But the statements of this section are almost limited to the deity of Jesus in distinction from Father and Spirit. As a consequence, God's action in Jesus' history is certainly not bypassed, but it still does not become thematic as God's action'; 404–5.

[80] Wright contends: 'One of the things for which Schweitzer has become most famous is now increasingly questioned: "apocalyptic" was for him, and for the ninety years since he wrote, almost synonymous with the end of the space-time universe, but it is now clear that this is a bizarre literalistic reading of what the first century knew to be thoroughly metaphorical.' *Victory*, 81.

The demise of the grand narrative that sought to explain everything within the terms of some universal frame of reference has cast a shadow over the all-encompassing tendencies of history and has now been replaced by the postmodern condition of 'incredulity toward metanarratives'. So, for instance, Jean François Lyotard has argued that any over-arching theory of universal history is really a form of cultural imperialism. It is the way one dominant culture supplants and overcomes the legitimacy of another in the vain search for universal meaning.[81] Within the confines of postmodern theory, universality has given way to particularity and the recognition of the importance of cultural contexts as critical evidence of the sociological and political conditioning of all our knowledge, both of the past and the present:

> Claims to objectivity, neutrality or empirical truth are subverted by showing the problematic status of 'facts', the need of the historian always to impose some plot and order are taken as facts, and the inevitable bias to towards particular cultures, groups, and political interests.[82]

Even within contemporary theology there are those who are suspicious of the claim that history mirrors reality. Rather, it is claimed that history merely portrays ideological self-interest and the inevitable bias of one cultural aspiration over and against another.[83]

Moltmann is one theologian who has voiced a similar concern. He notes that the ascendancy of the modern paradigm of history has aided and abetted the ruthless subjugation of nature by technology. By making ourselves the sole subjects of history, we have severed the connection between the history of the natural world and ourselves. It is only the ecological crisis that has alerted us to this fact and so revealed the considerable limitations of the modern investment in our own historical destiny:

> The more human beings put themselves above nature the less they know who they really are. The modern crisis of identity and humanity are an inescapable result of the self-isolation of human beings from nature.[84]

Moltmann advocates a theology of mutual interdependence, or *perichoresis*, where the history of nature and human beings are put on an equal footing within a new covenantal relationship.

---

[81] J.F. Lyotard, *Missive on Universal History*, 43–64.

[82] Ford (ed.), *Modern Theologians*, Vol. 2, 292.

[83] See for instance M.C. Taylor, 'Terminal Faith', in P. Heelas, D. Martin & P. Morris (eds), *Religion, Modernity and Postmodernity*.

[84] Moltmann, *Way*, 271.

Other critical voices have come from within the circle of feminist thought. Here the concern has been over the identification of history with *his* story, to the virtual exclusion of *her* story. The modern paradigm of history has been exposed as a particular version of the 'androcentric fallacy'. We shall investigate both these concerns in due course. At this stage, however, it is sufficient to note that the history of the modern world has been the history of the dominance of the masculine psyche.[85]

What then of the modern economic conception of history as that which has been driven largely by the engine of two competing ideologies, i.e. capitalism versus communism? The origins of this dispute go back to Hegel and Marx, and both ideologies espouse a developmental, progressive notion of historical evolution:

> For both of these thinkers, there was a coherent development of human societies from simple tribal ones based on slavery and subsistence agriculture, through various theocracies, monarchies, and feudal aristocracies, up through modern liberal democracy and technologically driven capitalism. This evolutionary process was neither random nor unintelligible, even if it was possible to question whether man was happier or better off as a result of historical 'progress'.[86]

It is also the case that both thinkers, operating within the parameters of these premises, posited a possible end to universal history when our most basic and fundamental socio-political needs and aspirations were realised in a universal form of human society. For Hegel, this was the liberal democratic state, and for Marx it was egalitarian communism.

According to Francis Fukuyama, it is Hegel who has won the day. Despite the deep pessimism about the possibility of historical progress that has accompanied the continuing atrocities of this century of 'mass death', and the intellectual bombardment of the notion of progress by contemporary philosophers and historians, what we have actually witnessed in recent history is the near total collapse of both military authoritarian Right regimes and their Leftish counterparts (totalitarian communism). Fukuyama argues that the Hegelian notion of the end of history has been realized in the victory of liberal democracy over its ideological and economic counterpart. Obviously, in some sense history continues. Historical events, patterns of succession and development, the conflict of competing ideologies, the rise of religious fundamentalism and political nationalism are all part of the historical and cultural fabric of contemporary life. However, it does seem that in the spread of liberal democracy throughout the world we have arrived at an inherently stable form of society that protects, nourishes and satisfies our basic socio-political needs. According

---

[85] Cf. Tarnas, *Passion of the Western Mind*, 441.

[86] F. Fukuyama, *The End of History And The Last Man*, xii.

to Fukuyama, this is based on the realisation of two prior underlying prerequisites. The first is the development of modern natural science and technology, which in turn has led to the realisation of the capitalist ideal of continued economic expansion bolstered by the rise of the global economy.[87] Fukuyama does concede that there is no necessary inner connection between advanced economic industrialisation and liberal democracy. While economic expansion and development may have led inexorably to the victory of capitalism over communism, the logic of modern natural science is insufficient to account for this fact.

Returning to Hegel and Nietzsche, Fukuyama asserts that the second crucial determinant is the desire for recognition or self-esteem which creates the basis for equality and the mutual recognition of human and civil rights, which in turn is central to the development of modern liberal democracy:

> Recognition is the central problem of politics because it is the origin of tyranny, imperialism, and the desire to dominate. But while it has a dark side, it cannot be simply abolished from political life, because it is simultaneously the psychological ground for political virtues like courage, public-spiritedness, and justice. All political communities must make use of the desire for recognition, while at the same time protecting themselves from its destructive effects. If contemporary constitutional government has indeed found a formula whereby all are recognised in a way that nonetheless avoids the emergence of tyranny, then it would indeed have a special claim to stability and longevity among the regimes that emerged on earth.[88]

Fukuyama's thesis can be contested and he himself argues for a more robust form of social democracy than has hitherto been exhibited in international affairs. However, what is common to the nature versus history, men versus women, and capitalism versus communism interpretations of history is the postmodern ambivalence about power relations. Nietzche and Foucault's conviction that all human knowledge, value judgements and the rise of historical consciousness is ideologically controlled, driven by the will to power, has become firmly situated in the postmodern psyche and, indeed, in the contemporary evaluation of the nature of history. Before we assess the integrity or otherwise of this claim it would seem apposite to enquire first into the nature and practice of contemporary historiography.

The making of history

Here we need to ask not what does the historian presume his or her task might be, but how do they actually practise their task? How does the historian go

---

[87] Ibid., xiv–xv.
[88] Ibid., xxi–xxii.

about making or constructing history? This involves the interconnectivity of a number of crucial factors:

1. The historian brings herself to the task – her values, prejudices, self-evaluation, academic position, ideological interests, and personal preferences.
2. They bring with them their epistemological presuppositions and preferences, be that Marxist, empiricist, feminist, positivist, idealist, progressive, liberationist, postmodernist etc., or a range of these possibilities. We are referring here to the educational, political, cultural and economic situatedness of the historical interpreter.
3. They bring with them their research skills or lack of them, the use of various techniques or methods of enquiry and the application of certain consensus driven 'tools of the trade'. Here theory and practice mutually inform one another. It matters a lot whether we think of history as a universal interconnected nexus of events or just one damn thing after another. Similarly how do we evaluate the importance of cause and effect or the notion of the fundamental homogeneity of all events, or the psychological mechanism of empathy, or the interpretation of history by use of analogous or anachronistic criteria?
4. The historian works with, interprets, deconstructs and evaluates both primary and secondary material, although this does not imply a value judgement in regard to the importance of one in relation to another. The historian may have a preference for original artefacts, primary sources or he or she may attribute equal value to biographical and therefore already interpreted accounts of such information and data.
5. The historian is required to write up their research and so evolve their own, or borrow some other, interpretative framework. Again, epistemological, ideological, methodological and personal factors clearly come into play.
6. There is the consumption of such constructed histories by other academics, or the scholarly community, or, indeed, the populace at large. Here we are indebted to the literary critics who remind us that no two readings need be literally the same. There is always the '*différence*' between one interpretative horizon and another. There are always aporias to be discerned. There is always the potential to misunderstand, misapply, wrongly judge or categorise, or deconstruct the text as it is read in a new context. Similarly, there is still some sense of scholarly consensus or the testing and refining of historical hypotheses among a community of interested and committed historians.

History as a cultural construct

In terms of the common coinage of all six factors, nowadays it is difficult to ignore the prominence of the word ideological. How we learn to read history depends on how we interpret those who construct history and they, largely, are the product of the dominant cultural ideology that has produced such history in the first place. George Steiner expresses the nature of the problem we face:

> Croce's dictum 'all history is contemporary history' points directly to the ontological paradox of the past tense. Historians are increasingly aware that the conventions of narrative and implicit reality with which they work are philosophically vulnerable. The dilemma exists on at least two levels. The first is semantic. The bulk of the historian's material consists of utterances made in and about the past. Given the perpetual process of linguistic change not only in vocabulary and syntax but in meaning, how is he to interpret, to translate his sources ... Reading a historical document, collating the modes of narrative in previous written history, interpreting speech-acts performed in the distant or nearer past, he finds himself becoming more and more of the translator in the technical sense ... And the meaning thus arrived at must be the 'true one'. By what metamorphic magic is the historian to proceed?[89]

In terms of the dominant cultural ideologies that have controlled the construction of history in Western civilisation, there are three variations on a single theme, i.e. realist or empiricist, idealist, with a new contender recently appearing on the scene, postmodern. The single theme that unites all three is the conviction that the truth is basically out there in some form or another waiting to be discovered. It is either out there empirically in the real world to which we can gain genuine epistemic access, provided we use the right 'tools' of investigation; or it is out there in someone's mind, be that the mind of God or the problem of 'other minds' and, therefore, must be disclosed to us; or it is out there in somewhat disconnected and interrupted form waiting to be deconstructed or reconstructed by ourselves. As Whitehead remarked, the history of Western philosophy is still a series of footnotes to Plato.[90]

The fundamental question remains: what is the nature of truth and how is the truth mediated to us and in what form is it discovered or appropriated by us? Is truth mediated to us through the eternal forms, or through the self-disclosure of the eternal God in and through the unfolding events of history, or through the universal application of reason to the traditions, discourses, narratives and still resonating evidences of the past, or through the acceptance that truth is largely our own ideological construction?

---

[89] G. Steiner, *After Babel: Aspects of Language and Translation*, 134–6.
[90] A.N. Whitehead, 'Introduction', in *Process and Reality: An Essay in Cosmology*.

In the empiricist tradition, history is correspondingly the way we gain access through the application of critical reason to the various forms of knowledge we have about the past. In the idealist tradition, history is the way we gain entry to the divine mind or the mind of others through the critical application of both reason and empathy. The material we investigate may be largely the same, e.g. artefacts, documents, archaeological data, census information, maps. However, for the realist-empiricist that information does and can inform us about the world of the past. For the idealist, it informs us about what other minds thought about themselves and the world of the past. In both traditions, certain cultural factors dominate the interpretation of the past.

History is organised along a value scale that, with a few critical reservations, has been positivistic, programmatic, progressive and liberal. There are still apparently such things as ascertainable facts granted that they arrive replete with ready made interpretations, which, it is the historians task to assess, evaluate and interpret, usually by venturing a particular hypothesis or interpretative framework which tries to make sense of the available information in as parsimonious and convincing a way as possible. To achieve this the historian must accept the inevitability of progressive development because they work within a developing tradition of scholarship and enquiry, and usually it is granted that they should avoid prejudicing the evidence through bias or wanton misrepresentation.

For the postmodernist there is no such thing as the past. We are in fact cut off from the past by an ontological gap, a version of Lessing's ditch. Thus there is only the way we construct the past and we do so inevitably through our own ideological and epistemological preferences, and through critical exposure to socially constructed texts. In terms of this latter perspective and

> in these arguably postist days ... the old centres barely hold, and the old meta-narratives no longer resonate with actuality and promise, coming to look incredible from late twentieth-century sceptical perspectives.... Possibly no social formation we know of has so systematically eradicated intrinsic value from its culture so much as liberal market capitalism, not through choice, but through the 'cultural logic of late-capital' ... it is this collapse, more or less complete, more or less conscious, of those hierarchical, definitional value gradients (and can there be value without hierarchy?) which is now the major fact of our intellectual and social circumstances.[91]

Consequently, the postmodernist readily accepts that there is really a smorgasbord of historical perspectives because 'from Nietzsche to Freud to Saussure to Wittgenstein to Althusser to Foucault to Derrida'[92] we have ransacked our various disciplines and found them all variously devoid of foundations. It is

---

[91] K. Jenkins, *Re-thinking History*, 63.

[92] Ibid., 64.

interesting that in terms of the political processes of intellectual discourse, it is liberalism that has again won the day. From the perspective of postmodern discourse, the integral relationship between the modern dogma of progress and the development of modern historical critical study of the Bible, witnesses precisely to the reality of ideological construction:

> Humanity does not gradually progress from combat to combat until it arrives at universal reciprocity, where the rule of law finally replaces warfare; humanity installs each of its violences in a system of rules and thus proceeds from domination to domination.[93]

In relation to Christology, there is obviously no historical Jesus nor indeed a Christ of faith, nor any historical evidence for a clear delineation of the relationship between them. There is only Bultmann's, Schweitzer's, Käsemann's, Pannenberg's, Wright's or Crossan's constructed histories of the narratives, stories and loose causal identities that form our perception of the past. The only way to avoid this conclusion is to accept on the basis of some sort of philosophy of universal history that it is possible to arrive at a theology of history where both the unity and the end of history are centrally related to christological convictions.

This is what Pannenberg, again with the help of the Idealist tradition, endeavoured to achieve. The choice in modern biblical scholarship appears to range evenly across the critical realist, idealist and postmodern options. Should we be surprised that theology must owe its debt to a philosophy of history. The failure to do so leads to the same positivistic, progressive and liberal pursuit that has recently eventuated in yet another attempt to build a modern flyover across Lessing's ditch.[94]

Implications for the New Quest

The new 'New Quest' to unearth the historical Jesus seems destined to dress up an old scarecrow in modern designer clothes. In the process all the old fallacies, fables and fictions of post-Enlightenment biblical scholarship are simple revisited or repositioned in a schema that cannot relinquish the old positivistic myth of progress.

---

[93] M. Foucault, *Language, Counter-memory, Practice: Selected Essays and Interviews*, 151.

[94] For an intriguing survey see Wright, *Victory*, 28–78; For an equally interesting account of similar developments in the field of Old Testament studies see I. Provan, 'Ideologies, Literary and Critical: Reflections on Recent Writing On the History Of Israel', *JBL* 114/4 (1995), 585–606.

> The renewed New Quest works ... with an overall picture of Christian origins that
> ought now to be abandoned. It is the Bultmannian picture, with variations: a de-
> Judaised Jesus preaching a demythologised, 'vertical' eschatology; a crucifixion with
> no early theological interpretation; a 'resurrection' consisting of the coming to faith,
> sometime later, of a particular group of Christians; an early sapientiel gnostic group,
> retelling the master's aphorisms but uninterested in his life story; a Paul who
> invented a Hellenistic Christ-cult; a synoptic tradition in which rolling aphorisms, as
> they slowed down, gathered the moss of narrative structure about themselves, and
> gradually congealed into gospels in which the initial force of Jesus' challenge was
> muted or lost altogether within a fictitious pseudo-historical framework. This
> modern picture ... is the real fiction.[95]

The above carries merit, however, if it is not based on the presupposition that a
faculty called good historical judgement is somehow immune to ideological
control or influence. Such a position is, in our view, equally a fiction and the
continual infiltration of historical science by the myth or dogma of human
progress demonstrates the point. Laws of history, or ideological shifts in the
construction of history are easy to discern because we create them, and in the
end we destroy them when they no longer support the reigning plausibility
structure by which we measure our place in the order of things.

> Was not 'the law of progress' so much in evidence thanks to powers sufficiently
> skilful, resourceful and unscrupulous or callous to make the 'progressive' live and
> spread and the 'backward' shrink and die? Was it not the case that laws of history
> and progress came to rule thought when such powers came to rule the world? And
> is it not the case that, short of the return of such powers, the modern certainty of
> progress and, more generally, of historical direction, are unlikely to rise from the
> postmodern ashes?[96]

Similarly, the idea of the unity of history easily lends itself to ideological control
because at the end of the day the victors always write history. The subjugated
voices of history can only be remembered or retrieved in a way that does not
permit the accurate record of what happened but as Moltmann contends, leads
only to a new hoped for beginning. Such was the experience of the Israelites
after the catastrophe of the exile, and every subsequent catastrophe that has
overtaken countless peoples and nations and erased their memory from the
trajectory of history calls for redemption and recognition.

> History understood as a continuum, as development and progress, can only be the
> history of the victors, who wish to secure and expand their own power. History as it

---

[95] Wright, *Victory*, 79–80.
[96] Bauman, *Postmodernity*, 200.

is experienced by the defeated, the subjugated and the enslaved is the experience of catastrophe and the hope for redemption, the experience of an enforced end and a longed-for new beginning, a downfall suffered and a new dawn hoped for. The catastrophe permits hope only for the overthrow of conditions as they have come to exist.[97]

We have been engaged in an extensive investigation of the Jesus of history versus the Christ of faith debate, and the diverse and troublesome issues surrounding the hermeneutical recovery of the person of Jesus in the context of contemporary culture. Paradoxically, this has alerted us to the almost total dominance of the modern consciousness of history during the post-Enlightenment period and the interesting phenomena that this regnant paradigm is showing signs of breaking up in the midst of the rough waters of postmodern interrogation. What happens, however, when human history and progress is subsumed within an even more comprehensive narrative, that of the evolution and unification of the whole created cosmos? What takes place when Christology is no longer controlled by the constraints and demands of historiography but by the notion that the whole of reality bears the imprint of the odyssey of the divine mind, to abrogate and find itself in the other? It is to this particular metanarrative that we must now turn.

---

[97] Moltmann, *Way*, 24.

6.

Christology and Self-transcendence

PARADIGM THREE: THE MYTH OF TRANSCENDENTALISM

The world and its history are moving, i.e. are in evolution, towards a unity of matter and spirit, which Rahner (like Hegel) conceives as a becoming higher. The capacity for becoming something higher is called the capacity for 'self-transcendence.'[1]

Introduction

A major thesis of our study of Christology has been the contention that Christology cannot afford to remain immune from developments in human thought and culture. Where this has largely been the case, for instance in Roman Catholic Christology from the time of Aquinas to arguably the middle of the twentieth century, the person of Christ has ceased to influence modernity, becoming instead a relic of the past. Developments in human culture provide a set of moving images and metaphors which serve to illuminate our experience of reality: 'We need language to be human, to become self-conscious and to communicate and form relationships, but we are as much a text written by culture as we are subjects of our own thoughts.'[2] At the same time, some concepts and ideas fall by the intellectual wayside because they can no longer adapt to the rapid changes in science and our experience of the world.[3] Thus, a major question that has arisen in modern Christology relates to the adequacy or otherwise of the terminology deployed in the two-nature Christology of Chalcedon. The theological concepts used were borrowed from Greek philosophical logic. As such, they betray the influence of a particular metaphysic that, it is claimed, is no longer appropriate to inhabitants of the modern world. Let us examine this contention in more detail.

---

[1] R.P. McBrien, *Catholicism*, 473.

[2] J.M. Hopkins, *Towards a Feminist Christology: Jesus of Nazareth, European Women and the Christological Crisis*, 13.

[3] Cf. A.N. Whitehead, *Science and the Modern World*, 142.

Christology and metaphysics

We have noted previously that from the second century onwards the concept of the *Logos* provided the basis for a cosmological Christology that was to have an abiding influence in the history of christological debate. A major reason for the success of *Logos* Christology was its ability to cross-fertilize metaphysical and theological concerns. The metaphysical superstructure was Neoplatonism, from which the early church borrowed both ontological and epistemological categories in order to construct the doctrine of the Trinity and the two–nature Christology of Chalcedon.[4] However, in the process of constructing the specifically Christian doctrine of God, the adequacy of the metaphysical infrastructure was at times called into question or qualified. For example, the Neoplatonic idea of divine emanation, with its inevitable subordinationist tendencies, was rejected in favour of an ontological compatibility between the Father and the Son (i.e. *homoousius*, of one substance). It became clear in the midst of this debate that any clarification of the christological issues, such as how to conceive adequately of the meaning of the incarnation, would take place within the context of this ongoing dialogue between an appropriate doctrine of God and the Neoplatonic metaphysic.

Ontological or functional Christology

But what happens to Christology when the metaphysical superstructure is no longer in place and the ontology of substance on which much of its logical consistency was based has been consigned to the philosophical dustbin? John Robinson raised this important question in *The Human Face of God*. He contended that the Enlightenment provides an unavoidable philosophical impasse that prevents any return to the old metaphysics as a point of entry into 'a super-world of divine objects'.[5] We can no longer make sense of the static ontology of substance, nor can we avoid the 'dissolution of the Absolute', which is a typical feature of our modern worldview. In a manner that anticipated some of the tenets of postmodernity, Robinson argued that there is

---

[4] Hence the reliance on the ontology of substance expressed through the use of terms like *ousia* (substance), used at Nicea to describe the solidarity of being or identity of essence between the Father and the Son or *Logos*. Other terms such as *hypostasis* (concrete actuality or particularity) were used to differentiate the three persons of the Trinity and the person of the Son from the two natures conjoined in his own being; *phusis* (nature) described the totality of attributes or qualities needed to designate a particular entity or person and so delineate it from members of another logical class. Given such a definition, it is not difficult to see why Schleiermacher claimed that the idea that one person could be the unity of two natures was logically absurd.

[5] Cf. J.A.T. Robinson, *Human Face of God*, Introduction.

nowadays a fundamental distaste for all-encompassing philosophical systems that seek to explain the structures of the universe or the essence of being.[6]

Another way to approach this problem is to find an alternative metaphysic, which enables us to reconstruct the doctrine of God and similarly find a suitable Christology that is consonant with our experience of the contemporary world. Arguably, the most successful example of such a position has been the transcendental Christology of Karl Rahner.

Karl Rahner and Roman Catholic Theology

If Karl Barth is justifiably hailed as the father of twentieth-century Protestant theology then a similar acclamation must go to Karl Rahner as his Roman Catholic counterpart. In terms of sheer intellectual rigour, theological comprehensiveness and published output both theologians have few rivals in the history of modern theology. Again, like Barth, Rahner saw the need for radical reform in terms of his own theological heritage. He, more than any other Roman Catholic theologian of his time, accomplished what in the nineteenth century seemed almost unthinkable, i.e. a wholesale recasting of the theological and philosophical parameters of Roman Catholic theology in terms of the dialogue with modernity.

As a Jesuit layman, Rahner's influence stretched well beyond the academy and it was the persistence and subtlety of his theological voice that could clearly be heard amidst the excitement and at times acrimonious debate of the Second Ecumenical Council convened by Pope John XXIII in 1959. By the time the Council ended in 1965, the theological imprint of Rahner could be discerned in its deliberations on the church, the episcopacy and the sacraments, history and tradition, revelation and reason, the church and the modern world, and the relationship between salvation and those of other faiths. Towards the end of his life Rahner was asked by some colleagues to explicate the meaning of his philosophy; his reply, '*ich habe keine Philosophie*' ('I do not have a philosophy'), indicated his intense desire (like Barth) to break through what he regarded as the epistemological restrictions of modernity.

The challenge and the complexity of Rahner's theology is the way in which his evolutionary view of reality links together anthropology and Christology in one impressive synthesis. As we shall see, Rahner developed a sophisticated

---

[6] The dissolution of this metaphysical superstructure also explains the rush for alternative paradigms that has been a recurring feature of modern Christology: Schleiermacher's phenomenology of God-consciousness, Tillich's religion of existentialist estrangement, Pannenberg's theology of history all provide alternative epistemological frameworks which, it is hoped, will establish a new cogency to christological convictions.

approach to Christology that sought to pay due attention to the traditional incarnational model and yet recast this within an evolutionary framework.

Transcendental Thomism

The philosophical basis of Rahner's thought was Transcendental Thomism (an attempted synthesis of the philosophical outlook of Thomas Aquinas and German Idealism). Aquinas discerned both a passive and active element in the process of acquiring knowledge. The passive element referred to the fact that all our knowledge occurs through a genuine encounter with objective reality mediated to us through our senses and is not derived from innate ideas. The active element is that self-presence, or awareness of ourselves as knowing subjects, which undergirds our engagement with the real world.

It was the latter element, the turn towards the knowing subject that became the focus of investigation in Kant's *Critique of Pure Reason*. In Kant's transcendental epistemology (theory of method, or grounds of knowledge), the transcendent element is supplied by the a priori categories of thought, which enable the human subject to make intelligible the information that comes to us from the world of phenomena – hence the designation transcendental idealism.

Transcendental method

Kant's enquiry into the transcendental conditions of human knowledge that make our experience of the world both coherent and possible was re-appropriated by Rahner and functioned as a fundamental aspect of his theological method. He frequently used the transcendental argument to enquire into the philosophical conditions for the possibility of human knowledge and experience of God and, indeed, the conditions of human receptivity to divine revelation. In fact, Rahner developed his own account of the nature of human knowledge, one that ran counter to the prevailing scientific model of knowledge as largely an exercise in cognitive domination and rational dissection. For Rahner, knowledge is as much 'a capacity to be grasped', to stand before an incomprehensible mystery, as it is to advance by deduction and analysis. Here we find one of the basic tenets of the Idealist tradition standing at the forefront of the account of what it actually means to know, i.e. that knowledge which encompasses both faith and wisdom tends to be disclosed to us, rather than plucked from the morass of extraneous detail about the world, if only we could recognise it as such.

Acknowledging his debt to Kant, Heidegger and Joseph Maréchal, Rahner's fundamental theology endeavours to sketch out a philosophy of religion where both theology and philosophy are complementary moments in the search to find the rationally justifiable epistemological basis to all human knowledge.

In his groundbreaking work *Hearer of the Word*, Rahner focuses on the act of cognition whereby human beings not only perceive, intuit, or remember objects, but also seek to classify and describe them. In such abstraction we conceptualise both the distinctiveness and the inherent inter-relatedness of particulars in the known world. Rahner's contention is that through such abstraction we transcend not only the object concerned, but also ourselves. This is only possible if we presuppose a relationship to absolute being, or the totality of reality, as the necessary metaphysical basis to all human cognition and classification. This infinite horizon of meaning and reality could remain, as Wittgenstein postulated, merely an external linguistic limit beyond which we cannot venture, unless this inherently mysterious infinity is somehow revealed to us. Without the self-disclosure, or co-giveness, of the 'whole of reality' in the act of human cognition, our enquiry into the act of human understanding and the transcendental conditions of knowledge, remains a futile and meaningless exercise. We must hold before us the possibility of a plenitude of being. Indeed, we must attend to it in our entire epistemo-logical enquiry and in so doing we stumble upon a *potentia oboedientialis*, an obediential potency to hear a word or receive a revelation from the divine mystery. Rahner – like his Protestant contemporary, Pannenberg – was careful not to describe this capacity as a natural knowledge of God from which we can deduce God's existence. Rather, this intrinsic inbuilt relationship to the infinite horizon of meaning and reality is viewed as an unthematic, non-reflexive and, therefore, in some way, preconscious aspect of human nature.[7]

It is even more important that we do not deduce the nature of God's self-disclosure in Christ from this basis. Rather, the reverse is the case. It is only because we perceive the answer to our innate religious quest in the person of Christ that we can fully understand the nature of ourselves as the existential question that is referred beyond itself to the absolute ground of being.

> Metaphysics, which is already a philosophy of religion, must acknowledge God as the one who is free and unknown; it must understand human persons as beings who, in our innermost spirit, live in history; it must refer us to our history and bid us listen in it to an eventual revelation of this free unknown God. Such meta-physics will view God as one who is free and unknown, and who cannot be clearly grasped by human groping. It will not make bold to decide *a priori* how this free, personal, unknown God will behave towards us, and in what guise this God will be and can be revealed, how God will establish the relation between God and humanity.[8]

---

[7] Pannenberg, *Systematic Theology*, Vol. 1, 63–107.

[8] K. Rahner, *Hearer of the Word*, 8.

God the absolute mystery

Rahner's conception of God as absolute Mystery or absolute Being is broadly
Hegelian, in that he accepts the Idealist designation of God as Absolute Subject.
Hegel, like the Romantics, sought to overcome the Kantian bifurcation of
the real world (*noumena*) and the world of experience (*phenomena*). He did so by
conceiving of the real world as the product of the divine Mind or *Geist*. For
Hegel, the structure of thought and the rational order of the world are one and
the same thing because both are the process whereby the divine, rational Subject
is realised in the other. *Geist* is not the deist notion of transcendence outside
nature, but the Absolute idea that is realised in the whole historical process as
both its dynamic inner-being and the truth of reality itself. In that sense, 'the
eternal life of God is to find himself, coincide with himself'[9] so that history itself
becomes the self-realisation, or manifestation of this 'odyssey of mind'.[10] Because
of the contention that everything stems from the activity of the divine Mind,
Hegel's philosophy is another form of Transcendental Idealism, one that was
controlled and understood in terms of this itinerary of the Spirit or *Geist*.

Rahner's concept of the transcendental was akin to Hegel's. It referred to the
dynamic openness of the human subject to the infinite horizons of being and
knowledge that constitute our experience of historical existence. There is
always a beyond and a more to our experience, a continual questing and self-
transcending that drives us onwards in search of what, for Rahner, was
ultimately a search for the Infinite ground of reality itself. Like Hegel, Rahner
understood this transcendental element as the elevation of the finite to the
infinite, which is the ground of everything that exists. He emphatically denied
that self-transcendence was reducible to a merely human potentiality. Rather, it
is a function of that which constitutes our essential creatureliness. In the tension
that exists between a person's autonomy and self-possession and the mediated
immediacy of the absolute Mystery, we are ultimately referred or orientated
beyond ourselves to both the source and the future of our existence.[11] This is
ultimately only possible because reality itself is the dynamic evolutionary
process that constitutes the self-communication or revelation of God in the
other. The self-realisation of God in history occurs because the divine mystery
is expressed in and through Another (i.e. the *Logos*), through whom God is
manifest to the world as both its hidden source and final fulfilment.

> The *Logos* did not merely become (statically) man in Christ: he assumed a human
> history. But this is part of an entire history of the world and of humanity before and

---

[9] G.W.F. Hegel, *Introduction to the Lectures on the History of Philosophy*, 79–80.
[10] P. Singer, *Hegel*, 45.
[11] Cf. K. Rahner, *Foundations of Christian Faith: An Introduction to the Idea of Christianity*, 80.

after it, and, what is more, the fullness of that history and its end. But if we take at all seriously the unity of this history as centred upon Christ, it follows that Christ has always been involved in the whole of history as its prospective entelechy.[12]

Transcendental anthropology or ascending Christology

From one point of view, as Rahner puts it himself, Christology is transcendent anthropology and anthropology is deficient Christology.[13] This should not lead us to conclude that Rahner ignored the historical Jesus in favour of a general philosophical anthropology. Like many modern theologians, Rahner was critical of the Christology from above practised by the early church because it tended to bypass the historical Jesus.[14] This is not, however, where Rahner began.

He accepted the need for a culturally attuned Christology that took seriously our experience of the world as an evolutionary process with a beginning and a possible end. This is no mere accommodation to the spirit of the age but an attempt to put in context what the cosmic Christology and Adam typology of the New Testament sought to achieve, i.e. a theological justification of how the particular history of the man Jesus of Nazareth relates to history and humanity in general. Rahner, however, made this link by means of a theology of self-transcendence. If all life and creaturely existence are part of this process of elevation to something more, it must be clear just what this something more actually is. In that sense, Rahner sought to show how 'The God-Man is the initial beginning and the definitive triumph of the movement of the world's self-transcendence into absolute closeness to the mystery of God.'[15] This confluence of the historical process of self-transcendence with the person of Jesus of Nazareth is based on three fundamental presuppositions.

Transcendental revelation
The first is the unity of spirit and matter in the sense of an evolutionary movement of the material world into spiritual existence. There is no Carthesian dualism in Rahner's thought between matter and spirit. Rather, matter and spirit share a common origin as part of God's good creation; they have a common history as complementary, yet also disparate, elements in the total evolutionary process. Everything in creation shares in the self-transcending movement of becoming, not because of its own innate possibilities of growth

---

[12] K. Rahner, *Theological Investigations*, Vol. 1; 167.

[13] Rahner, *Foundations*, 178.

[14] Cf. Rahner, *Theological Investigations*, Vol. 13; 201.

[15] Rahner, *Foundations*, 181.

and development, but because of 'Gods creative and co-operative presence as the ground of his creation'.[16]

The imminent presence of the divine is located in the emergence of spirit from more primitive inanimate life forms. The relationship of temporal duration between spirit and matter entails that human beings are the self-transcendence of living matter, i.e. the unity of matter and spirit whereby we become self-consciously aware of our relation to the rest of creation, and our ability to transcend and go beyond its limitations. The emergence of the spiritual itself ensures that humanity is defined in terms of our openness to the divine. We are matter when we are aware of our concrete embodiedness as an individual and our solidarity with all living things. We are spirit when we accept that we are not an enclosed finitude, but part of a limitless process of transcendence towards the infinite because the process of becoming issues forth from a plenitude of being and, consequently, must always be understood as a becoming more.[17] The essence of religion is not the intuitive feeling of dependence upon God (Schleiermacher), but a continual transcending movement out towards union with God.

Supernatural existential

This unity of spirit and matter, as complementary elements in the history of creation, is analogous in Rahner's thought to the unity of nature and grace. He referred to this unity as the *supernatural existential*, i.e. God's gracious presence in the world through the Spirit. Heidegger used the term 'existential' to designate those features that distinguished a human being from other forms of life. If God created humanity so that he could share his own life of love and grace with us, then that possibility of loving relationship is part of what constitutes our fundamental humanity. We are creatures orientated towards the transcendent possibilities of grace. Creation or nature is consequently ordered towards the supernatural life of grace as its deepest purpose and goal. It is a *supernatural* existential because it is part of our human existence only through the free and gracious act of God. Openness to the divine mystery may be a constitutive aspect of our nature but elevation towards the divine mystery is a free and gratuitous action of God that is a pre-given in human experience. While sin distorts our nature, it does not obliterate the presence of God within the created orders of reality. Rather, the purposes of creation are maintained, and so the transcendence of human life beyond alienation and hostility to God, to participation in God's own life and self-knowledge, is part of the history of God's self-revelation.[18] Consequently, it is impossible to think of

---

[16] W.V. Dych, *Karl Rahner*, 71.
[17] Cf. Rahner, *Foundations*, 184.
[18] Ibid., 190–1.

salvation in an atomistic or individualistic sense. We are not redeemed out of the world but as part of the world. We share now in its fractured and perishing existence and will share in its unified and consummated existence when all things are made new in the future kingdom of God.

Categorical revelation

History begins when the evolutionary process reaches the stage of human consciousness and freedom. Human freedom and hope then become a constitutive element in the process. The unity of our transcendentality and historicity are mediated to us through the concrete actualisation of human existence in time and space. It is in this context of free inter-dependence and response to God that Rahner saw the real significance of Christology. While God's self-communication is an existential that pervades the whole of history, it can only be met by an actual free response from individuals in history. Whenever this takes place and humans acknowledge and appropriate the gracious self-communication of God, as well as actualise their own transcendental elevation towards the absolute mystery, then religion becomes a genuine dialogue between God and humanity.

Such 'anonymous Christianity' pertains in all religions, however partial and corrupted their cultural forms and manifestations may be. However, the most complete and, therefore, normative form of revelation takes place in the dialogue between God and humanity that is contained in the witness of the prophets and the apostles. Jesus is the person who, in his complete openness to God, appropriates God's life of grace, or his self-communication, in an attitude of free response. In Jesus' life, death and resurrection the history of grace reaches its irreversible and unsurpassable triumph over the history of sin and alienation from God.

> Since the history of sin is the history of separation and alienation from God, the perfect union of God that [Jesus] achieved in his free response is the undoing of sin and the entrance into the history of its opposite, that is, salvation. He is salvation and saviour in his very being, and not just in his actions.[19]

The absolute Saviour

It was at this juncture that Rahner introduced the notion of the absolute Saviour. While it is obviously the case that the divine self-manifestation existed prior to the historical subjectivity of the man Jesus, it is entirely conceivable 'to employ the notion of an event through which this self-communication and acceptance reaches a point in history which is irrevocable

---

[19] Dych, *Rahner*, 72–3.

and irreversible'.[20] The justification of the notion of an absolute Saviour cannot simply be based on the fact that such an event has occurred in the person and destiny of Jesus and is capable of being unambiguously recognised as such, although there are times when Rahner appears to suggest just this.[21] Rather, in a manner reminiscent of Pannenberg, Rahner had recourse to the philosophical presupposition of universal history.

Given that history is (a) a single process which implies both a unity and an end as yet hidden in the openness of the future, and (b) is the self-communication of God, it makes sense to think of at least one occasion where this self-communication and the existential acceptance of it reaches a climax. The Christ-event must be eschatologically conceived as just such a prolepsis of the end of history.[22] Similarly, it is in the coming together of these two movements – the human complete openness and free response to God and the gracious free communication of God himself – that we find the meaning of the *hypostatic union*, the unity of the divine and the human in the unique personhood of Jesus.

Rahner frequently asserted that the incarnation could not be conceived as the coming of the *Logos* disguised in human flesh, as if it were the assumption of something essentially alien, foreign and extrinsic to God. Rather, it is the coming to concrete historical expression of a graced reality that is intrinsic to who and what we are:

> Jesus is truly man, he has absolutely everything which belongs to a man, including a finite subjectivity in which the world becomes conscious in its own unique, historically conditioned and finite way, and a subjectivity which has a radical immediacy to God in and through God's self-communication in grace, just as it is also present in us in the depths of our existence.[23]

But the other side of the equation must also be maintained. Jesus is not just the unsurpassable finite mediation of God. He is not simply a uniquely, spiritually responsive human being. Jesus is, in his own being, the historical realisation of the divine self-communication; he is both very God and very man. With Jesus, therefore, we arrive at a unique moment in the history of the world's

---

[20] Rahner, *Foundations*, 194.

[21] For instance, 'The more difficult question is *how* and *where* and *when* one may give an earthly name to him who is such a being. But if one seeks *him*, to whom one can bring the eternal mystery of the pure fullness of one's own being for fulfilment, one can see very simply, if one seeks 'quietly', that is, in meekness and with the eyes of innocence, that is only in Jesus of Nazareth that one can dare to believe such a thing has happened and happens eternally'; see, *Theological Investigations* Vol. 4, 111.

[22] Cf. Rahner, *Foundations*, 194–5.

[23] Ibid., 196.

self-transcendence towards God and the history of God's self-communication towards the world, the latter making the former possible.

The intrinsic relationship of the *hypostatic union* to the grace of God's self-communication to everyone requires careful delineation. Traditionally, theology has had recourse to the representative status of the God-man. In Christ, God's unconditional offer of salvation to all people is both unequivocally expressed and received. In a manner reminiscent of Barth, Rahner asserts that self-manifestation does actually entail that in the incarnation we have the unabrogable subjectivity of God. Put simply, God discloses God-self. Such a true unveiling of the divine mystery in human form can only happen once. To deny this is to deny the actual self-manifestation of the ineffable mystery of God in the Christ-event.

Descending Christology

Rahner sought to demonstrate that his ascending Christology is perfectly compatible with the descending Christology that utilised the incarnational model of the divine *Logos* assuming or becoming a human being.[24] Indeed, he viewed both as simple two sides of the same coin. What is meant then by the confession that the Word became a *man*? Rahner started with the part of the formula with which we are most familiar and asked what do we mean by the expression 'human nature'.

In line with his transcendental anthropology, Rahner viewed humanity as a reality that cannot be defined and classified as if it were simply one biological species among many. Rather, human nature is unbounded, ultimately indefinable, because it is both undisclosed mystery and, 'an indefinability come to consciousness of itself'.[25] So if God assumes a human nature it is the unique and fullest actualisation of the very essence of the nature that is always on its way and open to union with God:

> If this is human nature, we begin to understand more clearly – always of course within the framework of the basic mystery which is God and we – what it means to say: God takes on a human nature as his own. The indefinable nature, whose limits – 'definition' – are the unlimited reference to the infinite fullness of the mystery, has, when assumed by God as his reality, simply arrived at the point to which it always strives by virtue of its essence.[26]

Secondly, we have to ask what does it mean to say God 'becomes'. Does not the attribution of becoming to God radically contradict his immutability? A

---

[24] Rahner, *Theological Investigations*, Vol. 13, 213–23.

[25] Ibid., Vol. 4, 107.

[26] Ibid, 109.

basic affirmation of the Christian faith is that God does not change; he does not cease to be what in his eternal essence he has always been. Neither does he become more; his being is already infinite plenitude to which nothing extra can be added. Rahner resolved this by saying that God 'who is not subject to change in himself can *himself* be subject to change *in something else*'.[27]

Chalcedon asserted that the divine and human natures in Christ were distinct and unmixed, so affirming that the becoming took place within the humanity of Christ. Jesus was a man who knew human development and change; he experienced suffering and death. But the two natures are also without separation. So, it was the *Logos* himself who was the subject of this process of change and development. Do these two assertions simply have to remain intractable contradictions that we cannot resolve?

Rahner tried to shed light on this difficulty through the notion of *kenosis* (self-emptying). He asserted that God creates by assuming to himself that which is other than himself. But that otherness does not stand in contra-distinction to God. Rather, it is initiated through the process of self-emptying. God dispossesses himself so that there can be a reality distinct from him, but which is nevertheless united to him, and so can be understood as two distinct but related aspects of the same creative process. In other words, as Barth similarly acknowledged, the *Logos* is intrinsically the humanity of God; consequently, the incarnation need not be conceived as if the *Logos* assumed an already existing human nature. Rather, the man Jesus is brought forth through this process of *kenosis* whereby God, through the *Logos*, becomes the unity of his own self-giving and free human responsiveness.

Rahner endeavoured to preserve the dialectic of unity and distinction. The fact that God creates that which is both distinct from him, a genuine other (i.e. humanity) but nevertheless is still united with that reality as the source of it's being. He does so through the concept of *kenosis*. In this way, Rahner pre-served the essential truth that only the *Logos*, and not the Spirit, could become incarnate, because the *Logos* both noetically and ontologically is God's way of owning and undertaking a history with that which is other than God's self:

> The absolute, or, more correctly, the absolute One in the pure freedom of his infinite relatedness, which he always preserves, possesses the possibility of himself becoming the other, the finite. He possesses the possibility of *establishing* the other as his own re-ality by dispossessing *himself,* by giving *himself* away.[28]

This provides a deeper foundation to the concept of the *Logos*. Within the inner trinitarian life of God, the *Logos* is the self-expression of the Father. The

---

[27] Rahner, *Foundations*, 220. My italics for emphasis.
[28] Ibid, 223.

Father dispossesses himself (gives himself away) and the other, the Son, is both a distinct person within the life of God and united with the Father through the Spirit in essence. So this self-expression within the immanent trinity is the basis, indeed is identical to, the outward self-expression of God in the incarnation. This is the meaning of Rahner's controversial assertion that the immanent trinity and the economic trinity are the same process of becoming. The immanent Word within the Godhead is the ontological ground to the external Word who is expressed in the historical person of Jesus Christ.[29]

To think of the humanity of Jesus as the self-expression of God is to see it as the real symbol of God. The artist expresses himself symbolically in his work. In other words, something of his own being comes to expression in his creation. The Father expresses himself in the Son, but in such a way that he is only himself in that relationship. There is a real ontological union – the Father would not be the Father without the Son. Similarly, the Word or the Son only exists as the symbol or self-expression of the Father. In his freedom, God speaks this Word (*Logos*) outward and so the Son becomes, or comes to expression, in the humanity that is assumed: 'The immanent self-expression of God in its eternal fullness is the condition which makes possible God's self-expression outwards and outside himself, and the latter is the identical revelation of the former.'[30]

Jesus of Nazareth

In his analysis of transcendental Christology, Rahner deliberately focused upon the idea of the God-man, or the logical possibility of an 'absolute Saviour'. He then turned his attention to the fundamental question that he had hitherto left unresolved. In moving to an enquiry into the nature of the biblical sources concerning Jesus of Nazareth, Rahner did not wish to resurrect the old christological dispute between the Jesus of history and the Christ of faith. As we have noted already, that particular dilemma is more apparent than real and largely revolves around false notions of historical objectivity.[31] Rather, Rahner was asking the question has the unsurpassable offer of salvation present in the notion of an absolute Saviour actually come to historical expression in the history of Jesus of Nazareth? This question raised the issue of the accountability and historical justification of both the individual's and the church's faith in Jesus as the absolute self-manifestation of the divine mystery.

---

[29] Cf. Jones' discussion of this aspect of Rahner's thought in *Critical Theology*, 74.
[30] Ibid., 222.
[31] Evans, *Historical Christ*.

We are posing the Christological question ... about Jesus the Christ as a question about the accountability of each one's own faith in Jesus as the Christ. [It is a] question about the accountability of faith, which implies a free decision, [it is] a question about my faith ... a question which places every individual in his concrete existence as a man and as a believer ... and demands an answer.[32]

There are many interesting similarities between Rahner's approach to the historical justification of the Christian faith and that of Wolfhart Pannenberg, which are worth noting. Both theologians reject any retreat into fideism openly acknowledging that christological assertions necessarily imply some degree of historical verification. While there will always be an inevitable incongruence between the probability, uncertainty and obscurity that surround such historical events and the absolute commitment which faith demands, this is in principle no different from the numerous faith decisions we make which are similarly based on historical presuppositions we cannot theoretically verify. Life is from beginning to end a venture of faith seeking understanding. Similarly, if we agree with John's Gospel that the *Logos* did actually become flesh we fully embrace the historicity of our own existence and accept that christological enquiry cannot escape the burden of history.

The evangelists knew their faith was founded on real historical events, just as we accept that all our knowledge of God, the world and ourselves is historically conditioned and mediated. For Rahner and Pannenberg this entailed that there can be no escape from the rigours of historical-critical investigation of the different portrayals of Jesus we find in the New Testament. While the divergent brush strokes of the various faith communities are discernible in such impressionistic portraits, this does not mean that there is either an inevitable disjunction, or a correlation, between the self-understanding of Jesus and that of the early church. This allows more latitude for genuine historical enquiry given that the determining event for Christology remains the resurrection.

Rahner summarised what he considered were the reliable findings of scientific historical exegesis into the gospel traditions:

1. Jesus must be located within a particular historical and religious situation that in general he accepted as the good will and purpose of God. He took part in the religion of contemporary Judaism 'which included temple and synagogue, law and customs, feasts and holy scriptures, priests and teachers'.[33] While Jesus was not a politico-religious revolutionary, he was a reformer of his own inherited religious tradition.

---

[32] Rahner, *Foundations*, 230.
[33] Ibid., 247.

2. The nature of that reform was deeply challenging to the religious authorities. He dissented from the lordship of the law opposing all forms of legalism in favour of a new security and intimacy with the God whose coming kingdom he both proclaimed and provisionally inaugurated. That kingdom reached out to all the lost sheep of Israel, especially those whose social status excluded them from the rights and privileges of their native religion.

3. While at first Jesus hoped his own mission would lead to the conversion of his people, he gradually came to accept that some form of confrontation with the religious and political establishment was inevitable. As the Gospels contend, he set his face towards Jerusalem.

4. Jesus faced death resolutely as the consequence of fidelity to his mission and as an expression of his radical subordination to the vocation to which he had been called and freely assented.

5. His exhortations of reform were manifested in the gathering of disciples as the representatives of the new social order encapsulated in the message of the imminent arrival of the Kingdom. While this created a political context to his life and vocation it did not necessarily involve a preferential option for the poor and marginalised as a condition of following in the way of the Messiah. Rather the unconditional offer of salvation to everyone was expressed in the proximity of God's kingdom and was appropriated through a radical act of repentance.

6. From a historical point of view we should be justifiably wary of attributing to Jesus an explicit Messianic self-consciousness recognising that all the christological titles already contain elements of post-resurrection faith and belief.

7. We should be similarly cautious about viewing the miracles of Jesus as confirmations of his divine status or temporary suspensions of the laws of nature. Given the intrinsic relationship between nature and grace and the reality of God's self-manifestation throughout the whole self-transcending movement of creation, we should understand miracles in terms of a sign or a call to which people must respond.[34]

Given the complexity of the historical investigation involved in the enquiry into the historical grounds of faith, Rahner isolated what he regarded as the essential connection between the historical Jesus and the church's affirmation that Jesus is the absolute Saviour:

> First, Jesus saw himself not merely as one among many prophets who in principle form an unfinished line which is always open to the future, but understood himself rather as the eschatological prophet, as the absolute and definitive saviour, although

---

[34] Ibid., 263.

the more precise question of what a definitive saviour does and does not mean requires further reflection.

Secondly, this claim of Jesus is credible for us when, from the perspective of our transcendental experience in grace of the absolute communication of the holy God, we look in faith to that event which mediates the saviour in his total reality: the resurrection of Jesus.[35]

Rahner adroitly tackled the vexed question of the relationship between the objective historical grounds of faith and the subjective confession of faith in Jesus as Lord and Saviour. He recognised the role played in all our knowledge of historical events by the presuppositions and existential interest of the knower. Similarly, he noted that the Gospels are books of faith in that they reflect the coming to faith in Jesus of individuals and whole communities.

While he would have agreed with Pannenberg that there is no bare, unprejudiced factual history, only interpreted events, Rahner avoided some of the acrimonious dissent which Pannenberg incurred in his earlier writing when he contended that faith does not add anything new to what history can or cannot verify.[36] The issue here is not whether the attribution of faith in Jesus as absolute Saviour adds another cognitive or confirmatory element to the historical record. Rather, it has to do with the socially conditioned religious framework of belief within which both the evangelists and believers today interpret the significance of Jesus as the Christ. The former context was that of a politically chastened and apocalyptically orientated Judaism; the latter is the culturally mediated, religious, secular or pagan alternatives that make up our contemporary horizons of faith and belief. All our knowledge is both an act of discovery and of recognition and it is the latter that is to a certain extent dominant in the minds of the New Testament writers.

The death and resurrection of Jesus

The New Testament does not present the death and resurrection of Jesus as if they were wholly disconnected events. Rather, there is an intimate and intrinsic relationship between the two that is determinative for any adequate Christology. Rahner endeavoured to construct the biblical basis of his Christology from this essential foundation. Beginning with the resurrection, he asserts that this metaphor does not refer to the resuscitation of a dead corpse, nor does it mean the survival of the cause for which Jesus gave his life; neither does it mean entry into the newfound faith of the disciples in the continued existence of Jesus.

---

[35] Ibid., 245–6.
[36] Cf. Pannenberg, *Revelation as History*, and J.M. Robinson and J.B. Cobb Jr, *Theology as History*.

Again, interesting similarities between Rahner and Pannenberg appear. Both theologians sought to protect the real historicity of the resurrection against those who would dissolve the resurrection narratives, ambiguous and mutually contradictory as they are, into the visions, or faith experiences, of the disciples. However, neither theologian was content to leave their defence of the resurrection with just the bare historicity of the event. Rather, they spoke of an openness beyond death or, as Rahner described it, 'the transcendental hope of resurrection' which links our horizon with that of the disciples.[37] Everyone possesses a longing that our lives do ultimately have some enduring validity and significance. It is this 'phenomenology of hope' (Pannenberg) that pushes our search for meaning out beyond death.

Pannenberg made much of the fact that from within the context of apocalyptic Judaism resurrection could only refer to the general resurrection from the dead at the end of history. Rahner, on the other hand, simply notes that the confession 'he is risen' is the core element of Easter faith and as such it points to the fact that this man is now vindicated in his claim to be the eschatological prophet and the bearer of a new immediacy with God, which transcends the demands of the law and the temple. However, both Pannenberg and Rahner were united in their conviction that the resurrection stands as the irrevocable basis of all later christological affirmations about the significance and status of Jesus. In that sense, there is no necessary disagreement between the exaltation or functional Christology of the New Testament and the later translation of these ideas into more metaphysical and ontological categories.[38]

It is true that only in the light of the resurrection can we affirm the universal relevance of the salvation Jesus procured. However, we also have to determine what actually was the nature of the redemption his death achieved. While the New Testament utilises a variety of metaphors, Rahner perceives the dominant thread as that of a sacrifice or satisfaction for sin. Not surprisingly, as a Roman Catholic theologian, Rahner was working almost wholly from within what Gustaf Aulen referred to as the Latin doctrine of atonement.[39] However, Rahner did appear to agree with others that in the context of the contemporary world sacrifice is largely a redundant metaphor.[40] He accordingly understood the causality that underlies the death of Jesus as both eschatological and personal:

---

[37] Rahner, *Foundations*, 268–9.

[38] Pannenberg would proceed with more caution in this regard, especially in respect to the unification and disjunction Christologies which culminated in the council of Chalcedon.

[39] Aulen, *Christus Victor*.

[40] Cf. C.E. Gunton, *The Actuality of Atonement: A Study of Metaphor, Rationality and the Christian Tradition*, 115–35.

The single history which we all share has already entered into eschatological salvation in the person and history of Jesus, who is thus the first moment and the inauguration of the final, eschatological stage of history for all of us.[41]

Taking his lead from John's Gospel, Rahner affirmed a symbolic personal union between the believer and Jesus. This he referred to as an existential Christology that takes shape and form in the life of discipleship. In a manner similar to Jürgen Moltmann, Rahner insisted that Christology is not primarily a metaphysical theory about Jesus but a way of life, a praxis, a response to the real categorical imperative, 'Follow me'.[42]

Assessment

Although sophisticated, Rahner's Christology, which was based on a traditional incarnational model recast within an evolutionary framework, has been, not surprisingly, the subject of a number of criticisms.

Serious misgivings have surrounded Rahner's identification of Jesus as absolute Saviour. A number of Rahner's contemporaries, for instance, have concluded that Rahner's insistence on the natural aptitude of human beings for a 'transcendental' revelation in and through the structures of their own spiritual dynamism effectively obviates the need for the categorical revelation present in Jesus, who consequently cannot be understood normatively as the absolute Saviour.[43] G. Vass, one of Rahner's students, warned 'the weight and emphasis [Rahner] attributes to this anthropological approach could prejudice man's genuine listening to the genuine word of God that surprises him in history'.[44] Is God's self-disclosure in Christ subject to the precondition of human transcendentalism? Is the categorical revelation dependent on our concept of it? Did Rahner consequently 'run the risk of the same radical immanentism that plagued the theologies of Schleiermacher and Tillich'?[45]

Rahner endeavoured to counter such criticisms when he acknowledged that 'he who is essentially open to being cannot by his own capacities set limits

---

[41] Dych, *Rahner*, 60.

[42] This was why, with his brother Hugo, Rahner maintained a lifelong interest in the spiritual exercises of St Ignatius of Loyola, the founder of the Jesuit order to which Rahner belonged. The exercises seek to establish the relationship between Jesus and ourselves not solely in terms of our intellectual grasp of the faith, but also based on the daily reality of contemplative prayer and the imaginative entry into the Gospel narratives. Cf. H. Rahner, *Ignatius the Theologian*, 59.

[43] H. Urs von Balthasar, *The Moment of Christian Witness*.

[44] G. Vass, *A Theologian in Search of a Philosophy*, Vol. 1, 20.

[45] Grenz and Olson, *20th Century Theology*, 244.

to the possible object of revelation'.[46] The central tenet of his transcendental method was that human spirituality, in its radical openness to the loving self-communication of the Absolute Mystery, is a universal *praeparatio evangelica*. This enables us to recognise both our own need of salvation and the fulfilment of that need in the absolute Saviour, the one who lives out unreservedly and unconditionally our vocation to surrender ourselves to God in love, trust and obedience.

Whether this is recognised by humanity or not, Rahner did make it clear that it is the historical Jesus, as the divine *Logos*, who is both the supernatural existential and the categorical revelation of God. Although these aspects of revelation are distinct, they, nevertheless, belong intrinsically together and are the necessary conditions for revelation to exist at all.[47] Rowan Williams puts the issue succinctly: 'just as knowledge is one, revelation is one. "Transcendental" and "categorical" revelation have the same content and the same purpose, God's gracious giving of himself'.[48]

From within the parameters of Rahner's trinitarianism it is also true that an absolute event of salvation must be an event in the very life of God:

> it still remains true that the *Logos became* man, that the history of the becoming of this human reality became *his own* history, that our time became the time of the eternal One, that our death became the death of the immortal God himself.[49]

Consequently, from this perspective, Rahner's enquiry into human transcendental experience, that searching for the God-man within history, must be an intrinsic human activity, and therefore transcendental Christology provided a point of contact between anthropology and the basic Christian affirmation that Jesus is the Saviour of the world. Perhaps the best way of putting this issue is to note that, 'We cannot "deduce" Jesus of Nazareth from our anthropology, although we can demonstrate from the transcendental analysis of spirit that he does fulfil the conditions there apprehended for a concrete manifestation of the absolute.'[50]

Doubts, however, remain. Rahner has to address an important question. Is it the case that Jesus in his own self-identity as a particular person fulfils the conditions of what constitutes the absolute Saviour? To deal adequately with

---

[46] Rahner, *Hearer of the Word*, 114.

[47] Rahner, *Foundations*, 61.

[48] R. Williams notes in passing that on the rare occasions that Rahner ventures into the domain of the other religions, this relationship is not so intrinsic as it first seems; see, 'Balthasar and Rahner', in J. Riches (ed.), *The Analogy of Beauty: The Theology of Hans Urs von Balthasar*, 18.

[49] Rahner, *Foundations*, 220.

[50] Williams, 'Balthasar', 17.

this issue Rahner had to consider what constituted the necessary predicates of an absolute Saviour, and whether Jesus could be the only person in whom these conditions are met.

Bruce Marshall, in his analysis of the differing christologies of both Rahner and Barth, contends that an absolute Saviour must be *heilsbedeutsam*, a Rahnerian term which means 'significant for salvation'.[51] He interprets this further as 'meaningful, intelligible and existentially accessible',[52] but challenges what he describes as Rahner's rather negative formulation of the assumption that it has to be Jesus that is the absolute Saviour[53]. Marshall argues that the notion of absolute Saviour 'as that which is ultimately significant for us, cannot be conceived in such a way that it could apply to someone else as readily as to Jesus'.[54] He contends that this is what Rahner's transcendental Christology implies because 'it seems thoroughly conceivable that Socrates or Martin Luther King Jr could be absolute Saviour'.[55] They could also be the actualisation of 'that for which all persons are necessarily on the lookout'.[56] Marshall concludes:

> The question reasonably can be raised whether in Rahner's Christology it must finally be false to say that 'Jesus Christ is the absolute saviour', although this proposition can be saved by giving it a forced sense which fits with the overall argument, (forced, that is, because 'Jesus Christ', an expression which introduces a particular person, must be treated as though it does not). This suggests that there is a serious, perhaps fatal, equivocation in Rahner's central and most characteristic christological argument. Belief in Jesus Christ as the absolute saviour, which it has been shown functions like a 'minor premise' in Rahner's Christology, ends up meaning one thing as the Christian conviction which is the presupposition and norm of christological argument, and quite another thing in the context of the argument itself.[57]

Rahner argued that the essence of Jesus' *heilsbedeutsam* resides in his historical self-consciousness and his resurrection. Rahner asked us to imagine the resurrection but without the presupposed knowledge 'in faith' of the 'metaphysical' divine sonship, so that the resurrection of Jesus would be at most the actual conclusion of his life.[58] Rahner acknowledges that this was not really possible because 'according to the New Testament the experienced

---

[51] B. Marshall, *Christology in Conflict: The Identity of a Saviour in Rahner and Barth*, 20.
[52] Ibid., 145.
[53] Ibid., 58.
[54] Ibid., 58.
[55] Ibid., 11.
[56] Ibid., 11.
[57] Ibid., 60.
[58] Rahner, *Foundations*, 279.

resurrection contributed to the content of the interpretation of the essence of the person and work of Jesus, and was not merely the divine confirmation of a knowledge already clearly expressed by Jesus before the resurrection.'[59] Consequently, 'the claim that there is present with [Jesus] a new and unsurpassable closeness of God [the coming and arrival of God's kingdom] which on its part will prevail victoriously' is inseparable from Jesus' self-identity.[60] Jesus is vindicated as the absolute Saviour by the resurrection; he is the final prophet, the 'one who brings a word of God to concrete historical existence over and beyond all "eternal truths" '.[61]

The comparison between Rahner and Schleiermacher has already been made, perhaps unfairly. However, is it the case that Rahner, like Schleiermacher, because of his commitment to a particular philosophical anthropology, was really unable to do justice to the biblical traditions and sources concerning Jesus as the Christ? In that sense, transcendental Christology prejudiced Rahner's investigation of the biblical narrative.

This is the thrust of W. Thüsing's misgivings about Rahner's approach. Thusing notes quite rightly, that Rahner's Christology pays scant attention to the antecedents of Christology found in the Old Testament.[62] He argues that the Old Testament witness to the election of Israel is simply purloined by Rahner as a prolegomena to the Christ-event.[63] Thusing asserts, however, that such an approach undervalues the central theological content of the Old Testament, which is Yahweh's continual engagement with humanity as the God of hope and not just the one who is the bringer of salvation.[64] Furthermore, this means that the notion of Jesus as the absolute Saviour lacks specific biblical content:

> In any attempt to achieve a collaboration between dogmatic theology and exegesis, the concept of the absolute bringer of salvation must ... be given a concrete content and meaning from the Bible, because it is too abstract in the transcendental approach and yet indispensable to this approach because it is abstract.[65]

Thusing argues that, because of this lack of biblical content, Rahner's Christology contained an *a priori* necessity that God's absolute self-communication automatically implies the incarnation.

---

[59] Ibid., 279.
[60] Ibid., 279.
[61] Ibid., 279.
[62] K. Rahner, W. Thüsing, D. Smith & V. Green, *A New Christology*, 63–4.
[63] Ibid., 64.
[64] Ibid., 64.
[65] Ibid., 65.

Could God not have conceived his communication of himself in a different way? Could he not have brought it about in continuity with Hosea's proclamation of the radical and unfathomable love of Yahweh as an unmediated gift, that is, as a gift not mediated by a God-man? Is it not possible to think of God's communication of himself, as Buber did (i.e. that God commits himself to his people and the world immediately, that is, without mediation, and in this way completes the line that has begun by Hosea and the other prophets), and therefore have a transcendental view of that self-communication as a possible way in which God's freedom might have been realised?[66]

While all of this is most certainly conceivable, Thusing misses the essential trinitarian structure of Rahner's Christology. If, as Rahner asserted, the immanent trinity and economic trinity are one and the same process within the life of God and the world, then the God-man was always within the eternal life of God the bringer and bearer of God's self-communication to the world.[67]

Thusing also asks the fundamental question: 'Is it possible to regard the cross, within a transcendental Christology, as the object towards which the incarnation (in Johannine theology) and God's plan (in Paul's theology) are orientated?'[68] In terms of the internal logic of Rahner's Christology the answer to this question, despite his insistence on an expiatory framework to soteriology, is probably no. 'It is possible to develop other christologies into which the cross, the social implications of man's relationship with Jesus (the church or the community) and eschatology can be integrated more adequately and given a more central position.'[69]

Thusing's basic conviction is that Rahner's connection between transcendental Christology and an evolutionary view of the world is inherently problematic because it simply cannot do justice to the pluriform nature of the New Testament witness to the significance of Jesus as the God-man. Taking all these considerations together, it is justifiable to contend that Rahner's investigation of the New Testament traditions concerning the belief in Jesus as the Christ lacked a sufficiently coherent biblical interpretative framework, because he did not pay enough attention to the antecedents

---

[66] Ibid., 65.

[67] This does not, however, refute the claim that there is a necessitarian element to Rahner's Christology. According to J.A. Di Noia, it only serves to confirm it because it is linked to Rahner's ontology of the symbol which not only expresses the intent of a personal action but actually embodies it; see, 'Karl Rahner', in D. Ford (ed.), *The Modern Theologians: An Introduction to Christian Theology in the Twentieth Century*, 129.

[68] Rahner et al, *New Christology*, 66.

[69] Ibid., 66.

of Christology in the eschatological and apocalyptic Judaism of the Old Testament which forms Jesus' own context of self-understanding. As N.T. Wright indicates, there is a story to be told here which links Jesus' message, his actions, lifestyle and his death and resurrection to the motif of the return from exile of God's elected people.[70] To a certain extent then, the charge that Rahner, like Schleiermacher, collapses Christology into an already presupposed ontology of religion, is justifiable, although as Jones makes clear, this remains a contentious issue amongst Rahner's interpreters.[71]

Thusing's comment that transcendental Christology lacks an adequate socio-political content is interesting because if forms the background of Sobrino's hesitation with Rahner's approach. To a certain extent this is a reason why Roman Catholic liberation theology has reacted with some equivocation to Rahner's Christology. 'To put it concretely, it must ask itself whether or not its conception of God, sin, liberation, and transcendence are derived from Jesus and hence christological, or whether they are viewed as realities already known logically from some other source quite independent of Jesus' appearance in history. How radically rooted in Christ are all the realities considered by theology?'[72] Thus, from within the perspectives of liberation Christology, Sobrino raises similar objections to those we have already noted. 'Is Jesus merely a privileged example and embodiment of things that can be learned quite independently of him?'[73]

In his comparison of the respective christologies of Rahner and Moltmann, Jones makes the same basic point:

> Unlike Moltmann ... Rahner is unwilling to answer explicitly social or political questions in any length; he does not go on to develop, as Moltmann does ... the material and liberating implications of this understanding of the Christ event. On the contrary, Rahner determinedly shies away from such statements, preferring to locate his resources and significance in the area of fundamental, speculative theology.[74]

What Jones fails to realise, however, is that this preference for what he calls 'speculative theology' is itself a political statement, but this time one that relativises the importance and significance of the socio-political sphere in favour of a evolutionary framework which links nature and grace. Indeed, a few pages further on Jones is almost forced, against the logic of his argument, to concede this point himself.[75]

---

[70] Wright, *Victory*.
[71] Jones, *Critical Theology*, 78.
[72] J. Sobrino, *Christology at the Crossroads: A Latin American Approach*, 350.
[73] Ibid., 350.
[74] Jones, *Critical Theology*, 74.
[75] Ibid, 78.

Rahner's evolutionary perspective is clearly different to that of Teilhard de Chardin's. The latter was a scientist and a theologian who utilised scientific data to construct his own particular neo-Darwinian worldview. While he related his theology of nature to philosophical principles, his main concern was to detail the course of historical evolution from matter to life, mind and society, and ultimately to its consummation in Christ the Omega point. His philosophy was consequently a carefully constructed synthesis of evolutionary biology and the Christian tradition.[76] The source of Rahner's evolutionary theory was not the dialogue with neo-Darwinism, but the metaphysics of transcendentalism he derives ultimately from Kant, Fichte, Hegel, Heidegger and Maréchal. It is here deeply embedded in this idealist tradition, based as it is on the philosophy of subjectivity, where we encounter the myth of evolution that has dominated much scientific theory. This persuasive metanarrative views the evolution of the universe as the product of that 'odyssey of Mind' which begins with the metaphysics of the Absolute subject.

The Romanticism of the late eighteenth and nineteenth century developed Kant's transcendentalism in a decidedly Idealist direction. Fichte, Schelling and Hegel sought to overcome Kant's denial of metaphysics by asserting that the *a priori* cognitive categories of the mind were, in some way, also the ontological categories of the universe. Human knowledge did not, therefore, point to a divine reality beyond itself, but was part of that reality whereby the universe is able to become self-consciously aware of itself. Kant's 'transcendental ego' (the idea of the self that imposed heuristic categories upon experience to render knowledge possible) was in fact transposed onto a cosmic framework and became a feature of the absolute Spirit or Subject that determines the nature of reality itself.

Kant's careful distinction between the manifold or content of experience, which is ultimately derived from the real world and the ordering concepts of the mind, is obliterated in favour of the all encompassing Mind, so that the real world becomes an image or cipher of the absolute Ego or Self. With the emergence from the evolutionary process of human self-consciousness the universe learns to think itself, consequently, the primary metaphysical principle is pure self-conscious Spirit. This narrative is one that effectively subjugates and subordinates the contingency and particularity of the real world in favour of the 'metaphysics of Presence'. The ubiquitous presence of the divine rationality or divine spirit is both the absolute source and the end of the historical process. Such a totalitarian ontology ultimately traces everything back to the Fichtean notion of the self-postulating absolute subject. The human mind is conceived analogously to the divine mind.

---

[76] P. Teilhard de Chardin, *The Phenomenon of Man*; also, *Man's Place in Nature: The Human Zoological Group*, and *Christianity and Evolution*.

In Rahner's transcendental epistemology there was a real affinity with this idealist tradition. For instance, through the process of abstraction whereby we conceptually impose order on the particulars of the world there is a strong sense that the particularity of the other is not valued or recognised in and for itself, but is instead primarily a means toward transcendental experience, the elevation of the self-consciousness subject toward the absolute horizon of being. It is through the subject's mastery or overcoming of the other that transcendental experience becomes possible. This metaphysical tradition, albeit often unwittingly, nevertheless displaces the freedom, contingency and fragile originality of real particulars in favour of an all-encompassing and ultimately imperialistic plenitude of being. In such a system, there is an all too smooth transition from human transcendentalism to its highest, unsurpassable manifestation in Christ the absolute Saviour. 'In Jesus Christ there is achieved in a unique and fundamental way that "unity of reality" to which the human spirit is, as such, always oriented, and which it can therefore find only in – explicit or anonymous – relation to Jesus Christ'.[77] In effect, Christ becomes the highest realisation of totalitarian metaphysical realities.

This is the source of Von Balthasar's criticism that Rahner is unable within the confines of this form of transcendentalism to develop an adequate *theologia crucis*. The cross presents us with the radical and deeply disturbing otherness of the Saviour whose absoluteness is manifest in godforsakenness, abandonment and annulment. Von Balthasar bids us look in silence and horror into the abyss of Holy Saturday before we can hear a fresh and evocative word from God through Easter to Pentecost.[78] As Rowan Williams perceptively notes:

> The heart of the difference here seems to be that Rahner thinks of human frustration in terms of incompletion, Balthasar in terms of tragedy. Freedom is not simply a smooth trajectory of finite towards infinite; it is more importantly, the possibility of self-deceit, self-destruction, refusal.[79]

These are questions to which we will have to return at a latter stage in our considerations. Sufficient to note at this stage how one impressive and highly nuanced Christology has, nevertheless, become irresistibly linked to a philosophical tradition which effectively undermines it at source and cannot sustain the sheer tantalising fecundity of the rich biblical vein out of which fresh resources for Christology must continually be quarried.

---

[77] M. Kehland & W. Loser, *The von Balthasar Reader*, 19.

[78] Cf. H. Urs von Balthasar, *Mysterium Paschale*.

[79] Williams, 'Balthasar'; 32. See also L. Gardner, D. Moss, B. Quash and G. Ward, *Balthasar at the End of Modernity*.

We have again been dealing with a philosophical tradition of mythic proportions, one of those gargantuan ideas that the postmodern philosopher Richard Rorty claims continually infiltrates the modern philosophy of subjectivity. It is surely one of the most ironic aspects of the early Enlightenment preference for a rationalist natural religion, that it continually denigrated the category of myth. Myth was inevitably described as a primitive stage in the growth of religious and philosophical consciousness, prior to the philosophy of self-consciousness that characterised the intellectual ethos of Enlightenment. What we have discovered, however, is that hidden in the recesses of modern thought myths abound. Many of them are designed to protect one of the most cherished ideals of modernity, the primacy of the universal human subject. In Rahner's thought, an original and at times compelling theory of self-transcendence bolstered this same ideology.

We must now turn our attention to another of these attendant myths, in many ways the most powerful and persuasive of them all, for without it the primacy of the individual self all but dissolves, as indeed it does in postmodern theory, in either the acidic mire of nihilism, or the equally destructive power discourses of contemporary culture.

7.

Christology and Human Liberation

PARADIGM FOUR: THE MYTH OF EMANCIPATION

Emancipation is to be seen as a kind of epochal catchword for our present experience of the world and as an historico-philosophical category for the process of enlightenment and freedom in the modern era, in the circumstances (and not just the conditions) of which we have to articulate and represent the Christian message of redemption. In that case it is a fundamental question for modern Christology to decide the relation between redemption understood in a Christian perspective and emancipation understood as the modern age understands it.[1]

Introduction

There is no story or great idea that has been so compelling to the modern mind than the narrative of human emancipation. In their influential and revealing analysis of contemporary American culture, the authors of *Habits of the Heart* trace the origins and influence of this narrative through the earliest traditions of American civic and political life. From this, Robert Bellah and his colleagues have been able to trace the evolution of the notion of human emancipation, from its roots in biblical communitarianism to its modern form of individual self-expression and achievement. In the course of this development the social and political meaning of human freedom as that which can only be adequately achieved in relation to other civic and ethical virtues such as justice, equality and fraternity, has been abrogated in favour of a highly attenuated notion of freedom as the sole right or prerogative of the individual.[2] Such a cultural evolution of the concept of human freedom is based on the Enlightenment distinction between church and State, a political expediency, which, as we

---

[1] Kasper, *Jesus*, 42.

[2] For a helpful and illuminating analysis of similar themes, see R. Bauckham, *God and the Crisis of Freedom*.

have already noted, is itself founded on an equally convenient epistemological dichotomy between fact and value. Here ethics and religion are banished from the public square and the notion of freedom is conceived almost entirely in terms of emancipation from either external or internal constraint. It is precisely at this juncture that we encounter repeatedly the Enlightenment myth of emancipation and it is not difficult to define some of its credal affirmations.

1. The realisation of the freedom of the individual from outside constraint and domination by the exercise of critical reason.
2. The acquisition of new knowledge in the natural and social sciences to free people from the shackles of superstition and the errors of received dogma.
3. The development of technological expertise and know-how to expand the horizons of human freedom and to allow us to manipulate the natural world for our own advantage.
4. The critical historical investigation and interrogation of the past to enable us to better understand the present and to free us to make more informed decisions about the future.
5. The emancipation of the proletariat from the domination of repressive social and economic structures.
6. The search for the one truth that underlies all religious traditions to emancipate us from the fear and prejudice that fuels fanaticism and fundamentalism.

Ironically, this apparent fascination with the ideal of emancipation sees the delight of autonomy gradually turn into the terror of abandonment.[3]

The Enlightenment challenged almost all extraneous authorities in the name of human emancipation and liberation, but there are those who argue that it failed to deliver what it promised. Liberation theologians such as David Boesak and Munas Buthelezi (both from Africa) and Gustavo Gutierrez and Juan Luis Segundo (both from South American) claim that Enlightenment ideologies have given rise to situations of systemic injustice, oppression and racism, which are perpetuated in the economic and social divisions that divide the first world from the rest of the world's inhabitants. It is therefore not surprising that in such a context the question of what we mean by this process of liberation and how it is best achieved should in recent years become one of the most dominant and insistent christological paradigms.

In this chapter we will concentrate on the work of Jon Sobrino, with reference to Leonardo Boff, because it is here that we find the most sustained christological reflection aimed at the articulation of a comprehensive form of human emancipation.

---

[3] R. Lundin, 'Interpreting Orphans', 5.

Two Stages of the Enlightenment

Today no Christology can sidestep the challenge posed by the Enlightenment. If it
does not respond to the challenge, no Christology is credible or relevant. But every
Christology must take cognisance of the underlying interest that motivates it. Is it
trying to show that the truth of Christ can be justified before the bar of reason or is
it trying to show that it can be justified before the demands and yearnings for a
transforming praxis?[4]

Stage 1

Both Sobrino and Boff discern two stages to the Enlightenment. The first,
associated with Immanuel Kant, is concerned with the liberation of human
reason from theological domination. Naturally, this meant that Christology had
to justify its claim to speak of the unique status of Christ '*before the bar of reason*'.
This was particularly urgent in the face of the atheistic critique of religion that
began with Ludwig Feuerbach, Karl Marx and Friedrich Nietzsche. According
to liberation theologians, however, this has been the main preoccupation of
European theologians; it was epitomised by the apologetic Christology of
Wolfhart Pannenberg, which emphasises the priority of establishing rational
and historical grounds for belief in Jesus as the Christ.

　　Gustavo Gutierrez refers to modern European theology as progressive theology. He argues that it operates within the confines of the Enlightenment
dichotomy between reason and faith or belief. Its concern is to justify religion
as a reasonable form of belief, so the modern bourgeois non-believer is its ubiquitous subject. Liberation theology, on the other hand, focuses on the poor and
oppressed, those who are historically the victims of the domination of the
bourgeois subject.[5] Consequently, it is asserted, liberation theology is not only
different in kind from its European counterpart, it is actually opposed to it.

---

[4] Sobrino, *Christology*, 348.
[5] Arturo Paoli makes a similar point concerning the difference between European and
　Latin American theology: 'It may well be possible that Latin American and European
　theologians … agree on the definition of faith as intrinsically political. The substantive
　difference between them is to be found in their completely different concrete situa-
　tions. Latin America does not have any theological tradition to defend, nor any
　commitment to apologetics. Its people have already rejected certain ideologies, not
　through a process of controversy and debate but through an inability to assimilate
　them. Here theology really is in a position to become a biblical, prophetic theology. It
　has no need of a theology of revolution, or a theology of violence, or a theology of
　secular realities, as we are wont to encounter these lines of thought. Latin American
　theology centres around reflection on real happenings in the light of God's word. It
　seeks to discover God in the people, in taking cognisance of dependence and political

It may be the case that epistemological issues dominate Western Christology because it emerges from a political and cultural situation that is avowedly secular. A culture that implicitly accepts globalisation will be shaped in the image of secular technological humanism. Technological humanists retain an instinctive faith in the capacity of critical reason to deliver reliable information about the world. This enables us to make the necessary political and social adjustments that will guarantee the continued prosperity and stability of Western democratic capitalism. For liberation theologians, 'The enemy of humanity is not nature (as is the case in technological humanism), but one structure of human power which exploits and destroys the powerless.'[6]

Western theology, particularly Roman Catholic theology, is also accused of espousing an optimistic evolutionary philosophy; it is either apolitical or orientated towards the maintenance of the status quo. The ideal of self-transcendence, or the elevation of the finite toward the infinite, is the theology of the rich and powerful. As such, Western theology easily disguises the real forces of economic and political exploitation and oppression that hold countless people captive; this is nowhere more apparent than in the failure of developmentalism.[7]

Stage 2

Consequently, liberation theology aligns itself with the second phase of the Enlightenment, which is encapsulated in Marx's famous phrase: 'The philosopher only seeks to understand the world; the revolutionary intends to change it.' The influence of Marxism on liberation theologians such

---

[5] *(continued)* initiatives on behalf of liberation.' See, 'Latinoamerica: Explosivo continente del futuro', quoted in A. Perez-Esclarin, *Atheism and Liberation*, 117.

[6] Bosch, *Transforming Mission*, 439.

[7] Developmentalism was the economic system undertaken by governments in the First and Second world to try and eliminate Third-World poverty and other social ills by pouring money and resources into ambitious development projects. It assumed that all our poorer neighbours needed was Western technological expertise plus the necessary injection of cash. Developmentalism created a system of economic dependency where the only beneficiaries where small cartels of the rich, or oppressive totalitarian oligarchies and military regimes who continued to oppress the masses of the poor in the name of western business interests. The rich got richer the poor got poorer. Mostly, the project failed disastrously. On the socio-political level, developmentalism was replaced by revolution; theologically it was replaced by the call for liberation and espousal of the preferential option of the poor. Roman Catholics articulated these fundamental concerns at the Second and Third General Conferences of Latin American Bishops at Medellin, Columbia (CELAM II, 1968) and Puebla, Mexico (CELAM III, 1979).

as Gutierrez, Miguez Bonino, Jose P. Miranda, Sobrino and Boff has been considerable, but not uncritical. Overall liberation theology has been characterised by a rejection of capitalism in favour of socialism. Liberation theologians have also accepted that the law of history is not the inevitable progress of development, but the social dynamics of revolution. As Marx claimed, this is a phenomena that is not subject to the human will because it exposes, critiques and eventually overthrows political and economic systems of injustice.[8] Accordingly, a liberation perspective does not begin with the question 'Does God exist?, but 'Whose side is God on?' Similarly, its fundamental epistemological principle is not establishing rational grounds for belief, but the liberating praxis of the kingdom embodied in Jesus of Nazareth.

> Christological reflection in Latin America seeks to respond to the second phase of the Enlightenment ... It seeks to show how the truth of Christ is capable of transforming a sinful world into the kingdom of God.[9]

Orthopraxis Over Orthodoxy

To espouse a Christology which is radically contextualised means that liberation Christology begins not with a 'dialogue with other theologies, philosophies, or cultural movements', but with the 'basic Latin American reality of underdevelopment and oppression'.[10]

> Universal statements are not enough; they must be verified in the very texture of human life. Without such mediation they are unreal and ideological, and they end up bolstering the powers that be. When we inquire about Christ's liberation and meaningfulness in terms of the liberation process now going on in Latin America, we are already pointing the response in a certain direction and setting up a viewpoint through which we will scan the words, life, and historical journey of Jesus Christ.[11]

This remarkably candid statement constitutes what has become an almost universal tenet of liberation theology, i.e. the primacy of orthopraxis over orthodoxy.

---

[8] For a helpful analysis see J.A. Kirk, *Theology Encounters Revolution*; J. Miguez Bonino, *Christians and Marxists: The Mutual Challenge to Revolution.*

[9] Sobrino, *Christology*, 349.

[10] Ibid., 33. Similar concerns were at the heart of the 'black theology' that emerged from the African experience of colonialism. For a useful summary see J.W. de Gruchy, 'African Theology (2)', in Ford (ed.), *Modern Theologians*, 445–55.

[11] L. Boff, 'Christ's Liberation via Oppression: An Attempt at Theological Construction from the Standpoint of Latin America'; in R. Gibellini (ed.), *Frontiers of Theology in Latin America*, 101.

Rebecca Chopp offers a helpful analysis of what is meant by the term praxis in liberation theology. She discerns three crucial but interrelated dimensions to the use of this important concept.[12] First, there is the recognition that human beings are constituted by the social and political factors that are part of their historical context. Issues such as class, socio-economic status, gender and race and access to power are determinative factors in understanding human nature. Secondly, over and against the Enlightenment stress upon the independence and objectivity of reason, praxis affirms that human subjectivity is unequivocally interpersonal. The essence of what and who we are and will become is dependent upon our relationships with other persons and other social factors. Thirdly, the freedom of human beings is realised in our inherent ability to transform reality and so create history. We are not the hapless victims of a predetermined historical process, but participants in the struggle to create a just and humane society. Thus Christologies that do not liberate human beings from conditions of servitude and oppression must be rejected.[13]

Hugo Assmann recognises that there are many vestiges of Enlightenment Christology in Latin America:[14]

1. There is the Christ of old Catholicism, shrouded in mystery and technical theological terms. This is the Christ of Chalcedon, supposedly apolitical, a Christ who has power because he is the union of humanity and divinity in one person, but he does not exercise his power, at least not in the kingdoms of this world.
2. There is the imperialist Christ of the oppressors, backed up by the church hierarchy that accepts the division between the political and religious spheres. But to opt for the expediency of peaceful coexistence allows the politics of divide and rule to persist and so puts Jesus on the side of the big battalions.
3. There is the sorrowful, suffering Christ of the oppressed and exploited peoples, the Christ who images the impotence and defeat of a subjugated people and so similarly baptises the divisions between the rich and the poor, the exploited and the exploiter.
4. There is also the revolutionary Christ of socialist and Marxist ideology who promises eternal renown in the annuls of history for all those martyred in the cause of liberation.[15]

---

[12] R.S. Chopp, 'Latin American Liberation Theology', in Ford, *The Modern Theologians*, Vol. 2, 177.

[13] Cf. R. Radford Ruether, *To Change the World, Christology and Cultural Criticism*, 25.

[14] H. Assmann, 'The Power of Christ in History: Conflicting Christologies and Discernment', in R. Gibellini (ed.), *Frontiers of Theology in Latin America*, 133–51.

[15] Ibid., 133–51.

His analysis reveals that no human knowledge, least of all Christology, is free from ideology. All our knowing and imaging of reality arises out of our encounter with social, historical and political factors. Liberation Christology accepts that knowledge is socially conditioned. It is impossible to think christologically in some ideological neutral zone.

Boff warns against 'ideologising the titles of Christ' in a way that appears to justify 'social and religious status'.[16] Rather, one must make a prior commitment to liberating praxis and develop a Christology that arises out of the experience of oppression and systemic injustice that dominates the lives of ordinary people. The perpetual reminder of liberation theologians to those living in a European or American context is clear and unequivocal: 'Those reflecting theologically on experience outside Europe have shown us how salvation, unrelated to liberation and participation in a just society, as God intended, means little to the struggling majority of the world who live in grinding poverty.'[17]

There is a further theological justification to this view: the only way to know Christ is to follow the way of the suffering servant of God. 'Only in and through the process of conversion and practical change do we have access to the God of Jesus Christ.'[18] Right knowledge (orthodoxy) is impossible without right doing (orthopraxis). In that sense, wisdom is located in what the Bible refers to as 'the fear of the Lord', which is the practice of living skilfully in obedience, faith and trust. Similarly, it is the primacy of orthopraxis that can act as a check against the degeneration of doctrine into ideology. By subjecting our beliefs to the test of whether they lead to liberation or further oppression, we expose the ideological control that often masquerades in the name of orthodoxy.

Christological Factors: Where to Begin?

The priority of orthopraxis means that Sobrino rejects the Chalcedonian formula that Christ is the union of divinity and humanity in one person as a starting point for Christology, because:

1. It is a summary dogmatic statement that is both chronological and logically posterior to the reality of the historical Jesus.
2. It is couched in reified metaphysical terminology, such as *hypostasis* and *phusis*, which require radical reinterpretation in today's context. In the

---

[16] L. Boff, *Jesus Christ the Liberator: A Critical Christology for our Time*, 229–31.
[17] Doctrine Commission of the Church of England General Synod, 'The Mystery of Salvation' 172.
[18] Boff, *Liberator*, 279.

history of dogma it stands as a 'limit-concept'; this means that it defines the limits of doctrinal adequacy concerning the person of Christ. But the only access we have to the actual reality of Christ that lies behind such conceptual formulations is to follow the actual course of Jesus' life as it is recorded for us in the Gospels.[19]

3. It presupposes a Christology of descent. Its subject is already a divine figure, i.e. the eternal *Logos*, whereas Scripture begins with the human person Jesus of Nazareth.

4. It is couched in the conceptuality of Neoplatonism, which is basically an epiphany religion.[20] The Bible, however, speaks of a God who acts, who is involved in history in the struggle for justice, in the alleviation of human suffering and the bringing of good news to the poor.

In addition to his critique of Chalcedon, Sobrino also rejects other starting points from European christological reflection. These include:

1. The sacramental experience of Christ in the liturgy and the eucharist, which amounts to a christological reflection on the real presence of Christ[21] – a point of departure for much Roman Catholic Christology – however in the cultic history of Christianity much distortion and misrepresentation has occurred which has been 'directly contrary to the reality of Jesus himself'.[22]

2. The christological titles (such as Messiah, Son of God, Logos, Saviour, etc.) that are also the result of later theological reflection. As such, they point to a christological pluralism that is part of the biblical testimony to Jesus. The underlying unity and ultimate justification of the suitability or otherwise of these titles remains, however, the historical Jesus.

3. The preached Christ, or the Christ of the *kerygma*, as advocated by Martin Kähler and Rudolf Bultmann. Sobrino does not deny that the proclamation of the gospel should move us from inauthentic to authentic existence, to use the existential terminology, but this is much too individualistic a concept of what Christian existence entails because it fails to take note of the social and political realities that continually fragment and distort our humanity and make us either victims of, or contributors to systems of oppression and injustice. To begin with the teaching of Jesus or his moral

---

[19] Here Sobrino remains wedded to one of the fundamental presuppositions of modern European Christology, i.e. that it is possible to gain access to the Jesus of the Gospels by way of historical critical investigation. Cf. Jones, *Critical Theology*, 106.

[20] Moltmann has made much of the fact that Greek theology concentrates on the epiphany of the eternal now, the unveiling of the divine in the human sphere. See, *Theology of Hope: On the Ground and the Implications of a Christian Eschatology*, 95–133.

[21] Cf. G. O'Collins, *Christology: A Biblical, Historical, and Systematic Study of Jesus*.

[22] Sobrino, *Christology*, 6.

example, as was the wont of liberal Protestantism, is similarly to miss the mark, because it presents a Jesus who 'was the model of bourgeois morality and citizenship in the nineteenth century'.[23]

4. The experience of Jesus as the Redeemer or Saviour. While the decisive importance of soteriological concerns is recognised as an essential aspect of Christology, it is rejected as a methodological starting point. To begin here is to risk constructing a Jesus who is a mere symbol or cipher of our own values and self-interest.

5. The resurrection of Jesus. This is a major break with European Christology. Sobrino's reasons for doing so reflect anxieties that are particularly pertinent to the Latin American situation. His main concern is that this will perpetuate the dichotomy between the Christ of faith and the Jesus of history that has dogged the history of modern Christology. When the risen Christ becomes our main focus of attention, he easily becomes associated with expressions of religious and political power that are oppressive and totalitarian. Such was the case with the imperial Christology of Constantianism. The same was true with the monarchical concepts of priesthood and episcopacy that in the medieval period were associated with the presence of the risen Christ in the eucharist.

The Priority of the Historical Jesus

In light of this analysis, Sobrino argues that liberation Christology must make the historical Jesus the starting point of all its endeavours. It must begin with 'the person, proclamation, activity, attitudes, and death by crucifixion of Jesus of Nazareth insofar as all of this can be gathered from the New Testament texts – with due respect for all the precautions imposed by critical exegesis'.[24] In this way, as previously explained, we respond to Jesus' call to know him by following him. It is the praxis of Christian discipleship that allows us to retrace the historical course of Jesus' life. Furthermore, concentration on the historical Jesus reveals that there is a structural similarity between his situation of religious and political oppression, and the attendant yearning for liberation and the situation that faces people in the Two-Thirds world today.

At this juncture we encounter a crucial move in much liberation theology. The primacy of the historical Jesus for the renewal of liberation Christology has as much, if not more, to do with the conviction that there is a material correspondence between the socio-political situation of first-century Palestine and that of contemporary Latin America, than it has to do with the

---

[23] Ibid., 8.
[24] Ibid., 352.

hermeneutical consistency of the contemporary theologian. The danger here is that a pragmatic politicising will replace genuine exegesis.

A Christology that is founded on the historical Jesus also reveals that he only discovered his sonship through the actual course of his earthly existence. In a manner similar to Pannenberg, Sobrino explains that this is the reason why Christology cannot begin with the relationship of Jesus to the pre-existent *Logos*. To do so is to assume that Jesus' sonship was already defined, or at least prescribed for him, even if he was unaware of it. Rather, we must accept that it is Jesus' relationship with the Father that constitutes his person. What Chalcedon described in ontic terms (i.e. in terms of nature) Sobrino transcribes into relational terms. The divinity of Jesus flows out of his concrete obedience and faithfulness to the will of the Father. Sobrino recognises that this is only possible if we also accept that it is the trinitarian self-definition of God, which forms the ontological and epistemological framework that allows this assertion not to degenerate into mere adoptionism. Then we are also at liberty to suggest that Jesus does not simply reveal the Father, he also reveals the way of sonship.

At this point, Sobrino tries to rehabilitate the neglected Pauline notion of Jesus as the firstborn of a new humanity as a christological motif. This means that part of Jesus' divinity includes his relationship to us, as well as his relationship to the Father. Jesus points the way to our incorporation into the life of sonship:

> The path of Jesus is the revelation of the Son's path. If it were incapable of incorporating others into it, then Jesus would not be the Son. Hence being the "firstborn" is part and parcel of Jesus' divinity. He traverses the way to God and makes it possible for his brothers and sisters to do the same.[25]

Jesus and the poor

Attention to the actual ministry of Jesus reveals his preferential option for the poor. This is not merely a reflection of his compassion and understanding of the plight of the poor and marginalized (i.e. this was not just a question of ethics). Rather, Jesus reveals that this is a theological issue. He preaches good news to the materially poor (e.g. Lk. 4): 'Once we recognise the identification of Jesus with the poor, we cannot any longer consider our relation to the poor as a social ethics question; it is a gospel question.'[26] God is revealed in the plight of the poor. Throughout biblical history God chooses the poor, he is on the side of the poor and marginalised. Jesus embraces a particular lifestyle and speaks of

---

[25] Ibid., 107.
[26] Bosch, *Transforming Mission*, 437.

entry into the kingdom in terms of our identification with and response to the poor. He lives and ministers amongst the poor and marginalised, demonstrating that here is the critical loci of God's action in history.

The question remains, however, who are the poor? They are not simply the deprived, understood in material terms, they are the marginalised, the socially ostracised, those at the bottom of the pile lorded over by others, those who are excluded from full participation in society and therefore denied access to the God of hope:

> When we opt for the poor in a commitment to liberation, we are forced to realise that we cannot isolate oppressed people from the social class to which they belong. If we were to do that, we would simply be sympathising with their own individual situations. Poor and oppressed people are members of a social class which is overtly or covertly exploited by another social class.[27]

This analysis, however, remains on the level of social and Marxist theory because it lacks specific biblical content. In the Gospels, particularly Luke, it is the poor and oppressed (understood as the under-classes of society) who are included in the kingdom and given full rights of inheritance and citizenship in the realm of God's ordinances. We cannot therefore advocate a Jesus who simply appears to occupy a particular place within the normal realm of social prejudice and class division, this time in solidarity with the poor and disenfranchised. Rather, we need specific theological categories to enunciate what should be our understanding and response to this situation. In other words, we need a more comprehensive doctrine of sin:

> There is poverty because the rich do not share their wealth. There is religious oppression because the priests impose intolerable burdens on people. There is ignorance because the Levites have carried off the keys to knowledge. There is political oppression because the rulers rule despotically. In short the sinfulness of these people is not something which affects only the subjective life of the individual; it is visibly crystallised in the social realm.[28]

All of this makes it imperative that we again hear the summons of conversion and entry into the kingdom. The preferential option for the poor is contained in Jesus' message of the coming kingdom and liberation theology will not allow an other worldly spiritualising of this message. Rather, the good news of the kingdom must be understood in socio-political terms.

---

[27] Gutierrez, 'Liberation Praxis and Christian Faith', in R. Gibellini (ed.), *Frontiers in Theology in Latin America*, 8.

[28] Sobrino, *Christology*, 120.

Jesus and the kingdom

At the centre of Jesus' proclamation and, indeed, at the heart of liberation Christology, stands the metaphor of the kingdom. The kingdom of God refers to the saving rule of God. Consequently, it unites the spiritual and the physical, the personal and the social, the individual and the political realms of life:

> The theme of Christ's preaching was neither himself nor the Church but the king-dom of God. 'Kingdom of God' signifies the realisation of a utopia cherished in human hearts, total human and cosmic liberation. It is the new situation of an old world, now replete with God and reconciled with itself. In a word, it could be said that the kingdom of God means a total, global, structural revolution of the old order, brought about by God and only by God.[29]

In Jesus' ministry, the kingdom breaks in as the liberating grace and love of God that frees people from physical affliction, sin and injustice. In christological terms, Jesus' proclamation of the kingdom demonstrates that the centre of his existence lay outside himself. He receives his identity as the Son only in the service of the kingdom. Sobrino discerns two stages in Jesus proclamation of the kingdom.

The prophetic tradition

In the first stage, Jesus stands firmly within the prophetic tradition that viewed the kingdom as the fulfilment of the Torah. The only adjustment to that tradition was the assertion that the kingdom was now present in his person and ministry. The signs of the kingdom typify this initial stage. Miracles, healings and deliverances reveal the *dunamis* (power) of the kingdom.

From this analysis Sobrino picks out four salient issues which define the nature of eschatology, as evidenced in Jesus' proclamation of the coming kingdom:

1. It issues in a crisis, it is both judgement and opportunity.
2. It reorientates us to the future as that which is determinative of the present.
3. It poses the question of God again but in a radically new way to that which is typical of secular ideologies. God requires no exegetical or epistemological proof of his existence. Rather, he is discovered in the phenomena of radical hope.
4. Theology is itself refocused around different issues, no longer nature and grace, God and creation, faith and works, but church and kingdom, injustice and liberation, the gracious disclosure of the kingdom versus our

---

[29] Boff, *Liberator*, 63–4.

feeble attempts to reconstruct it from a humanistic basis. Here Sobrino is at his most strained. Once again we hear the familiar tone of a well-worn theme, the priority of praxis over belief.

This is straightforward enough, but Gareth Jones complains that Sobrino utilises kingdom theology in a very exclusive and illegitimate sense:

> The issue of the place or locus of the kingdom of God serves simply to confirm this analysis: the kingdom, like Jesus himself, is placed directly in a world defined by the social and cultural concerns of Latin America, a process of theological redefinition which mirrors the Christian life of people in this world.[30]

Given that Sobrino has already claimed a material correspondence between the socio-political situation that determined the nature of Jesus' message about the kingdom, and the situation of economic and social injustice that gripped Latin America, one wonders what precisely is Jones' point. Furthermore, regarding the biblical material, the kingdom equals God's reign, which is synonymous with shalom – a vision of human flourishing – directed towards the healing of the nations, and so by necessity involving socio-political existence.

It would appear that Jones misses both these points. He accuses Sobrino of hoisting in via the back door ecclesial authoritarianism or a political pragmatism that is only loosely attached to Jesus' message of the kingdom. This is manifestly not the case.[31] It would have been more to the point to ask if Sobrino, like his European counterparts, had really understood the nature of biblical eschatology. An over-literal rendition of the metaphor of the coming kingdom regards it as a reference to the end of the space-time continuum. However,

> it is possible ... to take the idea in quite a different sense: that Jesus and some of his contemporaries expected the end of the present world order, i.e. the end of the period when the Gentiles were lording it over the people of the true god, and the inauguration of the time when this god would take his power and reign and, in the process, restore the fortunes of his suffering people.[32]

---

[30] Jones, *Critical Theology*, 99. See also J. Sobrino, 'Central Position of the Reign of God in Liberation Theology', in J. Sobrino and I. Ellacura, *Liberation Theology*.

[31] 'What one finds in *Christology at the Crossroads*, then, is a very pragmatic image of Jesus presented as factual: it serves a function, before retiring gracefully and being replaced by an incipient – and socially coercive rule. And this is the problem with objectivism: people – theologians expecially – turn towards it when they want a form of modern authority to underpin a specific programme or course of action'. Ibid., 107. In our opinion, this is simply nonsense.

[32] Wright. *Victory*, 95.

Jesus' warnings about impending judgement are a call to national repentance and the socio-political content of the kingdom metaphor is preserved.

Galilean crisis

The second stage of Jesus' proclamation of the Kingdom was initiated by the crisis in Galilee (Mt. 13; Mk. 8). In a manner reminiscent of Schweitzer, Sobrino claims that at this juncture Jesus' understanding of the kingdom undergoes a radical change. Jesus realises that power must be subordinated to the reality of sacrificial love. He feels compelled to surrender everything – his life, his future and even his conception of God – in the service of the coming kingdom:

> For Sobrino, the paradox of the life of Jesus lies in the fact that in the last phase of his life in the service of justice he was in ignorance of the coming of the Day of the Lord and the future of his own mission, but nevertheless entrusted himself fully to God the Father, who was to abandon him on the cross.[33]

Two stages of faith and discipleship correspond to the two stages of Jesus' understanding of the nature of the kingdom. In the first stage, the content of faith and discipleship flows naturally out of the proclamation of the just and gentle rule of God with the preferential option for the poor and ostracised members of society clearly in focus.[34] In the second stage of Jesus' consciousness of the kingdom, the scandal of his apparent failure to bring in the kingdom becomes the focus of attention. Correspondingly, faith and discipleship must take the form of a radical trust in Jesus himself as he journeys toward the cross. Here we move from what is known to the dark night of the unknown.

Jesus and the cross

Martin Luther remarked that all our thinking about God ends with the cross. He recognised that there was an iconoclastic dimension to the cross that shattered all our previous conceptions of God's power and transcendence.[35] In an interesting analysis, Sobrino plots the course whereby the cross was more or less robbed of its scandalous and iconoclastic elements. He sees in the different Gospel accounts a levelling-down process that moves from the stark sense of abandonment, which is present in Mark's Gospel, to the triumph of Jesus'

---

[33] T. Witvliet, *A Place in the Sun: Liberation Theology in the Third World*, 135.

[34] Sobrino, *Christology*, 360.

[35] P.T. Forsyth made a similar theological observation: 'Christ is to us just what his cross is. All that Christ was in heaven or on earth was put into what he did there ... You do not understand Christ till you understand his cross.' See, *The Cruciality of the Cross*, 44–5.

death, which is typical of John's Gospel. It is doubtful if this analysis could withstand the rigour of recent exegesis of the Gospel accounts of Jesus death,[36] but Sobrino is on firmer ground when he notes that in Acts the death of Jesus is being interpreted as an event which conformed to some preconceived divine plan. Similarly, there can be no doubt that atonement theology with its attendant emphasis upon the vicarious satisfaction of Jesus' death removed much of that sense of godforsakenness and abandonment we find in the Gospels. Finally, Sobrino takes due note of the Greek preference for the *apatheia* of God, the refusal to countenance any direct influence or attack upon the impassability of God by linking the being of God to historical events, such as Jesus' crucifixion.

Sobrino's theology of the cross owes much to the influence of Moltmann, who contended that the cross radicalises our experience and knowledge of God. Natural theology constructs a knowledge of God based on 'the positive elements in creation, e.g. nature, history, and human subjec-tivity'.[37] Natural theology is based on the epistemological principle of analogy, like is known by like. From the basis of the creation we assume a powerful creator. A theology of the cross, however, utilises the principle of dialectical knowledge of God. God is revealed in his opposite, i.e. suffering, godforsakenness and death. Thus, the cross is a question of theodicy. It is concerned not solely with the justification of the sinner and the godless, but with the justification of God in the face of human sinfulness and oppression. The dialectic of cross and resurrection express the dialectic of the absence and the presence of God. This corresponds to the contradictions of history, the reality of a world caught in the grip of systems that exploit and condemn peoples and nations to a life of suffering, servitude and misery. By and large, liberation theologians have sought to counteract the image of the impotent, suffering Jesus with the trinitarian theology of the cross that was first developed by Moltmann.[38]

Jesus and the resurrection

Sobrino comprehends the significance and import of the resurrection from a triple perspective. In all three respects, he reveals how dependent he is upon the very Christology he seeks to distance himself from.

First, concerning the historical investigation of the resurrection event, Sobrino recognises the enormity of the task and the tendency of many

---

[36] Cf. Brown, *Death of the Messiah*, Vol. 1 & 2.

[37] Sobrino, *Christology*, 370.

[38] Ibid., 371. Also J. Moltmann, *The Crucified God: The Cross of Christ as the Foundation and Criticism of Christian Theology*, and *Way*.

theologians to retreat from the affirmation of the full historicity of the resurrection to the mere acceptance of the changed perspective of the disciples.
The realism of the cross suggests that the disciples' hopes and expectations
concerning Jesus must have been shattered. Their newfound faith, belief and
certainty could not simply be tied to the mere fact of the empty tomb; they had
to be linked to the traditions concerning the appearances of Jesus. Sobrino
accepts that these traditions are both ancient and authentic, and that ultimately
this is as far as historical science can take us. What remains is not science, but
the legitimacy, or otherwise, of prejudices or presuppositions about dead men
being raised from the dead.

Secondly, and very importantly for Sobrino's purposes, the theological
significance of the resurrection is that it redefines the nature of God as
'liberative power' and 'historicised love'. Sobrino also takes due note of the
early exaltation Christology that links Jesus with the heavenly Son of Man
figure in Daniel 7, and the move from this, reflected in the christological traditions of the New Testament, to the notion of pre-existence. This entailed that
the honorific titles (such as *Logos*, *Kyrios* and Son of God) took precedence over
the older adoptionist titles (such as Prophet, Servant of God and High Priest).
The importance of these titles is their relational meaning and not just the mere
attribution of divinity and authority to the risen Lord. Jesus is vindicated
through his resurrection as the one who discloses to us both the nature and the
mission of the Father.

Finally, in a manner clearly reminiscent of Rahner, Pannenberg and
Moltmann, Sobrino links the resurrection hermeneutically to the phenomenology of hope, which allows us to move beyond death and embrace history as
a history of promise that now takes shape in the mission and vocation of the
church:

> Our hope and praxis of love must be kept alive and operational at every moment.
> Only in that way can Jesus' resurrection be grasped not only as something that
> happened to him alone but as the resurrection of the "firstborn" and a promise that
> history will find fulfilment.[39]

Jesus the liberator

David Bosch contended that liberation theology has resurrected the prophetic
element within the Jewish–Christian tradition. It has affirmed a biblical faith
that looks to a God who is righteous and just, and so is actively involved in
history, championing the cause of the poor and oppressed:

---

[39] Ibid., 381.

The prophets declared first of all that what really offended God were the moral evils of injustice, cruelty, violence, oppression of the poor; and all the sacrifices in the world would be unacceptable to God so long as these evils continued.[40]

Israel's liberation from slavery and oppression in Egypt was the dominant theological paradigm and motif in the liberation theology of the 1960s. Not surprisingly, Jesus was viewed as the one who still liberates humankind from all false ideologies and the 'principalities and powers' that hold us in bondage. Salvation cannot be reduced to a purely personal or individual dimension of emancipation from sin and guilt. Rather, our concern must be to recognise that salvation is integral liberation that operates on three levels. It is liberation from:

- social and political situations of oppression and marginalisation.
- every kind of personal servitude and ostracism.
- sin that ruptures our relationship with God and other human beings.

The salvation that Jesus' death and resurrection obtains must embrace all three dimensions.[41]

In recent years we have seen the emergence of a more chastened and sober form of liberation theology that rejects some of the false utopianism of the early rhetoric of liberation. For example, Segundo accepts that not everything about our common humanity is reducible to the socio-political dimension. Similarly, all liberation must be subject to the criterion of the cross of Christ, where the awful apostasy of human sin in all its dimensions assaults and crucifies the Son of the living God. The cross relativises all triumphalist expectations concerning liberation. Total liberation from oppression and sin is not possible in history: 'Liberation and salvation overlap with each other to a significant degree, but they do not overlap totally. We should not deceive ourselves into believing that everything lies in our grasp.'[42]

Christianity should never lose its counter-cultural and world transforming role. If it does, as we have seen in the West, other forces will take its place. The salvation that both Jesus and Paul proclaimed bore the seeds of hope and resurrection. As Moltmann affirmed, the dynamics of hope continually undermine the politics of the status quo.[43] Hope refuses to remain indifferent to exploitation, poverty and human suffering.

---

[40] J. McIntyre, *The Shape of Soteriology: Studies in the Doctrine of the Death of Christ*, 112.
[41] Boff, *Liberator*, 275.
[42] Bosch, *Transforming Mission*, 446.
[43] Moltmann, *Theology of Hope*.

Assessment

Liberation Christology has been welcomed as a positive and important alternative to the apolitical christologies of Western culture. It contains an explicit critique of all anthropological Christologies that reduce the significance of Jesus to the merely personal or interpersonal realms of life. Similarly, it has offered a more comprehensive theology of salvation understood as integral liberation, which must embrace the political, economic and social realities of power, particularly those power structures that oppress and exploit the poor and under-privileged.[44]

To be fair, liberation theology has also contained the seeds of its own critical self-evaluation. More recently, liberation theologians have distanced themselves from some of the false utopianism of the early Marxist cries for total liberation and political revolution, which not surprisingly incurred the wrath of the more traditional elements within the Roman curia. In 1984 and 1986, Cardinal Joseph Ratzinger, head of the Sacred Congregation for the Defence of the Faith, criticised liberation theologians for failing to distinguish adequately between 'authentic' theologies of liberation rooted in the word of God, and those that are based on 'concepts uncritically borrowed from Marxist ideology'.[45] With some justification, Ratzinger cites examples where liberation theologians appear to combine biblical themes with Marxist analysis. Thus, he asserts that the poor in the Bible are identified with Marx's notion of the proletariat: the 'people of God' are understood as a movement engaged in a class struggle with hierarchical elements within the church's leadership, and the history of salvation is equated with the dialectical history of Marxist materialism. In other words, there is a tendency for everything to be politicised (e.g. the Pharisees often become the political scapegoat in liberation theology; a thesis that has now been all but discounted).[46] In particular, Ratzinger claims that Sobrino's interpretation of the kingdom of God and the significance of Jesus' death and resurrection are heavily influenced by Marxist propaganda. Given that Sobrino rarely refers to Marx in *Christology at the Crossroads* this would appear to be a heavily prejudicial reading of the evidence. At times, Ratzinger seems barely aware of that which liberation theology should have alerted him to, namely, the fact that no realm of human enquiry, least of all theological reflection, is free from ideological constraints and concerns. It is little wonder therefore that, from his position of affluence and influence,

---

[44] Cf. O. O'Donovan, 'Political Theology, Tradition and Modernity', in C. Rowland (ed.), *The Cambridge Companion to Liberation Theology*, 239.
[45] Cf. A.F. McGovern, *Liberation Theology and Its Critics Toward an Assessment*, 47–60.
[46] See, Sanders, *Jesus and Judaism*, and *Historical Figure*.

Ratzinger reinforces the traditional apolitical view of emancipation as that which is mediated through the sacramental system of the church.

Segundo, on the other hand, criticises both Boff and Sobrino for failing to advance a genuinely Latin American equivalent to European Christology; they are not political enough. Segundo considers in detail the political dimension of Jesus' life and ministry, and concludes that the post-resurrection church downplays this in favour of the spiritual. Similarly, a genuine hermeneutic will need to transpose much of Jesus' concern for the poor, for social relationships, and his integration of politics and theology into the contemporary world. To do so is to embrace the political elements of Christology in all their full vigour.[47]

John Millbank offers a more nuanced but, nonetheless, trenchant criticism of liberation theology.[48] He asserts that, despite their protestations, liberation theologians have largely taken over the Rahnerian version of integralism. In other words, the notion of salvation is confined to an essentially apolitical sphere of self-transcendence, which leaves the artificial distinction between the individual and the social realms virtually intact. Given the liberation theologians' insistence on integral liberation, this seems to be a surprising conclusion.[49]

Millbank believes that there is deceptive plausibility to the schema of integral liberation disguised in the juxtaposition of the three levels of liberation – socio-political, personal servitude and ostracism, and sin. These do not undermine or critique the validity or otherwise of the autonomous secular realm on which they are based. Millbank argues that liberation theologians have completely taken over the Marxist-Weberian presupposition that the social, ethical and political sphere should remain independent of any religious or theological interference. In so doing, they have also effectively accepted the thesis that secularisation is to be welcomed as the practical and pragmatic extension of human freedom.

> By viewing modern secularisation and politicisation in a favourable, or, at least, resigned light, political and liberation theology sunder all their previous ties to previous Christian socialism. For even the Christian socialists who have most influenced the public affairs of our time … persistently connected the dominance of the 'free market', privately owned wealth, a bureaucratic politics, and an unrestrained centralised sovereignty, with a secular age, where religion no longer supplied common values, common measures and standards.[50]

---

[47] J.L. Segundo, *The Historical Jesus of the Synoptics*.
[48] J. Millbank, *Theology and Social Theory: Beyond Secular Reason*.
[49] Ibid., 233.
[50] Ibid., 243.

A basic thesis of this chapter seems to be underscored by Millbank's analysis, i.e. liberation theologians like Assmann, Segundo, Gutierrez and Sobrino remained trapped within a post-Enlightenment dialectic of human emancipation. Liberation and the secular notion of emancipation are insufficiently distinguished. Consequently, liberation remains either (i) the Kantian notion of autonomous practical reason that requires theology only to support its existing presupposition rather than expose the collapse of religion into morality upon which it is based; or (ii) it refers to a process of secularisation that is supposed to guarantee political autonomy when, in fact, it has all but removed the genuine political context for freedom in favour of an unbridled individualism.

Similar concerns come to the fore when evaluating the much-vaunted elevation of orthopraxis over orthodoxy. Many theologians now regard this as a false antithesis that obscures rather than illuminates the distinctive aspects of liberation theology. For instance, in the following quote from Gutierrez we can see how a firm commitment to liberation praxis can also lead to an equally firm embrace of traditional christological orthodoxy:

> liberation theology ... involves a direct and specific relationship with historical praxis; and historical praxis is liberation praxis. It implies identification with oppressed human beings and social classes and solidarity with their interest and struggles. It involves immersion in the political process of revolution, so that from there we may proclaim and live Christ's gratuitous and liberative love. That love goes to the very root of all exploitation and injustice: the break up of friendship with God and other people. That love enables human beings to see themselves as children of their Father and brothers and sisters to each other.[51]

It would appear unnecessary and misleading to postulate a priority that is in name only, which only serves to distance liberation theology from its antecedents in the Christian tradition. Max Stackhouse makes this point forcibly when he notes that numerous metaphysical and moral visions or perspectives in fact undergird all contextualised theology that develops out of a particular orientation to praxis.[52] He concludes that *theoria* (theory) and praxis also require the dimension of *poiesis* (beauty). The sense of the numinous, the transcendent mystery of life and the imaginative entry into this domain through a proper recognition of the role of the aesthetic, as indeed Kant recognised, militates against any simplistic juxtaposition of theory and praxis.[53]

One wonders if liberation theologians, and especially those who have sought alternative Christologies, have really attended effectively enough to the

---

[51] Gutierrez 'Liberation Praxis', 24.

[52] I. Stackhouse, *Apologia: Contextualisation, Globalisation, and Mission in Theological Education*.

[53] I. Kant, *Critique of Judgement* and *Groundwork of the Metaphysics of Morals*.

realism of the Pauline discourse about the principalities and powers. Walter Wink's thorough analysis of this biblical tradition raises a fundamental question for some of the more facile espousals of liberation that have eventuated from those who remain committed to contextualised theology and praxis.[54] Might it be the case that deep within the social fabric of life there are forces and anarchic tendencies that lead to the eruption of violence and social disintegration, and they cannot be expunged through the process of social change and revolution? The eschatological perspective of the Christian faith recognises that the kingdoms of this world are always passing away. Consequently, our hope is in another kingdom where truth, justice and love will find their resolution in a new world order.

Finally, it must be conceded that there is a stark contrast between the political Christology of the Constantinian era and that of modern-day liberation theory. The former was articulated as a means of legitimating the existing political system; the latter serves the purpose of exposing political ideologies that lead to oppression and injustice. On the other hand, the imperial Christology of Eusebius was formulated from the basis of a shared metaphysic, and that is precisely what current liberation theology lacks. Quite apart from the inadequacy of the former, it could be the case that without such a metaphysic liberation theology falls victim to merely echoing the call for emancipation and freedom that lies at the heart of the Enlightenment, without a critical recasting of this *crie d'couer* in the light of new christological convictions.

In its Latin American context, liberation theology seeks to discover a genuine indigenous Christology that is integrally related to the socio-political situation of oppression and subjugation to the economic dominance of the West. However, it does not radically change the discourse of Christology that it has inherited from Western Europe. Liberation theology deploys many of the exegetical and hermeneutical manoeuvres that are typical of its Western counterpart to try and reconstruct a Christology from below, which remains more or less in the tradition of christological reconstruction begun by Schleiermacher. By and large, liberation theologians accept the autonomy of the nation-state and the secular. As a consequence, they undermine their schema of integral salvation at source. Inevitably, they have to borrow their political categories from the social sciences. Once this move is made, liberation remains a catchword for socio-political rhetoric rather than a genuine theological concept.

After a period of relative stagnation when many Western theologians were prepared to write it off as a passing fad, liberation theology is now showing signs of recovering some of its earlier prophetic impulses and passion. In the face of the continuing inequalities and monetary vicissitudes of the global

---

[54] Cf. W. Wink's trilogy on the powers. See Bibliography for details.

market, there have been calls for a renewed liberation theology that will resist the temptation to adapt religion to the consumerist requirements of the market. Jerjes Castro (a Nicaraguan theologian) and Fr Peter-Hans Kolvenbach (the former general of the Jesuits) have called for a more self-critical and reflective liberation theology; one that will develop new and tangible forms of living in solidarity with the poor that firmly resists the continued elevation of economic necessities over human dignity and rights. The new situation is well described by Jorge Pixley:

> When liberation theology emerged, it was expected that societies could be transformed under the protective umbrella of a socialist bloc. Taking power is no longer an option. But the pastoral aim of building an alternative vision of reality in which the poor become subjects rather than objects – this remains as valid as ever.[55]

It is to be hoped that a new reinvigorated liberation theology could address some of the theological infelicities and weaknesses that have dogged its history so far and develop a truly indigenous Christology that can radically break with the Enlightenment myth of human emancipation.

---

[55] J. Luxmoore, 'New Options for the poor', *The Tablet*, 8 July 2000, 918–19.

8.

Christology and Gender

PARADIGM FOUR: THE MYTH OF EMANCIPATION (CONTINUED)

Almost all theology in the Christian tradition, including liberation theology done from the perspective of the poor and oppressed, has been done by male theologians. In our day we are witnessing the phenomenon that all over the world the 'other half' of the human race, women, are waking up to their own dignity and finding their own voice … The christological question 'Who do you say that I am?' receives a response with yet another dimension when answered from the experience of believing women.[1]

Introduction

Although feminist theology is a relative newcomer on the theological scene, it is clear that a number of feminist theologians have embarked on a bold and imaginative reconstruction of the basic tenets of Christology. The sources of feminist theology, and its critique of society and the Christian tradition, however, lie in the 'emancipatory ideas of the Enlightenment'.[2] Ann Loades, for instance, distinguishes three broad streams of feminist thought that correspond with three of the main traditions of cultural criticism spawned by the Enlightenment – the liberal tradition, Marxist feminism and Romantic feminism.[3] All three aspects of feminist thought have helped to identify the 'androcentric fallacy', which has prevailed throughout out the history of Western civilisation.[4] Men and women not only differ physiologically; they also differ in their experience, perception and appropriation of reality. But these differences have been masked in the development of Western culture. Consequently, what has become normative and representative of humanity in

---

[1] E.A. Johnson, *Consider Jesus: Waves of Renewal in Christology*, 97.
[2] Hopkins, *Feminist Christology*, 1.
[3] A. Loades, *Feminist Theology: A Reader*.
[4] G. Lerner, *The Creation of Patriarchy*, 236–7.

general are, by and large, the experiences, values and conceptual constructs of males. Thus only half the story has been told. The contribution to society and culture of female experience has been both ignored and repressed. The result has been the oppression of patriarchy, the exclusion of women from all the main facets of cultural and social formation.

Against the background of the patriarchal social and cultural norms of Western society, how can women achieve genuine subjectivity and fashion a symbolic form of discourse that makes room for what is genuinely female? According to Luce Irigaray, there are two possibilities – either she allows herself to become masculinised and subservient to the dominant symbolic order, or she adopts a strategy of subversion identifying the gaps and the lacunae in the dominant forms of discourse and listening to the voices from the margins. The problem with the latter strategy as Steven Connor notes is that in our previous cultural context:

> The exploration of the marginal in feminist writing projects the female as the place of patriarchy's Other, identified with the dark and discredited negative side of every polarity, as body to mind, nature to culture, night to day, matter to form and madness to reason.[5]

To subvert this tendency women must develop their own distinctive ways of conceiving and of being. In other words, both ontology and epistemology must change because in the history of Western thought both reflect the male Promethean attempt to dominate and control the other. Not surprisingly, in such a context it is the religious symbolic forms of discourse that have bolstered patriarchy and permeated our corporate intersubjectivity; so it is here where the disruption and transformation must begin.

Irigaray connects with many feminist theologians when she observes that the god of Western culture has been constructed according to the male gender:

> We have no female trinity. But as long as woman lacks a divine made in her image she cannot establish her subjectivity or achieve a goal of her own. She lacks an ideal that would be her goal or path in becoming ... If she is to become woman, if she is to accomplish her female subjectivity, woman needs a god who is a figure for the perfection of *her* subjectivity.[6]

The fact that Irigaray accepts the Feuerbachian analysis of religion as largely a projection of our own subjectivity also entails that it is this male god that inevitably construes a woman's subjectivity according to the pattern of the generic

---

[5] S. Connor, *Postmodernist Culture. An Introduction to Theories of the Contemporary*, 229.
[6] L. Irigaray, 'Divine Women' in her *Sexes and Genealogies*; quoted in G. Jantzen, 'Luce Irigaray', in G. Ward (ed.) *The Postmodern God: A Theological Reader*, 194.

male. Within the terms of such an analysis the inevitable question must arise, does a male Jesus have the same adverse effect? Similarly, does this mean that salvation or liberation must inevitably embrace the healing and transfiguration of this fractured or stunted subjectivity that has been the means by which women have been rendered second-class citizens in Western culture?[7]

The Origins and Rise of Feminist Theology

Mary Daly attributes the origins of a feminist critique of the Christian tradition to remarks make by the suffragette, Elizabeth Cady Stanton:

> Take the snake, the fruit tree and the woman from the tableau, and we have no fall, no frowning Judge, no Inferno, no everlasting punishment – hence no need of a Savior. Thus the bottom falls out of the whole Christian theology. Here is the reason why in all the biblical researches and higher criticisms, the scholars never touch the position of women.[8]

Here the assumption is that the whole of Christian theology and ministry remains trapped or, indeed, helps to bolster a cultural gender dichotomy that is regarded as essential and common sense. In other words, women are inferior because sin originated with a woman, but it was expiated and over-come by a man.

Feminist theology did not begin to emerge in the mainstream circles of Christian theology until the 1960s. Valerie Goldstein's article, 'The Human Situation, a Feminist View', was published at the beginning of the decade.[9] In this article, she criticised the traditional doctrine of sin, because it was largely based on male experience of self-assertion and self-aggrandisement, and argued for a reconsideration of the categories of sin and redemption to include woman's experience of loss and negation of self. Twenty years later, Judith Plaskow published her Yale dissertation *Sex, Sin and Grace*, which was a critique of the theologies of Reinhold Niebuhr and Paul Tillich. Plaskow argued that both theologians unwittingly gave priority to the openness of male experience to the transformational and redemptive grace of God. What becomes representative of the whole human race is, in fact, the experiences and insights of only one part of humanity. Once again, the voices and testi-monies of women had been effectively silenced to the impoverishment of theological endeavour in general. In both studies the Christian tradition and

---

[7] Cf. G. Ward, *Divinity and Sexuality: Luce Irigaray and Christology*.
[8] Quoted in M. Daly, *Beyond God the Father: Toward a Philosophy of Women's Liberation*, 69.
[9] V. Goldstein, 'The Human Situation, a Feminist View'.

theological reflection were accused of conforming to cultural values which prescribe certain roles for women and suppress the differences between the experience of women and that of men.

In 1968 the publication of Mary Daly's *The Church and the Second Sex* continued this tradition of critical exposure and interrogation of what Fiorenza refers to as the 'malestream' Christian tradition.[10] Daly described the woman's movement as an exodus community for those women who were seeking an authentication of their role and experience presently not available to them within the Christian church. Already she was articulating the fundamental concern that traditional Christian symbols were wedded to patriarchy – perhaps irretrievably so as far as women were concerned. This process of parting company with Christianity was completed with the publication in 1973 of Daly's *Beyond God the Father*. Here her infamous questioning of the Christian tradition ('if God is male then male is God') took the form of a strident insistence that patriarchy and the worship of the male lay at the heart of the Christian faith. This idolatry eventuated in the subjugation and oppression of women at the hands of a misogynistic religion.[11]

Feminist thought is now a worldwide phenomenon that unites women from every race and culture in an attempt to 'eliminate the androcentric fallacy'.[12] The most detrimental and oppressive ideology of Western culture is, it is claimed, androcentrism, the fundamentally erroneous worldview whereby 'men possess all dignity, virtue, and power in contrast to women who are seen as inferior, defective, less than fully human, the alien or "other" in relation to the male human norm'.[13]

---

[10] E.S. Fiorenza, *Jesus: Miriam's Child, Sophia's Prophet: Critical Issues in Feminist Christology*.

[11] Daly now refers to herself as post-Christian and searches among other religious traditions where, for instance, the worship of the Goddess allows room for genuine feminine experience. Daphne Hampson remains unconvinced by such manoeuvres, finding the Goddess devotees guilty of the same anthropomorphic misconception of God as Christian patriarchy. Others like Fiorenza, L. Russell and R. Radford Ruether remain within the Christian tradition but exhibit a dialectical relationship to its central texts and dogmas. Their task is both to deconstruct the ideology of patriarchy and to retrieve those elements within the tradition that witness to the role and status of women as a genuine expression of both the human and the divine. Other significant feminist voices and contributors to this burgeoning field of study include L.M. Russell, *Human Liberation in a Feminist Perspective – A Theology*, P. Trible, *God and the Rhetoric of Sexuality* and *Texts of Terror*, E.S. Fiorenza, *Memory* and *Jesus*, R. Radford Ruether, *Sexism and God-Talk* and *Women-Church: Theology and Practice of Feminist Liturgical Communities*, S. McFague, *Models of God*, and D. Hampson, *Theology and Feminism*.

[12] Loades, *Feminist Theology*, 2.

[13] A.E. Carr, *Transforming Grace. Christian Tradition and Woman's Experience*, 136.

Feminism and the Christian Tradition

According to Margaret Farley there are four main problems in relation to the Christian faith and feminist concerns.

1. The failure to find femininity in God.
2. The belief that woman is derivative from and hence secondary to man.
3. The assumption that woman is characterised by passivity.
4. The tendency to identify woman with bodiliness as opposed to transcendent mind.[14]

Perhaps the most comprehensive attempt to recover the hidden and subversive role and status of women in the origins of early Christianity is offered by Fiorenza.[15] She discerns a dichotomy in the sources of early Christianity between the more egalitarian Jewish cultural setting of the Gospel writers (where structures of ministry and lifestyle were characterised by a 'discipleship of equals') and the patriarchy of the later Pauline and Pastoral epistles (where in order to maximise their evangelistic impact Christians had conformed to Greco-Roman patterns of patriarchal household order, so that leadership increasingly became a male prerogative):

> The Christian community, as the household of God, has become stratified according to the age/gender divisions of the patriarchal household. Ministry and leadership are dependent upon age/gender qualifications, not primarily upon one's spiritual or organisational resources or giftedness.[16]

In a significant review of *In Memory of Her*, Irigaray remains unconvinced that the Jewish origins of Christianity were quite as egalitarian as Fiorenza presents. Irigaray suspects that the dichotomy between the same and the Greco-Roman cultural context is more apparent than real.[17] Nevertheless, an examination of the Christian tradition soon reveals that it was patriarchy that solidly won the day. Such a situation begs the question, what was the social and political context that allowed such a cultural development to take place?

From the second century onwards the role, status and experiences of women were often prescribed and distorted in three particular ways. First, woman was the temptress or seductress, whose erotic sexuality was deployed to deflect man from the paths of righteousness. This was the view held by Tertullian:

---

[14] Quoted in Loades, *Feminist Theology*, 5.
[15] See, Fiorenza, *Memory*.
[16] Ibid., 289.
[17] L. Irigaray, 'Equal to Whom' in Ward (ed.) *Postmodern God*, 198–213.

Do you not realise that you are each an Eve? The curse of God on this sex of yours lives on even in our times. Guilty, you must bear its hardship. You are the devil's gateway; you desecrated the fatal tree; you first betrayed the law of God; you softened up with your cajoling words the one against whom the devil could not prevail by force. All too easily you destroyed the image of God, Adam. You are the one who deserved death, and yet it was the Son of God who had to die.[18]

It was just such a misogynistic religion of female sinfulness, deception and guile that was identified and quite rightly repudiated by Stanton.

Secondly, woman is the man's helpmate. The Hebrew term (*'iššâ*) actually means 'corresponding to' or 'fit for'; it's a term of equality. However, it came to mean an assistant or subordinate to. The subjugation of women that this view upheld was well expressed by Augustine:

Woman does not possess the image of God in herself, but only when taken together with the male who is her head, so that the whole substance is one image. But when she is assigned the role as helpmate, a function that pertains to her alone, then she is not the image of God. But as far as the man is concerned, he is by himself alone the image of God just as fully and completely as when he and the woman are joined together into one.[19]

In similar vein, Thomas Aquinas, utilising Aristotelian biology, viewed the female child as a misadventure or a misbegotten male. She could not be a true reflection of either the divine or the human.

Another reason why the woman was assigned the role of helpmate was due to the fact that she was regarded as woolly minded, incapable of rational thought and, therefore, not fit for leadership or responsibility.[20] Fiorenza located the socio-political context for this view in the Greco-Roman notion of the *polis*. Here it was only free, propertied, educated men who were regarded as those capable of exercising political leadership and responsibility. Similarly, she claimed that:

Modern political philosophy continues to assume that propertied, educated elite Western man is defined by reason, self-determination, and full citizenship, whereas women and other subordinated peoples are characterised by emotion, service and dependence. They are seen not as rational and responsible adult subjects but as emotional, helpless, and childlike.[21]

---

[18] Tertullian, *Ethical Treatises* in *The Anti-Nicene Fathers*, Vol. III. *Tertullian Parts I–III*.

[19] Augustine, *De Trinitate*, 417/ 1953: 7.7.10 in *Augustine: Later Works*.

[20] Richard Hooker, one of the founders of Anglicanism, claimed that the reason a man gave the woman away at her wedding was to remind her of her imbecility!

[21] Fiorenza, *Jesus*, 37.

Fiorenza's analysis, if correct, explains why this view of women has been so perniciously maintained during the long history of Christian cultural domination and influence.

Finally, we have the idealised picture of the female cast in the image of the Virgin Mary. This spiritualising of femininity in terms of virginal purity and passive docility offers an essentially sanitised picture of womanhood. It is the woman devoid of sexuality, her bodily existence reduced to being the perfect icon of female passivity. Irigaray most fervently objects to all such forms of androgynous Christianity that endeavour to minimize sexual difference.

Feminism and kyriarchy

While some feminists are content to rest their case with the exposure, denunciation and deconstruction of androcentrism, others view patriarchy in a more inclusive sense. For Rosemary Radford Ruether it involves all relationships of domination and hierarchy.

> By patriarchy we mean not only the subordination of females to males, but the whole structure of Father-ruled society: aristocracy over serfs, masters over slaves, kings over subjects, racial overlords over colonised people. Religions that reinforce hierarchical stratification use the Divine as the apex of this system of privilege and control.[22]

Fiorenza has now broadened the parameters of debate even further and in the process coined a new word, 'kyriarchy', for what was previously called patriarchy.[23] While appreciative of the attempt to isolate the socio-politcal contexts of domination, Fiorenza is critical of Ruether because she believes Ruether's analysis remains trapped within the pre-constructed cultural sex/gender system that reinforce the male/female stereotypes. Accordingly, Fiorenza wants to emphasise the importance of the ideological and cultural constructs that have maintained these distinctions as that which is supposedly essential to, or biologically prescribed by human nature: 'Since kyriocentrism replaces the category of androcentrism, it is best understood as an intellectual

---

[22] Ruether, *Sexism*, 61.

[23] 'Because feminist discourses continue to use the term "patriarchy" in the sense of gender dualism, I introduced in *But She Said* the neologism "kyriarchy", meaning the rule of the emperor/master/lord/father/husband over his subordinates. With this term I mean to indicate that not all men dominate and exploit all women without difference and elite Western educated propertied Euro-American men have articulated and benefited from women's and other "non-persons" exploitation.' See, Fiorenza, *Jesus*, 14.

framework and cultural ideology that legitimates and is legitimated by kyriarchal social structures and systems of domination.'[24]

Woman's experience, a theological norm

Given this hermeneutic of suspicion towards Scripture and the Christian tradition, feminist theologians see woman's experience as a new, legitimate focus of theological concern and enquiry. It is, however, difficult to define what is meant by woman's experience. Most feminist theologians are also contextualists: they recognise and accept that all our experience is mediated through specific cultural and historical contexts (e.g. the experience of a white middle-class European woman living in a First World capitalist country is radically different from her Two-Thirds World counterpart). Similarly, all attempts to generalize female experience utilising terms such as person-centred relationality, commonality and mutuality, non-dualism and ecological or intuitive and non-coercive seem destined to promote another fallacy, i.e. that there is such a thing as universal woman's experience. Jacquelyn Grant, an African-American theologian, makes this criticism. What in fact is taken as universal and normal is the experience of white European American women.[25] Thus, a universalised notion of women's experience unwittingly promotes racism. The postmodernist feminists N. Fraser and L. Nicholson also radically object to any suggestion that there is anything pertaining to a notion of essential woman's experience. Rather, there is only the social constructedness of gender discourses and expectations relative to women of different cultures and historical periods.[26]

Pamela Young is on safer ground when she distinguishes five aspects of woman's experience, which she claims differ noticeably from that of men.

1. Women's bodily existence is more closely related to the cycles of nature.
2. Women's experience of culture and society is one where they are taught to be subordinate to men and to appeal to them sexually.
3. Women are now much more conscious of structures of oppression and gender related issues that restrict their aspirations, dehumanise and demonise them as objects of male domination.

---

[24] Fiorenza seeks to demonstrate how the sex/gender system operates on four interactive levels, the socio-political level, the ethical-symbolic level, the biological-natural level and the linguistic-grammatical level. Ibid., 35–43. In so doing, she endeavours to reinforce Irigaray's contention that the sex/gender system has dominated the way women perceive their relationships to the world and other persons.

[25] J. Grant, *White Woman's Christ, Black Women's Jesus*.

[26] N. Fraser and L. Nicolson, 'Social Critisism Without Philosophy'.

4. Women now experience history as no longer just *his* story but that which has recovered the lost memory of *her* story.
5. Women have different individual experiences that can be harnessed as the liberating praxis of change.[27]

The problem with such a classification is that, with the exception of the first and the last characteristics (both of which may be open to dispute), so-called woman's experience is not based on anything intrinsic to female nature as such. Rather, it is based on a historical and cultural experience of gender discrimination and oppression. There are now an increasing number of feminist theologians, like Fiorenza, who reject all purely anthropological classifications of nature, female or otherwise, in favour of the postmodern analysis of human nature as largely a socio-political cultural construct. Hence, feminist theology shares with liberation theology the same fundamental concern, the liberation of one group of people from the false ideologies and structures of oppression imposed upon them by another party (the 'kyriarchal relations of domination' as Fiorenza puts it).[28]

Feminist Christology and the Historical Jesus

In light of feminist theology's concentration on liberation from structures and systems of domination, it is not surprising that feminist Christology initially focused its concern on the liberating praxis of the historical Jesus. Here, feminist Christology shares with almost all forms of modern Christology the exegetical desire to retrieve the historical Jesus as the basis of christological reflection.[29] Elizabeth Johnson provides an informative summary of some of the main elements of such a Christology. We will incorporate into her analysis hermeneutical issues that actually often challenge some of her conclusions.

Jesus' proclamation of the kingdom

In Jesus' proclamation of the kingdom we find a vision of the just and compassionate reign of God that is inclusive of all people. The kingdom reverses the hierarchies of the normal social order. Entry into the kingdom is not based on moral righteousness or social and religious privilege. Quite the reverse: first

---

[27] P.D. Young, *Feminist Theology/Christian Theology: In Search of Method*, 53–6.

[28] Fiorenza, *Jesus: Miriam's Child*, 14.

[29] Like Liberation Christology, the subversive memory of the historical Jesus is retrieved, which, it is claimed, contains an explicit critique of all systems of oppression, particularly patriarchy.

into the kingdom are the sinners, the lowly, the marginalised and the poor. In Luke's Gospel in particular it is women and the poor, representing the marginalised, who are given pride of place in the kingdom.[30]

Addressing God as Abba

It is Johnson's contentious conviction that Jesus' designation of God as *Abba* was also a liberation from the domination of patriarchy. This form of address emphasised intimacy and mutuality of relationship. There is an important link between addressing God as *Abba* and the rejection of structures of dominating leadership referred to in Matthew 23:9–12.

Despite the intimacy of the term, *Abba* still represented God in essentially male terms, albeit as a loving heavenly Father rather than an oppressive and dominant one. The metaphors of Fatherhood and Sonship, it is asserted, effectively exclude the feminine from being able to represent God. This either calls for a revision of these traditional terms of address to include Motherhood and sisterhood, or points to the limitations of the parental model as a way of conceiving of the relationship between the divine and ourselves. All too often, the parental model is interpreted in terms of a static, imperialistic and wholly other God who keeps human beings in a state of cowering dependence, rather than encouraging their growth into responsibility and freedom.

Sally McFague looks toward other models such as God as lover or companion, friend and liberator.[31] Ruether is also critical of the traditional parental imagery for God as being both dualist and hierarchical. She believes that it reinforces patriarchy rather than undermines it and engenders a form of spiritual infantilism in our relationship to the divine: 'Perhaps the parental language for transcendence and immanence itself should be relativised by some metaphor other than parent or child to better state this relationship between God transcendent and God manifest in creation and history.'[32] Fiorenza argues that the male metaphors used to describe Godself are mere

---

[30] Ruether has consequently emphasised how Jesus' message of the kingdom contains an explicit rejection of all hierarchical structures of domination, especially patriarchy.

[31] McFague has much in common with the process model of God; see, *Models of God.*

[32] Ruether, *Sexism and God Talk*; quoted in Loades, *Feminist Theology*, 147. In her more recent work, Ruether looks to Tillich's theology of immanence that reconceived God as the Ground of Being. Tillich advocated that such a designation for the being of God is best symbolised in female terms, that is, the mother quality of giving birth and reciprocity. Ruether deploys such terms as, 'primal matrix', or 'God/ess' (she believes this form of address helps us avoid a dualist and hierarchical concept of God). See R. Radford Ruether, *Can Christology be Liberated from Patriarchy in Reconstructing the Christ Symbol?*, 7–30. R.N. Brock argues for a more extreme renunciation of the parent–child model on the basis of her own work among the abused. See 'Losing

socio-cultural linguistic constructs that reflect the hegemony of the androcentric Western tradition. Feminist theologians must accordingly replace
these with other more versatile images and symbols that allow the divine
reality to reflect the legitimacy of woman's experience.[33]

Jesus' relationships with women

Jesus' relationships with women and his behaviour towards them is another
source of feminist critique of androcentrism. Jesus afforded women respect
and dignity. This also undermined the patriarchal model of human relationships. Jesus gathered together an egalitarian community of men and women
who re-enacted the eschatological reality of the kingdom in their communal
lifestyle and table fellowship: 'They rejected the current patriarchal social
structures and eschewed external religious and familial obligations and formed
a new sort of extended family based upon the belief that they were brothers
and sisters, "a discipleship of equals".'[34]

The preferential position of woman in the Gospels

If liberation Christology has rediscovered the significance of Jesus' preferential
option for the poor, then feminist Christology has also isolated a certain
preferential position of women contained in the Gospels. For instance, the
women do not desert Jesus but are united with him in his crucifixion and death.
Similarly, all the Gospels record that it was the women who were the first
witnesses of the resurrection and the first to receive the apostolic commission
to go and tell others.

Elizabeth Green charts the course whereby the words remain but the
women disappear through the process of redaction by the Gospel writers.
According to Mark, the women remained silent and told no one what they
had seen and heard, 'they said nothing to anyone for they were afraid' (Mk.
16:9). In Luke, the women did speak on their own initiative, but it is classified
as mere gossip: 'these words seemed to them an idle tale, and they did not
believe them' (Lk. 24:11). Matthew, however, omits to inform us whether or
not the women spoke about Jesus' resurrection appearance. John is the one
Gospel that does afford an influential position to women, but even John carefully circumscribes the testimony of Mary Magdalene with that of Peter and
the beloved disciple. In terms of the early church's record of the resurrection

---

[32] (*continued*) your Innocence but not your Hope' in M. Stevens (ed.), *Reconstructing
the Christ Symbol: Essays in Feminist Christology*, 38.

[33] Fiorenza, *Jesus*, 162.

[34] Hopkins, *Feminist Christology*, 34; building on the work of Fiorenza.

appearances, 1 Corinthians 15:5–8 is an important benchmark in New Testament scholarship, but no women are mentioned:

> While it is clear from the various Gospel accounts that the news of the resurrection was entrusted to the women disciples (and that the risen Lord appeared to them), the early writers all tend to minimize the authority of the women's words and thus perhaps disqualify any female claim to be numbered amongst the apostles. This means that while the words remain, the women disappear from the nascent church.[35]

The cross of Christ

The cross of Christ is also reclaimed as a potential critique of all forms of patriarchy and androcentric religion. Here Jesus' maleness is important because it is a male who exhibits the vulnerability and brokenness of self-sacrificial love. This would have been nothing new if the Messiah had been Jesa Christa (i.e. female). Similarly, it is a male saviour who enters into the godforsakenness of suffering and abuse, which is a reality women have been well acquainted with throughout the history of patriarchal domination.[36]

There has, however, been a strident feminist reaction to all such attempts to reconceive the cross as a deconstruction of patriarchy. Atonement theology, with its central notion of the vicarious suffering of an innocent victim and an angry father who requires recompense, is denounced as a doctrine that reinforces rather than ameliorates patriarchy and the abuse of women:

> Christianity is an abusive theology that glorifies suffering. Is it any wonder that there is so much abuse in modern society when the predominant image or theology of the culture is of 'divine child abuse' – God the father, demanding and carrying out the suffering and death of his own son … This bloodthirsty God is the God of the patriarchy who at the moment controls the whole Judeo-Christian tradition.[37]

---

[35] E. Green, 'Women's Words: Sexual Difference and Biblical Hermeneutics', *Feminist Theology* 4 (1993), 64–78.

[36] In a passage that owes much to Moltmann's theology of the crucified God, Hopkins expresses this insight in moving terms: 'This God is wholly involved in human life and shares the consequences of human creativity and perversity. This God has abdicated power and chosen loving identification with the poor, the sick, the outcasts and the sinners. This God did not rise up in sublime justice and take Jesus down from the cross or strike his oppressors with thunderbolts from heaven. But this God felt the pain of Jesus and the grief of forsakenness.' See, *Feminist Christology*, 62.

[37] J.C. Brown, R. Parker and C.R. Bohn, *Christianity, Patriarchy and Abuse: A Feminist Critique*, 26; quoted in Fiorenza, *Jesus*, 99.

One would have to say that by any account this is an extreme over-literal rendition of atonement theology. It does not do justice to either the *Christus Victor* tradition or the Anselmic account of the meaning of Jesus' death, although such a criticism could apply to the Reformed theology of penal substitution. Similarly, there is a particular contextual issue at stake here that is by no means universally accepted by feminist theologians. The claim, from those working mostly in the West amongst the abused, that the religious symbol of the suffering, obedient and abused Christ inexorably reinforces similar notions of vicarious suffering and obedience to authority figures among abuse victims is challenged by those working in other contexts. For instance, Chung Hyun Kyung, a Korean feminist theologian, claims that the figure of the suffering servant of God intrinsically connects with the everyday experience of Asian women: '[They] are discovering with much passion and compassion that Jesus takes sides with the silenced Asian women in his solidarity with all oppressed people. This Jesus is Asian women's new lover, comrade and suffering servant.'[38]

It must be conceded that such a remark comes from a more compliant culture that is much more at home with hierarchy and submission in the sphere of both politics and gender. It is for this reason that Western theologians like Fiorenza and Regula Strobel[39] are extremely uneasy with such sentiments because, in their view, it reinforces rather than deconstructs the dominant system of kyriarchy:

> By ritualising the suffering and death of Jesus and by calling the powerless in society and church to imitate Jesus' perfect obedience and self-sacrifice, Christian ministry and theology do not interrupt but continue to foster the circle of violence engendered by kyriarchical social and ecclesial structures, as well as by cultural and political discourses.[40]

There have also been attempts to reconstruct the theology of the cross in a manner that is consonant with women's experience and utilises feminist symbols. For example, Mary Grey argues that it is possible to theologise about the cross of Christ utilising concepts like 'at-one-ment' and 'redemptive mutuality' that avoids the destructive fixation with death and violence.[41]

This excursus into the divergent perspectives within feminist theology regarding the significance and meaning of Jesus' death reflects the

---

[38] H.K. Kyung, *Struggle to Be the Sun Again: Introducing Asian Women's Theology*, 56.
[39] R. Strobel, 'Feministische Kritik an traditionellen Kreuzestheologien'; see Fiorenza, *Jesus*, 217.
[40] Fiorenza, *Jesus*, 106.
[41] M.C. Grey, *Redeeming the Dream: Feminism, Redemption and Christian Tradition*. See also Moltmann-Wendel, *Fiorenza*, 216.

hermeneutical pluralism of contextualised theology. For some, mainly in the Two-Thirds World, the cross of Christ remains an invocation of women's experience of suffering and abuse. For others, mainly in the West, it must be repudiated because it sanctions and legitimises abuse and violence. Other feminists want to reconstruct the theology of the cross according to the variety of biblical frames of reference, or to other feminist symbols and forms of discourse.

Wisdom Christology

Of key significance for many feminist theologians is the recovery of the *Sophia* (Wisdom) Christology of both John and Paul. In the Old Testament *Sophia* is the female personification of God who creates and redeems, establishes justice, protects the poor, gives life and expresses the hidden wisdom of God. In John's Gospel the long discourses of Jesus are modelled on the wisdom literature of the Old Testament and the Pauline corpus utilises the wisdom tradition to develop the theology of the cosmic Christ. Moltmann concedes that *Logos* Christology was originally wisdom Christology, and, as we shall see in due course, combines this with a Spirit Christology, which he hopes addresses some of the feminist concerns.

Ruether, on the other hand, uses this insight to mount a devastating attack on the androcentric *Logos* Christology of the early church. She is mindful of the importance of the *Logos* concept in preventing the split between creation and redemption that gnosticism encouraged. So the Word active in creation is also the Word who became incarnate in the person of Jesus. Nevertheless, Ruether's main criticism is that the Stoic and Neoplatonic background to the concept of the *Logos*, which understood the *Logos* as the rational soul of the universe, possessed an inevitable androcentric bias. In a patriarchal society, rationality and sovereignty are characteristics attributed to the divine and reflected in the male of the species only. This meant that when the *Logos* concept was associated with the metaphor Son of God, then both God and the *imago Dei* (the image of God in humanity) were conceived in largely andro- centric fashion.[42]

Fiorenza has also subjected orthodox Chalcedonian Christology to a similar socio-political critique. She claims that from the Council of Nicea (AD 325) through Ephesus (AD 431) to Chalcedon (AD 451) we observe doctrinal formulation under the imperial control of the Emperor:

---

[42] R. Radford Ruether leveled the same basic criticism at the imperial Christology of Eusebius of Ceasarea. See, *To Change the World: Christology and Cultural Criticism*, 48–9.

While bitter struggles over meaning are inscribed in the writings of the Christian Testament, these writings bespeak internecine "sectarian" struggles more than they assert ruling power. The christological dogmas of the fourth and fifth centuries, to the contrary, are generally recognised as articulated under Roman imperial pressures. They exercise normalising functions by which the increasingly imperialised church establishes its rule, sanctions its violence, and sacralizes its power. This shift in theological process and politics of meaning is clearly inscribed in the Chalcedonian council document.[43]

Fiorenza makes much of the fact that the Greek term *oikonomia* – one of the words used to refer to the incarnation in the council document of Chalcedon – is an amalgam of *oikos* (house/household) and *nomos* (law/order/management). Consequently, Fiorenza claims that the mystery of the incarnation is derived from kyriarchal systems of household management and control. She notes that the Chalcedonian statement attributes the divinity of Jesus to the begetting of the Father and his humanity to the passivity of the Virgin Mary, thereby reinforcing gender discrimination and domination.

W e have already taken note of the political processes that surrounded and to a certain extent controlled the Chalcedonian settlement, and, indeed, the transfer of imperial titles originally attributed to the Emperor to Christ, which remodelled the rule of Christ according to the image of the Emperor. However, a number of comments can and should be made at this juncture in response to Fiorenza's analysis. First, she shows little sympathy with the history of doctrinal dispute and schism which preceded Chalcedon and required some kind of theological and ecclesial agreement. Secondly, Fiorenza seems unaware of developments in linguistic philosophy which demonstrate that the meaning of a word changes with use. Terms that are transferred from their original context to another do not necessarily carry the same linguistic freight because the meaning of a word is changed by the new context the term occupies. Finally, it is surprising that Fiorenza ignores the title *theotokos* (mother of God), which was used to refer to the Virgin Mary, because this honorific title introduces feminine characteristics into the very being and divinity of God. Indeed, both Irigaray and Leonardo Boff have explored this tradition and reinstated Mary as co-redeemer with her son Jesus.[44]

In conclusion, if *Logos* Christology was originally wisdom Christology, then the retrieval of the *Sophia*/Wisdom tradition undermines its androcentric bias. It serves as an important foil to gender discrimination determining our relationship to the divine.

---

[43] Fiorenza, *Jesus*, 21.

[44] Boff, see notes 28 and 30, pages 14 and 15 in E. Green's article 'Musing on maleness: The Maleness of Jesus Revisited', *Feminist Theology* 20 (1999), 10–27.

Jesus the liberator

All these factors combine to help women rediscover Jesus as the liberator from oppression and abuse. Elisabeth Johnson, Jacquelyn Grant and Rita Nakashima Brock underline the connection here between a liberationist and a feminist approach to Christology.[45]

> The actual experience and observable impact of oppression is where we begin. Victims are not to be liberated from oppression because the oppressed are good. Women will shatter patriarchy because misogyny in all its aspects – rape, the denial of power over our bodies, institutionalised poverty, and systematic limitation of access to the decision-making structures of society – harm us.[46]

Elisabeth Amoah and Mercy Amba Oduyoye point to the rediscovery of Jesus the liberator in the experiences of African women.[47] Chung Hyun Kyung makes the same point in relation to the contemporary experience of Asian women:

> The reason why Jesus as liberator is the most prominent new image among Asian women is a consequence of their historical situation. The liberation from colonialism, neo-colonialism, poverty, and military dictatorship, as well as from the overarching patriarchy, has been the major aspiration of twentieth-century Asian women.[48]

Ruether is insistent that what is important about the particularity of the man Jesus is not the biological fact of his maleness, but the iconoclastic, prophetic and liberating praxis of his ministry toward the marginalised and oppressed:

> Jesus as the Christ, the representative of liberated humanity and the liberating Word of God, manifests the kenosis of patriarchy, the announcement of the new humanity through a lifestyle that discards hierarchical caste privilege and speaks on behalf of the lowly.[49]

---

[45] See M. Stevens, *Reconstructing The Christ Symbol: Essays in Feminist Christology*.

[46] R.N. Brock, 'The Feminist Redemption of Christ' in J.L. Weidman (ed.), *Christian Feminism – Visions of a New Humanity*, 63.

[47] E. Amoah & M.A. Oduyoye, 'The Christ for African Women', in V. Fabella & M.A. Oduyoye, (eds), *With Passion and Compassion: Third World Women Doing Theology: Reflections from the Women's Commission of the Ecumenical Association of Third World Theologians*, 43–6.

[48] Kyung, *Struggle*, 62.

[49] Ruether, *Sexism*, 137. Hampson misrepresents Ruether when she claims that this is simply a 'message Christology' which either ignores or side-steps the significance of Jesus' personhood; cf. *Theology and Feminism*. For Ruether both the person and the message are integral to the new humanity Jesus represents. Her claim that the

The Representative Function of Christ's Humanity

'Can a male saviour redeem and save women'? This was the fundamental question Ruether articulated in response to the whole christological tradition. By and large there have been two ways in which feminist theologians have endeavoured to circumvent this apparent conundrum.

First, many feminists have taken due note of the fact that there have been a number of alternatives to patriarchal Christology within the Christian tradition which stress the representative function of Christ's humanity as that which unifies male and female. Both Ruether and Elisabeth Moltmann-Wendal have stressed the importance of these androgynous Christologies as a corrective to the androcentric *Logos* Christology of Chalcedon.[50] Most of these christologies, with the exception of pietism, have been either condemned as heretical or suppressed by the church. They are all based on the Pauline affirmation that 'in Christ ... there is neither ... male nor female' (Gal. 3:28) and so the way is open to view Christ's humanity as that which includes both female and male roles, and characteristics. The limitation of such androgynous Christologies is that they do not alter the ontological status of the divinity of Christ, which remains tied to patriarchal imagery. Christ is still in being and essence the only begotten *Son* of the Father.

Mindful of this crucial issue, Daly has suggested that traditional incarnational Christology is actually a form of 'christolatry':

> Christian idolatry concerning the person of Jesus is not likely to be overcome except through the revolution that is going on in woman's consciousness. It will ... become increasingly evident that exclusively masculine symbols for the ideal of "incarnation" or for the ideal of the human search for fulfilment will not do.[51]

In response to this accusation, some feminists have sought to relativise the maleness of Jesus as that which is not definitive of the new humanity he represents. Jesus is depicted as the new person or 'God's re-presentation of the humanity of God'[52] and not necessarily as the new Adam. Jesus is distinctive not because of his sex or race, but because he both expresses and represents inclusive, redeemed humanity.

---

[49] *(continued)* maleness of Jesus is unimportant in comparison to the new humanity he establishes and represents reflects another approach to the concern to find a Christology that is compatible with feminism.

[50] Ruether, *To Change the World*, 49. See also E. Green, *More Musings on Maleness: The Maleness of Jesus Revisited.*

[51] Daly, *Beyond God*, 71.

[52] Russell, *Human Liberation*, 136.

Fiorenza used to continually emphasise the 'discipleship of equals', which the Jesus movement enshrined.[53] Here is a community of people where gender discrimination no longer operates. Such egalitarian social relationships, which were integral to Jesus' earthly pilgrimage, are part of the liberty of the sons and daughters of God, which the world is still waiting in longing and anticipation to see. In her most recent writing, however, Fiorenza has revised her previous viewpoint. The problem with generic terms, such as Ruether's 'new humanity', and the reason why such androgynous Christologies have been largely rejected by feminist theologians, is they do not 'challenge the Western cultural sex/gender system and its androcentric language, according to which the male Man is the paradigm of being human, whereas woman is either his inferior or complementary other'.[54] In other words, what pertains on the ontological level in terms of Jesus' divinity and the link with patriarchal imagery exists also on the socio-cultural level with regard to his humanity. The same criticisms can be levelled at the attempt to relativise the maleness of Jesus by concentrating on the liberating praxis of his ministry among the poor and marginalised. Inadvertently what can actually take place is the valorisation of Jesus as the perfect expression of the new humanity, the great hero to which women can continue to relate in feminine expressions of love, personal devotion and self-sacrifice.

In opposition to this tendency to relativise the maleness of Jesus, Hopkins has argued that both Jesus' race and his gender constitute the distinct, historical particularity of the man, Jesus of Nazareth, and this is precisely what the traditional Christology of Chalcedon seeks to protect.

> The Church Fathers in spite of their grounding in neo-Platonic philosophy, realised that in order to affirm the reality of the incarnation of God in the flesh, it was necessary to stress the sex of Jesus. The humanity of God in Christ took a personal form through the human male Jesus of Nazareth.[55]

Ruether, in particular, has recognised the anti-Semetic tendencies that accompany any attempt to dislocate Jesus from his antecedents in Judaism. It seems strange and inconsistent when the same logic is not applied to the issue of gender. Is it the case then, as both Hampson and Daly conclude, that the christological dogma of Chalcedon, which declares that Jesus was very *Deus* and very *Homo*, is both idolatrous and sexist? This apparent conundrum has led

---

[53] Cf. Fiorenza, *Memory*.

[54] Fiorenza, *Jesus*, 47.

[55] Hopkins, *Feminist Christology*, 91–2. Karl Barth made substantially the same point in regard to Jesus' integral relationship with the nation of Israel. Cf. Barth, *Church Dogmatics*, 4/1, 166.

to a form of feminist Christology that seeks to explore a different approach to the incarnation.

Relational Christologies: Truly God and Truly Female

There is, as yet, no universally agreed strand that unites feminist Christologies. In the light of our critical investigation of the main paradigms of modern Christology, perhaps this is too much to expect. What we do have, however, is a number of explorative possibilities that seek to open up traditional Christology to a feminist perspective. Relational Christologies, for example, try to broaden the concept of the incarnation. Thus, the coming of God into our midst is no longer exclusively tied to an individual male:

> This feminist christological discourse uses key concepts such as redemptive connectedness, power–in–relation, dynamic mutuality, erotic creativity, the language of lovers, mutual interdependence, passionate creativity, inclusive wholeness, healing energy of existence, and the ontological priority of relationality. These terms and many more have become the coinage of the christological discourse of relationality.[56]

Carter Heyward demonstrates how many feminists have struggled with this issue. It is her contention that the feminist concentration upon the historical Jesus has not been helpful because it has tended to reinforce the maleness of Jesus and has not been able to get beyond the duality of divinity and humanity that bedevilled traditional Christology. Heyward argues that the modern equivalent to this dichotomy is the dualism of the Jesus of history versus the Christ of faith. Thus, 'The christological task of Christian feminism is to move the foundations of Christology from the ontology of dualistic opposition toward the ethics of justice making. This happens only in a praxis of relational particularity and co-operation.'[57]

   In a perceptive analysis, Julie Hopkins argues that Heyward has not really rejected the Chalcedonian formula, although she has rejected it as the test of orthodoxy. In so doing she has also 'begun to explore what incarnation as an experience of God rather than as a doctrine about the unicity of Christ might mean'.[58] To understand the incarnation in terms of the experience of God it encapsulates is to move beyond the uniqueness of Jesus as the incarnate *Logos*, the *Kyrios*, Son of God or the New Adam and to affirm the uniqueness of the

---

[56] Fiorenza, *Jesus*, 50.
[57] C. Heyward, *Speaking of Christ: A Lesbian Feminist Voice*, 21.
[58] Hopkins, *Feminist Christology*, 87.

Christic experience. Heyward describes this Christic experience in terms of a passionate, liberating, Christian humanism.[59]

While applauding the move away from the fixation on Jesus the 'heroic individual', Fiorenza is nevertheless critical of Heyward. Fiorenza believes Heyward does not critically reflect on the inherent tension between all existentialist Christologies, which are based on the language of relationality and the attempt to also embrace a liberationist perspective. Fiorenza comments: 'Without question we are all born into relationships and connections; these relations, however, are power structures that not only situate the self but also shape and define it'.[60]

Patricia Wilson-Kastner seeks to understand Christ not in terms of his particularity but as 'the agent of wholeness and reconciler of fragmentation in the world'.[61] She subordinates the particular human individual, Jesus of Nazareth, to the Christ who overcomes all dualisms and forces of alienation and domination in the world. Her Christ is a feminist version of the cosmic Christ who reconciles and unites all things through the healing and redemptive agency of his death and resurrection. Once again, Hampson claims that this is really sidestepping the main issue:

> The fact that [Wilson-Kastner] is basically thinking in terms of the resurrected, cosmic Christ again tends to minimize any distinction which there might be between a woman and Christ in regard to sex. Thus the question which confronts Christian feminists – how should they deal with the fact that the basic symbol of their religion is that of a male Christ – does not really impress her.[62]

By relativising the particularity of Jesus of Nazareth, Wilson-Kastner also relativises the particularity of women's experience, be it white, black, Asian or European. Her Christology becomes another version of that universalising tendency that obliterates the distinctive individuality of particular forms of human experience.

Rita Nakashima Brock, an Asian Puerto Rican feminist, builds her Christology from the real experiences of both First and Two-Thirds World women. She argues for a Christology of inter-connectedness and relation but utilises the metaphor of 'broken-heartedness'.[63] The source of such inter-relatedness is not an undifferentiated vision of wholeness, but the acknowledgement of the power of the erotic. Brock is indebted to Andre Lorde.[64] He describes the

---

[59] Heyward, *Speaking of Christ*, 21.

[60] Fiorenza, *Jesus*, 51.

[61] P. Wilson-Kastner, *Faith, Feminism and the Christ*.

[62] Hampson, *Theology and Feminism*, 60.

[63] R.N. Brock, *Journeys by Heart: A Christology of Erotic Power*.

[64] A. Lorde, 'Uses of the Erotic: the Erotic as Power', in *Sister Outsider*, 53–9.

erotic as the celebration of intimacy and union with others, the power that creates, sustains and enlarges relationships; it protests against all forms of oppression and domination because it is the principle and power of inter-connectedness. Thus, the erotic is clearly not being confined to the sexual dimensions of life and shunned as the very opposite of the spiritual.[65]

Armed with this new natural theology of the erotic, Brock turns her attention to Christology:

> If Christology is to be reclaimed in feminist visions, the image of an exclusive divine presence in a 'perfect' man called Jesus who came to be called the Christ is disallowed. The doctrine that only a perfect male form can incarnate God fully and be salvific makes our individual lives in female bodies a prison against God and denies our actual, sensual, changing selves as the locus of divine activity.[66]

While seeking to construct a Christology of relation and connectedness, Brock is also critical of Wilson-Kastner's attempt to relativise the particularity of Jesus in favour of her vision of cosmic wholeness. For Brock, we only experience ourselves as individual persons, not as abstract principles or in terms of general religious symbols and metaphors. It is out of our particular experience, what-ever it might be, that interconnectedness develops. Consequently, she rejects Wilson-Kastner's feminist version of the cosmic Christ and Ruether's prefer-ence for the iconoclastic, liberator Christ in favour of what she refers to as 'Christa/Community': 'Christ is … Christa/Community. Jesus participates centrally in this Christa/Community, but he neither brings erotic power into being nor controls it. Christa/Community is described in the images of events in which erotic power is made manifest.'[67]

Brock seems to be suggesting that we view the incarnation not solely in terms of a single divine act or as the emergence of a divine/human person, but as a continual divine event. The power and presence of divine love and justice making cannot be limited to individuals. Rather, it takes communal shape and form. Is this a Christology of the real presence of Christ in the community of believers? Or has the real person of Jesus been abandoned in favour of a new Christ symbol understood in terms of the interconnectedness, mutuality and vulnerability of our own sacred humanity?

In Britain, Mary Grey has sought to construct a relational Christology utilising images and metaphors similar to those used by Brock. Concepts such as 'brokenness', 'woundedness', 'creative love' and 'wholeness' enable Grey to discern in the messianic Christian community a deeper reality of mutuality and

---

[65] Brock, 'Feminist Redemption', 64.
[66] Ibid., 68.
[67] Brock, *Journeys*.

interconnectedness, which is itself redemptive and moves beyond the conflict of power relations. Fiorenza remains unconvinced by this new 'canonical' position of christological reconstruction based on the interpersonal realities of shared community and redemptive mutuality. Such christologies do not deconstruct the socio-political sex/gender schema and so they reinscribe within their own frames of reference the traditional feminine roles of women as in personal relationship with Jesus and one another. The norm is still the dominant male and 'hegemonic heterosexual love relationships'.[68]

Assessment

In recent decades, feminist theologians have struggled to reconstruct traditional Christology in a way that is consonant with their own experience and embraces the perceptions, values, aspirations and embodiedness of what it means to be a female in today's world. Most feminist Christology shares with modern Christology in general, a preference for a Christology from below. There has been a fierce and fervent attempt to recover the historical Jesus, particularly in the social context of his relationships with men and women, as the one who deconstructed all oppressive hierarchies of race, status and gender. Jesus is interpreted as the person who represents and incarnates the iconoclastic, prophetic praxis of liberation. He has been rediscovered as the liberator of the oppressed, the friend and companion of the abused and marginalised, the lover and vulnerable mystic who breaks apart all dualisms and binary opposites. The inevitable stumbling block that feminist Christology of this genre encounters, however, is Jesus the man, God incarnate in a male persona:

> The serious problem for many contemporary Christians which resides in the seemingly indisputable historical 'fact' that Jesus of Nazareth, who is worshipped as Christ and Lord is/was a real male person. Further, this male Christ, symbolised religiously, has been used to subordinate, to dehumanize, and to render women invisible and voiceless.[69]

There can be and will be a number of reactions to this incontrovertible reality. One is the conservative response that says this is just the way things are. The parental imagery of Father and Son is no mere metaphor of convenience. It is ontologically true. As such, it expresses the hierarchy of headship and voluntary

---

[68] Fiorenza, *Jesus*, 55.
[69] E. McLaughlin, 'Feminist Christologies: Re-dressing the Tradition', in Stevens (ed.), *Reconstructing*, 130.

subordination that distinguishes the trinitarian relationships and is reflected in the natural order by the gender divisions of male and female. Graham Leonard, the former Anglican bishop of London, admirably expresses this position:

> The Scriptures speak of God as Father, that Christ was incarnate as a male, that he choose men to be his apostles … not because of social conditioning, but because in the order of creation headship and authority is symbolically and fundamentally associated with maleness. For the same reason the highest vocation of any created being was given to a woman, Mary, as representative of mankind in our response to God because symbolically and fundamentally, the response of sacrificial giving is associated with femaleness.[70]

There is also the liberal reaction that tends to espouse a representative Christology. Here Jesus' humanity is understood in the generic sense as that which transcends gender and is therefore inclusive of both male and female.

Such laudable manoeuvres, however, tend to dilute rather than solve the problem, for several reasons. First, there is the indisputable fact that this so-called generic humanity has been reconstructed in the cultural symbols of maleness, within a largely androcentric Christian tradition.[71] Secondly, and more importantly, many feminists do not want to be subsumed within this undifferentiated, generic humanity. Rather, they want a Jesus who relates specifically and salvifically to what it means to be a woman:

> If there is to be found or constructed a feminist Christology which includes woman as well as man in the icon of God, the male hegemony must be deconstructed such that the image of God made Flesh is seen and experienced as female as well as male.[72]

Thirdly, some feminists, such as Hampson, seem to be unaware that the apparently laudable concern for equality of the sexes still operates within the terms of Enlightenment epistemology. At the centre of this concern are the rights and privileges of the so-called autonomous, human subject. Many advocates of postmodernity now regard this notion of self-determination as a spurious invention of modernity. Nor does it satisfy those feminists who are more

---

[70] Quoted in Hampson, *Theology and Feminism*, 66.

[71] This is evidenced in the anger and outrage what greeted Edwina Sandy's sculpture of the 'Christa', exhibited in the cathedral of St John the Divine, New York (1984) and other such depictions of a female crucified Christ, for instance, that of Almuth Lutkenhaus-Lackey, also created for the International Year of the Woman and put on display in a parish in Toronto during Holy Week in 1979. A further example of such iconoclastic art was the sculpture by James M. Murphy of the crucified Christa put on display in the Chapel of Union Theological Seminary in New York 1984.

[72] McLaughlin, 'Feminist Christologies', 121.

concerned with developing a Christology that takes seriously the 'discovery of woman-self, woman voice and woman in relation as woman made in God's image'.[73]

What are we to make of Fiorenza's attempt to redefine the scope of feminist Christology in terms of the sex/gender dichotomy she identifies as kyriarchy? It is the critical exposure of this all-pervasive socio-political cultural phenomenon that allows her to perceive feminist criticism as a kind of agent provocateur, destabilising the so-called free enquiry of the academy and exposing the patriarchy of the church in the name of liberation. But, what kind of liberation does Fiorenza envision? In line with her general theory that all relationships of whatever kind are power relations, Fiorenza assesses christological discourses in terms of their ability to 'make possible a critical mode of thought, radical democratic politics, and committed solidarity in the struggles for economic justice and global well-being'.[74]

In every respect, therefore, Fiorenza aligns herself with liberation Christology and commits the same fallacy: her concept of liberation remains on the level of mere socio-political theory devoid of any genuine theological content. This is because she has removed her notion of liberation from any contaminating contact with a male Jesus understood as a heroic liberator. In the place of a possible christological concept of salvation, Fiorenza substitutes the empty rhetoric of Marxism and liberal democracy. Liberation becomes synonymous with emancipation when manifestly it is not. It is for this reason that Fiorenza's attempts to construct a theology of the cross, which does not reinforce abusive patriarchy and retrieve the *Sophia*/Wisdom tradition, remain curiously detached from her continual attempt to deconstruct the sex–gender dualism of kyriarchy.

A candid assessment of both Marxism and liberal democracy must accept that the abolition of hierarchy and its replacement by egalitarianism does not guarantee justice for all, nor does it necessarily enhance individual freedom. Rather, hierarchies of another kind, which are mainly economic, come into play, creating widespread injustice and prima facie divisions between the 'haves' and the 'have nots'. We should thus heed the warning of Thomas Mann: 'the reconciliation of liberty and equality is never finally completed but remains a humanitarian task to be solved often in the context of competing ideologies'.[75] If the concept of emancipation is to mean anything in a theological sense it must be reinserted within a biblical communitarian narrative of covenantal social and political ethics, otherwise it languishes among the tawdry slogans of socio-political discourse. Worse still, it is reduced to utilitarian and

---

[73] Ibid., 125.
[74] Fiorenza, *Jesus*, 8.
[75] Quoted in Bauman, *Postmodernity*, 206.

expressive individualism. The same criticism could be directed towards the other feminist theologians who casually allow the concept of liberation to become detached from its biblical roots and reduce Christology to the rhetoric of social justice.

In light of these considerations, there may be more to be gained from a high Christology, or a Christology from above, which interprets the incarnation in terms of the enfleshing of the *sophia*/wisdom of God. The woman-ness of God actually takes historical shape in the person of Jesus of Nazareth. Jesus in his embodied existence expresses the intimate, seeking, embracing, longing, passionate consummating lure of the divine Wisdom of God. As Elisabeth Johnson suggests, such a Christology has the potential not only to relativise androcentric alternatives, but also to present a Jesus who is both male and female:

> The fluidity of gender symbolism in Jesus–Sophia breaks the stranglehold of androcentric thinking which fixates on the maleness of Jesus, the male metaphors of *Logos* and Son. This leads to the situation where gender is decentered, where it is not constitutive for the Christian doctrine of incarnation or for speech about Christ.[76]

Such an ability to cross gender boundaries is not unknown in the Christian tradition. Clement of Alexandria, for instance, could use female imagery to speak of both the Father and Jesus the divine *Logos*. Here we discover those 'care banishing breasts', offering to us 'the milk of love given by the Word who is father and mother, teacher and nurse'.[77] Similarly, Julian of Norwich celebrates and extols a Jesus who is our Mother and friend:

> We see that Jesus is the true Mother of our nature, for he made us. He is our Mother, too, by grace, because he took our created nature upon himself. All the lovely deeds and tender services that beloved motherhood implies are appropriate to the Second Person.[78]

Teresa Berger cites other examples where gender distinctions were much more fluid than Fiorenza's notion of kyriarchy would allow. Berger quotes the example of a woman crucified in Lugdunum in Gaul (AD 177) who was perceived by the witnesses as an image of the crucified Christ:

> Blandina was hung on a post and exposed as food for the wild beasts let loose in the arena. She looked as if she was hanging in the form of a cross, and through her ardent

---

[76] Johnson, 'Wisdom was made flesh and pitched her tent among us', in Stevens (ed.), *Reconstructing*, 108.

[77] Quoted in McLaughlin, 'Feminist Christologies', 133.

[78] Julian of Norwich, *Revelations of Divine Love*, 168.

prayers she stimulated great enthusiasm in those undergoing their ordeal, who in their agony saw with their outward eyes in the person of their sister the One who was crucified for them.[79]

Berger also refers to Lukardis of Oberweimar (c.1274–1309), a medieval nun who, like St Francis, received the stigmata and so carried the marks of the crucified Christ. Berger summarises the female images of Christ that are found in much medieval devotional literature:

> First, the sacrificial death of Jesus on the cross is described as a birth, that is to say, Christ is seen as a woman in the travail of childbirth. Such is the case with the Carthusian mystic, Marguerite d'Oingt (d. 1310). Second, Christ's love is described as the love of a mother, for example, by Julian of Norwich. Third, Christ's self-sacrifice in the Eucharistic meal is imaged as breast-feeding, that is to say, Christ is seen as a mother who feeds her children at the breast.[80]

What is important in all these images is not gender per se, but the way the believer is irradiated into the image of the suffering Christ. It is not, however, appropriate to claim, as Fiorenza does, that such devotional images do not deconstruct the socio-political sex/gender relations of exploitation and domination typical of what she classifies as kyriarchy. Clearly, power relations were operative in most eras of church history. However, if one is of a mind to interpret social and cultural history through the postmodern lens, which perceives everything in terms of the Nietzscherian will to power, then one will selectively rewrite history according to this particular canon of interpretation as the following demonstrates:

> The Hellenistic paradigm of kyriarchal submission encoded in Christian Scriptures – together with the Roman imperial paradigm – developed into the hierarchical cultic structures of the Roman church in the second and third centuries. This conjunction of ancient kyriarchal structures determined the self-understanding of the post-Constantinian 'othodox' church.[81]

Fortunately, cultural history is rarely as ossified and reified as this would suggest and there are clearly patterns of relations in the history of christological reflection that do not conform to these apparent structures of domination. Similarly, as Berger acknowledges in terms of the inculturation of the gospel,

---

[79] Berger, 'A Female Christ Child in the Manger and a Woman on the Cross, Or: The Historicity of the Jesus Event and the Inculturation of the Gospel', *Feminist Theology* 11 (1996), 40.

[80] Ibid., 41.

[81] Fiorenza, *Jesus*, 16.

the particular *Logos ensarkos*, or the incarnate person of Christ can deconstruct race, gender and ideological distinctions that had hitherto pertained:

> Why can Christ bear the face of a Campesino, the eyes of an Asian, the skin colour of an African, but not the physical characteristics of a woman? In other words: is it really impossible to show the conviction that Jesus redeemed not only human existence in general, but also the specific particularity of African or Asian or female existence, by pointing to a picture of a crucified African or Asian woman?[82]

We shall be investigating the contours of postmodernity in our next chapter. However, at this juncture one would have to admit that there are other perspectives from this stable which would allow a further deconstruction of the sex–gender system of domination Fiorenza describes. For instance, the literary turn of postmodernity permits a variety of readings of the text according to the interpreters' experience. Consequently, Elizabeth Green suggests:

> If we read the recurring Christian motifs of God as creator, sustainer and provider, as purifier, cleanser and deliverer, as accompanying presence, teacher and guide, as giver of new life and vanquisher of death, from women's experience, the text will take on new meaning. We will read *Logos* from the perspective of Sophia and we will see, for example, in Mary of Bethany's act, the royal anointing. The Word will take on flesh and the martyred bodies of women and men will at last acquire meaning and words.[83]

We will return to some of these themes and considerations in our final chapter; however, enough has already been said to indicate that the sex–gender cultural construct which Fiorenza claims inhibits, dehumanises and silences women can be relativised and overcome by critical christological reflection. The incarnation cannot be prescribed or delimited by gender descriptors, just as it could not be wholly adequately described by Neoplatonic philosophical categories.

Irigaray has alerted us to the ontological and epistemological requirement to redefine divinity so that it makes space for the development of female subjectivity. So again, our deliberations have shown that ontological issues cannot be sidestepped or avoided in Christology. Who Jesus is in his essential being and personhood must be integral to the being and nature of the God he both reveals and represents. In that sense, Mary Daly's pertinent remark, 'if God is male then male is God', needs to be taken seriously if the Christian faith is to be rescued from its compromising alliance with various forms of patriarchy and androcentrism.

---

[82] Berger, 'A Female Christ Child'.
[83] Green, 'Women's Words', 77.

Both feminist and liberationist christologies are a welcome and important development within the christological tradition. We have been charting, however, the ease with which both have become too readily aligned with the spurious story of human emancipation and liberation spawned by the Enlightenment. It is now time to make our way into a new cultural landscape that is no longer illuminated by the light of these previous cultural paradigmatic stories and narratives. Whether this is the dawning of a new era or evidence of further cultural decay and collapse is a question already implied in our previous chapters.

THE ENGAGEMENT WITH POSTMODERNITY

DECONSTRUCTING THE CULTURAL PARADIGMS

9.

Christology and the End of the Enlightenment

Post-modern theories are part of a culture of 'unmaking' whose key principles include: decreation, disintegration, deconstruction, decentrement, displacement, difference, discontinuity, disjunction, disappearance, decomposition, de-definition, demystification, de-totalization, delegitimation.[1]

Introduction

It has been our contention that the crisis of modern Christology is almost entirely due to the way in which successive theologians and the theological trends spawned by their work have become aligned with the dominant socio-political paradigms of modernity. In one way this is hardly surprising because of the inevitable conversation that must take place between biblical interpretation, the christological tradition and the interrogation of both by successive cultural trends and horizons. The new cultural fissure that we are presently trying to negotiate, however, which we will consider in more detail below, has undermined the intellectual and sociological cogency of every one of those paradigms that previously supported and expanded the thralldom of modernity.

In the process, paradigms become myths because they fail to convince as suitable plausibility structures that illuminate our present experience of reality. The socio-political strategies that were devised to provide ontological and epistemological security for the now hard-pressed universal human subject were based on a tendentious misrepresentation of the nature and function of religion. It is true of the Judeo-Christian faith, at least, that it is cut off at the knees once it is depoliticised, or indeed once a bifurcation between metaphysics and mysticism is expedited in the name of human progress. It is indeed fascinating and ironic that postmodernity should promulgate such a fierce attack on the politics, anti-metaphysics and anti-mysticism of the modernity

---

[1] I. Hassan, *The Postmodern Turn: Essays in Postmodern Theory and Culture*, 92.

project, because in so doing it has exposed a lacuna in the modernity project once occupied by the phenomena of religion.

The question therefore remains, what place for religion in the context of postmodernity? It is here where the conspiracy of the Enlightenment began. So, has postmodernity eventuated in a more favourable cultural climate with regard to the religious question, or have all the old prejudices and misrepresentations been simple re-inscribed within the new cultural fabric? An answer to this crucial question we will have to postpone until the concluding chapter.

Modernity Versus Postmodernity – The Rise of Cultural Theory

It is not difficult to contend that we are presently in the midst of a vast, complex and at times disorientating period of cultural transition. It is, however, much more difficult to know how to describe it. Has the great scientific, political and economic project of modernity, the brilliant 'sacred canopy' of secular humanism that replaced the fading memory of Christendom, genuinely come to an end, or has it merely moved into another mode of operation? Should we agree with Jürgen Habermas that modernity is an incomplete project that presently merely requires a new sense of direction,[2] or should we accept that we have moved beyond the grand illusions and rationalist pretensions of modernity into the semiotic, language and discourse theory orientated world of postmodernity?

For some cultural commentators the designation postmodernity refers to the dying gasps of the Enlightenment's attempt to redefine reality from the vantage point of the emancipated human subject. The revolt into subjectivity, with its consequent belief in the omnicompetent human reason, is adjudged to have resulted in a misrepresentation of the real world and our place in it, the consequences of which have proved nearly disastrous. We are now inhabitants and 'resident aliens'[3] in a world that is facing numerous 'boundary situations',[4] many of which seem to be distinctly resistant to the power of human reason. The secular replacement of the vision that inspired Christendom – the 'scientific and technological human experiment'[5] – has ceased to offer a viable plausibility structure in terms of our understanding and perception of reality. Others, like Alastair MacIntyre, speak more in terms of the 'crisis of

---

[2] Habermas, 'Modernity – An Unfinished Project' in *Modernity Versus Postmodernity*.

[3] Cf. S. Hauerwas and W.H. Willimon, *Resident Aliens: A Provocative Assessment of Culture and Ministry for People who Know that Something is Wrong*.

[4] K. Jaspers, *General Psychopathology*; quoted in J. Macquarrie, *Existentialism*, 242.

[5] Moltmann, *Way*, 56.

modernity', interpreting the concerns of postmodernity as simply the critical exposure of the fallacies and ideologies that controlled the Enlightenment agenda.[6] David Lyon concludes that postmodernism is 'the exhaustion of modernity'.[7] So, 'Is postmodernity the dusk of the Enlightenment? Or is postmodernity "the dawning of the Age of Aquarius", when the true change – a change in consciousness – finally occurs?'[8]

It is inevitably the case that any fundamental shift in cultural values and allegiances begins with a critique of the major dogmas and ideologies that supported the previous cultural regime. A critical realignment of cultural norms begins almost imperceptibly. The first task is a certain blessed rage for disorder,[9] the attempt to discern what exactly has gone wrong before we can suggest how to put things right (if indeed there is enough clarity and vision to attempt such a resolution in the first place). Consequently, as David Bosch suggests, we could presently be in an interim state, juggling with two paradigms.[10] One contains the old Enlightenment quest for knowledge and certainty, and is still absorbed by epistemological issues. The other 'has to do with putative social changes' and so is presently immersed in radical social and cultural analysis.[11] If this is the case, then:

> Either a new kind of society is coming into being, whose contours can already be dimly perceived, or a new stage of capitalism is being inaugurated. In both cases, previous modes of social analysis and political practice are called into question.[12]

In terms of the continuing and at times acrimonious debate between those who confidently declare the continuing resilience of modernity and those who have gladly heralded its demise, there would appear to be three official positions.

The new cultural phase: the collapse of modernity

The first speaks boldly and without regret of the death or near extinction of modernity, and therefore postulates a total rupture with the past and the arrival of a new phase of cultural development – referred to variously as post-modernity, postmodernism or, more simply and, indeed, more starkly,

---

[6] MacIntyre, *After Virtue*, 111.
[7] D. Lyon, *Postmodernity*, 6.
[8] P. Lakeland, *Postmodernity: Christian Identity in a Fragmented Age*, 7.
[9] This is a deliberate misquote of Tracy's fine study, *Blessed Rage for Order: The New Pluralism in Theology*.
[10] Bosch, *Transforming Mission*, 349.
[11] Lyon, *Postmodernity*, 7.
[12] Ibid.

the end of modernity.[13] There is obviously an ambiguity about the use of the prefix 'post' which permits a certain vacillation between whether or not postmodernity is a positive or negative element in the transition from modernity to its 'postist' counterpart.

Those who insinuate or welcome the death of modernity do so because they view the Enlightenment project as either exhausted or, more seriously, as an oppressive ideology of domination and exploitation which must be repudiated. Consequently, most postmodernists incorporate some element of a break or rupture with modernity into their respective systems. Jacques Derrida, for instance, who is really a post-structuralist rather than an advocate of post-modern cultural theory, concentrates his critique on that logocentrism and the metaphysics of presence that he claims have dominated the epistemological concerns of modernity.[14] This attempt to create a foundationalist structure to knowledge (metaphysics of presence) inevitably privileged the individual, autonomous subject as the prime source of our unmediated epistemic access to reality.[15]

The metaphysics of presence, with its logocentric discourses, thus works to positively privilege reality over appearance, subject over object, speech over writing, reason over nature, men over women and philosophy over literary theory. Consequently, Derrida seeks to continue the post-structuralist deconstruction of modern epistemology and attempts to arrive at a radical alternative that explores the diffuse and decentred space created by the *différence* between text and meaning, sign and signifier. Similarly, other French theorists such as Michel Foucault assailed secular humanist ethics and political discourses proclaiming the inevitable rejoinder to Neitzche's death of God, i.e. the 'death of man', and so at the same time proffering new directions in cultural theory, politics and ethics.[16] Perhaps the most post-postmodern of theorists Jean Baudrillard, embracing a form of technological determinism, talks in terms of the end of industrial production in favour of a new period of simulation and information technology dominated reality, where cybernetics,

---

[13] See for instance, B. Smart, 'Modernity, Postmodernity and the Present' in B.S. Turner (ed.), *Theories of Modernity and Postmodernity*.

[14] J. Derrida, *Of Grammatology*.

[15] Following Nietzsche, Heidegger, Wittgenstein, James, Dewey, Rorty, Bataille, Foucault and others Derrida has claimed that such an attempt to postulate binary opposites such as appearance and reality, subject and object, speech and writing, sign and signifier etc, have constructed an oppressive hierarchy of values that function as an ideology of domination which excludes or nullifies supposedly inferior alternatives.

[16] M. Foucault, *Madness and Civilization: A History of Insanity in the Age of Reason; Power/Knowledge: Selected Interviews and Other Writings, 1972–1977; The Subject and Power*.

computerisation and the media take over as the prime brokers of the new *semiurgic* society.[17]

The temporary demise of modernity

At the other end of the spectrum are those who are convinced that what we are presently experiencing is merely the diminution or temporary demise of modernity. Consequently, what is urgently required is a reinvigoration of the emancipatory, progressive and democratic ideals that inspired the Enlightenment vision of a new society.

Jürgen Habermas, perhaps the most accomplished exponent of the Frankfurt school of critical theory, has emerged, to a certain extent, as the self-appointed custodian of the modernity project. He has no taste for the excesses of irrationalism he discerns in the anti-modernity lobby. On the contrary, 'The New Critique of Reason' – advanced by Foucault, Baudrillard, Lyotard, Gilles Deleuze and the other doyens of postmodernity – 'suppresses that almost 200-year-old counter-discourse inherent in modernity itself.'[18] Habermas believes modernity still contains resources which could help us get beyond our present epistemological impasse.

In his major work, *The Logic of the Social Sciences, Theory and Practice, Knowledge and Human Interests*, Habermas seeks to salvage certain aspects of the work fore-grounded by his predecessors in the Frankfurt school of critical theory. He endeavours to discern the emancipatory logic latent in a combination of empirical social investigation and critical social theory. It is at this juncture that Habermas seeks to defend the project of modernity against those who endeavour to repudiate or reject it entirely.

Habermas recognises and accepts the domination of scientific and technological rationality that typified modernity, but is highly critical of the 'false programmes of the negation of culture', accusing the anti-modernity lobby of imbibing an explosive cocktail of subjectivist irrationalism mixed with not a little pre-modern nostalgia and mysticism.[19] He defends the development of autonomous areas of knowledge (such as morality and law, art, social and political theory and, indeed, philosophy)[20] and seeks to develop his own variation of a post-Kantian epistemology, which he refers to as communicative rationality.[21] In this way, he hopes to rescue the emancipatory ideals of the Enlightenment. With the development of an intersubjective epistemology

---

[17] J. Baudrillard, *Simulation* and *In the Shadow of the Silent Majorities*.
[18] J. Habermas, *The Philosophical Discourses of Modernity: Twelve Lectures*, 294.
[19] Habermas, *Modernity versus Postmodernity*, 14.
[20] Ibid., 9.
[21] J. Habermas, *Theory of Communicative Action*, Vol. 1 & 2.

of communicative action, Habermas connects with some aspects of the feminist reconstruction of the modernity project undertaken by Irigaray,[22] Fraser and Nicholson[23] and Sabina Lovibond.[24] The linkages between feminism, multiculturalism and postmodernity are a pertinent aspect of the new cultural landscape.

A dialectic of discontinuity and continuity

Somewhere in the middle of these two extremes are those who espouse a dialectic of discontinuity and continuity between modernity and postmodernity, which does not permit, as yet, a valorisation of one over the other. For instance, Foucault never accepted the notion of a radical disjunction between modernity and postmodernity, and opposed all interpretations of his work that construed his criticisms of the modernity project along such lines. He warned that 'one of the most harmful habits in contemporary thought is the analysis of the present as being ... a present of rupture'.[25] Similarly, Derrida, who is often interpreted as the prophetic voice of the notion of a radical break or schism with the past, categorically states: 'I do not believe in decisive ruptures, in an unequivocal "epistemological break", as it is called today. Breaks are always, and fatally, reinscribed in an old cloth that must continually, interminably be undone.'[26]

As we have noted in another context, the neo-Marxist, Fredric Jameson, who has somewhat ingeniously linked postmodern theory with a reinvigorated Marxist theory of cultural transformation, has similarly repudiated the notion of a radical break between modernity and postmodernity. He prefers to view this development in terms of a reordering of cultural priorities and emphases.[27]

We have already hinted that the more likely explanation of our present cultural situation is that of transition, the appearance of a borderline state or a new terrain, where existing alongside one another are both familiar species and new mutations requiring more astute explanation and classification. In such a situation, it is always unwise to claim a total rupture with the past because that inevitably disguises the extent to which the new theorists are still invested in the cultural capital of the previous regime (e.g. the reappearance of

---

[22] L. Irigaray, *The Sex Which is Not One*.

[23] N. Fraser and L. Nicholson, *Social Criticism Without Philosophy: An Encounter Between Feminism and Postmodernity*.

[24] S. Lovibond, *Feminism and Postmodernism*; see also, J. Flax, *Thinking Fragments: Psychoanalysis, Feminism, and Postmodernism in the Contemporary*.

[25] Foucault in L.D. Kritzman (ed.), *Michel Foucault: Politics, Philosophy, Culture*, 35.

[26] J. Derrida, *Positions*, 24.

[27] F. Jameson, *Postmodernism and Consumer Society*, 123.

a typically Romantic anti-rationalism, or the extension of Nietzscherian nihilistic individualism, or indeed the inevitable Marxist obsession with a critique of new modes of capitalist expansion).[28]

Similarly, the rejection of all supposedly imperialist metanarratives and totalising theories either leads to the rejection of any possibility of representative forms of political, social and cultural theory, or more insidiously, just as Derrida warned, the reintroduction of such macro theories in somewhat covert and coded form.[29] Consequently,

> It is ironic that despite the war against totality by Lyotard and others, theorists identified as postmodern like Foucauld and Baudrillard have produced extremely totalising theories which are often abstract, overly general, and sometimes over-simplify complex historical situations.[30]

If one has rejected outright the notion of historical continuity and development is it legitimate to still invest in the discourse of a radical disjunction or break with the past, which presupposes the reality of that which one denies, i.e. the possibility of continuity, as well as discontinuity, with past modes of thought and epistemological enquiry? One way to try and map out the new cultural territory of this intermediary state, lacuna, or transition period, is to investigate the socio-political, historical and theological continuities and discontinuities that exist between modernity and postmodernity.

The Causes of the Collapse of the Enlightenment

Socio-political evaluations

The idea of discussing the collapse or implosion of the Enlightenment project in such a fashion invites dissension and, indeed, ridicule from those within the postmodernist lobby who eschew all such historical analysis. There are, however, those who do espouse a socio-political description of the transition from modernity to postmodernity.

Fredric Jameson has sought to engage the rhetoric of postmodern theory from the perspective of neo-Marxist political analysis.[31] He relativises some of

---

[28] A similar thesis is ventured by G. Graff in 'The Myth of the Postmodernist Breakthrough'.

[29] Derrida, *Positions*.

[30] S. Best and D. Kellner, *Postmodern Theory: Critical Interrogations*, 280; cf. also C. Norris, *What's Wrong with Postmodernism?: Critical Theory and the Ends of Philosophy*, 164–94.

[31] F. Jameson, *Marxism and Form: Twentieth-century Dialectical Theories of Literature*; and *The Prison House of Language: A Critical Account of Structuralism and Russian Formalism*.

the more extreme claims of postmodernists by situating it within the evolution
of capitalism that started with the emergence of the bourgeoisie in the
eighteenth century and the advent of the Industrial Revolution in the nineteenth century. Not unlike Habermas, Jameson views postmodernity as a new
stage in the 'cultural development of the logic of late capitalism'.[32] Economics,
and particularly Marxist social and economic theory, predominate in Jameson's
vision.[33] He regards the genesis of postmodernity as a specific political manifestation of the growth and rapid expansion of global multinational capitalism. As
such, it contains both progressive and potentially catastrophic elements that
manifest themselves in different ways.[34] Relying heavily on Ernest Mandel's
Late Capitalism, Jameson argues that the distinctive difference between modernity and postmodernity is the migration of commodity driven economics to
embrace all aspects of culture, including knowledge, values, art and aesthetics,
and even the subconscious itself. Each stage in the expansion of capitalism
results in a corresponding cultural style, hence 'realism, modernity, and
postmodernism are the cultural levels of market capitalism, monopoly capitalism, and multinational capitalism'.[35]

Not surprisingly, for Jameson the logic of late capitalism and its global
manifestation in multinational conglomerates are viewed as both an oppressive system of domination and a dangerous ideology. It renders individual
decision making problematic as more and more of us are stranded in a kind of
decentred, postmodern hyperspace.[36] According to Jameson, a new cognitive
mapping, which will enable individuals to relocate themselves within two
referential systems, is required. The first element is an acceptance of the value
of narratives that reconnect individuals with events and circumstances that are
contextualised within broader totalities. Individuals are rehabilitated within
'the lost unity of social life'. This, in turn, 'demonstrates that widely distant
elements of the social totality are ultimately part of the same global historical
process.'[37] The second element is to listen carefully to the voices from the
margins and so engage with the micro-politics of resistance. Minority and
traditionally oppressed groups, such as blacks, gays and women, become the
'new subjects of history', a new proletarian class struggle that flourishes

[32] F. Jameson, *Postmodernism, or the Cultural Logic of Late Capitalism*, 85.
[33] Best and Kellner, *Postmodern Theory*, 183.
[34] Ibid., 184.
[35] Ibid., 185.
[36] F. Jameson, *Cultural Logic*, 83.
[37] F. Jameson, *The Political Unconscious: Narrative as a Socially Symbolic Act*, 226.
   Jameson's privileging of the concept of totality as the necessary social dynamic to
   revolutionary rather than merely reformist politics, is a clear break with the normal
   postmodern assault upon all such totalising narratives or systems of discourse.

through political alliances which subvert the established social order.[38] Jameson's depiction of postmodernity as a culture of fragmentation, pastiche, images and simulacra connects strongly with Baudrillard's inventory of postmodern culture games.

As we have already noted, Baudrillard, in his earlier work, also sought to offer a socio-political rendition of the transition from pre-modernity to modernity to postmodernity. He claimed that pre-modern societies were characterised by a system of symbolic exchange. With the advent of market capitalism, however, a political economy replaced the older system, which was based on a wholly different system of exchange value.[39] Capitalism is characterised by exchange value (based on money and capital), use value (based on production and commodity) and sign value (based on prestige, social significance and power).[40]

Baudrillard argued for a return to symbolic exchange value systems to overcome the domination of political economy. Like Jameson, Baudrillard connected this concept of symbolic exchange value with the marginalised and oppressed groups who advocate revolutionary lifestyles and values as a form of political subversion. Here he makes contact with Foucault, Lyotard, Deleuze and Félix Guattari who similarly valorise a micropolitics of desire where revolutionary change is associated with alternative lifestyles, sexuality, bodiliness and image, which, once again, is supposed to articulate a new logic of emancipation from domination and control.[41]

In his later work, Baudrillard abandons the attempt to forge a new political theory and adopts the discourses of postmodernity as a way of signalling the end of production and industrial capitalism. Instead, he claims that in the passage from a metallurgic to a *semiurgic* society we are entering the realm of hyper-reality. Here the boundaries between image, simulation and reality implode, as do the distinctions between politics, entertainment and public relations. This is the world of Disney where computer graphics, cybernetics, media simulation and simulacra diminish and displace reality and become themselves more real, i.e. hyper-real. In the world of hyper-reality image is all that matters.[42]

If modernity was characterised by explosion (i.e. the rapid expansion of market and monopoly capitalism, widespread commercialisation, the eventual triumph of global economics and the wholesale dominance of science and

---

[38] F. Jameson, *History and Class Consciousness as an Unfinished Project*, 71. See also 'Periodising the 60s' in S. Sayres (ed.), *The 60s Without Apology*, 209.

[39] J. Baudrillard, *For a Critique of the Political Economy of the Sign*, 63ff.

[40] Best and Kellner, *Postmodern Theory*, 115.

[41] Ibid., 116.

[42] Norris, *What's Wrong with Postmodernism?*, 171. A number of writers refer to the election victories in America and Britain in 1988 as a prime example of the relentless exploitation of public opinion by the mass media.

technology) then postmodernity is defined by implosion (i.e. the dominance of media simulation and information technology, the collapse of traditional boundaries between the public and private domains, the marginalisation of science and the commodification of culture, the ossification of meaning, the overwhelming of religion and philosophy by consumerism and endless bland entertainment). The bleak picture painted by Baudrillard deserves careful consideration because the end result of such an implosive trajectory is social entropy and resentment:

> The apathetic masses ... become a sullen silent majority in which all meaning, messages, and solicitations implode as if sucked into a black hole. The social ... disappears and with it distinctions implode between classes, political ideologies, cultural forms, and between media semiurgy and the real itself. Baudrillard is not only describing a series of implosions (that is, between politics and entertainment, capital and labour, or high and low culture) but is claiming that the society in its entirety is implosive.[43]

An important common feature to the analysis of postmodernity provided by Habermas, Jameson and Baudrillard is the collapse of the intellectual and cultural distinctions, which the Enlightenment sought to preserve, between science, philosophy, economics, art and literature, politics and ethics, law and religion. These distinctions were based on the belief that a universal common religion could be replaced by an equally universal common humanity. However, once the death of man succeeds the death of God, no such common humanity is believed to exist, and all such convivial and convenient intellectual dichotomies are exposed as mere power plays that lead to domination and exclusion. In the process, knowledge is no longer located within such supposedly foundational disciplines, but is transcribed within the very social processes that sought to create such normative disciplines in the first place. For instance, in law and ethics the concept of justice was understood to refer to a real state of affairs that could be observed in different societies, defined by law and maintained by the judiciary. For the postmodernist all of this is illusory. There is no independent reality we can refer to as justice; there is simply the representation of justice in texts and other coded forms which are the direct result of social configurations, which, it is claimed, tend to be based on self-interest, privilege and power. Not surprisingly, therefore, postmodernity is characterised by the dominance of social and cultural theory fuelled by an almost ubiquitous hermeneutic of suspicion. Similarly, the dominant genre of cultural investigation is no longer philosophical critiques, but socio-political genealogies and archaeologies.[44]

---

[43] Best and Kellner, *Postmodern Theory*, 121.

[44] See for instance, M. Foucault, *The Archaeology of Knowledge; and On the Genealogy of Ethics*.

Historical evaluations

In terms of historiography, we are dealing with the rapid coalescence of wide-spread cultural factors that began to take shape over a thirty-year period and it is problematic to try to identify any particular historical moment or schism as a decisive indication of the transition from modernity to postmodernity. However, one of the first instances of the category postmodern occurs in Arnold Toynbee's epic account of human civilisation, *A Study of History*. Toynbee's historicist and idealist presuppositions clearly underlie his description of modernity as the era of middle-class bourgeoisie ascendancy, social stability, scientific rationalism, and intellectual and economic progress. This ideal picture he contrasted with the postmodern age of social disintegration, widespread anti-rationalism, relativism and socio-political revolution.[45] On the other hand, the cultural historian Bernard Rosenberg chooses to describe the postmodern cultural landscape in terms of the arrival of a mass-marketed social identity and conformity.[46] In a similar fashion, Peter Drucker identifies postmodern society with post-industrialism, which he defines in terms of the decline of the nation-state, the rapid rise in living standards associated with the increase in modernisation and the arrival of the post-ideological age.[47]

The postmodernity issue began to emerge in cultural theory in the 1970s with typically polemical positions being embraced. Susan Sontag,[48] Leslie Fiedler[49] and Ihab Hassan[50] eulogised the postmodern break with the oppressive and imperialist mores of modernity. However, George Steiner lamented the arrival of the postmodern culture of anti-foundationalism and anti-humanism rhetoric.[51] In short,

> The term 'postmodern' gradually came into expanded use in the 1970s. Ihab Hassan, who would become one of postmodernism's most well known spokesmen, connected literary, philosophical, and social trends under the term in 1971. Charles Jencks applied it to architecture in 1975. Postmodernism as a cultural phenomenon was attacked by Daniel Bell in 1976. In the late 1970's, three books galvanised postmodernism as a movement: Jencks's *The Language of Post-Modern Architecture*

---

[45] A.J. Toynbee, *A Study of History*, Vol. VIII and IX.

[46] Cf. Best and Kellner, *Postmodern Theory*, 7.

[47] P.F. Drucker, *Landmarks of Tomorrow*. The use of the expression post-ideological age is taken from D.J. Bosch, *Believing In The Future: Toward a Missiology of Western Culture*.

[48] S. Sontag, *Against Interpretation*.

[49] L.S. Fiedler, *The Collected Essays of Leslie Fiedler*, Vol. II.

[50] I. Hassan, *The Dismemberment of Orpheus: Toward a Postmodern Literature*; *Right Promethean Fire*; and *The Postmodern Turn*.

[51] G. Steiner, *In Bluebeard's Castle: Some Notes Towards the Re-definition of Culture*.

(1979); Jean-François Lyotard *La Condition postmoderne: rapport sur le savoir* (1979; English translation: *The Postmodern Condition: A Report on Knowledge*, 1984); and Richard Rorty's *Philosophy and the Mirror of Nature* (1979). The last, while not discussing postmodernism per se, argued that the developments of post-Heideggerian European philosophy and post-Wittgensteinian analytic philosophy were converging on a kind of pragmatic anti-foundationalism. Rorty thereby became an American representative of postmodernism, albeit in pragmatic garb. It was partly through Rorty's influence that in the 1980s postmodernism came to have a meaning for most American philosophers and not just architectural and literary critics. Simultaneously the term came into general use as a label for the current era, our own *fin de siecle* (end of century) mood.[52]

To this inventory of cultural trends and moods should be added the significance of the1968 student and workers protests for French postmodernists. The revolutionary impulses that marked this particular episode of social unrest were ostensibly directed toward the inherent conservatism and nepotism of the French intellectual establishment. However, this also served to hasten the rupture that was taking place in French philosophical and political theory. For some, this was a decisive test of the nihilism that had dominated the post-war years in France (Jean-Luc Marion). For others, it marked a final break with the metaphysics of reason and freedom (Cartesian rationalism) and the metaphysics of humanism (Sartre and Merleau-Ponty), which, as we shall shortly see, also accompanied the increasing influence of Martin Heidegger upon the French intellectual scene.

Philosophical evaluations

Reason without the bounds of religion
If Descartes and Kant stand head-and-shoulders above their contemporaries as the philosophical architects of modernity, then it is Nietzsche and, to a certain extent, Heidegger, who perform the same function for postmodernity. It was Descartes and Kant who founded modernity on a negotiated compromise between first philosophy and theology. Nietzsche and Heidegger have exposed that compromise as not merely untenable, but fundamentally mendacious.

In both Descartes and Kant's philosophical systems, religion functions as a necessary guarantor of the validity of the rational subjects cognitive and moral capacities. If knowledge of ourselves, the external world and morality is to be founded on the consciousness of ourselves as a rational, experiencing subject, then the existence of God is only required as a metaphysical sanction that this is the way things are and always have been. The marriage of convenience that takes place here between the philosophy of origins and theology is not only

---

[52] Cahoone, *Modernism to Postmodernism*, 9.

extremely tenuous, but also deeply problematic. It was Nietzsche's genius to find a way to not only prise them apart, but also to try to destroy the basis upon which both were based.

The abiding legacy of Nietzsche

It is important to realise that Nietzsche's first line of attack was the Judeo-Christian God upon which both morality and the philosophy of consciousness were founded. Nietzsche announced the demise of this God with undisguised exultation:

> The most important of more recent events – that 'god is dead', that the belief in the Christian God has become unworthy of belief – already begins to cast its first shadows over Europe … In fact, we philosophers and 'free spirits' feel ourselves irradiated as by a new dawn by the report that the 'old God is dead'; our hearts overflow with gratitude, astonishment, presentiment and expectation. At last the horizon seems open once more, granting even that it is not bright; our ships can at last put out to sea in face of every danger; every hazard is again permitted to the discerner; the sea, *our* sea, again lies open before us; perhaps never before did such an 'open sea' exist.[53]

Nietzsche's starting point was the non-existence of God. It is to his credit that he recognised that if this fundamental bulwark is removed then everything else collapses like a house of cards, hence the madman in *The Gay Science* announces an apocalyptic event, because if God is dead then the whole tradition of Western morality, metaphysics and culture also disintegrates.

As Brian Ingraffia contends, there have been many readings of Nietzsche and this continues to be the case for the advocates of postmodernity.[54] Some, like the influential studies of Karl Jaspers and Walter Kaufman,[55] sought to blunt the vitriolic substance of Nietzsche's attack on Christianity as both hypocritical and puerile. They valorise Nietzsche as a crypto-Christian who, like Kierkegaard, directed his scorn and bile toward the diminishing shadows and vain glories of Christendom, rather than at the founder of Christianity itself. Such an interpretation of Nietzsche is not only disingenuous it is an invention. Nietzsche makes no distinction between Christendom and Christianity. It is clear, particularly in his latter years, that Nietzsche regarded the Judeo-Christian faith as a mendacious conspiracy that sought to blind humanity to its true greatness and destiny. The source of this misunderstanding is Heidegger's portrayal of Nietzsche as the last great metaphysician of the West.

---

[53] F.W. Nietzsche, *The Joyful Wisdom*, No. 343, 275.

[54] Ingraffia, *Postmodern Theory*, 19–33.

[55] K. Jaspers, *Nietzsche and Christianity*, and W.A. Kaufman, *Nietzsche: Philosopher, Psychologist, Antichrist.*

Heidegger claims that Nietzsche's 'madman' proclaims the death of meta-physics or onto-theology, rather than the death of the Christian God.

> The pronouncement 'God is dead' means: the suprasensory world is without power. It bestows no life. Metaphysics, i.e. for Nietzsche Western philosophy understood as Platonism, is at an end. Nietzsche understands his own philosophy as the counter-movement to metaphysics, and that means for him a movement in opposition to Platonism.[56]

Again, it is not difficult to see why Heidegger chose to emphasise this aspect of Nietzsche's critique, because Nietzsche scorned Christianity as Platonism for the people. It is not, however, the death of Platonism that heralds in the great age of nihilism and unbelief. Rather,

> According to Nietzche, the reason that the rebound from Christianity is so great, the reason that one moves from complete faith to total despair, is the fact that Western society invested so much into this interpretation: 'the untenability of one interpretation of the world, upon which a tremendous amount of energy has been lavished, awakens the suspicion that *all* interpretations of the world are false' (WP 1). This is the negative response to the loss of faith in Christianity, to the death of the Christian God.[57]

It is true, however, that Plato is regarded by Nietzsche as the originator of the fiction that has held Western culture spellbound for countless generations. He is the author of that fateful dualism, the root of all idealism, the philosophical genus who sought a theory of origins and so divided the universe into a mere world of appearances and an eternal world of heavenly archetypes.

Plato did, however, as we have noted, maintain a real ontological connection between both worlds via the instrumentality of the *Logos* through which the world of eternal ideas is mirrored in the particularities of the world of appearances. Nevertheless, the denigration of the natural, material world in favour of an ideal, eternal world was a pernicious aspect of Plato's metaphysics. According to Nietzsche, Christianity not only took over this metaphysical dualism, it bolstered the dichotomy through a moral re-evaluation of the natural world as a vale of tears, a world smitten and afflicted with sin, suffering and corruption.

> The places of origin of the notion of 'another world': the philosopher, who invents a world of reason, where reason and the logical functions are adequate: this is the

---

[56] M. Heidegger, *The Question Concerning Technology*, 61 quoted in Ingraffia, *Post-modern Theory*, 26.

[57] Ingraffia, *Postmodern Theory*, 27.

origin of the 'true' world; the religious man, who invents a 'divine world': this is the origin of the 'denaturalised, antinatural' world; the moral man, who invents a 'free world': this is the origin of the 'good, perfect, just holy' world.[58]

Not surprisingly, for Nietzsche the modern representative of idealism is Kant, whom he condemned as an 'underhanded Christian', just as he regales against the main purveyors of Western metaphysics for having 'theologians blood in their veins'.[59] Kant re-inscribed the distinction within the framework of the new philosophy of subjectivity, but it is still the old sun of the Platonic–Christian-moral ideal.[60] This time, however, due to the demise of Christian metaphysics the ideal world (*noumena*) is not only unattainable but also unknowable. So, asked Nietzsche, what use is it, how does it serve our practical needs? Here, Nietzsche ruthlessly exploited that tenuous compromise between natural theology and the rationality of the autonomous subject upon which modernity constructed its new philosophical edifice.

> It is true, there could be a metaphysical world; the absolute possibility of it is hardly to be disputed ... Then that possibility still remains over; but one can do absolutely nothing with it, not to speak of letting happiness, salvation and life depend on the gossamer of such a possibility – for one could assert nothing at all of the metaphysical world except that it was a being-other, an inaccessible, incomprehensible being-other; it would be a thing with negative qualities. Even if the existence of such a world were never so well demonstrated, it is certain that knowledge of it would be the most useless of all knowledge.[61]

When it comes to an evaluation of the source of this religious instinct to create a bifurcated reality, Nietzsche is less original. In fact, he followed Hegel in viewing religion as a primitive stage in human development and he follows Feuerbach in terms of the latter's theory of psychological projection. Nietzsche, the quasi-anthropologist, claimed that primitive animism demonstrates that ancient peoples recoil in terror and horror at the mercurial unpredictability and apparently arbitrary nature of natural occurrences and so invent a perfect world as a form of psychological compensation.[62] In the process, human beings belittle themselves, dividing themselves and their world in two, attributing weakness, vulnerability and mortality to themselves and strength, invincibility and immortality to their gods.[63]

---

[58] F.W. Nietzsche, *The Will to Power*, 586 quoted in Ingraffia, *Postmodern Theory*, 35.
[59] F.W. Nietzsche, *The Antichrist*, 8.
[60] See Ingraffia, *Postmodern Theory*, 39.
[61] F.W. Nietzsche, *Human, All Too Human*, 9 quoted in Ingraffia, *Postmodern Theory*, 39.
[62] F.W. Nietzsche, *The Gay Science*, 343.
[63] F.W. Nietzsche, *Twilight of the Idols*, 484 and *The Antichrist*, 15.

Whereas Feuerbach thought it possible to expose the nature of this psychological projection, deny the existence of God and then salvage Christian morality as that which was now founded on the ennobling of the human spirit,[64] Nietzsche was both more ruthless and consistent. The projection of an omnipotent deity is far from harmless. Rather, for Nietzsche, it is a crime against life itself:

> What has been revered as God and as godlike is denounced by Nietzsche because it has for the most part been the product of the *decadent* or sickly imagination … What he opposes is the type of gods and ideals created by slave morality, by the weak and sick who create these ideals in opposition to the actual world in which they are oppressed.[65]

According to Nietzsche, the invention of the gods is a projection of either a people's power or weakness. It is a manifestation of either a master or a slave mentality and Nietzsche believes he can chart the course of this conspiracy in terms of the origin and development of the Judeo-Christian faith.[66] Accordingly, the religion of the slave mentality is erected upon the shaky foundations

---

[64] L. Feuerbach, *Essence of Christianity*, in this regard see the introductory essay by Karl Barth.

[65] Ingraffia, *Postmodern Theory*, 49.

[66] To begin with, the Israelites create a god based on their own positive assessment of the natural world and their own political achievements. This god symbolises and represents the will to power. With the exile, the loss of the land, the temple and the monarchy, all this changes. Instead of abandoning their belief in a god who has obviously failed them a new god is invented, a denatured moral absolute that must simply be obeyed on fear of punishment. This process of reinvention is due to resentment, the resentment of the Jewish priests toward their Babylonian oppressors.

For Nietzsche, the 'moral world order' based on the absolute will of God for all people at all times, is a fiction based on political and social impotence. As such, it requires a metaphysic that postulates a degenerate world of corruption held in check by a perfect world of God-given moral imperatives. Ibid., 52. It is not difficult to see how these views, combined with Nietzsche's thesis of the superman, fuelled the demonic anti-Semitism of Hitler's National Socialism.

Upon this 'false soil' of Judaism, Christianity sprouted forth and flourished, which, according to Nietzsche, was 'a form of mortal enmity against reality that has never yet been surpassed'. Ibid., 53, Ingraffia highlights the way in which Nietzsche differs from idealism in ascribing a basic continuity between Judaism and Christianity rather than the latter's preference for the degenerate versus the true system of belief. Again, the dichotomy between the natural and supernatural world is based on impotence, fear and resentment, but this time directed toward the Roman oppressors.

Jesus is not exempt from Nietzsche's tendentious reading of Christian origins. Rather, he is regarded as one who possessed a pathological fear of reality, a man of decadence and resentment, further propped up by the twin pillars of free will and moral responsibility. If the individual subject is free then he or she is also morally accountable; accountable, however, for all that transgresses our basic instincts and desire to flourish. Consequently, the concept of sin is the manifestation of a bad conscience designed to create guilt and so curb our most fundamental and powerful drives.[67]

So how must this fiction be overcome? By reversing the re-evaluation and taking back for ourselves all that has been invested in God, i.e. our natural will to power. In that way, no longer trapped in the prison of absolute responsibility to an absolute God, humanity can grow bigger and thence comes the *Ubermensch*; the one who has courageously appropriated the most basic drive which lies at the heart of the natural world, the will to power, the master mentality. This is much more than the mere Darwinian instinct for self-preservation. It is the will to dominate, to transform our environment so that it serves our purposes and reflects our aims. If there is no objective, transcendent moral order, then there are no indisputable moral facts. There are only moral interpretations that serve either to promote the master mentality or to invent its counter ego. Once this state of affairs is embraced and accepted then we are beyond good and evil, and are in fact merely inhabitants of the natural world.[68]

---

[66] (*continued*) devoid of the capacity to espouse the path of resistance and in possession therefore of a decadent physiology. Encapsulated in the Sermon on the Mount is this fateful transvaluation where poverty, meekness and impotence become a virtue, founded on the notion of an inner reality, the kingdom of God within you, a world of pure fiction, that is 'rooted in hatred of the natural'. Ibid., 54.

[67] Ibid., 55 Ingraffia is correct to draw attention to Neitzsche's dependence upon Schopenhauer for his understanding of the doctrine of creation. The latter demonstrates the essentially negative attitude to the material and the particular that typified idealism.

[68] It is not difficult to challenge or refute most, if not all, of the tenets upon which Nietzsche's defamation of religion is based. Much of what he confidently asserted is both historically inaccurate and woefully inadequate in terms of the sociology of religion. Christianity is not Platonism for the people because it grew out of the soil of Jewish eschatology and apocalyptic. The latter is antithetical towards Greek dualism because it advocates a good creation, most certainly tainted and skewed from its original intention, but nevertheless still orientated toward a material future consummation and fulfilment. Those who studied the phenomenology and sociology of religion have seriously contested Feuerbach's thesis; it would appear that it is the encounter with the non-manipulable, non-coercive, unbounded, numinous divine reality that preceded ancient people's awareness of their own subjectivity. Through such an experience of that which is beyond them, they caught a glimpse of similar numinous and impenetrable characteristics about their own being as personal subjects. Cf. W. Pannenberg, *Theology and the Kingdom of God*, 57–8. Similarly, the

Having denied that there are foundations to morality, Nietzsche readily did the same to epistemology. In this way, he mounted an attack on all sides designed to demolish the pretensions of modernity. When it comes to truth, knowledge and certainty, the same pertains. There are no facts, only interpretations. Truth is but a convention, that apparently indisputable *interpretation* of the world that allows a particular group of people to thrive and be successful. In typically ironic tone, Nietzsche contended that 'Truth is that sort of error without which a particular class of living creatures could not otherwise live'.[69] Truth is but common sense evaluation and is therefore only one of any number of possible 'interpretations' of the world.

Nietzsche's attack on the philosophy of consciousness with its attendant notion of the primacy of the ego or the self-conscious subject follows a similar pattern. Reason imports the notion of the ego as a being or a subject underlying our self-consciousness from the experience of causation or activity and then projects this belief unto everything. This entails that the primary notion of being construed as a cause is 'shoved under' things. The concept of being is derived from that of the ego.[70] All that we are in fact doing is inferring the concept of an acting ego or subject from something that happens, supposing that an active agent lies behind all that we think or do. However, under scrutiny we discover that much of our thinking and doing is involuntary, it wills rather than I will. Much of what goes on in our minds and bodies we are barely aware of, nor do we need to be, so what purpose does self-consciousness serve? Nietzsche offered an 'extravagant hypothesis':

---

[68] *(continued)* primary source of the Jews self-identity both as a nation and as the covenant people of God was the displacement and disaster of the exile. If the prime motive behind their theological reflections on this traumatic event had been frustration, resentment and political impotence that would be discernible in the prophetic, wisdom and Torah traditions that express their sense of national identity as well. Finally, if Jesus had demonstrated a pathological fear of reality he would hardly have set his face toward Jerusalem in the knowledge of the likely outcome of that particular re-evaluation of his nation's Messianic traditions. Nor does Nietzsche seem aware of Augustine's discourses on the nature of sin which have precious little to do with guilt inducement, but much more to do with our disordered relationship with the world around us and therefore the forfeiting of that very freedom which mediates to us a sense of moral responsibility. While it is legitimate to challenge the genealogy of Nietzsche's attack upon Christian faith and morality in such a manner, nevertheless, his basic contention that belief in the Christian God had become unsustainable and that widespread nihilism would devastate the Christian landscape of his native Europe is much more difficult to refute.

[69] Neitzsche, *Nachlass*, 814; quoted in D.J. O'Connor (ed.), *A Critical History of Western Philosophy*, 387.

[70] O'Connor, *Critical History*, 390.

> The strength and subtlety [of self-awareness] stand in proportion to the capacity for communication of a man (or an animal). The capacity for communication is in turn proportional to the *necessity to communicate.*[71]

Thus, the ego or self-consciousness is not a private necessity, but a social indulgence; it satisfies our need for communication. Just as Nietzsche reduced rationality, truth and knowledge to the logic of language, so he reduces the philosophy of subjectivity to social psychology.

Here lies the source of Nietzsche's anti-foundationalism and in its stead we discover a novel perspectivism. Nietzsche is very far from being an anti-rationalist. He simply believed that when we talk about reason and ascribe to it a cognitive or metaphysical capacity to intuit such things as unity, identity, permanence, substance, cause, thinkhood and being, all apparently actually existing in something called the real world, we are actually referring to features that constitute the nature of our language. In this way, Nietzsche anticipates later developments in the philosophy of language, claiming that Kant's a priori categories of the mind are in fact not structures of subjectivity at all but aspects of speech. The realist in Nietzsche, however, could accordingly remark, 'I am afraid we shall not get rid of God because we still believe in grammar.'[72]

It is Nietzsche's conviction that in the end common sense would prevail, the herd instinct always wins through, that which the philosophers accept as foundational, as known, is 'that which we are accustomed to, so that we no longer wonder at it. It is the commonplace, is any kind of rule that is fixed, whatever we are at home with.'[73] In that sense Nietzsche felt his untimely ideas were for a generation as yet unborn. He would no doubt have approved that his pragmatic notions about reason and the use of language should form the substance of Wittgenstein's *Philosophical Investigations.*

Heidegger's via media

Amidst the profusion of postmodern thought it is often possible to get straight from Nietzsche to the issues which dominate the new cultural territory. This is certainly true for Foucauld, Deleuze, Guattari and Lyotard. However, Derrida, E. Lévinas, Irigaray, J. Kristeva and G. Vattimo are fascinated by another link in the chain, i.e. the existentialist anti-metaphysics of Heidegger. Again, Ingraffia deftly handles the singular, subtle and intense influence of Neitzsche upon Heidegger. Other commentators have similarly noted that Nietzsche's influence on Heidegger is discernible before the latter's prolonged engagement with the former between 1936–46.

---

[71] Ibid., 391.
[72] F.W. Neitzsche, *Twilight of the Idols* III, 5; O'Connor, *Critical History*, 388.
[73] Neitzsche, *Gay Science*, 355; O'Connor, *Critical History*, 392.

However rarely cited in *Being and Time,* Nietzsche may well be the regnant genius of the work – Nietzsche, who exposes the anthropomorphic base of metaphysical projections and the evanescence of Being understood as permanence of presence, supplies genealogical accounts of time and eternity in such a way that the latter appears as vengeance wreaked on the former; confronts with subterfuge human existence as irredeemably mortal, bursting with possibility yet bound to fatality.[74]

Heidegger, the one-time conservative Catholic theologian and erstwhile supporter of Hitler, later relinquished both ideologies in favour of a prolonged philosophical pilgrimage to finally bring Western metaphysics to an end, consequently following Aristotle in the belief that atheism is indigenous to philosophy. Throughout his particular philosophical sojourn, Heidegger argued repeatedly that metaphysics began with Platonism and culminated in Nietzsche. Consequently, surprising as this conclusion may seem, he remained convinced, as did Nietzsche, that metaphysics is largely a theological exercise; it is in fact onto-theology.

The fundamental error of all such metaphysics is the forgetting of Being, the failure to think Being beyond its absorption in the Being of beings. In this way, Being remains trapped by its shadow and is always thought of as the permanence of presence within things.[75] Heidegger contended that Nietzsche does not escape from the dichotomy of the real world versus the world of appearances because he merely affirms one and denies the other. It is in this sense that Heidegger referred to Nietzsche as the last metaphysician because the latter does not think beyond this fundamental dualism, he merely says yes to the flourishing finitude of becoming and no to the brooding infinity of Being. Just as he inverts the dualism of Being and becoming, asserting the priority of the latter over the former, leaving the residual problem of metaphysics intact, so he does the same with the modern philosophy of the self-conscious subject. Whereas Descartes grounded the certainty of truth, rationality and knowledge in the thinking subject, Nietzsche grounded it in the will to power of the *overman.*[76] Accordingly, Nietzsche created yet another form of the dominance of the subject, this time grounded in a naturalistic concept of the fundamental human will for power and domination. In an illuminating analysis of the Enlightenment project, Heidegger affirmed that:

What is new about the modern period as opposed to the Christian medieval age consists in the fact that man, independently and by his own effort, contrives to become certain and sure of his human being in the midst of beings as a whole. The

---

[74] D.F. Krell, *Intimations of Mortality: Time, Truth and Finitude in Heidegger's Thinking of Being,* quoted in Ingraffia, *Postmodern Theory,* 103.

[75] Cf. Ingraffia, *Postmodern Theory,* 103–6.

[76] Ibid., 107.

essential Christian thought of the certitude of salvation is adopted, but such "salvation" is not eternal, other-worldly bliss, and the way to is not selflessness. The hale and the wholesome are sought exclusively in the free self-development of all the creative powers of man … In the context of man's liberation from the bonds of revelation and church doctrine, the question of first philosophy is 'In what way does man, on his own terms and for himself, first arrive at a primary, unshakeable truth, and what is that primary truth?'[77]

It is common knowledge that Heidegger's 'universal phenomenological ontology'[78] originated with his prolonged encounter with the theology of the apostle Paul. The methodology comes from Brentano and Husserl, and the content from the New Testament, although it is the New Testament interpreted through the lens of liberal Protestant exegesis, with the inevitable tendency to resolve the eschatological tension between the now and the not yet in favour of a realised eschatology. As both Paul Ricoeur and Moltmann note, in the process the eschatological dimensions of the New Testament are evacuated in favour of the philosophy of the eternal present.[79] Consequently, biblical theology is transposed into ontology, the uncertainty and fragility of our creaturely existence before God becomes the facticity, temporality and finitude of *Dasein*.

It is at this point that Heidegger believed he had thought beyond the Being of beings, locating the primordial ontological reality, and thus ending the dependence of first philosophy upon theology that has characterised the unhappy conscience of modernity. So, what is the nature of *Dasein*?

> If to Interpret the meaning of Being becomes our task, *Dasein* is not only the primary entity to be interrogated; it is also that entity which already comports itself, in its Being, towards what we are asking about when we ask this question.[80]

Being comports itself, it is a plenitude manifest in the clearing that emerges between itself and other beings. In one sense, it is an existential or, as Sartre later explained, existence precedes essence. This is only so because Being is concealed in the other and so is beyond representation:

> The difference of Being and beings, as the differentiation of overwhelming and arrival, is the perdurance (*Austrag*) of the two in *unconcealing keeping in*

---

[77] Heidegger, *Neitzsche* volume iv: *Nihilism*, 89 quoted in Ingraffia, *Postmodern Theory*, 108.

[78] Ingraffia, *Postmodern Theory*, 125.

[79] P. Ricoeur, *Freedom in the Light of Hope*; *The Conflict of Interpretations: Essays in Hermeneutics*, 407; Moltmann, *Theology of Hope*, 95–102.

[80] Heidegger, *Being and Time*, 35; quoted in Ingraffia, *Postmodern Theory*, 124–5.

concealment. Within this perdurance there prevails a clearing of what veils and closes itself off.[81]

Two things follow from the thinking of this difference, the intuition of a space between Being and beings but that nevertheless remains hidden. First, Being cannot be thought of as a substance and described in categories or properties that analogously define it as a reality presently at hand. Secondly, this inevitably entails that we can only think Being as that which is manifest in contingent particulars and existentials (*Dasein*). To be more specific, and this is not easy when dealing with fundamental ontology, *Dasein* is Being thrown down in the world without an explanation, i.e. it is devoid of theological interpretation. It is intentional Being that reaches out toward other objects and so can lose its self, forget the perdurance when the human subject is dislocated due to 'the transitivity of Being'[82] or, indeed, has become inauthentic through its assimilation to the world of others, and so its very becoming is lost in everydayness.

On the other hand, it is Being that can find itself, tentatively enter the clearing of Being, become authentic as it reaches out in anticipation of death and so assuage the anxiety and guilt of finitude. Whether or not this is a mere secularisation of Pauline anthropology, as Ingraffia continually complains,[83] is to a certain extent beside the point, because what is really at stake for Heidegger is the ending of two fundamental trajectories of metaphysical reflection that always thought of Being only in relation to the other form of being. The first, idealism, starts with consciousness, reaches out to the external world, and so postulates the essential subject/object dichotomy. The second, theism, starts with the external world (e.g. that of cause and effect) and derives a concept of Being from this basis. We understand *Dasein*, however, as being in the world or we have not grasped it at all.

Did Heidegger succeed in his task? Clearly, he did not. For a start, he never satisfactorily defined why some concepts are primary and others are not. Secondly, the near fatal solipsism of Heidegger's primordial ontology, a Being largely impervious to the socio-political context of human life, makes *Dasein* almost as vacuous as Kierkegaard's concept of inwardness. Should we be surprised, therefore, that Heidegger's fascination with the temporality, finitude and facticity of Being could not alert him to the fascism and anti-Semitism of Hitler's National Socialism? Thirdly, *Dasein* is as laden with philosophical

---

[81] Heidegger, 'Identity and Difference' trans Joan Stambaugh 65; quoted in Ward (ed.), *Postmodern God*, xxxiv.

[82] The phrase is that used by G. Vattimo in *The Adventure of Difference: Philosophy after Neitzsche and Heidegger*, trans Cyprian Blamires et al. (Oxford: Polity Press, 1993), 177; quoted in Ward, *The Postmodern God*, xxxiv.

[83] Cf. Ingraffia, *Postmodern Theory*, Chapter 9.

content and metaphysical implications as is the philosophy of phenomenology from which it is ultimately derived.

In *What is Metaphysics? The End of Philosophy and the Task of Thinking* and numerous other writings Heidegger smuggled in an inventory of intentional relationships peculiar to *Dasein* that lay the foundation for a new regnant meta-physical paradigm.[84] Consequently, *Dasein* is 'being projected into Nothing' whereby it can negotiate 'the totality of what is'. In the process, *Dasein* can stand outside the totality of reality (i.e. experience transcendence), and so create a 'clearing' in which Being manifests itself.[85] And what kind of Being is this, if not some grandiose mythic or metaphysical reality, another form of what Richard Rorty refers to as the 'big' ideas that continually comport them-selves amongst the tangled philosophical undergrowth of onto-theology?

Furthermore, Heidegger's re-appropriation of the Kierkegaardian dynamics of *Angst* (dread) as a means of delineating the reality of Being in the world intro-duced another troubling metaphysical theme to the already overloaded super-structure of this primordial ontology. It is difficult not to conclude that had Nietzsche had access to Heidegger's concept of *Dasein*, burdened as it is with the problematics of *Angst* – or, indeed, had he been aware of Sartre's later notion of *being-in-itself* all but overwhelmed by nausea and anxiety in the face of the apparent meaninglessness of life – he would have asserted that all this was another return to that slave mentality and sick conscience that is unable to come to terms with the uncomfortable reality of the will to power.

In his critique of Heidegger, Theodor Adorno claims there is a direct line of descent from Heidegger's mystified ontology of being and his endorsement of pro-Nazi politics. Adorno regards Heidegger's entire philosophy of *Dasein* as but another example of a bankrupt metaphysical tradition from which he was unable to break free.

> For Adorno's whole case must be seen to rest on a principled resistance to such vacuous (but all too beguiling) talk of essences, primordial truths, concealments of Being, historical *Dasein* and other such quasi-mystical absolutes dressed up in an oracular jargon that claims some priviledged access to truths beyond reach of argued critique.[86]

---

[84] See D. Farrell Knell (ed.), *Basic Writings: Martin Heidegger*.

[85] M. Heidegger, *Existence and Being*, 325–61.

[86] Norris, *What's Wrong With Postmodernism?*, 231. Philippe Lacoue-Labarthe flatly denies Adorno's thesis. He claims that Adorno fails to take account of Heidegger's own critique of Nazism that can be quarried from his writing, i.e. that Hitler's national socialism was a form of national aestheticism that wrongly conflated the realms of politics and arts. Cf. P. Lacoue-Labarthe, *Heidegger, Art and Politics: The Fiction of the Political*. By any account one would have to contend against Lacoue-Labarthe that this is a highly attenuated and theoretical postulation that could simply

The reappraisal of Nietzsche that characterises postmodernity also entails that the *via media* of Heideggerian existentialism, replete with the bourgeoisie notions of authentic and inauthentic existence, exemplifies a cleavage between those postmodernists who still wish to explore the debris left by Nietzsche and Heidegger's implosion of metaphysics (and others such as Foucauld, Deleuze, Lyotard and Baudrillard, who not only abandoned Hegelian dialectics, but also the subsequent outworking of this tradition in Marxism, existentialism and the phenomenology of Husserl, which culminated in the thought of Heidegger and Merleau-Ponty).

> Nietzsche's critique of representation … has two different components: (1) an attack on realist theories that claims subjects can accurately reflect or represent the world in thought without the mediations of culture, language, and physiology; (2) a *Lebensphilosophie* which privileges the body and its forces, desires, and will over conscious existence and representational schemes.[87]

One salutary and common feature of postmodernity is the way in which its main exponents have intensified Nietzsche's attack on the autonomous, rational subject of modernity. Many postmodernists appear to have accepted that the death of God was Nietzsche's achievement, but the 'infantile omnipotence' of the human subject – that which Hegel referred to as finitude bearing an impossible burden – he left merely mortally wounded. Consequently, their task is to accomplish another act of genocide, the final execution of the universal human subject with an obituary included in their various publications.

The linguistic turn

During the transition from modernity to postmodernity philosophical theory has taken a decidedly 'linguistic turn'.[88] Marxism, existentialism and phenomenology have given way to structuralism, where the modernist obsession with holistic systems was transferred to the world of language and semiotic theory. Systems are now analysed in terms of the relationships between parts and the whole, or the language constituted system of binary opposites, or the internal rules of systems of discourse. This is exemplified in the kinship theories of Levi-Strauss, the dream theories of Jacques Lacan, or the new political theory of Louis Althusser:

> The aim of all structuralist activity, in the fields of both thought and poetry, is to reconstitute an object, and, by this process, to make known the rules of functioning,

---

[86] *(continued)* be guilty of ignoring the obvious. Cf. Norris, *What's Wrong With Postmodernism?*, 254.

[87] Best and Kellner, *Postmodern Theory*, 83.

[88] R. Rorty (ed.), *The Linguistic Turn: Recent Essays in Philosophical Method*.

or 'functions', of this object. The structure is therefore effectively a *simulacrum* of the object which … Brings out something that remained invisible, or, if you like, unintelligible in the natural object.[89]

Structuralism sought to eliminate from philosophical enquiry the dominance of the self-conscious rational subject and replace it with the efficacy of the symbolic system, the subconscious and social relations. Subjectivity became a function of language, the subject was constituted by the relationship between *parole*, the use of language by individual subjects, and *langue*, the internal rules of the system of discourse. In this regard, the semiotic theory of Ferdinand de Saussure became highly influencial.[90]

Saussure analysed language in terms of a system of binary opposites, the synchronic and the diachronic, *la langue* and *la parole*, the signifier and the signified. However, he emphasised the apparent arbitrariness between the system of signs and that which is signified. Signs do not refer to external objects but are governed by the internal rules of the signifying system. The relationship between a sign or signifier and the idea or concept is established through the principle of iteration or repetition, which entails that the meaning of the sign is not stable but alters according to use. Once a sign is transferred to a different symbolic system the meaning alters accordingly.

Saussure's work combined with that of Wittgenstein to create an 'intra-textual' worldview.[91] Within any symbolic system the inter-relationship of signs and the signified creates the phenomenon of semiotic difference and the possibility of a highly attenuated fluidity of meaning. Post-structuralists such as Derrida, Barthes, Kristeva, Levinas and Irigaray, exploit this reality of semiotic difference and the consequent possibility of the deferral of meaning, in the process dismantling the demarcation lines that previously existed between separate symbolic systems, such as the linguistic, the psychological, the literary, the philosophical and the theological. Consequently, according to Derrida,

The meaning of meaning is infinite implication, the indefinite referral of signifier to signified … Its force is a certain pure and infinite equivocality which gives signified meaning no respite, no rest … it always signifies again and differs.[92]

Theological evaluations

To seek to delineate theological reasons for the demise of the Enlightenment and the arrival of postmodernism would appear to fly in the face of all these

---

[89] Barthes, *Essais Critiques*, quoted in Best and Kellner, *Postmodern Theory*, 18.

[90] F. de Saussure, *Course in General Linguistics*.

[91] Ward (ed.), *Postmodern God*, xxxvi.

[92] J. Derrida, *Speech and Phenomena, and Other Essays on Husserl's Theory of Signs*, 58.

developments in philosophy and cultural theory we have been examining. However, it has been our contention throughout this study that theological judgements, both correct and erroneous, pertain in all aspects of human life because, to a certain extent, they are the way we seek to articulate our relationship to the world at large and our own place within that wider scheme of things. Similarly, it has been our primary thesis that the crisis of modern Christology is largely due to the way successive forms of christological reconstruction have become aligned with the socio-political myths spawned by the Enlightenment. Whether it is the myth of a universal humanity (which replaced universal religion), the myth of human progress, the myth of transcendentalism or the myth of political and social emancipation, they all ultimately find their source in that legacy of philosophical reflection referred to as idealism. In that sense, our basic thesis and critical engagement with this tradition has much in common with the work of one of the great exponents of the Frankfurt school of critical theory, Theodor Adorno.

The critique of idealism

In his groundbreaking book, *Negative Dialectics*, Adorno anticipated much of the postmodern conflict with idealism. He described the idealism that originated with Kant and culminated in Husserl as a form of philosophical rage that endeavoured to obliterate all difference and otherness, and subsume everything within its imperialistic, all encompassing categories of thought. This is nowhere more admirably exemplified than in Hegel's phenomenology of Spirit:

> On the one side, actual self-consciousness through its externalisation, passes over into the actual world, and the latter back into actual self-consciousness. On the other side, this same actuality – both person and objectivity – is superseded; they are purely universal. This alienation is *pure consciousness* or *essence*. The *present* actual world has its antithesis directly in its *beyond*, which is both the thinking of it and its thought-form, just as the beyond has in the present world its actuality, but an actuality alienated from it.[93]

In Hegel's dialectic we discover that 'theory of aggression' that George Steiner claimed resided at the heart of European culture. Why? Because, as is true for any major cultural transition, the cultural sojourn from Christendom to modernity was not without considerable cost. It was Adorno's contention that this particular cultural revolution was characterised by a search for absolute spiritual or ontological security,[94] i.e., the retreat into foundationalism. Similar to the thesis advocated by Erich Fromm in *Escape from Freedom*, Adorno

---

[93] G.W.F. Hegel, *Phenomenology of Spirit*, 295.
[94] T.W. Adorno, *Against Epistemology: A Metacritique Studies in Husserl and the Phenomenological Antinomies*, 15.

claimed that the new bourgeoisie emerged from feudalism existentially triumphant, but epistemologically insecure. In the midst of rapid social change, political and economic upheaval and the new social and moral dilemmas spawned by industrialisation, the educated middle-classes sought intellectual and epistemological security through the search for unshakeable philosophical foundations. Descartes' philosophy of consciousness, Kant's transcendentalism, Hegel and Fichte's idealism of the self-postulating Absolute Subject, Schelling's dialectics of existential estrangement and Husserl's transcendental phenomenology all manifest the same fantasy, the philosophical search for archetypal foundations. Adorno claimed that *prima philosophia*, or the philosophy of first principles, seeks to assuage epistemological insecurity through the discovery of indubitable foundations to knowledge.[95]

The shaking of the foundations

The source of such foundationalism is the ubiquitous, universal subject abstracted from the contamination of particular socio-political or cultural circumstances. Here, in the unsullied substratum of pure self-consciousness, the rational subject supposedly gains epistemic access to the external world. What in fact transpires is an unwarranted philosophical pre-emptive strike, whereby the reified autonomous subject creates a mirror image of itself.[96] It does so through an act of epistemological aggression, subsuming all difference, particularity, non-identity and otherness within the boundaries of its own totalising intellectual constructs. In the process, as we have already noted, a philosophical, idealist, totalitarianism emerges whereby 'spirit confiscates what is unlike itself and makes it the same, its property. Spirit inventories it. Nothing can slip through the net.'[97] Such a philosophical lust for security and certainty is far from politically neutral. Rather, the converse is the case:

> The 'desire to vindicate for truth a superhuman objectivity which must merely be recognised' might also promote recognition and obedience of a superhuman social authority, a superior *Führer*.[98]

It is surely not a historical accident that it is the apparently epistemologically emancipated bourgeois subject who has invented all the grand ideologies such as National Socialism, Fascism, Marxism and its corollary totalitarian communism. In the name of such imperialistic ideologies, we have justified the subjugation,

---

[95] Ibid., 15.

[96] Nietzsche argued that when philosophy felt compelled by its own vision it always reverses the account of Genesis i.e., it creates a mirror image of itself.

[97] Adorno, *Against Epistemology*, 9.

[98] Best and Kellner, *Postmodern Theory*, 231.

domination and extermination of countless non-identifiable others and so turned the twentieth century into one of mass death.

Similarly, the fetishisation of conceptual constructs replicates the dynamics of monopoly capitalism in the Academy. Foundational ideas become the intellectual property of the educated classes who are not economic producers, but who, nevertheless, own the title deeds to such concepts thereby guaranteeing their own epistemological security and enhancing their authority.[99] So, like the commodities of capitalism, a new system of exchange and consumption, based on the fetishisation of intellectual property, is established. Even the most apparently abstract ideas are the product of the social processes that produced them and so are inevitably freighted with social content. It is this articulation of negative dialectics, a combination of philosophy and socio-political theory that both anticipates many of the discourses of post-modernity, and constitutes a telling theological critique of the philosophical presuppositions of modernity.

Adorno explains why this is so. Foundationalism represents a 'tendency to regression, a hatred of the complicated, that is steadily at work in a theory of origins, thus guaranteeing its affinity with lordship'.[100] Thus, as was true of modernity and science, so it is also with the philosophy of first principles, a new jealous monotheism of ideas emerges which regards all non-identifiable particularity and otherness with distrust and suspicion. Unlike the mono-theism of Scripture, this one makes no room for dissent and the multi-culturalism of the nations. The lordship of the universal subject is maintained by the socio-political strategies of domination and exclusion we have already investigated. Religion is depoliticised and privatised, history is identified with social, intellectual and cultural progress. Reality becomes the self-referential narrative of the evolution of matter to self-conscious spirit, the elevation of the finite to the infinite and the rhetoric of emancipation and individualism becomes the basis to the new political settlement and contractual politics. Consequently, when Christology is superimposed on such an intellectual framework it replicates both the same futile search for absolute foundations, as demonstrated for instance in the endless search for the elusive historical Jesus, and renders the discourse of salvation nothing more than a carbon copy of the rhetoric of socio-political emancipation. Hence, inadvertently and almost imperceptible, Christianity capitulates to the cultural aspirations and mores of modernity.[101]

---

[99] Adorno, *Against Epistemology*, 14–15.

[100] Ibid, 20.

[101] It is of course possible to contend that it was this kind of intellectual accommodation that Colossians 2:8 warns against.

Assessment

The deconstruction of the transcendental subject and the nature of power

We have noted already that the construction of the transcendental-self, understood as the autonomous thinking subject who occupies a position of epistemological privilege in relation to the world, was largely the work of Descartes and Kant. The former's search for indubitable knowledge arrived at the apparently unassailable certainty of 'I think, therefore I am'. The *res cogitans* (humanity and the human mind) became the focal point of departure for all knowledge of the world, morality, God and ourselves.

Kant's attempt to adopt a more constrained approach to human knowledge and so map out the limits of critical reason to make room for faith, did, in fact, further consolidate the epistemological priority of the thinking subject. The transcendental subject was now in possession of a cognitive grid (namely, the a priori categories of the mind) through which all our interaction with the external world was processed, organised and conceptualised,. It was Nietzsche's firmly held conviction, however, that the modern autonomous subject was an ideological construct designed to deflect our attention away from the unpalatable reality of the sovereignty of the will to power, domination and control. Not surprisingly, therefore, a central theme in postmodern theory is the analysis and dissection of the nature of power.

The first to develop this analysis beyond Nietzsche was Foucault. 'We had to wait until the nineteenth century before we began to understand the nature of exploitation, and to this day, we have yet to fully comprehend the nature of power.'[102] We have already noted that modernity tended to represent power structures in terms of macro-theories and totalising systems such as the power of the nation-state or the conflict between monopoly capitalism and Marxism. Foucault believed there have been two dominant models for analysing power in modernity both of which, he claims, are laden with erroneous and outmoded assumptions. The first is the Marxist economistic model, which reduces power to systems of class domination and its antidote, economic emancipation. The second is the juridical model, a descendent of the divine right of kings, which defines power in terms of the law, moral rights and political sovereignty, representing power in largely hegemonic, restrictive and oppressive modes. Foucault rejected the macro-theories of power in favour of a non-totalising, non-representational and non-humanistic theory of power as that which is essentially highly dispersed, indeterminate, subjectless and potentially productive.[103] The

---

[102] Foucault, *Language*, 213.
[103] M. Foucault, *The History of Sexuality*, 136.

transition from modernity to postmodernity represents the proliferation of power centres and distribution networks, 'never have there existed more centres of power … more circular contacts and linkages … more sites where the intensity of pleasures and the persistency of power catch hold, only to spread elsewhere'.[104] Consequently, Foucault defined power as 'a multiple and mobile field of force relations where far-reaching, but never completely stable effects of domination are produced'.[105]

Knowledge is a function of these socially dispersed coercive relationships. It is part of that 'normalisation' process in society that both invests power in certain self-interest groups, and constructs sophisticated surveillance and control mechanisms to exclude and dominate the other, all in the name of emancipation. Foucault sought to demonstrate this by means of his genealogy of the human sciences,[106] a process whereby society privileges the soul over the body, reason over nature, subject over object and so subjects the individual to the tyranny of the 'psyche, subjectivity, personality, consciousness … and the moral claims of humanism'.[107] Accordingly, society creates new surveillance disciplines, for instance psychiatry, sociology and criminology bolstered by the appropriate correctional institutions such as asylums, hospitals, prisons and police forces. These dispersed centres of power are maintained by the myth of the universal subject, a myth Foucault sought to expose by illustrating the ambiguities inherent in the threefold doubling the subject undergoes in relation to the external world.

First, there is the I, who, as that prodigious self-consciousness, mentally constitutes the world of objects, but is at the same time an object of scrutiny in the world. Secondly, there is the I who is both a product of unknown forces and yet somehow transcends such limitation by being aware of this necessary inconvenience. Thirdly, there is the I from which history unfolds as I acknowledge a past, present and future in relation to myself; however, I am also part of a history that antedates me and will also eventually supersede myself.[108]

According to Foucault, modernity resolved these antinomies of the subject by investing in the mastery of the transcendental self. Once again we encounter the theory of aggression and domination that lies at the heart of the Enlightenment conspiracy, masquerading in the language of epistemological emancipation. How do we disabuse ourselves of such fantasy? Through the destruction of the subject as a political expediency, 'One has to dispense with the constituent subject, and to get rid of the subject itself, that is to say, to

---

[104] Ibid., 49; quoted in Best and Kellner, *Postmodern Theory*, 51.
[105] Ibid., 102; Best and Kellner, *Postmodern Theory*, 51.
[106] Cf. M. Foucault, *Discipline and Punishment: The Birth of the Prison*.
[107] Ibid., 29–30.
[108] Cf. Lakeland, *Postmodernity*, 21.

arrive at an analysis which can account for the constitution of the subject within a historical framework.'[109] In so doing, we listen again to the subjugated and suppressed voices of history and overcome the politics of domination.

> It seems to me that the real political task in a society such as ours is to criticise the working of institutions which appear to be both neutral and independent; to criticise them in such a manner that the political violence which has always exercised itself obscurely through them will be unmasked, so that one can fight them'.[110]

Like other postmodernists who have sought an explication of human society largely in terms of power relations, Foucault, at this stage in his intellectual sojourn, was unable to refute the charge of having conceded to a debilitating presentism. If everything is reducible to power then in effect nothing is because we possess no standard or criteria through which we could extrapolate a possible remedy.[111]

In his later work, Baudrillard developed an ironic metaphysics whereby the subject simply looses the battle to dominate and domesticate the object. Ironically, playing with Descartes' notion of the malevolent genius that could be deceiving the thinking subject if it were not for a good and gracious God, Baudrillard casts the world of objects in this role. In *Fatal Strategies*, the self must surrender to the high tech-world of objects that now assume autonomous

---

[109] Foucault, *Power/Knowledge*, 117.

[110] M. Foucault, *Human Nature: Justice Versus Power*, 171; quoted in Best and Kellner, *Postmodern Theory*, 57.

[111] Other notable representatives of postmodernity continue the intense assault upon the autonomous, rational subject. For instance, Deleuze and Guattari attempt to radically de-centre the univocal subject through a process of schzoanalysis. Whereas psychoanalysis privileges the despotic self-conscious subject, schzoanalysis seeks out the subliminal and unconscious levels of desire that do not operate according to such stratified hierarchies. Promulgating a materialistic theory of desire akin to Nietzsche's theory of the will to power, Derrida's notion of dissemination, Foucault's conception of productive power, and Lacan's striking notion of libidinal instability, Deleuze and Guattari postulate a non-representational, monistic theory of the individual as essentially a desiring machine. See G. Deleuze and F. Guattari, *Anti-Oedipus: Capitalism and Schizophrenia*, and *Kafka: A Thousand Plateaus*. 'Where psychoanalysis neuroticises, producing subjects who conform to authority and law and are repressed in their desire, schizoanalysis schizophrenicises, opening up the lines of movement of desire away from hierarchical and socially imposed forms'; quoted in Best and Kellner, *Postmodern Theory*, 91.

To a certain extent Foucault, Deleuze and Guattari seek to discover alternative forms of subjectivity that replace the idealist subject with a materialist libidinal dynamics. However, Baudrillard and Lyotard endeavour to obliterate all traces of this malign legacy of modernity altogether.

powers independent of social relationships. In this strange world the tables are truly turned and it is individual subjects who become the alienated flotsam on the ever-increasing ocean of their own fetishised objects and simulations.[112] In *The Differend*, Lyotard seeks to banish the metaphysics of the subject through a Wittgensteinian theory of language games and 'regime of phrases'. Again, we discover a philosophy developing a preferential option of the weak, marginalised minorities, articulating the fundamental postmodern themes of difference, otherness and plurality. Similarly, Lyotard followed Adorno in asserting that the myth of the universal subject died in the holocaust. After Auschwitz, there can be no common humanity and consequently an agonistic politics is inevitable.[113]

Reconstruction of the human subject

Not surprisingly, postmodernity has also spawned a counter movement to this near total annihilation of the personal subject. Foucault's work moved from an archaeological focus on systems of knowledge in the 1960s, to a genealogical focus on modalities of power in the 1970s, to an emphasis on technologies of the self that form the basis for both a personal and social ethics of liberty in the 1980s. Through his study of pre-modern Greek, Roman and Christian cultures, Foucault arrived at a modified theory of subjectivity. The subject is no longer viewed as purely a product of power relations, but also a relation of self-awareness, discipline and to a certain extent, self-mastery the individual has with oneself. Ethics is constituted by such technologies of the self, practices

> which permit individuals to effect by their own means or with the help of others a certain number of operations on their own bodies and souls, thoughts, conduct, and a way of being, so as to transform themselves in order to attain a certain state of happiness, purity, wisdom, perfection of immortality.[114]

Foucault constructed a *via media* between the wholly self-constituting, or self-postulating subject of idealism and phenomenology, and the self who is a mere product of discourses of power and systems of domination. The subject is still socially situated and vulnerable to political manipulation and coercion, but now the self is also capable of obtaining a measure of self-identity and forging certain practices of freedom:

---

[112] J. Baudrillard, *Fatal Strategies*, 259ff.

[113] Cf. Best and Kellner, *Postmodern Theory*, 170.

[114] M. Foucault, *Technologies of the Self*, 18; quoted in Best and Kellner, *Postmodern Theory*, 61.

> if now I am interested…in the way in which the subject constitutes himself in an active fashion, by the practices of the self, these practices are nevertheless not something that the individual invents by himself. They are patterns that he finds in his culture and which are proposed, suggested, and imposed on him by his culture, his society and his social group.[115]

In his *Theory of Communicative Action*, Habermas endeavoured to develop a post-Kantian theory of inter-subjectivity that he believes can rescue the subject from the twin mires of the Enlightenment philosophy of consciousness and postmodern anti-foundationalism. His is a re-constructive, rather than a de-constructive agenda.

Habermas aligned himself over and against what he regarded as two essentially reductionist traditions of postmodern thought. The first was the anti-metaphysical, anti-subjectivity lobby which originated with Nietzsche, moved through Heidegger to Derrida and ended up with either a mysticism of Being (Heidegger) or a mysticism of language (Derrida). The second also began with Nietzsche, but this time the trajectory moved via Georges Bataille to Foucault culminating in an irrationalist aestheticism that can provide no substantial basis for ethics or political action. Habermas also faulted the Wittgensteinian–Frege philosophy of language school for being locked into the same subject/object dichotomy as its idealist opponents. Consequently, he wanted to begin with the ego/alter (self/other) model of communication favoured by Martin Buber's philosophy of personalism, thus enabling him to concentrate on the efficacy of speech-acts. Habermas accused the postmodern theorists of intensifying the problematics of instrumental reason, a reason fixated on technological control and domination. The extension of this form of reason into the life-world of social and communicative action has transformed reason into an instrument of terror and all but obliterated any foundation to ethics or politics. For Habermas, the art of inter-subjective communicative action rested on certain formal, if not constitutive, foundational principles:

> Intersubjective communication can only occur because there is an assumption on both parts that the speaker is comprehensible, sincere, truthful, and exhibits recognisable ethical norms. Deceit, lying, manipulation are possible only because the speaker can take advantage of the hearer's assumption that the rules of discourse are operative.[116]

The speech-act relies on rules of discourse that require openness to the other, commitment to certain democratic ends and ideals and mutual participation in

---

[115] M. Foucault, *The Ethic of Care for the Self as a Practice of Freedom*, 11; quoted in Best and Kellner, *Postmodern Theory*, 65.

[116] Lakeland, *Postmodernity*, 22.

such essentially emancipatory processes. It would appear, however, that Habermas valorised the ideal speech-act and the suspicion is that he is guilty of universalising what in the fragmented, heterogeneous world of postmodern micro-politics rarely happens. This would be the substance of Lyotard's critique that different language games and 'regimes of phrases' deploy different rules, many of which do not advocate consensus but dissent and subversive resistance. It is not difficult to agree with Lyotard. For instance the discourses of multinational global capitalism are often highly instrumental and commercially manipulative. Similarly, the media both popularises and indulges in its own form of highly alluring and seductive advertising propaganda. If one analyses the development of modern management theory, one discerns a movement from highly domineering and abrasive forms of discourse too much more consensus driven programmes of mutual accountability. Clearly, it all depends which system of discourse is operative and what rules govern our participation in the particular language game before we can assume Habermas' laudable theory of intersubjective communicative action will apply.

Incredulity toward metanarratives and the end of history

We have noted already that one of the primary texts of postmodernity is Jean-Francois Lyotard's *The Postmodern Condition: A Report on Knowledge*, commissioned by the Canadian Government. In this influential study, Lyotard not only named the postmodern condition but also sets out to analysis its constituent ingredients. His focus was knowledge. Thus he did not describe modernity as a historical process, but as the odyssey of reason that began with the rise of the natural sciences.

According to Lyotard, there are three conditions that define the nature of modern knowledge; an appeal to metanarratives to legitimise foundational claims and assertions; the development of criteria of legitimisation that consequently delegitimise and exclude others; and the consequent preference for homogeneous epistemological and moral frameworks of meaning. Postmodern knowledge, on the other hand, is the product of a post-industrial society dependent upon computerisation and advanced systems of information technology. Consequently, it demonstrates an incredulity toward metanarratives, eschews foundational systems of legitimisation, prefers heterogeneous plurality, revels in constant innovation and relies on pragmatic rules of discourse and consensus morality.

In an ironic exposé of modern science and its reliance on apparently objective claims for truth and legitimisation, Lyotard claimed that science is intrinsically opposed to other forms of knowledge, such as narrative, myth and story, which rely on other criteria of legitimisation and possess a sociological function in defining the ethos, traditions and identity of a particular group or culture. Ensconced in the supposedly neutral modern university system, science in effect becomes the esoteric language game of the expert advancing claims to knowledge based on agreed truth claims and the current consensus of scientific knowledge. In the process, science becomes 'actively opposed to the language game of narrative, which it associates with ignorance, barbarity, prejudice, superstition and ideology'.[117]

The irony of all this is that science is exposed as that which relies on two dominant Enlightenment metanarratives as its founding legitimisation, both of which constitute the underlying political and philosophical justification of the whole scientific enterprise. Not surprisingly, one of these, as we have had many opportunities to note, is the Enlightenment myth of progress and emancipation. Science and technology, it was claimed, would liberate us from superstition and ignorance and secure a safe passage to truth, progress and economic prosperity.[118]

The other complementary totalising theory is the philosophical grand-narrative ultimately derived from Fichte, Schelling and Hegel. Here the whole history of humanity is conceived as the adventure of the 'divine Life' and knowledge is a product of that evolution of self-conscious mind from inanimate matter that discovers how to think itself:

> German idealism has recourse to a metaprinciple that simultaneously grounds the development of learning, of society, and of the State in the realisation of the 'life' of a Subject, called 'divine Life' by Fichte and 'Life of the spirit' by Hegel. In this perspective, knowledge first finds legitimisation with itself, and it is knowledge that is entitled to say what the State and what Society are. But it can only play this role by changing levels, by ceasing to be simply the positive knowledge of its referent (nature, Society, the State, etc.), becoming in addition to that the knowledge of the knowledge of the referent – that is, by becoming speculative. In the names of 'Life' and 'Spirit', knowledge names itself.[119]

Both of these metanarratives are examples of what Emmanuel Levinas refers to as unethical totalitarianism. They both demand consent and exclude the other. In submission to either the emancipatory ideals of science or the imperialistic philosophies of history, be that Hegelianism, Marxism, Positivism or Liberal-ism, we give licence to ourselves, in the name of progress and knowledge, to use the other either as a means toward our own self-transcendence or as the

---

[117] Connor, *Postmodernist Culture*, 29.

[118] Cf. Lyotard's use of the proposals of Fichte, Schleiermacher and Wilhelm von Humboldt concerning the foundation of Berlin University (1807–10), a university that became a model for others throughout Europe. J.F. Lyotard, *The Postmodern Condition: A Report on Knowledge*, 32.

[119] Ibid., 34–5.

extension of our own lust for power and control. What has happened since the end of the Second World War, according to Lyotard, is the terminal decline of both of these metanarratives as the external legitimisation of the whole scientific endeavour. The reasons for this state of affairs are supposed to have something to do with the expansion of international capitalism, the demise of state communism and the emergence of the post-industrial society, and here we are amongst the familiar themes of postmodern cultural theory. With the demise of the grand-narratives, we have the advent of scientific pragmatism. Science is no longer orientated toward legitimating myths such as progress, emancipation and the elevation of the human spirit and degenerates instead into a mass of unrelated specialisations, none of which has recourse any longer to foundational narratives of legitimisation. 'We have seen, therefore, a shift from the muffled majesty of grand narratives to the splintered autonomy of micro-narratives.'[120]

Not surprisingly, others have taken their lead from Lyotard's analysis. For instance, Gianni Vattimo contends in *The End of Modernity* that the rejection of metanarratives that seek to impose some order, unity and cohesion to the historical process inevitably means the end of history. It is not just that postmodernity signals the arrival of the post-metaphysical age or the post-industrial age, it is that history itself can no longer be understood in terms of a universal, foundational narrative. History is always someone's story, his story rather than her story, the story of the rise and fall of particular cultures and civilisations, the story of European conquests and expansionism, and always it is a story told from the perspective of the winners rather than the losers. As we have already contended, the rise of historical science itself in modern times was a positivistic science driven by the myth of progress and development. Consequently, in terms of the political explanation of the nature of history, the end of history has arrived.[121]

Baudrillard also joined the chorus of voices announcing the end of history. He referred repeatedly to Canetti's remarks that at a certain moment in time the human race decided to drop out of history.[122] What we are now witnessing is the ecstasy of history; history disappears as the abiding form of social existence:

> For modernity, history was its substance and ethos: modernity was a process of change, innovation, progress, and development. Moreover, history was the repository

---

[120] Connor, *Postmodern Culture*, 32.

[121] A neo-Marxist like Jameson begs to differ and while he agrees that history is only accessible to us in textual form, he asserts against Lyotard that history is 'not a text, not a narrative, master or otherwise, unfortunately history is what hurts and its alienating necessities will not forget us, however much we might prefer to ignore them'. Jameson, *Political Unconscious*, 102.

[122] E. Canetti, *The Human Province*.

of hopes of the epoch; it would bring democracy, revolution, socialism, progress and well-being for all. All of this has now disappeared, Baudrillard suggests, with the end of history'.[123]

Embracing his own version of Nietzsche's theory of eternal recurrence, Baudrillard postulated a number of possible ends to history. Borrowing from cosmology he sees the universe expanding at ever increasing speed until eventually history vanishes 'into a hyperspace where it looses all meaning'[124] Moving back into more familiar territory he revisited his earlier concern that the masses satiated with endless bland entertainment could arrive at such a state of boredom and entropy that history will implode into a state of social and political inertia.[125] Finally, he postulated the possibility that technological and media simulation will reach such a level of sophistication that nothing is real and all that awaits us is a futureless future of infinite repetition.[126]

These are very bleak scenarios, but then we must remember that

With Baudrillard and other postmodernists, theory itself is 'postmodernised', adapting to the speed, fashions, superficiality, and fragmented nature of the contemporary era. Theory thus becomes a hypercommodity, geared to sell and promote the latest fashions in thought and attitudes.[127]

---

[123] Best and Kellner, *Postmodern Theory*, 133.

[124] J. Baudrillard, 'The Year 2000 Has Already Happened' in Arthur and Marilouise Kroker (eds), *Body Invaders: Panic Sex in America*, 35–44 (36); quoted in Best and Kellner, *Postmodern Theory*, 134.

[125] Ibid., 37.

[126] Ibid., 40.

[127] Best and Kellner, *Postmodern Theory*, 140. Baudrillard is clearly on the far left as far as the prophets of the end of history are concerned. However, perhaps it is as well to note that that apparently most historicist of philosophers, Karl Marx, in the satirical tract *Eighteenth Brumaire of Louis Bonaparte*, sounded his own strongly suspicious note in regard to the efficacy of historical science. The best known of his remarks from the *Eighteenth Brumaire* is his parody of Hegel: 'Hegel remarks somewhere that all facts and personages of great importance in world history occur, as it were twice. He forgot to add: the first time as tragedy, the second as farce'. K. Marx, *The Eighteenth Brumaire of Louis Napoleon*, in *Karl Marx and Friedrich Engels: Collected Works* Vol 2, 108, quoted in Norris, *What's Wrong With Postmodernism?*, 30. Similarly, Marx notes that some of the most farcical episodes of history are the direct result of repetitive and seemingly regressive tendencies in human beings that render the whole historical process apparently devoid of meaning, significance or coherence:

'Men make their own history, but they do not make it just as they please; they do not make it under circumstances chosen by themselves, but under circumstances directly encountered, given and transmitted from the past ... And just when they seem engaged in revolutionising themselves and things, in creating something that

Postmodernity remains for our time the age of criticism; its deconstructionalist agenda has all but obliterated the powerful political and cultural paradigms of modernity and launched us into a new era of chastened self-reflection. Before we may be able to see the next stage in the cultural evolution of late capitalism, we may have to listen to the prophets who similarly sought to overthrow the aggressive totalitarian epistemological imperialism of the modernity project. It is precisely to such a prophet that we now turn in search of a Christology that sought to remain its own paradigmatic witness to a gracious and loving God.

---

[126] (*continued*) has never yet existed, precisely in such periods of revolutionary crisis they anxiously conjure up the spirits of the past to their service and borrow from them names, battle-cries and costumes in order to present the new scene of world history in this time-honoured disguise and this borrowed language.' Ibid., 103–4; quoted in Norris, *What's Wrong With Postmodernism?*, 34–5.

10.

Jesus Christ the True Paradigm

Karl Barth is really an initiator, indeed the main initiator, of a 'postmodern' paradigm of theology that was already dawning at that time ... But, for uncritical admirers of Barth: Karl Barth is an initiator and not a perfecter of such a paradigm.[1]

Introduction

In light of the genealogical and archaeological investigations of postmodern cultural theory that seek to expose the regnant power structures and ideological constraints of all forms of human knowledge, should theology, and more specifically Christology, forsake the dialogue with human culture altogether? Is it possible to privilege the biblical norms of faith and belief, and the later history of christological interpretation in such a way that the constant danger of cultural accommodation and contamination is removed from the theological agenda and replaced by a positive science of revelation? Has God given us sufficient clues to his existence and saving purposes for humankind that theology can simply become the obedience of faith seeking understanding? If so, then Christology would effectively become the construction of an independent paradigm of revelation that protects the sanctity and integrity of the church's ecclesial existence in the world?

It is this journey of reorientation that was taken by probably the greatest theologian of the modern era. Consequently, Christology is not one particular aspect of Karl Barth's theological system. Rather, as Robert Jenson notes, the whole of the massive and highly original *Church Dogmatics* represents nothing less than the attempt to construct a christological metaphysics or a christological vision of reality:

> In Barth's interpretation of reality, the life-history of one human person has taken the place held in the West's traditional metaphysics by – to use perhaps familiar language – the Ground of Being. The *Church Dogmatics* casts a metaphysical vision of

---

[1] Küng, *Great Christian Thinkers*, 198.

temporal reality bracketed not by Timelessness but by one of the temporal entities it contains, the Crucified and Risen.[2]

This intense concentration upon Christology led G. Berkouwer in his book, *The Triumph of Grace in the Theology of Karl Barth*, to accuse Barth of developing an extreme Christomonism.[3] If this were true, Barth's theology would be analogous to an imploding star: the sheer power of the christological gravitational forces would eventually drag everything into the 'black hole' of the eternal person and being of Christ.

It is, however, more accurate to use the analogy of a christological prism. The iridescent light that shines from the person of Christ is refracted through that prism to illuminate the landscape of Christian theology in a way not previously attempted. In that respect, as H. Hartwell recognised:

> The *Church Dogmatics* is wholly christological in the sense that in it, generally speaking, every theological proposition has as its point of departure Jesus Christ, the Son of God and the Son of Man, in the unity of his person and work. This christological concentration of the *Church Dogmatics* and indeed of Barth's theology as a whole is unparalleled in the history of Christian thought.[4]

Hartwell's observation makes the point that Barth's famous christocentrism did not result in any constriction in theological analysis or definition. Rather, it stands for a total reconstruction of what we might term the basic topography of Christian theology, in such a way that nothing remains independent or dislocated from this central axis.[5]

Barth's Christology represented a consistent attempt to overturn the popular tide of theological opinion both in regard to what Christology is and how, methodologically, it should be approached. In both respects he is his own best advocate:

> For me thinking is christological only when it consists in the perception, comprehension, understanding and estimation of the living person of Jesus Christ as attested by Holy Scripture, in attentiveness to the range and significance of his existence, in openness to his self-disclosure, in consistency in following him as is demanded ...

[2] R. Jenson, 'Karl Barth', in D. Ford (ed.), *The Modern Theologians: An Introduction to Christian Theology in the Twentieth Century*, Vol. 1, 41.

[3] G.C. Berkouwer, *The Triumph of Grace in the Theology of Karl Barth*. Christomonism is the assertion that Jesus Christ remains the sole subject and definitive expression of God's salvation, which, consequently eliminates any possibility of human response. For Barth's response to this accusation see *Church Dogmatics* 4\4 (fragment), 20–33.

[4] H. Hartwell, *The Theology of Karl Barth: An Introduction*, 15–16.

[5] Also Johnson, *Mystery*, 102–3.

We are not dealing with a Christ-principle, but with Jesus Christ himself as attested by Holy Scripture.[6]

This entails that, almost alone in modern theology, Barth practised and consistently advocated a Christology from above, which began not with the historical Jesus, but with the pre-existent *Logos*, the second person of the Trinity, and also, as we shall see, because of the actualism of revelation, the man Jesus of Nazareth.[7]

Barth's Christology also attempted to unite the person and work of Christ within the parameters of a dynamic doctrine of reconciliation. Incarnation and atonement are one and the same movement of God to humanity in the person of Christ the Mediator. Consequently, the 'humiliation' and 'exaltation' of Jesus Christ cannot be understood, as they were in Reformed theology, as two sequential states. Rather, they are one simultaneous movement of God that embraces the whole of humanity. In all respects, both in Germany (where he is still much admired), and in Britain and North America (where, until recently, he was rarely read), Barth is a problem to his interpreters.[8]

Barth and his Interpreters

That Barth is the father of modern twentieth-century theology, in the way Schleiermacher was for nineteenth-century liberal Protestantism, is difficult to dispute.[9] That fact was recognised by one astute commentator as early as 1937: 'With Barth we have incontestably the greatest figure in Christian theology that has appeared for decades.'[10] Barth's systematic contribution to modern theology may be much admired, but he is often adjudged, however, to have

---

[6] Barth, *Church Dogmatics*, 4\3, 174.

[7] One could say that Karl Rahner's Christology is also a Christology from above. However, Rahner's preference for the evolutionary paradigm immediately moves his christological considerations into an idealist framework of interpretation whereas the structure for Barth's Christology is much more that of a critically realistic position, as Bruce McCormack has sought to argue in his highly influential book, *Karl Barth's Critically Realistic Dialectical Theology: Its Genesis and Development, 1909–1936*.

[8] For an analysis of this particular problem see R.H. Roberts, 'The Reception of the Theology of Karl Barth in the Anglo-Saxon World: History, Typology and Prospect' in *A Theology on Its Way: Essays on Karl Barth*, 95–154.

[9] Cf. J. Baillie, *The Sense of the Presence of God*, 254.

[10] H.R. Mackintosh, *Types of Modern Theology*, 263.

failed in the attempt to present viable alternatives to the pressing issues that still haunt the modern mind.

The usual attempts to put Barth in historical context often eventuates in the portrayal of him as some sort of theological dinosaur, with his particular brand of *neo-orthodoxy* being viewed as a largely unsuccessful attempt to turn the theological clock back. Alister McGrath, for example, thinks Barth's Christology largely evades the issue in relation to one of the classic post-Enlightenment conundrums: the relation of faith to history. Instead, McGrath claims Barth's Christology belongs to the pre-modern period. It is really a kind of throwback to concerns that were appropriate to the sixteenth and seventeenth centuries, but not to the modern era.[11] According to Bruce McCormack, a thesis with which we largely agree, the main reason for this standard, and somewhat dismissive interpretation of Barth in the Anglo-American world as a *neo-orthodox* theologian, is due to the long ascendancy of the 'von Balthasar paradigm' regarding the development and interpretation of Barth's theological career. Hans Urs von Balthasar promulgated the thesis that Barth underwent two significant theological conversions that changed the direction of his whole theological pilgrimage.[12]

The first, which remains incontestable, was Barth's rejection of his liberal theological heritage mediated to him directly by his theological teacher, Wilhelm Herrmann. Due to the considerable post-First World War socio-political, cultural, pastoral and theological pressures that bore down on Barth while serving as a pastor in the country parish of Safenwil, he underwent a complete theological transformation that eventuated in the publication of the first and second editions of the *Römerbrief*.[13] According to von Balthasar, Barth experienced another 'radical change' sometime in the 1930s when he largely rejected the dialectical theology of his younger years in favour of a christologically grounded doctrine of analogy, the *analogia fidei* (analogy of faith): 'The content of this shift was ... described in terms of a "turn from dialectic to analogy" – a formula which has exercised a tremendous influence in scholarly reflection on Barth's development'.[14] Von Balthasar, following Barth, interpreted the 'turn to analogy' as largely due to Barth's study of Anselm and the publication in 1931 of Barth's little book *Fides Quaerens Intellectum* (*Faith Seeking Understanding*). Hans Frie and Tom Torrance reinforced this thesis in

---

[11] McGrath, *Modern German Christology*, 143. Cf. Macquarrie, *Modern Thought*, 282.

[12] H. Urs von Balthasar, *The Theology of Karl Barth: Exposition and Interpretation*.

[13] The significance of the socio-political and cultural influences upon Barth during this important period of his life has been explored in Germany by F.W. Marquardt, *Theologie und Sozialismus: Das Beispiel Karl Barth*, and Helmut Gollwitzer, *Reich Gottes und Sozialismus bei Karl Barth*, see McCormack, *Dialectical Theology*, 26.

[14] McCormack, *Dialectical Theology*, 2.

the English-speaking world through the influence of their respective studies on Barth's theology.[15]

In addition, Paul Tillich and Dietrich Bonhoeffer argued that Barth persistently practised a supra-naturalism or a 'positivism of revelation'. Thus, the thesis seemed secure that Barth's whole theological programme represented a form of neo-orthodoxy that was inherently resistant to historical-critical study of the Bible or other so called 'significant developments' in modern theology. Understandably, 'The perception was widespread among liberals that Barth was a theological reactionary who wanted to overthrow the fruits of scientific theology since the 1780's (or thereabouts) in order to return to the theology of a former age.'[16]

In terms of the systematic exegesis of Barth's theological development, the basis of this assessment (i.e. the dominance of von Balthasar's thesis) has been substantially challenged by McCormack's groundbreaking endeavours. Building on the more nuanced assessments of Barth's theology in Germany by Eberhard Jüngel, I Spieckermann, and M. Beintker, McCormack makes two substantial points:[17]

1. Although Barth rejected the 'dialectical method' of his earlier period, the famous *analogia fidei* is itself 'an *inherently dialectical concept*'.
2. The *Realdialektik* (real dialectic) *of* the 'divine veiling and unveiling', upon which the analogy of faith was based, was never rejected or abandoned by Barth as he undertook the massive task of writing the *Church Dogmatics*.[18]

McCormack's work has not only changed the understanding and interpretation of Barth's theological development, it has also contributed to the changing perception of Barth's significance in the context of postmodernity.[19]

The transition from modernity to postmodernity, with its acerbic critique of most of the revered tenants of the Enlightenment agenda, sheds new light on the importance of Barth's theology. Instead of being judged by the standards of

---

[15] H. Frei, 'The Doctrine of Revelation in the Thought of Karl Barth, 1909 to 1922'; and T.F. Torrance, *Karl Barth: An Introduction to his Early Theology, 1910–31*.

[16] McCormack, *Critically Realistic Dialectical Theology*, 25.

[17] E. Jüngel, 'Von der Dialekit zur Analogie: Die Schule Kierkegaards und der Einspruch Petersons', in idem, *Barth-Studien*; I. Spieckermann, *Gotteserkenntnis: Ein Beitrag zur Grundfrage der neuen Theologie Karl Barths*; M. Beintker, *Die Dialektik in der 'dialktischen Theologie' Karl Barths*.

[18] McCormack, *Dialectical Theology*, 16–17.

[19] Küng, *Great Christian Thinkers*; Jenson, 'Karl Barth', 23–49; Johnson, *Mystery of God*; G. Ward, *Barth, Derrida And The Language Of Theology*, T. Rendorff, 'Radikale Autonomie Gottes: Zum Verstandnis der Theologie Karl Barths und ihre Folgen', in idem, *Theorie des Christentums*, 161–81, for a similar assessment of Barth.

modernity as a theological reactionary, he is being rediscovered as a prophetic voice, the initiator of a new paradigm in the constant attempt by theology to both critique and draw nourishment from its cultural context:

> In the face of the crisis of the modern paradigm, Karl Barth called for and encouraged a fundamentally new orientation of theology. Earlier than others – in a theological critique of ideology– his theology saw through the despotic and destructive forces of modern rationality, relativised the claim of Enlightenment reason to absoluteness, and showed Enlightenment reason where it was deceiving itself; in short, earlier than others, his theology recognised the 'dialectic of the Enlightenment' and worked for an Enlightenment beyond the Enlightenment.[20]

Barth and Postmodernity

So, how are we to read Barth's theological proposals in the context of postmodernity? Barth's whole theological programme was a conscious attempt to overturn the inherent limitations and epistemological imperialism of modernity. We have not understood Barth if we consign his theological programme to the grave of the recent past and place over it an epitaph labelled neo-orthodoxy. Instead, we should take note of the alternative vision of reality he offers: one where the emancipated human subject is replaced by the sovereign freedom of God to be with us and for us in the Word made flesh; where the elevation of human reason is replaced by the inherent rationality of the object of faith, which, even in the act of theological exposition, remains incontestably beyond our intellectual grasp and control. There are at least four influential aspects of Barth's theological programme that, to a certain extent, anticipate some of the main tenets of postmodernity.

The theological task and the mystery of God

The first relates to Barth's conception of what constitutes the theological task when theology is reoriented toward the unfathomable mystery of God. Successive interpreters of Barth's theology have often highlighted the evocative and sustaining power of a particular image or metaphor that reoccurs throughout his voluminous writings. For instance, Richard Roberts has written extensively on the significance of Barth's dialectic of time and eternity that occupied Barth from the time of the *Römerbrief* through to the *Church Dogmatics*.[21]

---

[20] Küng, *Great Christian Thinkers*, 201.

[21] R.H. Roberts, 'Barth's Doctrine of Time: Its Nature and Implications' in S.W. Sykes (ed.) *Karl Barth-Studies of his Theological Methods*, 88–146. McCormack has now challenged the apparent dominance of this metaphor in Barth's later writing at

Likewise, William Johnson draws our attention to the metaphor of the wheel with an open space at the centre, an image used frequently by Barth throughout his theological career.[22] According to Johnson, this metaphor enabled Barth to practise his own particular brand of apophatic theology that involved a radical decentring of the theological task. From the *Romerbrief* to the *Church Dogmatics*, Barth was engaged in a thorough ground-clearing exercise that was inherently non-foundational and always vigilant and aware of the inherent limitations, or inevitable distortions, of all our conceptual frameworks and attempts at theological exposition:

> To 'centre' upon God is to converge upon the untamed and the uncoercible. It is to focus upon that which calls us fundamentally into question, upon that which brings about a shaking of the foundations, an overturning of all that was previously considered stable and secure. The mystery of God, far from safeguarding (*Sicherung*) theology, precipitates an act of endangerment (*Entsicherung*), like removing the safety pin from a loaded gun.[23]

The metaphor of the empty space at the centre of the wheel[24] expressed Barth's continual opposition to all forms of theology, Christocentric or otherwise, that sought to read off the substance of theology from some historical, empirical or anthropological given. Whether that datum be the co-givenness of the divine reality in the intuition of the infinite (Schleiermacher), the historical and empirical study of religion (Troeltsch), or an idealist metaphysics (Hegel) – all represent different forms of foundationalism – the illegitimate attempt to gain epistemological purchase on some posited or presupposed basic data that is, in one form or another, representative of the ultimate. As we shall see, in his earlier years Barth protected this open space (*Hohlraum*) at the centre of theology through a *diastatic* Christology that would not allow for any 'points of contact' (*Anknupfungspunkt*), or analogies of being (*analogia entis*), between God and humanity. The God who is 'wholly other' is a God who remains completely beyond our comprehension.

Jüngel claims that Barth's constant attempt to maintain this theological open space where only the unfathomable mystery of God could endure,

---

[21] (*continued*) least, emphasising in its stead the dialectic of veiling and unveiling, which, McCormack claims, serves the same purpose, i.e. that of locating God beyond any ready made human conceptuality. See, McCormack, *Dialectical Theology*, 248.

[22] Johnson, *The Mystery of God*, 11–43; See also S.W. Sykes, 'Barth on the Centre of Theology' in Sykes (ed.) *Karl Barth – Studies of his Theological Methods*, 17–55.

[23] Johnson, *Mystery*, 14.

[24] As we noted in the last chapter, this is akin to Heidegger's notion of a clearing at the centre of our thinking where the essence of Being can appear.

represents Barth's sustained attempt to overcome the 'metaphysical concept of God' that 'had to be thought as one who is absolutely present'.[25] So, it would appear that Barth was engaged in his own war against the same enemy of Neitzsche, Heidegger and Derrida, i.e. the 'metaphysics of presence'.

In recent years, both Walter Lowe and Graham Ward have sought to draw comparisons between Barth's concerns in this regard and the deconstructionalist agenda of Derrida.[26] Derrida's philosophy of *différence* offers a hermeneutical reflection on the nature of language that privileges both otherness and postponement in all attempts at referral and the inferral of meaning:

> On the one hand, there is an ineluctable unlikeness and dissimilitude that attends all efforts to make language refer to an object. Everything is caught up on 'difference'. On the other hand, our very efforts to speak this unlikeness are ceaselessly 'deferred'.[27]

As we have already noted, Derrida's 'indeterminate play of difference'[28] was aimed at the structuralist account of language that sought to delineate the relationship between sign and signifier in terms of the internal rules of the symbolic system. For Derrida, the meaning of any signifier is never secure; signifiers only operate with reference to other signifiers. Consequently, language is inherently unstable. All our words must be written 'under erasure' because there is a continual flux or overflow of meaning.

Foundationalism seeks to avoid this impasse, or indeterminacy, by positing a self-sufficient centre or the 'singularity of a presence'[29] to which we have direct and unmediated access – whether that centre be the 'sense data' of the empiricists; the self-positing universal subject of the idealists, or the transcendental *Logos* or reason of the Neoplatonists that signifies the presence of the divine.[30] Derrida did not advocate pure scepticism or the sheer relativity of language. He understands the search for a foundation in terms of a moral imperative. Nevertheless, he seeks to 'problematise' any suggestion of an arrival because the arrival always goes via binary opposition – an arrogant dualism that seeks to privilege men/women, transcendence/immanence, and reason/language at the expense of the other.

---

[25] E. Jüngel, *God as the Mystery of the World: On the Foundation of the Theology of the Crucified One in the Dispute between Theism and Atheism*, 182; see also Johnson, *Mystery*, 21

[26] W.J. Lowe, *Theology and Difference: The Wound of Reason*, and Ward, *Language*.

[27] Johnson, *Mystery*, 21.

[28] Ibid., 22.

[29] Ibid., 22.

[30] All are examples of logocentrism; the presumption of having arrived at the ontological centre of reality through the advocacy of our innate reason, which, in turn, is independent of the structure of our language.

However, the fundamental question that arises in any interrogation of Barth's theological method is whether he always did theology *under erasure*, or whether he eventually succumbed to his own form of logocentrism[31] by privileging church over culture and finally locating the centre of theology in the Christology of the enfleshed *Logos*. The issue is this:

> At first glance one might think that Karl Barth's theology offers a prime example of the very foundationalist "logocentrism" that Derrida so roundly rejects. Does not Barth consider the divine "*Logos*" or "Word" to be the present possession of a privileged community, the church? And is it not given with unrestrained clarity in the texts of Scripture?[32]

It might well be that the *aporia* that finally rescues Barth from such found-ationalism is his own dialectic of difference, which aligns him with Derrida's cause.[33] This is a critical area of Barth's Christology on which we will ultimately have to adjudicate.

The human subject

To a certain extent, there is a formal similarity between postmodernity's deconstruction of the transcendental self and that which Barth affects by other means. In his debate with Heidegger and Husserl, Derrida transcribes the phi-losophy of subjectivity into semiotics. According to Derrida, there is no tran-scendental self prior to the indeterminate play of signs and language. Instead, 'Consciousness is always already invaded by alterity.'[34] The inability to fore-close on meaning, the requirement to postpone or defer the meaning of the signifier, interrupts the apparent self-sufficiency or solipsism of the self, which, in turn, is shown to be trapped within the same antinomies of language.

Barth, on the other hand, had come to his own decision regarding the ultimate fate of the idealist, universal human subject relatively early on in his theological career. The inherent danger of idealism, which rightly recognises the constructive possibilities of the human subject, is that it reduces theological reflection to a synopsis of the cultural values and aspirations of a particular era.[35] To safeguard against such a possibility, theology must both assert its own independence and maintain its own integrity over and against any form of cultural accommodation. Thus Barth's verdict on the eighteenth-century

---

[31] Note Bonhoeffer's accusation of a positivity of revelation, *Letters and Papers from Prison*, 280, 286, 329.

[32] Johnson, *Mystery*, 25.

[33] Cf. Ward, *Language*, 247.

[34] Ingraffia, *Postmodern Theory*, 179.

[35] Cf. Johnson, *Mystery*, 29.

concept of the autonomous, transcendental human subject: it was but an example of hubris and self-deception:[36]

> The would be autonomous subject, self-contained over against every instance by which his/her intention or judgement might be relativised, is precisely the person 'curved in on him/herself' of Reformation teaching, the person 'who wants to be Lord himself, the judge of good and evil, who wants to be his own helper – the *Church Dogmatics* primary description of sin.[37]

Theology and ethics

One of the most interesting aspects of Barth's *Church Dogmatics* is the way he combines theology and ethics. Thus, we find 'an open-ended ethics of otherness' which aligns Barth's concerns with that of Emmanuel Levinas:[38]

> Since both God and human beings have their being in activity, theological reflection is only worthwhile when pursued as a prelude to action. Who we are, our identity as Christians, Barth would say, is validated in reference to our own love in freedom.[39]

If both the being of God and humanity are consummated in action, then ethics is not a separate domain from theological reflection. In fact, the latter implies the former.[40]

Barth conceived of theological ethics not in terms of epistemological moral theory but as the autonomy of obedience to the command or will of God given in each particular situation. For some critics who accused Barth of 'occasionalism' (the failure to produce a consistent moral theory that was not radically orientated to particular situations), this rendered his ethics highly unsatisfactory.[41] However, as Johnson recognises, 'To conceive of theological ethics as a ready-made system would constitute an infringement upon the

---

[36] Barth used Fichte's notion of the self-determining subject who apparently knows no limitation as his chief example. Cf. *Church Dogmatics* 3\2, 121.

[37] Jenson, 'Karl Barth', 27.

[38] E. Levinas, *Otherwise than Being: Or Beyond*.

[39] Johnson, *Mystery*, 153.

[40] Barth intended to complete each of the four major foci of the *Church Dogmatics* – God, Creation, Reconciliation and Redemption – with major sections on theological ethics. He completed only two, 'The Command of God' (2\1) and 'The Command of God the Creator' (3/4). Barth started and almost finished the projected third volume, 'The Command of God the Reconciler', but he died before 'The Ethics of Redemption' could even be sketched out.

[41] Johnson, *Mystery*, 154. For a considered response to such accusations see J. Webster, *Barth's Ethics of Reconciliation*, and N. Biggar, *The Hastening That Waits: Karl Barth's Ethics*.

freedom of God'.[42] Ethics would, of course, also immediately become detached from its grounding in the event of God's self-disclosure in the person of Jesus.

Detachment from history

Barth's much criticised detachment from history was also, like some post-modernists, politically motivated. He saw how the liberal ideal of 'reverence before history' led straight to the endorsement of the Kaiser's war policy and was, therefore, an example of cultural imperialism.[43] Barth could no longer follow the ethics, dogmatics, the understanding of the Bible and history of any of his theological teachers, whom he had previously venerated.[43] For Barth, this was the end of *Kulturprotestantismus* (cultural Protestantism), the identification of Protestant Christianity with European culture, or the *enculturisation* of the Christian gospel within the intellectual mores of nineteenth-century bourgeois society. The great task of rebuilding theology on a more secure footing had begun and who else to take as one's *bête noire* in such a venture than the great exponent of liberal Protestantism itself, Friedrich Schleiermacher.[45]

Barth and Schleiermacher

Like the theology of crisis it inspired, Barth's relationship to the man he much admired was always a dialectical one. He understood well the extent of Schleiermacher's achievement:

> Schleiermacher has succeeded, above all in his great work on the doctrine of faith but also in his shorter works and in his explicitly philosophical efforts as well, in giving to dogmatics, indeed to science in general, something that the great theologians before him (Augustine, Thomas, Melanchthon, Zwingli and Calvin) have failed to manage despite their corresponding efforts, which are so neatly marked off

---

[42] Johnson, *Mystery*, 154.

[43] Cf. K. Barth, *The Humanity of God*, 14. For a helpful and illuminating discussion of the political implications of Barth's theology see G. Hunsinger, *Disruptive Grace: Studies in the Theology of Karl Barth*, 21–128; also T.J.Gorringe, *Karl Barth Against Hegemony*.

[44] Barth, *Humanity of God*, 14. See also G.J. Dorrien, *The Barthian Revolt in Modern Theology: Theology Without Weapons*.

[45] From the time of his great theological revolution in the parish of Safenwil, through to his lectures on Schleiermacher during the winter semester of 1923–24 at Göttingen, on to his famous lectures on the history of modern theology at Munster in 1926, Barth never let Schleiermacher far out of his sights.

with chapters, articles, loci, sections, and so forth. Only Schleiermacher managed to provide an utterly amazing and thorough overview of the scattered limbs (*disjecta membra*) of the historical Christian faith.[46]

However, Barth remained implacably opposed to the premises upon which Scleiermacher's theological tour de force was constructed. Barth turned all the main tenets of Schleiermacher's theology on their head.

The point of entry into Schleiermacher's system is the subjective religious experience of 'absolute dependence'. For Barth, it was the objective reality of the *Deus dixit*, the God who had spoken in AD 1–30, and who, on that basis alone, continued to speak. For Schleiermacher, the unity of God and ourselves is realised through the phenomena of God-consciousness, exemplified and mediated to us through the church's corporate experience of the Redeemer. For Barth, that unity is only achieved in one concrete historical person, Jesus Christ, and is then mediated to us through the presence of the Holy Spirit. So, where Schleiermacher locates a phenomenological link between God and humanity, Barth sees only an existential and ontological chasm. Whereas Schleiermacher relativised the claims of reason by locating within the human subject an intuitive and non-negotiable domain of religious experience, Barth relativised the claims of both reason and religion by claiming that the self-communication of God is wholly focused in the person of Christ. We can never, asserts Barth, imagine we have genuinely spoken of God 'simply by speaking of man in a loud voice'.[47] Finally, like Schleiermacher, Barth also wished to construct a proper theology of culture, but whereas Schleiermacher looked to the world of our creation, Barth fixed his gaze in the opposite direction, towards the world of God's good creation, both revealed and restored in Christ.[48] In short, where Schleiermacher operates from below, concentrating on the phenomenon of religion; Barth operates from above, concentrating on the person of Christ:[49]

A Christology of *Diastasis* (Separation)

Barth's first attempt to smash the idols of cultural Protestantism resulted in his notorious *The Epistle to the Romans*. This commentary assaults the reader time and time again with a polemical dialectic of negation.

---

[46] K. Barth, *Die Theologie und die Kirche*, 165–6.
[47] K. Barth, *The Word of God and the Word of Man*, 196.
[48] E.g. K. Barth, *Theology and Church: Shorter Writings, 1920–1928*, 334–54.
[49] Cf. J.C. Pugh, *The Anselmic Shift: Christology and Method in Karl Barth's Theology*, 156.

Having learnt from his reading of both Kierkegaard and Plato how Socrates sought to break down the claim of Athens to be the upholder of truth and justice, Barth deploys the same tactic to dismantle the pretensions of *Kulturprotest-antismus*. He takes aim at what he regards as the most detrimental aspects of his liberal heritage – individualism, historicism, any attempt to lay a foundation for theology upon religious experience, and idealistic epistemology and ethics:

> Barth's new theology represented an assault on a central feature of late nineteenth-century bourgeois culture: the understanding of the human individual as the creative subject of culture and history (and even of her own being and worth). Against the divisive individualism which had given rise to class warfare and world war, Barth posited a divine 'universalism': the God who is complete and whole in Himself prior to all knowledge of Him, stands over and against the whole of so-called "reality" judging it, condemning all so that He might elect all.[50]

In short, Barth's main object of attack was a form of religious affectation that provided ideological support and justification for bourgeoisie culture and social aspirations.

In the foreground remains Kierkegaard's 'infinite qualitative distinction' between time and eternity. God is in heaven and all is not well with humanity. Rather, a crisis has occurred. There is a vast separation between God and us, which means that the domestication of God due to the elevation of humanity is judged to be idolatrous. God remains *totaliter aliter*, i.e., wholly and totally removed from us. There is a huge crevasse, a fixed gulf we cannot cross, which disallows any attempt to construct a god from the debris of human culture and religiosity. Barth replaces Lessing's historical ditch with the chasm that exists between time and eternity. When caught between so great a gulf, 'so-called history' flounders. On the other hand, 'real history' remains, but only as a punctiliar event, a 'breakthrough' that remains hidden and so cannot become the object of historical correlation or investigation.[51]

Next, particularly in the second edition of the *Römerbrief*, Barth approaches the issue from the high terrain of the recently rediscovered eschatological dimensions of the preaching of Jesus. Liberal Protestantism had refused to scale these precarious heights discovered by Weiss and Schweitzer. Barth, however, announces that 'A Christianity which is not totally and utterly eschatology, has totally and utterly nothing to do with Christ!'[52] But, again, it is only the negative aspects of eschatology that Barth deploys. The distance between God and humanity is further radicalised as that which exists between our time and the eschatological recesses of eternity:

---

[50] McCormack, *Dialectical Theology*, 141; see also Dorrien, *Barthian Revolt*, 47–71.
[51] K. Barth, *Der Römerbrief Unveränderter Nachdruck der ersten Auflage von 1919*, 46, 98, 106.
[52] Ibid., 314.

Barth abandoned the process eschatology of Romans 1 in favour of a radically futurist 'consistent' eschatology according to which the kingdom of God is understood as that which brings about 'the dissolution of all things', the cessation of all becoming, the passing away of the world's time.[53]

This dialectic of time and eternity is mirrored in the Adam–Christ dialectic that underscores the same total disjunction between the old world and the new. In Christ the old world of sin and death has been vanquished; the new order has come in his death and resurrection. A real transformation has occurred; there can be no oscillation back and forth, no juxtaposing of the old and new as if they were of equal value or import. This is not, however, a movement that is discernible in the vagaries or contingencies of history:

> The movement is a movement which has taken place 'in eternity', not in time. That is to say, the turn which has occurred was accomplished by the raising of Jesus from the dead, which is an 'unhistorical' event. But the fact that this dialectic is eternal does not mean that it is unreal. What has taken place in Christ is the 'real reality', not reality as it appears to us.[54]

In the second edition of the *Römerbrief*, Barth's pressing concern is the question how can the unknowable, eternal God actually become known without theology lapsing into a *Glaubenslehre*, a mere teaching about the subjective dimensions of faith? How does the 'impossible possibility of faith' become reality without the miracle of the epistemic relationship being wrenched from God's control?[55] Already the move toward a theology of revelation where God is revealed indirectly – and, therefore, concealed through the means of a particular medium – can be discerned. However, the crucial question remained, what place could Christology have in such a violent theology of *diastasis*?

Theoretically and practically it could only be one that underscored that separation and maintained that only at one point do the two worlds meet or the two planes intersect. But this is not a point of intersection that is in conformity with our domain of existence. Rather, it drops vertically from above, as a tangent intersects a circle. It is a bomb that explodes, demolishing our towers of Babel. All we see is the crater or shell hole, which reminds us of our precarious existence. There remains a 'glacial crevasse', a 'polar region', a 'desert zone' between time and eternity, history and eschatology, humanity and God:

> The seeing of the line of intersection is not self-evident. The point of the line of intersection – where it is to be seen and is seen – is *Jesus*, Jesus of Nazareth, the

---

[53] McCormack, *Dialectical Theology*, 208.
[54] Ibid., 269.
[55] Barth, *Der Romerbrief*, 114.

'historical' Jesus … That point of the line of intersection itself, however, like the entire unknown plane whose presence it announces, has no extension on the plane known to us. The emanation or much rather, the astonishing bomb-craters [*Einschlagstrichter*] and empty spaces [*Hohlraume*] through which it makes itself noticeable within the realm of historical intuitability are, even if they are called the 'life of Jesus', not the other world which in Jesus comes into contact with our world. And in so far as this, our world, is touched in Jesus by another world, it ceases to be directly intuitable as history, time, or thing.[56]

The point of intersection is in fact the cross and resurrection, an event that Barth makes clear by no means opens up a pathway to the historical Jesus; rather, it discloses a 'paradox', a 'victor', who remains outside history, and who cannot therefore be grasped by historical investigation. He remains the end of history.

The problem with such a Christology is that, ironically, it repeats the error of its liberal forebears.[57] It has nothing material to say about the real Christ, except that he discloses to us the unknowable God, who is present paradoxically in the God-forsakenness and dereliction of the cross and, therefore, present in his absence from the human realm. The dissolution of religion had taken Barth precariously close to the maxim mistakenly attributed to Tertullian, *credo quia absurdum* ('I believe it because it is absurd'). It is little wonder that Paul Althaus complained that Barth had assimilated both Nietzsche's and Franz Overbeck's radical scepticism concerning the possibility of any knowledge of God. Barth's dialectic of time and eternity turned the living God of the Bible into a mere limit concept, a boundary and a crisis that disallowed any genuine relationship between God and humanity. McCormack and Beintker are correct to stress that the distinction is not absolute, there is a point of intersection where eternity interrupts or encounters time, nevertheless, at this juncture Barth's theology possesses only the most attenuated Christology and he is dangerously close to a form of theological irrationality.[58] For Barth, the route back to a proper christological rationale, so received wisdom used to confidently announce, went via his theological encounter with Anselm's *Proslogion*.

Christ the True Paradigm

In October 1921 Barth was appointed Professor of Reformed Theology at Göttingen. The *Göttingen Dogmatics*, which eventuated from his labours, have always presented a problem for Barth's interpreters, because Barth later abandoned them in favour of *Die christliche Dogmatik im Entwurf*, which he also

---

[56] Ibid., 5, quoted in McCormack, *Dialectical Theology*, 252–3.
[57] Cf. Jenson, 'Karl Barth', 33.
[58] See, McCormack, *Dialectical Theology*, 262–6. Beintker, *Die Dialektik*, 53–4.

referred to as a 'false start'. Thus, by implication, both were subsequently superseded by the *Church Dogmatics*. McCormack contends that Barth never relinquished the real dialectic of the *Deus revelatus* and the *Deus absconditus*, a dialectic which is still clearly discernible in the first volumes of the *Church Dogmatics*, and that von Balthasar overemphasised the importance of Barth's engagement with Anselm. This inevitably means that McCormack must look for evidence of a more naunced christological grounding of Barth's central dialectic in the *Göttingen Dogmatics*. He finds this in Barth's discovery (in the work of two interpreters of the Reformed tradition, Heinrich Schmid and Heinrich Heppe) of a little known christological formula *anhypostatos–enhypostatos*.[59]

The development of this subtle distinction is usually traced to Leontius of Byzantium, but is, in fact, largely the work of 'the great compiler of the patristic tradition', John of Damascus.[60] This formula takes us back to a central aspect of the Alexandrian, *Logos/sarx* tradition of christological reflection. As we noted, *enhypostatos* entails that it is the pre-existent *Logos* who assumes a whole human nature and so is the personalising subject of the historical person, Jesus of Nazareth. For Barth, the Alexandrian position maintained the dialectic of divine veiling and unveiling but this time in christological terms.[61] God is genuinely revealed through the incarnation of the *Logos*, but he also simultaneously remains incognito, or hidden, in human form.[62] The incarnation is accordingly a 'unity in differentiation' or 'a strictly dialectical union' whereby the *kenosis* of the *Logos* does not mean a relinquishment, abandonment or a diminution of divinity, but the veiling of the eternal *Logos* in the life history of Jesus.[63] The *Logos* becomes *enhypostatos*, the personal centre of the assumed humanity, which entails that the person of Jesus is *anhypostatos*, i.e., possesses no personal identity or subsistence outside his union with the *Logos*:

> This individual in which the human nature is embodied has never existed as such. The humanity of Christ (although it is body and *soul*, although it is *Individuum*) is nothing subsistent or real in itself. It did not, for example, exist *before* its union with the *Logos* ... *The human nature of Christ has no personality of its own; it is anhypostatos* ...

[59] See, McCormack, *Dialectical Theology*, 327–9.
[60] V.M. Lang, 'Anhypostatos-enhypostatos: Church Fathers, Protestant Orthodoxy And Karl Barth', *Journal of Theological Studies* 49/2 (Oct 1998), 630–57.
[61] For an analysis of Barth's Christology and its adherence to the Alexandrian as opposed to the Antiochene positions see, C.T. Waldrop, *Karl Barth's Christology: Its Basic Alexandrian Character*; also Hunsinger, *Disruptive Grace*, 131–47.
[62] Cf. McCormack, *Critically Realistic Dialectical Theology*, 327.
[63] K. Barth, *The Göttingen Dogmatics: Instruction in Christian Religion* Vol. 1, 139.

Or, positively expressed, it is *enhypostatos; it has personality,* subsistence, reality, *only in its union with the Logos of God.*[64]

This was a substantial advance:

No longer did Barth need to reduce the 'site' of revelation to a single 'mathematical point' – the event of the cross. Now, the dialectic of veiling and unveiling on its objective side could comprehend the whole of the incarnate existence of the Mediator.[65]

Accordingly, as McCormack makes clear, the eschatological reservation of the second edition of *Romans* was maintained, but now the dialectic of time and eternity is superseded by a substantial christological equivalent. More importantly, Barth moved from a Christology of *diastasis* – where only the cross and resurrection constitute the tenuous intersection point between God and humanity – to a position that takes the reality of the incarnation seriously.[66]

What then are we to make of Barth's claim that both *The Göttingen Dogmatics* and *Die christliche Dogmatik* represent a false start and that *a real turning point* in his theological pilgrimage occurred through his investigation of Anselm's *Proslogion?*[67] A firmer and more confident grasp of the fundamental nature of

---

[64] Barth, *Göttingen Dogmatics,* 157. Barth's return to christological orthodoxy in its Alexandrian form also entailed that the doctrine of the Virgin Birth maintained the validity of the *anhypostatos–enhypostatos* distinction. Similarly, he rejected the Lutheran doctrine of the *communio naturarum* because it rested on a confusion of the concepts of person and nature. Divinity and humanity do not intermingle, neither are the properties of one attributed to the other because this is to expurgate the distinction between God and humanity. Rather, the union of the natures is mediated indirectly through the concrete life history of the incarnate *Logos.*

[65] McCormack, *Dialectical Theology,* 328.

[66] What we find in *The Göttingen Dogmatics* is a sophisticated prolegomena to dogmatics based on the threefold reality of the Word of God – the Word Incarnate, the Word attested to in Scripture and the Word proclaimed or announced in the act of preaching. All three forms constitute the event of the *Deus Dixit,* the God who speaks and so is revealed in the threefold linkage of the Word and who now *chooses* to become the Subject of a contingent history AD 1–30. The same God whom Barth would later describe as commandeering human language, the God who establishes a real analogy between the Word who assumes a 'qualified history' and so can come to expression in 'qualified words'. The *analogia fidei* was already at this stage an implicit presupposition of Barth's threefold theology of the Word of God, if not yet a fully developed doctrine of analogy.

[67] K. Barth, *How I Changed my Mind,* 42–4; see also Barth, *Anselm: Fides quaerens intellectum, Anselm's Proof of the Existence of God in the Context of his Theological Scheme,* 11; and von Balthasar, *Theology of Karl Barth,* 93.

theological rationality certainly eventuates from Barth's study of Anselm. It was his intense engagement with a genre of thought other than German idealism and his enquiry into the nature of Anselm's theological method that enabled Barth to underscore the priority of the ontological rationality, the *ratio veritatis*, that is identical with the Word who is consubstantial with the Father, over and against the noetic rationality, the knowledge of the knower, that is itself hidden in the *ratio fidei*, which constitutes the Credo of faith.[68]

McCormack contends that, since the *Romerbrief*, Barth had always endeavoured to do theology from above, i.e. stressing the priority of the Word of God over and against the human subject.[69] However, what *is* new, as Jüngel, Torrance and Spieckermann acknowledge, is the refinement of theological rationality that allows Barth to state that theological exposition is always a following after the event of God's self-disclosure. Theology is consequently the obedience of prayer and faith, undertaken not as a logical proof of God's existence, but as faith seeking understanding, a seeking after that hidden correspondence with the Subject of faith, the inherent ontological rationality of God. It is the deeper precision in the dialectical relationship between the ontic and noetic levels of theological reflection that comes to the fore in Barth's exegesis of Anselm's theological method, and this deserves recognition.

This raises the issue of how to both protect the ontological rationality of the Word of God from distortion and yet nevertheless declare the wisdom of God to the generations. The *analogia fidei* – Barth also referred to this as the *analogia relationis* (analogy of relation) or indeed, the *analogia revelationis* (analogy of revelation) – establishes Jesus Christ as the only true correlation between God and humanity. Through this event of revelation God establishes a correspondence whereby he is, in the Word made flesh, what he is in his own being and nature. In Jesus Christ we find the *self-disclosure* of God, the correspondence in human form of the God who had previously been veiled in ineffable mystery: 'The analogy which is established in a revelation event is an analogy between God's knowledge of Himself and human knowledge of Him in and through human concepts and words.'[70] There is consequently only one paradigm for our knowledge, experience and speech about God, Jesus Christ the *Logos* of God, who is veiled in human form. Nevertheless, in humble submission to the inherent rationality of that self-disclosure, we are able to think God's thoughts after him.[71]

---

[68] Ibid., 45–7.
[69] McCormack, *Dialectical Theology*, 14–20.
[70] Ibid., 17.
[71] Here Barth comes very close, at least in formal structure, if not in content, to Hegel's dialectic, a point that has been recognised by other Barth interpreters. In this regard see, R.H. Roberts, *A Theology on Its Way*, 95–154.

The *analogia fidei* was Barth's riposte to any attempt to ground knowledge of God in the structures of the cosmos or our own self-understanding. For Barth, the *analogia entis* (analogy of being), the misguided attempt to postulate a fundamental similarity between the world, or ourselves, and God, is an anathema to true theology because the *analogia entis* is orientated towards analogous structures of being rather than the event of revelation. Thus, it constantly underestimates the biblical realism concerning human sinfulness, which asserts that all our engagement with God is polluted by our own self-interest and tends to lead to idolatry.

Such theological convictions have political implications. It was this tarnished self-interest, in the form of a resurgent German nationalism, which led to the German church's official support of the national socialism of Hitler. Against this, in the Barmen declaration of 1943, Barth raised the banner of Jesus Christ, the 'one word of God, whom we have to hear, and whom we have to trust and obey in life and death'.[72] Similarly, there can be no predisposition – no pre-understanding, no *anknupfungspunkt* (point of contact), which resides in the human subject and helps to bring about this analogy, or correspondence – between human language and the event of revelation.

It was this central conviction that led to Barth's fierce repudiation of his former friend and ally, Emil Brunner. Brunner sought to argue that there must be a preliminary to dogmatics, which he called *eristics*. Eristic theology takes place on the battlefield of anthropology because located in the *imago dei* is a 'bridge to faith'. As Gogarten had also endeavoured to demonstrate, the inherent questionableness of human existence, the shattering of the theoretical possibility that human beings are theological neutral, raises again the question of the 'addressability' of men and women who, to be sure, only respond to the gospel through the grace of Christ, but, nevertheless, know that they have heard a *genuine* word of God.[73]

For Barth, this was to return again to the old well-worn track travelled by *homo religiosus*, the question of the innate religiosity of human beings that supposedly prepared them for the grace of the gospel. Barth replaces this belief with the actualism of revelation. Men and women come to faith only in so far as the grace of God establishes a genuine correspondence between the event of revelation and the frail, weak and inadequate vessel of human language. That it happens we can be certain, how it happens remains the prerogative of the Holy Spirit.[74]

---

[72] See E. Jüngel, *Christ, Justice and Peace: Toward a Theology of the State*, xxi–xxix. Also Gorringe, *Barth Against Hegemony*, 130–3; Hunsinger, *Disruptive Grace*, 78–83, 95–6, 101–2.

[73] McCormack, *Dialectical Theology*, 403.

[74] Ibid., 17.

Finally, *Fides quaerens intellectum* enabled Barth to move closer to the ideal, supposedly enshrined in the *Church Dogmatics*, of developing a self-authenticating theology of the Word of God that expunged from the theological agenda all correlation or dialogue with, or indeed indebtedness to, alien philosophical conceptualities. It is clear that his target was still the kind of philosophical anthropology to which, with dismay, he watched his previous associates Bultmann and Gogarten capitulate.[75] It was this factor that led Barth to eventually disassociate himself from the cortege of supposedly 'dialectical theologians' who had since the time of its inception been associated with the publication *Zwischen den Zeiten*. In a letter to his long-standing friend Eduard Thurneysen, Barth expressed his frustration with

> Bultmann's 'theology of believing existence', which derived its legitimation from an existential philosophy; Gogarten's stress on historicity and anthropology; and Brunner and Schumann, in their belief that they were able to make unbelieving man and women 'unsure' of themselves. Barth could not see in any of these attempts anything other than a renewal of the relationship of theology to philosophy which had prevailed in the nineteenth century.[76]

McCormack correctly points out that all of these particular emphases can be located in Barth's earlier work. Nevertheless, their accumulated affect appears, to us at least, to lend substantial support to Barth's claim that his little book on Anselm signalled a move, if not a new departure, toward a much more substantial theological rationality. This, in turn, paved the way for the christocentrism of the *Church Dogmatics*.

There is more than a hint of suspicion that McCormack, swayed by the apparent clarity of his own vision, indulges in his own form of historical postivism by discounting the plain sense of Barth's own testimony to the significance of *Fides quaerens intellectum*. McCormack's claim that Barth exaggerated the differences between the *Göttingen Dogmatics*, the *Die christliche Dogmatik* and the initial volumes of the *Church Dogmatics*, and that the real factor at work here was the desire to distance himself from the other dialectical theologians, suggests that his laudable attempt to render Barth's critically realistic dialectic entirely intact, does at times require some special pleading.[77]

---

[75] In the *Church Dogmatics* 1\1, Barth later expressed amazement that he could have written a statement such as the following that appeared in *Die christliche Dogmatik*; 'The hearing human is included in the concept of the Word of God just as much as the speaking God. He is "co-posited" in it, as Schleiermacher's God is in the feeling of absolute dependence.' See Barth, *Church Dogmatics*, 1\1 140; see *Die christliche Dogmatik in Entwurf*, 148.

[76] McCormack,, 409–10.

[77] McCormack, *Dialectical Theology*, 412–48.

Christology From Above

> I had to learn that Christian doctrine, if it is to merit its name and if it is to build
> up the Christian church in the world as she must needs be built up, has to be
> exclusively and conclusively the doctrine of Jesus Christ – of Jesus Christ as the
> living Word of God spoken to us men and women … I should like to call it a
> christological concentration.[78]

Both McCormack and Johnson rightly recognise that Barth's 'christological
concentration' entails that every doctrine of the Christian faith must be centrally
related to the event of God's self-disclosure in the person of Jesus Christ. There
could, for instance, be no independent doctrine of creation or, as in so much
natural theology, an independent doctrine of God constructed from the wreck-
age of philosophical speculation. Rather, every doctrinal loci must be materially
related to the manner in which God chooses to make himself known to us.
Thus, Barth's threefold doctrine of revelation which, in line with the Church
Fathers, developed out of a dynamic doctrine of God presented in terms of the
trinitarian self-determination of the divine being, also systematically remained
christocentric. According to Barth, that is no mere formal theological proce-
dure, but is in fact what the witness of Scripture demands. There we read about
the God who reveals himself as Lord (*Kyrios*). This simple biblical affirmation
alerts us to the structure of revelation. It informs us that God is the Revealer
(*Offenbarer*) because only God can reveal God. Similarly, such a statement tells us
that God is the content of his revelation (*Offenbarung*). God reveals himself in the
person of his Son, and in the event of revelation God remains free as the lord of
his own self-disclosure. He is his own revealedness (*Offenbarsein*).

Jesus Christ the electing God and elected person

The concentration on Christology in and for its own sake occurs in volume 1\2
of the *Church Dogmatics* under the Doctrine of God and in 4\1 and 2 under the
Doctrine of Reconciliation. In the former volume, Barth made his conception
of the dogmatic task in theology irrevocably clear:

> A church dogmatics must, of course, be christologically determined as a whole and
> in all its parts, as surely as the revealed Word of God, attested by Holy Scripture and
> proclaimed by the church, is its one and only criterion, and as surely as this revealed
> Word is identical with Jesus Christ. If dogmatics cannot regard itself and cause itself
> to be regarded as fundamentally Christology, it has assuredly succumbed to some
> alien sway and is already on the verge of losing its character as church dogmatics.[79]

---

[77] Barth, *Mind*, 43.
[79] Barth, *Church Dogmatics* 1\2, 123.

In many ways, however, the best approach to Barth's Christology is via his highly original christological regrounding of the doctrine of election that occurs in 2\2. There were of course interesting and important historical reasons for this emphasis. These amounted to nothing short of another momentous theological discovery by Barth.

In June 1936 Barth travelled to take part in a congress to celebrate the four-hundreth anniversary of the Reformation in Geneva. The theme of the conference was the Reformed doctrine of predestination, particularly Calvin's doctrine of double predestination. At the conference Barth heard a significant and influential address by Pierre Maury entitled 'Election and Faith', which was as significant for the *Church Dogmatics*, as was his study of Anselm's *Proslogion*:

> Most of those present at the Calvinist Congress were hardly prepared to accept with their hearts, or even to register with their minds, what Pierre Maury was saying to them then. There were but few who realised the implications of his thesis in the course of the years that followed … But I remember one person who read the text of that address with the greatest attention – myself! … One can certainly say that it was he who contributed decisively to giving my thoughts on this subject their fundamental direction.[80]

Maury presented a christological reorientation of the doctrine of predestina-tion that was to become for Barth the 'very centre' of the event of God's self-revelation. In truth, it was 'the sum of the gospel', a fundamental aspect of the dialectical mystery of God's veiling in unveiling.[81] From thereon Barth abandoned the foundation of election in soteriology, which had been the way he had dealt with the subject in the *Göttingen Dogmatics*, and made election the core concept to both his doctrine of God and his Christology.

In *Church Dogmatics* the doctrine of election moved into the centre of Barth's understanding of revelation and indeed of his understanding of the self-determination of the divine being. If it is the case that 'God is who He is in the act of His revelation', that God's being is a 'being in act',[82] then the divine election does not constitute God's eternal decree or choice, but his eternal determination (*Bestimmung*) to be who he is only in relation with and for another. To put it another way, 'God is gracious enough *not* to be God without humanity. God has claimed a stake in humanity's future, for election is God's primordial resolution to be "for" human beings no matter what the cost.'[83] In

---

[80] Karl Barth, Foreword in P. Maury, *Predestination and Other Papers*, 456–7; quoted in McCormack, *Dialectical Theology*, 456–7.
[81] Barth, *Church Dogmatics* 2\2, 159.
[82] Barth, *Church Dogmatics* 2\1, 257, 262.
[83] Johnson, *Mystery*, 59.

terms of Christology, Jesus Christ, in the unity of his person, is both the electing God and the elected person.

There are three aspects to Barth's doctrine of election that define the heart of his Christology. They show how Christology and soteriology are linked by the same gracious action of God towards humanity.

First, Jesus Christ is the electing God:

> From the very first [Jesus] participates in the divine election; that that election is also His election; that it is He Himself that posits this beginning of all things; that it is He Himself who executes the decision which issues in the establishment of the covenant between God and man; that He too, with the Father and the Holy Spirit, is the electing God.[84]

This necessarily entails that in terms of the Christian faith, at least, we are not dealing with abstract notions of divinity and humanity. Rather, we are thinking in terms of their concrete unity and relatedness. This is the eternal basis to the incarnation as expressed in the New Testament idea of pre-existence. We are not permitted, therefore, to think in terms of a *Logos asarkos* (without humanity) but only of a *Logos ensarkos* (enfleshed in humanity). This does not mean that there was a man Jesus of Nazareth existing eternally before creation and incarnation. It does mean, however, that because of election (the fact that God has freely chosen to be a God in relationship with us) and, as a result of the incarnation (the fact that God has embodied that relationship in a particular individual), we cannot think of the *Logos* in isolation from his historical manifestation in the person of Christ:

> In Jesus Christ, as he is attested in Holy Scripture, we are not dealing with man in the abstract; not with the man who is able with his modicum of religion and religious morality to be sufficient unto himself without God and thus himself to be God. But neither are we dealing with God in the abstract; not with one who in his deity exists only separated from man, distant and strange and thus a non-human if indeed an in-human God. In Jesus Christ there is no isolation of man from God or of God from man. Rather, in him we encounter the history, the dialogue, in which God and man meet together and are together.[85]

Secondly, the content of this election can only be the Son of God who freely chose to become the Son of Man. Once again, we are thinking in terms of the pre-existent unity between God and humanity that the incarnation expresses. Election and incarnation are two sides of the same coin. They confirm who

---

[84] Barth, *Church Dogmatics* 2\2, 105. See also J. Thompson, *Christ in Perspective in the Theology of Karl Barth*, 1–58.
[85] Barth, *Humanity*, 43.

God is, the one who freely chose to be with us eternally, and so also chooses to act for and on behalf of us within history. The incarnation is accordingly the voluntary condescension and self-humiliation of the Son – the way of the Son into the far country – and the way God enters our domain. Election implies incarnation. Incarnation, in turn, takes up within itself atonement and all together constitute the grace of the eternal God in the act of reconciliation:

> Since the incarnation means God with us and with us as we actually are, God with us as one of us and acting for us in our place, it must be understood as atoning reconciliation between God and man and man and God at work from the very birth of Jesus, reaching throughout his earthly life and ministry, to its consummation in his death and resurrection as one continuous indivisible saving and sanctifying act of God.[86]

Consequently, the atonement can be understood in terms of Jesus the 'Judge judged in our place'. He is Judge because he brings the kingdom of righteousness into our midst, which exposes our own inherent lack of righteousness, i.e. that we are lost in sin,.

Jesus is also the one elected to bear the pain and penalty of sin in our place. He is, as Barth controversially puts it, the only really rejected person, the way God chooses to take upon himself the cost and calamity of our disobedience and also, consequently, our disenfranchment from the benefits of the covenant. Just as he is the only one who comes and acts among us as Judge, so he is the only one who is judged, condemned and rejected on our behalf.[87] Reconciliation is, so to speak, the gracious expression of the logic of election.[88]

Thirdly, Jesus Christ is the elected human being, the exaltation of the Son of Man and so also the homecoming of the Son of Man; there is a man, a royal man, enthroned in Heaven:

> God humbles Himself to man, even to the final and most radical depth of becoming man, not to deify man, but to exalt him to perfect fellowship with Himself. We have tried to see and understand the event of the Incarnation in the special light of this scope and *telos*. This exaltation comes to human essence in the person of Jesus of Nazareth who is the Son of God. It does so once, but once and for all, in this One. It does so in Him in a way which is valid and effective for all who are also of human essence, for all His brothers. It is to be seen only in this One. But in Him it is revealed as the divine decision which has been made and is declared concerning all men.[89]

---

[86] T.F. Torrance, *Karl Barth Biblical and Evangelical Theologian*, 201.
[87] Barth, *Church Dogmatics* 4\1, 237–8. See Thompson, *Christ in Perspective*, 61–71
[88] Barth, *Church Dogmatics* 2\2, 164.
[89] Barth, *Church Dogmatics* 4\2, 117.

This statement shows that Barth has not simply deconstructed the autonomous human subject. He has arrived at an alternative, christological re-grounding of the derived worth and freedom of human beings. Barth does not think of humanity in isolation from or independent of God, but from the vantage point of our fundamental determination as God's covenant partner. This is not something God accomplishes after his trinitarian self-determination, which would reduce our status to something of an after thought; it is contained within God's trinitarian existence as that which constitutes the humanity of God. Put simply, when God elects the Son to be his partner in eternity, all of humanity is included in that covenant relationship. The ontological status of humanity is not defined, therefore, by recourse to our own subjectivity, but in terms of our being in relationship with God and one another.

Assessment

The christological contours of the *Church Dogmatics* map out in immense detail the vast topography of Barth's christological metaphysics. We consistently return to the person of Christ as the unsurpassable revelatory presence of the eternal God who transfigures and transforms our precarious and perishing existence. This concept of the revelatory presence of God in the human destiny of the Son has been further developed in the Christology of Wolfhart Pannenberg.

Pannenberg endorses Barth's concern to demonstrate that the concept of God's self-revelation implied the divinity of Christ,[90] but is critical of the manner in which Barth's Christology proceeds. By adopting a Christology from above and remaining content to deduce the divinity of Christ from the concept of revelation, Barth has effectively assumed the divinity of Christ without providing an adequate exegetical basis for this confession in the actual life and destiny of the man Jesus of Nazareth. When one attends to the vast exegetical material contained in the long footnotes and elsewhere in the *Church Dogmatics*, one wonders if this criticism is either entirely fair or accurate.

Pannenberg's own contribution to this debate has been to show how a basis for acknowledging the divinity of Christ can be located in the historical relationship of self-differentiation that Jesus has with the God to whose royal rule and reign he subordinated all other concerns. The validity of this relationship and the endorsement of Jesus as the Son of God is provided by the resurrection. In this way Pannenberg seeks to show that Jesus cannot be properly understood in isolation from this fundamental relationship. Consequently, a Christology from below that concentrates solely on the historical

---

[90] Cf. Pannenberg, *Jesus—God and Man*, 130.

Jesus is inadequate. However, a Christology from above that begins with the pre-existent *Logos* or divine Son, without demonstrating how a firm basis for acknowledging the divinity of the Son can be found in the mission and vocation of Jesus, is also inadequate.

Another related criticism of Barth's Christology is that it is really a retreat into fideism. Ever since Bonhoeffer accused Barth of revelatory postivism, the suspicion has been that Barth's so-called self-authenticating theology of the Word of God lapses into the same subjectivism that beset liberal Protestantism. Again, it is Pannenberg who claims that Barth's theology collapses back into a Schleiermacherian subjectivism, because it ultimately rests on the inner testimony of faith and not public historical or philosophical grounds that can be disputed and debated.[91] McCormack rightly acknowledges that Barth is always going to be vulnerable to this accusation, but also points out that in Barth's view

> the only adequate safeguard against the threat of subjectivism will be found in the objectivity of a God who discloses Himself in such a way that He remains Lord of the epistemic relation. And that means, the objectivity of a God who veils Himself in human flesh and bears witness to Himself in and through the veil of human words and does not give Himself over to the control and management of human beings.[92]

In one sense, Pannenberg and, indeed, Brunner (with his concern for theological *eristics*), are right in that no theology can effectively expunge from its agenda the dialogue with philosophy and the other sciences and still remain catholic or ecumenical in scope. It is only in conversation with what the other sciences say about human nature, culture and society that the universality of Christ, as the saviour and Lord of all these concerns, can be credibly articulated, if not finally demonstrated.

In defence of Barth, it appears that it was a particular type of philosophical anthropology – one that violated the sovereignty of God by reducing theology to some historically or empirically presupposed *datum*, which then functioned as a foundation to which all else must refer – that he was endeavouring to exorcise from *Church Dogmatics*. More importantly, it is clear from any systematic investigation of Barth's theology that he remained indebted to the idealist tradition of philosophy throughout his lifetime. As McCormack acknowledges, the very dialectic of veiling and unveiling that supposedly constituted Barth's anti-foundationalism remained wedded to the basic tenets of Kantian epistemology.[93]

---

[91] Pannenberg, *Systematic Theology*, Vol 1, 45.

[92] B. McCormack, 'Barth in Context: A Response to Professor Gunton' *Scottish Journal of Theology* 49/4 (1996), 497.

[93] McCormack, *Critically Realistic Dialectical Theology*, 466.

Foundationalism revisited

It is time to return to the vexed question of whether or not Barth succumbed to his own brand of foundationalism and so, to use his metaphor, filled in the empty space at the centre of theology with a form of christological determinism. It is our conviction that it is almost impossible to arrive at a satisfactory answer to this question simply by underscoring the centrality and cruciality of the dialectic of the *Deus revelatus* and the *Deus absconditus* throughout the Barthian corpus (McCormack), or refer Barth's concerns at this juncture to a postmodern theory of language (Ward). Rather, we need to attend to the kind of foundationalism in theology that Barth rejects and replaces with his own viable alternative.

Barth fiercely repudiated the attempt, by his liberal forebearers, to create a form of scientific theology that operated from the basis of an indisputable essence or basic given, be that the pious self-consciousness of the individual subject or von Harnack's notion of the simple religion of Jesus. All such forms of theological exposition violated the freedom of the Word of God in its three-fold form to both create and manage its own conditions of cognitive possibility. But Barth also rejected the dogmatic method of Protestant orthodoxy to which he is often accused of returning, a fact that is not always recognised. He would not allow that dogmatics was ultimately reducible to the exegesis and systematic explication of supposedly foundational creeds and dogmas:

> In dogmatics we cannot presume to know and declare in advance, as a more than hypothetical certainty, what is and what is not fundamental. Traditional notions as to what is fundamental or not, central or peripheral, more or less important, have to be suspended, so that they can become a matter for vital new decision by the Word of God itself.[94]

Barth's *Church Dogmatics* demonstrates a braver theological method than mere conformity to the doctrinal and dogmatic loci that supposedly lie at the heart of the church's credal tradition. Instead, he contends that a theologian must be prepared in obedience to the dynamic interaction of the Word of God with the church community, to challenge both the preaching of the church and the ethical practice of faith and discipleship in the name of that Word attested to in Scripture, and revealed in the sacramental reality of the humanity of Christ. In both of these factors there is a self-effacing hiddeness that cannot be violated through recourse to dogmas, creeds and doctrinal formulae.

What then does Barth put at the centre of the dogmatic task? It is our contention that at the centre, and it may well be that this means only the inner

---

[94] Barth, *Church Dogmatics* 1\2, 865.

periphery of the hub, is the narrative logic of election, the gracious reconciling action of God whereby, through the instrumentality of the *Logos*, the broken covenant is healed and our salvation procured:

> The whole being and life of God is an activity, both in eternity and in worldly time, both in Himself as Father, Son and Holy Spirit, and in His relation to man and all creation. But what God does in Himself and as the Creator and Governor of man is all aimed at the particular act in which it has its centre and meaning. And everything that He wills has its ground and origin in what is revealed as His will in this one act. Thus it is not merely one amongst others of His works as Creator and Governor. Of course, it can and must be understood in this way, in accordance with the general will and work of God. But within this outer circle it forms an inner. The one God wills and works all things, but here He wills and works a particular thing: not one with others, but one for the sake of which He wills and works all others.[95]

It is clear that when Barth referred to that which forms the inner circle, he is referring to the sovereign activity of God in atoning action on our behalf, not a christological dogma or doctrine. Most certainly, christological doctrines or preferences of the Alexandrian variety do ensue from Barth's dogmatic endeavours, but nevertheless the centre remains the ultimate mystery of God's reconciling action for us and with us, without which we would know neither our predicament nor the solution to that apostasy and existential dilemma.

But what does this open space at the centre actually express? It could well be, as Stephen Sykes contends, that it merely and unavoidably demonstrates Barth's commitment to a particular ecclesial identity.[96] There is, however, more at stake here than mere ecclesial preferences and loyalty. It is our judgement that we have to go beyond one particular metaphor and look at the combined effect of Barth's actualism of revelation, his dialectic of veiling and unveiling, his use of the *analogia fidei*, his rejection of all points of contact and his apophatic theology of a cloud of unknowing at the centre of the dogmatic task to perceive that here is a theologian who is at least endeavouring to be christocentrically non-foundational.

Much criticism has centred on Barth's apparent flight from, or disregard for, the issues to do with the historicity of the events that supposedly undergird the foundations of Christology. This concern is well illustrated in the correspondence between Barth and von Harnack. Von Harnack put fifteen questions to the 'despisers of scientific theology' and the fourteenth clearly expresses the dilemma:

---

[95] Barth, *Church Dogmatics* 4\1, 7.
[96] Sykes, *Karl Barth*, 52.

If the person of Jesus Christ stands at the centre of the gospel, how else can the ba-sis for reliable and communal knowledge of this person be gained but through critical-historical study so that an imagined Christ is not put in place of the real one? What else besides scientific theology is able to undertake this study?[97]

Barth's reply was equally uncompromising:

The reliability and communality of the knowledge of the person of Jesus Christ as the centre of the gospel can be none other than that of God-awakened *faith*. Critical-historical study signifies the deserved and necessary end of *those* 'foundations' of this knowledge which are no foundations at all since they have not be laid by God himself.[98]

Similarly, much has been made of the fact that, as early as 1916, Barth wrote to his close friend and colleague Eduard Thurneysen ruefully admitting 'how frightfully indifferent historical questions have become to me'.[99] In this respect, Pannenberg is also critical of Barth. In his own work, Pannenberg has sought to show that, as Troeltsch recognised, such a confrontation with historical–critical method could not be avoided:

Barth escaped [historical relativism], but I don't think he really overcame the problem. He chose to neglect it, to turn his back on it. My feeling concerning Barth and Troeltsch is that when I read Troeltsch, I read all the questions with which theology still has to wrestle. Troeltsch could have written last year or the year before. When I read Barth it is as if I were reading a church father of the fifth century.[100]

In light of the postmodern analysis that, in many respects, we now inhabit the post-historical era (or our contention, that very few biblical historians have truly understood the political and ideological motives that lie behind their own historical investigations), Barth's indifference to the results of historical criticism can appear more sanguine than previously recognised. In Barth's defence, he did take the historicity of our existence very seriously, but it is history qualified and circumscribed by the history of Christ, rather than the other way round. He was not prepared to allow the self-disclosure of God in the person of his Son to be subject to the canons and criteria of critical-historical interrogation.

Barth is now a real force to be reckoned with in the postmodern world. He does appear to have almost unwittingly anticipated some of the main criticisms

---

[97] M. Rumscheidt, *Revelation and Theology, An Analysis of the Barth-Harnack Correspondence of 1923*. See also Hunsinger, *Disruptive Grace*, 319–39

[98] Ibid., 35.

[99] The main substance of Alister McGrath's criticism of Barth's Christology is that he never repented from this cardinal error. See, *Modern German Christology*, 140.

[100] W. Pannenberg, *A Theological Conversation with W Pannenberg*, 294–5.

and objections of postmodern theory to the modernity project. In that sense, there is, in Barth's writing, a refreshing candour and alertness to the reality of changing historical and cultural circumstances that can easily render any theological programme obsolete. In our judgement this is what has transpired in regard to the theology of Paul Tillich, and yet Tillich, more than most theologians, alerted us to that continual dialogue and interchange with culture that we have sought to explore and develop.

Barth was too suspicious of culturally attuned theological programmes to allow to cultural analysis the role that we have been prepared to maintain. But it is here that our main criticism should be directed. All theology must seek to serve, encourage and consolidate the life and witness of the Christian church, and it is for this reason that it cannot remain a church dogmatics. The distinction kergymatic theology – as opposed to apologetic theology or indeed the attempt to mediate between the two by calling for a dialogical theology – seems to us largely redundant.[101] This is because theology continually breaks out of such categories and distinctions as it engages in the threefold discussion that, as we have maintained throughout this study, mediates to us a sense and awareness of the presence of Christ in the world. Scripture, church and culture continually interpenetrate. To opt for a preference of one over the other is to cut short the conversation that could actually liberate the church from its own cultural internment and isolation.

In a postmodern world, alien philosophical and theological conceptualities abound, but like the prodigal son, sometimes it is only when we have picked our way through the husks and refuge of them that we desire to return to more nourishing food. Similarly, occasionally we happen upon a tasty morsel that we bring with us because we recognise its ability to actually flavour and enhance our theological palate.

We must now turn to another theological pilgrimage that owes much to Barth's influence and direction but that has also recognised that every theology requires the help of other disciplines and cultural influences if it wants to remain a theology with an eschatological proviso and an unfinished agenda.

---

[101] See, for example, D.J. Hall, *Professing the Faith*.

11.

The Engagement with Postmodernity – Christology on the Way

That theology is based on God's self-revelation in his Word in the biblical history and has its determining centre in the cross and resurrection of Jesus Christ are the methodological convictions which link Moltmann's work with Barth's, though he came to differ from Barth in opening both to an eschatological perspective.[1]

Introduction

Jürgen Moltmann's book, *The Way of Jesus Christ*, has been hailed as 'probably the most important work on Christology for a decade at least'.[2] In his Christology, Moltmann sought to incorporate the strengths and achievements, and overcome the weaknesses, of the two dominant models in the history of Christology – the cosmological and the anthropological. In so doing, he developed a post-liberal narrative Christology, which retained strongly messianic and eschatological perspectives.

Moltmann's Christology speaks into the context of postmodernity and helps us draw together many of the inter-related themes with which we have been concerned in our study. Moltmann's debt to Barth is present at every level of his theology, even when he attempts to distance himself from Barth. Unlike Barth (whose Christology was ahead of its time in endeavouring to overturn the epistemological constrictions of modernity), Moltmann has the distinct advantage of being able to see just where the obsession with the power of human reason and ourselves has led us. Consequently, with this baleful legacy in mind, Moltmann constructs a Christology that postulates a universal soteriological situation of the end times, which threatens the very existence of humanity.

---

[1] R. Bauckham, *Moltmann: Messianic Theology In The Making*, 23.
[2] R. Bauckham, 'Moltmann's Messianic Christology', *SJT* 44.4 (1991), 519.

Moltmann and Barth

Both Barth and Moltmann's deepest theological convictions and concerns arose out of the crucible of war, and the cataclysmic events and forces that were shaking European civilisation to its very core during and after the First and Second World Wars. Moltmann's conversion to the Christian faith and the early seeds of his dynamic theology of hope emerged out of these experiences:

> As I continue to look back I see a young prisoner of war interned in an English camp. His horizon there is the barbed wire, even though the war has been over for some time. His path is one which curves in a circle around the edges of the barbed wire. Freedom lies beyond – out there were people live and laugh ... Hope rubbed itself raw in the barbed wire! A man cannot live without hope! The prisoner experienced an inner conversion when he gave up hope of getting home soon, and in his yearning he discovered that deeper 'hope against hope.'[3]

If the symphonic scope of Barth's theology can be encapsulated in a single melody,[4] then Moltmann's theological overture is the overwhelming dynamic of hope revealed in the God of the promise who raises Jesus from the dead.

Similar contexts often lead to similar emphases and Moltmann's theology has retained the strong political and ethical dimensions found in Barth's *Church Dogmatics*. In both cases, their theology 'has never been a neutral scientific study or an objective doctrine, but an existential experience, which must be personally suffered, digested and understood'.[5] Consequently, while there are real and important differences, Barth's and Moltmann's respective theologies have nevertheless been directed toward the praxis of discipleship and the mission of the church in and to the world.[6]

Like Barth, Moltmann's early theology derived much of its passion and fury from an intense dialogue with certain crucial philosophical influences, as well as a rediscovery of the eschatological dimensions of biblical faith. For both of them, this eventuated in a sharply attenuated theological dialectic that under-scored the radical disjunction between the sin and suffering of humanity and the transcendent God of the Bible. Indeed, Richard Bauckham notes that in

---

[3] M.D. Meeks, *Origins of the Theology of Hope*, 10–11.

[4] For instance, the sheer triumph of God's grace in vicarious love and self-sacrifice. Cf. G. Berkouwer, *Triumph of Grace*.

[5] Bauckham, *Moltmann*, vii.

[6] 'If I were to attempt to sum up the outline of my theology in few key phrases, I would have at the least to say that I am attempting to reflect on a theology that has ... a biblical foundation ... an eschatological orientation ... [and] a political responsibility.' J. Moltmann, *History and the Triune God: Contributions to Trinitarian Theology*, 182.

The Theology of Hope Moltmann simply transposed Barth's infinite qualitative distinction between time and eternity into an eschatological distinction between the turmoil of the present and God the power of the future.[7]

Regarding the philosophical dialogue, Barth initiated a fierce debate between Pauline theology and Kiergaardian existentialism, whereas Moltmann commenced an ongoing discussion between biblical apocalyptic and the futurist utopianism of the Marxist philosopher, Ernest Bloch. It was this intense dialogue that produced the eschatological Christology or christological eschatology of Moltmann's earlier theology.

The origins of this eschatological perspective are found in the Old Testament history of promise. These messianic expectations provide a necessary presupposition for Christology and find their fulfilment in the resurrection of Jesus from the dead: 'The promise that announces the *eschaton*, and in which the *eschaton* announces itself, is the motive power, the mainspring, the driving force and the torture of history.'[8] Christ is not the end of the promise, but its liberation and validation;[9] the dialectic of cross and resurrection reveals the incongruence between the sin and suffering of the present era, and the hope, freedom and eventual victory of the future. The resurrection assures us that the future is not constructed out of the latent tendencies of the present; neither is it a totally nebulous future devoid of all specific content. Rather, it directs us to the eschatological lordship of Christ over the creation.[10] Consequently, the resurrection is the christological basis for hope and transforms history into the universal mission of the church.[11]

Just as Barth's theology moved toward a new christocentric focus, so 'Moltmann moved from an early stress on the wholly future God who contradicts present reality to a later emphasis (in *The Crucified God*) on the incarnate God who identifies with the suffering of the present'.[12] In a manner reminiscent of Barth (in the *Church Dogmatics*), Moltmann links the inner trinitarian relationships with the incarnation and the cross of Christ in a way that underscores the radical identification of God with the suffering history of the

---

[7] Cf. Bauckham, *Moltmann*, 41: 'Moltmann substitutes a transcendent future for Barth's transcendent eternity, but the dialectic is otherwise similarly conceived.'

[8] Moltmann, *Hope*, 17.

[9] Ibid., 145.

[10] R. Bauckham, *The Theology of Jürgen Moltmann*, 9.

[11] Here it is clear that what was lacking in Barth's early theology, i.e. a more positive and nuanced utilisation of the eschatological dimensions of biblical faith, received both due note and a new christological focus in Moltmann's theology of hope. As we shall see, this concern has remained central to Moltmann's theological development, the mature flowering of which can be discerned in the final volume of his systematic theology, J. Moltmann, *The Coming of God: Christian Eschatology*.

[12] Bauckham, *Moltmann*, 41.

world.[13] The largely functional and representative Christology of *Theology of Hope* was augmented with a dialectical Christology of the cross that represented

> a shift from the God who has future as his essential nature and moves history forward by his promise, to the God who enters history and suffers it, makes godless and god-forsaken humanity the sphere of his presence, and moves history forward by the power of suffering love.[14]

In *The Crucified God*, the links between Martin Luther's *theologia crucis* and Horkheimer and Adorno's 'dialectic of Enlightenment', constituted (like Barth's earlier alliances with Kierkegaard and Overbeck) Moltmann's attempt to overcome the metaphysics of presence as he observed it operating in the analogical principle of knowledge:

> The knowledge of God in the crucified Christ takes seriously the situation of man in pursuit of his own interests, man who in reality is inhuman, because he is under the compulsion of self-justification, dominating self-assertion and illusion-ary self-deification. For this reason, the crucified Jesus is the 'image of the invisible God'. Thus because of its subject, the theology of the cross, right down to its method and practice, can only be polemical, dialectical, antithetical and critical theory.[15]

By broadening his soteriology so that it unites 'both the question of human guilt and man's liberation from it, and also the question of human suffering and man's redemption from it',[16] Moltmann again moves beyond Barth.

In *The Crucified God*, Moltmann subsumed the justification of the sinner and the traditional concerns of theodicy within the wider question of God's righteousness in the world. Godlessness and godforsakenness refer both to humanity lost in sin and alienation, which God judges and reconciles to God, and the suffering, abandonment and dereliction that human beings experience, like the crucified Christ, with which God identifies and so redeems. Instead of a political theology based on the revolutionary power of the future, Moltmann thought in terms of Christian discipleship and identity defined by our relationship to the crucified God.

While Moltmann has always repudiated any claim to subsume his theology within a total programme, be that a church dogmatics or a fortress-like systematic theology, he nevertheless explored and developed his own

---

[13] Moltmann, *Crucified God*.
[14] Bauckham, *Moltmann*, 58.
[15] Moltmann, *Crucified God*, 69.
[16] Ibid., 134.

pilgrimage in messianic theology in a manner that is certainly reminiscent of the great unfinished task of Barth's particular theological and dogmatic concerns. There are several parallels. For example, in *The Trinity and the Kingdom of God*, Moltmann further develops Barth's renewal of trinitarian theology; he provides Barth's covenantal theology of creation in *God in Creation*, with a new ecological focus; in *The Way of Jesus Christ*, the christocentrism of Barth's mature theology is taken into the wider parameters of Moltmann's messianic theology; finally, the doctrine of redemption and a proper development of the theology of the Spirit in the church and the world as both move toward their consummation in the coming kingdom of God (the unfinished agenda of Barth's *Church Dogmatics*) receives due attention in *The Spirit of Life* and *The Coming of God*.

Messianic Christology

The symbol of the 'way' is both an evocative and crucial metaphor for Moltmann's christological purposes; it allowed him to develop his narrative approach to Christology by:

1. Enabling Christology to become a retelling of the story of Jesus from his birth to his baptism, from his ministry amongst the poor and marginalised to his journey to Jerusalem; and from his cross and resurrection to his cosmic rule and eventual *parousia*.
2. Establishing from the beginning the historically conditioned and therefore epistemologically limited nature of all our christological reflections. 'Every human christology is a "christology of the way", not yet a "christology of the home country", a christology of faith, not yet a christology of sight.'[17]
3. Becoming an invitation to both believe in Christ (Christology) and follow that way in lifestyle and discipleship (christopraxis) and so facilitates the link between Christology and ethics.
4. Being oriented toward the goal of the process and therefore simultaneously messianic, eschatological and apocalyptic. The latter three adjectives interpreted in the light of the one who announces and embodies God's hoped for reconciliation of the cosmos.
5. Being oriented to the Jewish–Christian question, beginning with the messianic promise of the old covenant and moving on to its fulfilment in the new covenant. Consequently, it begins with the path leading from

---

[17] Moltmann, *Way*, xiv.

the Jewish messianic hope to the Jesus of the Gospels and the Christ of the NT.[18]

Throughout this study, we have noted the fracture in Christology that takes place when Jesus the Jew is severed from his religious and cultural roots in Judaism. Clearly, the hope in and for the coming Messiah links the theological perspectives of the Bible. Moltmann's messianic Christology affords us the opportunity to explore biblical and christological resources that we have, hitherto, left underdeveloped. Similarly, it directs us to the real hiatus in Jewish–Christian relationships, i.e. that although Christology is a particular form of the Jewish hope for the Messiah, it is still a real stumbling block for those who cannot find in the crucified Jesus the hoped for liberator of Israel or indeed the redeemer of the world (Lk. 24:21).

Moltmann explores the biblical dimensions of messianism, 'the idea which Israel gave the world'.[19] The eschatological history of Jesus begins, therefore, not in the notion of his pre-existence which formed the starting point of the incarnational Christology of the ancient church, but with Israel's messianic hopes and expectations. Born out of Israel's ambivalent experience of monarchy, the coming Messiah was to be the one who fulfilled the Davidic kingship, a royal rule open to prophetic correction and expressed through priestly office. The spirit-filled life of the anointed one would establish God's just and gentle rule among the nations.

What divides Jewish messianism from its Christian equivalent? Moltmann quotes Martin Buber, Schalom Ben-Chorin and Gershom Scholem, all of whom are united in their indefatigable protest that Judaism knows only one form of the promise of salvation, one that is public, transformational and complete (i.e. the irradication of all pain, suffering and evil before the universal unveiling of the kingdom of God).[20] There cannot be for Jews a private salvation that takes the entire public, prophetic, biblical acclamations concerning the future of the world and applies them to the destiny of the individual soul. It will be some kind of answer to this heartfelt and searching interrogation of Christian faith that will form the substance of Moltmann's Christology on the way.

---

[18] This does not imply a radical reduction in the scope of Christology because 'People who restrict the Christian faith to "the historical Jesus" or – more recently to "Rabbi Jesus", dispensing with the allegedly 'high christology' of Paul, John and the ancient church – do not only lose the Christian faith in the resurrection. At the same time, they cast away the faith in God that is specifically Christian. And they do not surmount all possible theological anti-Judaism just by doing so.' Cf. *Way*, xvi-xvii.

[19] Ibid., 2.

[20] Ibid., 2.

Paul postulated an interim solution where Israel's vocation remained intact although her hope is delayed so that the Gentiles can also become heirs of the promise. The Jewish 'No!' to Jesus may have launched the mission to the Gentiles, and necessarily involved the fracturing of the original promise into two diverse forms, but it should always be remembered that the Jewish–Christian question is ultimately irreconcilable until there is an answer to that original question upon which the two faiths can agree.

The Search for a New Paradigm

Moltmann is concerned to develop a new christological paradigm that is sensitive to the changing soteriological situation of the modern world, or as he puts it: 'Christology in the contradiction of scientific and technological civilisation'.[21] In the process, Moltmann hopes to surmount the limitations and restrictions of the cosmological and anthropological paradigms. Consequently, he affirms what we have identified as the basic intent of modern Christology, and continues the search for an appropriate paradigm whereby the universal salvific significance of Christ can be interpreted afresh in the context of our modern experience of reality.

Moltmann contends that we need a fresh paradigm that is able to address a new soteriological context, where the very survival of human civilisation is seriously threatened. Because of the dissolution of modernity and the transition to postmodernity, a universal soteriological context has emerged. On the positive side, this could unite Jew and Christian, or those of any faith, in a common experience of the perilous nature of the end times. On the negative side, Moltmann has to address a key philosophical query of postmodernity: namely, our present experience of reality is both inherently fractured and multifaceted, and thus incorrigibly resistant to all universal contexts of meaning and interpretation. Similarly, Moltmann's Christology remains vulnerable to our main criticism that all such christologies that venture down the soteriological route will inevitably align themselves with one or a number of the socio-political myths of the Enlightenment that are designed to support the lordship of the universal subject.

Critique of cosmological and anthropological Christologies

Cosmological Christology
We have already noted that the cosmological Christology of the early church originated within the cosmocentric world of Neoplatonism. Within such a worldview an intractable dualism easily developed between the immutable

---

[21] Ibid., 63.

world of divine, eternal reality and the transient, perishable world of material-ity.[22] The soteriological concern was to discover how to break free from what was perceived as the wretchedness of the human condition (the doctrine of physical redemption).

Within the general metaphysical framework of this Christology, Jesus' unity with God is not established from the basis of the resurrection, but from the principle of incarnation. The mystery of the incarnation involves the divine *Logos* assuming human nature and so becoming the unity of divinity and humanity in the person of Jesus. As we noted in the previous chapter, the twin formulations of *anhypostatos* and *enhypostatos* safeguarded the Chalcedonian affirmation that it is the eternal *Logos* who is the personal centre of the man Jesus of Nazareth:

> This union (*unitio*) takes place in such a way that the eternal *Logos*, the second person of the Trinity, the eternal Son, assumes non-personal human nature in the womb of Mary, absorbing it into the unity and independence of his person, and into the fellow-ship of his divine nature. In the eternal *Logos*, the divine nature is a nature determined by personhood; the human nature that is assumed is a non-personal nature.[23]

Moltmann raises a number of crucial objections to the two-nature Christology of the early church.

First is the classical objection that this Christology inevitably moves in a docetic direction. How are we to think of a divine *Logos* assuming a non-personal human nature, as if the humanity of Jesus was some kind of fleshly garment housing a divine subject? Could the notion of a human nature, where the personalising element is the pre-existent *Logos*, ever be understood as a properly historical existence? Is it not the case, as the process theologians have complained, that here we have a divine visitor from another sphere, which consequently introduces a schism between our humanity and that of Christ, however the latter is conceived?[24]

Secondly, if the divine *Logos* is the personalising centre to the man Jesus do we have a human nature that is in fact immortal? Similarly, is this a human nature without any propensity toward sin, and if so, how are we to make sense of the crucifixion as a real death within the being of God rather than merely a death in sympathy with ourselves?[25]

---

[22] J. Moltmann, *Twilight of the Idols*, 484.

[23] Moltmann, *Way*, 50.

[24] Ibid., 51.

[25] It is surprising that Moltmann does not refer to the concerns of Barth's doctrine of election at this point. If the eternal *Logos* is already, in some sense, the humanity of God then historical existence is not something inimical to the being of God. Simi-larly, we cannot think of divinity or humanity in isolation from the incarnation in

Thirdly, conflating Moltmann's third and fourth points, we would agree that the metaphysical superstructure of the two-nature Christology inevitably minimises the importance of the real lowliness, humanity, suffering and godforsakenness of the man Jesus and his coming to grief in the socio-political cauldron of events his own actions in the Temple may have initiated. Similarly, when Christology is fixated upon the relationship of the *Logos* to the man Jesus, it easily misses the intimacy and indeed the christological significance of Jesus' relationship to the God he called 'Abba':

> The passion of his love and its capacity for suffering can no longer be stated. 'The God of history', 'the coming God', disappears in favour of the eternal presence of the heavenly Lord.[26]

Finally, Moltmann takes note of the political situation whereby the *Logos* Christology of the church became the imperial Christology of the Byzantine Empire. His main point, with which we have concurred, is that this is a political context that no longer exists in the modern world.[27]

Anthropological Christology

The cosmocentric world of the early church was replaced by the anthropo-centric world of the modern era:

> The modern era no longer asks the question about God in the context of cosmology – if it asks it at all. It asks the question in the context of anthropology. For us, the human being is the starting point from which we ask about the meaning of the whole, and from which we ask the question about Jesus Christ also.[28]

The fateful turn inwards towards the human subject changed our relationship with the external world. Put simply, human beings no longer viewed themselves as embedded in the structures of the cosmos, but as isolated, autonomous human subjects who could control and manipulate the natural world for their own gainful purposes. This process of emancipation led to the permanent identity crisis of the modern human subject.[29] A clear understanding of our

---

[25] *(continued)* which case what transpires in the history of Jesus belongs both in principle and essence to the trinitarian life of the eternal God. Both of these factors would mitigate some of the substance of Moltmann's criticism of cosmological Christology.

[26] Moltmann, *Way*, 53.

[27] Ibid., 54.

[28] Kasper, *Theology*, 103–4.

[29] This fundamental sense of anomie, disorientation, dislocation and loss of meaning and direction has been documented by many sociologists of religion. Emile Durkheim refers to the 'pluralization of lifeworlds' that typified modernity causing a

own definitive humanity remains oblique and uncertain to us. Human rights and human dignity, ethical concerns to which Moltmann devotes a lot of attention, have become the foundation of the European and American human-itarian liberal tradition.[30] However, that has not stopped us behaving in inhumane and barbarous ways toward our fellow human beings. This contra-diction was recognised by Theodor Adorno and Max Horkheimer as early as 1947 when they asked 'why mankind, instead of entering into a truly human condition, is sinking into a new kind of barbarism'.[31]

In such a context, the old incarnational Christology – which understood Jesus as the God-man, the unity of divinity and humanity in his own person, and so the guarantor of our redemption from the world of transience and decay – no longer makes soteriological sense. Instead, modern Christology is domi-nated by the desire to recover the historical Jesus as the perfect, or ideal, example of human existence:

> Jesus was no longer understood against a theological background, as the God-human being. He was now viewed in an anthropological foreground, as God's human being. What was stressed now was not his incarnation and – as its physical sign – the virgin birth, but his human perfection in its correspondence to the divine and – as its sign – his sinlessness. Salvation was no longer to be found in the deifica-tion of human beings and creation. It was now seen in the inner identity of the self-divided human being, who has become a stranger to himself – an inner identity which would then make it possible to arrive at a moral humanity.[32]

In a similar vein, incarnation and resurrection were regarded as intrusive miracles that no longer cohered with the new scientific worldview. All our knowledge, including Christology, was now directed towards practical ends. Metaphysical speculation was deemed of no import to the practical organisa-tion of human society. As we have noted, in such a context Jesus easily became the guarantor of our practical morality; or the great moral educator of the human race; or the prototypical manifestation of the God-conscious human

---

[29] (*continued*) consequent dislocation from tradition. Peter Berger talks in terms of 'the homeless mind' of the modern individual. Max Weber and, to a certain extent, Jürgen Habermas, viewed the fascination with instrumental rationality typical of modernity, as leading to the 'disenchantment of the world'. Herbert Marcuse speaks bitingly of the modern subject as 'one-dimensional man' and Jacques Ellul has docu-mented the modern obsession with 'technique' alone, as but another retreat from the apparent meaninglessness of the modern world. Lyon, *Postmodernity*, 30.

[30] Cf. J. Moltmann, *On Human Dignity: Political Theology's Ethics*.

[31] T.W. Adorno and M. Horkheimer, *Dialectic of Enlightenment* Vol. 2, xi; see also Lyon, *Postmodernity*, 28–36.

[32] Moltmann, *Way*, 57–8.

being; or the existential expression of the New Being; or the superlative realisation of the self-transcending openness of human nature; or the fullest expression to date of the evolutionary process of becoming or, of course, the great liberator from cultural and ideological oppression. Moltmann's criticism of anthropological Christology moves in a similar direction.

First, at the centre of all such christologies is the alienated and self-divided human subject.

> Right down to the present day, this modern Jesuology has made the human Jesus of Nazareth the projection screen for all the different fantasies of the true humanity which alienated men and women are seeking – men and women who have become strangers to themselves: Jesus offers pure personhood, absolute humanity, the faith that gives certitude, and so forth.[33]

Secondly, the soteriological focus of this form of Christology is an abstraction, i.e. the individual human soul, or personal subject, or existential individual, or our innate ability for self-transcendence. Through a brief look at the respective christologies of Schleiermacher and Rahner, Moltmann concludes that this type of anthropological Christology extrapolates human nature, or individual subjectivity, from the political, social and cultural contexts that really control our destiny. As such, it bolstered the privatisation of religion that has been such a deleterious feature of modernity:

> A theology which with its Christology goes along with the modern experience of subjectivity, and now conveys the content of the Christian doctrine of salvation only in so far as this is related to the individual subject of experience, is no longer willing – and no longer able – to call in question the social conditions and political limitations of this experience of subjectivity. This theology fits without any conflict into the requirements of the 'civil religion' of modern society.[34]

Thirdly, Jesus must be understood as more than just the prototypical human being. He is, first and foremost, the messianic human being still on his way to the redeeming future.

Who is Jesus Christ for us today?

At this juncture, Moltmann analyses the congenital defects of the modern scientific and technological project that has brought human civilisation perilously close to virtual extinction. The three factors he isolates provide the

---

[33] Ibid., 61.
[34] Ibid., 63.

context in which we have to answer the question: who really is Jesus Christ for us today.[35]

The first relates to the concerns of Liberation Christology, i.e. the continued economic exploitation of the Two-Thirds World and the subjugation of its peoples to the capitalist self-interest of the First World. This is nothing less than an iniquitous system of global injustice and inequality. Secondly, despite the end of the Cold War and the first major attempt at international disarmament, Moltmann believes that the nuclear threat still exists. We cannot unlearn what science has given us. Consequently, we inhabit a world that has produced its own apocalyptic scenario of global destruction. Moltmann identifies nuclearism as a crypto-religion, a self-made blasphemy that offers both total power and threatens total annihilation. Finally, the continued expansion of technological self-interest has also produced the ecological crisis, with the potential threat of the wholesale destruction of our natural habitat. In a manner that echoes the prophets of postmodernity, Moltmann views the controlling values of modern society as the acquisition of power, the consolidation of power and the pursuit of profit. Such values have now supplanted the previous metanarratives of science and have led to the equally ruthless subjugation and exploitation of the natural world.[36]

In such a context, Moltmann contends that we should abandon the superficial distinction of Christology from above and below. Both take their respective points of departure from general metaphysical or anthropological perspectives that are insufficiently related to the message and history of Jesus as the Christ. A preference for a Christology from above easily leads to a theological Christology without Jesus, and a mere Christology from below produces an anthropological Jesuology without God.[37] In contrast to Christology from above and below we need a new paradigm that is a 'Christology in the eschatological history of God'.[38] Such a framework will develop a narrative Christology that tells the story of the Christ in terms of the future redemption of the whole created cosmos:

> We shall begin with the messianic mission of Jesus, the prophet of the poor, go on to the apocalyptic passion of Jesus, the Son of the Father, and then arrive at the transfiguring raising of Jesus from the dead. We shall devote particular attention to his reconciliation of the cosmos, as the Wisdom of creation. In the future of Christ in judgement and kingdom, we then find the completion of salvation in the glory of God, and the fulfilment of the promise of reconciliation in the redemption of the world.[39]

---

[35] Ibid., 64.
[36] Cf. Ibid., 67–8.
[37] Ibid., 69.
[38] Ibid., 70.
[39] Ibid., 71.

Eschatological Christology, it is hoped, will provide a broader frame of reference for anthropological Christology, integrating the history of human beings with the history of nature, and it takes up within this eschatological perspective the cosmic concerns of the earlier cosmological and political christologies of the ancient church.

Spirit or Logos *Christology*

A decisive step in Moltmann's Christology is the way he substitutes a pnuematological Christology in place of the incarnational *Logos* Christology of the early church. His reasons for doing so are threefold.

First, it preserves the efficacy of his messianic Christology that views the historical Jesus as the fulfilment of the Old Testament history of promise. Jesus is the promised messiah, the bearer of the eschatological Spirit in unique measure and the one who bestows the Spirit upon all flesh. Moltmann is able to include the messianic mission of Jesus as part of the narrative structure of his Christology, a perspective that the traditional incarnational schema tended to lose:

> We are starting with a *pneumatological christology*, because we discover that the efficacy of the divine Spirit is the first facet of the mystery of Jesus. In this way we are taking up Israel's messianic history of promise as the presupposition of every New Testament Christology, and are developing Christology out of the Jewish contours of the messianic promise.[40]

Secondly, pnuematological Christology enables Moltmann to engage with the concerns of feminist Christology because Spirit Christology is also Wisdom Christology; both are feminine modes of the divine appearance. Spirit Christology is a useful foil to the androcentric Son of God and *Logos* christologies that have dominated the doctrinal tradition.

> Spirit or Wisdom Christology is the premise for every Son of God christology; for according to messianic tradition, the messiah who is anointed with the Spirit of God is 'the son of God'.[41]

Thirdly, it allows us to think of Jesus' history as that which flows out of the trinitarian history of God. Jesus' person, vocation and history are determined by his being in relationship with the God whose fatherly love he embodies and whose eschatological kingdom he proclaims; and his being in relationship with

---

[40] Ibid., 73–4.
[41] Ibid., 74.

the Spirit who is the very presence and life of God within him, and so provides a basis for affirming his divinity:

> If Christology starts by way of Pneumatology, this offers the approach for a trinitarian Christology, in which the Being of Jesus is from the outset a Being-in-relationship, and where his actions are from the very beginning interactions, and his efficacies co-efficacies.[42]

In developing a preference for a Spirit Christology, Moltmann follows a tradition recently explored in Britain by G. Lampe[43] and in Germany by Walter Kasper and Hendrik Berkhof.[44] As we have noted, Paul Tillich also moved in this direction in the third volume of his *Systematic Theology*. For all of these theologians, the uniqueness of Jesus is found in his spirit-filled existence and it is this reality that distinguishes him from his predecessor, John the Baptist.

In a way similar to Kasper, Moltmann views the presence of the Spirit in Jesus as the connecting link between the earthly Jesus and the post-Easter proclamation of him as the risen Lord. Moltmann accepts that the resurrection must be understood as both a historical and an eschatological event: 'It is the Easter event that prompts the confession of faith: "Jesus is the Christ of God"'.[45] However, Moltmann rejects Pannenberg's notion of the retroactive ontological force of the resurrection that takes up Jesus' pre-Easter path into his essential unity with God. In its place he substitutes a pneumatological Christology:

> The experience of the Spirit evidently provides a differently supported logic of correspondence between the experience of Christ's presence and the remembrance of his history. If Christ is present now in the eternal Spirit of God, then his history must have been determined by this Spirit from the very beginning.[46]

In the NT Jesus' relationship to the Spirit is one which is both pervasive and crucial for his identity as the promised Messiah. He is conceived through the Spirit, baptised in the Spirit and so empowered by the Spirit for his ministry of deliverance, healing and proclamation. Paul asserts in Romans 1:3–4 that Jesus was raised through the instrumentality of the Spirit. After his exaltation, Jesus is the one who now bestows the Spirit on the community of his people (Acts 2:33). Moltmann explores all these exegetical sources and finally arrives at the

---

[42] Ibid., 74.
[43] Lampe, *God as Spirit*.
[44] Kasper, *Jesus*. H. Berkhof, *Christian Faith: An Introduction to the Study of the Faith*.
[45] Moltmann, *Way*, 76.
[46] Ibid., 77.

suggestion that it is the *kenosis* of the divine Spirit that establishes a basis for the confession of Jesus' divinity:

> If we talk about a 'condescending' of the Spirit, we have also to talk about a kenosis of the Holy Spirit, which emptied itself and descended from the eternity of God, taking up its dwelling in this vulnerable and mortal human being Jesus.[47]

It is clear that Moltmann either believes that a Spirit Christology is able to fulfil all the ontological requirements of that usually ascribed to a *Logos* Christology, or, as Richard Bauckam suggests:

> At this point Moltmann's focus on pneumatological Christology evidently enables him to side step a classic christological issue; it is less clear that his own trinitarian theology ought to allow him to evade it.[48]

The issue at stake is a fundamental one. It is the question of how, on the basis of a Spirit Christology, we are to understand the pre-existence of the Son in the eternal fellowship of God? The issue, as Moltmann acknowledges, is contained in the notion of Sonship.[49] Put simply, what fundamentally *constitutes* Jesus' self-identity as the son is his relationship to the God he acknowledged as a loving Father, and not his relationship to the Spirit accepting the inherently metaphorical nature of all our language about God. The relationship of the Son to the Spirit is how that self-identity as the Son of the Father is *mediated*, both to the earthly Jesus and within the eternal fellowship of the eternal God.

The problem, as it arises within Moltmann's Christology, stems from his rejection of what he regards as the traditional monarchical view of the Trinity. He substitutes the notion of a social Trinity constituted through *perichoresis* in its place:

> Relationships of rule and subjection have no final validity either within the Trinity or in God's relationship to the world, since in himself God is a fellowship of love and in his relationship to the world it is not in the last resort his lordship so much as loving fellowship which he seeks.[50]

It is our conviction that here Moltmann introduces a near fatal error, both to his Christology and his doctrine of God. We can illustrate this point by a comparison of the way this issue is handled by Moltmann and Pannenberg.

---

[47] Ibid., 93.
[48] Bauckham, *Theology*, 208.
[49] Moltmann, *Way*, 143.
[50] Bauckham, *Theology*, 162.

The pre-existence of the Son

At this juncture, is worth quoting Pannenberg at length, not least because of the clarity he obtains with regard to the notion of the Son's pre-existence:

> If the relation to the historical person of Jesus of Nazareth in eternity characterises the identity of God as Father, then we must speak of a pre-existence of the Son, who was to be historically manifested in Jesus of Nazareth, even before his earthly birth. Then we also must view the earthly existence of Jesus as the event of the incarnation of the pre-existent Son. Certainly we may not think of this Son in isolation from the historical filial relation of Jesus to the Father if the affirmation of his pre-existence is grounded on this alone. Theologically the eternal relation of the Father to the Son may not be detached from the incarnation of the Son in the historical existence and work of Jesus. Nevertheless, we are to understand this relation as part of the eternal identity of the Father. We can thus speak of a state of pre-existence of the Son of God, who was manifested in the history of Jesus, even before his earthly birth, just as for the same reason we may speak of an abiding relation of the Crucified and risen Lord to the Father in consequence of his exaltation to fellowship with the Father and to participation in his lordship.[51]

In his christological considerations Pannenberg constantly affirms that sonship implies a relationship of differentiation and subordination. This is not to be derived from some general metaphysical principles concerning the eternal generation of the Son from the Father, but from the actual relationship of Jesus of Nazareth to his God. Jesus did not make himself equal with God, but clearly differentiated himself from him as the one God to whose coming rule and reign he subordinated all other concerns. In doing so, Jesus recognised that his own identity and vocation were determined by this primary relationship: 'I tell you the truth, the Son can do nothing by himself; he can only do what he sees his Father doing, because whatever the Father does the Son also does' (Jn. 5:19). This also constitutes the nature of the intra-trinitarian relationships because, as Athanasius recognised, the Father cannot be the Father without the Son.

In his ministry, Jesus claimed authority as the one who represented and realised the rule of God amongst his people. This led to the ambivalence that surrounded his identity as the Son of God. For the religious authorities he was a blasphemer who made himself equal with God. The charge resulted in his execution:

> The upshot was that on account of the supposed arrogance of making himself equal with God, he was put to death. Death exposed his finitude as distinct from his alleged equality with God (Mt. 27:40–43 par.) It was a punishment for the sinner and his delusion of being God's equal. It showed his finitude. The light of his resurrection

---

[51] Pannenberg, *Systematic Theology*, Vol. 2, 368.

revealed, however, that he had not deserved this sinner's death. This means, then, that in truth he suffered in our place as sinners. In the light of the Easter event the transgressors are those who rejected his message and ministry and contributed to his death.[52]

So, through the resurrection, God endorses Jesus' obedience and the voluntary subordination of his life to the kingdom.

Sonship also reveals a relationship of unity in distinction that, unless we are to lapse into adoptionism, entails that this is a relationship which belongs to the eternal God.

> The relation of the Son to the Father is characterised in eternity by the subordination to the Father, by the self-distinction from the majesty of Father, which took historical form in the human relation of Jesus to God.[53]

This self-distinction of the Son, or *Logos*, from the Father is also the basis of the distinction of all creaturely existence from God and so also of Jesus' human existence. Here, Pannenberg's Christology is very similar to Rahner's. Both view the importance of the concept of the *Logos*, or the pre-existent Son, as that which points to an integral relationship of differentiation and subordination within the eternal life of God, which includes the freedom and independence of the creation.

Barth worked out these relationships in terms of the doctrine of election. When the Father elects the Son as his covenant partner, the whole creation, and therefore our existence as creatures is included within that covenant relationship. Rahner, in a somewhat Hegelian fashion, viewed the *Logos* as the person who was brought forth from the *kenosis*, or self-emptying, of the Father. This relationship also formed the basis of God's unity in distinction with his creation.

Pannenberg, on the other hand, views the relationship of the Father to the Son in terms of a voluntary differentiation and subordination that similarly includes within it the freedom of the creation. Indeed, in the differentiation of the Son from the Father there is a moving out of the Son from the divine life that comes to partial realisation in the independence of the creation and the election of Israel. The Son was always on his way towards his manifestation as the promised messiah. 'He was in the world, and though the world was made through him, the world did not recognise him' (Jn. 1:10). The incarnation means that this relationship which formed the basis of the creation's differentiation from the Creator, comes to actual human and historical embodiment in

---

[52] Ibid., 374.
[53] Ibid., 377.

the person Jesus of Nazareth. 'He came to that which was his own, but his own did not receive him' (Jn. 11):

> By distinguishing the Father from himself as the one God, the Son certainly moved out of the unity of the deity and became man. But in so doing he actively expressed his divine essence as the Son. The self-emptying of the pre-existent is not a surrender or negation of his deity as the Son. It is its activation.[54]

It is this type of *Logos*, Son of God or Wisdom Christology, in whatever shape or form, which has been central to the Christian tradition since the time of Irenaeus, Origen and Athanasius. It alerts us to the fact that it took time to properly conceptualise the ontological differentiations that are born out of Jesus' witness to the coming God and his own resurrection from the dead, and as such, these distinctions cannot be abandoned without impunity.[55]

Similarly, if the *Logos* is already the generative principle of life, the basis of all creaturely independence in relation to the Creator, then the incarnation of the *Logos* does not need to be viewed as the entry of something alien or foreign

---

[54] Ibid., 377.

[55] This also has repercussions for our understanding of the vexed issue of the two natures adhering in one person. The starting point in this development was the early Christian twofold evaluation of Jesus 'after the flesh' and 'after the Spirit' (1 Tim. 3:16 and 1 Pet. 3:18), which Moltmann also considers. This twofold schema originally referred successively to Jesus' earthly pilgrimage and his exaltation after the resurrection. Here it is still the resurrection that forms the basis of Jesus' unity with God. However, when this formulation gave way to the notion of two natures or substances simultaneously adhering in the one person (which was certainly the case from the time of Tertullian onwards) then it was the birth of Jesus, rather than the Easter event, which became determinative for the union of deity and humanity in the person of Jesus. Once this step is taken we arrive at all the insoluble problems of Alexandrian and Antiochene Christology. Either at the incarnation the eternal *Logos* united with an already complete human being (as in Appollinarianism) Jesus becomes a hybrid figure made up of the compilation of two distinct natures; or if the Alexandrian position is preferred, then the human nature taken from the womb of Mary was fashioned into a human being only at the incarnation. Here Jesus is less than fully human because he possessed no specific human individuality or independence.

The only way to counteract these problems, if not necessarily to completely overcome them, is to view the union of divinity and humanity in the Christ, not as something that was completed at the incarnation, but as a process which took shape throughout the life history of the man Jesus. At this point we are moving close to Theodore of Mopsuestia's notion of *prosopic* union. Humanity and deity cannot therefore be conceived as two ontological substances that somehow cohere or inter-penetrate in the person of Jesus; rather, it describes a process whereby the eternal Son of God takes historical form and reality as a distinct human being.

into the human sphere. Rather, as both Rahner and Pannenberg affirm, human nature is ordained for the incarnation of the eternal Son.[56] Human nature is already related and open to the *Logos* as its source of origin in the self-distinction of the Son from the Father. Consequently, the life history of Jesus can be viewed as the historical manifestation of that which had been taking shape since the moment of creation and throughout the long history of Israel's election. This process was brought to completion in the resurrection of Jesus from the dead, which is the eschatological fulfilment of human life in fellowship with the eternal God.

These considerations do answer some of the objections to cosmological Christology raised by Moltmann. They also show how a Spirit Christology is unable to provide a viable alternative to *Logos* Christology and does, in fact, arise from a confusion of the trinitarian relationships. We can illustrate this by reference to some troubling comments in *The Spirit of Life* where Moltmann deals with the inherent limitations of the filioque clause as it is traditionally understood by reference to the Nicaeno–Constantinopolitan creed:

> It is not a matter of two separate acts, when the Son proceeds from the Father, and the Spirit is breathed out by the Father. On the contrary, the eternal birth of the Son from the Father and the eternal issuing of the Spirit from the Father are, in spite of all the differences, so much one that the Son and the Spirit must be seen, not as parallel or successive to one another, but *in* one another.[57]

Quite apart from the difficulty of making any plain sense out of this statement, it must be said that here we are not referring to successive acts within the trinitarian being of God, but relational differentiations that enable us to both understand the nature of the respective persons and their interaction. A theologian is not at liberty to simply interchange such differentiations at will without ending up in the sort of theological confusion Moltmann's preference for a Spirit Christology demonstrates. Similarly, as Bauckham notes, Moltmann's embrace of a social Trinity where relationships are apparently interchangeable at will does not lead to a clarification of the nature of the person of the Spirit, but to further exegetical difficulties and antinomies.[58]

A metaphysical or a social Christology

As we have noted, modern Christology has retreated from the metaphysical issues that dominated the cosmological Christology of the early period. The

---

[56] Ibid., 385–6.
[57] Moltmann, *Spirit of Life*, 72.
[58] Bauckham, *Theology*, 166–70.

complaint is often made that this Christology utilised categories that tended to conceive of Jesus' person as that which was the union of static or self-enclosed essences. The modern concept of person is defined in terms of our openness to others and the external world and not as enduring essence. As the feminist theologians have stressed, Jesus must also be understood, not just as an individual person, but also in terms of his being in relationship with others. Moltmann sought to address these concerns with a social Christology that underscores the three-dimensional character of Jesus' personal existence.

First, Jesus is the *messianic person*. By this Moltmann meant the eschatological reality of the person of Jesus, i.e. he is still on his way to his messianic rule over the whole creation. In a rather convoluted fashion, he seeks to relate this insight to the issue of the messianic secret: did Jesus see himself as Israel's messiah? Moltmann concludes that Jesus did not possess his messiahship, but grew into it. In the process, he redefined the nature of the Messiah as the suffering servant of God and eschatological judge of the nations.

Secondly, Jesus is the *theological person*. In his filial dependence upon the Father, Jesus redefines the nature of person as a being in relationship. The stress is not on the masculinity of sonship but on his willing participation in the Father's mission. In line with his earlier trinitarian considerations, Moltmann views the relationship between the Father and the childlike Jesus as one of mutual indwelling; both define the nature of the other. These considerations are hardly likely to satisfy the more radical feminists who object to the parental imagery when applied to God, as another instance of the dominance of patriarchy.

Thirdly, Jesus is the *social person*. Here Moltmann concentrates on the important social dimensions of Jesus' ministry: his preferential option for the poor and marginalised members of society; the special significance afforded to women; his link through the twelve disciples with the community of Israel; and, finally, his solidarity with the multitudes, the under-classes of society with no special privileges or rights.

In all three respects we discover the public dimensions of Christology. We are brought within the fellowship of the *christic* experience (Carter Heyward) or the Christa/ community (Rita Natishima Brock). Moltmann believes that messianic Christology, as opposed to incarnational Christology, is better able to embrace the feminist concern for a social Christology that does not tie the union of divinity and humanity exclusively to an individual male:

> Traditional Christology stressed only the theological person of the God-man Jesus Christ. Modern eschatological theology stressed the eschatological person of Jesus Christ. The most recent contextual christologies have disclosed the social

person of Jesus Christ. These last two developments have again begun to take seriously the messianic and social mission of Christ.[59]

The centrality of the cross and resurrection to Christology

Our exploration of modern Christology has revealed one persistent defect in many so-called christologies from below. That is the failure to make the cross and resurrection central and therefore constitutive for the identity of Jesus as the divine Son of God. This is often the case because it is the anxious search for the self-identity of the alienated modern subject which occupies centre stage in all such christologies. This goes hand-in-hand with the attempt to retrieve the historical Jesus as the ideal expression of a healed and restored humanity open to God. In fact, the error of the old quest for the historical Jesus reappears; he becomes the focus of wider anthropological and ideological concerns that effectively disguise the distinctiveness of his own personhood.

Schleiermacher's Christology, which revered a Jesus who was the proto-typical expression of the God-conscious human being, could make little of the significance of the cross and resurrection as the central matrix of interpretation with regard to who this Jesus actually was. Rahner's vision of Jesus as the summation of the evolutionary process exemplified similar deficiencies. This problem is less apparent in Liberation and Feminist christologies, because here the cross at least becomes central as the revelation of the suffering love and vulnerability of the passionate God; one whose voluntary self-sacrifice both exposes and deconstructs the dehumanising power of all oppressive ideologies. Nevertheless, it is still the soteriological concern of salvation, or integral libera-tion, understood as a process of greater humanisation that is central to this form of Christology. There is the same failure to find an integrative framework of meaning that demonstrates why the cross and resurrection occupy such a central position in the Gospel narratives. In other words, the unity of cross and resurrection as the disclosure of the one who suffers, dies and is raised on our behalf, must be preserved:

> Where he himself is concerned, the cross and resurrection are mutually related, and they have to be interpreted in such a way that the one event appears in the light of the other. The cross of Christ is the cross of the Lord who was raised by God and exalted to God.[60]

Many of the old atonement theories concentrated on the soteriological signifi-cance of the cross to such an extent that the meaning of the resurrection was

---

[59] Moltmann, *Way*, 149–50.
[60] Ibid., 213.

lost from view. On the other hand, it can also be the case that the resurrection becomes the dominant factor in the equation and the meaning of the cross is reduced to an unfortunate mistake by the religious establishment. This was certainly the case in Pannenberg's earlier Christology, although he rectified this deficiency in his *Systematic Theology*.[61]

In this respect, Moltmann's Christology fares better than most. In his earlier theology, Moltmann maintained the unity of the cross and resurrection by viewing both as the eschatological transition from the old to the new creation. In his later work, he develops this notion further in terms of the apocalyptic context from which the concept of resurrection is derived. He asserts that the meaning of the cross must be understood within the context of the Judeo–Christian apocalyptic expectation of unprecedented suffering and universal turmoil that marks the birth pangs of the new aeon. If the resurrection must be understood in terms of an anticipation of the general resurrection from the dead that heralds the end of history, then the cross is the anticipation of that universal context of death, sorrow and suffering which immediately precedes the end. In that sense, the unity of the cross and the resurrection mark the transition from a world passing away to one reborn in the future of God.

We have taken due note of the fact that this interpretation of apocalyptic is by no means universally shared by biblical scholars, although some would accept that Moltmann's thesis is consonant with recent research into the earliest interpretations of Jesus' passion and resurrection within the NT. For instance, Dale Allison concludes that Matthew, Mark, John, Paul and Revelation:

> Preserve an interpretation of the passion and resurrection of Jesus according to which the sufferings of the Messiah marked the inauguration of the messianic travail and his resurrection the onset of the general resurrection of the dead.[62]

Moltmann refers to the extraordinary signs which accompanied Jesus' death on the cross – the overwhelming darkness, the temple veil split in two, the rocks split and sundered, the graves opened – as the metaphorical depiction of the cross in terms of the signs of the end times. In such a context, Jesus'

---

[61] Pannenberg, *Systematic Theology*, Vol. 2, 397–454. Certainly, in his earlier monograph on Christology, Pannenberg used distinct categories to exegete the meaning of the cross and resurrection: the former being the ultimate expression of the Son's self-distinction from the Father and the latter being the prolepsis of the end-times. Here it is also difficult to maintain the unity of the cross and resurrection as the essential revelation of the person of the messiah.

[62] D.C. Allison, *The End of the Age Has Come: An Early Interpretation of the Passion and Resurrection of Jesus*, 80.

suffering becomes the vicarious suffering of the end times inclusive of all suffering throughout history.[63]

This apocalyptic context of meaning also entails that the resurrection contains an implicit critique of the modern paradigm of history. The secular transformation of history into the history of the human subject has always led to the resurrection being misunderstood in terms of a divine intrusion into human affairs. Barth's retreat into the category of divine or primal history, Bultmann's notion of existential history and Pannenberg's attempt to redefine the resurrection within the context of universal history are all taken as examples of a wider problem. The resurrection must now be interpreted within an ecological framework, which Moltmann believes will eventually supplant the modern paradigm of history. It is the history of the whole created cosmos that is our natural habitat. If that cannot be sustained and preserved, due to our profligate interference with its inbuilt harmonies and structures, then our own historical destiny will also be severely curtailed:

> This means that Christian theology is not going far enough if – as in the last one hundred and fifty years – it discusses belief in the resurrection only in the framework of the paradigm 'history' and in critical acceptance of the corresponding historical sciences. Theology must go deeper than this, and look beyond the world of history to the ecological conditions of history in nature.[64]

The cosmic Christ

In many ways the most disappointing aspect of Moltmann's Christology is his attempt to integrate the legitimate concerns of cosmological Christology within his own eschatological framework. Given the socio-political, nuclear and ecological apocalyptic scenario that Moltmann isolates, this is a theological necessity. Unfortunately, there is little that is new or original in Moltmann's diverse and, at times, fanciful handling of this theme.

He is correct to go back to Joseph Sittler's much talked about address on this theme to the General Assembly of the World Council of Churches in New Delhi in 1961, and, indeed, pick up on Barth's tantalising suggestions that there could be a third form of Christ's existence in the world, i.e. as the *Pantocrator* who is in all and through all and so rules the cosmos.[65]

Similarly, Moltmann rightly points to the abundance of exegetical material there is to hand in developing and exploring this theme:

---

[63] Moltmann, *Way*, 155.
[64] Ibid., 247.
[65] Ibid., 276–80.

Yet in its original, biblical form Christianity was by no means personal, anthropo-
centric and historical in the modern Western sense. It was much more a way and a
moving forward, in the discovery of 'the always greater Christ'. Christ is the first-
born among many brethren – Christ is the first-born of the new humanity – Christ
is the first-born of the whole creation: Jesus is Israel's Messiah – Jesus is the son of
Man of the nations – Jesus is the head of the reconciled cosmos: the body of Christ is
the crucified and raised body of Jesus – the body of Christ is the church – the body of
Christ is the whole cosmos.[66]

The theological differentiation of Moltmann's cosmic Christology is limited,
however, to his dialogue with and critique of the respective evolutionary
christologies of Teilhard de Chardin and Rahner. He applauds the breadth
of their respective christologies, but remains critical of their dependence on
the modern evolutionary paradigm. In its place, he substitutes a universal
eschatology of redemption. The consummation of all things in the kingdom
does not happen as the result of a process of teleological development or historical progress, but as a glorious eschatological transformation:

> What has to be called eschatological is the movement of redemption, which runs
> counter to evolution. If we want to put it in temporal terms: this is the movement
> which runs from the future to the past, not from the past to the future. It is the
> divine tempest of the new creation, which sweeps out of God's future over history's
> fields of the dead, waking and gathering every last being. The raising of the dead, the
> gathering of the victims and the seeking of the lost bring a redemption of the world
> which no evolution can ever achieve.[67]

Richard Bauckham correctly observes that the eschatological dualism between
evolution and eschatology present in Moltmann's theology corresponds to the
christological dialectic of cross and resurrection that links the cross of Jesus with
the apocalyptic suffering of the creation and the resurrection with the eschatological dawn of the new creation.[68]

So, to the question posed by the believing Jew to his fellow Christian: why
is the world still unredeemed? The answer, as it has always been, is to point to
the anticipatory arrival of the kingdom in the history of the crucified and risen
Christ who is still on his way to the eradication of all that contradicts God's
promised sabbath rest with the creation.

> Rather the kingdom is anticipated within the world from which evil, suffering and
> death have not yet disappeared. It is this concept of anticipation which now allows

[66] Ibid., 275.
[67] Ibid., 303.
[68] Bauckham, *Theology*, 194–8.

Moltmann to see in the evolutionary process in nature, as well as in human history, 'parables and hints, anticipations, and preparations for the coming of the messianic new creation'.[69]

Assessment

For some contemporary theological commentators, the gains in Moltmann's Christology are impressive and convincing. He quarries from the rich vein of the messianic and eschatological traditions of biblical faith. In so doing, he creates a novel narrative approach to Christology that postulates a universal end-time soteriological context within which a genuinely therapeutic Christology and christopraxis must operate.

We have referred to Moltmann's Christology as a post-liberal narrative approach to christological issues. Others have also noticed Moltmann's proximity in this regard to the Yale school of narrative theology,[70] represented by Hans Frei, George Lindbeck and Ronald Theimann.[71] In fact, there are close similarities between Moltmann's narrative approach in *The Way of Jesus Christ* and the claims made by Frei that it is the function of biblical narrative to reveal and render the identity of an active agent.[72] In other words, the identity of the person of Jesus, and through him the triune God, is disclosed to us through attention to the appropriate christological narratives. What we can then discern is the unity of intention and enactment that characterises the gospel story:

> This is what the gospel story does at one or two crucial points; but it does so in exceedingly spare terms that do not search out the personality, inner motivation, or even the ethical quality of Jesus. The glimpse we are provided within the story of Jesus' intentions is just sufficient to indicate the passage of intention into enactment.[73]

It seems at best odd, or at worst a reflection of a certain insularity that characterises some aspects of German scholarship, that Moltmann did not acknowledge these obvious similarities. In fact, we could go further and say that the inclusion in *The Way of Jesus Christ* of biographical material, such as the correspondence Moltmann draws between Jesus' martyrdom and contemporary martyrs

---

[69] Ibid., 197–8.

[70] E.g. Lakeland, *Postmodernity*, 48.

[71] H.W. Frei, *The Identity of Jesus Christ: The Hermeneutical Bases of Dogmatic Theology* and *Eclipse*; G. Lindbeck, *Nature of Doctrine*; G. Thiemann, *Revelation and Theology: The Gospel as Narrated Promise*.

[72] Frei, *Identity*.

[73] Ibid.

(e.g. Schneider, Bonhoeffer, and Romero),[74] invites comparisons between Moltmann and the Californian school of narrative theology,[75] which concentrates specifically on the importance of biography.[76] Again, however, there is no acknowledgement of such synergies in the index. Moltmann is, however, able and willing to take on board some of the concerns of the most recent contextualised christologies and relativise the previous dominance of the paradigm of history within an ecological and eschatological perspective that is always open to the future of the coming kingdom. For us, however, the losses are also substantial and militate against the likelihood of Moltmann's Christology becoming a lasting contribution to the future of Christology within a postmodern context.

Obviously, Moltmann's Christology represents an alternative approach to Barth's in terms of how we might address the concerns of postmodernity. Whereas Barth took as his sole point of reference the person of Christ as attested by scripture and developed a christological metaphysics from above, Moltmann starts from what he considers is a universal soteriological context and constructs an alternative Christology from below. This is clearly the case despite Moltmann's protestations concerning the irrelevancy of the distinction, Christology from above and below. His rejection of any metaphysical foundation to Christology,[77] manifested in his inability to deal adequately with the indispensable concerns of *Logos* Christology, and his attempt to replace it with a Spirit Christology, means that the kind of balance which is present (e.g. in Pannenberg's Christology, where it is clearly and exegetically demonstrated how one implies the other) is missing from Moltmann's work.

Similarly, while Moltmann's engagement with the Frankfurt school of critical theory, particularly that of Adorno and Horkheimer, was a welcome sign, it appears to have come to a halt after the publication of *The Crucified God*. His later work is consequently often characterised by a lack of philosophical clarity and subtly that can lead to the kind of hermeneutical irresponsibility others have noted.[78] For instance, it seems incredible that Moltmann consistently fails to give due importance to the fact that linked to the notion of God's kingdom is the complementary idea of rule, dominion, or authority over, expressed not only in the monarchy of the Father over the creation, but also in the eternal fellowship of the Father with the Son. Pannenberg is clear about this:

[74] Moltmann, *Way*, 196–203.
[75] See Stiver, *Philosophy*, 154–9.
[76] See for instance James Wm McClendon Jr. *Biography as Theology: How Life Stories Can Remake Today's Theology*; M. Goldberg, *Theology and Narrative: A Critical Introduction*; and T.W. Tilley, *Story Theology*.
[77] In this regard see Jones, *Critical Theology*, 62.
[78] Bauckham, *Theology*, 210–12.

The monarchy of the Father had been actualised already in the eternal fellowship of the Trinity. It did not need the existence of a world. In all eternity the Son gives the Father the honour of his kingly rule. The rule thus is eternal – not, of course, without the Son and Spirit, but through them. But it now applies to creation as well. The rule of the Father is set up and brought to acknowledgement in creation through the Son and the Spirit.[79]

The royal rule of the Father is manifested in the world through the mission of the Son in and through the Spirit. Here we can discern relationships of mutual differentiation and subordination because through the transference of power to the Son the Father makes his deity dependent on the success of the mission of the Son:

His deity is tied to the sending of the Son, who with the Spirit is already present to all creatures from creation, but who himself also took creaturely form in order that by his message the future of God might be present to the world, to its salvation and not its judgement. In this way the Son glorifies the Father in the world and completes the work of creation.[80]

Many have enthusiastically welcomed the dialogical character of Moltmann's theology exemplified by his thorough attempt to develop his christological proposals in the context of the Jewish-Christian question. We have been able to use Moltmann's Christology as a way of reviewing and revisiting some of the unresolved issues we have encountered in our own study hitherto. At times, however, this laudable attempt to address issues that have emerged from other theological contexts leads to a peculiar lack of focus in Moltmann's own christological considerations. The specific nature of this new christological paradigm, Christology that seeks to move beyond the contradictions of scientific and technological humanism, proves elusive. Is that because we have a Christology that is again controlled by soteriological issues, thus it easily looses its distinctiveness amongst the competing claims and assertions of other socio-political paradigms?

Similarly, one wonders at times whether or not Moltmann really has the perspectives of postmodernity in view. One searches in vain for much evidence of radical engagement with postmodern thinkers and, of course, universal soteriological contexts of expectation and meaning, and other totalising systems of discourse are inherently vulnerable to the claim that there is a semiotic plasticity of meaning to the representational content of language that defies such categorisation. In this regard, it is hardly conceivable that a messianic Christology, which looks forward to Christ's universal rule, would have

---

[79] Pannenberg, *Systematic Theology*, Vol. 2, 390.
[80] Ibid., 392.

so little to say about the particular context of religious pluralism and the competing truth claims among the religions that some have claimed is one of the dominating horizons of postmodernity.

Finally, it is interesting that Pannenberg moved away from his earlier dependence on a particular interpretation of apocalyptic.[81] Moltmann, on the other hand, has embraced it more fully. The consensus since Schweitzer that biblical apocalyptic should be interpreted in terms of the end of the historical space-time continuum has been seriously challenged. This is an issue we will take up more fully in our concluding chapter. However, it is worth saying at this stage that it is this over literal interpretation of the metaphor of apocalyptic that allows Moltmann to lose touch with some of the political persuasiveness of his earlier theology.

Clearly there is much to be gained from a Christology that is so passionately alive to the eschatological and messianic perspectives that underscore the biblical narrative concerning the mission of the divine Son. There are, however, metaphysical and socio-political concerns that are similarly part of the biblical witness to the crucified and risen Christ. In our concluding chapter we will try to construct a Christology that seeks a resolution of what are often regarded as competing themes within Christology. Once again, however, we will have to reckon with the perplexing genre of literature we call apocalyptic.

---

[81] Cf. Panneneberg, *Systematic Theology.*

12.

And Where to Now?

What then does our foundational myth say? ... it locates Jesus, as the focus of faith, within a very specific context of ethnic, religious and political history: the title 'Christ' is the almost indecipherable archaeological trace of his involvement in the story of Israel.[1]

Introduction

We are nearing the end of our journey. Along the way we have joined many fellow pilgrims who represent ancient and honourable traditions of thought, reflection and wisdom, and have taught us much about the topography and landscape of Christology. We have sought to be guided by the bright star of the person and continuing enigma of the man from Nazareth who breaks apart all our categories and classifications. In our search for wisdom and insight, we have followed three horizons of interpretation that continually interpenetrate, mutually inform, but also, at times, challenge and contradict one another. It has been our contention that the hermeneutical recovery of the person of Jesus from the contingencies, fading memories and aporia's of the past is only possible when we listen intently to the continuing conversations, which have developed through the centuries, between the biblical horizons of faith and belief, the doctrinal traditions of christological enquiry and interpretation, and the mediation and interrogation of both through successive historical and cultural contexts. Only in this way does our vision actually correspond to the universal claims and perspectives that guided the NT writers in their explication of Christology. The various and diverse NT christologies all find their focus of unity in Jesus Christ Lord of the nations and the cosmos who is still set on reconciling all things to God (2 Cor. 18–19). For this reason we are not permitted to limit our enquiry to a mere 'worldly point of view' (v. 16) – which is precisely what many current representatives of Jesus research appear determined to do.

---

[1] R. Williams, *On Christian Theology*, 95.

The language and grammar of such a three-way conversation is both *glossalia* (a doxology of praise and worship through the Spirit to the eternal Wisdom of the triune God) and, simultaneously, Christ-*Logos* (meditation reflection and disputation concerning the significance and import of the promised Messiah who will set the nations free from their warfare and dishonour [Isa. 49:1–7; Amos 9:11–12: Mic. 4:1–5]). It is a language and a theology, the terms of reference of which remain in continuity with Israel's covenant and hope. It is also a language where meaning is deferred or postponed until the purposes of God for the Gentiles and the nations are fulfilled, but that is to anticipate.

With the benefit of hindsight, we will briefly look back on the contours and vistas of our journey. We discovered two maps to guide us both of which began at the same location but directed us to two different destinations.

Review

The first way – cosmological Christology

The cosmological Christology of the patristic era possessed two complementary foci. The first was the affirmation of the equal divine status and unity of substance, or essence, of the Son with the Father. This, in turn, led inexorably to the conviction that the historical career and vocation of the man Jesus must be understood in terms of the incarnation of the pre-existent Son or *Logos*.[2] Thus the Nicene Creed followed the affirmation of the divinity of Christ with a statement concerning the divine economy (God's plan of salvation). If the pre-existent divine *Logos* had become incarnate 'for our sakes and the purpose of our salvation', it became incumbent upon the early church's theologians to articulate correctly the connection between this divinity and our humanity. Only then could believers, sceptics and unbelievers comprehend their eternal destiny, the promise and hope that our mortal and perishable nature could be redeemed and so share in the immortal and imperishable nature of the eternal Son.

Justin, Irenaeus, Clement, Tertullian, Origen, Athanasius through to Cyril of Alexandria, Theodore of Mopsuestia, Gregory of Naziansus and Augustine all recognised that any deficient Christology would eventuate in an equally deficient soteriology. Surprising as it may seem, this is well-expressed by Apollinarius:

---

[2] As previously indicated we are also of the opinion that the distinction Christology from above and below does not help us much when it comes to the explication of Christology in its concrete historical reality.

We declare that the *Logos* of God became man for the purpose of our salvation, so that we might receive the likeness of the heavenly One and be made God after the likeness of the true Son of God according to nature and the Son of man according to the flesh, our Lord Jesus Christ.[3]

We then traced the disputes and controversies that beset the Alexandrian and Antiochene traditions and were never fully resolved by the settlement of Chalcedon. However, in an historical and cultural context where existential anxiety was experienced and expressed in terms of cosmic alienation or reconciliation, both traditions were linked by two decisive elements, namely, mysticism and metaphysics. Both the history of biblical interpretation and the Neoplatonic cosmology, within which the Alexandrian and Antiochene traditions operated, entailed that mystical experience and metaphysical speculation remained in close contact with one another, the twin linkages being the mediatory role of the *Logos* and the understanding of salvation in terms of deification or assimilation to the divine. The eschatological horizons and perspectives that Christianity inherited from Judaism were translated into another philosophical and metaphysical language that was more culturally attuned to the ethos and mindset of the new hearers of the gospel,[4] which directs our attention to the inherent instability of worldviews.

Cosmological Christology eventually developed into the *Kyrios*/political Christology of the Christendom era. In the midst of a more favourable political and cultural context, dogma and political expediency became inextricably linked. The imperial Christology of Eusebius, through which the divine right of the emperor to rule in the name and authority of the *Rex Gloria* was carefully explicated, was a direct descendent of both the mystical and metaphysical *Logos* Christology of Origen. With the advent of Christendom, liturgy, dogma and the political consolidation of the Empire became the tradition of orthodox Catholicism, that was cherished and revered in both the East and the West until the eventual division between the two in the fourteenth century:

In many ways the most representative spokesman for catholic orthodoxy in the East was Justinian – not only because a Christian emperor was regarded as "Christ loving", but because in Justinian, "as hardly ever again in a Byzantine emperor, politics, administration, and theology are combined ... Nevertheless, certain areas can be identified in which the theologian won out over the ruler and the politician".[5]

---

[3] *Apoll. Fid. sec. pt. 31*; quoted in Pelikan, *Christian Tradition* Vol. 1, 233. Here it should be noted that the interchangeability of the christological titles clearly delineated the full scope of our salvation.
[4] Cf. Pelikan, *Christian Tradition*, Vol. 1, 123–32.
[5] Ibid., 341.

Particularly in the West, theologians did, however, begin to outmanoeuvre rulers and politicians. The authority and rule of the church began to displace the authority and monarchy of the emperor, and ecclesiology began to supplant the role previously exercised by Christology. It is our contention, radical enough in itself, that it was not the theological conclusions and deliberations of the various ecumenical councils that sustained the Christology of both the East and the West, but the combination of mysticism, metaphysics and a socio-political settlement which guaranteed the survival of Chalcedonian orthodoxy up until the Reformation and the religious wars that followed in its wake. Here, a common religion, a common culture and a common doctrinal heritage maintained a christological vision of reality that was a compelling, albeit very different, expression of the apocalyptic hopes of early Christianity that somehow the lamb of God slain on our behalf would continue to hold sway over the nations.

None of these developments was free from theological contradictions, compromises and, some would claim, manifest error, but there is no other way in which the three-way conversation between the Bible, dogma and culture can proceed. Those who would seek to find some unsullied, uncontaminated arena of theological and doctrinal purity and truth would never embark on that adventure of faith that could actually express in tangible and practical ways the powerful christological confession first articulated in Peter's Pentecost sermon: this Jesus whom *we* have crucified, God has made both Lord and Christ (cf. Acts 2:36).[6]

The second way – anthropological Christology

Taking our bearings from the new Adam Christology of the NT, and with the help of the Apostle Paul, Irenaeus and Athanasius, we traced the linkages between this representative Christology and the Logos Christology of the same period. The idea of Jesus Christ as the prototype and purveyor of a new humanity (the new Adam), hard won through suffering and obedience and appropriated by the believer through the saving reality of the eschatological Spirit, directed our attention to the epistemological and soteriological significance of religious experience. It was here, and not, as Jürgen Moltmann contends, in the various post-Enlightenment Jesuologies, that we found an alternative map to guide us, one that we labelled anthropological Christology

---

[6] Unless the notion of kingship and reign is understood in terms of a totally heavenly and other-worldly aspiration, Christology will inevitably remain inextricably linked with ethical and political considerations manifest in differing and at times competing cultural forms.

because it took as its point of departure a form of Christ-mysticism rooted in the believer's union with the incarnate and risen Christ.

Through this form of Christology the combination of mysticism and doctrine carried on unabated from the sixth century to the fourteenth, particularly through the profound influence of the writings of Pseudo-Dionysius the Areopagite. Attributed with quite erroneous biblical status, the decisive and some would claim, malign influence, of this form of Neoplatonic apophatic mysticism was quite out of proportion to the rigor or the quality of the theology. However, through the work of Maximus Confessor and the tradition of Hesychast spirituality epitomised by Symeon '(the new theologian'), this form of mysticism remained firmly rooted in the monasticism of the East. In the West, particularly in the monastic traditions, detailed attention to the Song of Songs as the biblical basis to such Christ-mysticism led to an intense concentration on what we could call the vicarious humanity and suffering of Jesus. During the medieval period this, in turn, developed into a vigorous Christopraxis, which centred around personal identification with the life, ministry and death of the suffering servant of God, Jesus the man of sorrows.

From the twelfth century onwards, through the mediation of Aristotelianism in the thought of both Aquinas and the Islamic philosopher Averroes, and the consequent development of scholasticism, the subtle synthesis of metaphysics and mysticism that underpinned orthodox Christology began to break apart. Here, an early form of empiricism developed from Aquinas through Dun Scotus to William of Occam that sanctioned the epistemological validity of direct sensory experience of the external world. The influence of Aristotle overturned the Neoplatonic consensus and, severed from its metaphysical roots, Christopraxis consequently moved in a decidedly exemplarist direction. Christology suffered a critical reduction in scale as soteriology took centre stage.

From Anselm, Abelard and Bernard of Clairvaux through to Luther and Calvin, atonement theologies proliferated and the essential *pro nobis* structure of soteriological concerns dominated theological considerations. In that sense, Christology suffered an anthropological constriction, was largely displaced by soteriology and the confession of Jesus as the Christ of God was based almost wholly on a mystical theology of religious experience manifest in both Catholic and Protestant guise; the first concentrating on the phenomena of mystical ascent to God and the other on the details and interpretation of the *ordu salutis* (order of salvation).

The third way

The Renaissance and the Reformation ushered in new intellectual and cultural challenges, but the religious wars that dominated the early part of the seventeenth century tore apart the socio-political settlement of Christendom. This, in turn, hastened in the economic, political and cultural forces that eventuated in the Enlightenment. The three pillars of orthodox Christology (mysticism, metaphysics and a socio-political settlement), upon which both a common religion and a common culture were built, collapsed. Consequently, Christology suffered a series of ignominious defeats, the most obvious of which was the equivocation that now surrounded the socio-political status and function of religion. The privatisation of religion and the construction of a new political settlement, based on the persuasive idea of the social contract, entailed that a universal common religion (i.e. one, holy, catholic and apostolic church) gave way to the notion of a universal common humanity. At the same time, the Enlightenment repudiated mysticism, ransacked, banished and all but obliterated the great traditions of metaphysics, and transformed religion into practical morality. Christology, unfortunately, but inevitably, again degenerated into exemplarism – Jesus was reduced to either a moral exemplar or a sophist cum teacher of religion. The lordship of the human subject was now firmly in place. With religion depoliticised it became possible to believe in the continued social, economic and intellectual progress of the human race, and to construct historiography and an idealist evolutionary philosophy around these premises, while at the same time maintaining that this would eventuate in further forms of political and cultural emancipation.

It has been our contention that the crisis in Christology that has dominated modernity is almost entirely due to the way successive theologians, and the theological trends inspired by their work, were aligned with the particular paradigms that sanctioned the legitimacy of the new worldview. But, when do paradigms become myths? Only when their plausibility structures wane and the ideological sub-text that authorised their legitimacy is exposed, repudiated, or denounced. This is postmodernity's achievement.

If modernity displaced God from the warp and woof of social, political and cultural life, postmodernity has done the same for the universal human subject.[7] All epistemological and ontological foundationalism, particularly that based on the bourgeois self-conscious or self-postulating Absolute subject, has crumbled under the withering storm of Neitzsche's constructivist rhetoric; Heidegger's determined attempt to finally end metaphysics; Foucault's recognition of the nature and extent of capillary power; Wittgenstein and Derrida's hermeneutics of language; Jameson's discourses concerning the logic of late capitalism and the commodification of culture; Baudrillard's ruminations on the persuasive influence of media induced simulation and hyper-reality; Lyotard's incredulity

---

[7] In regard to the former, i.e. the dispersal of the God issue by modernity see, C.E. Gunton, *The One, The Three And the Many: God, Creation And The Culture of Modernity*.

toward metanarratives; and Freud, Lacan, Deleuze and Guattari's mystification of libidinal instability and flow.

Hitherto, postmodernity has been almost entirely an exercise in radical deconstruction, decentring and the wholesale dethroning of usurpers and pretenders to the throne of absolute power and truth. The resulting epistemological *blitzkrieg* has devastated the intellectual landscape of modernity beyond repair including the ideological interment camp to which religion had been banished. If this analysis is correct, then the opportunity is there to try to construct again a sustainable, credible and intellectually convincing christological vision of reality. However, both the intellectual and spiritual energy required will be enormous and few are probably equal to the task.

We are in search of a new theological rationality that will once again hold mysticism, metaphysics and socio-political praxis together in creative tension (this is not necessarily to generate a common culture, which always runs the risk of imperialism). Quite simply, this is the nature of religion and none of the alternative definitions examined hitherto have convinced us otherwise. Religion may be more than this, but in its classical Christian form it is certainly not less. Unfortunately, the ardent secular liberalism and consumerism of the post-Enlightenment period, hardwired as it is into the contemporary *Voltgeist*, has made it much less, with the consequent catastrophic collapse of most of the forms of traditional Christianity.

Christology Reconstructed

It is time now to attempt the task of christological reconstruction, bearing in mind the acknowledged results of our investigation of Christology both past and present. At this stage in the proceedings it would be possible to simply argue for the consistency and historical veracity of the church's story concerning the person of Jesus, which is articulated in the historic creeds and can be referred to as the traditional incarnational narrative.[8]

It is our conviction, however, that a contemporary Christology must endeavour to relocate the origins of Christology in the apocalyptic and messianic expectations of Second Temple Judaism. This yields some surprising results. First, it underscores the singular importance of the eschatological and apocalyptic context of Jesus' life, ministry, mission, death and resurrection, and so refuses any attempt to translate such cultural and religious hopes and aspirations into a more convient modern terminology. Secondly, as the originators of the second quest for the historical Jesus sought to do, it constructs a link

---

[8] Cf. C.S. Evans, *The Historical Christ and the Jesus of Faith: The Incarnational Narrative as History*.

between apocalyptic as a particular subspecies of eschatological expectation and Jesus' teaching and embodiment of the imminent kingdom of God. Thirdly, it draws out the cultural horizons of crisis and catastrophe, which is where apocalyptic in all its myriad forms originated. Fourthly, the commonality of these eschatological horizons of faith, belief and practice present in Second Temple Judaism, the teaching and expectations of Jesus and that of the early church hold together the essential ingredients of religion (i.e. mysticism, metaphysics and socio-political praxis); which need to be retrieved if there is to be a substantial renaissance of Christian faith in the context of the modern world. Fifthly, attention to the essentially metaphorical and symbolic nature of apocalyptic and eschatological language offers a route beyond both the positivism of modernity and the pragmatism of postmodernity that has bedevilled their respective accounts of the nature of history, language and religion. Finally, in all of this it is the integral, but nevertheless asymmetrical, relationship of the narrative of cross and resurrection that begins to construct an appropriate Christology for the postmodern situation, where any alliance with epistemological foundationalism will inevitably corrupt the Jesus story at source.[9]

Apocalyptic and the metaphor of the kingdom of God

In the course of the last 150 years, this biblical and theological debate has caused much ink (if not blood) to be spilt! Schweitzer first raised the issue of the enigmatic character of biblical apocalyptic in the modern mind[10] and so opened the way to attempts to dymythologise and demystify it. Like many others, we remain unconvinced by translation processes that eventuate in a realised or horizontal eschatology (Bultmann) or a moralising equivalent (Dodd, Harnack and Ritschl). But we do want to embrace, as far as historical reconstruction will permit, the original first-century or Second Temple Jewish meaning of apocalyptic. Thus, we are not prepared, like Robert Funk, Burton Mack, Dominic Crossan and some other representatives of 'the renewed new Quest' for the historical Jesus to translate apocalyptic into an ethical eschatology.[11] They assert that, while Jesus' ministry, sayings and sense of vocation appear to be housed within an apocalyptic worldview, his real intention was to offer a less bombastic, cynically debunking, amusingly fun poking form of radical social critique aimed at generating a new egalitarian

---

[9] Cf. C.J.D. Greene, ' "Starting a Rockslide": Deconstructing History and Language via Christological Detonators', in C. Bartholomew et al. (eds.), *After Pentecost: Language and Biblical Interpretation*, 195–223.
[10] Schweitzer, *Quest*.
[11] R.W. Funk and R.W. Hoover (eds), *The Five Gospels: The Search for the Authentic Words of Jesus*; Mack, *Myth*; Crossan, *Historical Jesus* and *Jesus*.

reform movement within first-century Judaism. This simply does not fit the worldview of early Christianity – riddled as it is with eschatological hopes and horizons.[12]

Instead, we want to begin with a realist eschatology (and by that we do not mean literalist) that ties eschatology into the basic storyline that lay behind Israel's self-identity as a nation. The more critically realistic the eschatology, the more difficult it will be to extract Jesus from this context and transpose him into an alien worldview (e.g. the modern secular notion of an atemporal wandering mystic, cynic or teacher of religion). Accordingly, there is a lot of sense to Wright's conviction that the phrase the kingdom of God did not refer to some heavenly domain where the dead could rest in peace. Rather, it articulated Israel's basic storyline and hope that YHWH would once again return to Zion and establish himself as King of the nations:

> God's kingdom, to the Jew-in-the-village in the first half of the first century, meant the coming vindication of Israel, victory over the pagans, the eventual gift of peace, justice and prosperity. It is scarcely surprising that, when a prophet appeared announcing that this kingdom was dawning, and that Israel's god was at last becoming king, he found an eager audience.[13]

In Wright's opinion, a worldview cannot be understood as a history of ideas project, but refers instead to an overarching metanarrative in which a central defining story, symbols and subversively realised praxis are inextricably linked.[14] YHWH and Israel's eventual return to Zion from exile links together temple, land and torah (symbols and praxis) and Israel's sense of national identity in one 'reinforcing narrative of hope'.[15]

Wright provides evidence for this interpretation of the eschatology of Second Temple Judaism by noting other substantial retellings of the story with which Jews would have been familiar.[16] Most important of all was Jesus' subversive retelling of the story with the signs of the kingdom breaking in through his own symbolic re-enactment of the basic storyline. This was a man who was in some sense unafraid to see his own vocation and calling as deeply messianic, because he believed he personified in himself and his actions the long-awaited return of YHWH and Israel to Zion. Similarly, Jesus identified

---

[12] E.g., Wright, *Jesus*, 210–14.

[13] Ibid., 204.

[14] See Wright, *People of God*, 243.

[15] Ibid., 243.

[16] E.g. Josephus' essentially idolatrous version ends with the Temple in ruins and Vespasian enthroned as the new world ruler; the author of the Habakkuk commentary sought to reverse the tables with the elect few now representing Israel and executing YHWH's judgement over the nations. Ibid., 199.

the real enemy – the great Satan, not pagan puppet regimes – who must be defeated before YHWH could once again be King. Marcus Borg suggests, however, that Jesus could also have been suffering from delusions of grandeur, unless, of course, he was in some mysterious fashion installed as Messiah by YHWH and no one else.[17]

The meaning of apocalyptic and eschatology within recent biblical scholarship

When eschatology is inserted into a storied universe, it functions as an essential structural element to the whole worldview and is capable of being adapted to different, if at times conflicting, versions of the central metanarrative. Wright outlines the main alternatives and offers a useful sliding scale of eschatological expectation, or a grid that allows us locate most of the theologians who have deployed eschatological expectations in their christological deliberations:

1. Eschatology as the end of the world, i.e. the end of the space-time universe (or the transformation of the space-time universe into a new heaven and a new earth where there are both continuities and discontinuities between the former and the latter).
2. Eschatology as the climax of Israel's history, involving the end of the space-time universe.
3. Eschatology as the climax of Israel's history, involving events for which end-of-the-world language is the only set of metaphors adequate to express the significance of what will happen, but resulting in a new and quite different phase *within* space-time history.
4. Eschatology as major events, not specifically climactic within a particular story, for which end-of-the-world language functions as metaphor.
5. Eschatology as 'horizontal language' (i.e., *apparently* denoting movement forwards in time) whose *actual* referent is the possibility of moving 'upwards' spiritually into a new level of existence.
6. Eschatology as critique of the present world order, perhaps with proposals for a new order.
7. Eschatology as critique of the present socio-political scene, perhaps with proposals for adjustments.[18]

---

[17] See Borg's critique of Wright in N.T. Wright and M. Borg, *The Meaning of Jesus: Two Visions*, part 2.

[18] Wright, *Jesus*, 208. Schweitzer obviously set the scene with 1 and 2; both positions are apparent in the respective christologies of Pannenberg and Moltmann. Bultmann, and to a certain extent Tillich, with the help of the anti-metaphysical mysticism of Heidegger, largely invented 5. Crossan and many of the other leading representatives

With due respect to all those, we have taken different trajectories on the roller-coaster of eschatological expectation, we would like to offer an alternative viewpoint, which might be closer to the original intention of both Second Temple Judaism and Jesus;

8. Eschatology does not refer to the literal end of the space-time universe, nor necessarily to the climax of Israel's history, although it most probably does contain elements of this within it. Rather, it uses a set of metaphors that refer to climactic events (most notably the exile and the crucifixion/resurrection) that *tear the fabric of history apart*. Consequently, they offer proposals and possibilities for a new social order.

We can test this hypothesis, as Wright indicates, by asking whether such an eschatological perspective would make sense in the context of Second Temple Judaism. To do this, we need to return to the origin of eschatology in cataclysmic socio-political events upon which Israel's whole history was both predicated and decided. Jewish scholars such as Gershom Scholem, Walter Benjamin and Martin Buber have argued that Jewish messianism was by its origin and nature a theory about a catastrophe; a theory that 'stressed the revolutionary, subversive element in the transition from every historical present to the messianic future'.[19] The catastrophe was, of course, the exile and included the defeat, subjugation and enslavement of Israel by the Assyrian Empire. As Wright recognises, this was the hinge upon which Israel's covenant hope and election turned. Is it any wonder that Nietzsche postulated that such an event was in fact the end of Israel's dream, the zero point in her history that demanded a complete reassessment of her covenant relationship to YHWH and unfortunately eventuated in a new religion of moral and spiritual servitude born out of defeat and resentment?[20] In a more restrained fashion, whilst still granting the traumatic theological and political catastrophe of the exile, Gerhard von Rad emphasised that the exile involved the complete breakdown of the traditions and institutions through which Israel's national identity had been sustained. The central symbols of the overarching meta-narrative (temple, monarchy, land and, to a large extent, the practice of the torah) had all perished. Thus, a serious question arose: how was it possible to be Israel in such a situation?[21]

---

[18] (*continued*) of the third quest find themselves at home with some combination of 6 and 7. Borg and interestingly enough the early Barth fit into category 4 and Wright and Meier endorse different versions of 3.

[19] Quoted in Moltmann, *Way*, 22.

[20] F.W. Nietzsche, *The Antichrist*, 24–5; see also, *On the Genealogy of Morals: A Polemic*, 34–5.

[21] So for instance Psalms 74, 79, and particularly 137.

Von Rad pointed to the resilience of Israel's prophetic traditions that put this whole catastrophe under the proviso of the former things that had now perished and apparently disappeared (Isa. 43:18), and in compassionate and compelling language pointed to the new thing whereby both covenant and election would be preserved. What was new was the eschatological and, to a certain extent, the messianic:

> The eschatological phenomenon is simplified once more; it is reduced to the ex-tremely revolutionary fact that the prophets saw Jahweh approaching Israel with a new action which made the old saving institutions increasingly invalid since from then on life or death for Israel was determined by this future event.[22]

Of course, the prophets could only envision this new event in terms of a reappropriation of the old saving traditions. So, for Hosea it is a new entry into the land, for Isaiah a new Davidic monarchy and a new Zion, for Jeremiah a new covenant, and for Deutero-Isaiah a new exodus. Similarly, this new event revisited Israel's hope concerning the day of YHWH, his return to Zion, and the instigation of a new holy war when all his enemies would be routed and all nations, indeed creation itself, would pay homage to the King of Kings.[23]

But what happens when the old dies? This is the nub of the issue. It tumbles into the abyss caused by the cataclysmic rupture of the fabric of history, and what is new cannot just be predicated on the basis of the old. Israel's future after the exile remained undecided, unfulfilled and essentially an interim experiment. Brueggemann notes that:

> Whereas the 'storyline' before the exile is clear and singular, the 'plot' of Judaism after the exile is much less clear and singular, no doubt reflecting the tentative situation of a community scarred and sobered by displacement.[24]

It was, therefore, not surprising that shadowy, ill-defined, eschatologically oriented, messianic expectations emerged and, more importantly, that another perplexing literary genre we call apocalyptic appeared.

Apocalyptic involved a theological rereading and retelling of Israel's political history – past, present and future – through the lens of highly metaphori-cal language. But while metaphorical, the language is not gnostic or dualist (unless, like von Rad, Schweitzer and much biblical scholarship since, it is taken literally as the language of cosmic meltdown). Apocalyptic is a profound speculative hope born out of a powerful combination of mystical experience,

---

[22] G. von Rad, *Old Testament Theology*, II, 118.

[23] Ibid., 119–25.

[24] W. Brueggemann, 'A Journey: Attending to the Abyss', *The Bible in Transmission* (Bible Society, Spring, 2000), 6–8.

socio-political impotence, metaphysical representation, and historical realism and perplexity. It is, therefore, all too aware that history fractures, skews off in different directions and even, at times, due to the pressure of apparently absurd occurrences, appears to turn back on itself. At times of catastrophe, history rips apart, and both the judgement and salvation of YHWH rain down upon Israel and the nations. Many of the former things are washed away, while all Israel waits for the new day of salvation – however and whenever it will come.

Other retellings of the central story similarly combine contemporary political events with theological interpretation, because the future remains the future of the unpredictable kingdom. Apocalyptic could not be expressed in anything other than deeply symbolic and metaphorical language, because it refers to decisive, cataclysmic historical events and yet renders them part of a wider cosmic drama – which means, not surprisingly, that meaning is both postponed and deferred.[25]

Jesus, apocalyptic and the kingdom of God

Can this thesis make any sense of Jesus' vocation, ministry and eventual fate? That is a difficult question to answer because it depends, at least in part, on two further questions:

1. Do we believe that all we have access to in the New Testament is the early Christian representation or misrepresentation of the Jesus phenomenon?
2. Is there some real continuity between Jesus' awareness of his vocation and calling and that which his followers ascribed to him?

On the basis that what we find throughout the period from the exile to the sacking of Jerusalem in 70 AD, however, is realistic, hardwired eschatology, we should ask a third question:

3. How can both Jesus and the early Christian communities be understood within such a context?

---

[25] This does not mean, however, that eschatological language or apocalyptic cannot be taken literally. So, for instance, there is a real sense contra Wright that such eschatological hopes went beyond the return of YHWH to Zion and set Israel's history within the context of the history of the cosmos. We have been reminded recently how literally some Jews did take such language particularly through the practice of keeping the bones of the dead in ossuaries to be ready for the final resurrection. Metaphors allow for a fluidity of meaning, but this does not happen by cancelling out the referential and cognitive aspect to such linguistic usage.

John the Baptist came preaching a baptism of repentance for 'the forgiveness of sins' into just such a context. Why? Because another fiery judgement, maybe even another exile, but certainly another substantial tear in the already overloaded tissue of history, was on the way; the axe was even now laid at the root of the tree.[26] How then did Jesus, the one who would baptize with the Holy Spirit and fire (metaphorical language that heralded another apocalyptic event), understand his own role in such a situation, particularly after the arrest of John?

We know that Jesus' preaching and embodiment of the kingdom was new and distinctive because it was somehow both present and future. *Both* dimensions expressed the *imminence* of the kingdom, which entailed that the *signs* of the kingdom were already breaking in through his jubilee ministry of good news for the poor, release for the captives and recovery of sight for the blind (Lk. 4:14–30).[27] Nevertheless, Wright argues that Jesus' announcement must be understood as a basic variation on the same central storyline:

> We must stress, again, that this message is *part of a story*, and only makes sense as such. And there is only one story that will do. Israel would at last 'return from exile'; evil would be defeated; YHWH would at last return to 'visit' his people. Anyone wishing to evoke and affirm all this at once, in first-century Palestine, could not have chosen a more appropriate and ready-made slogan than 'kingdom of god'.[28]

Based on this thesis, however, Jesus had a very particular idea of messiahship in mind, and all the essential symbols of the story required radical, subversive reinterpretation; the important metaphors could have one and only one set of referents, namely, the climax of Israel's history, the return of YHWH to Zion.

We accept that it would be hard for a first-century Jew proclaiming the arrival of the kingdom not to be intimately aware of this basic storyline. But they would also be poignantly aware that with regard to history it had never quite worked out like that, nor was there yet any substantial burden of evidence that it was going to. Similarly, we contend that they would also have been aware that within the variegated and deeply mysterious corpus of apocalyptic writings there were more than just variations on a single theme; there were whole new overtures and melodies that may have been written to

---

[26] The Gospels are not only redolent with the creative use of metaphors and illusion to past events in salvation history; they also provide us with striking instances of rhetoric – particularly in John's Gospel. In what follows we deliberately adopt a more rhetorical style as a way of untapping the reservoir of meaning that metaphors hold.

[27] These were the signs John the Baptist was asked to acknowledge as an indication that his own enigmatic predictions concerning one greater than himself were being fulfilled, and therefore in Jesus the time was ripe.

[28] Wright, *Jesus*, 227.

find a way of dealing with the torture and fragility of a hope that seemed so often out of sync with real politics and history.[29]

So, what if Jesus *was* or *may have been* operating within some notion of the basic metanarrative of exile and restoration, but also had no way of predicting what shape that restoration would take? YHWH's triumphant return to Zion was one and, in some sense, the ultimate possibility, but there could be, if past history was anything to go by, other possible avenues of exploration. There was even possibly a penultimate extension to the storyline about to take place that involved his own unique and distinctive contribution to this chequered history between Israel and her covenant God.

And what was this distinctive calling? To be the conduit, the focus whereby that clearing, that tensile space referred to as the kingdom, would arrive and hold long enough for YHWH to save and comfort his people Israel. And is this not what his baptism on behalf of Israel implied? His vocation, to demonstrate and incarnate that saving reality in the praxis of his preaching, lifestyle, healing and liberating actions and deeds, in turn indicated that even now the febrile fabric of history was being stretched to breaking point by the imminent arrival of the kingdom in his own personage. Indeed, another cataclysmic fissure could appear at any moment when the evil and tyranny that resided in all the dispersed centres of power within a compromised Judaism were flushed out and exposed. Is this not just what the temptations and the infamous temple incident imply?

That was why the time of both judgement and salvation had arrived, because you could not have one without the other. And the evidence was there, the signs of the new age were already tumbling in, fracturing the space–time continuum that supported the rumble tumble of events we call history, making the miraculous commonplace. That was why the call was out to be the new Israel, to create the clearing of the kingdom, so that YHWH could gather his lost sheep to himself, so that like the waiting Father he could run to embrace all those returning from exile.

Could this not be why Jesus, like the early Christians, appeared to hold so loosely to the central defining symbols of Judaism? As we have indicated, temple, monarchy, land and even to a certain extent torah (certainly the Pharisaical interpretation of the law that sought holiness from the outside in) belonged to the old regime. Consequently, such an apparently cavalier attitude to these once central and cherished symbols was, therefore, *bound* to bring him into conflict with the religious establishment; a conflict that mirrored the apostasy of Israel's former leaders who thought that politics and religion could be expedited separately which, Jesus well knew, had heralded in the catastrophe of

---

[29] For instance, the apocalyptic visions of Daniel, 1 Enoch, 2 Esdras, 2 & 3 Baruch, and the Apocalypse of Abraham.

the exile. This was why it was imperative that he seek out the lost, the marginalised and ostracised members of society, and call them to repentance and faith. Jesus' focus was justifiably sinners, not those whose apparent righteousness blocked their entrance to the kingdom. It was, therefore, incumbent upon him, together with the disciples who represented the twelve tribes of Israel, to establish an egalitarian community based on the jubilee principle. This was also why Jesus, like the prophets, embraced a restoration theology of love, mercy and forgiveness, but would not identify himself with any of the expectations of what was, after all, a fairly confused notion of messiahship.[30] Finally, this was why Jesus used the image of the suffering servant of Deutero-Isaiah as his way of personifying Israel, because, as Jesus acknowledged to Peter, to be this kind of prophet, to become the meeting place between heaven and earth, was to take the reality of sin, suffering and exile upon your own fragile frame (Mk. 8:27–29; Mt. 16:13–16; Lk.9:18–20). It was to weep over the sins of Jerusalem, to seek the spiritual and therefore also the political and moral regeneration of his nation, and so, when the chasm appeared, to fall into the abyss of godforsakenness in one final act of surrender and atonement.[31]

Mysticism revisited

One can readily see that within such a view of what the kingdom represents we find, once again, the integration of mysticism, metaphysics and politics. This does not imply that Jesus or anyone else for that matter thought in such apparently abstract terms. Here we can also locate a genuinely Jewish and Christian strand of mysticism that is quite different from the Neoplatonic model of ascent and absorption that dominated the apophatic theology of later centuries, at least in the East. Thus we find some common ground with Borg's contention that with Jesus we have a Jewish mystic, a term that encompasses the complementary notions of (1) spirit person; (2) healer; (3) wisdom teacher; (4) social prophet; and (5) movement founder.[32]

This is a refreshingly broad definition of the mystic. It refers to someone who exemplifies an intimate relationship with God, experiences the world differently through that relationship, possesses an openness to the ecstatic, or spirit-filled dimensions of life and worship, and demonstrates a certain

---

[30] In this regard, see the discussion between Wright and Borg, *Meaning*, part 2. For a more substantial investigation of Jewish messianic hopes and expectations see Charlesworth, 'From Messianology to Christology: Problems and Prospects'.

[31] The nature of metaphor is to marry history with hope and so create the possibility of fluidity of meaning, to defy any one set of referents, to introduce a 'semantic impertinence' (Ricœur) and so set the imagination free to linger long enough in an act of attestation that names the proper object of faith – that is, the love and mercy of the covenant God.

[32] Wright and Borg, *Meaning*, 62–4.

authority and wisdom in their relationships with others. Mysticism of this nature is often deeply counter-cultural, socially and politically subversive and has a tendency to lead to martyrdom. Moltmann describes this form of mysticism that unites the experiences of Jesus and Paul and contemporary followers of 'the way' in moving terms:

> God in the cell, God in the interrogation, God in the torture, God in the body's agony, God in the darkness that has descended on the soul – that is the political mysticism of the martyrs. It is not going too far to say that today prison is a very special place for the Christian experience of God. In prison Christ is experienced in the Spirit. In prison the soul finds the *unio mystica*.[33]

This is also the political mysticism that allowed Tertullian to define the early church as that which was founded on the blood of the martyrs.[34]

The early Christian communities, apocalyptic and the kingdom of God

We must also ask whether our rendition of the nature of eschatology coheres with the Christian version of the story, which began with the cataclysmic events of the cross and resurrection – they must be taken together as complementary, if not symmetrical, aspects of the one saving event. As such they define the true identity of Jesus of Nazareth, and that is both their narrative and metaphorical intent. The crucifixion was a catastrophic event for Jesus' first followers; as catastrophic as the exile was for Israel.[35] It precipitated a crisis that left the storyline, symbols and praxis of the fledgling Jesus movement in tatters. The disciples' confusion, disarray and desertion expressed in tangible form the same question that faced the Jews in exile: how was it possible to be this egalitarian reform movement after this tumultuous event? A new exile, a new torture of history seemed imminent.

The apocalyptic signs and language that surround the Synoptic Gospels' account of the crucifixion event require explanation. In contradistinction to Moltmann, we are not convinced that these apocalyptic metaphors necessarily refer to the foreshadowing of the universal suffering that hasten the end

---

[33] Moltmann, *Spirit of Life*, 209.

[34] Tertullian, *Apology*; see, O. O'Donovan and J.L. O'Donovan, *From Irenaeus to Grotius: A Sourcebook in Christian Political Thought 100–1625*, 23–6.

[35] I am not suggesting that there is a direct comparison between the central defining elements of Israelite religion and those of the fledgling Jesus movement. Rather I am simply drawing attention through analogical language to the complete disarray that overtook this 'discipleship of equals', to use Fiorenza's phrase, that Jesus appears to have tried to construct as a way of practically representing the new Israel under the aegis of the kingdom.

times.[36] Nor do we believe that this is figurative language used to denote the inexplicable. Apocalyptic language describes an apocalyptic event, namely, the sundering of the connection and continuity between the Jesus phenomenon and the messianic future. The crucifixion may have been on the cards as far as Jesus' behaviour in Jerusalem was concerned, but it still represented the *terminus ad quem* of anyone purporting to be a national leader, a prophet, and most certainly a Messiah.

If this was the climax this new reform movement was building up to, then it was a maniac leap into the abyss. Unless, of course, that was precisely what it was intended to achieve. So, like the sundered temple veil, it severed the jugular of history as the judgement of God upon the nations has a tendency to do and the resulting haemorrhage of meaning rendered history a dead end. Another apparently disastrous, but certainly decisive, break in the space-time continuum appeared and the hopes and fears of the generations spilled out into an empty crevasse which no form of historicism could possible bridge.

The asymmetrical relationship between cross and resurrection is due to the fact that one does not automatically imply the other. Neither the disciples nor scholarship can extrapolate a resurrection event out of the fracture and torture of Good Friday. This is what all the evocative stories and narratives at the end of John's Gospel imply – a complete *novum*, a totally unexpected development of the storyline that no one, least of all the disciples, were predicting. Rowan Williams makes basically the same point when he invokes the category of risk:

> It is a story of 'risk'; and only at Easter are we able to say, 'he comes *from* God just as he goes *to* God', and to see in the contingent fact of the resurrection – the limited events of the finding of an empty tomb and a scatter of bewildering encounters – that which is not contingent, the life of God as Father and Son together.[37]

Consequently, in line with all that has been said so far, we would contend (contra Pannenberg) that resurrection is not just a metaphor that refers solely to the prolepsis of the end of the space–time universe.[38] Neither is it shorthand for the disciples' vision of the continued 'aliveness' of Jesus;[39] nor does it merely refer to their corporate experience of faith.[40] Instead, we would affirm that resurrection refers primarily to the installation or enthronement or exaltation of Jesus as the Messiah. The same God whose kingdom Jesus sought to inaugurate has installed him, and no other, as the Christ. Only in this way does the exalted Messiah now rule so that what is done in heaven can become reality on

---

[36] Moltmann, *Way*, 151–95.

[37] Williams, *On Christian Theology*, 159.

[38] Pannenberg, *Jesus–God and Man*.

[39] Schillebeeckx, *Jesus*.

[40] Macquarrie, *Christology Revisited*.

earth. All socio-political principalities and powers are now subject to Jesus the Christ who is King of Kings (Rev. 17:14). As Peter announced, this crucified Jesus has now been confirmed as both Messiah and *Kyrios*.[41] Most certainly this would have led eventually, as we see in the Pauline corpus and John's Gospel, to some notion of pre-existence, but what it eventuated in first of all was something quite different.

Throughout the NT we encounter passages that inform us that the kingdom is no longer the sole prerogative of YHWH but now also belongs to the Messiah. This is explicit, for instance, in Ephesians 5:5 (the kingdom of the Messiah and of God).[42] More importantly, we learn in 1 Corinthians 15:20–28 that the Messiah, the first fruits of both the new resurrection life and the new humanity, has been charged with rescuing the whole creation from its bondage to futility, death and decay. The Messiah is still 'on his way' to realising the kingdom in the affairs of this world and will have only achieved his purpose when the final enemy, death, has also been destroyed.

Again, we encounter the distinctively Christian contribution to the history of eschatological hope. The present and future dimensions of the kingdom interlock. In other words, the *imminence* of the kingdom has not retreated or gone away. It is steadily at hand, ready at any moment to break in again, buckle and splay the fibrous layers of the mean play of history and let the signs of the kingdom break out once again. The exalted Messiah is now the new broker of the kingdom who possesses the power and authority to pour out the eschatological Spirit on all his followers and companions so that they too are kingdom people, visible signs and portents of a new age.[43] Pentecost becomes the new baptism in the Holy Spirit because the installation of Jesus as the Messiah instigates a radically new understanding of the nature of the kingdom and indeed of discipleship.

At this point, as Wright concedes, we discover the most audacious redefinition of the Jewish hope of the kingdom, the almost total absence of any association with the essential symbols and praxis that defined Second Temple Judaism:

> The story of the new movement is told without reference to the national, racial or geographical liberation of Israel. The praxis of the kingdom (holiness) is defined without reference to Torah. The answers to the worldview questions can be given in terms of a redeemed humanity and cosmos, rather than in terms simply of Israel and her national hope.[44]

---

[41] Acts 2:36.

[42] See also Colossians 1:13; 2 Peter 1:11; John. 18:36f.

[43] Romans 8:18–27; 2 Corinthians 5; Revelation 21.

[44] Wright, *Jesus*, 218.

Wright offers a useful cameo of the evidence. John distinguishes the kingdom 'not from this world' from that espoused by the Jewish revolutionaries of the time. Paul disassociates the kingdom of 'righteousness, peace and joy in the holy spirit' from a kingdom tied into dietary restrictions and other such ceremonial rituals. Luke emphasises that this kingdom is no longer territorially defined but spans the whole world. And the Apocalypse directs our attention to the heavenly Jerusalem, where the lamb is on the throne and no temple is required. What does all this imply?

> Even at a surface reading, this early Christian kingdom-language has little or nothing to do with the vindication of ethnic Israel, the overthrow of Roman rule in Palestine, the building of a new Temple on Mount Zion, the establishment of Torah-observance, or the nations flocking to Mount Zion to be judged and/or to be educated in the knowledge of YHWH.[45]

Precisely so and to try and surmount what others would view as a serious if not mortal threat to his whole thesis concerning the central meaning of eschatology, Wright has recourse to the role of metanarratives. In other words, what we locate here is not a new story, but a new moment in the old story, we are in Act 5 of the overarching dramatic rendition of the one central story.[46]

At this point we must again demur and exercise a certain incredulity toward metanarratives, particularly those that can become totalising forms of discourse that imperialistically exclude and deny the validity or viability of other metaphorical referents (although this is most certainly not Wright's intention). This looks impecuniously like a new story and one that recognises, perhaps reluctantly, an inevitable parting of the ways, because now the Gentiles, and not solely Israel, are YHWH's target and focus. While this dimension of the story may well have been in place well before AD 70, Judaism was redefining its story dramatically after Jerusalem and the temple were razed to the ground. In other words, it is at this point that the central story splits into two perplexing and conflicting discourses of controversy and disputation, because both the Jewish and Christian stories are ecclesiologically separated and eschatologically unfulfilled.

No doubt this is, at least in part, something of what Paul is struggling with in Romans 9 to 11. He recognised, with great personal pain and perplexity, which Israel had, at least temporally, refused the invitation to stay within the Christian version of the overarching metanarrative. For the Jew, the Christian belief in the resurrection of Jesus and the enthronement of him as the Messiah did not create a new act within their story. Instead, it founded a new story based

---

[45] Ibid., 219.
[46] The acts being creation, fall, Israel, Jesus and the church. Ibid., 219.

on a new movement with a new mission.[47] In other words, a metanarrative gave way to a continuing history of disputation and religious controversy, because the understanding of the kingdom peculiar to both Jesus and the early Christians has to do with the interpenetration of both the present and the future that brings the kingdom within reach of the nations and consequently can no longer be defined solely through Israel's symbols of national identity.

While Christians affirmed this interpretation of events post-70 AD, overall Jews did not. To ignore this hiatus and simply conclude that the church is the new Israel is to collude in the kind of religious imperialism that would inevitably produce the baleful legacy of anti-Semitism that emerged once Christianity became the first great world religion. This is what happens continually within history, because history cannot bear the weight of metanarratives. The vagaries, distortions, silences, misrepresentations, tragedies, downright absurdities and inexplicable farce of history, as Karl Marx (that apparently most historicist of thinkers) realised, elude the meaning imposed upon it by totalising metanarratives.[48] It is also for this reason that we see no point in trying to apply Troeltsch's criteria of historical verifiability to an event like the resurrection. This is not because it is a unique historical event of which there are no analogues; all events are in some sense unique and not simply the result of causal interconnections. Cataclysmic events, however, that rupture the tissue of history itself cannot be judged by criteria that presuppose that history is a seamless robe based on the fiction of the homogeneity of all events.[49]

Metaphysics revisited

The kingdom that Jesus proclaimed and represented and the kingdom the early Christians knew was still imminent implies the interconnectivity of mysticism (a space, a clearing where God is present and his company can be enjoyed), metaphysics (a way of understanding the linkages between the nearness of the kingdom and the fragility of history) and politics (the praxis of kingdom living that undermines and subverts the domination systems of this present evil age). In all of this, we must accept what we have been at pains to demonstrate throughout this study, namely, the dangerously unstable and potentially ideologically destructive nature of worldviews. The second and third generation of Christians were already in the perilous grip of another

---

[47] The original trace of which was the redefinition of Christians as the followers of a new way.

[48] K. Marx, 'The Eighteenth Brumaire of Louis Napoleon', in *Karl Marx and Friedrich Engels: Collected Works*, II, 103–50.

[49] See E. Troeltsch, 'Uber historische und dogmatische Methode in der Theologie' (1898), 'Historical and Dogmatic Method in Theology', in *Religion and History*, 11–32.

worldview when they decided to exploit the apologetic, ontological and epistemological fecundity of the concept of the *Logos*.

According to Ingraffia's thesis, they had moved from biblical eschatology to onto-theology (nowadays, we are informed, we must embrace the former and reject the latter).[50] In our opinion, such a position is a fiction. Apocalyptic was already metaphysics, a cosmic drama of colossal proportions, and the kingdom language of the NT brokered the transition to the *Logos* Christology of the patristic era, which, in turn, reappropriated the language of the Messiah/ Christos/*Kyrios* in the context of a new political praxis. Such is the opportunism of mission and we should be thankful for it because it continually alerts us to the resilience of religion.

It is, however, at this juncture where we need to exercise a certain christological caution. The immense significance and importance of *Logos* Christology cannot be underestimated and we have already refused to follow those who would seek to supplant it with a supposedly more parsimonious Spirit Christology.[51] We do, however, agree with Pannenberg that the route from the historical figure of Jesus to the pre-existent *Logos* is not only fraught with theological tensions, but can only be expedited indirectly.[52]

If, to use Pannenberg's thesis, the resurrection can be understood to exercise a certain retroactive ontological power subsuming the whole of Jesus' pre-Easter path within the parameters of his status as the exalted *Christos*, this can only be on the basis that what is real, present and active in Jesus' career and ministry is the reality of the kingdom and not solely the second person of the Trinity veiled in human form. It is here where we enter the domain yet again of christological metaphysics and in so doing we redefine the nature of the metaphysical task. This is no idle speculation concerning ontological origins that, as Ingraffia and John Caputo correctly argue, is the form of onto-theology Kierkegaard, Neitzsche, Heidegger and now also Derrida continually mistake for genuine Christian faith.[53]

Christological metaphysics deals with cosmological linkages. It concerns the mediation of the kingdom through the prevenient grace of the triune God. In other words, Christology cannot be reduced to a two-term equation or relation, that of the relationship between the pre-existent *Logos* and the incarnate Lord. Contra Barth, the divinity of Jesus cannot be adequately, or we might add, convincingly explained, simply in terms of the *enhypostatic* union of the pre-existent *Logos* with the human Jesus. Both Jesus' personal identity as the

---

[50] Ingraffia, *Postmodern Theory*, 225–37.
[51] E.g. Kasper, Moltmann, Berkoff, and Tillich.
[52] Pannenberg, *Jesus–God and Man*, 334–44.
[53] Ingraffia, *Postmodern Theory*; see also J.D. Caputo, *Radical Hermeneutics: Repetition, Deconstruction, and the Hermeneutic Project*.

son of the Father and his mediation of the kingdom of God are expropriated and experienced through the mutual collaboration of the other two persons of the Godhead.[54] It is precisely as Jesus willingly subjugates himself to the will, purpose and mission of the Father in and through the presence and power of the Spirit that the reality of the kingdom breaks in twisting and fracturing the space-time continuum. In other words, time and eternity intersect.

At this point in the discussion, Christology inevitably becomes a subset of trinitarian theology. However, the obverse is also the case. If Christology cannot be successfully explicated solely in terms of a two-term set of relationships, a conclusion forcefully arrived at due to the logical difficulties of the two-nature language, then neither can Christology be reduced to being a function of a three-way set of relations. The latter may be entirely appropriate in terms of Jesus' self-identity as the Son/*Logos* or Wisdom of God, but there is more to his divinity than this, which must be established on the basis that he both proclaims and embodies the interpenetration of the presence and the future of the kingdom. In Jesus' ministry of deliverance and liberation, the distance between what is present and what is promised collapses; here, the glory of God is revealed to those who have eyes to see and can witness the transparency of history to the proximity of the kingdom.

If Jesus' divinity hinges on the question of whether or not in his person, ministry, death and resurrection the kingdom is actually manifested, then the same is true in regard to the vexed issue of how we can possibly understand the question of his pre-existence. If the Wisdom/*Logos* of God was there when God 'set the heavens in place, when he marked out the horizon on the face of the deep, when he gave the sea its boundary ... and when he marked out the foundations of the earth' (Prov. 8:27–29), then one possible interpretation of such evocative language is that it was always the task of the Wisdom/*Logos* of God to stretch out the boundaries and mark out the horizons, to create a space–time continuum where both the freedom and integrity of the creation could be preserved and the glory of God revealed. In that sense, as we have already argued, the creation, the election of Israel and the incarnation express in history the desire of the personified Wisdom of God to move out of the unity of the Godhead and create a space where the covenant God can sojourn with his people. That space, as the ancient Greeks recognised, also constitutes the ontological foundation of the universe for without it chaos would once again have ensued. Indeed, the present wisdom of cosmology reminds us that without the perdurance of the kingdom chaos and collapse will indeed be the eventual fate of the space–time continuum, as we understand it.

What we are trying to articulate cannot be adequately expressed in terms of the notion of the self-differentiation of the *Logos* or the Son from the Father

---

[54] See Pannenberg, *Systematic Theology*, Vol 1.

(contra Pannenberg). As we argued throughout this study, both Christology and trinitarian theology enter into a perilous compromise through appropriating the language of idealist philosophy. God cannot be understood by analogy with the project of the human subject and postmodernity renders all such terms as self-realisation, self-differentiation, self-emptying when applied to God hugely problematic. These terms also inevitably privilege the two-term relationship of Father and Son at the expense of the trinitarian identity of the Christian God. The realisation of the kingdom and the glory of God in the world is not the sole prerogative of the Father and the Son.[55] Rather, the *Logos/Son/Wisdom* creates the clearing where the glory of the Father can be expressed but it is the ecstasy of the Spirit, in and through the Son, who manifests the signs of the kingdom in our midst and so glorifies both the Father and the Son.

We have arrived at a point where Christology dares to go no further, except, as we have indicated, when it is subsumed within a trinitarian exposition of the doctrine of God and that is not our particular task. We can, however, explicate our central thesis in relation to a number of peculiarly modern problems that have hitherto shown resistance to theological and christological explanation.

History Reconstructed

We are clearly departing from a broad consensus in terms of how history has been understood both by the exponents of modernity and by those who have appropriated their insights in theology. Put starkly, if somewhat simplistically, for most of the modernity project history has remained an over-inflated positivistic myth, at times of gargantuan proportions, extolling the virtues, values and progress of the human spirit, while at the same time masquerading under the guise of historical objectivity. To substantiate this thesis, we refer to the latest addition to the modern industry of Jesus research by Dominic Crossan, *The Birth of Christianity: Discovering what Happened in the Years Immediately after the Execution of Jesus.*

In an entirely commendable fashion, Crossan develops an interdisciplinary approach to critical-historical investigation of both the intra- and extra-canonical sources, which he postulates formed the bedrock of early Christianity. This amounts to a three-pronged analysis of the evidence. First, utilising cross-cultural anthropology, Crossan seeks to demonstrate that ancient agrarian societies undergoing a period of extensive commercialisation inevitably provoked serious peasant unrest, particularly when encouraged by members of a

---

[55] John 14:15–21; 16:5–16.

retainer class. Secondly, historical analysis of Greco-Roman involvement in first-century Palestine points to a bitter conflict between traditional Jewish values and Roman commercialisation. Finally, both of these conclusions are apparently supported by archaeological evidence. Taken together, Crossan asserts that these three historical factors would have inspired a Jesus resistant movement centred on opposition to commercial exploitation aided and abetted by disaffected retainer scribes. This, in turn, supposedly demonstrates that Jesus advocated an ethical eschatology based on Jewish covenantal traditions of justice and the preferential option for the poor and marginalised.

Crossan's thesis, however, breaks down in a number of significant ways. Most notably, the interdisciplinary approach unravels in favour of overtly theological judgements concerning equally problematic historical sources. These include judgements about the significance of a common sayings tradition upon which both Q and the Gospel of Thomas are supposedly based – a common meal tradition that apparently links together Jesus' pre-Easter itinerant rural ministry and the early Christian, Jerusalem-based, urban passion and resurrection story; and, even more incredulously, a Cross gospel located within the second-century Gospel of Peter.

To be fair, Crossan does not agree with positivistic accounts of history. Rather, he claims that all history is story, that it requires reconstruction of the past through critical interaction with the present, and that this interactivism is the same as Wright's critical realism.[56] What remains in dispute, however, is the problematic status of history, reconfigured according to an equally tendentious theory of reconstructed sources that automatically privileges the epistemological scope of the historian. It is this error that is always the source of the pernicious fallacy that undergirds all positivism.

History telling is always also history making and therefore, to a certain extent, history remaking. In other words, imaginative portrayals and conjectures, which are based on some ascertainable and recoverable historical sources and accounts, but which, nevertheless, can only amount to a probable construal of what the available evidence might suggest, or the direction *we* might be orientated towards in our investigations. It is, in fact, this dissimilitude that makes history interesting.

As Paul Ricœur acknowledges, historical reconstruction most certainly owes a debt to the past; we are not at liberty to fictionalise. However, that does not and cannot absolve us from the risk of interpretation and the test of appropriation.[57] Neither can it guarantee immunity from the possible contamination of ideological reconstruction of the past in the light of perceived religious or

---

[56] J.D. Crossan, *The Birth of Christianity: Discovering what Happened in the Years Immediately after the Execution of Jesus*, ch. 2.

[57] Ricœur, *Time and Narrative*, III, 142–3.

epistemological threats and challenges the historian is facing in the present. Even when a historian allows sufficient credence to the uncertainty, probability and vexing disputability surrounding events, actions, speech acts and interpretations of the past, he or she may not recognise the equally problematic status of the cultural, sociological and historical situatedness of the interpreter in the present. Nor may a historian necessarily be clear about the philosophical relationship between the 'two horizons', to use Gadamer's suggestive phrase.

So, against the positivism and historicism of modernity, are we opting for the more austere landscape of postmodernity? Apparently, we have been confidently informed that we stepped off that particular trajectory of history some time ago, rejecting it as an imperialistic metanarrative of self-delusion and domination. Hence, we can no longer believe in history as anything other than an ideological construct, rather than the universal carrier of truth and meaning.[58] In contemporary theology, the relativist and consumerist approach to biblical and theological exploration[59] provides a good example of this approach to history.

Interestingly, there is a parallel here with Crossan's thesis concerning the socio-political reality of first-century Palestine. For now a new postmodern ethic of commercialisation has subverted the old Enlightenment foundational values of truth and meaning, and all we can do is let the market decide which Jesus we should seek to valorise; a Jesus who could not be counter-cultural but, instead, inevitably baptises the consensus morality of the hapless victims of postmodern kitsch and simulacra.

We wish to repudiate both extremes, while, at the same time, put forward the thesis that the reason for their apparent persuasiveness resides in the privatisation of religion. Once the ability of religion to provide 'public' meaning, truth and vision had been both seriously truncated and elided, something had to take its place. In our view, the modern impostor has been the philosophies and theologies of universal history. We have argued in our study that most philosophies of history – including those espoused by Hegel, Dilthey, Rahner and Pannenberg, with the possible exception of Heidegger – subsume the meaning of the particular within the metanarrative of the universal. Once this step is taken, the contingency, particularity, and sheer strange otherness of events is forgotten and the fragility of history, which cannot bear the imprint of totalising discourses, is ignored.

This does not entail that we should scorn or reject the important discoveries, illuminating hypotheses and occasional refreshing demythologising of those involved in history telling and writing. But we come back to our conclusion above:

---

[58] See J. Baudrillard, *Forget Foucault*, 67ff.; 'The Year 2000 Has Already Happened', in A. Kroker and M. Kroker (eds), *Body Invaders: Panic Sex in America*; and *Cool Memories*.

[59] See D.J.A. Clines, 'Possibilities and Priorities of Biblical Interpretation in an International Perspective', *Biblnt*, 1.1 (1993), 67–87; also *The Bible and the Modern World*.

history telling is always a case of history remaking, because the space–time continuum that supports the intoxicating dance and revel of past, present and future events knows no inherent supporting logic or immanent entelechy;[60] or if it does, we submit that it is a dangerous move to connect this with a full-blown theology of revelation. So, for instance, John Goldingay, in commenting on Daniel 11 (a passage where history is reconceived and reconstructed through the medium of apocalyptic), is quite sanguine about the implications of all this for those who want to claim history as the most comprehensive category of revelation:[61]

> The details of Persian and Hellenistic history have no constructive theological meaning. Events unfold as a pointless sequence of invasions, battles, schemes, and frustrations, a tale of selfishness, irrationality, and chance. History is neither the implementation of human purposes, the outworking of a principle of order and justice, the unfolding of a plan formulated in heaven, nor the reflection of the sovereign hand of God at work in the world. Often it seems to be the tale of human beings' unsuccessful attempts to be like God, though for the most part the true God appears to be sitting in the gallery watching history go nowhere.[62]

In reality, we make our own history and obliterate that of others. We tell stories that are by no means an idle fiction. Rather, they are often freighted with ideological constraints and tantalisingly persuasive and potentially destructive worldviews.[63] They are powerful articulations of how we believe things are or should be. In the process, we often deliberately ignore the aporias that should require us to look again at the evidence.

It is indeed ironic that for those who have sought to integrate or develop their Christology from the basis of some overarching theory of history, apocalyptic has been a favourite hunting ground.[64] It is our contention that this confidence has been misplaced, because it is apocalyptic that directs us to the fundamental aporia and dispersal of meaning that continually breaks apart the fragile continuities and interconnectivities of history. Apocalyptic remains the torture of history. Under the pressure of cataclysmic events, the earthen vessel of history shatters and the meaning of the past evaporates, spilling out into the sands of time.

---

[60] See, e.g., the ill-fated attempt by Pannenberg to rewrite human history from the perspective of the doctrine of election in *Human Nature, Election and History* – a project he thankfully abandoned.

[61] See, e.g., Pannenberg, *Redemptive Event*, 15.

[62] J. Goldingay, *Models for Scripture*, 305.

[63] A good example of which in recent history has been the nationalistic ideology of Slobadan Milosovich, by which he dragged the Serbian people into three catastrophic ethnically motivated wars.

[64] So, for instance, both Pannenberg and Moltmann in their respective christologies.

How, then, should we articulate a theology of history which in turn would have a radically new bearing on how we understand the nature of language? We suggest a christological alternative based on the assymetrical relationship between the cross and resurrection of Jesus. To use an analogy developed by Hans Urs von Balthasar in his atonement theology, history stands under the judgement and mercy of God explicated by the Easter events.[65] Good Friday, if it was indeed the crucifixion and death of the eternal Wisdom of God, symbolises the end of history – history as we could possibly know and experience it; history as the forward thrust of a continuous, seemingly random and disjointed, yet also interconnected series of events; history as representatively encompassed in the body of the dying and tortured Jesus, fractures, loses its meaning and momentum and suffers the judgement of God. Cast into the abyss of Holy Saturday, history, like the Son, dies and descends into the depths. All that remains is a dark and foreboding crevasse, and both the promise and the failure of the past is consigned to its meaningless depths. The mean power play of history, that which is subject to sin, chaos and futility, and so, for many, 'still remains nasty, brutish and short',[66] is dissipated and destroyed. If the Son is dead, his future denied, lost in Hades, then everything mortal and human (including the debris of history) suffers the same fate.

There it would and should remain, and if it were not for Easter Sunday we would have no interest in, or contemplate any glory to, the bacchanalian revel we call history. It is here that the kingdom praxis of the Messiah is fulfilled, verified and exonerated, because the hollow shell of history has been broken open. The two 'arms of God' outstretched upon the cross in love and forgiveness – his judgement and mercy – grasp again the past and the future folds of the robe of history. The Father, through the ecstasy of the Spirit, raises the Son; history is reborn. Now, and only now, can we say 'comfort, comfort my people', and claim that the warfare of history has ended (Isa. 40:1). The only meaning or purpose to history that could possible be perceived is through the lens of the resurrection. Without the resurrection, without this particular space and peace in the midst of time, history would remain what to a certain extent it always is. It is at worst a bitter tragedy of failed projects, the destructive menace of ideological conflict, the coercive reality of futile domination systems; or, at best, it is a positive reminder that the distance from the finite to the infinite is always infinite.

Let us be clear about the theological claims we are making. The asymmetrical relationship between cross and resurrection does not permit a seamless

---

[65] Von Balthasar, *Mysterium Paschale*. For a similar way of approaching the mystery of the Passion through a metaphorical appropriation of the chronology of the Easter events see the fine study by Alan E. Lewis, *Between Cross and Resurrection: A Theology of Holy Saturday*.

[66] Hobbes, *Leviathan*.

transition from one to the other. Revelation is God's judgement and mercy, both of which are manifest in the fissures, fractures and frustrations of history in every era and we must learn to live with this discordance. Neither do we wish to understand the judgement of God in a purely punitive sense. We do not want to return to the old Reformation juxtapositioning of the wrath and love of God. Judgement and mercy are twin expressions of the enduring love of God for creation. The judgement of God is manifest in the equivocation, uncertainty and obstinate refusal of the past to be subsumed within some inflexible law of historical determinism. The past is protected in the eternity of God from both our arbitrary interference and our abject fear of reaping its consequences. We most certainly owe a debt to the past, but we are not circumscribed or controlled by it. Nor are we at liberty to ignore the past and become immersed in a debilitating 'presentism' that typifies some aspects of postmodernism. To a certain extent, the judgement of God also relativises the perspective of the interpreter in the present because we must acknowledge the epistemological scope of the future to deconstruct and reinterpret the actions of history makers in the present. Consequently, there can be no overarching, totalising metanarrative to history understood in the postmodern sense as a grand theory that seeks to legitimise foundational claims for knowledge and truth.

The same is true for the biblical account of God's actions in creation and history. Most certainly, there is a compelling story to be told that moves from creation to eschaton. However, none of the crucial episodes in this story are necessarily implied in what precedes it. Creation does not necessarily imply a cataclysmic fall into non-being. The fractured contingencies of a creation now seriously out of sync with its creator most certainly do not imply election. The total shock, displacement and meaning under erasure of the exile were never intended to be part of the election narrative, and the tentative experiments in restoration could not have anticipated the inevitable renegotiation of the incarnation. In fact, every episode in the storyline comes up for constant renegotiation because of the shock and pressure of developments that appear to break away from the past with ever-greater intensity, eluding the totalising discourses that would seek to explain each episode as an inevitable part of the whole scheme of things. Only the person who stands at the end of history can understand the real meaning of its fragile contingencies and scarred and wounded trajectories. Only from this perspective would the enormous resilience of those who in faith, hope and love continually sift through its debris make sense, as they find their eternal rest and peace in the embrace of the kingdom.

Language Reconstructed

It is no coincidence that the positivistic modernity myth of history was accompanied by equally positivistic approaches to the philosophy of language. When philosophies of universal history were in the ascendancy, a unilateral philosophy of language also became fashionable, although the connections were not always recognised.

Logical positivism – as represented by such important figures as the early Wittgenstein, Bertrand Russell, G.E. Moore and A.J Ayer – effectively reduced the world and our understanding of it to a series of logical relationships between ascertainable facts.[67] Language, it was claimed, mirrors reality and so the limits of our language constitute the limits of our world. Not surprisingly, metaphysics, religion and, indeed, ethics were not well suited to such cognitive positivism. The high priests of logical positivism, the Vienna circle, sought to demolish all three:[68]

> It was a revolutionary force in philosophy, for it stigmatised metaphysical, theological, and ethical pronouncements as devoid of cognitive meaning and advocated a radical reconstruction of philosophical thinking which should give pride of place to the methods of physical science and mathematical logic ... Today logical positivism no longer exists as a distinct movement, yet its effects, direct and indirect, recognised and unrecognised, continue to be felt.[69]

The notion of a univocal language based on 'protocol' statements that apparently mirrored demonstrable and measurable facts was a theory of language that understandably worshipped at the high altar of the verification principle.[70]

At heart, logical positivism reflected the Enlightenment bifurcation of the world, undertaken by Hume and Kant, into 'hard facts', where science is the only credible form of knowledge, and 'soft beliefs', or values, that apply to just about everything else, including art, religion and morality. Thankfully, the verification principle died the death of its own empirical unverifiablity! However, due to the work of Karl Popper and Anthony Flew, it was mysteriously brought back to life again in the equally positivistic mode of

---

[67] L. Wittgenstein, *Tractatus Logico-Philosophicus*; A.J. Ayer, *Language, Truth and Logic*.

[68] For instance, philosophers A.J. Ayer, Rudolph Carnap and Moritz Schlick (Freidrich Waisman, Hans Hahn, Karl Mengar and Kurt Gödel were primarily mathematicians), Otto Neurath (sociologist), Victor Fraft (historian), Felix Kaufmann (lawyer), and Philipp Frank (physicist); See O'Connor, *A Critical History of Western Philosophy*, 492–3.

[69] Quoted in Stiver, *Philosophy*, 42.

[70] See Stiver, *Philosophy*, 42–7.

the falsification principle.[71] Due in large part to the influence of the later Wittgenstein, the non-cognitive theory of religious language fell into disrepute. However, if positivism dominated the philosophy of language espoused by the proponents of modernity, then pragmatism is the postmodern equivalent.

In his celebrated book *Philosophy and the Mirror of Nature*, Richard Rorty rejects what he regards as the foundational pretensions of philosophy since Hume, Descartes and Kant, which sought to make knowledge the result of a cognitive match between the real world, or states of affairs, and the concepts of pure understanding.[72] Rorty claims that the privileged metaphors of Enlightenment epistemology were the source of its power – particularly the persuasive notion of the mind or rationality, or pure consciousness, as the mirror of reality. The result was a story or a narrative that concentrated on the unearthing of unreal solutions to unreal problems, most noticeably the entire post-Kantian debate about the limits of human knowledge.

Rorty also claims that Kant's privileging of the a priori categories of the understanding are merely transcribed into the equally privileged equivalents of analytic and linguistic philosophy. So, for instance, most noticeably in the interminable debates about how far language mirrors reality and so can be judged and tested by the equally vacuous criteria of verification or falsification. The exchange of one technical vocabulary for another simply serves to distance philosophy from any semblance of social relevance. The holy grail of post-Enlightenment epistemology, the search for pure concepts of understanding and its linguistic equivalents, should now be abandoned in favour of a wider cultural conversation where we accept that no revered group of metaphors can ever cut the world at its joints. So what is real, true and, for all practical purposes, life giving, is in the end what Nietzsche recommended – that which can serve the purposes of society's best interest.

Here the old Enlightenment dichotomy of knowledge versus belief, or fact versus value, has been reversed. Now it is knowledge and fact that prove to be the illusory self-serving candidates, while belief, opinion and value strike a more reasonable chord amidst the postmodern cacophony of pragmatic possibilities:

> On the Nietzschean view that Rorty adopts, this process (*i.e. the search for indubitable knowledge*) started out with the victory of Socratic rationalism and achieved its bad apotheosis with Descartes, Kant and their successors. Its last major episode was the rise of Anglo-American analytical philosophy, a movement that has now lost its way among the competing (and wholly undecidable) claims and counter claims. So our best option is to drop the old metaphors – especially those that still trade on ideas of

---

[71] K. Popper, *The Logic of Scientific Discovery*; A. Flew, 'Theology and Falsification', in A. Flew and A. MacIntyre (eds), *New Essays in Philosophical Theology*.

[72] Rorty, *Philosophy*.

privileged epistemic access, or the mind as a mirror of nature – and try out whatever promising substitutes now come to hand.[73]

Rorty's postmodern pragmatism is echoed in Baudrillard's deconstruction of Marxist theory in favour of a media-induced, consumerist-driven vision of hyper-reality. What Rorty does to epistemology, Baudrillard does to political theory.[74] The Marxist mirror of production is denounced as another version of the post-Kantian mirror of reality metaphor, which is again based on an illusory search for a theory of truth that can separate fact from fiction and knowledge from ideologically tainted forms of belief.[75] Add to this Derrida's post-structuralist exploitation of the lacuna between signifier and the signified in the name of *différence*, his equally punishing deconstruction of the metaphysics of presence and his preference for 'grammatology' over 'logocentrism', and the possibilities seem endless.

It is, however, worth remembering that the route from positivism to pragmatism was expedited via the later Wittgenstein's ruminations about language games and the general hermeneutical theory of Heidegger, Gadamer and Ricœur. As Jean Grondin recognises, the latter in particular were part of that transition from a metaphysical to a hermeneutical universe that travelled via Kant, Jacobit and Schopenhauer.[76] In the process, theories that promoted the respective notions of univocal language and universal history that supposedly mirrored reality were superseded by the idea that everything, including, of course, the human subject, is a culturally and historically conditioned 'text', in which meaning is no longer found 'behind', but 'in front' of, our engagement with and interpretation of reality.[77] We have thus moved from an understanding of reality and language based on the natural sciences to one modelled on the human sciences, to one apparently constructed around the vertiginous pluralism of cultural theory. In terms of the latter, however, we should take note that not all the representatives of postmodernism espouse the designation relativist, pragmatic or nihilist. Derrida, for instance, categorically rejects such labels:

> There have been several misinterpretations of what I and other deconstructionists are trying to do. It is totally false to suggest that deconstruction is a suspension of reference. Deconstruction is always deeply concerned with the 'other' of language. I never cease to be surprised by critics who see my work as a declaration that there is

---

[73] Norris, *What's Wrong with Postmodernism?*, 168.

[74] J. Baudrillard, *The Mirror of Production* and *Critique*.

[75] Ibid., see also *Simulacres and Simulations*, and *Simulations*.

[76] J. Grondin, *Sources of Hermeneutics*, chapters 1 and 2.

[77] P. Ricœur, 'The Model of the Text: Meaningful Action Considered as a Text', in J.B. Thompson (ed.), *Hermeneutics and the Human Sciences: Essays on Language, Action and Interpretation*; and *Essays on Biblical Interpretation*.

nothing beyond language, that we are imprisoned in language; it is, in fact, saying the exact opposite. The critique of logocentrism is above all else the search for the 'other' and the 'other of language'.[78]

The difficulty for the poststructuralists, however, is that they are often hoisted on their own petard; it simply depends on how you read or play with the text. So, for instance, a pertinent critique of the deconstructionalist agenda is to ask how their concern for the 'other' could ever be anything more than an arbitrary assertion or meaningless foil. If meaning is always deferred, then the 'other' is also constantly destabilised, decentred and deconstructed. There simply is no basis in language for establishing the legitimacy of the 'other' over and against the acerbic deconstruction of the interpreter, who, in turn, is vulnerable to the same epistemological destabilising.[79]

Once again we suggest a Christological equivalent that avoids the postmodern slide toward pragmatism, constructivism and relativism but nevertheless respects the alterity and instability of language and so the inevitable superfluity of meaning that accompanies all forms of discourse. The verification principle is this: we simply must not balk at the holocaust of the cross. The death of the *Logos* incarnate means that everything is broken. Primarily, the eternal fellowship of the triune God is broken. The space–time continuum, which is itself dependent on the *Logos* marking out the horizons of the creation, is therefore broken; ontology and the possibility of metaphysical representation is broken; history and the ability to link past, present and future as a meaningful episode of human endeavour is broken; epistemology, the heuristic efficacy of mental constructs, and the desire to know aright is broken. hermeneutics and the promise of imaginative interpretation is broken; the structure of language and the meaning of meaning is broken; semiotics and the relationship between signifier and the signified is broken. As the creation story suggests, nothingness hovers at the margins and meaning is constantly deferred.

After the cross and the death of the *Logos*, nothing remains the same. Here we meet God's judgement in all its finality, the eternal act of deconstruction that relativises and marginalises all our *epistemes*. It is the ultimate *aporia* that exposes the naked ideology and power play of the human text. Once again, the asymmetrical relationship between cross and resurrection means that one does not imply the other and so the whole human project still limps. The complete *novum* of the resurrection, the unpredictable brokerage of the kingdom, God's penultimate 'Yes' to the human situation, is, after all, only partial repair

---

[78] J. Derrida, 'Jacques Derrida', in R. Kearney (ed.), *Dialogues with Contemporary Continental Thinkers: The Phenomenological Heritage*, 123.

[79] Prof. Andrew Lincoln of the University of Gloucestershire helpfully alerted me to this critique of the deconstructionalist preference for a constant postponement and instability of meaning.

and reconstruction that consequently entails an eschatological elasticity of meaning. We who experience the first fruits of the Spirit and the privileges of adoption still groan inwardly as we long for our redemption (Rom. 8:23).

But in this epistemological and linguistic gap, this historical lacuna, this textual instability that requires constant imaginative renegotiation, we encounter the hermeneutics of hope. Hope that all our striving after truth, knowledge, beauty and meaning is a reflection of, or referral to, the only transcendental signifier – the cross and resurrection of the incarnate *Logos*. Everything is broken and so truth, meaning, wisdom and knowledge constantly elude us because of the cross, and the judgement of God upon the human text. But where hope breaks forth from the power of the resurrection, then the kingdom is still near, the signs of the kingdom still break in, all things are under reconstruction according to the image of the Son, and the liberation of our language to speak the truth in hope and love is still possible.

The whole of reality is cast into this dialectical relationship so we should not be surprised that our language alerts us to this heuristic possibility. Where modernity preferred a *theologia gloria* and proclaimed the indubitable reality of foundationalism, postmodernity locates the debris of a false hubris and opts instead for a *theologia crucis*. The former leads to a vacuous triumphalism and the latter to an equally debilitating nihilism. The NT holds both in tension and so refuses either option. This entails that the instinctive feel for referral can and does stem from closure and the desire to assuage our ontological anxiety by the construction of some illusory epistemological foundation. However, as Kierkegaard recognised, this merely reflects humanity turned in upon itself. On the other hand, the constant negation of referral and the preference for an epistemological and linguistic vacuum is, after all, simply an exercise in bad faith.

The eschatological horizon of cross and resurrection is the transcendental foundation to which everything is ultimately referred. Only here do we discover the mystery of the other, the meaning of meaning, the fallible yet genuine possibility that we have spoken truthfully and aright, and the necessary erasure of all those mean power plays whereby we seek to exclude, dominate and subjugate our neighbour.

Religion Reconstructed

Religion belongs to a family of curious and often embarrassing concepts which one perfectly understands until one wants to define them. The postmodern mind, for once, agrees to issue that family, maltreated or sentenced to deportation by modern scientific reason, with a permanent residence permit. The postmodern mind, more tolerant (since it is better aware of its own weaknesses) than its modern predecessor and critic, is soberly aware of the tendency of definitions to conceal as much as they reveal and to maim and obfuscate while pretending to clarify and straighten up. It also accepts the fact that, all too often, experience spills out of the verbal cages in which one would wish to hold it, that there are things of which one should keep silent since one cannot speak of them, and that the ineffable is as much an integral part of the human mode of being-in-the-world as is the linguistic net in which one tries (in vain, as it happens, though no less vigorously for that reason) to catch it.[80]

It is our contention that at the present time, religion has emerged from the lengthening shadows of modernity where it languished in decrepitude due to lack of regular nourishment, to find itself with some bewilderment, an indefinable ingredient of the postmodern drama. The time is ripe to declare a moratorium on all definitions of the essence of religion, despite the modernist obsession with calculation continually displayed by those engrossed in the sociology of religion.

With the demise of the universal subject, all attempts to define the essence of religion in relation to this particular usurper appear all the more lamentable. Religion as the *mysterium tremendum et fascinans* (Otto); or as the feeling of absolute dependence (Schleiermacher); or the basis of our ultimate concern (Tillich); or the self-transcendence of the finite to the infinite (Hegel and Rahner); or the anthropological reality of openness to the world (Pannenberg); or the relationship to our own solitariness (Whitehead); or the 'recognition of all our duties as divine commands' (Kant); or the projection of our own inner self-consciousness (Feuerbach); or the repression of libidinal energies (Freud) – are all exposed as foundational-less, leaky vessels with meaning spilling out all over the place.

We should be grateful for some relief from the tyranny of the definition, because it is an acknowledgement of the inter-changeability of systems of discourse, something that the foundational classifications of modernity would not allow. What then is religion if it is not reducible to some innate or natural capacity within the human species? Bauman refers to the seminal work of Kalakowski:

Religion is indeed the awareness of human insufficiency, it is lived in the admission of weakness ... The invariable message of religious worship is: 'from the finite to the infinite the distance is always infinite' ... We face two irreconcilable ways of accepting the world and our position in it, neither of which may boast of being more 'rational' than the other ... Once taken, any choice imposes criteria of judgement which infallibly support it in a circular logic: if there is no God, empirical criteria alone have to guide our thinking, and empirical criteria do not lead to God; if God

---

[80] Bauman, *Postmodernity*, 165.

exists, he gives us clues about how to perceive His hand in the course of events, and with the help of those clues we recognise the divine sense of whatever happens.[81]

Looking at this analysis from one perspective, Nietzsche would appear to be right: religion stems from human weakness. However, Nietzsche was wrong in denigrating such weakness as moral turpitude or servility. So, despite the valorisation of Nietzsche as the prophet of postmodernism, he still exemplified a stubbornly resistant characteristic of modernity. His embrace of the Prometheam will to power was another example of that 'infantile omnipotence' that typified the exponents of the expansionist vision of the Enlightenment, many of whom apparently failed to recognise that in the context of an infinite universe the finite will always meet with insufficiency, weakness and limitation.

Many of the proponents of postmodernity have as little stomach for Nietzsche's *overman* as they do for the Christian God; hence, nihilism seemed the only option. From our point of view, however, there are some significant benefits to this analysis of the cultural and sociological function of religion. The admission of such insufficiency opens up a 'clearing' (to use Heidegger's language) where mysticism can flourish. It is a space that could be filled with fear and repulsion, or indeed with denial and deception, but also, thankfully, with grace and revelation. It is a space that either defies description or invites metaphysical and theological exploration. Similarly, it is a space that recognises the place of the other and so must be protected by a political vision with an ethical agenda.

This is also a 'clearing' that down through the centuries the religions have sought both to examine, colonise and exploit. Consequently, if, as Bauman suggests, an observation with which we agree, the contention that there are natural, innate, or ready made answers to this dilemma simply due to our being-in-the-world, is a case not yet proven, then by implication answers, suggestions or observations, regarding this state of affairs, are 'relentlessly insinuated'.[82] This, by necessity, also entails that not every experience of human finitude and being-in-the world is indelibly religious, i.e. infused with a sense of inevitable human limitation or lack. As Nietzsche persistently argued, there are other ways of explaining this reality and there are other ways of ignoring it all together. The great strategy of modernity was to construct a world orientated mainly to problems and concerns we ourselves could solve because, as Marx explained, 'no historical era sets itself tasks it cannot fulfil'.[83] Accordingly,

---

[81] L. Kalakowski, *Religion If there is no God ... On God, the Devil, Sin and other Worries of the so-called Philosophy of Religion*, 194, 199, 202; quoted in Bauman, *Postmodernity*, 168.

[82] Bauman, *Postmodernity*, 169.

[83] Ibid., 171.

religion and morality were removed from the public domain and allowed only that extracurriculum time and activity that a few, and as production and consumption became more and more intense, even fewer, people were able to enjoy.

The demise of Christendom, as we have already noted, was the dissolution of a pre-ordained order of things and the response of modernity was simply to create another agenda, one which this time was directed to that which we wanted to become, rather than that which we were informed we already were. Consequently, the demise of religion in the modern world was related to the ability of the Enlightenment project to interrupt and undermine three classical functions of religion:

- The first was to bind us to the inviolable natural or supernatural rhythm of life. In this regard, medieval theologians continually affirmed that God provided two books to read: nature *and* Scripture.
- The second was to incorporate us into a clearly stratified social order, be that church or community or membership of both.
- The third was to align us with 'the apprehension of human destiny, existence and death'. Sober attention to which in this life prepared us for survival in the next.[84]

In their place, modernity constructed another agenda; science, technology and economics dispensed with pre-ordained natural rhythms and orders. Increased social mobility untied the bonds of social stratification, the privatisation of religion transformed issues to do with human destiny into a leisure pursuit, and death became the sanitised domain of the care professions. Similarly, with the increase in living standards, the advances of modern medicine and the life prolonging predictions of genetics, death, the once perennial and absolute experience of human limitation, has experienced a number of significant defeats in the context of the modern world that tend to relativise its existential impact altogether.[85]

The effect of all this is to undermine one of the chief ways in which religion and onto-theology was inserted into the *Lebenswelt*. The anticipation of death as the way to live authentically without the obliteration of *Dasein* in everydayness (Heidegger), or the religious recognition of death as the final frontier which must be met with fortitude and hope, has limited appeal to those who are engrossed in the adventures of the modern consumer story (or, indeed, those who now regard death as simply the final episode in *their* story which may or may not have anymore meaning than that).

---

[84] Ibid., 172–3.
[85] Ibid., 174.

Religion and human identity

Neitzsche sought the transcendence of the human, but redefined it in favour of the apparent infinity of the will to power. In the process, ontological insecurity was to be assuaged by our own constructivist possibilities. In the transition from modernity to postmodernity we have gone on producing and constructing and now the human, the all-too-human, is experienced again, but this time at the radical existential edge of identity formation:

> It is the uncertainties focused on *individual identity*, on its never complete construction and on the ever attempted dismantling-in-order-to-reconstruct, which haunt modern men and women, leaving little space and time for the worries arising out of the *ontological* insecurity. It is in this life, on this side of being (if there is another side at all), that existential insecurity is entrenched, hurts most and needs to be dealt with. Unlike the ontological insecurity, the identity-focused uncertainty needs neither the carrot of heaven nor the stick of hell to cause insomnia. It is all around, salient and tangible, all-too-protruding in the rapidly ageing and abruptly devalued skills, in human bonds entered until further notice, in jobs that can be taken away without *any* notice, and the ever new allures of the consumer feast, each promising untried kinds of happiness while wiping the shine off the tried ones.[86]

Neitzche's self-reliant constructivism was no doubt to some degree an expression of the new expansionism of market capitalism. Against this cultural context, Bauman suggests that the producer/soldier entrepreneurial role became one of the most formative matrixes of social identity, at least for the male section of the species. An altogether more egalitarian model of the pleasure or sensation-gatherer has emerged in the context of postmodernity, which no doubt could also be aligned with the global reality of multi-national capitalism and the expansion of consumerism to invade culture itself.

Utilising the work of Abraham Maslow, Bauman concurs that the sensation-gatherer is socially conditioned to search for 'peak experiences'. In the pre-modern situation, this used to be the domain of the religious mystics and luminaries, where, as we have noted, apophatic theology constructed an elaborate technique of generating mystical experience. In that sense, the ecclesiastical institution can also be viewed as the attempt by organised religion to communicate peak-experiences to non-peakers'![87] Does the search for peak experiences have any religious significance in the context of postmodernity as the renaissance in made to measure spirituality might suggest? To quote Bauman:

---

[86] Ibid., 178.
[87] Ibid., 179.

I propose that the postmodern cultural pressures, while intensifying the search for 'peak-experiences', have at the same time uncoupled it from religion-prone interests and concerns, privatized it, and cast mainly non-religious institutions in the role of the purveyors of relevant services. The 'whole experience' of revelation, ecstacy, breaking the boundaries of the self and total transcendence, once the privilege of the selected 'aristocracy of culture' – saints, hermits, mystics, ascetic monks, *tsadiks* or dervishes – and coming either as an unsolicited miracle, in no obvious fashion related to what the receiver of grace has done to earn it, or as an act of grace rewarding the life of self-immolation and denial, has been put by postmodern culture in every individual's reach, recast as a realistic target and plausible prospect of each individual's self-training, and relocated at the product of life devoted to the art of consumer self-indulgence.[88]

This insightful analysis corresponds with our contention that it is the consumer metanarrative of endless satisfaction or 'peak-experiences' that has replaced the outmoded progress and socio-political emancipation equivalents that dominated the aspirational horizons of modernity.

Again, as Bauman notes, this metanarrative is constructed upon two residual premises of modernity, one that individual freedom is the ultimate value of worth, two that in order to encourage the former, religion should continue to be marginalised and privatised. In the process, transcendence becomes a totally this-worldly experience encouraged and promoted by the postmodern philosophies of libidinal flow and extension, where the human being is no more than a avatar of desire and ecstasy (Delueze and Guattari). The human person could, consequently, exemplify a tendency to self-destruct, then all that is required is the self-help remedies and correctional procedures advocated by Foucault's technologies of the self. Problems in experience, in the ever-increasing intensity of pleasure seeking sensation-gatherers, are diagnosed as technological hitches that simply require more sophisticated training techniques.[89]

After Bauman's analysis, one wonders what form of religion has been given a 'permanent residence permit' within the cultural parameters of postmodernity, because avid sensation-gatherers do not seem to be particularly receptive to the message of human insufficiency and weakness. We do not have to wait long for an answer. The specific religion of postmodernity born out of the internal contradictions of a culture bathed in endless consumer enticements with its inevitable corollary of infinite choice, is *fundamentalism* (in French *intégrisme*). Consequently, Bauman agrees with Gilles Kepler's findings: fundamentalism in all its forms – Jewish, Christian, Islamic, racial or national – is not a throwback to the pre-modern period, nor

---

[88] Ibid., 180.
[89] Ibid., 181.

is it a manifestation of the endemic irrationalism of the human species; it is, in fact, a very contemporary form of religious persuasion that accepts all the benefits of the postmodern era without paying the price.[90] 'The price in question is the agony of the individual condemned to self-sufficiency, self-reliance and the life of never fully satisfied and trustworthy choice.'[91] As was always the case, fundamentalism recruits its members from among the ranks of the poor, the marginalised and the needy. But the poor of today are *flawed consumers*, those who for whatever reason cannot take their place at the consumer feast of infinite variety and who are consequently left with a bitter taste in their mouths:

> The bitter experience in question is the experience of freedom: of the misery of life composed of risky choices, which always mean taking some chances while forfeiting others, or incurable uncertainty built into every choice, of the unbearable, because unshared, responsibility for the unknown consequences of every choice, of the constant fear of foreclosing the future and yet unforeseen possibilities, of the dread of personal inadequacy, of experiencing less and not as strongly as others perhaps do, of the nightmare of not being up to the new and improved formulae of life which the notoriously capricious future may bring.[92]

The message incubated by fundamentalism is not the insufficiency and weakness of the whole human race, but the insufficiency and lonely peril of the individual when faced with radical freedom and the notoriously uncertain consequences of its effects. The emancipation offered by fundamentalism is relief from the unbearable burden of a risk-contaminated individual freedom of choice. The price paid is the amputation of the infected organ, the removal of the uncertainty and insecurity of individual freedom, and the imposition of a new totalitarian authoritarianism.

Fundamentalism does, of course, abandon the modernist conspiracy of a privatised and depoliticised religion thrusting religion once again into the public domain, because it offers an alternative rationality to the rampant individualism born out of the liberal separation of church and state.[93] The new authoritarian rationality offered can be the authority of the book (Torah,

---

[90] See G. Kepel, *The Revenge of God: The Resurgence of Islam, Christianity, and Judaism in the Modern World*.

[91] Bauman, *Postmodernity*, 182.

[92] Ibid., 183.

[93] 'If the market-type rationality is subordinated to the promotion of freedom of choice and thrives on the uncertainty of choice-making situations, the fundamentalist rationality puts security and certainty first and condemns everything that undermines that certainty – the vagaries of individual freedom first and foremost.' Ibid., 185.

Bible or Koran), the authority of the group (nation, race, community, church or sect), the authority of tradition, or, indeed, the authority of history. In all respects the message is the same: there are limits imposed on human freedom in the name of some higher court of appeal or some alternative rationality.

We appear to have arrived at a non-negotiable impasse. One either accepts the radical constructivism of postmodernity where there is no relief from the perils and dilemmas of individual freedom, or one seeks an alternative rationality where the individual, freedom of choice, self-invention and self-gratification are not the ultimate values, nor the inevitable destiny of human life.[94] It would appear, however, that this apparent impasse is in fact nothing more than that legacy of voluntarism that has beset the liberalism of late modernity and now, also, postmodernity. On various occasions throughout this study we have traced the route whereby a genuinely Christian concept of freedom, which is realised as the objective correlate of authority, dissolves into the Romantic notion of the liberation of the individual through freedom of choice or the arbitrary exercise of free will.[95] The origin of this erroneous notion of freedom, we have contended, lies in Rousseau's and Locke's account of society as the product of the social contract. As Thomas Mann has indicated, such an account renders any possibility of a genuine reconciliation between the objective poles of freedom and equality nil and void. Similarly, with others we have taken due note of the unhistorical character of the myth that simply undermines the notion of the community or society as both a prior and logical good:

> So obviously is this myth unhistorical that it is easy to underestimate its hold on the modern mind. It means that society's demands are justified only in so far as they embody what any individual might be expected to will as his or her own good. It rejects the Christian paradox of freedom perfected in service.[96]

---

[94] We could of course assert that the opposite to fundamentalism is the old liberal strategy of adapting one's theological clothes to the new cut of the postmodern cultural fabric, but this would not be particularly new. In fact, this agenda dominated the dialogue that took place between theology and modernity. That is why those who take this particular route look increasingly like relics from a bygone era. Cultural accommodation stands no one in good stead when a new basis to theological rationality needs to be found. For a good example of this old and thoroughly redundant liberal strategy see D. Cupitt, *Taking Leave of God*; *Only Human*; *Life Lines*; *The Long Legged Fly: A Theology of Language and Desire*; *What is a Story?*; *The Time Being*; *After All. Religion Without Alienation*. For an insightful critique of the whole Sea of Faith movement see Thiselton, *Interpreting God*, 81–111.

[95] See Chapter 7.

[96] O'Donovan, *Desire*, 275.

O'Donovan goes on to note that this radical reorientation of society around the notion of individual freedom makes suffering unintelligible and the ordering of civil society more and more an exercise of sheer arbitrary pragmatism.

We would also contend that it produces precisely the inadequate account of religion to which Baumen subscribes. One where the individual replete with the terrorising possibility of infinite freedom of choice is inevitably and mercilessly pitted against the alien authority of the community or the state, which, in turn, knows no internal legitimisation. The narrative of cross and resurrection that reveals the identity of the *Kyrios*, however, witnesses to the surrender of absolute freedom for the sake of the world. The traumatic experience of Jesus in the garden of Gethsemane was that total and therefore also world denying freedom was in fact within his grasp. The greater will and authority to which he surrendered not only transformed the nature of suffering but also reconstituted society as that which ultimately and therefore also penultimately must acknowledge his victory over sin, death and evil. It is his judgement and mercy that alone can establish society's greater good, not as that which realises the greatest happiness for the greatest number, but as that which protects the vulnerable, the weak and the disadvantaged. The resurrection invests divine power and authority in one Lord only and every society that refuses to acknowledge this lordship, like modernity itself, inevitably becomes the antichrist. The socio-political task of a contemporary Christology is to relate all notions of freedom to the eternal Lordship of the crucified and risen Christ and so dispense with the illusory metanarrative of human emancipation.

Bibliography

Adorno, T.W., *Against Epistemology: A Metacritique Studies in Husserl and the Phenomenological Antinomies* (Oxford: Basil Blackwell, 1982)

Adorno, T.W. & M. Horkheimer, *Dialectic of Enlightenment* (tr. J. Cumming; London: Verso, 1979)

Allison, D., *The End of the Age Has Come: An Early Interpretation of the Passion and Resurrection of Jesus* (Edinburgh: T. & T. Clark, 1987)

Amoah M. & M.A. Oduyoye, 'The Christ for African Women', in V. Fabella & M.A. Oduyoye (eds.), *With Passion and Compassion: Third World Women Doing Theology: Reflections from the Women's Commission of the Ecumenical Association of Third World Theologians* (New York: Orbis Books, 1988), 43–6

Assmann, H., 'The Power of Christ in History: Conflicting Christologies and Discernment' (translation of *La Nuova Frontiera Della Teologia in America Latina* originally published by Maryknoll: Orbis Books, 1979), in R. Gibellini (ed.), *Frontiers of Theology in Latin America* (London: SCM Press, 1980), 133–51

Augustine, *De Trinitate* in *Augustine: Later Works* (The Library of Christian Classics; ed. J. Burnaby; Philadelphia: Westminster, 1980)

Aulen, G., *Christus Victor: An Historical Study of the Three Main Types of the Idea of the Atonement* (London: SPCK, 1965)

Ayer, A.J., *Language, Truth and Logic* (New York: Dover Publications, 1946)

Balthasar, H Urs von, *The Theology of Karl Barth: Exposition and Interpretation* (San Francisco: Communio Books, Ignatius Press, 1992)

——, *Mysterium Paschale* (tr. A. Nichols; Edinburgh: T. & T. Clark, 1990)

——, *The Moment of Christian Witness* (tr. R. Beckley; Glen Rock, NJ, Newman Press, 1969)

Barth, K., *Die Theologie und de Kirche* (Zollikon-Zürich, Evangelischer, 1928)

——, *The Word of God and the Word of Man* (tr. D. Horton; London, 1928)

——, *Church Dogmatics* (eds. G.W. Bromiley & T.F. Torrance; Edinburgh: T. & T. Clark, 1936–77)

——, *Protestant Thought: From Rousseau to Ritschl* (New York: Harper, 1959)

——, *Anselm: Fides Quaerens Intellectum, Anselms Proof of the Existence of God in the Context of his Theological Scheme* (tr. I.W. Robertson; London: SCM Press, 1960)

——, *The Humanity of God* (London: Collins, 1961)

———, *Theology and Church: Shorter Writings, 1920–1928* (London: SCM Press, 1962)

———, *The Epistle to the Romans* (tr. E.C. Hoskyns, from sixth edition of *Der Römerbrief*; Oxford: Oxford University Press, 1968)

———, *How I Changed my Mind* (Edinburgh: Saint Andrew Press, 1969)

———, *The Theology of Schleiermacher: Lectures at Göttingen, Winter Semester of 1923/ 24* (Edinburgh: T. & T. Clark, 1982)

———, *The Göttingen Dogmatics: Instruction in Christian Religion* Vol. 1 (Edinburgh: T. & T. Clark, 1991)

Bauckham, R., *Moltmann: Messianic Theology In The Making* (Basingstoke: Marshall Pickering, 1987)

———, 'Moltmann's Messianic Christology', *SJT* 44.4 (1991), 519–31

———, *The Theology of Jürgen Moltmann* (Edinburgh: T. & T. Clark, 1995)

———, *God and the Crisis of Freedom: Biblical and Contemporary Perspectives* (Louiseville: Westminster John Knox Press, 2002)

Baudrillard, J., *The Mirror of Production* (St Louis: Telos Press, 1975)

———, *For a Critique of the Political Economy of the Sign* (St Louis: Telos Press, 1981)

———, *Simulacres et Simulation* (Paris: Galilee, 1981)

———, *Simulations* (New York: Semiotexte, 1983)

———, *In the Shadow of the Silent Majorities* (New York: Semiotexte, 1983)

———, *Cool Memories* (Paris: Galilee, 1987)

———, *Forget Foucault* (New York: Semiotexte, 1987)

———, 'The Year 2000 Has Already Happened', in A. Kroker & M. Kroker (eds.), *Body Invaders: Panic Sex in America* (Montreal: The New World Perspectives, 1988), 35–44

———, *Jean Baudrillard: Selected Writings* (ed. M. Poster; Cambridge/Stanford: Polity/Stanford University Press, 1988)

———, *The Ecstasy of Communication* (tr. B. & C. Schutze; ed. S. Lotringer; New York: Autonomedia, 1988)

———, *Fatal Strategies* (New York/London: Semiotext/Pluto, 1990)

Bauman, Z., *Postmodernity And Its Discontents* (Cambridge: Polity Press, 1997)

Bebbington, D.W., *Patterns in History: A Christian Perspective on Historical Thought* (Leicester: Inter-Varsity Press, 1979)

Beintker, M., *Die Dialektik in der 'Dialktischen Theologie' Karl Barths* (Munich: Kaiser, 1987)

Bellah, R.N., *Habits of the Heart: Individualism and Commitment in American Life* (London: University of California Press, 1985)

Berger, P.L., *The Heretical Imperative: Contemporary Possibilities of Religious Affirmation* (London: Collins, 1980)

Berkhof, H., *The Doctrine of the Holy Spirit: The Annie Kinkead Warfield Lectures, 1963–1964* (London: Epworth, 1965)

——, *Christian Faith: An Introduction to the Study of the Faith* (tr. S. Woudstra; Grand Rapids: Eerdmans, 1979)

Berkouwer, G.C., *The Triumph of Grace in the Theology of Karl Barth* (tr. H.R. Boer; Grand Rapids: Eerdmans, 1956)

Bernard of Clairvaux, 'Sermon on the Song of Solomon', in *On Loving God: And Selections from Sermons* (ed. H. Martin; London: SCM Press, 1959)

——, *Letters*, in L.W. Grensted, *A Short History of the Doctrine of the Atonement* (Manchester: University of Manchester Press, 1962)

Best, S & D. Kellner *Postmodern Theory: Critical Interrogations* (London: Macmillan, 1991)

Bettenson, H., *Documents of the Christian Church* (London: Oxford University Press, 1947)

Biggar , N., *The Hastening that Waits: Karl Barth's Ethics* (Oxford Studies in Theological Ethics; Oxford: Clarendon Press, 1993)

Bockmuehl, M., *This Jesus: Martyr, Lord, Messiah* (Edinburgh: T. & T. Clark, 1994)

Boff, L., 'Christ's Liberation via Oppression: An Attempt at Theological Construction from the Standpoint of Latin America'; in R. Gibellini (ed.), *Frontiers of Theology in Latin America* (London: SCM Press, 1980), 100–32

——, *Jesus Christ Liberator: A Critical Christology for our Time* (London: SPCK, 1980)

Bonhoeffer, D., *Letters and Papers from Prison* (London/New York: SCM Press/ Macmillan, 1967)

——, *Lectures on Christology* (London: Fount, 1978)

Bonino, J. Miguez, *Christians and Marxists: The Mutual Challenge to Revolution* (London, 1975)

Borg, M., *Conflict, Holiness and Politics in the Teachings of Jesus* (Lewiston, Lampeter: Edwin Mellen, 1984)

——, 'A Temperate Case for a Non-Eschatological Jesus', *Foundations and Facets Forum* 2.3 (1986), 81–102

——, *Jesus: A New Vision* (San Francisco: Harper Row, 1987)

——, 'An Orthodoxy Reconsidered: The "End-of the-World Jesus"', in L.D. Hurst & N.T. Wright (eds.), *The Glory of Christ in the New Testament: Studies in Christology in Memory of George Bradford Caird* (Oxford: Oxford University Press, 1987)

Bornkamm, G., *Jesus of Nazareth* (tr. F. & I. McLuskey, with J.M. Robinson; London: Hodder & Stoughton, 1973)

Bosch, D.J., *Transforming Mission: Paradigm Shifts in Theology of Mission* (New York: Orbis Books, 1991)

——, *Believing In The Future: Toward a Missiology of Western Culture* (Valley Forge, PA/Leominster: Trinity Press International/Gracewing, 1995)

Braaten, C.E., *Justification, the Article by which the Church Stands or Falls* (Minneapolis: Augsburg-Fortress, 1990)

———, *No Other Gospel: Christianity Among the World's Religions* (Minneapolis: Augsburg-Fortress, 1992)

Braaten, C.E. & P. Clayton (eds.), *The Theology of Wolfhart Pannenberg* (Minneapolis: Augsburg-Fortress, 1988)

Braaten, C.E. & R.W. Jenson, *Reclaiming the Bible for the Church* (Edinburgh: T. & T. Clark, 1995)

Brock, R.N., 'The Feminist Redemption of Christ', in J.L. Weidman (ed.), *Christian Feminism – Visions of a New Humanity* (San Francisco: Harper & Row, 1984), 72–89

———, *Journeys by Heart: A Christology of Erotic Power* (New York: Crossroad, 1988)

———, 'Losing your Innocence but not your Hope', in M. Stevens (ed.), *Reconstructing the Christ Symbol: Essays in Feminist Christology* (New York: Paulist Press, 1993), 30–53

Brown, C., *The Death of Christian Britain: Understanding Secularisation 1800–2000* (London: Routledge, 2001)

Brown, R.E., *The Death of the Messiah: From Gethsemane to the Grave: A Commentary on the Passion Narratives in the Four Gospels* (2 Vols; London: Geoffrey Chapman, 1994)

Brox, N., *A History of the Early Church* (London: SCM Press, 1994)

Brueggemann, W., *Theology of the Old Testament: Testimony, Dispute, Advocacy* (Minneapolis: Augsburg-Fortress, 1997)

———, 'A Journey: Attending to the Abyss', *The Bible in Transmission* (Bible Society, Spring, 2000), 6–8

Bultmann, R.K., *Theology of the New Testament* (2 Vols; London: SCM Press, 1952–55)

Butterfield, H., *Christianity and History* (London: Collins/Fontana, 1957)

Byrne, J.M., *Glory, Jest and Riddle: Religious Thought in the Enlightenment* (London: SCM Press, 1996)

Cahoone, L.E. (ed.), *From Modernism to Postmodernism: An Anthology* (Cambridge, MA/Oxford: Basil Blackwell, 1996)

Caputo, J.D., *Radical Hermeneutics: Repetition, Deconstruction, and the Hermeneutic Project* (Bloomington: Indiana University Press, 1987)

Carr, A.E., *Transforming Grace: Christian Tradition and Woman's Experience* (San Francisco/London: Harper & Row, 1988)

Casey, M., *From Jewish Prophet to Gentile God: The Origins and Development of New Testament Christology* (London: Clarke & Co, 1991)

Charlesworth, J.H., 'From Messianology to Christology: Problems and Prospects', in J.H. Charlesworth (ed.), *The Messiah: Developments in Earliest Judaism and Christianity* (Minneapolis: Augsburg-Fortress, 1992), 3–35

Chopp, R.S., 'Latin American Liberation Theology', in D. Ford (ed.), *The Modern Theologians: An Introduction to Christian Theology in the Twentieth Century* (2nd edn.; Oxford: Basil Blackwell, 1997), 409–25

Christian, C.W., *Friedrich Schleiermacher* (Waco: Word, 1979)

Clayton, J.P., *The Concept of Correlation: Paul Tillich and the Possibility of a Mediating Theology* (Berlin: Walter de Gruyter, 1980)

——, *The Problem of God in Modern Thought* (Grand Rapids: Eerdmans, 2000)

Clements, K.W., *Friedrich Schleiermacher: Pioneer of Modern Theology* (London: Collins, 1987)

Clines, D.J.A., 'Possibilities and Priorities of Biblical Interpretation in an International Perspective', *BibInt* 1.1 (1993), 67–87

——, *The Bible and the Modern World* (Sheffield: Sheffield Academic Press, 1997)

Coakley, S., *Christ Without Absolutes: Study of the Christology of Ernst Troeltsch* (Oxford: Clarendon Press, 1988)

Comte, A., *The Positive Philosophy* (New York: AMS Press, 1974)

Condorcet, A.N. de, *Sketch for a Historical Picture of the Progress of the Human Mind* (tr. J. Barraclough; London, 1955)

Connor, S., *Postmodernist Culture: An Introduction to Theories of the Contemporary* (Oxford: Basil Blackwell, 1989)

Crossan, J.D., *Jesus: A Revolutionary Biography* (San Francisco: Harper San Francisco, 1994)

Crossan, J.D., *The Historical Jesus: The Life of a Mediterranean Jewish Peasant* (Edinburgh: T. & T. Clark, 1991)

——, *The Birth of Christianity: Discovering what Happened in the Years Immediately after the Execution of Jesus* (Edinburgh: T. & T. Clark, 1999)

Cullmann, O., *The Christology of the New Testament* (London: SCM Press, 1963)

Cupitt, D., *Taking Leave of God* (London: SCM Press, 1980)

——, *Only Human*, (London: SCM Press, 1985)

——, *Life Lines* (London: SCM Press, 1986)

——, *The Long Legged Fly: A Theology of Language and Desire* (London: SCM Press, 1987)

——, *What is a Story?* (London: SCM Press, 1991)

——, *The Time Being*, (London: SCM Press, 1992)

——, *After All: Religion Without Alienation* (London: SCM Press, 1994)

Daly, M., *Beyond God the Father: Toward a Philosophy of Women's Liberation* (London: Women's Press, 1986)

Davie, G., *Religion in Modern Europe: A Memory Mutates* (Oxford: Oxford University Press, 2000)

——, *Europe: The Exceptional Case: Parameters of Faith in the Modern World* (London: Darton, Longman & Todd, 2002)

Davies, S., *Jesus the Healer: Possession, Trance and the Origins of Christianity* (London: SCM Press, 1995)

Deleuze, G. & F. Guattari, *Anti-Oedipus: Capitalism and Schizophrenia* (London: Athlone Press, 1983)

——, *Kafka: Toward a Minor Literature* (tr. D. Polan; Minneapolis: University of Minnesota Press, 1986)

——, *A Thousand Plateaus: Capitalism and Schizophrenia* (tr. B. Massumi; Minneapolis: University of Minnesota Press, 1987)

Derrida, J., *Speech and Phenomena, and Other Essays on Husserl's Theory of Signs* (Evanston: Northwestern University Press, 1973)

——, *Margins of Philosophy* (tr. D. Bass; Chicago: University of Chicago Press, 1981)

——, *Positions* (Chicago: University of Chicago Press, 1981)

——, 'Jacques Derrida', in R. Kearney (ed.), *Dialogues with Contemporary Continental Thinkers: The Phenomenological Heritage* (Manchester: Manchester University Press, 1984), 123–4

——, *Of Grammatology* (Baltimore/London: Johns Hopkins University Press, corrected edn., 1997 [1976])

Di Noia, J.A., 'Karl Rahner', in D. Ford (ed.), *The Modern Theologians: An Introduction to Christian Theology in the Twentieth Century* (2 Vols; Oxford: Basil Blackwell, 1987), 118–33

Dillistone, F.W., *The Christian Understanding of Atonement* (London: SCM Press, 1968)

Dorrien, G.J., *The Barthian Revolt in Modern Theology: Theology Without Weapons* (Louisville: Westminster John Knox Press, 2000)

Dowey, E.A., *The Knowledge of God in Calvin's Theology* (New York: Columbia University Press, 1952)

Downing, F.G., *Cynics and Christian Origins* (Edinburgh: T. & T. Clark, 1992)

Dunn, J.D.G., *Jesus and the Spirit* (London: SCM Press, 1975)

——, *Christology in the Making: A New Testament Inquiry into the Origins of the Doctrine of the Incarnation* (London: SCM Press, 1980)

——, *Unity and Diversity in the New Testament: An Inquiry into the Character of Earliest Christianity* (2nd edn.; London: SCM Press, 1990)

——, 'Messianic Ideas and Their Influence on the Jesus of History', in J.H. Charlesworth (ed.), *The Messiah: Developments in Earliest Judaism and Christianity* (Minneapolis: Augsburg-Fortress, 1992), 365–81

Dych, W.V., *Karl Rahner* (Collegeville, MN: Liturgical Press, 1992)

Eliade, M., 'Paul Tillich and the History of Religions', in J.C. Brauer (ed.), *The Future of Religions* (New York: Harper & Row, 1966), 84–116

Eusebius, *Life of Constantine* (tr. and commentary A. Cameron & S.G. Hall; Oxford: Clarendon Press, 1999)

Evans, C.S., *The Historical Christ and the Jesus of Faith: The Incarnational Narrative as History* (Oxford: Clarendon Press, 1996)

Farrow, D., *Ascension and Ecclesia: On the Significance of the Doctrine of the Ascension for Ecclesiology and Christian Cosmology* (Edinburgh: T. & T. Clark, 1999)

Feuerbach, L., *The Essence of Christianity* (tr. G. Eliot; New York: Harper Bros, 1957)

Fiddes, P.S., *Past Event and Present Salvation: The Christian Idea of Atonement* (London: Darton, Longman & Todd, 1989)

Fiedler, L.S., *The Collected Essays of Leslie Fiedler* (New York: Stein & Day, 1971)

Fiorenza, E.S., *In Memory of Her: A Feminist Theological Reconstruction of Christian Origins* (London: SCM Press, 1983)

——, *Jesus: Miriam's Child, Sophia's Prophet: Critical Issues in Feminist Christology* (London: SCM Press, 1995)

Flew, A., 'Theology and Falsification', in A. Flew & A. MacIntyre (eds.), *New Essays in Philosophical Theology* (London: SCM Press, 1955), 96–130

Ford, D. (ed.), *The Modern Theologians: An Introduction to Christian Theology in the Twentieth Century* (2nd edn.; Oxford: Basil Blackwell, 1997)

Forsyth, P.T., *The Person and Place of Jesus Christ* (London: Independent Press, 1909)

——, *The Cruciality of the Cross* (London: Independent Press, 1948)

Foucault, M., *Madness and Civilization: A History of Insanity in the Age of Reason* (London: Tavistock Publications, 1967)

——, *The Archaeology of Knowledge* (London: Tavistock Publications, 1972)

——, *Language, Counter-memory, Practice: Selected Essays and Interviews* (Oxford: Basil Blackwell, 1977)

——, *Discipline and Punish: The Birth of the Prison* (New York: Vintage Books, 1979)

——, *The History of Sexuality* (London: Allen Lane, 1979)

——, *Power/Knowledge: Selected Interviews and Other Writings, 1972–1977* (Brighton: Harvester, 1980)

——, *The Care of the Self* (New York: Vintage Books, 1983)

——, 'What is Enlightenment?', in P. Rabinow (ed.), *The Foucault Reader* (New York: Pantheon Books, 1984)

——, 'The Ethic of Care for the Self as a Practice of Freedom', in J. Bernauer & D. Rasmussen (eds.), *The Final Foucault* (Cambridge, MA: MIT Press, 1988)

Fraser W. & L. Nicholson, 'Social Criticism Without Philosophy: An Encounter Between Feminism and Postmodernity', *Theory, Culture and Society* 5 (2–3), 373–84

Frei, H.W., 'The Doctrine of Revelation in the Thought of Karl Barth, 1909 to 1922' (PhD dissertation, Yale University, 1956)

——, *The Eclipse of Biblical Narrative: A Study in Eighteenth and Nineteenth Century Hermeneutics* (New Haven: Yale University Press, 1974)

——, *The Identity of Jesus Christ: The Hermeneutical Bases of Dogmatic Theology* (Philadelphia: Fortress Press, 1975)

Fukuyama, F., *The End of History And The Last Man* (London: Hamish Hamilton, 1992)

Fuller R.H. & P Perkins, *Who Is This Christ?* (Philadelphia: Fortress Press, 1983)

Funk, R.W. & R.W. Hoover (eds.), *The Five Gospels: The Search for the Authentic Words of Jesus* (New York: Macmillan, 1993)

Gadamer, H.-G., *Truth and Method* (New York: Crossroad, 1982 [1975])

Gallagher, M.P., *Clashing Symbols: An Introduction to Faith & Culture* (London: Darton, Longman & Todd, 1997)

Gardner, L., D. Moss, B. Quash & G. Ward, *Balthasar at the End of Modernity* (Edinburgh: T. & T. Clark, 1999)

Gerrish, B.A., *A Prince of the Church: Schleiermacher and the Beginnings of Modern Theology* (London: SCM Press, 1984)

Giddens, A., *Modernity and Self-Identity: Self and Society in the Late Modern Age* (Cambridge: Polity, 1991)

Goldberg, M., *Theology and Narrative: A Critical Introduction* (Nashville: Abingdon, 1982)

Goldingay, J., *Models for Scripture* (Carlisle/Grand Rapids: Paternoster Press/ Eerdmans, 1994)

Goldstein, V.S., 'The Human Situation, a Feminist View', *Journal of Religion* 40 (April 1960), 100–12

Gollwitzer, H., *Reich Gottes und Sozialismus bei Karl Barth* (München: Kaiser, 1972)

Goodacre, M., 'The Quest to Digest Jesus: Recent Books on the Historical Jesus', in *RRT* 7.2 (2000), 156–61

Gorringe, T., *Karl Barth: Against Hegemony: Christian Theology in Context* (Oxford: Oxford University Press, 1999)

Graff, G., 'The Myth of the Postmodernist Breakthrough', *Tri-Quartley* 26 (1973), 383–417

Grant, J., *White Woman's Christ, Black Women's Jesus* (Atlanta: Scholars Press, 1989)

Green, E., 'Women's Words: Sexual Difference and Biblical Hermeneutics', *Feminist Theology*, 4 (Sept 1993), 64–78

Greene, C.J.D., 'Is the Message of the Cross Good News for the Twentieth Century?', in J. Goldingay (ed.), *Atonement Today* (London: SPCK, 1995), 222–39

——, 'Consumerism and the Spirit of the Age', in C. Bartholomew & T. Moritz (eds.), *Christ and Consumerism* (Carlisle: Paternoster Press, 2000), 13–33

——, '"In the Arms of Angels": Biblical Interpretation, Christology and the Philosophy of History', in C. Bartholomew, C. Greene & K. Möller (eds.), *Renewing Biblical Interpretation* (SAHS Vol. 1; Carlisle/Grand Rapids: Paternoster Press/Zondervan, 2000), 198–239

——, '"Starting a Rockslide" – Deconstructing History and Language via Christological Detonators', in C. Bartholomew, C. Greene & K. Möller (eds.), *After Pentecost: Language and Biblical Interpretation* (Sahs Vol. 2; Carlisle/Grand Rapids: Paternoster Press/Zondervan, 2001), 195–223

——, 'Revisiting Christendom: A Crisis of Legitimization', in *A Royal Priesthood: A Dialogue with Oliver O'Donovan* (SAHS Vol. 3; Carlisle/Grand Rapids: Paternoster Press/Zondervan, 2002), 314–43

Grenz, S.J., *A Primer on Postmodernism* (Grand Rapids: Eerdmans, 1996)

Grenz S., & R.E. Olson, *20ᵗʰ Century Theology: God & the World in a Transitional Age* (Exeter/Downers Grove: Paternoster Press/InterVarsity Press, 1992)

Grey, M.C., *Redeeming the Dream: Feminism, Redemption and Christian Tradition* (London: SPCK, 1989)

Grillmeir, A., *Christ in Christian Tradition* (London: Mowbray, 1975)

Grondin, J., *Sources of Hermeneutics* (Albany, NY: State University of New York Press, 1995)

de Gruchy, J.W., 'African Theology (2)', in D. Ford (ed.), *The Modern Theologians: An Introduction to Christian Theology in the Twentieth Century* (2ⁿᵈ edn.; Oxford: Basil Blackwell, 1997), 445–55

Gunton, C.E., *Yesterday and Today: A Study of Continuities in Christology* (London: Darton, Longman & Todd, 1983)

——, *The Actuality of Atonement: A Study of Metaphor, Rationality and the Christian Tradition* (Edinburgh: T. & T. Clark, 1988)

——, *The One, The Three And the Many: God, Creation And The Culture of Modernity* (Cambridge: Cambridge University Press, 1993)

——, 'Bruce McCormack's Karl Barth's Critically Realistic Dialectical Theology: Its Genesis and Development 1909–1936', *SJT* 49.4 (1996), 483–91

Gutierrez, G., *A Theology of Liberation: History, Politics and Salvation* (Maryknoll: Orbis Books, 1973)

——, 'Liberation Praxis and Christian Faith', in R. Gibellini (ed.), *Frontiers in Theology in Latin America* (London: SCM Press, 1980), 1–33

Habermas, J., 'Modernity Versus Postmodernity', *New German Critique* 22 (1981), 3–14

——, *Theory of Communicative Action* (Cambridge: Polity, 1984–1987)

——, *The Philosophical Discourses of Modernity: Twelve Lectures* (Cambridge: Polity, 1990 [1987])

——, *The Structural Transformation of the Public Sphere: An Inquiry into a Category of Bourgeois Society* (tr. T. Burger, with the assistance of F. Lawrence; Cambridge, MA: Polity, 1989)

Haight, R., *Jesus: Symbol of God* (Maryknoll, NY: Orbis Books, 1999)

Hall, D.J., *Thinking The Faith* (Minneapolis: Augsburg-Fortress, 1991)

——, *Professing The Faith* (Minneapolis: Augsburg-Fortress, 1993)

——, *Confessing The Faith* (Minneapolis: Augsburg-Fortress, 1998)

Hamilton, W., *A Quest for the Post-Historical Jesus* (London: SCM Press, 1993)

Hampson, D., *Theology and Feminism* (Oxford: Basil Blackwell, 1990)

Harnack, A. von, *History of Dogma* (7 Vols; tr. N. Buchanan; Gloucester, MA: Peter Smith, 1976)

Harrisville, R.A. & W. Sundberg, *The Bible in Modern Culture: Theology and Historical-Critical Method from Spinoza to Käsemann* (Grand Rapids: Eerdmans, 1995)

Hartwell, H., *The Theology of Karl Barth: An Introduction* (London: Duckworth, 1964)

Harvey, V.A., *The Historian and the Believer: The Morality of Historical Knowledge and Christian Belief* (London: SCM Press, 1967)

Hassan, I., *The Dismemberment of Orpheus: Toward a Postmodern Literature* (New York: Oxford University Press, 1971)

——, *Right Promethean Fire: Imagination, Science, and Cultural Change* (Urbana: University of Illinois Press, 1980)

——, *The Postmodern Turn: Essays in Postmodern Theory and Culture* (Columbus: Ohio State University Press, 1987)

Hauerwas, S., *After Christendom: How the Church is to Behave if Freedom, Justice, and a Christian Nation are Bad Ideas* (Nashville: Abingdon Press, 1991)

——, *With the Grain of the Universe: The Church's Witness and Natural Theology* (Gifford Lectures, 2001; Grand Rapids/London: Brazos Press/SCM Press, 2001/2002)

Hauerwas, S., & W.H. Willimon, *Resident Aliens: A Provocative Assessment of Culture and Ministry for People who Know that Something is Wrong* (Nashville: Abingdon Press, 1989)

Hegel, G.W.F., *Phenomenology of Spirit* (Oxford: Oxford University Press, 1979)

——, *The Christian Religion* (tr. P.C. Hodgson; Montana: Scholars Press, 1979)

——, *Introduction to the Lectures on the History of Philosophy* (tr. T.M. Knox & A.V. Miller; Oxford/New York: Clarendon Press/Oxford University Press, 1987)

Heidegger, M., *Existence and Being* (London: Vision Press, 1968 [1949])

——, *Basic Writings from 'Being and Time' (1927) to 'The Task of Thinking' (1964)* (ed. D.F. Krell; revised and expanded edn.; London: Routledge, 1993)

Hengel, M., *Judaism and Hellenism: Studies in their Encounter in Palestine During the Early Hellenistic Period* (London: SCM Press, 1974)

——, *Studies in Early Christology* (Edinburgh: T. & T. Clark, 1995)

Heron, A.I.C., *A Century of Protestant Theology* (Guildford: Lutterworth Press, 1980)

Heyward, C., *Speaking of Christ: A Lesbian Feminist Voice* (New York: Pilgrim Press, 1989)

Hopkins, J.M., *Towards a Feminist Christology: Jesus of Nazareth, European Women and the Christological Crisis* (London: SPCK, 1995)

Horsley, R.A., *Jesus and the Spiral of Violence: Popular Jewish Resistance in Roman Palestine* (San Francisco: Harper & Row, 1987)

——, *Sociology and the Jesus Movement* (New York: Crossroad, 1989)

Horsley, R.A. & J.S. Hanson, *Bandits, Prophets and Messiahs: Popular Movements at the Time of Jesus* (Minneapolis: Winston Press, 1985)

Horton, W.M., 'Tillich's Role in Contemporary Theology', in C.W. Kegley & R.W. Bretall (eds.), *The Theology of Paul Tillich* (New York: Macmillan, 1952), 26–47

Howard, W.A., *Religion and the Rise of Historicism: W.M.L. de Wette, Jacob Burckhardt, and the Theological Origins of Nineteenth-Century Historical Consciousness* (Cambridge: Cambridge University Press, 2000)

Howard-Brook, W. & A. Gwyther, *Unveiling Empire: Reading Revelation Then and Now* (New York: Orbis Books, 1999)

Hume, D., *Essay on Miracles* (London: J. Watson, 1852)

——, *Hume's Dialogues Concerning Natural Religion* (ed. N.K. Smith; London: Thomas Nelson & Sons, 1962 [1947])

——, *A Treatise of Human Nature* (ed. L.A. Selby-Bigge; Oxford: Oxford University Press, 1967)

——, *An Enquiry Concerning Human Understanding* (Buffalo, NY: Prometheus Books, 1988)

Hunsinger, G., Disruptive Grace: Studies in the Theology of Karl Barth (Grand Rapids: Eerdmans, 2000)

Ingraffia, B., *Postmodern Theory and Biblical Theology: Vanquishing God's Shadow* (Cambridge: Cambridge University Press, 1995)

Irigaray, L., *The Sex Which is Not One* (Ithaca: Cornell University Press, 1985)

——, 'Equal to Whom', in G. Ward (ed.) *The Postmodern God: A Theological Reader* (Oxford/Cambridge, MA: Basil Blackwell, 1998), 198–213

Jameson, F., *Marxism and Form: Twentieth-century Dialectical Theories of Literature* (Princeton: Princeton University Press, 1971)

——, *The Prison House of Language: A Critical Account of Structuralism and Russian Formalism* (Princeton: Princeton University Press, 1972)

——, 'Postmodernism and Consumer Society', in H. Foster (ed.), *The Anti-Aesthetic: Essays on Postmodern Culture.* (Seattle: Bay Press, 1983), 111–25

——, *The Political Unconscious: Narrative as a Socially Symbolic Act* (London: Methuen, 1983)

——, 'Periodizing the '60s', in S. Sayres et al (eds.), *The '60s Without Apology* (Minneapolis: University of Minnesota Press, 1984)

——, '"On History and Class Consciousness" as an "Unfinished Project"', in *Rethinking Marxism* 1.1 (1989), 49–72

——, *Postmodernism or the Cultural Logic of Late Capitalism* (London: Verso, 1991)

Jantzen, G.M., 'Luce Irigaray', in G. Ward (ed.) *The Postmodern God: A Theological Reader* (Cambridge, MA/Oxford: Basil Blackwell, 1998), 191–7

Jaspers, K., *Nietzsche and Christianity* (tr. E.B. Ashton; Chicago: H. Regnery Co., 1961)

——, *General Psychopathology* (Manchester: Manchester University Press, 1962)

Jenkins, K., *Re-thinking History* (London: Routledge, 1991)

Jenson, R.W., *Essays in Theology of Culture* (Grand Rapids: Eerdmans, 1995)

——, 'Karl Barth', in D. Ford (ed.), *The Modern Theologians: An Introduction to Christian Theology in the Twentieth Century*, Vol. 1 (2nd edn.; Oxford: Basil Blackwell, 1997), 21–36

Jeremias, J., *The Problem of the Historical Jesus* (tr. N. Perrin; Philadelphia: Fortress Press, 1964)

Johnson, E.A., *Consider Jesus: Waves of Renewal in Christology* (London: Geoffrey Chapman, 1990)

——,'Wisdom Was Made Flesh and Pitched Her Tent Among Us', in M. Stevens *Reconstructing the Christ Symbol: Essays in Feminist Christology* (New York: Paulist Press, 1993), 95–117

Johnson, W.S., *The Mystery of God: Karl Barth and the Postmodern Foundations of Theology* (Louisville: Westminster John Knox Press, 1997)

Jones, G.S., *Critical Theology: Questions of Truth and Method* (Cambridge: Polity, 1995)

Jonge, M. de, *Jesus, the Servant-Messiah* (New Haven/London: Yale University Press, 1991)

Julian of Norwich, *Revelations of Divine Love* (tr. C. Wolters; ed. E.V. Rieu; Harmondsworth: Penguin, 1966)

Jüngel, E., 'Von der Dialektik zur Analogie: Die Schule Kierkegaards und der Einspruch Petersons', idem., *Barth-Studien* (Zurich/Cologne: Benziger/ Gutersloh, 1982), 127–79

——, *God as the Mystery of the World: On the Foundation of the Theology of the Crucified One in the Dispute between Theism and Atheism* (Edinburgh: T. & T. Clark, 1983)

——, *Christ, Justice and Peace: Towards a Theology of the State* (tr. D.B Hamill & A.J. Torrance; Edinburgh: T. & T. Clark, 1992)

Justin Martyr, *First Apology* (Ante-Nicene Christian Library; Grand Rapids: Eerdmans, 1978)

Kähler, M., *The So-called Historical Jesus and the Historic, Biblical Christ* (Philadelphia: Fortress Press, 1964)

Kant, I., *The Critique of Practical Reason* (tr. L.W. Beck; Chicago, 1949)

——, *Critique of Judgement* (Oxford: Clarendon Press, (1952)

——, *Groundwork of the Metaphysics of Morals* (tr. H.J. Paton; New York: Harper Row, 1964)

——, *The Critique of Pure Reason* (tr. N.K. Smith; London: Macmillan Press, 1973)

——, *Was ist Aufklarung: Aufsätze z. Geschichte u. Philosophie* (Göttingen: Vandenhoeck und Ruprecht, 1967, 1975; Hamburg: F. Meiner, 1999)

Kasper, W., *Jesus the Christ* (London/New York: Burns & Oates/Paulist Press, 1976)

——, *Theology and the Church* (London: SCM Press, 1989)

Kaufman, W.A., *Nietzsche: Philosopher, Psychologist, Antichrist* (Princeton: Princeton University Press, 1950)

Kaylor, R.D., *Jesus the Prophet: His Vision of the Kingdom on Earth* (Louisville: West-minster John Knox Press, 1994)

Kehland M. & W. Löser (eds.), *The Von Balthasar Reader* (tr. R.J. Daly & F. Lawrence; Edinburgh: T. & T. Clark, 1982)

Kelsey, D.H., *The Fabric of Paul Tillich's Theology* (New Haven/London: Yale University Press, 1967)

Kepel, G., *The Revenge of God: The Resurgence of Islam, Christianity, and Judaism in the Modern World* (Cambridge: Polity, 1994)

Kerr, F., *Immortal Longings: Versions of Transcending Humanity* (London: SPCK, 1997)

——, 'Thomas Aquinas', in G.R. Evans (ed.), *The Medieval Theologians* (Oxford: Basil Blackwell, 2001), 201–21

Kierkegaard, S., *Concluding Unscientific Postscript to Philosophical Fragments* (Princeton: Princeton University Press, 1992)

Kirk, J.A., *Theology Encounters Revolution* (Leicester: Inter-Varsity Press, 1980)

Knox, J., *The Humanity and Divinity of Christ* (Cambridge: Cambridge University Press, 1967)

Kreider, A., *The Change of Conversion and the Origin of Christendom: Christian Mission and Modern Culture* (Harrisburg, PA: Trinity Press International, 1999)

Kritzman, L.D. (ed.), *Michel Foucault: Politics, Philosophy, Culture* (New York: Routledge, 1988)

Kuhn, T.S., *The Structure of Scientific Revolution* (Chicago: University of Chicago Press, 1996)

Küng, H., *On Being a Christian* (tr. E. Quinn; London: Collins, 1977)

——, *The Incarnation of God* (Edinburgh: T. & T. Clark, 1987)

——, *Christianity and World Religions: Paths of Dialogue with Islam, Hinduism, and Buddhism* (tr. P. Heinegg; Maryknoll, NY: Orbis Books, 1993)

——, *Great Christian Thinkers* (London: SCM Press, 1994)

——, *Christianity: The Religious Situation of Our Time* (London: SCM Press, 1995)

Küng, H. & D. Tracy (eds.), *Paradigm Change in Theology: A Symposium for the Future* (tr. M. Köhl; Edinburgh: T. & T. Clark, 1989)

Kyung, H.K., *Struggle to Be the Sun Again: Introducing Asian Women's Theology* (London: SCM Press, 1991)

Lacoue-Labarthe, P., *Heidegger, Art and Politics: The Fiction of the Political* (tr. C. Turner; Oxford: Basil Blackwell, 1990)

Lakeland, P., *Postmodernity: Christian Identity in a Fragmented Age* (Minneapolis: Augsburg-Fortress, 1997)

Lampe, G.W.H., *God as Spirit* (Oxford: Clarendon Press, 1977)

Lang, V.M., Anhypostatos-enhypostatos: Church Fathers, Protestant Orthodoxy And Karl Barth', *JTS* 49/2 (Oct 1998), 630–57

Lerner, G., *The Creation of Patriarchy* (New York/Oxford: Oxford University Press, 1986)

Lessing, G.E., *Lessing's Theological Writings: Selections in Translation* (ed. H. Chadwick; London: Adam & Charles Black, 1956)

Levinas, E., *Otherwise Than Being, Or, Beyond Essence* (tr. A. Lingis; The Hague/London: Nijhoff, 1981)

Lewis, A.E., *Between Cross and Resurrection: A Theology of Holy Saturday* (Grand Rapids: Eerdmans, 2001)

Lindbeck, G.A., *The Nature of Doctrine: Religion and Theology in a Postliberal* (London: SPCK, 1984)

Loades, A., *Feminist Theology: A Reader* (London: SPCK, 1990)

Lohse, B., *A Short History of Christian Doctrine* (tr. F.E. Stoeffler; Philadelphia: Fortress Press, 1966)

Lorde, A., 'Uses of the Erotic: the Erotic as Power', in *Sister Outsider: Essays and Speeches* (Trumansburg, NY: Crossing Press, 1984), 53–9

Lovibond, S., 'Feminism and Postmodernism', *New Left Review* 178 (1989), 5–28

Lowe, W.J., *Theology and Difference: The Wound of Reason* (Bloomington: Indiana University Press, 1993)

Luckmann, T., *The Invisible Religion* (London: Macmillan, 1967)

Lundin, R., C. Walhout & A.C. Thisleton (eds.), *The Promise of Hermeneutics* (Grand Rapids/Carlisle: Eerdmans/Paternoster Press, 1999), 1–64

Luxmoore, J., 'New Options for the Poor', *The Tablet*, 8 July, 2000, 918–19

Lyon, D., *Postmodernity* (Buckingham: Open University Press, 1994)

Lyotard, J.F., *The Postmodern Condition: A Report on Knowledge* (Theory and History of Literature Vol. 10; tr. G. Bennington & B. Massumi; Manchester: Manchester University Press, 1984)

——, 'Missive on Universal History', in *Postmodernism Explained to Children: Correspondence 1982–1985* (Paris: Editions Galilée, 1986), 43–65

——, *Peregrinations: Law, Form, Event* (New York: Columbia University Press, 1988)

——, *The Differend: Phrases in Dispute* (Minneapolis: University of Minnesota Press, 1988)

——, *The Lyotard Reader* (ed. A. Benjamin; Oxford/Cambridge, MA: Basil Blackwell, 1989)

MacDonald, N.B., 'Illocutionary Stance in Hans Frei's The Eclipse of the Biblical Narrative: An Exercise in Conceptual Redescription and Normative Analysis', in C. Bartholomew, C. Greene & K. Möller (eds.), *After Pentecost: Language & Biblical* (SAHS Vol. 2; Carlisle/Grand Rapids: Paternoster Press/Zondervan), 312–27

MacIntyre, A.C., *After Virtue: A Study in Moral Theory* (London: Duckworth, 1985)

Mack, B., *A Myth of Innocence: Mark and Christian Origins* (Philadelphia: Fortress Press, 1988)

Mackintosh, H.R., *The Person of Christ* (London: SCM Press, 1912)

——, *Types of Modern Theology* (London, 1937)

MacMullen, R., 'Christianity Shaped Through its Mission', in A. Kreider (ed.), *The Origins of Christendom in the West* (Edinburgh/New York: T. & T. Clark, 2001)

Macquarrie, J., *Existentialism* (Harmondsworth: Penguin, 1976)

——, *Jesus Christ in Modern Thought* (London: SCM Press; Philadelphia: Trinity Press International, 1990)

——, *Christology Revisited* (London: SCM Press, 1998)

Marina, J., 'Schleiermacher's Christology Revisited: A Reply to his Critics', *SJT* 49.2 (1996), 177–99

Marquardt, F.W., *Theologie und Sozialismus: Das Beispiel Karl Barth* (München: Kaiser, 1985)

Marshall, B. *Christology in Conflict: The Identity of a Saviour in Rahner and Barth* (Oxford: Basil Blackwell, 1987)

Marshall, I.H., *The Origins of New Testament Christology* (Leicester: Inter-Varsity Press, 1990)

Marx, K., 'The Eighteenth Brumaire of Louis Napoleon', in *Karl Marx and Friedrich Engels: Collected Works*, II (London: Laurence & Wishart, 1979), 103–97

Matera, F.J., *New Testament Christology* (Louiseville: Westminster John Knox, 1999)

Maury, P., *Predestination and Other Papers* (tr. E. Hudson; London: SCM Press, 1960)

McBrien, R.P., *Catholicism* (London: Geoffrey Chapman, 1984)

McClendon Jr., J.W., *Biography as Theology: How Life Stories Can Remake Today's Theology* (Nashville: Abingdon Press, 1974)

McCormack, B., *Karl Barth's Critically Realistic Dialectical Theology: Its Genesis and Development, 1909–1936* (Oxford: Clarendon Press, 1995)

——, 'Barth in Context: A Response to Professor Gunton', *SJT* 49/4 (1996), 491–8

McFague, S., *Models of God: Theology for an Ecological Nuclear Age* (London: SCM Press, 1987)

McGinn, B. & J. Meyendorff, *Christian Spirituality: Origins to the Twelfth Century* (London: SCM Press, 1989)

McGovern, A.F., *Liberation Theology and Its Critics Toward an Assessment* (Maryknoll: Orbis Books, 1989)

McGrath, A.E., *The Making of Modern German Christology: From the Enlightenment to Pannenberg* (Oxford: Basil Blackwell, 1986)

——, *The Genesis of Doctrine: A Study in the Foundations of Doctrinal Criticism* (Bampton Lectures, 1990; Oxford/Grand Rapids: Basil Blackwell/Eerdmans, 1990)

McIntosh, M.A., *Mystical Theology: The Integrity of Spirituality and Theology* (Oxford: Basil Blackwell, 1997)

McIntyre, J., *The Shape of Soteriology Studies in the Doctrine of the Death of Christ* (Edinburgh: T. & T. Clark, 1992)

McKelway, A.J., *The Systematic Theology of Paul Tillich: A Review and Analysis* (London: Lutterworth Press, 1964)

McLaughlin, E., 'Feminist Christologies: Re-dressing the Tradition', in M. Stevens, *Reconstructing the Christ Symbol: Essays in Feminist Christology* (New York: Paulist Press, 1993), 118–49

Meeks, M.D., *Origins of the Theology of Hope* (Philadelphia: Fortress Press, 1974)

Meier, J.P., *A Marginal Jew: Rethinking the Historical Jesus* Vol. 1. *The Roots of the Problem and the Person* (2 Vols; New York: Doubleday, 1991)

——, *A Marginal Jew: Rethinking the Historical Jesus* Vol. 2. *Mentor, Message, and Miracles* (2 Vols; New York: Doubleday, 1994)

Melanchthon, P., *Loci Communes Theologici* (London: SCM Press, 1969)

Millbank, J., *Theology and Social Theory: Beyond Secular Reason* (Oxford: Basil Blackwell, 1990)

Mollegen, A.J., 'Christology and Biblical Criticism in Tillich', in C.W. Kegley & R.W. Bretall (eds.), *The Theology of Paul Tillich* (New York: MacMillan, 1952), 230–45

Moltmann, J., *Theology of Hope: On the Ground and the Implications of a Christian Eschatology* (tr. J.W. Leitch; London: SCM Press, 1967)

——, *The Crucified God: The Cross of Christ as the Foundation and Criticism of Christian Theology* (London: SCM Press, 1976)

——, *On Human Dignity: Political Theology's Ethics* (London; SCM Press, 1984)

——, *The Way of Jesus Christ: Christology in Messianic Dimensions* (London: SCM Press, 1990)

——, *History and the Triune God: Contributions to Trinitarian Theology* (London: SCM Press, 1991)

——, *The Spirit of Life: A Universal Affirmation* (London: SCM Press, 1992)

——, *The Coming of God: Christian Eschatology* (London: SCM Press, 1996)

Moltmann-Wendel, E., *The Women Around Jesus* (New York: Crossroads, 1982)

——, 'Christ in Feminist Context', in H. Regan & A.J. Torrance (eds.), *Christ and Context: The Confrontation Between Gospel and Culture* (Edinburgh: T. & T. Clark, 1993), 105–16

Nestlehutt, M.S.G., 'Chalcedonian Christology: Modern Criticism And Contemporary Ecumenism', *Journal of Ecumenical Studies* 35.2 (Spring 1998), 175–96

Newbigin, L., *Foolishness to the Greeks: The Gospel and Western Culture* (London: SPCK, 1986)

——, *The Gospel in a Pluralist Society* (London: SPCK, 1989)

Newport, J.P., *Paul Tillich* (ed. B.E. Patterson; Waco: Word, 1984)

Nicholl, A., *The Pelican Guide to Modern Theology* Vol. 1 (Harmondsworth: Pelican, 1969)

Nichols, A., *Christendom Awake: On Re-energising the Church in Culture* (Edinburgh: T. & T. Clark, 1999)

Nicholson, E.W., *Interpreting the Old Testament: A Century of the Oriel Professorship* (Oxford/New York: Clarendon Press/Oxford University Press, 1981)

Nicholson, L., *Feminism/Postmodernism* (New York: Routledge, 1990)

Niebuhr, H.R. (ed.), *Schleiermacher on Christ and Religion* (London: SCM Press, 1965)

Niebuhr, H.R., *Beyond Tragedy* (London: Nisbet & Co., 1938)

——, *Christ and Culture* (London: Faber & Faber, 1952)

Nietzsche, F.W., *The Will to Power* (tr. W. Kaufmann & R.J. Hollingdale; ed. W. Kaufmann; New York: Vintage Books, 1968)

——, *The Gay Science*, Part Three, 'The Madman' with a prelude in rhymes and an appendix of songs (New York: Vintage Books, 1974)

——, *Thus Spake Zarathustra: A Book For All and None* (tr. W. Haufmann; New York: Penguin, 1978)

——, *The Antichrist* (Costa Mesa, CA: Noontide Press, 1980)

——, 'The Antichrist', in *The Portable Nietzsche* (ed. & tr. W. Kaufmann; New York: Penguin Books, 1982), 568–656

——, *On the Genealogy of Morals: A Polemic* (tr. W. Kaufmann & R.J. Hollingdale; New York: Vintage Books, 1989), 13–163

——, *Beyond Good and Evil: Prelude to a Philosophy of the Future* (tr. W. Kaufmann; New York: Vintage Books, 1989)

——, *Twilight of the Idols or How One Philosophizes* in *The Portable Nietzsche* (ed. & tr. W. Kaufmann & R.J. Hollingdale; New York: Vintage Books, 1989), 465–563

Norris, C., *What's Wrong with Postmodernism?: Critical Theory and the Ends of Philosophy* (London: Harverster Wheatsheaf, 1990)

Norris, R.A., *The Christological Controversy* (Philadelphia: Fortress Press, 1980)

O'Collins, G., *Christology: A Biblical, Historical, and Systematic Study of Jesus* (Oxford: Oxford University Press, 1995)

O'Connor, D.J. (ed.), *A Critical History of Western Philosophy* (Basingstoke: Macmillan, 1985, 1964)

O'Donovan, O., 'The Political Thought of the Book of Revelation', *Tyndale Bulletin* 37 (1986), 61–94

——, *The Desire of the Nations: Rediscovering the Roots of Political Theology* (Cambridge: Cambridge University Press, 1996)

——, 'Political Theology, Tradition and Modernity', in C. Rowland (ed.), *The Cambridge Companion to Liberation Theology* (Cambridge: Cambridge University Press, 1999), 235–47

O'Donovan, O. & J.L. O'Donovan, *From Irenaeus to Grotius: A Sourcebook in Christian Political Thought 100–1625* (Grand Rapids: Eerdmans, 1999)

Page, R., 'The Consistent Christology of Paul Tillich', *SJT* 36 (1993), 195–212

Pan-Chiu-Lai, *Towards a Trinitarian Theology of Religions: a Study of Paul Tillich's Thought* (Kampen: Kok Pharos, 1994)

Panikkar, R., *The Trinity and the Religious Experience of Man: Icon-Person-Mystery* (Maryknoll: Orbis Books, 1973)

Pannenberg, W., *Jesus—God and Man* (London: SCM Press, 1968)

——, *Revelation as History* (London: Sheed & Ward, 1969) American edition

——, *Theology and the Kingdom of God* (Philadelphia: Westminster Press, 1969)

——, 'Redemptive Event and History', in *BQIT* Vol. 1 (London: SCM Press, 1970), 15–80

——, *What is Truth?* in *BQIT* Vol. 2 (London: SCM Press, 1971), 1–28

——, *Human Nature, Election and History* (Philadelphia: Fortress Press, 1977)

——, *Christianity in a Secularized World* (London: SCM Press, 1988)

——, 'Hermeneutic and Universe History', in *BQIT* Vol. 1 (London: SCM Press, 1990), 96–136

——, *Systematic Theology* (3 Vols.; tr. G. Bromiley; Edinburgh: T. & T. Clark, 1991–8)

Patterson, L.G., *God and History in Early Christian Thought: A Study of Themes from Justin Martyr to Gregory the Great* (London: Black, 1967)

Pauck, W. & M., *Paul Tillich – His Life and Thought* Vol. 1 (London: Collins, 1979)

Pelikan, J., *The Christian Tradition: A History of the Development of Doctrine* (5 Vols.; Chicago: University of Chicago Press, 1971–1989)

——, *Jesus through the Centuries: His Place in the History of Culture* (New Haven/London: Yale University Press, 1985)

Pérez-Esclarín, A., *Atheism and Liberation* (London: SCM Press, 1980, 1978)

Pokorny, P., *The Genesis of Christology: Foundations for a Theology of the New Testament* (Edinburgh: T. & T. Clark, 1987)

Pope, A., *Essay On Man?* Epistle III? (London: J. Wilford, 1733)

Popper, K., *The Logic of Scientific Discovery* (New York: Basic Books, 1959)

Provan, I., 'Ideologies, Literary and Critical: Reflections on Recent Writing On the History Of Israel', *JBL* 114/4 (1995), 585–606

Pugh, J.C., *The Anselmic Shift: Christology and Method in Karl Barths Theology* (New York: P. Lang, 1990)

Quine, W. Van Orman, *From a Logical Point of View: 9 Logico-philosophical Essays* (New York: Harper Row, 1961)

Rad, G. von, *Old Testament Theology* (2 Vols; tr. D.M.G. Stalker; Edinburgh: Oliver & Boyd, 1962 & 1965)

Rahner, H., *Ignatius the Theologian* (London/Dublin: G. Chapman, 1968)

Rahner, K., *Theological Investigations* (13 Vols; London: Darton, Longman & Todd, 1961–75)

——, W. Thüsing, D. Smith & V. Green, *A New Christology* (London: Burns & Oates, 1980)

——, *Foundations of Christian Faith: An Introduction to the Idea of Christianity* (London: Darton, Longman & Todd, 1978)

——, *Hearer of the Word: Laying the Foundation for a Philosophy of Religion* (tr. J. Donceel; ed. A. Tallon; New York: Continuum, 1994)

Randall Jr., J.H., 'The Ontology of Paul Tillich', in C.W. Kegley & H.W. Bretall (eds.), *The Theology of Paul Tillich* (New York: Pilgrim Press, 1982 [1952]), 132–63

Rendorff, T., 'Radikale Autonomie Gottes: Zum Verstandnis der Theologie Karl Barths und ihre Folgen', *Theorie des Christentums* (Gutersloh: Gutersloher Verlagshaus Gerd Mohn, 1972), 161–81

Reventlow, H.G., *The Authority of the Bible and the Rise of the Modern World* (London: SCM Press, 1984)

Reventlow, H.G. & W. Farmer (ed.), *Biblical Studies and the Shifting of Paradigms, 1850–1914* (Sheffield: Sheffield Academic Press, 1995)

Richards, G., *Towards a Theology of Religions* (London: Routledge, 1989)

Riches, J.K, *The World of Jesus: First-century Judaism in Crisis* (Cambridge: Cambridge University Press, 1990)

Ricoeur, P., *The Conflict of Interpretations: Essays in Hermeneutics* (Evanston: Northwestern University Press, 1974)

——, *Essays on Biblical Interpretation* (tr. R. Sweeney; ed. L.S. Mudge; Philadelphia: Fortress Press, 1980)

——, 'The Model of the Text: Meaningful Action Considered as a Text', in J.B. Thompson (ed.), *Hermeneutics and the Human Sciences: Essays on Language, Action and Interpretation* (Cambridge: Cambridge University Press, 1981), 131–44

——, *Time and Narrative* (3 Vols.; tr. K. McLaughlin & D. Pellauer; Chicago: University of Chicago Press, 1984–1988)

——, *Figuring the Sacred: Religion, Narrative, and Imagination* (tr. D. Pellauer; ed. M.I. Wallace; Minneapolis: Augsburg-Fortress, 1995)

Ricœur, P., *Time and Narrative* (3 Vols; tr. K. McLaughlin & D. Pellauer; Chicago: Chicago University Press, 1984–88)

Roberts, R.H., 'Barth's Doctrine of Time: Its Nature and Implications', in S.W. Sykes (ed.) *Karl Barth-Studies of his Theological Methods* (Oxford: Clarendon Press, 1979), 88–146

——, *A Theology on its Way?: Essays on Karl Barth* (Edinburgh: T. & T. Clark, 1991)

Robinson, J.A.T., *The Human Face of God* (London: SCM Press, 1973)

Robinson, J.M. & J.B. Cobb, *Theology as History* Vol. 3 (New Frontiers in Theology Series; New York: Hayes & Row, 1967)

Rogerson, J., *Old Testament Criticism in the Nineteenth-Century: England and Germany* (London: SPCK, 1984)

Rorty, R. (ed.), *The Linguistic Turn: Recent Essays in Philosophical Method* (Chicago: University of Chicago Press, 1967)

Rorty, R., *Philosophy and the Mirror of Nature* (Oxford: Basil Blackwell, 1980)

Ruether, R. Radford, *To Change the World: Christology and Cultural Criticism* (London: SCM Press, 1981)

——, *Sexism and God-Talk: Toward a Feminist Theology* (London: SCM Press, 1983)

——, *Women-Church: Theology and Practice of Feminist Liturgical Communities* (San Francisco: Harper & Row, 1985)

——, 'Can Christology be Liberated from Patriarchy in Reconstructing the Christ Symbol', in M. Stevens (ed.), *Essays in Feminist Christology* (New York: Paulist Press, 1993), 7–29

Rumscheidt, M., *Revelation and Theology, An Analysis of the Barth–Harnack Correspondence of 1923* (Cambridge: Cambridge University Press, 1972)

Russell, L.M., *Human Liberation in a Feminist Perspective: A Theology* (Philadelphia: Westminster, 1974)

Sachs, J., *The Politics of Hope* (London: Jonathan Cape, 1997)

Saint-Simon, H. de, 'On the Reorganisation of European Society', in G. Ionescu (ed.), *The Political thought of Saint-Simon* (London: Oxford University Press, 1976)

Sanders, E.P., *Jesus and Judaism* (Philadelphia/London: Fortress Press/SCM Press, 1985)

——, *The Historical Figure of Jesus* (London: Allen Lane, 1993)

Saussure, F. de, *Course in General Linguistics* (London: Duckworth, 1983 [1974])

Schelling, F.W., *Of Human Freedom* (tr. J. Gutmann; Chicago: Open Court Publishing, 1936)

——, *System of Transcendental Idealism* (tr. P. Heath; Charlottesville: University Press of Virginia. 1978)

——, *The Unconditional in Human Knowledge: Four Early Essays (1794–1796)* (tr. and commentary F. Marti; Lewisburg/London: Bucknell University Press/ Associated University Presses, 1980)

Schillebeeckx, E., *Jesus: An Experiment in Christology* (tr. H. Hoskins; London: Collins, 1979)

Schleiermacher, F., *On Religion: Speeches to its Cultural Despisers* (New York: Harper & Row, 1958)

——, *The Life of Jesus* (tr. S. Maclean Gilmour; ed. J.C. Verheyden; Philadelphia: Fortress Press, 1975)

——, *The Christian Faith* (eds. H.R. Mackintosh & J.S. Stewart; Edinburgh: T. & T. Clark, 1976)

Schmemann, A., 'The Missionary Imperative in the Orthodox Tradition', in G.H. Anderson (ed.), *The Theology of the Christian Mission* (London: SCM Press, 1961)

Schnackenburg, R., 'Christology and Myth', in H.W. Bartsch (ed.) *Kerygma and Myth: A Theological Debate* (New York: Harper & Row, 1961), 336–55

Schoonenebrg, P.J.A.M., *The Christ* (tr. D. Couling; London: Sheed & Ward, 1972)

Schwarz, H., *Christology* (Grand Rapids: Eerdmans, 1998)

Schweitzer, A., *The Quest for the Historical Jesus: A Critical Study of its Progress from Reimarus to Wrede* (London: A. & C. Black, 1968)

Schweizer, E., *Jesus Christ: The Man from Nazareth and the Exalted Lord* (London: SCM Press, 1989)

Schwobel, C. 'Once Again, Christ and Culture: Remarks on the Christological Bases of a Theology of Culture', in C. Gunton (ed.), *Trinity, Time, And Church: A Response to the Theology of Robert W. Jenson* (Grand Rapids: Eerdmans, 2000), 103–26

Scruton, R., *An Intelligent Person's Guide to Modern Culture* (London: Duckworth, 1998)

Segundo, J.L., *The Historical Jesus of the Synoptics* (Maryknoll/London: Orbis Books; Sheed & Ward, 1985)

Shults, F. LeRon, *The Postfoundationalist Task of Theology: Wolfhart Pannenberg and the New Theological Rationality* (Grand Rapids: Eerdmans, 1999)

Singer, P., *Hegel* (Oxford: Oxford University Press, 1983)

Smart, R., 'Modernity, Postmodernity and the Present', in B.S. Turner (ed.), *Theories of Modernity and Postmodernity* (London: Sage, 1990), 14–30

Smith, A., *Inquiry into the Nature and Causes of the Wealth of the Nations* (Oxford: Clarendon Press, 1976)

Smith, W.C., *Towards a World Theology: Faith and the Comparative History of Religion* (London: Macmillan, 1989 [1981])

Sobrino, J., *Christology at the Crossroads: A Latin American Approach* (London: SCM Press, 1978)

——, 'Central Position of the Reign of God in Liberation Theology', in J. Sobrino & I. Ellacuria (eds.), *Systematic Theology: Perspectives from Liberation Theology* (London: SCM Press, 1996), 38–74

——, 'Systematic Christology: Jesus Christ the Absolute Mediator of the Reign of God', in J. Sobrino & I. Ellacuria (eds.), *Systematic Theology: Perspectives from Liberation Theology* (London: SCM Press, 1996), 124–45

Sontag, S., *Against Interpretation* (London: Vintage Books, 1994)

Spieckermann, I., *Gotteserkenntnis: Ein Beitrag zur Grundfrage der neuen Theologie Karl Barths* (Munich: Chr. Kaiser, 1985)

Stackhouse, I., *Apologia: Contextualisation, Globalisation, and Mission in Theological Education* (Grand Rapids: Eerdmans, 1988)

Stanton, G.N.S., 'Incarnational Christology in the New Testament', in M. Goulder (ed.), *Incarnation and Myth* (London: SCM Press, 1979), 150–65

Stark, R., *The Rise of Christianity: A Sociologist Reconsiders History* (Princeton, NJ: Princeton University Press, 1996)

Steiner, G., *In Bluebeard's Castle: Some Notes Towards the Re-definition of Culture* (London: Faber, 1971)

——, *After Babel: Aspects of Language and Translation* (London: Oxford University Press, 1975)

——, *Real Presences: Is There Anything in What we Say?* (London: Faber, 1989)

Stevens, M., *Reconstructing the Christ Symbol: Essays in Feminist Christology* (New York: Paulist Press, 1993)

Stiver, D.R., *The Philosophy of Religious Language: Sign, Symbol & Story* (Oxford: Basil Blackwell, 1996)

Strobel, R., 'Feministische Kritik an traditionellen Kreuzestheologien', in D. Strahm & R. Strobel, *Vom Verlangen nach Heilwerden: Christologie in feministisch-theologischer Sicht* (Fribourg: Edition Exodus, 1991), 52–64

Studer, B., *Trinity and Incarnation: The Faith of the Early Church* (ed. A. Louth; tr. M. Westerhoff; Edinburgh: T. & T. Clark, 1993)

Stuhlmacher, P. *Jesus of Nazareth – Christ of Faith* (Peabody, MA: Hendrickson, 1983)

Sykes, S.W., *Friedrich Schleiermacher* (Makers of Contemporary Theology Series; London: Lutterworth Press, 1971)

——, 'Barth on the Centre of Theology', in S.W. Sykes (ed.), *Karl Barth: Studies of his Theological Methods* (Oxford: Clarendon Press, 1979), 17–54

Tanner, K., *Theories of Culture: A New Agenda For Theology* (Minneapolis: Augsburg-Fortress, 1997)

Tarnas, R. *The Passion of the Western Mind: Understanding the Ideas that have Shaped Our Worldview* (London: Pimlico, 1996)

Taylor, C., *Sources of the Self: The Making of the Modern Identity* (Cambridge: Cambridge University Press, 1989)

Taylor, M.C., 'Terminal Faith', in P. Heelas, D. Martin & P. Morris (eds.) *Religion, Modernity and Postmodernity* (Oxford: Basil Blackwell, 1998), 36–54

Taylor, M.K., *Paul Tillich: Theologian of the Boundaries* (London: Collins, 1987)

Teilhard de Chardin, P., *The Phenomenon of Man* (London: Collins, 1959)

——, *Man's Place in Nature: The Human Zoological Group* (London: Collins, 1966)

——, *Christianity and Evolution* (London: Collins, 1971)

Tertullian, *Ethical Treatises* in A. Roberts & J. Donaldson (eds.), *The Ante-Nicene Fathers* Vol. 4 (Grand Rapids: Eerdmans, 1979)

Thatcher, A., *The Ontology of Paul Tillich* (Oxford: Oxford University Press, 1978)

Theissen, G., *Sociology of Early Palestinian Christianity* [English title: *The First Followers of Jesus*] (Philadelphia/London: Fortress Press/SCM Press, 1978)

——, *The Shadow of the Galilean: The Quest of the Historical Jesus in Narrative Form* (London: SCM Press, 1987)

Thiemann, R.B., *Revelation and Theology: The Gospel as Narrated Promise* (Notre Dame: University of Notre Dame Press, 1985)

Thiselton, A.C., *The Two Horizons: New Testament Hermeneutics and Philosophical Description* (Carlisle/Grand Rapids: Paternoster Press/Eerdmans, 1980)

——, *Interpreting God and the Postmodern Self: On Meaning, Manipulation and Promise* (Edinburgh: T. & T. Clark, 1995)

Thomas à Kempis, *The Imitation of Christ* (tr. with notes L. Sherley-Price; Harmondsworth: Penguin, 1973)

Thompson, J., *Christ in Perspective: Christological Perspectives in the Theology of Karl Barth* (Edinburgh: St Andrew Press. 1978)

Thornhill, J., *Modernity: Christianity's Estranged Child Reconstructed* (Grand Rapids: Eerdmans, 2000)

Tilley, T.W., *Story Theology* (Wilmington: Michael Glazier, 1985)

Tillich, P., *The Interpretation of History* (New York/London: C. Scribner & Sons, 1936)

——, 'A Reinterpretation of the Doctrine of the Incarnation', *Church Quarterly Review* CXLVII, 294 (Jan–Mar, 1949), 133–48

——, *The Protestant Era* (London: Nisbet, 1951)

——, *The Courage to Be* (London: Collins, 1962)

——, *Christianity and the Encounter of the World Religions* (New York/London: Columbia University Press, 1963)

——, *Ultimate Concern: Tillich in Dialogue* (London: SCM Press, 1965)

——, *On the Boundary: An Autobiographical Sketch* (London: Collins, 1967)

——, *Perspectives on 19th and 20th Century Protestant Theology* (London: SCM Press, 1967)

——, *Systematic Theology* (3 Vols; London: SCM Press, 1978)

——, 'Basic Principles of Religious Socialism', in M.K. Taylor (ed.), *Paul Tillich: Theologian of the Boundaries* (London: Collins, 1987), 54–67

——, 'Religion and Secular Culture', in M.K. Taylor (ed.), *Paul Tillich: Theologian of the Boundaries* (London: Collins, 1987), 119–26

Torrance, T.F., *Karl Barth: An Introduction to his Early Theology, 1910–31* (London: SCM Press, 1962)

—— (ed.), *The Incarnation: Ecumenical Studies in the Nicene-Constantinopolitan Creed ad 381* (Edinburgh: Handsel Press, 1981)

——, *Karl Barth Biblical and Evangelical Theologian* (Edinburgh: T. & T. Clark, 1990)

——, *The Mediation of Christ* (Edinburgh: T. & T. Clark, 1992)

Toulmin, S.E., *Human Understanding, The Collective Use and Evolution of Concepts* (Oxford: Clarendon Press, 1972)

Toynbee, A.J., *A Study of History* (2 Vols; New York/Oxford: Oxford University Press, 1987)

Tracy D., *Blessed Rage for Order: The New Pluralism in Theology* (New York: Seabury Press, 1975)

——, *The Analogical Imagination: Christian Theology and the Culture of Pluralism* (London: SCM Press, 1981)

——, 'Tillich and Contemporary Theology', in J.L. Adams, W. Pauck & R.L. Shinn (eds.), *The Thought of Paul Tillich* (San Francisco/London: Harper & Row, 1985), 260–77

Trible, P., *God and the Rhetoric of Sexuality* (Philadelphia: Fortress Press, 1978)

——, *Texts of Terror: Literary-Feminist Readings of Biblical Narratives* (Philadelphia: Fortress Press, 1984)

Troelsch, E., *The Absoluteness of Christianity and the History of Religions* (London: SCM Press, 1972)

——, 'Historical and Dogmatic Method in Theology' ('Uber historische und dogmatische Methode in der Theologie'), in R. Morgan & M. Pye (eds), *Religion and History. Ernst Troeltsch: Writings on Theology and Religion* (Atlanta: John Knox Press, 1977), 11–32

Vanhoozer, K. *Is There a Meaning in this Text?: The Bible, the Reader, and the Morality of Literary Knowledge* (Leicester/Grand Rapids: Inter-Varsity Press/Zondervan, 1998)

Vass, G. *A Theologian in Search of a Philosophy* (Westminster: Christian Classics, 1985)

Vermes, G., *Jesus the Jew: A Historian's Reading of the Gospels* (London: Collins, 1973)

——, *The Changing Faces of Jesus* (London: Allen Lane, 2000)

Waldrop, C.T., *Karl Barth's Christology: Its Basic Alexandrian Character* (Berlin: Mouton, 1984)

Walker, A., *Telling the Story: Gospel, Mission and Culture* (London: SPCK, 1996)

Wall, R.W. & E.E. Lemcio, *The New Testament as Canon: A Reader in Canonical Criticism* (JSNTSS 76; Sheffield: Sheffield Academic Press, 1992)

Ward, G., *Barth, Derrida And The Language of Theology* (Cambridge: Cambridge University Press, 1995)

——, 'Divinity and Sexuality: Luce Irigaray and Christology', *Modern Theology* 12.2 (April 1996), 221–37

——, *The Postmodern God: A Theological Reader* (Oxford/Cambridge, MA: Basil Blackwell, 1998)

Watson, F., *Church, Text and World: Biblical Interpretation in Theological Perspective* (Edinburgh: T. & T. Clark, 1994)

Webster, J., *Barth's Ethics of Reconciliation* (Cambridge: Cambridge University Press, 1995)

Wells, D.F., *The Person of Christ: A Biblical and Historical Analysis of the Incarnation* (Westchester/London: Crossway/Marshall Morgan & Scott, 1984)

Whitehead, A.N., *Process and Reality: An Essay in Cosmology* (New York/London: Free Press/Collier Macmillan, 1979)

——, *Science and the Modern World* (London: Free Association Books, 1985)

Williams, R., 'Balthasar and Rahner', in J. Riches (ed.), *The Analogy of Beauty: The Theology of Hans Urs von Balthasar* (Edinburgh: T. & T. Clark, 1986), 11–34

——, *On Christian Theology* (Oxford: Basil Blackwell, 2000)

Wilson-Kastner, P., *Faith, Feminism and the Christ* (Philadelphia: Fortress Press, 1983)

Wink, W., *Naming the Powers: The Language of Power in the New Testament* (Philadelphia: Fortress Press, 1984)

——, *Unmasking the Powers: The Invisible Forces That Determine Human Existence* (Philadelphia: Fortress Press, 1986)

——, *Engaging the Powers: Discernment and Resistance in a World of Domination* (Minneapolis: Augsburg-Fortress, 1992)

Witherington, B., *The Christology of Jesus* (Minneapolis: Augsburg-Fortress, 1990)

——, *Jesus the Sage: The Pilgrimage of Wisdom* (Minneapolis: Augsburg-Fortress, 1994)

——, *The Jesus Quest: The Third Search for the Jew of Nazareth* (Downers Grove/ Carlisle: InterVarsity Press/Paternoster Press, 1995)

Wittgenstein, L., *Tractatus Logico-Philosophicus* (tr. D.F. Pears & B.F. McGuiness; intro. B. Russell; London: Routledge & Kegan Paul, 1961)

Witvliet, T., *A Place in the Sun: Liberation Theology in the Third World* (London: SCM Press, 1985)

Wrede, W., *The Messianic Secret* (Cambridge: Clarke, 1971)

Wright, A., *Why Bother with Theology?* (London: Darton, Longman & Todd, 2002)

Wright, N.T., *The New Testament and the People of God* (Christian Origins and the Question of God Vol. 1; London: SPCK, 1992)

——, *Who Was Jesus?* (London/Grand Rapids: SPCK/Eerdmans, 1992)

——, *Jesus and the Victory of God* (Christian Origins and the Question of God, Vol. 2; London: SPCK, 1996)

——, 'Paul and Caesar: A New Reading of Romans', in C.G. Bartholomew, J. Chaplin, R. Song and A. Wolters (eds.), *A Royal Priesthood: The Use of the Bible Politically and Ethically: A Dialogue with Oliver O'Donovan* (SAHS Vol. 3; Carlisle/Grand Rapids: Paternoster Press/Zondervan, 2002), 173–93

Wright, N.T. & M. Borg, *The Meaning of Jesus: Two Visions* (London: SPCK, 1999)

Young, F.M., *From Nicaea to Chalcedon: A Guide to the Literature and its Background* (London: SCM Press. 1983)

Young, P.D., *Feminist Theology/Christian Theology: In Search of Method* (Minneapolis: Augsburg-Fortress, 1990)

Zahrnt, H., *The Question of God: Protestant Theology in the Twentieth Century* (London: Collins, 1969)

Scripture Index

Old Testament

New Testament

Names Index

Abelard, Peter 59, 65–6, 349
Adams, J.L. 131
Adorno, T.W. 271, 274–6, 320, 326, 342
Allison Jr., D.C. 157, 338
Althaus, P. 19, 301
Althusse, L. 272
Amoah, E. 233
Anselm 67, 301, 302, 349
Apollinarius of Laodicea 39–40, 346–7
Aquinas, Thomas 63–4, 65, 173, 223, 349
Aristides 33
Aristotle 64
Arnold, M. 24
Assman, H. 201
Athanasius 39, 53–4, 151, 346, 348
Athenagoras I 34
Augustine 223, 346
Aulen, G. 67, 186
Averroes 349
Ayer, A.J. 374

Bacon, F. 76, 78
Baillie, J. 289
Barth, K. 27, 85, 103, 109, 114, 126–7,
    127, 134, 150–1, 235, 287–316, 318–21,
    324–5, 342, 355
Barthes, R. 273
Bartholemew, C. 3, 26, 44, 45, 134
Bataille, G. 281
Bauckham, R. 196, 317, 318–19, 320, 331,
    335, 340, 342
Baudrillard, J. 79, 252, 257–8, 284–5, 350,
    370, 376
Bauman, Z. 66, 168, 241, 378–84, 386
Baur, F.C. 143–4
Bebbington, D.W. 134, 153

Beck, H.G. 56
Beintker, M. 291, 301
Bellah, R.N. 92
Ben-Chorin, S. 322
Benedict 59
Benjamin, W. 355
Berger, P.L. 91, 93, 326
Berger, Teresa 242–3, 244
Berkhof, H. 330
Berkouwer, G. 288, 318
Bernard of Clairvaux 57–8, 59, 65, 349
Best, S. 255, 256, 257, 258, 272, 275, 278,
    279, 280, 281, 285
Bettenson, H. 46
Blamires. C. 270
Bloch, E. 319
Blumenberg, H. 85
Bockmuehl, M. 11
Boesak, D. 197
Boff, L. 200, 202, 207, 212, 232
Bohn, C.R. 229
Bonhoeffer, D. 21, 85, 111, 291, 295
Borg, M. 4, 7, 8, 354, 355, 360
Bornkamm, G. 15, 152
Bosch, D. 32, 59, 60, 93, 199, 205, 211–12,
    251
Bousset, W. 144
Braaten, C.E. 69, 147, 152
Brauer, J. 131
Bretall, R.W. 115, 122, 128
Brock, R.N. 227–8, 233, 237–8, 336
Brown, C. 2, 210
Brown, J.C. 229
Brown, R.E. 8
Brox, N. 47
Brueggemann, W. 141, 151, 356

Subject Index

transcendental epistemology, and idealist
 tradition 193–4
transcendental method 173–4, 193–4
Transcendental Thomism 173
 see also ascending Christology; descending Christology
rationalism 55, 91–2
Reasonableness of Christianity (Locke) 136
Reformation
 and development of modernity 93
 enlightenment exponents, natural successors of 70–1
 'gracious saviour', Christ as 67–8
 mystical union with Christ 68–9
religion
 crisis of 96–7
 and culture 125
 dialogue with culture, repudiation
 of 114
 essence, estrangement of existence
 from 119–20, 128
 experience of the Ultimate, as mediated through the finite 119
 religion, dual role of 116
 essence of 99–101, 100, 378–9
 existential insecurity 382
 and human weakness 379–80
 individual freedom
 cross and resurrection and surrender
 of 386
 and fundamentalism 384–5
 and society 385–6
 insufficiency of, and creation of 'clearing' for mysticism 380–1
 nature and function in modern
 world 98–9, 111
 peak-experiences, religious significance
 of 383
 privatisation of 370
 undermining of classical functions
 of 381
Religion within the Limits of Reason Alone
 (Kant) 83
religions, positive element in all 101–2,
 131–2
resurrection
 as apocalyptic concept 157

as invented by disciples 141
kerygmatic theology and centrality
 of 18–19
and metaphor of exaltation of Jesus as
 Messiah 362–3
ontological significance of 158
and phenomenology of hope 186, 211,
 212
as real event in history 157–8, 186,
 210–11
revelation
 threat to primacy of 126–7
 threefold doctrine of 307
 transcendental and categorical 178,
 187–8
Revelation as History (Pannenberg) 156
Roman Catholic theology *see* Rahner, and
 Roman Catholic theology
Romanticism
 dualisms of Enlightenment, reuniting
 of 86
 and Enlightenment, differences
 between 86–7
 Fichte, and philosophical roots of 86
 and high culture as route to transcendence 23, 24, 87
 humanity as microcosm of universe 88
 Nature, as divine Subjectivity 87–8, 98
Römerbrief, Der (Barth) 290, 292, 299, 300

Schleiermacher, theology of
 atonement, doctrine of 127–8
 Chalcedonian Christology, reinterpretation of language of 107–8
 Christocentrism 104–5
 Christology from below, and humanity
 of Christ 107, 108
 critical reason, acceptance of limits
 of 97
 divinity of Jesus 108–10
 exemplarism, charge of 127
 experience, reduction of theology
 to 98, 103
 grace, faith founded on 97
 hermeneutics, founder of modern discipline of 97–8
 historical Jesus 105–6